Contemporary Theatre, Film and Television

ISSN 0749-064X

Contemporary Theatre, Film and Television

A Biographical Guide Featuring Performers, Directors, Writers, Producers, Designers, Managers, Choreographers, Technicians, Composers, Executives, Dancers, and Critics in the United States, Canada, Great Britain and the World

Thomas Riggs, Editor

Volume 81

THOMSON

GALE

Detroit • New York • San Francisco • New Haven, Conn. • Waterville, Maine • London

THOMSON

GALE

Contemporary Theatre, Film & Television, Vol. 81

Editor
Thomas Riggs

CTFT Staff
Erika Fredrickson, Mariko Fujinaka, Annette Petrusso, Susan Risland, Lisa Sherwin, Arlene True, Andrea Votava, Pam Zuber

Project Editor
Michael J. Tyrkus

Editorial Support Services
Ryan Cartmill

Composition and Electronic Capture
Gary Oudersluys

Manufacturing
Drew Kalasky

LIBRARY OF CONGRESS CATALOG CARD NUMBER 84-649371

ISBN-13: 978-1-4144-0021-1
ISBN-10: 1-4144-0021-7
ISSN: 0749-064X

This title is also available as an e-book.
ISBN-13: 978-1-4144-3794-1, ISBN-10: 1-4144-3794-3
Contact your Thomson Gale sales representative for ordering information.

Printed in the United States of America
10 9 8 7 6 5 4 3 2 1

Contents

Preface

Provides Broad, Single-Source Coverage in the Entertainment Field

Contemporary Theatre, Film and Television (*CTFT*) is a biographical reference series designed to provide students, educators, researchers, librarians, and general readers with information on a wide range of entertainment figures. Unlike single-volume reference works that focus on a limited number of artists or on a specific segment of the entertainment field, *CTFT* is an ongoing publication that includes entries on individuals active in the theatre, film, and television industries. Before the publication of *CTFT*, information-seekers had no choice but to consult several different sources in order to locate the in-depth biographical and credit data that makes *CTFT*'s one-stop coverage the most comprehensive available about the lives and work of performing arts professionals.

Scope

CTFT covers not only performers, directors, writers, and producers, but also behind-the-scenes specialists such as designers, managers, choreographers, technicians, composers, executives, dancers, and critics from the United States, Canada, Great Britain, and the world. With 180 entries in *CTFT 81*, the series now provides biographies on approximately 23,087 people involved in all aspects of theatre, film, and television.

CTFT gives primary emphasis to people who are currently active. New entries are prepared on major stars as well as those who are just beginning to win acclaim for their work. *CTFT* also includes entries on personalities who have died but whose work commands lasting interest.

Compilation Methods

CTFT editors identify candidates for inclusion in the series by consulting biographical dictionaries, industry directories, entertainment annuals, trade and general interest periodicals, newspapers, and online databases. Additionally, the editors of *CTFT* maintain regular contact with industry advisors and professionals who routinely suggest new candidates for inclusion in the series. Entries are compiled from published biographical sources which are believed to be reliable, but have not been verified for this edition by the listee or their agents.

Revised Entries

To ensure *CTFT*'s timeliness and comprehensiveness, entries from previous volumes, as well as from Gale's *Who's Who in the Theatre*, are updated for individuals who have been active enough to require revision of their earlier biographies. Such individuals will merit revised entries as often as there is substantial new information to provide. Obituary notices for deceased entertainment personalities already listed in *CTFT* are also published.

Accessible Format Makes Data Easy to Locate

CTFT entries, modeled after those in Gale's highly regarded *Contemporary Authors* series, are written in a clear, readable style designed to help users focus quickly on specific facts. The following is a summary of the information found in *CTFT* sketches:

- *ENTRY HEADING:* the form of the name by which the listee is best known.

- *PERSONAL:* full or original name; dates and places of birth and death; family data; colleges attended, degrees earned, and professional training; political and religious affiliations when known; avocational interests.

- *ADDRESSES:* home, office, agent, publicist and/or manager addresses.

- *CAREER:* tagline indicating principal areas of entertainment work; resume of career positions and other vocational achievements; military service.

- *MEMBER:* memberships and offices held in professional, union, civic, and social organizations.

- *AWARDS, HONORS:* theatre, film, and television awards and nominations; literary and civic awards; honorary degrees.

- *CREDITS:* comprehensive title-by-title listings of theatre, film, and television appearance and work credits, including roles and production data as well as debut and genre information.

- *RECORDINGS:* album, single song, video, and taped reading releases; recording labels and dates when available.

- *WRITINGS:* title-by-title listing of plays, screenplays, scripts, and musical compositions along with production information; books, including autobiographies, and other publications.

- *ADAPTATIONS:* a list of films, plays, and other media which have been adapted from the listee's work.

- *SIDELIGHTS:* favorite roles; portions of agent-prepared biographies or personal statements from the listee when available.

- *OTHER SOURCES:* books, periodicals, and internet sites where interviews or feature stories can be found.

Access Thousands of Entries Using *CTFT*'s Cumulative Index

Each volume of *CTFT* contains a cumulative index to the entire series. As an added feature, this index also includes references to all seventeen editions of *Who's Who in the Theatre* and to the four-volume compilation *Who Was Who in the Theatre.*

Available in Electronic Format

Online. Recent volumes of *CTFT* are available online as part of the Gale Biographies (GALBIO) database accessible through LEXIS-NEXIS. For more information, contact LEXIS-NEXIS, P.O. Box 933, Dayton, OH 45401-0933; phone (937) 865-6800, toll-free: 800-543-6862.

Suggestions Are Welcome

Contemporary Theatre, Film and Television is intended to serve as a useful reference tool for a wide audience, so comments about any aspect of this work are encouraged. Suggestions of entertainment professionals to include in future volumes are also welcome. Send comments and suggestions to: The Editor, *Contemporary Theatre, Film and Television,* Thomson Gale, 27500 Drake Rd., Farmington Hills, MI 48331-3535; or feel free to call toll-free at 1-800-877-GALE.

Contemporary Theatre, Film
and Television

ANDERSON, Melissa Sue 1962–
(Melisa Sue Anderson, Melissa Anderson, Melissa Anderson–Sloan)

PERSONAL

Born September 26, 1962, in Berkeley, CA; daughter of Marion Anderson; married Michael Sloan (a writer and producer), March 17, 1990; children: Piper Kathleen, Griffin Henry. *Education:* Studied dance; attended public schools in Los Angeles.

Career: Actress. Appeared in advertisements.

Member: Screen Actors Guild.

Awards, Honors: Emmy Award nomination, outstanding lead actress in a drama series, 1978, and TP de Oro (Spain), best foreign actress, 1980, both for *Little House on the Prairie*; Daytime Emmy Award, outstanding individual achievement in children's programming, 1980, for "Which Mother Is Mine?," *ABC Afterschool Specials*; Young Artist Award nomination, best young motion picture actress, Young Artist Foundation, 1982, for *Happy Birthday to Me*; named female star of the year, ShoWest Convention, National Association of Theatre Owners, 1984, for *Chattanooga Choo Choo*; named of the one hundred greatest teen stars, VH1, 2006.

CREDITS

Television Appearances; Series:
Mary Amelia Ingalls (later Mary Amelia Ingalls Kendall), *Little House on the Prairie* (also known as *Little House: A New Beginning, Det lille hus paa prae-*

rien, Domek na prerii, Het Kleine huis op de prairie, Huset paa praerien, La casa de la pradera, La casa nella prateria, La casita de la pradera, La familia Ingalls, La petite maison dans la prairie, Lilla huset paa praerien, Pieni talo preerialla, To mikro spiti sto livadi, Uma casa na pradaria, and *Unsere kleine Farm*), NBC, 1974–81.
Yvette Marcel, *The Equalizer*, CBS, 1987–88.

Television Appearances; Miniseries:
(In archive footage) Herself, *The Ultimate Hollywood Blonde,* E! Entertainment Television, 2004.
First lady Megan Hollister, *10:5 Apocalypse* (also known as *10.5: Apocalipsis* and *10.5—Apokalypse*), NBC, 2006.
(In archive footage) Herself, *I Love the 70s: Volume 2,* VH1, 2006.
Herself (teen star number fifty–six), *100 Greatest Teen Stars,* VH1, 2006.

Television Appearances; Movies:
Mary Amelia Ingalls (later Mary Amelia Ingalls Kendall), *Little House on the Prairie: The Lord Is My Shepherd,* NBC, 1974.
Nancy Rizzi, *The Loneliest Runner,* NBC, 1976.
Dana Lee, *Survival of Dana* (also known as *On the Edge: Survival of Dana*), CBS, 1979.
Mary Amelia Ingalls (later Mary Amelia Ingalls Kendall), *Little House Years,* NBC, 1979.
Vivian Sotherland, *Midnight Offerings,* ABC, 1981.
Molly Rush, *An Innocent Love* (also known as *One Starry Night*), CBS, 1982.
(Uncredited) Mary Amelia Ingalls (later Mary Amelia Ingalls Kendall), *Little House: Look Back to Yesterday* (also known as *Unsere kleine Farm—Alberts Wille*), NBC, 1983.
Toby King, *First Affair,* CBS, 1983.
(Uncredited; archive footage) Mary Amelia Ingalls (later Mary Amelia Ingalls Kendall), *Little House: The Last Farewell* (also known as *Unsere kleine Farm—Das Ende von Walnut Grove*), NBC, 1984.

Noelle Drake, *Dark Mansions*, ABC, 1986.

(As Melissa Anderson) Colleen McCloud, *The Return of Sam McCloud*, CBS, 1989.

(As Melissa Anderson) Marie Shapiro, *Forbidden Nights*, 1990.

(As Melissa Anderson) Dr. Marilyn Blake, *Earthquake in New York*, Fox Family Channel, 1998.

Tanya Ferguson, *Thin Ice*, [Great Britain], 2000.

Voice of mother, *Marco Polo*, 2007.

Television Appearances; Specials:

NBC team member, *Battle of the Network Stars*, ABC, 1976.

Host, *Circus Lions, Tigers and Melissas Too*, NBC, 1977.

Kate, "Beat the Turtle Drum" (also known as "Story Time" and "Very Good Friends"), *ABC Afterschool Specials*, ABC, 1977.

Alexandria "Alex" Benton, "Which Mother Is Mine?" (also known as "My Other Mother"), *ABC Afterschool Specials*, ABC, 1979.

Where Have All the Children Gone, 1980.

The All–Star Salute to Mother's Day, NBC, 1981.

Host, *Sex Symbols: Past, Present and Future*, syndicated, 1987.

(As Melissa Anderson) Herself, *Circus of the Stars #14*, 1989.

Herself, *Michael Landon: Memories with Laughter and Love* (also known as *Michael Landon: Memorias, risas y gran amor*), c. 1992.

Herself, *The '70s: The Decade That Changed Television*, ABC, 2000.

Herself, *Sagas: Melissa Sue Anderson*, 2002.

(As Melissa Anderson) Herself, *Favorite Stars: Then & Now*, 2003.

(In archive footage) Mary Amelia Ingalls (later Mary Amelia Ingalls Kendall), *Como estan ustedes?*, Television Espanola (TVE, Spain), 2006.

Television Appearances; Episodic:

Girl, "Tabitha's First Day at School," *Bewitched*, ABC, 1972.

(Uncredited) Marshal's daughter, "The Enforcers," *Shaft*, CBS, 1973.

(As Melissa Anderson) Millicent, "Never Too Young," *The Brady Bunch*, ABC, 1973.

Herself, *Dinah!* (also known as *Dinah* and *Dinah and Friends*), syndicated, 1975.

Jennifer "Chubs" Smith, "Till Death Do Us Part, Maybe/Chubs/Locked Away," *The Love Boat*, ABC, 1978.

Cindy Geo, "Cindy/Play by Play/What's a Brother For?," *The Love Boat*, ABC, 1979.

Lisa, "The Overcharge," *A New Kind of Family*, ABC, 1979.

Herself, "Melissa Sue Anderson visita Espana," *625 lineas*, 1979.

(Uncredited) Herself, "Roller Disco: Part 2," *CHiPs* (also known as *Chips* and *CHiPs Patrol*), NBC, 1979.

Amy Marson, "Rogues to Riches/Stark Terror," *Fantasy Island*, ABC, 1980.

Cathy Cummings, "Tell Her She's Great/Matchmaker, Matchmaker Times Two/The Baby Alarm," *The Love Boat*, ABC, 1980.

Host, "Treasure Island," *Special Treat*, NBC, 1980.

Mary Beth, "Princess," *Insight*, syndicated, 1980.

Vista Ford, "The Matadors/Mrs. Jameson Comes Out/Love's Labors Found/Marry Me, Marry Me: Parts 1 & 2," *The Love Boat*, ABC, 1980.

Voices of Katherine "Kitty" Pryde and Spryte, "The Origin of Iceman," *Spider–Man and His Amazing Friends* (animated), NBC, 1982.

Cassie Ray, "Lifelines," *Hotel* (also known as *Arthur Hailey's "Hotel"*), ABC, 1984.

Elizabeth, "Minor Miracle," *Glitter*, ABC, 1984.

Eve Crystal, "Hooray for Homicide," *Murder, She Wrote*, CBS, 1984.

Voices of Katherine "Kitty" Pryde and Spryte, "The X–Men Adventure," *Spider–Man and His Amazing Friends* (animated), NBC, 1984.

Herself, *The Phil Donahue Show* (also known as *Donahue*), syndicated, 1984.

Anne Goldman, "Imperfect Union," *Hotel* (also known as *Arthur Hailey's "Hotel"*), ABC, 1985.

Laura Donovan, "VCR—A Very Careful Rape," *Alfred Hitchcock Presents* (also known as *Alfred Hitchcock esittaeae*, *Alfred Hitchcock presenta*, *Alfred Hitchcock presente*, and *Alfred Hitchcock zeigt*), USA Network, 1988.

(As Melissa Anderson) Julie Fenton, "Murder in Mind," *Alfred Hitchcock Presents* (also known as *Alfred Hitchcock esittaeae*, *Alfred Hitchcock presenta*, *Alfred Hitchcock presente*, and *Alfred Hitchcock zeigt*), USA Network, 1989.

Voice of Snowbird, "Repo Man," *X–Men* (animated; also known as *Insuperabili X–Men*), Fox, 1993.

Michelle, "Who Killed Alexander the Great?," *Burke's Law*, CBS, 1994.

Voice of Snowbird, "Phoenix Saga, Part 5: Child of Light," *X–Men* (animated; also known as *Insuperabili X–Men*), Fox, 1994.

Herself, "Brandon Lee," *The E! True Hollywood Story* (also known as *Brandon Lee: The E! True Hollywood Story* and *THS*), E! Entertainment Television, 1997.

(As Melissa Anderson–Sloan) Herself, "Michael Landon," *The E! True Hollywood Story* (also known as *Michael Landon: The E! True Hollywood Story* and *THS*), E! Entertainment Television, 1997.

(In archive footage) Herself, *Intimate Portrait: Melissa Gilbert*, Lifetime, 1998.

(As Melissa Anderson) Cheryl Darrin, "Always," *Partners* (also known as *Socios*), CBS, 1999.

(As Melissa Anderson) Cheryl Darrin, "A Beautiful Day," *Partners* (also known as *Socios*), CBS, 1999.

(As Melissa Anderson) Cheryl Darrin, "Never Say Never Again," *Partners* (also known as *Socios*), CBS, 1999.

Herself, "David Strickland," *The E! True Hollywood Story* (also known as *David Strickland: The E! True Hollywood Story* and *THS*), E! Entertainment Television, 2000.

Herself, "Scott Baio," *Celebrity Profile* (also known as *E! Celebrity Profile*), E! Entertainment Television, 2000.

Herself, "Melissa Gilbert," *Biography* (also known as *A&E Biography: Melissa Gilbert*), Arts and Entertainment, 2001.

Herself, *Intimate Portrait: Melissa Sue Anderson*, Lifetime, 2001.

(In archive footage) Student, *El informal*, 2001.

Herself, *Intimate Portrait: Young Hollywood*, Lifetime, c. 2002.

Herself, "Melissa Gilbert," *Biography for Kids*, Biography, 2004.

Herself, "Scream Queens," *The E! True Hollywood Story* (also known as *Scream Queens: The E! True Hollywood Story* and *THS*), E! Entertainment Television, 2004.

Herself, "1974: Melissa Gilbert," *Class of ...*, 2005.

(In archive footage) Mary Amelia Ingalls (later Mary Amelia Ingalls Kendall), *Corazon, corazon*, Television Espanola (TVE, Spain), 2006.

Herself, "Les producteurs de stars," *Nice People*, 2007.

Herself, *eTalk Daily* (also known as *eTalk* and *e-Talk Daily*), CTV (Canada), 2007.

(In archive footage) Mary Amelia Ingalls (later Mary Amelia Ingalls Kendall), *Today* (also known as *NBC News Today* and *The Today Show*), NBC, 2007.

Also appeared in other programs, including "Melissa Gilbert," an episode of *Celebrity Profile* (also known as *E! Celebrity Profile*), E! Entertainment Television.

Television Appearances; Pilots:

Mary Amelia Ingalls, *Little House on the Prairie* (also known as *Little House: A New Beginning*, *Det lille hus paa praerien*, *Domek na prerii*, *Het Kleine huis op de prairie*, *Huset paa praerien*, *La casa de la pradera*, *La casa nella prateria*, *La casita de la pradera*, *La familia Ingalls*, *La petite maison dans la prairie*, *Lilla huset paa praerien*, *Pieni talo preerialla*, *To mikro spiti sto livadi*, *Uma casa na pradaria*, and *Unsere kleine Farm*), NBC, 1974.

Lacey Stevens, *James at 15*, NBC, 1977.

Maureen Tyler, *Advice to the Lovelorn*, NBC, 1981.

That's TV, NBC, 1982.

Nikki Gatos, *Finder of Lost Loves* (also known as *Maxwell, Ltd.: Finder of Lost Loves Pilot*), ABC, 1984.

Television Work; Movies:

(As Melissa Anderson) Associate producer, *Where Pigeons Go to Die* (also known as *Where the Pigeons Go to Die* and *Der Letze Flug der Taube*), 1990.

Film Appearances:

A Different Approach (short film), 1978.

Skatetown, U.S.A. (Also known as *La fiebre del patin*), Columbia, 1979.

Virginia "Ginny" Wainwright, *Happy Birthday to Me* (also known as *Ab in die Ewigkeit*, *Compleanno di sangue*, *Cumpleanos mortal*, *Feliz cumpleanos para mi*, and *Onnellista syntymaepaeivaeae*), Columbia, 1981.

(In archive footage) Herself, *Hollywood's Children* (documentary), Janson Media, 1982.

Jennie, *Chattanooga Choo Choo*, April Fools Distribution, 1984.

(As Melisa Sue Anderson) Kukki, *Goma–2* (also known as *Killing Machine* and *La maquina de matar*), 1984.

Tommy Pratter's girl, *Marie* (also known as *Marie: A True Story*, *Es ... jugar con fuego*, *Maria—A verdade de uma mulher*, *Marie—Die Unbestechliche*, *Marie—Eine Mutter in Angst*, *Marie—Eine wahre Geschichte*, *Marien taistelu*, and *Una donna, una storia vera*), Metro–Goldwyn–Mayer/United Artists, 1985.

Laura Donovan on television, *The Suicide Club* (also known as *Clube do suicidio*, *Il club dei suicidi*, *Klub samobojcow*, *Tod oder Joker*, and *Vaarallinen leikki*), Angelika Films, 1988.

(As Melissa Anderson) Young nurse, *Far North* (also known as *A casa de Kate e um caso*, *Far North, estremo Nord*, *Norte lejano*, *Ordem de execucao*, and *Sukulaisrakkautta*), Alive Films, 1988.

Looking Your Best, 1989.

Manuel, le fils emprunte (also known as *Manuel* and *Manuel, karkulainen*), Claire Films, c. 1990.

(As Melissa Anderson) Dulcie Niles, *Dead Men Don't Die* (also known as *Un cadavru printre noi*), 1991.

Voice of snake, *Animated Stories from the Bible: Music Video—Volume 1* (animated), 1994.

American lady, *Killer Lady* (also known as *Dama mortal*), 1995.

Herself, *The Joy of Natural Childbirth* (documentary), Universal, 1997.

Herself, *Buckle Up* (short documentary), 1998.

(Uncredited; in archive footage) Herself, *Dickie Roberts: Former Child Star* (also known as *Dickie Roberts: (Former) Child Star*, *Dickie Roberts: Entinen lapsitaehti*, *Dickie Roberts: Ex–enfant star*, and *Dickie Roberts: Ex nino prodigio*), Paramount, 2003.

(In archive footage) Virginia "Ginny" Wainwright, *Going to Pieces: The Rise and Fall of the Slasher Film* (documentary), THINKFilm, 2006.

Stage Appearances:
To Grandmother's House We Go, Toronto, Ontario, Canada, 1992.

RECORDINGS

Videos:
(In archive footage) Mary Amelia Ingalls (later Mary Amelia Ingalls Kendall), *A Little House Conversation,* 2006.

Herself, *Exclusive Interview with Melissa Sue Anderson* (short), 2006.

OTHER SOURCES

Periodicals:
People Weekly, June 1, 1981, p. 93.

ANDERSON, Sarah Pia 1952–

PERSONAL

Born July 19, 1952, in St. Albans, Hertfordshire, England; daughter of Stewart Angus and Eldina Pia Anderson. *Education:* University of Wales, University College of Swansea, B.A. (with honors), 1973. *Avocational Interests:* Photography, tennis, swimming.

Addresses: *Agent*—Bradley Glenn, Kaplan Stahler Gumer Braun Agency, 8383 Wilshire Blvd., Suite 923, Beverly Hills, CA 90211. *Manager*—Andrea Simon, Andrea Simon Entertainment, 14011 Ventura Blvd., Suite 101S, Sherman Oaks, CA 91423.

Career: Director. Crucible Theatre, Sheffield, England, trainee director, 1975–76, director, 1978–81; BBC–TV, director, 1978–85; Royal Shakespeare Company, director of a small–scale tour, between 1979 and 1983; also worked as stage manager for Traverse Theatre, Edinburgh, Scotland, and for Royal Shakespeare Company. University of California, Davis, professor of dramatic arts; former teacher at Royal Academy of Dramatic Arts and Central School of Art and Design, London. Susan Smith Blackburn Award, London, judge, 1986.

Member: Directors Guild of Great Britain (member of council, 1985–88; vice chair, 1987–88), British Academy of Film and Television Arts, Directors Guild of America, Women in Film.

Awards, Honors: Samuel Beckett Award, 1983, for *A Woman Calling;* grant from Arts Council of Great Britain.

CREDITS

Stage Director:
These Men, Bush Theatre, London, 1981.
Waiting, Lyric Studio Theatre, London, 1982.
The Nest, Bush Theatre, 1986.
Rosmersholm, Cottesloe Theatre, National Theatre, London, 1987, then La Mama Experimental Theatre Club Annex, New York City, 1988.
Derek, Royal Shakespeare Company, London, 1987.
Old Year's Eve, Royal Shakespeare Company, Pit Theatre, London, 1987–88.
Carthaginians, Peacock Theatre, Dublin, Ireland, 1988, then Hampstead Theatre, London, 1989.
Mary and Lizzie, Royal Shakespeare Company, Pit Theatre, 1989.
Across Oka, Royal Shakespeare Company, Pit Theatre, 1989.
Mary Stuart, Folger Shakespeare Theatre, Washington, DC, 1989–90.
Hedda Gabler, Roundabout Theatre Company, Criterion Center Stage Right Theatre, New York City, 1994.

Director of *Ashes, Caucasian Chalk Circle, Hello and Goodbye,* and *What the Butler Saw,* all Crucible Theatre, Sheffield, England; *Blisters, The Estuary, First Blush, Gin Trap,* and *Last Resort,* all Bush Theatre, London; *Indigo* and *Lizzie,* both Royal Shakespeare Company, London; *Saint Joan,* Folger Shakespeare Theatre, Washington, DC; and *The Winter's Tale,* Shakespeare Festival, Santa Cruz, CA.

Television Work; Specials:
Creator, "Shaping Up," *BBC2 Playhouse,* BBC, 1980.
Director, "A Silly Little Habit," *BBC2 Playhouse,* BBC, 1982.
Director, "Wayne and Albert," *Play for Today,* BBC1, 1983.

Television Director; Series:
The Bill, Thames, between 1990 and 1993.

Television Director; Episodic:
"A Man Lay Dead," *Inspector Alleyn Mysteries* (also known as *Alleyn Mysteries, Inspector Alleyn, Mystery!,* and *Ngaio Marsh's "Alleyn Mysteries"*), broadcast in United States on *Masterpiece Theatre,* PBS, 1993.
"Burning Bridges," *Doctor Finlay,* broadcast on *Masterpiece Theatre,* PBS, 1994.

"Secrecy," *Doctor Finlay,* broadcast on *Masterpiece Theatre,* PBS, 1994.

"In Arcadia," *Doctor Finlay,* broadcast on *Masterpiece Theatre,* PBS, 1994.

"Shattered Silence," *Profiler,* NBC, 1996.

"Unsoiled Sovereignty," *Profiler,* NBC, 1997.

"Roman Catholic Holiday," *Nothing Sacred,* ABC, 1997.

"Do You See What I See?," *ER,* NBC, 1997.

"To Serve and Protect," *Profiler,* NBC, 1999.

"The Long Way Home," *Profiler,* NBC, 2000.

"The Face," *Secret Agent Man,* UPN, 2000.

"Drug Interactions," *Strong Medicine,* Lifetime, 2000.

"Surveillance," *The District,* CBS, 2000.

"Rory's Birthday Parties," *Gilmore Girls* (also known as *Gilmore Girls: Beginnings*), The WB, 2000.

"Out," *Dark Angel* (also known as *James Cameron's "Dark Angel"*), Fox, 2001.

"Tom Dooley," *Ally McBeal,* Fox, 2002.

"Just a Formality," *Ed,* NBC, 2003.

"The Shallow End," *Dead like Me,* Showtime, 2004.

"Always," *Dead like Me,* Showtime, 2004.

"Return of the Kane," *Veronica Mrs.* UPN, 2004.

"Save Me," *Grey's Anatomy,* ABC, 2005.

"The Sample Closet," *Huff,* Showtime, 2005.

"Versatile Toppings," *Veronica Mars,* UPN, 2006.

"Sweet Release," *Huff,* Showtime, 2006.

"So … What Brings You to Armageddon?," *Huff,* Showtime, 2006.

"Tapping the Squid," *Huff,* Showtime, 2006.

"Four Thanksgivings and a Funeral," *Ugly Betty,* ABC, 2006.

"Skobo and Alice Hooked Up," *Big Day,* ABC, 2006.

"What about Temptations …," *What about Brian,* ABC, 2007.

"The Writing on the Wall," *Big Love,* HBO, 2007.

Directed episodes of *The Division,* Lifetime, *Leaving L.A.,* and *Level 9,* UPN.

Television Director; Other:
A Woman Calling, 1983.
Pity in History, BBC, 1985.
Prime Suspect 4: Inner Circles (movie), PBS, 1995.
Plastic Man (miniseries), M–Net, 1999.
Women's Murder Club (pilot), ABC, 2007.

Also director of *Blisters, Gran, Stepping Out, Summers Awakening,* and *This Is History.*

Film Director:
The Concord Peace Council (documentary), British Council, 1981.

OTHER SOURCES

Electronic:
Sarah Pia Anderson Official Site, http://www.sarahpiaanderson.com, August 25, 2007.

ANDREWS, David 1952–

PERSONAL

Born in 1952 in Baton Rouge, LA. *Education:* Attended Louisiana State University.

Addresses: *Agent*—Abrams Artists Agency, 9200 Sunset Blvd., Suite 1130, Los Angeles, CA 90069. *Manager*—Kass and Stokes Management, 9229 Sunset Blvd., Suite 504, Los Angeles, CA 90069.

Career: Actor.

Member: Screen Actors Guild.

Awards, Honors: Annual CableACE Award nomination, best actor in a dramatic series, National Cable Television Association, 1989, for *Pulaski.*

CREDITS

Television Appearances; Series:
Larry Summers (Pulaski), *Pulaski* (also known as *Pulaski: The TV Detective*), 1987.
Jack Scarlett, *The Antagonists,* CBS, 1991.
Detective Bobby Mann, *Mann & Machine,* NBC, 1992.
William "Billy" Monroe, *The Monroes,* 1995.
Major General Gordon "Biff" Cresswell, *JAG,* CBS, 2004–2005.

Television Appearances; Movies:
Wimpy Hughes, *The Burning Bed,* NBC, 1984.
Dean Ellis, *Wild Horses,* CBS, 1985.
Midas Valley, ABC, 1985.
Wayne O'Kelley, *A Son's Promise* (also known as *Fire in the Heart, The O'Kelley Brothers,* and *The Terry O'Kelley Story*), ABC, 1990.
Lonnie, *Living a Lie,* 1991.
Paul Davis, *Deconstructing Sarah,* 1994.
Shame II: The Secret, 1995.
Sophie & the Moonhanger, 1996.
Steve Carson, *Our Son, the Matchmaker,* 1996.
Reese Braverton, *Bad Day on the Block* (also known as *The Fireman* and *Under Pressure*), Cinemax, 1997.
Cal Spangler, *Fifteen and Pregnant,* 1998.
Gme3, *The Rat Pack,* 1998.
Philip Renfrew, *The Color of Courage,* USA Network, 1999.

James Barlow, *Switched at Birth* (also known as *Mistaken Identity* and *Two Babies: Switched at Birth*), CBS, 1999.
William Sanders, *Navigating the Heart*, Lifetime, 2000.
John Hytner, *The Dead Will Tell*, CBS, 2004.

Television Appearances; Miniseries:
Ricky Dunlap (some sources cite Dunbar), *Blind Faith*, NBC, 1990.
Frank Borman, *From the Earth to the Moon*, HBO, 1998.
(Uncredited) General Taylor, *Band of Brothers*, HBO, 2001.

Television Appearances; Episodic:
(Uncredited) "One Eyed Jack," *Miami Vice*, 1984.
Bodie Chase, *Lime Street*, ABC, 1985.
Mr. Simmons, "The Princess and the Weiner King," *L.A. Law*, 1986.
Del Larkin, "A Dance on the Dark Side," *The Equalizer*, CBS, 1988.
Dale Stevens, "Race Traitors," *The Equalizer*, CBS, 1989.
Jack Crockett, "Jack of All Trades," *Miami Vice*, 1989.
Michael Beiden, "Chapter Two, Year Two," *Murder One*, ABC, 1996.
Michael Beiden, "Chapter Four, Year Two," *Murder One*, ABC, 1996.
Michael Beiden, "Chapter Five, Year Two," *Murder One*, ABC, 1996.
Frank Conroy, "Bookworm," *Promised Land* (also known as *Home of the Brave*), CBS, 1997.
Jay Crew, "How the Finch Stole Christmas," *Just Shoot Me*, NBC, 1998.
Jim Sullivan, "With God As My Witness," *Touched by an Angel*, CBS, 2000.
Gus Weiner, "The Unusual Suspects," *Dawson's Creek*, The WB, 2000.
Dr. Washington, "I Know Why the Caged Rhino Sings," *Going to California*, Showtime, 2001.
Michael Piper, "The Plan," *Six Feet Under*, HBO, 2002.
Bayless, "With Honor," *Crossing Jordan*, NBC, 2002.
Judge Wilbur Stucky, "Final Judgement," *The Practice*, ABC, 2003.
Judge Wilbur Stucky, "Victims' Rights," *The Practice*, ABC, 2003.
Officer Fromansky, "All for Our Country," *CSI: Crime Scene Investigation* (also known as *C.S.I.*, *CSI: Las Vegas*, and *Les experts*), CBS, 2003.
Captain Silva, "Coyote," *Dragnet* (also known as *L.A. Dragnet*), ABC, 2003.
Captain Silva, "Slice of Life," *Dragnet* (also known as *L.A. Dragnet*), ABC, 2003.
Captain Silva, "Killing Fields," *Dragnet* (also known as *L.A. Dragnet*), ABC, 2004.
Officer Fromansky, "Paper or Plastic?," *CSI: Crime Scene Investigation* (also known as *C.S.I.*, *CSI: Las Vegas*, and *Les experts*), CBS, 2004.

Lorian, "E2," *Enterprise* (also known as *Star Trek: Enterprise*), UPN, 2004.
Animal control officer, *Surface*, NBC, three episodes, 2005.
Lloyd Wilkes, "False–Hearted Judges," *Law & Order: Criminal Intent* (also known as *Law & Order: CI*), NBC, 2005.
Richard Bowman, "Double Jeopardy," *CSI: Miami*, CBS, 2006.
Se'tak, "Counterstrike," *Stargate SG–1* (also known as *La porte des etoiles*), Sci–Fi Channel, 2006.
Donald Baxter, Jr., "The Round File," *The Closer*, TNT, 2007.

Also appeared in an episode of *Any Day Now*, Lifetime.

Television Appearances; Pilots:
Saxby Hall, *12 Miles of Bad Road*, HBO, 2007.

Film Appearances:
Foreman, *A Nightmare on Elm Street*, 1984.
Dean Moriarty, *Kerouac* (also known as *Jack Kerouac's America* and *Kerouac, the Movie*), Daybreak, 1985.
Sam Treadwell, *Cherry 2000*, Orion, 1988.
John Hall, *Graveyard Shift* (also known as *Stephen King's "Graveyard Shift"*), Paramount, 1990.
Intellectual, *The Pitch*, 1993.
James Earp, *Wyatt Earp*, Warner Bros., 1994.
The Waiter, 1994.
Pete Conrad, *Apollo 13* (also released as *Apollo 13: The IMAX Experience*), Universal, 1995.
Nathan, *The Whiskey Heir*, 1995.
Thomas at Remaining Men Together, *Fight Club*, Twentieth Century–Fox, 1999.
FBI Agent Clint Pearsall, *Hannibal*, Metro–Goldwyn–Mayer, 2001.
Brian McCauley, *Town Diary*, 2002.
Mr. Kelly, *A Walk to Remember*, Warner Bros., 2002.
James Kline, *A Touch of Fate*, PorchLight Entertainment, 2003.
Robert Brewster, *Terminator 3: Rise of the Machines* (also known as *T3* and *Terminator 3—Rebellion der maschinen*), Warner Bros., 2003.
Lieutenant Hogenbeck, *Two Soldiers* (short film), 2003, Westlake Entertainment Group, 2007.
Richard Finney, *The Last Summer*, D Productions/Film Artists Network/Michael Finney Productions, 2004.
Jerry, *The Rain Makers*, Image Entertainment, 2005.
Ray, *Stealth*, Columbia, 2005.

Stage Appearances:
(Off–Broadway debut) Eddie, *Fool for Love*, Circle Repertory Company, Douglas Fairbanks Theatre, c. 1985.

Stephen "Red" Ryder, *The Heart Outright,* Theatre for the New City, New York City, 1989.

Also appeared in *Friends in High Places* and *Safe Sex.*

RECORDINGS

Video Games:
Voice of Robert Brewster, *Terminator 3: Rise of the Machines,* Atari, 2003.
Voice of Robert Brewster, *Terminator 3: Redemption,* Atari, 2004.

ANDREWS, Peter
See SODERBERGH, Steven

ARCADE, Penny
See WORONOV, Mary

ARCHER, Lee
See ELLISON, Harlan

B

B, Melanie
  See BROWN, Melanie

BAY, Frances 1918–

PERSONAL

Born January 1, 1918, in Winnipeg, Manitoba, Canada; married Charles Bay (died, May, 2002).

Addresses: *Agent*—The McCabe Group, 8285 Sunset Blvd., Los Angeles, CA 90046.

Career: Actress. Appeared in commercials for Kodak Advantix cameras, 1997, and Little Debbie snacks, 1998.

Awards, Honors: Gemini Award, best guest actress, Academy of Canadian Cinema and Television, 1996, for *Road to Avonlea*; DramaLogue award, for *Uncommon Women and Others* and *Right of Way*; Los Angeles Drama Critics Circle Award nomination, for *The Man Who Came to Dinner*.

CREDITS

Stage Appearances:
Appeared in *Number Our Days; Uncommon Women and Others; Right of Way; The Man Who Came to Dinner; Sarcophagus; The Pleasure of His Company; The Caucasian Chalk Circle; Grease; Finnegans Wake; Genius.*

Film Appearances:
Mrs. Russel, *Foul Play,* Paramount, 1978.

Mrs. DeLillo, *Head Over Heels* (also known as *Chilly Scenes of Winter*), United Artists, 1979.
Librarian, *The Attic,* Hallmark Video, 1979.
Female patient, *Buddy Buddy,* Metro–Goldwyn–Mayer, 1981.
Mrs. Lewenowski, *Honky Tonk Freeway,* Universal, 1981.
Dream On!, 1981.
Old woman, *Double Exposure* (also known as *Model Killer*), Crown International Pictures, 1982.
Birdie Fallmouth, *Private School* (also known as *Private School for Girls*), Universal, 1983.
Lady with dog, *The Karate Kid,* Columbia, 1984.
Betty Gritz, *Movers and Shakers,* Metro–Goldwyn–Mayer, 1985.
Aunt Barbara, *Blue Velvet,* Metro–Goldwyn–Mayer, 1986.
Bertril, *Nomads,* Paramount Home Video, 1986.
Medium Rare, 1987.
Mrs. Haynes, *Big Top Pee–Wee,* Paramount, 1988.
Mother Superior, *Twins,* Argentina Video Home, 1988.
Mrs. Milo, *The Karate Kid, Part III,* Columbia, 1989.
Evelyn Metcalf, *Arachnophobia,* Buena Vista, 1990.
Madam, *Wild at Heart* (also known as *David Lynch's "Wild at Heart"*), Samuel Goldwyn, 1990.
Arizona motel clerk, *The Grifters,* Miramax, 1990.
Esmeralda, *The Pit and the Pendulum* (also known as *The Inquisitor*), JGM Entertainment, 1990.
Mrs. Menges, *Critters 3* (also known as *Critters 3: You Are What They Eat*), New Line Home Video, 1991.
Mrs. Tremond, *Twin Peaks: Fire Walk with Me* (also known as *Twin Peaks*), New Line Cinema, 1992.
Elderly neighbor, *Single White Female,* Columbia, 1992.
Grandma, *Inside Monkey Zetterland* (also known as *Monkey Zetterland*), IRS Media, 1992.
Aunt Sylvia, *The Neighbor,* Allegro Films, 1993.
Mrs. Rosemont, *The Paper Boy* (also known as *The Paperboy*), Allegro Films, 1994.
Mrs. Pickman, *In the Mouth of Madness* (also known as *John Carpenter's "In the Mouth of Madness"*), New Line Cinema, 1995.

Grandma Gilmore, *Happy Gilmore*, Universal, 1996.

Elisabeth Kronner, *Never Too Late* (also known as *Jamais trop tard*), Allegro Distribution, 1997.

Mitzi, *Mitzi & Joe*, 1997.

Midge, *Changing Habits*, A–Pix Entertainment, 1997.

Edith Proxmire, *Krippendorf's Tribe*, Buena Vista, 1998.

Raspy, *Sparkler*, Strand Releasing, 1998.

Old woman, *Goodbye Lover*, Warner Bros., 1999.

Storyteller, *The Storyteller*, 1999.

Thelma Burr, *Inspector Gadget*, 1999.

Rosa, *A Day in the Life* (also known as *Les lilas d'automne*), 2000.

Mrs. Steiner, *Stranger Than Fiction*, 2000.

Mrs. Sloan, *The Operator*, Black Wolf Productions, 2000.

Mrs. Dartmutter, *Finder's Fee*, 2000.

Harry's wife, *Cookies for Harry* (short), 2001.

Dottie, *The Wedding Planner* (also known as *Wedding Planner—verliebt, verlobt, verplant*), Columbia, 2001.

Mrs. Darmsetter, *Finder's Fee*, Lions Gate Films, 2001.

Grandma Julia Sposato, *Kiss the Bride*, Metro–Goldwyn–Mayer, 2002.

Wise Old Woman, *The Movie Hero* (also known as *Frame of Mind*), 2003.

Anna Freud, *A Freudian Image* (short), 2003.

Grandma Shallot, *In the Land of Milk and Money*, 2004.

Vivian Barry, *The Red Scarf* (short), 2005.

Fortune teller, *Edmond*, First Independent Pictures, 2005.

Nanna, *Ring Around the Rosie* (also known as *Fear Itself: Dark Memories*), Sony Pictures Home Entertainment, 2006.

Rosie Mcintyre, *Bare Knuckles*, 2008.

Television Appearances; Series:

Gideon Oliver, ABC, 1989.

Mrs. Fitch, *The Hughleys*, 1998–2000.

Television Appearances; Miniseries:

Myra Hill, *Murder in Texas*, 1981.

Annie Pyle, *By Way of the Stars* (also known as *Der lange weg des Lukas B.*), Disney Channel, 1992.

Television Appearances; Movies:

Mrs. Quincy, *Topper*, 1979.

Madame Zarona, *The Big Hex of Little Lulu*, 1981.

Mabel Simpson, *Callie & Son* (also known as *Callie and Son* and *Rags to Riches*), CBS, 1981.

Old woman, *Second Sight: A Love Story*, CBS, 1984.

Herbina Plum, *The President of Love*, 1984.

Lydia, *Amos*, CBS, 1985.

The Eagle and the Bear, 1985.

Convicted: A Mother's Story, 1987.

Mary, *Police Story: Monster Manor*, ABC, 1988.

Iva Ruth McKinney, *Grave Secrets: The Legacy of Hilltop Drive* (also known as *Grave Secrets*), CBS, 1992.

Martha Craddock, *Forever Love*, CBS, 1998.

Mrs. Lewis, *The Simple Life of Noah Dearborn*, CBS, 1999.

Maggie Winchester, *Oh, Baby* (also known as *Bratty Babies* and *Paroles de bebes*), 2001.

Older woman, *Annie's Point*, Hallmark Channel, 2005.

Also appeared in *Where Are My Children; LBJ.*

Television Appearances; Specials:

Mrs. Hamilton, *Christmastime with Mister Rogers*, 1977.

Madame Zarona, "The Big Hex of Little Lulu," *ABC Weekend Specials*, ABC, 1981.

Mrs. Timmins, *Wings*, PBS, 1983.

Elder Rosalie, *Rossini's Ghost*, HBO, 1996.

Television Appearances; Episodic:

Flower vendor, "With This Gun, I Thee Wed," *Hart to Hart*, 1979.

Cleaning lady, "What Murder?," *Hart to Hart*, 1981.

Mrs. Wilson, "My Hero," *The Jeffersons*, CBS, 1981.

"Hurricane," *Flamingo Road*, 1981.

"Bad Chemistry," *Flamingo Road*, 1981.

Aunt Hortense, "The Return of Hughie Hogg," *The Dukes of Hazzard*, CBS, 1981.

Title role, "Grandma Nussbaum," *Happy Days*, ABC, 1982.

Grandma Nussbaum, "Going Steady," *Happy Days*, ABC, 1982.

Alma Hubbard, "Eighty–Eight Keys to Happiness," *Father Murphy*, 1982.

Mother Trust, "Scene Steelers," *Remington Steele*, NBC, 1983.

"Charleston: The Spenders," *Lottery!*, 1983.

Grandmother, "Little Red Riding Hood," *Faerie Tale Theatre* (also known as *Shelley Duvall's "Faerie Tale Theatre"*), 1983.

Grandma Nussbaum, "Passages: Part 2," *Happy Days*, ABC, 1984.

Mrs. Menlo, "Keaton and Son," *Family Ties*, NBC, 1984.

Mrs. Gordon, "A Cold Night in Chicago," *E/R*, 1984.

Grandma George, "Who's Afraid of the Big Bad Wolf?," *Fame*, NBC, 1985.

Edna Kiss, "Violation," *Cagney & Lacey*, 1985.

Mrs. Santa Claus, "Santa '85," *Amazing Stories* (also known as *Steven Spielberg's "Amazing Stories"*), 1985.

Mrs. McRae, *Santa Barbara*, NBC, 1985.

Mrs. Enid Brubaker, "Take My Shirt … Please?" *Cheers*, NBC, 1986.

Mrs. Greene, "Taps for Officer Remy," *T. J. Hooker*, ABC, 1986.

Elizabeth Mies, "Larry of Arabia," *Hill Street Blues*, NBC, 1986.

Agnes Rich, "The Case of Don Diablo," *Simon & Simon,* 1986.

Librarian, "The Play's the Thing," *Riptide,* 1986.

"Requiem for Billy," *Mike Hammer* (also known as *Mickey Spillane's "Mike Hammer"* and *The New Mike Hammer*), CBS, 1986.

Sarah, "Grey Belts," *Sidekicks,* 1986.

Widow Kelsey, *The Cavanaughs,* 1986.

Mrs. Renninger, "Ewe Can't Go Home Again," *St. Else-where,* 1987.

Mrs. Zimmer, "Ike and Son," *The Oldest Rookie,* 1987.

"Vigilante," *Houston Knights,* 1988.

Miss Emma Parsons, "The Bogota Million," *Hunter,* 1988.

Claire, "The Days and Nights of Sophia Petrillo," *The Golden Girls,* CBS, 1988.

Becky, "Sudden Storm," *Simon & Simon,* 1988.

Mrs. Henderson, "Don't Worry Be Pregnant," *Newhart,* 1989.

Witch, "Rudy, You're Not Yourself Today," *Tales from the Crypt,* 1990.

Mrs. Tremond, "Coma," *Twin Peaks,* ABC, 1990.

"The Christmas Mysteries," *Father Dowling Mysteries* (also known as *Father Dowling Investigates*), 1990.

Mrs. Laskey, "Fatal Obsession: Parts 1 & 2," *Hunter,* NBC, 1991.

Eleanor, "Arthur," *Life Goes On,* ABC, 1991.

Rose Hayes, "The Defense," *Matlock,* NBC, 1991.

Samantha Bergstrom, "The Trial: Parts 1 & 2," *Matlock,* NBC, 1991.

Celia Lidner, "A Man's Best Friend," *Pacific Station,* 1991.

Miss Suzette, *Down the Shore,* 1991.

Mildred "Millie" Reynolds, "Moments to Live—May 4, 1985," *Quantum Leap,* NBC, 1992.

Mary DeBreeze, "Silence of the Lambskins," *L.A. Law,* NBC, 1992.

Sarah, "Love Letters," *Life Goes On,* ABC, 1992.

Candy, "Savor the Veal: Parts 2 & 3," *Who's the Boss?,* 1992.

"The Pig in the Python," *Middle Ages,* 1992.

Sylvia, "Charley for President," *Empty Nest,* 1992.

Agnes, "The Fracas in Vegas," *Empty Nest,* 1993.

Gertrude, *The Ben Stiller Show,* Fox, 1993.

Patricia Peters, "Pride and Prejudice," *Street Legal,* CBC, 1993.

Aunt Francine, "Alex, Then and N.O.W.," *The Five Mrs. Buchanans,* CBS, 1994.

Dorothy, "Excelsius Dei," *The X–Files,* Fox, 1994.

Daisy, "Lost Weekend," *Dave's World,* 1994.

The Crew, Fox, 1995.

Granny, "Snow Orchid," *The Marshal,* ABC, 1995.

Bella, "Sweet Denial," *Platypus Man,* UPN, 1995.

Ardith Cannon, "Off Broadway: Parts 1 & 2," *The Com-mish,* ABC, 1995.

Sarah McCoy, "Home Care," *Murder, She Wrote,* CBS, 1995.

Mrs. Henderson, "The Sugar Shack," *The Crew* (also known as *Cabin Pressure*), 1995.

Kate Downey, "Injustice for All," *Courthouse,* 1995.

Winnifred Ward, "After the Ball Is Over," *Road to Avon-lea* (also known as *Tales from Avonlea*), Disney Channel and CBC, 1996.

Elderly woman, "The Rye," *Seinfeld,* 1996.

Mabel Choate, "The Cadillac," *Seinfeld,* 1996.

Aunt Charlotte, "The Boxer Rebellion," *Life with Roger,* The WB, 1997.

Mrs. Davis, "Three of a Con," *Players,* NBC, 1997.

Mrs. Tidgely, "What a Card," *Suddenly Susan,* NBC, 1997.

Elderly Swiss jeweler, "Murder in the Air," *Diagnosis: Murder,* CBS, 1997.

Mrs. Elliot, *Social Studies,* 1997.

Opal, "Friends," *Clueless,* ABC, 1998.

Mabel Choate, "The Finale: Part 1," *Seinfeld,* 1998.

Miss Wilson, "The Art of War," *C–16: FBI,* ABC, 1998.

Elizabeth John, "Chelsea's Ex," *Style and Substance,* CBS, 1998.

Mildred Grayson, "The Gift," *Beyond Belief: Fact or Fic-tion* (also known as *Beyond Belief*), 1998.

Mrs. Fitch, *The Hughleys,* ABC, 1998.

Viola McKnight, "A Nice Home in the Country," *Da Vin-ci's Inquest,* CBC, 1999.

Georgia, "Witch Hunt," *ER,* NBC, 2001.

Evil old lady, *Passions,* NBC, 2001.

Laurie Evans, "Awards Bob," *Bob Patterson,* ABC, 2001.

Old Phoebe, "The Three Faces of Phoebe," *Charmed,* The WB, 2002.

"Make Over," *My Wife and Kids,* ABC, 2002.

Joan Hart, "This Baby's Gonna Fly," *Presidio Med,* ABC, 2002.

Cathy, "Debt It Be," *Hannah Montana,* Disney Channel, 2006.

Also appeared in *Touched by an Angel; Hill Street Blues.*

RECORDINGS

Music Videos:

Appeared in Jimmy Fallon's "Idiot Boyfriend."

BECK, John 1943–

PERSONAL

Born January 28, 1943, in Chicago, IL; married Tina Shillibeer, April 24, 1971; children: three.

Career: Actor.

CREDITS

Television Appearances; Series:

Sam Wilson, *Days of Our Lives* (also known as *Days* and *DOOL*), 1966.

Sam Curtis, *Flamingo Road,* NBC, 1981–82.
Mark Graison, *Dallas,* CBS, 1983–84, 1985–86.
Judge David Raymond, *Santa Barbara,* NBC, 1991–92.
Bruce, *Passions,* NBC, 2001–2003.

Television Appearances; Movies:
Billy Reed, *The Silent Gun,* ABC, 1969.
Gene Casey, *The Law,* NBC, 1974.
Nourish the Beast, 1974.
John Thornton, *The Call of the Wild,* NBC, 1976.
Neil Perry, *The Time Machine,* NBC, 1978.
Buzz Gregory, *Gridlock* (also known as *The Great American Traffic Jam*), NBC, 1980.
Dorian Blake, *Peyton Place: The Next Generation,* NBC, 1985.
Doug Vickers, *Perry Mason: The Case of the Lady in the Lake,* NBC, 1988.
Captain Edward Connors, *Fire and Rain,* USA Network, 1989.
Detective Les Zoeller, *Honor Thy Father and Mother: The True Story of the Menendez Murders* (also known as *Honor Thy Father & Mother: The Menendez Killings*), Fox, 1994.
Paul Cox, *Matlock: The Idol,* ABC, 1994.
CIA director, *Suspect Device* (also known as *Roger Corman Presents "Suspect Device"*), Showtime, 1995.
Jeremy, *Hart to Hart: Secrets of the Hart,* NBC, 1995.
Captain Strickland, *Black Scorpion,* Sci–Fi Channel, 1995.
Rebel general, *Dark Planet,* Sci–Fi Channel, 1997.
Dale Tucker, *Steel Chariots,* Fox, 1997.
President Fallbrook, *The Alternate* (also known as *Agent of Death*), Cinemax, 2000.
Simpkins, *Project Viper,* Sci–Fi Channel, 2002.

Also appeared in *Time Express.*

Television Appearances; Miniseries:
George Greg, *Attack on Terror: The FBI vs. the Ku Klux Klan,* CBS, 1975.
Peter Flodenhale, *Wheels* (also known as *Arthur Hailey's "Wheels"*), NBC, 1978.
Samson, *Greatest Heroes of the Bible,* 1978.
Robert Philips, *Trade Winds,* NBC, 1993.

Television Appearances; Pilots:
Micah Brucker, *Lock, Stock and Barrel,* NBC, 1971.
Luke, *Sidekicks,* CBS, 1974.
Colonel Frank "Buckshot" O'Connor, *Buffalo Soldiers,* NBC, 1979.
Sam Curtis, *Flamingo Road,* NBC, 1980.
Partners in Crime (also known as *50/50*), 1984.
Dan Gatlin, *Crazy Dan,* NBC, 1986.
Time Well Spent, ABC, 1995.

Television Appearances; Specials:
NBC team member, *Battle of the Network Stars IX,* ABC, 1980.

CBS team member, *Battle of the Network Stars XIV,* ABC, 1983.

Television Appearances; Episodic:
Sergeant, "Russian Roulette," *I Dream of Jeannie,* 1965.
Noogy Winkler, "The Ten Letterman," *Hank,* 1966.
Bill, "A Seat by the Window," *The Mod Squad,* 1969.
Boyes, "Color Her Missing," *Mannix,* CBS, 1969.
Harvey George Windsor, "Boomerang," *The F.B.I.,* 1969.
"Love and the Roommate," *Love, American Style,* ABC, 1969.
Walt Nagel, "The Medal," *Bonanza* (also known as *Ponderosa*), NBC, 1969.
Chad Lancer, "Chad," *Lancer,* CBS, 1970.
Chad Lancer, "Dream of Falcons," *Lancer,* CBS, 1970.
Albert Vail, "Kiowa," *Gunsmoke* (also known as *Gun Law* and *Marshal Dillon*), CBS, 1970.
Luke, "What Are Pardners For?," *Bonanza* (also known as *Ponderosa*), NBC, 1970.
Steve Phipps, "The Assassin," *Dan August,* 1971.
John Hecker, "The Missile," *Mission: Impossible,* 1971.
Moody Fowler, "The Tycoon," *Gunsmoke* (also known as *Gun Law* and *Marshal Dillon*), CBS, 1971.
Mark Bradbury, "The Bradbury War," *The Young Lawyers,* 1971.
Ketcham, "The Siege," *Nichols* (also known as *James Garner* and *James Garner as Nichols*), NBC, 1971.
Pilot, "Wings of an Angel," *Nichols* (also known as *James Garner* and *James Garner as Nichols*), NBC, 1972.
Ketcham, "Bertha," *Nichols* (also known as *James Garner* and *James Garner as Nichols*), NBC, 1972.
Walter Stark, "Nightmare in Blue," *Hawaii Five–0* (also known as *McGarrett*), CBS, 1974.
Mitch Hansen, "The Busters," *Gunsmoke* (also known as *Gun Law* and *Marshal Dillon*), CBS, 1975.
Clay Wesley, "The Scavengers," *How the West Was Won,* 1979.
Roy Culper, "Rodeo/Cop," *Time Express,* 1979.
Jack, "A Glowing Future," *Tales of the Unexpected* (also known as *Roald Dahl's "Tales of the Unexpected"*), 1980.
Dandy Randy Haines, "Killing Isn't Everything," *Matt Houston,* 1982.
"Candy Kisses/Operation Breakout," *Fantasy Island,* 1983.
Lieutenant Frank Logan, "Old Friends," *For Love and Honor,* 1983.
Ray Powell, "Portraits," *Finder of Lost Loves,* 1984.
Louis Upton, "Golden Opportunity," *Cover Up,* 1984.
Web McCord, "Sudden Death," *Murder, She Wrote,* CBS, 1985.
Peter Brackin, "Burn Out," *Scarecrow and Mrs. King,* CBS, 1985.
Tom Sherman, "Sleeping Dogs," *Hotel* (also known as *Arthur Hailey's "Hotel"*), ABC, 1985.
Brad Bingham, "The Seduction," *Matlock,* NBC, 1986.

Neil Jordan, "The Castro Connection," *Hunter,* NBC, 1986.

Carter Welles, "Shadow Play," *Hotel* (also known as *Arthur Hailey's "Hotel"*), ABC, 1986.

Edward T. Durant, "Limbo," *Magnum, P.I.,* CBS, 1987.

Major Alexander McAndrews, "The Wall," *The Twilight Zone,* 1988.

Matthew Grady, "Hard Choices," *Paradise* (also known as *Guns of Paradise*), CBS, 1989.

Matthew Grady, "Squaring Off," *Paradise* (also known as *Guns of Paradise*), CBS, 1989.

"Dangerous Cargo," *Paradise* (also known as *Guns of Paradise*), CBS, 1990.

Rupert Hill, "Based on a True Story," *Midnight Caller,* NBC, 1990.

Michael Hayworth, "Blind Ambition," *Hunter,* 1990.

Ben Olston, "Thursday's Child," *Murder, She Wrote,* CBS, 1991.

"Shrink," *Dark Justice,* 1992.

Roger Perry, "Wheel Man," *Renegade,* 1993.

Detective Eugene Vickers, "Vanishing Act: Parts 1 & 2," *Diagnosis Murder,* CBS, 1993.

Buzz Buchannon, "Coronado Del Soul: Parts 1 & 2," *Baywatch,* 1994.

"Gettysburg Change of Address," *Thunder in Paradise,* 1994.

Boone, "Tribunal," *Star Trek: Deep Space Nine* (also known as *Deep Space Nine, DS9,* and *Star Trek: DS9*), 1994.

Lyle Edwards, "Really Big Problems," *Models Inc.,* Fox, 1995.

Captain Meyers, "Trust," *Touched by an Angel,* CBS, 1995.

Carnie Matthews, *Extreme,* ABC, 1995.

Dr. Everett Carmichael, "Family Affairs," *Silk Stalkings,* USA Network, 1995.

Voice of Frank Castle (The Punisher), "Neogenic Nightmare Chapter 7: Enter the Punisher," *Spider-Man* (animated), 1996.

Voice of Frank Castle (The Punisher), "Neogenic Nightmare Chapter 8: Duel of the Hunters," *Spider-Man* (animated), 1996.

Voice of Frank Castle (The Punisher), "Partners in Danger Chapter 8: The Return of the Green Goblin," *Spider-Man* (animated), 1996.

Sergeant Lou Ross, "The Brotherhood," *Walker, Texas Ranger* (also known as *Walker*), CBS, 1996.

Max Elson, "Rainbow's End," *Walker, Texas Ranger* (also known as *Walker*), CBS, 1997.

Commander Keever, "Tight Spot," *Soldier of Fortune, Inc.* (also known as *SOF, Inc.* and *S.O.F. Special Ops Force*), 1998.

Al Craven, "Old Gold," *Air America,* syndicated, 1999.

Jake Foley, "Showdown at Casa Diablo: Part 1," *Walker, Texas Ranger* (also known as *Walker*), CBS, 2000.

Martin Deveaux, "Deathfist 5: Major Crimes Unit," *Martial Law,* CBS, 2000.

Mason Fawkes/Forrester Purdue, "Father Figure," *The Invisible Man* (also known as *I-Man*), Sci-Fi Channel, 2001.

Ted Granger, "Dead Heat," *Hunter,* NBC, 2003.

According to some sources, also appeared in an episode of *Arli$$,* HBO, and in *What Really Happened to the Class of '65?,* NBC, c. 1977.

Film Appearances:

Skinny, *Cyborg 2087* (also known as *Man from Tomorrow*), Features, 1966.

(Uncredited) Cowboy, *A Good Time with a Bad Girl* (also known as *A Good Time, a Bad Girl*), 1967.

Jake, *Three in the Attic,* American International Pictures, 1968.

Jason Bronson, *Lawman,* United Artists, 1971.

Sergeant Lulash, *Mrs. Pollifax—Spy,* United Artists, 1971.

Pov, *Paperback Hero* (also known as *Last of the Big Guns* and *Le coq du village*), Rumson, 1973.

John W. Poe, *Pat Garrett & Billy the Kid,* Metro-Goldwyn-Mayer, 1973.

Erno Windt, *Sleeper,* United Artists, 1973.

Lee, *Nightmare Honeymoon* (also known as *Deadly Honeymoon*), Metro-Goldwyn-Mayer, 1973.

The Bat People (also known as *It Lives by Night* and *It's Alive*), 1974.

Reverend Philip Norman, *Only God Knows,* Canart/Queensbury, 1974.

Moonpie, *Rollerball,* United Artists, 1975.

Ben, *Sky Riders,* Twentieth Century-Fox, 1976.

Shoulders O'Brien, *The Big Bus,* Paramount, 1976.

Larry Douglas, *The Other Side of Midnight,* Twentieth Century-Fox, 1977.

Bill Templeton, *Audrey Rose,* United Artists, 1977.

Alex Burton, *Deadly Illusion* (also known as *I Love You to Death* and *Love You to Death*), Cinetel Films, 1987.

Rudy, *In the Cold of the Night,* 1989.

Sheriff Kyle Shipp, *A Climate for Killing* (also known as *A Row of Crows*), 1991.

Joe Dolan, *Last Time Out,* 1994.

Paul Shuler, *A Place to Grow,* 1995.

Chief Morris Reed, *Black Day Blue Night,* 1995.

President Fallbrook, *The Alternate* (also known as *Agent of Death*), Replacement Productions, Inc., 1999.

Anderson, *Militia,* Cinetel Films, 2000.

Dr. Maurice Hunter, *Crash Point Zero* (also known as *Extreme Limits* and *Final Crash*), 2000.

(Uncredited) General Peterson, *Chain of Command,* 2000.

Deputy Director Anderson, *Militia,* 2000.

O'Rourke, *Timecop: The Berlin Decision* (also known as *Timecop 2*), Universal, 2003.

General McClaren, *Crash Landing,* Cinetel Films, 2005.

Stage Appearances:

The Collected Works of Billy the Kid, Center Theatre Group, Mark Taper Forum, Los Angeles, 1973.

Also performed in regional theatre productions.

RECORDINGS

Videos:
Himself, *Return to the Arena: The Making of "Rollerball,"* Metro–Goldwyn–Mayer/United Artists Home Entertainment, 2000.

OTHER SOURCES

Periodicals:
Cult Times, October, 1998, p. 11.

BELDONE, Phil "Cheech"
   See ELLISON, Harlan

BERESFORD, Bruce 1940–

PERSONAL

Born August 16, 1940, in Sydney, Australia; son of Leslie (in sales) and Lona (maiden name, Warr) Beresford; married Rhoisin Harrison (a graphic designer), 1965 (marriage ended); married Virginia Patricia Mary Duigan (a filmmaker and screenwriter), 1985; children: (first marriage) Benjamin, Cordelia, Adam; (second marriage) Trilby. *Education:* Sydney University, B.A., philosophy, 1962. *Avocational Interests:* Opera, skiing, Australian football, tennis, surfing.

Addresses: *Agent*—The Gersh Agency, 232 North Canon Dr., Beverly Hills, CA 90210; Steve Kenis and Company, 72 Dean St., London W1D 3SG United Kingdom.

Career: Director, screenwriter, and producer. Australian Broadcasting Commission, Sydney, film trainee, 1957–59; worked in advertising in Australia, c. early 1960s; teacher, London, England, c. 1962–c. 1964; East Nigerian Film Unit, film editor, 1964–67; British Film Institute Production Board, administrator, 1967–71; Arts Council of Great Britain, film advisor, 1967–70; HISK Productions, Los Angeles, CA, director of commercials, 1989. Also worked as a factory worker and cameraman.

Member: Directors Guild of America.

Awards, Honors: Australian Film Institute Award, best director, Golden Berlin Bear nomination, Berlin International Film Festival, 1977, both for *Don's Party;* Golden Palm nomination, Cannes Film Festival, Australian Film Institute Awards, best director and best screenplay—original or adapted (with Jonathan Hardy and David Stevens), 1980, Academy Award nomination (with Hardy and Stevens), best screenplay based on material from another medium, 1981, all for *"Breaker" Morant;* Australian Film Institute Award nomination, best director, 1981, for *The Club;* Golden Palm nomination, Cannes Film Festival, 1983, Academy Award nomination, best director, Golden Globe nomination, best director—motion picture, Directors Guild of America Award nomination, outstanding directorial achievement in motion pictures, 1984, all for *Tender Mercies;* Australian Film Institute Award (with Rhoisin Beresford), best screenplay—adapted, Australian Film Institute Award nomination, best director, and Golden Palm nomination, Cannes Film Festival, 1986, all for *The Fringe Dwellers;* Australian Neville Wran Award, for excellence in the film industry, 1986; Golden Palm nomination (with others), Cannes Film Festival, 1987, for *Aria;* Golden Berlin Bear nomination, Berlin International Film Festival, 1990, and Film Award nominations, best direction and best film (with Richard D. Zanuck and Lili Fini Zanuck), British Academy of Film and Television Arts, 1991, all for *Driving Miss Daisy;* Golden Berlin Bear nomination, Berlin International Film Festival, 1991, for *Mister Johnson;* Award for Best Opera Production, 1991, for *Elektra;* Genie Award, best achievement in direction, Academy of Canadian Cinema and Television, 1991, Australian Film Institute Award nomination, best director, 1992, both for *Black Robe;* Golden Berlin Bear nomination, Berlin International Film Festival, 1995, for *Silent Fall;* Film Critics Circle of Australia Award nominations, best director and best screenplay—adapted, 1998, both for *Paradise Road;* Golden Kinnaree Award nomination, Bangkok International Film Festival, best film, 2003, for *Evelyn.*

CREDITS

Film Director:
The Adventures of Barry McKenzie, Longford, 1972.
Barry McKenzie Holds His Own, Roadshow, 1974.
Side by Side, 1975.
Don's Party, Double Head, 1976.
The Getting of Wisdom, Roadshow, 1977.
Money Movers, Roadshow, 1978.
(Uncredited; additional footage) *Blue Fin,* 1978.
"Breaker" Morant (also known as *Breaker Morant*), New World, 1980.
The Club (also known as *David Williamson's "The Club"* and *Players*), Roadshow, 1980.
Fortress, 1981.
Puberty Blues, Twentieth Century–Fox, 1981.
Tender Mercies, Universal, 1982.
King David, Paramount, 1985.
The Fringe Dwellers, Atlantic, 1985.

Crimes of the Heart, De Laurentiis Entertainment Group, 1986.
"Die Tote Stadt," *Aria,* RVP–Virgin Vision, 1987.
Driving Miss Daisy, Warner Bros., 1989.
Her Alibi, Warner Bros., 1989.
Mister Johnson, Avenue Entertainment, 1991.
Black Robe (also known as *Robe noire*), Samuel Goldwyn, 1991.
Rich in Love, 1993.
A Good Man in Africa, Gramercy Pictures, 1994.
Silent Fall, Warner Bros., 1994.
Last Dance, Buena Vista/Touchstone, 1996.
Paradise Road, Twentieth Century–Fox, 1997.
Sydney: A Story of a City, Total Big Screen Productions, 1999.
Double Jeopardy (also known as *Doppelmord* and *Double condamnation*), Paramount, 1999.
Ataturk, 2000.
Bride of the Wind (also known as *Die Windsbraut*), Paramount Classics, 2001.
Boswell for the Defence, 2001.
Evelyn, Metro–Goldwyn–Mayer, 2002.
The Contract, First Look International, 2006.
Fever, 2007.

Film Work; Other:
Producer, *You're Human Like the Rest of Them,* 1967.
Cinematographer, *Magritte: The False Mirror,* 1970.
Producer, *Paradigm,* 1970.
Producer, *Barry McKenzie Holds His Own,* Roadshow, 1974.
Producer, *The Fringe Dwellers,* Atlantic, 1985.
Coproducer, *A Good Man in Africa,* Gramercy Pictures, 1994.
Executive Producer, *Curse of the Starving Class,* Trimark Pictures, 1994.
Producer, *Sydney: A Story of a City,* Total Big Screen Productions, 1999.
Co–executive producer, *Canvas* (documentary short), Screen Media Films, 2006.

Film Appearances:
(Uncredited) Man in pub, *The Adventures of Barry McKenzie,* Longford, 1972.
(Uncredited) Voice in Foureyes Fenton, *Barry McKenzie Holds His Own,* Roadshow, 1974.
Himself, *Miracles & Miracles* (documentary short), Anchor Bay Entertainment, 2002.
Himself, *"Miss Daisy"'s Journey: From Stage to Screen* (documentary short), Warner Home Video, 2003.
Himself, *Jessica Tandy: Theatre Legend to Screen Star* (documentary short), Warner Home Video, 2003.
Himself, *Evelyn: Behind the Scenes,* 2003.

Stage Director:
La Fancicella del West (opera; also known as *Girl of the Golden West*), Spoleto Festival, Charleston, SC, and Spoleto, Italy, 1985.

Elektra (opera), State Opera Company of South Australia, Adelaide and Melbourne, Australia, c. 1991.
The Crucible (opera), 1999.
Rigoletto, Los Angeles Opera, Los Angeles, 2000.
Cold Sassy Tree, Houston Grand Opera, Houston, TX, 2000.

Also directed *Sweeney Todd,* Portland Opera, Portland, OR; *Spoleto,* State Opera Company of South Australia, Adelaide and Melbourne, Australia.

Television Work; Series:
Executive producer and director, *Aria & Pasta,* Bravo, 2000.

Television Director; Movies:
Poor Fella Me, 1973.
The Wreck of the Batavia, 1974.
And Starring Pancho Villa as Himself, HBO, 2003.

Television Appearances; Episodic:
Mornings with Kerri–Anne, 2007.

WRITINGS

Screenplays:
(With Barry Humphries) *The Adventures of Barry McKenzie,* Longford, 1972.
(With Humphries) *Barry McKenzie Holds His Own,* Roadshow, 1974.
Side by Side, 1975.
Money Movers, Roadshow, 1978.
(With Jonathan Hardy and David Stevens) *"Breaker" Morant* (also known as *Breaker Morant*), New World, 1980.
The Fringe Dwellers, Atlantic, 1985.
"Die Tote Stadt," *Aria,* RVP–Virgin Vision, 1987.
(With William Boyd) *Mister Johnson* (adapted from a novel by Joyce Carey), Avenue Entertainment, 1991.
Curse of the Starving Class, Trimark Pictures, 1994.
Paradise Road, Twentieth Century–Fox, 1997.

Television Movies:
Poor Fella Me, 1973.

OTHER SOURCES

Books:
International Dictionary of Films and Filmmakers, Volume 2: *Directors,* St. James Press, 1996.

Periodicals:
American Film, January–February, 1987, pp. 36–40, 53.

BERNARD, Mary Ann
    See SODERBERGH, Steven

BIRD, Cord Wainer
    See ELLISON, Harlan

BIRNBAUM, Roger 1950–

PERSONAL

Born 1950, in Teaneck, NJ; married Pamela, c. 1985; children: one. *Education:* Attended the University of Denver.

Addresses: *Office*—Spyglass Entertainment Group, 10900 Wilshire Blvd., 10th Floor, Los Angeles, CA 90024.

Career: Producer. A&M Records, vice president of artists and repertoire, 1973–76; Arista Records, senior vice president of artists and repertoire, 1976–78; Robert Stigwood Organization, special assistant to chairman of the board of directors, 1978–80; Monument Pictures, president, 1980–85; Guber/Peters Co., president, 1985–87; United Artists, president of production, 1987–88; Twentieth Century–Fox, Los Angeles, CA, president of worldwide production, 1988–93, executive vice president, 1991–93; Caravan Pictures, chief executive officer, 1993–99; Spyglass Entertainment (a film production company), founder (with Gary Barber), co–chairman, chief executive producer, and producing partner, 1999—; Roger Birnbaum Productions, Los Angeles, CA, producer.

Awards, Honors: Daytime Emmy Award (with others), outstanding children's special, 1985, for "All the Kids Do It," *CBS Schoolbreak Special.*

CREDITS

Film Executive Producer:
Who's That Girl?, 1987.
Angie, Buena Vista, 1994.
Before and After, Buena Vista, 1996.
Maximum Risk (also known as *Bloodstone* and *The Exchange*), Columbia/Sony Pictures Entertainment, 1996.
The Beautician and the Beast, Paramount, 1997.
Overnight Delivery, New Line Cinema, 1998.

Keeping the Faith, Touchstone Pictures, 2000.
Unbreakable, Buena Vista, 2000.
Out Cold, Buena Vista, 2001.
Inspector Gadget 2 (also known as *IG2*), Walt Disney Pictures, 2003.
Bruce Almighty, Universal, 2003.
1 Love (also known as *The Supreme Court*), Spyglass Entertainment, 2003.
Seabiscuit, Universal, 2003.
The Legend of Zorro (also known as *Z*), Columbia, 2005.
Memoirs of a Geisha, Columbia, 2005.
Eight Below (also known as *8 Below*), Buena Vista, 2006.
Stay Alive, Buena Vista, 2006.
Stick It, Buena Vista, 2006.

Film Producer:
The Sure Thing, 1985.
Young Sherlock Holmes, 1985.
The Three Musketeers, Buena Vista, 1993.
Angels in the Outfield (also known as *Angels*), 1994.
A Low Down Dirty Shame (also known as *Mister Cool*), Buena Vista, 1994.
Houseguest, Buena Vista, 1995.
The Jerky Boys, Buena Vista, 1995.
Heavyweights, Buena Vista, 1995.
Tall Tale: The Unbelievable Adventures of Pecos Bill (also known as *Tall Tale*), Buena Vista, 1995.
While You Were Sleeping, Buena Vista, 1995.
The Big Green, Buena Vista, 1995.
Powder, Buena Vista/Hollywood Pictures, 1995.
Celtic Pride, Buena Vista, 1996.
First Kid, Buena Vista, 1996.
The Rich Man's Wife, Buena Vista, 1996.
Metro, Buena Vista, 1997.
Grosse Pointe Blank, Buena Vista, 1997.
Gone Fishin', Buena Vista, 1997.
G.I. Jane, Buena Vista, 1997.
Washington Square, Buena Vista, 1997.
Rocket Man (also known as *RocketMan*), Buena Vista, 1997.
Six Days, Seven Nights (also known as *6 Days 7 Nights*), Buena Vista, 1998.
Simon Birch (also known as *Angels and Armadillos*), Buena Vista, 1998.
Rush Hour, New Line Cinema, 1998.
Holy Man, Buena Vista, 1998.
Inspector Gadget, Buena Vista/Walt Disney, 1999.
Shanghai Noon, Buena Vista, 2000.
Rush Hour 2, New Line Cinema, 2001.
The Count of Monte Cristo (also known as *Alexandre Dumas' "The Count of Monte Cristo"*), Buena Vista, 2001.
Reign of Fire, Buena Vista, 2002.
Dragonfly (also known as *Im Zeichen der libelle*), Universal, 2002.
Abandon, Paramount, 2002.
The Recruit, Buena Vista, 2003.

Shanghai Knights, Buena Vista, 2003.
The Perfect Score (also known as *Voll gepunktet*), Paramount, 2004.
Connie and Carla, Universal, 2004.
Mr. 3000, Buena Vista, 2004.
The Pacifier (also known as *Gnome* and *La Pacifacteur*), Buena Vista, 2005.
The Hitchhikers' Guide to the Galaxy, Buena Vista, 2005.
The Lookout, 2007.
The Invisible, Buena Vista, 2007.
Evan Almighty, Universal, 2007.
Underdog, Buena Vista, 2007.
Rush Hour 3, New Line Cinema, 2007.
Balls of Fury, Rogue Pictures, 2007.
Flash of Genius, 2008.
27 Dresses, Fox 2000, 2008.
Bunny Lake Is Missing, Columbia, 2008.

Film Assistance:
Rain Man, Metro–Goldwyn–Mayer, 1988.

Film Appearances:
The Sure Thing, Embassy, 1985.
Hollywood type, *Making Sandwiches,* Fortis Films, 1998.
Himself, *A Piece of the Action: Behind the Scenes of "Rush Hour"* (documentary), 1999.
Himself, *Spy School: Inside the CIA Training Program* (documentary short), Touchstone Home Video, 2003.

Television Work; Series:
Producer (with Ervin Zavada) *Ryan's Four,* ABC, 1983.
Executive producer, *Miracles,* ABC and Vision/TV Canada, 2003.

Television Work; Movies:
Producer (with Ervin Zavada), *When Your Lover Leaves,* NBC, 1983.
Producer, *Scandal Sheet* (also known as *The Devil's Bed*), ABC, 1985.
Executive producer, *Bay Coven* (also known as *The Devils of Bay Cove, Strangers in Town, The Devils of Bay Cove,* and *Eye of the Demon*), NBC, 1987.
Executive producer, *Angels in the Endzone,* ABC, 1997.
Executive producer, *Flash,* 1998.
Executive producer, *Angels in the Infield,* ABC, 2000.
Executive producer, *The Ranch,* Showtime, 2004.

Television Work; Specials:
Executive producer, "All the Kids Do It," *CBS Schoolbreak Special,* CBS, 1984.
Producer, *Happily Ever After,* PBS, 1985.

Television Work; Episodic:
Producer, "Happily Ever After," *WonderWorks,* PBS, 1985.

Television Appearances; Episodic:
"Naked Hollywood," *A&E Premieres,* Arts and Entertainment, 1991.

BRIMLEY, Wilford 1934–
   (A. Wilford Brimley, Bill Brimley)

PERSONAL

Born September 27, 1934, in Salt Lake City, UT; father, a real estate broker; married Lynn, September 27, 1955; children: Jim, John, Bill.

Addresses: *Agent*—The Blake Agency, 1327 Ocean Ave., Suite J, Santa Monica, CA 90401; Cunningham, Escott, Slevin and Doherty Talent Agency, 10635 Santa Monica Blvd., Suite 140, Los Angeles, CA 90025.

Career: Actor. Worked as a riding extra and stuntman, beginning 1965; founding member of Los Angeles Actors' Theatre, 1976; appeared in television commercials for Quaker Oats, c. 1990, and Liberty Medical insurance, 1999—. Previously worked as a farmer, blacksmith, wrangler, ranch hand, horse trainer, rodeo rider, and bodyguard to Howard Hughes (late 1950s). *Military service:* Served in U.S. Marine Corps during Korean War.

Member: Screen Actors Guild.

Awards, Honors: CableACE Award nomination, actor in a movie or miniseries, 1987, for *Act of Vengeance; Advertising Age* Award, Star Presenter of the Year, 1988; Golden Boot Award, Motion Picture and Television Fund, 2005.

CREDITS

Film Appearances:
(Uncredited) *True Grit,* Paramount, 1969.
(As Bill Brimley) Marc Corman, *The Lawman,* United Artists, 1971.
Ted Spindler, *The China Syndrome,* Columbia, 1979.
Farmer, *The Electric Horseman,* Columbia, 1979.
(As A. Wilford Brimley) Scooter Jackson, *Borderline,* Associated Film Distributors, 1980.
Rogers, prison board member, *Brubaker,* Twentieth Century–Fox, 1980.
James A. Wells, Assistant U.S. Attorney General, *Absence of Malice,* Columbia, 1981.
(As A. Wilford Brimley) Sheriff, *Death Valley,* Universal, 1981.

(As A. Wilford Brimley) Blair, *The Thing* (also known as *John Carpenter's "The Thing"*), Universal, 1982.

Bill Long, *Tough Enough,* Twentieth Century–Fox, 1982.

Harry Silver, *Tender Mercies,* Universal, 1982.

Captain Malone, *10 to Midnight,* Cannon, 1983.

Bradley Tozer, *High Road to China,* Warner Bros., 1983.

George Jansen, *The Stone Boy,* Twentieth Century–Fox, 1983.

Tom, *Harry and Son,* Orion, 1984.

"Iowa Bob" Berry, *The Hotel New Hampshire,* Orion, 1984.

Otis Steward, *Country,* Buena Vista, 1984.

Pop Fisher, *The Natural,* TriStar, 1984.

(Archive footage) *Terror in the Aisles* (also known as *Time for Terror*), 1984.

Ben Luckett, *Cocoon,* Twentieth Century–Fox, 1985.

Harold Smith, *Remo Williams: The Adventure Begins ...* (also known as *Remo: Unarmed and Dangerous*), Orion, 1985.

Sheriff Mitchell, *Jackals* (also known as *American Justice*), Warner Bros., 1986.

Shadows on the Wall, 1986.

Will Haney, *End of the Line,* Orion, 1988.

Ben Luckett, *Cocoon: The Return,* Twentieth Century–Fox, 1988.

Eric/King, *Eternity,* 1990.

Grandpa Will, *Where the Red Fern Grows: Part Two,* 1992.

Uncle Douvee, *Hard Target,* Universal, 1993.

William Devasher, *The Firm,* Paramount, 1993.

Security guard, *Heaven Sent,* KOAN, Inc., 1994.

(Uncredited) Narrator, *Last of the Dogmen,* Savoy Pictures, 1995.

Jake, *A Place to Grow,* MTI Home Video, 1995.

Devro, *Mutant Species* (also known as *Bio–Force I*), Live Entertainment, 1995.

Joe Hollis, *My Fellow Americans,* Warner Bros., 1996.

Chief Danny Hawkins, *Chapter Perfect,* Vivafilm, 1996.

Frank Brackett, *In & Out,* Paramount, 1997.

The storyteller, *Lunker Lake,* 1997.

Grandpa Sam Ferrans, *Summer of the Monkeys* (also known as *L' te des singes*), BWE Distribution, 1997.

Charlie, *All My Friends Are Cowboys,* 1998.

Dr. David Wetherly, *The Progeny,* Fries Film Group, 1998.

Chief Hawkins, *Chapter Perfect,* 1998.

Jake, *A Place to Grow,* 1998.

Comance, 2000.

Benjamin Luckett, *Twentieth Century Fox: The Blockbuster Years,* 2000.

Sheriff Stu, *Brigham City,* Excel Entertainment, 2001.

PC and the Web, 2001.

Governor, *The Round and Round* (also known as *Cockfight*), 2002.

Morty, *Resurrection Mary* (short), 2002.

Harry, *Miracles & Mercies* (documentary short), Anchor Bay Entertainment, 2002.

Coach Weaver, *The Road Home* (also known as *Pitcher and the Pin–Up*), Screen Media Films, 2003.

Ted Spindler, *"The China Syndrome": A Fusion of Talent* (documentary short), Columbia TriStar Home Entertainment, 2004.

Ted Spindler, *"The China Syndrome": Creating a Controversy* (documentary short), Columbia TriStar Home Entertainment, 2004.

Film Work:

(Uncredited) Stunts, *Where the Red Fern Grows: Part 2,* 1992.

Television Appearances; Series:

(As A. Wilford Brimley) Horace Brimley, *The Waltons,* CBS, 1974–77.

Gus Witherspoon, *Our House* (also known as *My Grandfather's House*), NBC, 1986–88.

Bill Huntoon, *The Boys of Twilight* (also known as *Grey Guns* and *Cody and Bill*), CBS, 1992.

Television Appearances; Miniseries:

(As A. Wilford Brimley) Jude McWhirter, *The Awakening Land,* 1978.

Willie Clayton, *Roughnecks,* syndicated, 1980.

Admiral Troy Davis, *OP Center* (also known as *Tom Clancy's "OP Center,"* ABC, 1995.

Television Appearances; Movies:

(As Wilford A. Brimley) President Grover Cleveland, *The Wild Wild West Revisited,* CBS, 1979.

Bingo Gibbs, *Rodeo Girl,* CBS, 1980.

Pete Alberts, *Amber Waves,* ABC, 1980.

Dr. Andrew McCallister, *Murder in Space,* Showtime, 1985.

Noa, *Ewoks: The Battle for Endor,* ABC, 1985.

Tony Boyle, *Act of Vengeance,* HBO, 1986.

Red Haines, *Thompson's Last Run,* CBS, 1986.

Governor Lew Wallace, *Gore Vidal's "Billy the Kid"* (also known as *Billy the Kid*), TNT, 1989.

U.S. Marshal Winston Patrick Culler, *Blood River,* CBS, 1991.

Floyd Buckman, *Shadows on the Wall,* syndicated, 1991.

C. C. Tarpley, *The Good Old Boys,* TNT, 1995.

Joe Gill, *Crossfire Trail* (also known as *Louis L'Amour's "Crossfire Trail"*), TNT, 2001.

Deputy Sheriff Ambrose Scraggs, *The Ballad of Lucy Whipple* (also known as *California Gold*), 2001.

Television Appearances; Specials:

The Making of "The China Syndrome," 1979.

The Making of "Absence of Malice," 1982.

Voice of the Constitution, *Funny, You Don't Look 200* (also known as *Funny, You Don't Look 200: A Constitutional Vaudeville*), ABC, 1987.

Voice of Theodore Roosevelt, *The River of Doubt* (also known as *New Explorers*), PBS, 1992.

Charlie, *All My Friends Are Cowboys,* PBS, 1998.
Storyteller, *Keeper of the Flame,* 2005.

Television Appearances; Pilots:
Ludlow, *The Oregon Trail,* NBC, 1976.
Wally Haskell, *Joe Dancer: The Big Black Pill* (also known as *The Big Black Pill* and *Joe Dancer*), NBC, 1981.
Martin Barry, *The Firm,* NBC, 1983.

Television Appearances; Episodic:
(As A. Wilford Brimley) Blacksmith, "One Step to Darkness," *Kung Fu,* 1975.
"Hard Ride Home and the Last Game," *The Oregon Trail,* 1977.
Sheriff Daniels, "Hillary," *How the West Was Won,* 1979.
Harry Prentice, "See No Evil," *Homicide: Life on the Street* (also known as *Homicide*), NBC, 1994.
Storytime, PBS, 1994.
Burt Mueller, "War Zone," *Walker, Texas Ranger* (also known as *Walker*), CBS, 1995.
Henry Atkins, Postmaster General, "The Junk Mail," *Seinfeld,* NBC, 1997.
Larry King Live, CNN, 2003.

Also appeared in *Gunsmoke,* CBS; *Custer,* ABC; *Lancer,* CBS.

Stage Appearances:
The Petrified Forest, Off–Broadway production, 2001.

BROWN, Julie 1954(?)–
(West Coast Julie Brown)

PERSONAL

Born August 31, 1954 (some sources cite 1958), in Van Nuys (some sources cite Burbank), CA; daughter of Leonard Francis (a television technician) and Celia Jane (a secretary) Brown; sister of Paul Brown (a screenwriter); married Terrence E. McNally (an actor and comedian), June 11, 1983 (divorced, August, 1988); married Ken Rathjen, August 17, 1994; children: (second marriage) one son. *Education:* Los Angeles Valley College, A.A., 1977; trained at American Conservatory Theatre, San Francisco, CA. *Politics:* Democrat. *Avocational Interests:* Scuba diving, bicycling.

Addresses: *Agent*—Andy Patman, Paradigm, 360 North Crescent Dr. N., Beverly Hills, CA 90210. *Manager*—Billy Miller, Billy Miller Management, 8322 Ridpath Dr., Los Angeles, CA 90046.

Career: Actress, producer, director, composer, writer, and singer. Performed as standup comedian, 1980; MTV Music Television Network, worked as music video announcer, sometimes calling herself West Coast Julie Brown to distinguish herself from another MTV personality called Downtown Julie Brown.

Member: Writers Guild of America, Screen Actors Guild, American Federation of Television and Radio Artists.

Awards, Honors: Writers Guild of America Television Award (with Charlie Coffey), best variety–musical, award, tribute, or special event, 1993, for *Medusa: Dare to Be Truthful.*

CREDITS

Film Appearances:
Candy, *Any Which Way You Can,* Warner Bros., 1980.
Television commercial actress, *The Incredible Shrinking Woman,* Universal, 1981.
Beverly Brody, *Bloody Birthday* (also known as *Creepers*), 1981.
Chloe, *Police Academy 2: Their First Assignment,* Warner Bros., 1985.
Candy, *Earth Girls Are Easy,* Vestron, 1989.
Ms. Liberty, *The Spirit of '76,* Castle Rock, 1990.
Judy, *Shakes the Clown,* IRS Releasing, 1991.
(Uncredited) Waitress at Al's Diner, *Timebomb,* 1991.
Zoe, *The Opposite Sex and How to Live with Them,* Miramax, 1992.
Nancy Rudman, *Nervous Ticks,* 1992.
Voice of Lisa, *A Goofy Movie,* Buena Vista, 1995.
Ms. Stoeger, *Clueless* (also known as *I Was a Teenage Teenager* and *No Worries*), Paramount, 1995.
Mimi Hungry, *Plump Fiction,* Legacy Releasing, 1997.
Voice of Minerva Mink, *Wakko's Wish* (animated; also known as *Steven Spielberg Presents "Animaniacs: Wakko's Wish"*), 1999.
Connie Spheres, *Daybreak* (also known as *Rapid Transit*), 2000.
Samantha's mom, *Size 'em Up* (short film), 2001.
OutLoud receptionist, *The Trip,* TLA Releasing, 2002.
New Age mother, *Like Mike,* Twentieth Century–Fox, 2002.
Talker, *Intermission* (short film), 2004.
Special Thanks to Roy London (documentary), 2005.
Anny Neptune, *Boxboarders!,* Luminair Film Productions/Thunderhedd Productions, 2006.
Squeaky, *Fat Rose and Squeaky,* Hannover House, 2007.

Film Work:
Song producer, *Earth Girls Are Easy,* Vestron, 1989.

Television Appearances; Series:
Host, *Just Say Julie,* 1989.
Member of ensemble, *The Edge,* 1992–93.
Voice of Minerva Mink, *Animaniacs* (animated; also known as *Steven Spielberg Presents "Animaniacs"*), 1993–96.
Voice of Saleen, *Aladdin* (animated; also known as *Disney's "Aladdin"*), 1993.
Coach Millie Deemer, *Clueless,* ABC, 1996–97, UPN, 1997–99.
Tammi Tyler, *Strip Mall,* Comedy Central, 2000–2001.

Television Appearances; Movies:
Reporter, *Jane Doe,* 1983.
Tonya Hardly, "Tonya: The Battle of Wounded Knee," and Lenora Babbitt, "He Never Gave Me Orgasms," *Attack of the 5'2" Women* (also known as *National Lampoon's "Attack of the 5 Ft 2 Woman"*), 1994.
Joleen, *Out There,* 1995.
Rhonda, *Alien Avengers II* (also known as *Aliens Among Us, Roger Corman Presents "Alien Avengers II,"* and *Welcome to Planet Earth II*), 1997.

Television Appearances; Specials:
Montreal International Comedy Festival, 1989.
Medusa, *Medusa: Dare to Be Truthful* (also known as *Dare to Be Truthful*), Showtime, 1992.
Demented Top 20 Video Countdown, 1988.
I Was an MTV VJ, 1998.
Clueless: The E! True Hollywood Story, E! Entertainment Television, 2001.
Voice of Mom, *Elise: Mere Mortal,* Nickelodeon, 2002.
E! 101 Most Starlicious Makeovers, E! Entertainment Television, 2004.
E! 101 Most Awesome Moments in Entertainment, E! Entertainment Television, 2004.
50 Most Outrageous TV Moments, E! Entertainment Television, 2004.
Here to Remember, Here! Network, 2004.
101 Most Sensational Crimes of Fashion, E! Entertainment Television, 2004.
101 Even Bigger Celebrity Oops, E! Entertainment Television, 2005.
101 Craziest TV Moments, E! Entertainment Television, 2005.
Celebrity Autobiography: In Their Own Words, Bravo, 2005.
QTN Holiday Reel, 2005.

Television Appearances; Pilots:
Julie Brown: The Show, CBS, 1989.
Julie Robbins, *The Julie Show,* NBC, 1991.
Tammi Tyler, *Strip Mall,* Comedy Central, 2000.

Television Appearances; Awards Presentations:
Presenter, *The 42nd Annual Primetime Emmy Awards,* Fox, 1990.

The 17th Annual People's Choice Awards, CBS, 1991.
The 5th Annual American Comedy Awards, ABC, 1991.

Television Appearances; Episodic:
Gloria, "Ah, Wilderness," *Happy Days* (also known as *Happy Days Again*), 1980.
Patti, "The Note," *Laverne & Shirley* (also known as *Laverne & Shirley & Company* and *Laverne & Shirley & Friends*), 1982.
Secretary, "Rocky Ragu," *Laverne & Shirley* (also known as *Laverne & Shirley & Company* and *Laverne & Shirley & Friends*), 1982.
"Ratings," *Buffalo Bill,* 1983.
Cherry, "Who's the Fairest?," *The Jeffersons,* 1983.
Buffy Denver, "Co–Hostess Twinkie," *Newhart,* 1986.
Buffy Denver, "A Friendship that Will Last a Lunchtime," *Newhart,* 1988.
"MTV Celebrity Episode," *Remote Control,* 1988.
Wendy, "Small Blessing," *Monsters,* 1990.
Bunny O'Hare/Thelma Lou Dickey, "Maybe Baby—March 11, 1963," *Quantum Leap,* 1990.
Connie Bristol, "Terror on the Hell Loop 2000," *Get a Life,* 1990.
Voice of Julie Bruin, "Tiny Toon Music Television," *Tiny Toon Adventures* (animated; also known as *Steven Spielberg Presents ... "Tiny Toon Adventures"*), 1991.
Voice of Lily, "Eternal Youth," *Batman: The Animated Series* (animated; also known as *The Adventures of Batman & Robin* and *Batman*), 1992.
Voice of Zatanna Zatara, "Zatanna," *Batman: The Animated Series* (animated; also known as *The Adventures of Batman & Robin* and *Batman*), 1993.
Ms. Olivia Crawford, "To Party or Not to Party," *Clueless,* ABC, 1996.
Herself, "Goode Book," *Goode Behavior,* 1996.
Mrs. Heiner, "Family," *Tracey Takes On ...,* 1996.
Secretary number eighty–eight, "From the Terrace," *Murphy Brown,* CBS, 1997.
Lottie Bologna, "The Three Little Pigs," *Happily Ever After: Fairy Tales for Every Child,* 1999.
Late Night with Conan O'Brien (also known as *Conan O'Brien*), NBC, 2000.
"Comedians #3 Special," *The Weakest Link,* NBC, 2001.
Ms. Robbins, "No Small Parts," *Family Affair,* The WB, 2002.
Sissy Pasquese, "Time Flies," *Six Feet Under,* HBO, 2005.
Big Time (also known as *Steve Harvey's Big Time* and *Steve Harvey's Big Time Challenge*), The WB, 2005.
Cohost, *Queer Edge with Jack E. Jett & Sandra Bernhard* (also known as *Queer Edge* and *Queer Edge with Jack E. Jett*), multiple episodes, 2005.

Appeared in *An Evening at the Improv.*

Television Work; Movies:
Executive producer and director, *Medusa: Dare to Be Truthful* (also known as *Dare to Be Truthful*), Showtime, 1992.

Director, "Tonya: The Battle of Wounded Knee," *Attack of the 5'2" Women* (also known as *National Lampoon's "Attack of the 5 Ft 2 Woman"*), 1994.

Television Work; Series:
Coproducer, *Just Say Julie,* MTV, 1989.
Producer, *The Edge,* 1992.
Coproducer, *Clueless,* ABC, 1996–97, UPN, 1997–99.
Creator and executive producer, *Strip Mall,* Comedy Central, 2000–2001.

Television Work; Pilots:
Creator and executive producer, *Julie Brown: The Show,* CBS, 1989.
Creator and producer, *The Julie Show,* NBC, 1991.

Television Work; Episodic:
Director, "Cher and Cher Alike," *Clueless,* UPN, 1998.

Stage Appearances:
Performer of the solo show *Sluts—The Musical;* also appeared in the plays *Oklahomo* and *Space Therapy.*

RECORDINGS

Comedy/Musical Albums:
Goddess in Progress, Rhino, 1984.
(And co–songwriter) *Trapped in the Body of a White Girl,* Warner Bros., 1987.

Videos:
Performer and song composer, "The Homecoming Queen's Got a Gun," *Dr. Demento 20th Anniversary Collection,* 1991.

WRITINGS

Screenplays:
Script (with Charlie Coffey and Terrence E. McNally) and songs, *Earth Girls Are Easy,* Vestron, 1989.

Television Series:
Just Say Julie, 1989.
The Edge, 1992.

Television Pilots:
Julie Brown: The Show, CBS, 1989.
(And composer of main title theme song) *The Julie Show,* NBC, 1991.

Television Episodes:
"To Party or Not to Party," *Clueless,* ABC, 1996.
"Kiss Me Kip," *Clueless,* ABC, 1996.
"A Friend in Need," *The Big House,* ABC, 2004.

Also writer for *An Evening at the Improv* and *Quantum Leap.*

Television Writing; Other:
Script and musical score, *Medusa: Dare to Be Truthful* (special; also known as *Dare to Be Truthful*), Showtime, 1992.
Script and song lyrics, *Attack of the 5'2" Women* (movie; also known as *National Lampoon's "Attack of the 5 Ft 2 Woman"*), 1994.

OTHER SOURCES

Periodicals:
Details, April, 1989.
Femme Fatales, November, 2001, pp. 42–47.

Electronic:
Julie Brown Official Site, http://www.juliebrown.com, July 9, 2007.

BROWN, Melanie 1975–
(Mel B, Melanie B, Mel Brown, Mel G, Melanie G, Mel Gulzar, Melanie Gulzar, Scary Spice)

PERSONAL

Full name, Melanie Janine Brown; born May 29, 1975, in Leeds, West Yorkshire, England; married Jimmy Gulzar (an actor), September 13, 1998 (divorced, 2001); children: Phoenix Chi; (with Eddie Murphy) Angel Iris.

Addresses: *Agent*—Creative Artists Agency, 2000 Avenue of the Stars, Los Angeles, CA 90067. *Publicist*—The Outside Organization, Butler House, 177–178 Tottenham Court Rd., London W1T 7BY United Kingdom.

Career: Actress and singer. Member of the Spice Girls, 1994—; appeared in television commercial for Pepsi, 1997, and Commission for Racial Equality.

Awards, Honors: MTV Video Music Award (with the Spice Girls), best dance video, 1997, for "Wannabe"; MTV Europe Music Award (with the Spice Girls), best group, 1997; Blockbuster Entertainment Award nomination (with others), favorite actress—comedy, Blimp Award nomination (with others), Kids' Choice Awards, favorite movie actress, 1999, for *Spice World;* also won three American Music Awards with the Spice Girls.

CREDITS

Film Appearances:
Melanie B, *Spice World*, Columbia, 1997.
Herself, *Spice Power*, 1997.
Herself, *The Spice Girls in America: A Tour Story*, 1999.
Louise, *LD 50 Lethal Dose* (also known as *LD50* and *Lethal Dose*), First Look International, 2003.
Sandie, *The Seat Filler*, The Momentum Experience, 2004.
Maggie Thomas, *Telling Lies*, 2006.
Lonnie, *Love Thy Neighbor*, 2006.

Television Appearances; Series:
(As Melanie Gulzar) Herself, *Pure Naughty*, 1999.
Presenter, *This Is My Moment*, 2001.
Claire, *Burn It*, BBC, 2003.
Dancing with the Stars, ABC, 2007.

Television Appearances; Specials:
(With the Spice Girls) Performer, *Smash Hits Poll Winners Party 1997*, 1997.
(With the Spice Girls) Performer, *MTV Video Music Awards 1997*, MTV, 1997.
(With the Spice Girls) *44 edicion de los premios Ondas*, 1997.
Spice Up Your Life, 1997.
Comic Relief, 1997.
(With the Spice Girls) *MTV Europe Music Awards 1997*, MTV, 1997.
(With the Spice Girls) *Premios Amigo 97*, 1997.
An Audience with the Spice Girls, TIV, 1997.
Spice Girls: Too Much Is Never Enough, UPN, 1997.
(With the Spice Girls) Performer, *The 1997 Billboard Music Awards*, Fox, 1997.
(With the Spice Girls) *An Audience with Elton John*, ITV, 1997.
(With the Spice Girls) *Krede moder Spice Girls*, 1997.
(With the Spice Girls) *The BRIT Awards '97*, ABC, 1997.
(With the Spice Girls) *The 1997 World Music Awards*, ABC, 1997.
Dick Clark's New Year's Rockin' Eve '98, ABC, 1997.
The Brit Awards '98, ABC, 1998.
The 25th Annual American Music Awards, ABC, 1998.
(With the Spice Girls) *Spice Girls in Concert: Wild!* (documentary), pay per view, 1998.
Voice, *Creche Landing*, 1998.
Pavarotti and Friends, PBS, 1998.
(As Melanie G) Host, *The 1999 Malibu MOBO Awards*, 1999.
The 2000 MTV Europe Music Awards, MTV, 2000.
The 100 Greatest Pop Songs, MTV, 2000.
Spice Girls in Concert!, 2000.
Prince of Wales: Kings in Waiting, 2000.
Performer, *Brit Awards 2000*, 2000.
Solo Spice, 2001.
Geri Halliwell: Behind the Music (also known as *VH1's "Behind the Music"*), VH1, 2001.

(With the Spice Girls) *The New Royals*, 2001.
Wax Museum: History of Madame Tussaud's, 2001.
Performer, *Mgp 2001—de unges melodi grand prix* (also known as *M: G: P 2001—de unges melodi grand prix* and *Mgp 2001*), 2001.
Presenter, *The 2001 Top of the Pops Awards*, BBC, 2001.
The British Comedy Awards, ITV, 2001.
Melanie B: Voodoo Princess, 2002.
Seven Days That Shook the Spice World, 2002.
Presenter, *Party in the Park 2002*, Channel 5, 2002.
Bubblegum Babylon, VH1, 2002.
25 Years of Smash Hits, Channel 4, 2003.
Happy Birthday Oscar Wilde, BBC, 2004.
Avid Merrion's XXXmas Special, 2005.
(As Mel B) *Be My Baby: The Girl Group Story*, 2006.

Television Appearances; Episodic:
(Uncredited) Bettabuys worker, *Coronation Street*, ITV and CBC, 1993.
(With the Spice Girls) *Surprise! Surprise!*, 1996.
Die Harald Schmidt Show (also known as *Late Night Show mit Harald Schmidt*), 1996.
Guest presenter, *Top of the Pops* (also known as *All New Top of the Pops* and *TOTP*), 1996.
(With the Spice Girls) Musical guest, *Saturday Night Live* (also known as *SNL*), NBC, 1997.
(With the Spice Girls) *The National Lottery* (also known as *The National Lottery Live*), 1997.
(With the Spice Girls) "Wetten, dass …? aus Wien," *Wetten, dass?*, 1997.
(With the Spice Girls) "Wetten, dass …? aus Mannheim," *Wetten, dass?*, 1997.
"The Spice Girls," *Ruby Wax Meets …*, BBC, 1998.
(With the Spice Girls) "Titanic," *French and Saunders*, BBC, 1998.
(With the Spice Girls) *TFI Friday* (also known as *Thank Four It's Friday*), Channel 4, 1998.
(As Melanie B) *Top of the Pops* (also known as *All New Top of the Pops* and *TOTP*), 1998, 2000, 2001.
(As Melanie G) *Top of the Pops* (also known as *All New Top of the Pops* and *TOTP*), 1999.
(As Mel G) *Lamarr's Attacks*, BBC, 2000.
(As Melanie B) *Never Mind the Buzzcocks*, BBC, 2000.
Guest host, *TFI Friday* (also known as *Thank Four It's Friday*), Channel 4, 2000.
Mundo VIP, 2000.
So Graham Norton, Channel 4, 2001.
(As Mel B) *TV total*, 2001.
(As Melanie B) Singer, *Snurre Snups sondagsklub*, 2001.
The Kumars at No. 42, BBC2 and BBC America, 2001.
Friday Night with Jonathan Ross, BBC, 2002.
V Graham Norton, Channel 4, 2002.
(As Mel B) *Bo' Selecta!*, Channel 4, 2004.
(As Melanie B) *GMTV*, ITV, 2005.
Total Request Live, MTV, 2005.
Richard & Judy, Channel 4, 2005.
CD:UK, 2005, 2006.
Inside Edition, syndicated, 2006.

Also appeared (with the Spice Girls) *ABC in Concert,* ABC.

Stage Appearances:
Mimi, *Rent,* Nederlander Theatre, New York City, 2004.

Made stage debut in *The Vagina Monologues,* London, England.

RECORDINGS

Albums (with the Spice Girls):
Spice, Virgin, 1996.
Spiceworld, Virgin, 1997.
Forever, Virgin, 2000.

Albums (solo):
Hot, 2000.
L.A. State of Mind, 2005.

Music Videos (with the Spice Girls):
"Wannabe," 1996.
"Say You'll Be There," 1996.
"2 Become 1," 1996.
"Who Do You Think You Are," 1997.
"Mama," 1997.
"Spice Up Your Life," 1997.
"Stop," 1998.
"Viva Forever," 1998.
"Goodbye," 1998.
"(How Does It Feel) To Be On Top Of the World," 1998.
"Holler," 2000.

Music Videos (solo):
(With Missy Elliot) "I Want You Back," 1998.
"Word Up," 1999.
"Tell Me," 2000.
"Feels So Good," 2001.
"Lullaby," 2001.

Videos:
Spice Exposed (documentary), MVP Home Entertainment, 1997.
Spice Girls: Live in Istanbul, Virgin, 1997.
(As Scary Spice) *Spice Girls: One Hour of Girl Power* (also known as *Spice: The Official Video Volume One*), Warner Home Video, 1997.
Girl Power, 1997.
Spice Girls Live at Wembley Stadium, Virgin, 1998.
Spice Girls in America: A Tour Story, Virgin, 1999.
(As Spice Girls) *It's Only Rock 'n' Roll* (documentary short), 2000.
South Africa Freedom Day: Concert on the Square, Image Entertainment, 2002.

Video Games:
Voice of Scary Spice, *Spice World: The Game,* 1998.
(With Spice Girls) Herself, *SingStar Party,* 2004.

WRITINGS

Autobiography:
Catch a Fire, Headline, 2002.

OTHER SOURCES

Periodicals:
People Weekly, September 28, 1998, p. 11; March 8, 1999, p. 130; August 13, 2007, p. 21.

BURNS, Francis
    See GELBART, Larry

BURNS, Jere 1954–
    (Jere Burns II)

PERSONAL

Full name, Jere Eugene Burns II; given name is pronounced "Jerry"; born October 15, 1954 (some sources say October 5, 1956), in Cambridge, MA; son of a cap and gown manufacturer and a homemaker; married Melissa, 1982 (divorced, 1996); married Kathleen Kinmont, 1997 (divorced, 1999); children: (first marriage) Gillian, Jake, Luke. *Education:* University of Massachusetts, Amherst, B.A., comparative literature, 1980; studied acting at Tisch School of the Arts, New York University. *Avocational Interests:* Extreme skiing, wakeboarding, and surfing.

Addresses: *Agent*—Innovative Artists, 1505 Tenth St., Santa Monica, CA 90401.

Career: Actor. Appeared in television commercials for Panasonic Shaver, 1999. Worked as a lifeguard on Cape Cod and as a cab driver in Boston, MA, c. 1974–76.

Awards, Honors: Gemini Award nomination, best performance by an actor in a guest role in a dramatic series, Academy of Canadian Cinema and Television, 2000, for *Twice in a Lifetime.*

CREDITS

Film Appearances:
Levesque, *Touch and Go,* TriStar, 1986.
Washington aide, *Let's Get Harry* (also known as *The Rescue*), TriStar, 1987.
Lou, *Wired,* Taurus, 1989.
Jared Riley, *Hit List,* New Line Cinema, 1989.
Glen, *Greedy,* Universal, 1994.
Dr. Dan Yates, *Santa Fe,* Absolute Unequivocal Productions, 1997.
Weller, the movie director, *My Giant,* Columbia/Sony Pictures Entertainment, 1998.
Arnan Rothman, *Crocodile Dundee in Los Angeles,* Paramount, 2001.
Cemetery agent, *Mother Ghost,* Anthem Pictures, 2002.
Dixon Grain, *New Suit,* Trillion Entertainment, 2002.
Benjamin, *What's Up, Scarlet?,* 2005.
Jeffrey, *Two: Thirteen,* 2008.

Television Appearances; Series:
Eddie Green, *Ohara,* ABC, 1987.
Breugel, *Max Headroom* (also known as *Max Headroom: 20 Minutes into the Future*), ABC, 1987–88.
Kirk Morris, *Dear John* (also known as *Dear John USA*), NBC, 1988–92.
Pete Schmidt, *Bob,* CBS, 1993–94.
Tom Booker, *The Mommies* (also known as *Mommies*), NBC, 1994–95.
Jack Farrell, *Something So Right,* NBC, 1996–97, then ABC, 1997–98.
Michael, *Help Me Help You,* ABC, 2006.

Television Appearances; Miniseries:
Cade Dalton, *The Gambler Returns: The Luck of the Draw* (also known as *Luck of the Draw: The Gambler Returns*), NBC, 1991.

Television Appearances; Movies:
Steve, a therapy group member, *The Psychiatrist: God Bless the Children* (also known as *Children of the Lotus Eater*), 1970.
Junior Allen, *The Last Precinct,* NBC, 1986.
William Hawkins, *Turn Back the Clock* (also known as *Repeat Performance*), NBC, 1989.
Cliff Bartell, *Perry Mason: The Case of the Defiant Daughter* (also known as *Perry Mason: The Case of the Deadly Deal*), NBC, 1990.
Stephen Primes, *Eye of the Stalker* (also known as *Moment of Truth: "Eye of the Stalker"*), NBC, 1995.
Lewis Snow, *The Secret She Carried,* NBC, 1996.
Eddie Madden, *Road Rage* (also known as *Death Driver*), NBC, 1999.
Ben Stuart, *Life–Size,* 2000.

Television Appearances; Pilots:
Frank Alfano, *Good Morning, Miami,* NBC, 2002.
Michael, *Help Me Help You,* 2006.

Television Appearances; Specials:
Hal, "Mom's on Strike," *ABC Afterschool Special,* ABC, 1984.
Brother Vinnie, "God, the Universe, and Hot Fudge Sundaes," *CBS Schoolbreak Specials,* CBS, 1986.
Super Bloopers and New Practical Jokes, NBC, 1990.
Macy's Thanksgiving Day Parade, NBC, 1996.
All–Star TV Censored Show Me the Bloopers, 1997.

Television Appearances; Episodic:
James Fitzsimmons, "Watt a Way to Go," *Hill Street Blues,* NBC, 1984.
James Fitzsimmons, "Cookie Nookie," *Hill Street Blues,* NBC, 1984.
Eddie Watson, "Fire on the Wing," *Street Hawk,* 1985.
Greg Jones, "The Beach Boy," *Hunter,* NBC, 1985.
Rick "Badman" Badham, "Steele on the Air," *Remington Steele,* 1986.
(As Jere Burns II) "Little Girl Lost," *Crime Story,* NBC, 1987.
Eddie Green, *Ohara,* 1987.
Himself, "Blossom—A Rockumentry," *Blossom,* NBC, 1991.
Pete Collins, "We're Not Worthy," *Fantasy Island,* ABC, 1998.
Steven Jensen, "Friends," *Vengeance Unlimited* (also known as *Mr. Chapel*), ABC, 1999.
Roy, "Gina's Choice," *Just Shoot Me,* NBC, 1999.
Bob, "What about Bob?" *Odd Man Out,* ABC, 1999.
Thomas "Tom" Lasky, "The Trouble with Harry," *Twice in a Lifetime,* PAX–TV, 2000.
Andy Winston, "The Talented Mr. Ripoff," *For Your Love,* The WB, 2000.
Sam, "Legacy," *Touched by an Angel,* CBS, 2000.
Jake Worthy, "The Vessel," *The Outer Limits,* Showtime and syndicated, 2001.
Gabriel, "Time After Time," *Sabrina, the Teenage Witch* (also known as *Sabrina*), The WB, 2002.
John Carruthers, "Big Brother," *Family Law,* CBS, 2002.
Frank Alfano, "The New Good Morning, Miami," *Good Morning, Miami,* NBC, 2003.
Frank Alfano, "Good Morning, Manhattan," *Good Morning, Miami,* NBC, 2003.
Frank Alfano, "The Wait Problem," *Good Morning, Miami,* NBC, 2003.
Voice of Mego, "Go Team Go," *Kim Possible* (animated; also known as *Disney's "Kim Possible"*), Disney Channel, 2004.
Commissioner, "VolleyBrawl," *8 Simple Rules ... for Dating My Teenage Daughter* (also known as *8 Simple Rules*), ABC, 2005.
Dan Clayman, "One Nation, Under Surveillance," *Las Vegas,* NBC, 2005.
Brian Goodman, "So I Creep," *All of Us,* UPN, 2005.
Brian Goodman, "Movin' On Up," *All of Us,* UPN, 2005.
Brian Goodman, "Sail On," *All of Us,* UPN, 2005.
Howard, "Snow Job," *The War at Home,* Fox, 2006.

Keith, "Hartford Wailer," *The King of Queens,* CBS, 2006.

Assistant District Attorney Joe Issacs, "BL: Los Angeles," *Boston Legal,* ABC, 2006.

Man in cast, "The Finale," *Will & Grace,* NBC, 2006.

Voice of Mego, "Stop Team Go!," *Kim Possible* (animated; also known as *Disney's "Kim Possible"*), Disney Channel, 2007.

Also appeared in *Riptide,* NBC; as Norman the doorman, "Upper West Side Story," *Four Kings,* NBC.

Stage Appearances:

Member of ensemble, and understudy Don Carlos, *Don Juan,* New York Shakespeare Festival, Delacorte Theatre, New York City, 1982.

True West, Cherry Lane Theatre, New York City, 1982–83.

Egyptology, Other Stage, Public Theatre, New York City, 1983.

Cyclist, *Sarcophagus,* Los Angeles Theatre Center, Los Angeles, 1987–88.

Isaac Brooks, *Diva,* La Jolla Playhouse, La Jolla, CA, 2001.

The Exonerated, 45 Bleecker Theatre, New York City, 2002–2004.

Jack Boner, *The Scottish Play,* La Jolla Playhouse, 2005.

Bartender, Sherman, and Darryl, *After the Night and the Music,* Biltmore Theatre, New York City, 2005.

Wilbur, *Hairspray,* Neil Simon Theatre, New York City, 2007.

Also appeared in *Gillette,* La Jolla Playhouse, La Jolla, CA.

RECORDINGS

Videos:

Himself, *"Will & Grace": The Final Bow (Curtain Call)* (short), Lions Gate, 2006.

OTHER SOURCES

Periodicals:

People, April 10, 1989, p. 145.

C

CAMPBELL, Amelia 1965–

PERSONAL

Born August 4, 1965, in Montreal, Quebec, Canada; married Anthony Arkin (an actor). *Education:* Graduated from Syracuse University.

Addresses: *Agent*—Cornerstone Talent Agency, 37 West 20th St., Suite 1108, New York, NY 10011.

Career: Actress.

Awards, Honors: Antoinette Perry Award nomination, best actress in a featured role, 1991, for *Our Country's Good.*

CREDITS

Film Appearances:
Young girl in dream, *The Exorcist III* (also known as *The Exorcist III: Legion, Exorcist 3,* and *William Peter Blatty's "The Exorcist III"*), Twentieth Century–Fox, 1990.
Check cashier, *Single White Female,* Columbia, 1992.
Member of Murphy family, *Lorenzo's Oil,* Universal, 1992.
Robin, *The Paper,* Universal, 1994.
Mary Brandon Sherwood, *Mrs. Parker and the Vicious Circle* (also known as *Mrs. Parker and the Round Table*), Fine Line, 1994.
Marsha Swanson, *A Simple Twist of Fate,* Buena Vista, 1994.
Susan, *Picture Perfect,* Twentieth Century–Fox, 1997.
Toby, *The Definite Maybe* (also known as *No Money Down*), DJM Films/Kaufman Astoria Studios/Definite Maybe, 1997.

Anima, Other Pictures/Tangent Films, 1998.
Patty and stage manager, *Macbeth in Manhattan,* Asylum, 1999.
Cross Words (short), Bravo Networks/Goldheart Pictures, 1999.
Valerie, *Last Ball,* Sugar Pond Films, 2001.
Sandra Zeller, *A Dog Year,* Picturehouse Entertainment, 2008.

Also appeared in *Malcolm X.*

Television Appearances; Movies:
Margaret Truman, *Truman,* HBO, 1995.
The Prosecutors, NBC, 1996.
Corrina, *My Louisiana Sky,* Showtime, 2001.

Television Appearances; Specials:
Ida, "A Town's Revenge," *ABC Afterschool Special,* ABC, 1989.

Television Appearances; Pilots:
Barbara Boeck, *New Year,* ABC, 1993.

Television Appearances; Episodic:
New York Undercover, Fox, 1995.
Rachel, *Feds,* 1997.
Sandy Reynolds, "Abduction," *Homicide: Life on the Street,* NBC, 1998.
Mrs. Woodson, "Refuge: Part 1," *Law & Order,* NBC, 1999.
Leslie McDonald, "Letting Go," *Third Watch,* NBC, 2003.
Vicki Hale, "In the Dark," *Law & Order: Criminal Intent* (also known as *Law & Order: CI*), NBC, 2004.

Stage Appearances:
Frankie Adams, *The Member of the Wedding,* Union Square Theatre, New York City, 1989.

Lieutenant Will Dawes, Meg Long, and Duckling Smith, *Our Country's Good,* Nederlander Theatre, New York City, 1991.

Samantha, *A Small Family Business,* Music Box Theatre, New York City, 1992.

Meredith, *Five Women Wearing the Same Dress,* Lucille Lortel Theatre, New York City, 1993.

Sarah, *Translations,* Colonial Theatre, Boston, MA, then Plymouth Theatre, New York City, both 1995.

Woman, Angie, and Sis, *WASPs and Other Plays* (also known as *Steve Martin's "Wasp and Other Plays"*), New York Shakespeare Festival, New York City, 1995–96.

Acts of Providence, York Theatre at St. Peter's Church, New York City, 1996.

Hester Fletcher, *The Herbal Bed,* Eugene O'Neill Theatre, New York City, 1998.

Mercy, Vineyard Theatre, New York City, 1998–99.

Doreen, *Waiting in the Wings,* Walter Kerr Theatre, New York City, 1999–2000, then Eugene O'Neill Theatre, 2000.

Speaking Janis, *Love, Janis,* Village Theatre, New York City, 2001–2003.

Understudy Georgia Hayes, *The Exonerated,* 45 Bleecker Theatre, New York City, 2002–2004.

Abbie Putnam, *Desire Under the Elms,* American Repertory Theatre, Loeb Drama Center, Cambridge, MA, 2005.

Fools in Love, Culture Project, New York City, 2005–2006.

Adelaide Pinchin, *Tryst,* Promenade Theatre, New York City, 2006.

Arsinoe, *The Misanthrope,* New York Theatre Workshop, New York City, 2007.

Also appeared in *Fun; A Month in the Country,* Long Wharf Theatre, New Haven, CT; *My Mother Said I Never Should,* New York Stage and Film Theatre, New York City; *Our Country's Good,* Hartford Stage, Hartford, CT; *Revelers,* New York Stage and Film Theatre; *Smack the Birdie,* Nada 45 Theatre, New York City; "Tunnel of Love," *Marathon,* Studio Ensemble Theatre, New York City; *Wild Dogs,* Malaparte Theatre, New York City.

Stage Work:

Choreographer, *Fools in Love,* Culture Project, New York City, 2005–2006.

Radio Appearances:

Performed multiple voices for *The Night Kitchen Radio Theatre.*

CANTON, Mark 1949–

PERSONAL

Born June 19, 1949, in New York, NY; son of Arthur (a publicist, producer, and film importer) and Shirley Canton; brother of Neil Canton (a producer); married Wendy Finerman (a producer), 1985 (divorced, 1999); children: Dorothy, Henry, additional child. *Education:* Attended University of California, Los Angeles, 1978.

Addresses: *Office*—Atmosphere Entertainment MM LLC/Chiller Films, 4751 Wilshire Blvd., 3rd Floor, Los Angeles, CA 90010.

Career: Studio executive. Metro–Goldwyn–Mayer/Pathe, Culver City, CA, vice president and managing producer for motion picture development, 1978–79; Jon Peters Organization, Los Angeles, executive vice president, 1979; Warner Bros., Burbank, CA, vice president for production, 1980–83, senior vice president, 1983–85, president of worldwide theatrical production division, 1985–91, executive vice president, 1989–91; Columbia Pictures, Burbank, president, 1991–96; Columbia TriStar Motion Picture Companies, Culver City, chairperson, 1994–96; Canton Co., Burbank, producer, 1997–2002; Artists Production Group, partner, chairman, chief executive officer, 2002; Atmosphere Entertainment MM, Los Angeles, CA, co-founder, chairman, and chief executive officer, 2003—; Chiller Films, Los Angeles, CA, partner. American Film Institute, vice chairperson of board of trustees.

CREDITS

Film Work:

Production aide, *The Taking of Pelham One Two Three* (also known as *Pelham 1–2–3* and *El tomar de Pelham uno dos tres*), 1974.

Executive in charge of production, *Caddyshack,* Orion, 1980.

(With Robby Benson) Producer, *Die Laughing,* Warner Bros., 1980.

Producer, *Jack Frost* (also known as *Frost*), Warner Bros., 1998.

Producer, *Get Carter,* Warner Bros., 2000.

Producer, *Red Planet,* Warner Bros., 2000.

Producer, *Cherry Hills,* Canton Co./Original Film, 2000.

Producer, *Angel Eyes* (also known as *Ojos de angel*), Warner Bros., 2001.

Producer, *Six,* Franchise Pictures, 2001.

Executive producer, *Trapped* (also known as *24 Stunden Angst*), Columbia, 2002.

Producer, *Taking Lives,* Warner Bros., 2004.

Executive producer, *Godsend* (also known as *Adam*), Lions Gate Films, 2004.

Producer, *Land of the Dead* (also known as *George A. Romero's "Land of the Dead,"* *Land of the Dead—Le territoire des morts,* and *La terre des morts*), Universal, 2005.

Producer, *300,* Warner Bros., 2006.

Producer, *Full of It,* New Line Cinema, 2007.

Producer, *The Spiderwick Chronicles,* Paramount, 2008.

Film Appearances:
Himself, *"Caddyshack": The 19th Hole,* 1999.
Himself, *Shadows of the Bat: The Cinematic Saga of the Dark Knight—The Gathering Storm* (documentary short), Warner Home Video, 2005.
Himself, *Shadows of the Bat: The Cinematic Saga of the Dark Knight—The Road to Gotham City* (documentary short), Warner Home Video, 2005.
Himself, *Land of the Dead: Bringing the Dead to Life* (documentary short), Universal Studios Home Video, 2005.
Himself, *Shadows of the Bat: The Cinematic Saga of the Dark Knight—Dark Side of the Knight* (documentary short), Warner Home Video, 2005.
Himself, *Shadows of the Bat: The Cinematic Saga of the Dark Knight—The Legend Reborn* (documentary short), Warner Home Video, 2005.
Himself, *Undead Again: The Making of "Land of the Dead"* (documentary short), Universal Studios Home Video, 2005.
Himself, *Land of the Dead: A Day with the Living Dead* (documentary short), Universal Studios Home Video, 2005.

Television Work; Series:
Executive producer, *Jack and Jill,* The WB, 1999.

Television Appearances; Specials:
Mel Gibson's Unauthorized Video Diary, 1989.
Hello, He Lied & Other Truths from the Hollywood Trenches (also known as *Hello, He Lied*), AMC, 2002.

Television Appearances; Episodic:
"300," *HBO First Look,* HBO, 2007.

OTHER SOURCES

Periodicals:
Los Angeles, January, 1994, p. 62.
Premiere, December, 1991, p. 30.
Vanity Fair, December, 1991, p. 154.

CARON, Glenn Gordon 1954–
(Glenn Caron)

PERSONAL

Born April 3, 1954 in Oceanside, NY; both parents were salespeople; married, wife's name Mary; children: two. *Education:* State University of New York College, Geneseo, graduated; trained in New York City with Del Close and in Chicago, IL, at Second City.

Addresses: *Office*—Picturemaker Productions, 2000 West 57th St., Suite 1310, New York, NY 10019. *Agent*—Endeavor, 9601 Wilshire Blvd., 3rd Floor, Beverly Hills, CA 90210; Paul Haas, Hollywood Radio and Television Society, 13701 Riverside Dr., Suite 205, Sherman Oaks, CA 91423.

Career: Writer, producer, and director. Picturemaker Productions, New York City, founder and principal, 1985—. Also worked as an advertising copywriter, a gas station attendant, and a theater usher.

Member: Writers Guild of America, Directors Guild of America.

Awards, Honors: Emmy Award nominations, outstanding drama series (with others), 1986, 1987, and Writers Guild of America Award, all for *Moonlighting;* Emmy Award nomination, outstanding writing in a drama series, 1986, for "'Twas the Episode before Christmas," *Moonlighting;* Emmy Award nomination (with others), outstanding writing in a drama series, 1987, for "I Am Curious … Maddie," *Moonlighting.*

CREDITS

Television Work; Series:
Story editor, *Good Time Harry,* NBC, 1980.
Supervising producer, *Breaking Away,* CBS, 1980–81.
(As Glenn Caron) Supervising producer, *Remington Steele,* NBC, 1982–83.
Creator and executive producer, *Moonlighting,* ABC, 1985–88.
Creator and executive producer, *Now and Again,* CBS, 1999.
Creator and executive producer, *Fling* (also known as *When I Grow Up*), Fox, 2001.
Creator and executive producer, *Medium,* NBC, 2005–2007.

Television Work; Pilots:
Executive producer, *Concrete Beat,* ABC, 1984.
Producer, *Moonlighting,* ABC, 1985.
Director, *Now and Again,* CBS, 1999.
Director, *Medium,* NBC, 2005.

Television Director; Episodic:
"In Genes We Trust," *Fling* (also known as *When I Grow Up*), Fox, 2001.

Television Work; Movies:
Executive producer, *Long Time Gone,* ABC, 1986.

Television Appearances; Specials:
Hollywood Salutes Bruce Willis: An American Cinematheque Tribute, 2000.
Brilliant but Cancelled, Trio, 2002.
The Perfect Pitch (also known as *Brilliant but Cancelled: The Perfect Pitch*), Trio, 2002.
"Bruce Willis," *Biography,* Arts and Entertainment, 2005.

Television Appearances; Episodic:
Square Off, TV Guide Channel, 2006.

Film Director:
Clean and Sober, Warner Bros., 1988.
The Making of Me, 1989.
Wilder Napalm, TriStar, 1993.
Love Affair, Warner Bros., 1994.
Picture Perfect, Twentieth Century–Fox, 1997.

WRITINGS

Television Series:
Sweepstakes, CBS, 1979.
Good Time Harry, NBC, 1979.

Television Pilots:
Heaven on Earth, NBC, 1979.
Concrete Beat, ABC, 1984.
Moonlighting, ABC, 1985.
Now and Again, CBS, 1999.

Television Episodes:
Breaking Away, CBS, c. 1980.
"Alone in a Crowd," *Fame,* NBC, 1982.
(As Glenn Caron) "Signed, Steeled, and Delivered," *Remington Steele,* NBC, 1982.
(As Glenn Caron) "Hearts of Steele," *Remington Steele,* NBC, 1983.
(As Glenn Caron) "To Stop a Steele," *Remington Steele,* NBC, 1983.
"Brother, Can You Spare a Blonde?," *Moonlighting,* ABC, 1985.
"'Twas the Episode before Christmas," *Moonlighting,* ABC, 1985.
"The Straight Poop," *Moonlighting,* ABC, 1987.
"I Am Curious ... Maddie," *Moonlighting,* ABC, 1987.
"In Genes We Trust," *Fling* (also known as *When I Grow Up*), Fox, 2001.
"Suspicions and Certainties," *Medium,* NBC, 2005.
"A Couple of Choices," *Medium,* NBC, 2005.
"When Push Comes to Shove: Part 2," *Medium,* NBC, 2005.
"Four Dreams: Part 2," *Medium,* NBC, 2006.

Also writer for episodes of *Taxi,* ABC.

Television Writing; Other:
Long Time Gone (movie), ABC, 1986.
(With others) *The 58th Annual Academy Awards Presentation* (special), ABC, 1986.

Screenplays:
Condorman, Walt Disney, 1981.
The Making of Me, 1989.
(With Robert Towne and Warren Beatty) *Love Affair,* Warner Bros., 1994.
(With others) *Picture Perfect,* Twentieth Century–Fox, 1997.

Some sources also credit Caron as screenplays *Evita* (based on the stage musical) and *Knowing Damon.*

OTHER SOURCES

Periodicals:
Entertainment Weekly, November 26, 1999, p. 52.
Venice, April, 2000.

CARSEY, Marcy 1944–

PERSONAL

Original name, Marcia Lee Peterson; born November 21, 1944, in Weymouth, MA; daughter of John Edwin and Rebecca White (maiden name, Simonds) Peterson; married John Jay Carsey (a writer), April 12, 1969 (died April 5, 2002); children: Rebecca, John; stepchildren: Heidi, Riley, Kyre. *Education:* University of New Hampshire, B.A. (cum laude), 1966.

Addresses: *Office*—Carsey–Werner Distribution, 12001 Ventura Pl., 6th Floor, Studio City, CA 91604.

Career: Producer. Tomorrow Entertainment, Los Angeles, executive story editor, 1971–74; ABC–TV, Los Angeles, senior vice president for prime–time series, 1978–81; Carsey Co., Los Angeles, founder, 1981; Carsey–Werner Distribution (and predecessor companies), Studio City, CA, co–owner and partner (with Tom Werner), 1982–. University of Southern California, member of television executive advisory council for School of Cinema and Television. Previously worked as a tour guide at Rockefeller Center and in the programming department of an advertising agency in New York City; also acted in commercials.

Awards, Honors: Emmy Award, 1985, and Emmy Award nominations, 1986 and 1987, all outstanding comedy series (with others), for *The Cosby Show;* Image Award, best episode in a comedy series or special, National Association for the Advancement of Colored People, 1989, for "No Means No," *A Different World;* Crystal Award, Women in Film, 1990; nomination for Wise Owl Award (with others), television and theatrical film fiction, Retirement Research Foundation, 1993, for "Ladies' Choice," *Roseanne;* Golden Globe Award (with others), best television musical or comedy series, 1995, for *Cybill;* inducted into Academy of Television Arts and Sciences Hall of Fame and Broadcasting and Cable Hall of Fame, both 1996; Emmy Award nominations (with others), outstanding comedy series, 1997 and 1998, both for *3rd Rock from the Sun; The Cosby Show* chosen for Hall of Fame for Television Programs, Golden Laurel Awards, Producers Guild of America, 2000; Lucy Award, Women in Film, 2000; David Susskind Lifetime Achievement Award, Producers Guild of America, 2002.

CREDITS

Television Co–Executive Producer; Series:
Oh Madeline, ABC, 1983–84.
A Different World, NBC, 1987–93.
Chicken Soup (also known as *From This Moment On*), ABC, 1989–90.
Grand (also known as *Grosse Pointe*), NBC, 1990.
Davis Rules (also known as *The Principal* and *Spiral Bound*), ABC, 1991, CBS, 1991–92.
Frannie's Turn (also known as *Frannie* and *The Little Woman*), CBS, 1992.
You Bet Your Life, syndicated, 1992–93.
Grace Under Fire, ABC, 1993–98.
Men Behaving Badly, NBC, 1996–98.

Television Executive Producer; Series:
The Cosby Show, NBC, 1985–91.
Roseanne, ABC, 1988–97.
Cybill, CBS, 1995–98.
Townies, ABC, 1996–97.
Cosby, CBS, 1996–2000.
3rd Rock from the Sun (also known as *Life as We Know It* and *3rd Rock*), NBC, 1997–2001.
Damon, Fox, 1998.
That '70s Show, Fox, 1998–2006.
God, the Devil, and Bob (animated), NBC, 2000.
Normal, Ohio, Fox, 2000.
Dot Comedy, ABC, 2000.
Grounded for Life, Fox, 2000–2005.
You Don't Know Jack, ABC, 2001.
The Downer Channel, NBC, 2001.
That '80s Show, Fox, 2002.
Whoopi, NBC, 2003–2004.
The Tracy Morgan Show, NBC, 2003–2004.
(And creator) *Game Over,* UPN, 2004.
The Scholar, ABC, 2005.

Television Producer; Series:
She TV, Lifetime, 1994.

Television Executive Producer; Pilots:
Callahan, ABC, 1982.
I Do, I Don't, ABC, 1983.
Are We There Yet?, The WB, 2003.
These Guys, ABC, 2003.
Blue Aloha, Fox, 2004.
Peep Show, Fox, 2005.

Television Producer; Pilots:
The Mayor of Oyster Bay, ABC, 2002.

Television Executive Producer; Specials:
A Carol Burnett Special … Carol, Carl, Whoopi, and Robin, ABC, 1987.
Brett Butler: The Child Ain't Right, 1993.
The Cosby Show: A Look Back, NBC, 2002.
Until the Violence Stops, Lifetime, 2004.

Television Executive Producer; Movies:
Single Bars, Single Women, ABC, 1984.

Television Executive Producer; Episodic:
"Oh, Brother," *Good Girls Don't …* (also known as *My Roommate Is a Big Fat Slut*), Oxygen Network, 2004.

Television Appearances; Specials:
The 4th Annual Television Academy Hall of Fame, Fox, 1987.
An American Family and Television: A National Town Hall Meeting, 1997.
Brett Butler: The E! True Hollywood Story, E! Entertainment Television, 1999.

Television Appearances; Miniseries:
TV Land Moguls, TV Land, 2004.

Film Work:
Executive producer, *Let's Go to Prison,* Universal, 2006.

OTHER SOURCES

Periodicals:
Broadcasting & Cable, December 20, 1999, p. 49; January 19, 2004, p. 8A.
New York Times, November 25, 1990.
Time, September 23, 1996, p. 68.

CARTER, Jack 1923–

PERSONAL

Original name, Jack Chakrin; born June 24, 1923, in Brooklyn (some sources cite New York), NY; married Paula Stewart (a singer and actress; divorced); married, second wife's name Roxanne; children: (first marriage) Michael. _Education:_ Attended Brooklyn College (now of the City University of New York), and Feagin School of Dramatic Arts, New York, NY. _Avocational Interests:_ Music, tennis, golf.

Addresses: _Manager_—Michael Einfeld, Michael Einfeld Management, 10630 Moorpark, Ste. 101, Toluca Lake, CA 91602.

Career: Comedian and actor. Performed as standup comedian, with frequent appearances at clubs in Las Vegas. Worked as a commercial artist for advertising agencies. _Military service:_ U.S. Army Air Forces, entertainment division, served during World War II.

Awards, Honors: Emmy Award nomination, 1962, for _Dr. Kildare;_ Emmy Award nomination, outstanding actor in a daytime drama special, 1975, for "The Girl Who Couldn't Lose," _The ABC Afternoon Playbreak._

CREDITS

Television Appearances; Series:
Rotating host, _Texaco Star Theater_ (later known as _The Milton Berle Show_), NBC, 1948.
Host, _Pick and Pat,_ ABC, 1949.
Host, _American Minstrels of 1949,_ ABC, 1949.
Host, _Jack Carter and Company,_ ABC, 1949.
Host, _The Jack Carter Show,_ NBC, 1950.
The Dean Martin Show (also known as _The Dean Martin Comedy Hour_), NBC, multiple appearances, 1973–74.
Vaudeville, syndicated, 1975.
The People's Command Performance (also known as _The Second Annual People's Command Performance_), 1978.
Voice of Teiresias, _Hercules_ (animated; also known as _Disney's "Hercules"_), ABC and syndicated, 1998.
Mr. Rapowski, _Driving Me Crazy,_ 2000.

Television Appearances; Movies:
Freddie Farber, _The Lonely Profession,_ NBC, 1969.
McGee, _The Family Rico,_ CBS, 1972.
Poor Devil, 1973.
Manny Fox, _The Sex Symbol,_ ABC, 1974.

Jackie Leroy, "The Girl Who Couldn't Lose," _The ABC Afternoon Playbreak_ (also known as _ABC Matinee Today_), ABC, 1975.
Theo Weiss, _The Great Houdini_ (also known as _The Great Houdinis_), ABC, 1976.
George Jessel, _Rainbow,_ NBC, 1978.
The Gossip Columnist, syndicated, 1979.
Existentialist, _For the Love of It,_ ABC, 1980.
Chubby Waters, _Broadway Bound_ (also known as _Neil Simon's "Broadway Bound"_), ABC, 1991.
Matty, _Double Deception,_ NBC, 1993.

Television Appearances; Specials:
Atlantic City Holiday, 1956.
The Alan King Show, ABC, 1969.
The Bob Hope Show, NBC, 1969.
Plimpton! Did You Hear the One about …?, ABC, 1971.
The Rowan and Martin Special, NBC, 1973.
Joys (also known as _Bob Hope Special: Bob Hope in "Joys"_), 1976.
Sydney Wineberg, "Have I Got a Christmas for You," _Hallmark Hall of Fame,_ NBC, 1977.
Sam Weinberg, _The Last Hurrah,_ NBC, 1977.
The New and Spectacular Guinness Book of World Records, 1980.
Voice of Harold and Roy, "Bunnicula, the Vampire Rabbit" (animated), _ABC Weekend Specials,_ ABC, 1982.
George Burns Celebrates 80 Years in Show Business, NBC, 1983.
Himself (in archive footage), _The Great Standups_ (also known as _The Great Standups: Sixty Years of Laughter_), 1984.
Hanukkah: Let There Be Lights, PBS, 1989.
Search for Haunted Hollywood, 1989.
The Comedy Concert Hour, The Nashville Network, 1990.
"The World of Jewish Humor," _Great Performances,_ PBS, 1990.
The Ed Sullivan All–Star Comedy Special, 1995.
Make Me Laugh, Comedy Central, 1997.
Comedy Central Presents: The N.Y. Friars Club Roast of Drew Carey, Comedy Central, 1998.
Let Me In, I Hear Laughter, Cinemax, 1999.
Comedy Central Presents Behind–the–Scenes at the American Comedy Awards, Comedy Central, 1999.
Now That's Funny! The Living Legends of Stand–up Comedy, PBS, 2001.

Also appeared in other Bob Hope specials; host of the first televised Tony Awards show.

Television Appearances; Pilots:
Madhouse 90, ABC, 1972.
Robin Dennis, _Human Feelings_ (also known as _Miles the Angel_), NBC, 1978.
Mr. Mancuso, _The Hustler of Muscle Beach,_ ABC, 1980.

Television Appearances; Episodic:
Host, *Cavalcade of Stars,* Dumont, 1949.
Comedian, *Toast of the Town* (also known as *The Ed Sullivan Show*), CBS, multiple episodes, between 1951 and 1969.
This Is Show Business (also known as *This Is Broadway*), 1952.
Host from Chicago, *The Saturday Night Revue,* NBC, 1953.
"The Runaway," *Studio One* (also known as *Studio One in Hollywood, Studio One Summer Theatre, Summer Theatre, Westinghouse Studio One,* and *Westinghouse Summer Theatre*), 1954.
Guest panelist, *What's My Line?,* 1954.
Comedian, *The Colgate Comedy Hour* (also known as *Michael Todd Revue, Colgate Summer Comedy Hour,* and *Colgate Variety Hour*), 1954, 1955.
"Roberta," *The Colgate Comedy Hour* (also known as *Michael Todd Revue, Colgate Summer Comedy Hour,* and *Colgate Variety Hour*), 1955.
Host, *Stage Show,* CBS, 1956.
The Arthur Murray Party (also known as *Arthur Murray Party Time* and *The Arthur Murray Show*), 1957.
The Eddie Fisher Show, 1958.
The Perry Como Show (also known as *The Chesterfield Supper Club* and *Perry Como's Kraft Music Hall*), 1958.
Person to Person, 1958.
The Bob Crosby Show, 1958.
The Revlon Revue (also known as *Revlon Presents* and *Revlon Spring Music Festival*), 1960.
Guest host, *The Tonight Show,* NBC, 1962.
Stanley Towers, "Most Likely to Succeed," *Alfred Hitchcock Presents,* 1962.
Newspaper columnist, "The People People Marry," *The Roaring 20's,* 1962.
John Norton Jones, "Buttons and Bones," *Hennesey,* 1962.
Himself, "Danny's Replacement," *Make Room for Daddy* (also known as *The Danny Thomas Show*), 1962.
Panelist, Phyllis Newman vs. Jack Carter," *Password* (also known as *Password All–Stars*), 1962.
Ted Gallahad, "Guest Appearance," *Dr. Kildare,* NBC, 1962.
Willie Guy, "The Great Guy," *Dr. Kildare,* NBC, 1963.
The Judy Garland Show, 1963.
"Jack Carter Helps Joey Propose," *The Joey Bishop Show,* 1964.
Lyle Schenk, "Stretch Petrie vs. Kid Schenk," *The Dick Van Dyke Show* (also known as *The Dick Van Dyke Daytime Show*), 1964.
Red Dekker, "Who Killed April?," *Burke's Law* (also known as *Amos Burke, Secret Agent*), 1964.
Comedian or singer, *The Hollywood Palace,* ABC, multiple appearances, between 1964 and 1968.
Murphy, "Main Event," *Combat!,* 1965.
Host, premiere episode, *Hippodrome Show,* 1966.
"The Super Chief," *Mister Roberts,* 1966.

Fred Blaney, "Lullaby for a Wind–up Toy," *Ben Casey,* 1966.
(Uncredited) Hot Rod Harry, "Come Back, Shame," *Batman,* 1966.
(Uncredited) Hot Rod Harry, "It's How You Play the Game," *Batman,* 1966.
The Dean Martin Show (also known as *The Dean Martin Comedy Hour*), NBC, 1966.
Guest, *The Merv Griffin Show,* 1967, 1968, 1977.
Tallyl, "Never Chase a Rainbow," *The Road West,* 1967.
Beau Rees, "Is Charlie Coming?," *The Danny Thomas Hour,* 1967.
The Hollywood Squares, multiple appearances, 1967.
Personality, 1968.
The Jackie Gleason Show (also known as *The Color Honeymooners*), CBS, 1968.
James Ashley, "My Master the Ghostbreaker," *I Dream of Jeannie,* 1968.
Ernie Cori, "Witness," *The Name of the Game,* 1968.
Alan Thorpe, "The Night of the Janus," *The Wild, Wild West,* 1969.
"Love and the Comedy Team," *Love, American Style,* 1969.
Playboy after Dark, 1969.
You're Putting Me On, 1969.
The Movie Game, 1969, 1970.
The Barbara McNair Show, 1970.
It Takes Two, 1970.
Harry O'Toole, "One for the Lady," *Mannix,* 1970.
Himself, "I Love You, Billy Baker: Parts 1 & 2," *The Name of the Game,* 1970.
Bill Crail, "The Brass Ring," *The Name of the Game,* 1970.
Pete Olsen, "Edge of Violence," *Medical Center,* CBS, 1971.
"Operation: Heroin," *O'Hara, U.S. Treasury,* 1971.
Frank Gordon, "The Disposal Man," *McCloud,* 1971.
Mantrap, 1971.
Rowan & Martin's Laugh–In (also known as *Laugh–In*), NBC, 1972.
"Don Rickles," *This Is Your Life,* 1972.
Bennie Mitchell, "Ragged Edge," *Cade's Country,* 1972.
"Love and the Bachelor Party," *Love, American Style,* 1972.
Cunningham, "An Elementary Case of Murder," *McMillan & Wife* (also known as *McMillan*), 1972.
Montgomery, "Blues for Sally M," *McMillan & Wife* (also known as *McMillan*), 1972.
"Love and the Cryptic Gift," *Love, American Style,* 1973.
Sy Kleiner, "Syndrome," *Emergency!* (also known as *Emergency One* and *Emergencia*), NBC, 1973.
Harry Foxton, "Try to Die on Time," *Hawaii Five–0* (also known as *McGarrett*), 1973.
"Morey Amsterdam," *This Is Your Life,* 1973.
Match Game 73 (also known as *Match Game* and *March Game 74*), 1973, 1974.
The Joker's Wild, 1974.

The $10,000 Pyramid (also known as *The $20,000 Pyramid, The $25,000 Pyramid, The $50,000 Pyramid, The $100,000 Pyramid, The New $25,000 Pyramid,* and *The New $100,000 Pyramid*), 1974.

Rhyme and Reason, 1975.

Celebrity Sweepstakes, 1975.

Risky Ross/Joey Flanders, "The Adventure of Veronica's Veils," *Ellery Queen* (also known as *The Adventures of Ellery Queen*), 1975.

Joey Birney, "Your Mother Wears Army Boots," *The Odd Couple,* 1975.

Hogan, "The Star," *Cannon,* 1975.

Jackie, "Hello Poppa," *Big Eddie,* 1975.

Break the Bank, 1976.

Marvin, "Fred meets Redd," *Sanford and Son,* 1976.

Game announcer, "The Game," *Emergency!* (also known as *Emergency One* and *Emergencia*), NBC, 1976.

Marty Golden, "The Becker Connection," *The Rockford Files* (also known as *Jim Rockford, Private Investigator*), 1977.

"Welcome to Paradise," *Kingston: Confidential,* 1977.

Johnny Banks, "Man of the Year," *Insight,* 1977.

"Who Killed Lila Craig?," *Switch,* 1978.

Ray Foster, "The Business of Love/Crash Diet Crisis/I'll Never Fall in Love Again," *The Love Boat,* 1978.

Salesman, "Family Crisis," *CHiPs* (also known as *CHiPs Patrol*), 1978.

Kevin, "The Beachcomber/The Last Whodunit," *Fantasy Island,* ABC, 1978.

Danny Baker, "The Comic/The Golden Hour," *Fantasy Island,* ABC, 1979.

Premiere episode, *Big Shamus, Little Shamus,* 1979.

Louis the loan shark, "Building the Restaurant," *Archie Bunker's Place,* 1979.

Herman Dodge, "The Swinger/Terrors of the Mind," *Fantasy Island,* ABC, 1980.

Morgan Townsend, "Skater's Edge/Concerto of Death/The Last Great Race," *Fantasy Island,* ABC, 1980.

Charles Vicent, "My Brother's Keeper," *Beyond Westworld,* 1980.

Vic Fletcher, "The Searcher/The Way We Weren't," *Fantasy Island,* ABC, 1981.

Joey Jackson, "Here's Joey Jackson," *The Littlest Hobo,* 1981.

Bert, "Exit Line," *Darkroom,* 1982.

Telephone installer, "Nell Goes to Jail," *Gimme a Break!,* 1982.

Mr. Corelli, "The Emergency," *Gimme a Break!,* 1982.

Cliff Carpenter, "Dead Heat," *Murder, She Wrote,* CBS, 1985.

Glenn Wallace, *Santa Barbara,* 1985.

"The Sins of the Quarterback," *1st & Ten* (also known as *1st & Ten: The Bulls Mean Business, 1st & Ten: The Championship, 1st & Ten: Do It Again, 1st & Ten: Going for Broke, 1st & Ten: In Your Face!,* and *1st & Ten, Training Camp: The Bulls Are Back*), HBO, 1985.

Sonny Rando, "The Ugliest American," *Cover Up,* 1985.

Voice of announcer, "Carol's Article," *Growing Pains,* 1985.

Stanley Beckerman, "Leroy and the Kid," *Fame,* 1985.

True Confessions, syndicated, 1986.

"Murder in the Cards," *Mike Hammer* (also known as *Mickey Spillane's "Mike Hammer"* and *The New Mike Hammer*), CBS, 1986.

John Bluthener, "Miss Stardust," *Amazing Stories* (also known as *Steven Spielberg's "Amazing Stories"*), NBC, 1987.

Harry Finlay, "Just Another Fish Story," *Murder, She Wrote,* CBS, 1988.

Klaatzu, "Barter," *Tales from the Darkside,* 1988.

"The Legend," *They Came from Outer Space,* 1991.

"Only When I Laugh," *Blossom,* NBC, 1992.

Himself, "Final Analysis," *Empty Nest,* 1992.

Murray Brown, "I'm Looking through You," *Lois & Clark: The New Adventures of Superman* (also known as *Lois & Clark* and *The New Adventures of Superman*), ABC, 1993.

Bouncy's manager, "Oral Sex, Lies and Videotape," *Dream On,* HBO, 1993.

Old geezer, "Ren's Pecs/An Abe Divided," *The Ren & Stimpy Show* (animated; also known as *VH–1 Ren and Stimpy Rocks*), 1993.

"Who Killed the Host at the Roast?" *Burke's Law,* CBS, 1994.

Joey Miller, "The Lottery," *Time Trax,* syndicated, 1994.

Kenneth Trant, "The Big Crunch," *Cracker,* Arts and Entertainment, 1994.

Himself, "See Jeff Jump, Jump, Jeff, Jump!," *Cybill,* 1995.

"Resurrection/Niles and Bob/Harry Stenz," *The Watcher,* UPN, 1995.

Voice, "Research and Destroy," *Duckman: Private Dick/Family Man* (animated), USA Network, 1995.

Mr. Burns, "Kirk Unplugged," *Kirk,* 1995.

Sonny, "Bash at the Beach," *Baywatch,* syndicated, 1996.

Voice of old man, "Sleepless in Orlando," *Coach,* ABC, 1996.

Tony, "Something about a Family Photo," *Something So Right,* NBC, 1996.

Himself, "Caroline and the Comic," *Caroline in the City* (also known as *Caroline*), NBC, 1996.

Raymond "Ray" Kellum, "Compromising Positions," *Living Single* (also known as *My Girls*), Fox, 1996.

Raymond "Ray" Kellum, "Do You Take This Man's Wallet?," *Living Single* (also known as *My Girls*), Fox, 1996.

Voice of Harry, "Warrior Queen," *Superman* (animated; also known as *Superman: The Animated Series*), The WB, 1997.

Tony, "The Wrestler," *Beyond Belief: Fact or Fiction,* 1998.

"Been There, Done That," *L.A. Doctors,* 1999.

Gordon Gonza, "Retribution: Part 1," *Diagnosis Murder,* CBS, 1998.

Himself, "Cry and You Cry Alone," *Touched by an Angel,* CBS, 1998.

Uncle Abe, "Dick Solomon of the Indiana Solomons," *3rd Rock from the Sun* (also known as *Life as We Know It* and *3rd Rock*), NBC, 1999.

Oliver King, "Captain Crimestopper," *L.A. Heat,* TNT, 1999.

Rudy Steineger, "The Voice," *7th Heaven* (also known as *Seven Heaven* and *7th Heaven: Beginnings*), The WB, 1999.

"The Hypnotist," *Stark Raving Mad,* NBC, 2000.

"Unfunny Girl," *Hollywood Off–Ramp,* E! Entertainment Television, 2000.

Barnacle Bob, "Jane Cops Out," *One World,* 2000.

"As Others See Us," *Arli$$,* HBO, 2001.

Voices of Irwin Linker and Nate, "Yankee Hankee," *King of the Hill* (animated), Fox, 2001.

Voice of Irwin Linker, "Unfortunate Son," *King of the Hill* (animated), Fox, 2002.

Mickey, "The Maid Man," *Andy Richter Controls the Universe,* Fox, 2003.

Buddy Rivers, "The Comedy Stylings of Rivers & Red," *Just Shoot Me!,* NBC, 2003.

Voice of Sid, "This Little Piggy," *Justice League* (animated; also known as *JL* and *Justice League Unlimited*), Cartoon Network, 2004.

Man at bus stop, "Down the Drain," *CSI: Crime Scene Investigation* (also known as *C.S.I., CSI: Las Vegas,* and *Les experts*), CBS, 2004.

Voice of older Nathan, "Maybe–Sitting," *Phil of the Future,* Disney Channel, 2005.

Mickey Goldstein, "All about Christmas Eve," *ER,* NBC, 2005.

Kipke, "Reason to Believe," *ER,* NBC, 2006.

Also appeared as Friendly Freddie, *Gomer Pyle, U.S. M.C.;* and in episodes of *The Andy Williams Show* and *The Fall Guy,* ABC.

Television Director; Episodic:

Here's Lucy, CBS, 1971.

Film Appearances:

Lieutenant William "Billy" Monk, *The Horizontal Lieutenant,* Metro–Goldwyn–Mayer, 1962.

(Uncredited) Himself, *Viva Las Vegas* (also known as *Love in Las Vegas*), Metro–Goldwyn–Mayer, 1964.

Gunner's Mate Orville Toole, *The Extraordinary Seaman,* Metro–Goldwyn–Mayer, 1969.

Dwight Childs (some sources cite Chiles), *The Resurrection of Zachary Wheeler,* Vidtronics, 1971.

Herbie Dalitz, *Hustle,* Paramount, 1975.

Solly Kramer, *The Amazing Dobermans* (also known as *Lucky*), Golden, 1976.

Male journalist, *Won Ton Ton, the Dog Who Saved Hollywood* (also known as *Won Ton Ton*), Paramount, 1976.

Senator Caruso, *The Happy Hooker Goes to Washington,* Cannon, 1977.

Manny, *Record City,* American International Pictures, 1977.

Walter Stratton, *The Glove* (also known as *Blood Mad* and *The Glove: Lethal Terminator*), Pro International, 1978.

Mayor Ledoux, *Alligator,* Group 1, 1980.

Sharkey, *The Octagon* (also known as *The Man without Mercy*), American Cinema, 1980.

Rat vendor, *History of the World: Part I* (also known as *Mel Brooks' "History of the World: Part 1"*), Twentieth Century–Fox, 1981.

Barney Brodsky, *Separate Ways,* Crown International, 1981.

Voice of Catskill, *Heartbeeps,* 1981.

Philly Beekman, *The Funny Farm,* New World/Mutual, 1982.

Lester Burns, *Hambone and Hillie,* New World, 1984.

Sidney, *Love Scenes* (also known as *Ecstacy, Lovescene,* and *Love Secrets*) 1985.

Samsa, *The Trouble with Dick,* Frolix, 1987.

Frank Bower, *W.A.R.: Women Against Rape* (also known as *Death Blow, Death Blow: A Cry for Justice,* and *I Will Dance on Your Grave: Lethal Victims*), 1987.

Cal Farnsworth, *Sexpot,* 1988.

Evan Weiss, *Deadly Embrace,* 1989.

Mr. Castaglia, *Caged Fury,* 1990.

Robo–C.H.I.C. (also known as *Cyber–C.H.I.C.*), 1990.

Old priest, *Satan's Princess* (also known as *Malediction*), Paramount, 1991.

Senator Robertson, *Social Suicide* (also known as *Primadonnas: Rebels without a Clue*), 1991.

Announcer, *Arena,* Columbia/TriStar, 1991.

Stan, *In the Heat of Passion* (also known as *Heat of Passion*), Concorde, 1992.

Rabbi, *The Opposite Sex and How to Live with Them,* Miramax, 1992.

Honda Civic driver, *Killer per caso* (also known as *The Good Bad Guy*), 1997.

Pawnbroker, *October 22,* 1998.

Mr. Weintraub, *Pastry, Pain and Politics,* 1998.

Dante Solomon, *Play It to the Bone* (also known as *Play It*), Buena Vista, 1999.

Sid, *One Last Ride,* Eclectic Entertainment, 2004.

Also appeared in *Comics.*

Stage Appearances:

(Broadway debut) *Call Me Mister,* 1947.

Fred Campbell, *Mr. Wonderful* (musical), Broadway Theatre, New York City, 1956–57.

Guys and Dolls, Paper Mill Playhouse, Millburn, NJ, c. 1984.

A Funny Thing Happened on the Way to the Forum, 1991.

Sugar, Dorothy Chandler Pavilion, Los Angeles, c. 1992.

Legends of the Catskills, North Shore Center for the Performing Arts, Skokie, IL, 2000.

Also appeared in *Born Yesterday; Critic's Choice; A Hatful of Rain; The Last of the Red Hot Lovers; Little Me; The Odd Couple; A Thousand Clowns;* and *Top Banana.*

Major Tours:
Toured as Fagin, *Oliver,* Nederlander Company.

Stage Director:
Directed productions of *Mouth–Trap, Silver Anniversary,* and *A Thousand Clowns,* all at Drury Lane Theatre, Chicago, IL.

RECORDINGS

Video Games:
Voices of Barnabus, old male captive, and young male captive, *Lands of Lore III,* 1999.

Voice of uncle, *Jak and Daxter: The Precursor Legacy* (also known as *Jak and Daxter*), Sony Computer Entertainment America, 2001.

CASSIDY, David 1950–

PERSONAL

Full name, David Bruce Cassidy; born April 12, 1950, in New York, NY; son of Jack Cassidy (an actor) and Evelyn Ward (an actress and singer); half–brother of Shaun Cassidy (a singer, actor, and producer) and Patrick Cassidy (an actor); married Kay Lenz (an actress), April 3, 1977 (divorced, 1981); married Meryl–Amm Tanz (a horse breeder), December 15, 1984 (divorced, 1986); married Sue Shifrin, March 30, 1991; children: (third marriage) Beau Devon; (with Sherry Williams, a model) Katherine Evelyn Benedon/Katie Cassidy (an actress, singer, and model). *Education:* Studied psychology at Los Angeles City College; trained for the stage with David Craig and Milton Katselas. *Avocational Interests:* Breeding and racing thoroughbred horses.

Addresses: *Manager*—Billy Miller Management, 8322 Ridpath Dr., Los Angeles, CA 90046. *Publicist*—JAG Entertainment, 4265 Hazeltine Ave., Sherman Oaks, CA 91423.

Career: Actor, singer, and songwriter.

Member: Screen Actors Guild, American Federation of Television and Radio Artists, Actors' Equity Association, American Society of Composers, Authors, and Publishers.

Awards, Honors: Golden Apple Award, discovery of the year, Hollywood Women's Press Club, 1971; Emmy Award nomination, best actor in a dramatic role, 1978, for *Police Story;* TV Land Award, hippest fashion plate—male, TV Land Award nominations (with others), quintessential non–traditional family, 2003, and favorite singing siblings, 2006, all for *The Partridge Family;* eighteen Gold Record awards, Recording Industry Association of America; two Grammy Award nominations.

CREDITS

Stage Appearances:
The Pajama Game, Los Angeles Theatre Center, Los Angeles, 1960.
And So to Bed, Los Angeles Theatre Center, 1965.
(Broadway production) Billy, *The Fig Leaves Are Falling,* Broadhurst Theatre, New York City, 1969.
Sergeant Bill, *Voice of the Turtle,* Westport Country Playhouse, Westport, CT, 1979.
Title role, *Little Johnny Jones,* Dorothy Chandler Pavilion, Los Angeles, 1981.
Jud Templeton, *Tribute,* Stage West Dinner Theatre, Calgary, Alberta, Canada, 1982.
George M. Cohan, *Parade of Stars Playing the Palace,* Palace Theatre, New York City, 1983.
Title role, *Joseph and the Amazing Technicolor Dreamcoat,* Royale Theatre, New York City, 1983.
Jesus, *Jesus Christ Superstar,* Starlight Theatre, Kansas City, MO, 1984.
The rock star, *Time,* Dominion Theatre, London, 1987–97.
Mickey Johnston, *Blood Brothers,* Music Box Theatre, New York City, 1993–94, then Royal Alexandra Theatre, Toronto, Ontario, Canada, 1996.

Also appeared as Bobby Darin, *The Rat Pack,* Las Vegas, NV.

Major Tours:
Title role, *Little Johnny Jones,* U.S. cities, 1981.
Title role, *Joseph and the Amazing Technicolor Dreamcoat,* U.S. and Canadian cities, 1983–84.
Mickey Johnston, *Blood Brothers,* U.S. and Canadian cities, 1994–95.

Also appeared in *Tribute,* U.S. and Canadian cities.

Television Appearances; Series:
Keith Douglas Partridge, *The Partridge Family,* ABC, 1970–74.

Officer Dan Shay, *David Cassidy—Man Undercover*, NBC, 1978–79.
In Search of the Partridge Family, VH1, 2004.

Television Appearances; Movies:
David Greeley, *The Night the City Screamed,* ABC, 1980.

Television Appearances; Specials:
The Bob Hope Show, NBC, 1972.
The 16th Annual TV Week Logie Awards, Nine Network, 1974.
Keith Partridge, *Thanksgiving Reunion with the Partridge Family and My Three Sons,* ABC, 1977.
Celebrity Challenge of the Sexes, CBS, 1977.
Parade of Stars, ABC, 1983.
Presenter, *The 37th Annual Tony Awards,* CBS, 1983.
TV's Censored Bloopers, 1984.
The 1990 MTV Video Music Awards, MTV and syndicated, 1990.
Tom Arnold: The Naked Truth, HBO, 1991.
Voices That Care, 1991.
Idols, 1991.
The American Music Awards, ABC, 1991.
An American Saturday Night, 1991.
American Bandstand 40th Anniversary Special, 1992.
American Bandstand's Teen Idols, 1994.
Host, *VH-1's 8–Track Flash Back,* VH1, 1995–96.
Close to You: Remembering the Carpenters, 1997.
Mr. Vegas All–Night Party Starring Drew Carey, 1997.
The Viva in Vegas Special, 1998.
The WB Radio Music Awards, The WB, 1999.
The Partridge Family: The E! True Hollywood Story, E! Entertainment Television, 1999.
TV Guide's Truth Behind the Sitcoms, 1999.
David Cassidy: Behind the Music, VH1, 1999.
The Beth Littleford Interview Special, 1999.
Johnny Flamingo, *David Cassidy at the Copa,* 2000.
House on High Street, 2000.
The 2nd Annual Family Television Awards, CBS, 2000.
VH1 News Special: Listening to America, VH1, 2001.
Intimate Portrait: Shirley Jones, Lifetime, 2001.
Heart–throbs of the 70s, 2001.
Bubblegum Babylon, VH1, 2002.
We Are Family, BBC, 2003.
TV Land Awards: A Celebration of Classic TV (also known as *1st Annual TV Land Awards*), TV Land, 2003.
Comic Genius: The Work of Bernard Slade, 2003.
I Love the '70s, VH1, 2003.
The 6th Annual Family Television Awards, The WB, 2004.
When "The Partridge Family" Ruled the World, VH1, 2004.
100 Greatest Teen Stars, VH1, 2006.

Television Appearances; Pilots:
Keith Partridge, *A Knight In Shining Armor,* ABC, 1971.

Television Appearances; Episodic:
Mike, "Chapter 7," *The Survivors* (also known as *Harold Robbins' "The Survivors"*), ABC, 1969.
Billy Burgess, "The Law and Billy Burgess," *Bonanza* (also known as *Ponderosa*), NBC, 1969.
Gene Sanders, "In a Quiet Place," *This Is the Life,* 1969.
Danny Goodson, "Stolen on Demand," *Ironside* (also known as *The Raymond Burr Show*), NBC, 1970.
Larry Foster, "The Fatal Imposter," *The F.B.I.,* ABC, 1970.
Michael Ambrose, "Fun and Games and Michael Ambrose," *Marcus Welby, M.D.* (also known as *Robert Young, Family Doctor*), ABC, 1970.
Tim Richmond, "Log 24: A Rare Occasion," *Adam–12,* NBC, 1970.
Rick Lambert, "His Brother's Keeper," *Medical Center,* CBS, 1970.
Brad, "The Loser," *Mod Squad,* ABC, 1970.
"Shirley Jones," *This Is Your Life,* 1971.
The Glen Campbell Goodtime Hour, 1971.
Officer Dan Shay, "A Chance to Live," *Police Story,* NBC, 1978.
Ted Harmes, "The Oilman Cometh," *The Love Boat,* 1980.
Danny Collier, "Unholy Wedlock/Elizabeth," *Fantasy Island,* 1980.
John Gordon Boyd, "Joey's Here," *Matt Houston,* ABC, 1982.
Donald/David, "Heir Presumptuous," *Tales of the Unexpected* (also known as *Roald Dahl's "Tales of the Unexpected"*), 1982.
"The Songwriter," *Fantasy Island,* 1983.
Top of the Pops (also known as *All New Top of the Pops* and *TOTP*), 1985.
Joey Mitchell, "Career Move," *Alfred Hitchcock Presents,* USA Network, 1988.
Sam Scudder, "Done with Mirrors," *The Flash,* CBS, 1991.
"Blossom—A Rockumentary," *Blossom,* 1991.
Where In the World Is Carmen Sandiego?, 1991.
"Episode with Flea," *The Ben Stiller Show,* Fox, 1992.
Patrick Riley, "Falsches Spiel mit Patrick," *Ein SchoB am Worthesee* (also known as *Lakeside Hotel*), 1993.
"David Cassidy," *This Is Your Life,* 1994.
Jefferson Kelly, "Wrestling Matches," *The John Larroquette Show* (also known as *Larroquette*), NBC, 1995.
The Rosie O'Donnell Show, syndicated, 1996.
Sin City Spectacular (also known as *Penn & Teller's "Sin City Spectacular"*), ABC, 1998.
Wheel of Fortune, NBC, 1998.
"The Cassidys: C'mon, Get Happy," *Famous Families,* 1999.
"Sal Mineo: Hollywood's Forgotten Rebel," *Biography,* Arts and Entertainment, 1999.
"Shirley Jones: Hollywood's Musical Mom," *Biography,* Arts and Entertainment, 2000.
Host, "I Love 1972," *I Love 1970's,* 2000.
"Teen Idols," *VH–1 Where Are They Now?,* VH1, 2000.

Pajama Party, Oxygen, 2001.

The Late Late Show with Craig Kilborn (also known as *The Late Late Show*), CBS, 2001.

"70 Teen Idols," *VH–1 Where Are They Now?,* VH1, 2002.

Good Morning, America (also known as *G.M.A.*), ABC, 2002.

Everett Price, *The Agency,* CBS, 2002.

Hollywood Squares (also known as *H2* and *H2: Hollywood Squares*), syndicated, 2003.

GMTV, ITV, 2003.

Liquid News, BBC, 2003.

V Graham Norton, Channel 4, 2003.

"The Partridge Family," *Biography,* Arts and Entertainment, 2003.

Everett Price, "War, Inc.," *The Agency,* 2003.

Boone Vincent, "Vegas," *Malcolm in the Middle,* Fox, 2003.

Voice of Roland Pond, "Oh Boyz," *Kim Possible* (animated; also known as *Disney's "Kim Possible"*), Disney Channel, 2004.

Today (also known as *NBC News Today* and *The Today Show*), NBC, 2004.

The Paul O'Grady Show (also known as *The New Paul O'Grady Show*), ITV, 2004.

"David Cassidy: The Reluctant Idol," *Biography,* Arts and Entertainment, 2004.

Vince, "Playhouse," *Less Than Perfect,* ABC, 2005.

"Small Screen, Big Stars," *TV Land's Top Ten,* TV Land, 2005.

"Sexist Men," *TV Land's Top Ten,* TV Land, 2005.

Late Night with Conan O'Brien, NBC, 2005.

Strictly Come Dancing: It Takes Two, BBC2, 2006.

Loose Women, ITV, 2006.

"Danny Bonaduce: Tabloid's Bad Boy," *Biography,* Arts and Entertainment, 2006.

Richard and Judy, Channel 4, 2007.

"Locations," *TV Land Confidential* (also known as *TV Land Confidential: The Untold Stories*), TV Land, 2007.

Also appeared in *American Bandstand; The Merv Griffin Show.*

Television Work; Series:

Theme song performer, *The John Larroquette Show* (also known as *Larroquette*), NBC, 1993.

Creator, co–executive producer, and theme song performer, *Ask Harriet,* Fox, 1998.

Associate producer, *I Married ...* VH1, 2003.

Co–executive producer, *In Search of the Partridge Family,* VH1, 2004.

Producer, *I Married ...* VH1, 2004.

Television Work; Movies:

Executive producer, *The David Cassidy Story,* NBC, 2000.

Television Work; Specials:

Associate producer, *Bearing Witness,* Arts and Entertainment, 2004.

Co–executive producer, *The Partridge Family,* VH1, 2005.

Film Appearances:

Reno, *Instant Karma* (also known as *Almost a Virgin*), Metro–Goldwyn–Mayer, 1990.

Adam–11, *The Spirit of '76,* Columbia, 1990.

Grant, *Popstar,* Downtown the Movie LLC, 2005.

RECORDINGS

Albums (with the Partridge Family):

The Partridge Family Album, Bell, 1970.

Up to Date, Bell, 1971.

The Partridge Family Sound Magazine, Bell, 1971.

Partridge Family Christmas Card, Bell/Razor & Tie, 1971.

Partridge Family: At Home with Their Greatest Hits, Bell, 1972.

The Partridge Family Shopping Bag, Bell, 1972.

The Partridge Family Greatest Hits, Arista, 1989.

Albums (as a solo artist):

Cherish, Bell, 1972.

Dreams Are Nothin More Than Wishes, Bell, 1973.

Rock Me Baby, Bell, 1973.

David Cassidy's Greatest Hits, Bell, 1974.

Cassidy Live, Bell, 1974.

Forever, Bell, 1975.

The Higher They Climb, the Harder They Fall, 1975–76.

Home Is Where the Heart Is, RCA, 1976.

Gettin It in the Street, RCA, 1976.

Blood Brothers First Night, 1984.

Billy and Blaze, Caedmon, 1984.

Romance, Arista, 1985.

When I'm a Rock & Roll Star, Razor & Tie, 1986.

David Cassidy, Enigma, 1986.

Didn't You Used to Be ..., Scotti Bros., 1991.

The Best of David Cassidy, Curb, 1996.

Romantic Duets, 1998.

David Cassidy: Partridge Family Favorites, 1998.

Old Trick, New Dog, Slamajama, 1998.

The Definitive Collection, Arista, 2000.

Daydreamer, 2001.

Then and Now, Decca, 2001.

Touch of Blue, Universal Music TV, 2003.

Could It Be Forever: The Greatest Hits, Sony BMG, 2006.

Also performed on *Television's Greatest Hits,* TVT, 1996; *Andrew Gold's Halloween Howls: Fun and Scary Music,* Rhino, 1996; *EFX* (cast album), Metro–Goldwyn–Mayer, 1998; and *Sondheim: A Celebration,* 1998.

Videos:

Performer and producer, *David Cassidy Live in Glasgow,* Warner Music Vision, 2004.

Live In Concert, Image, 2004.

Greatest Hits Live, Standing Room Only, 2005.

Greatest Hits, Demon, 2007.

Music Videos:

Appeared in "Voices That Care."

WRITINGS

Books:

(With Chip Deffaa) *C'mon Get Happy: Fear and Loathing on the Partridge Family Bus* (autobiography), 1993.

Could It Be Forever, Headline, 2007.

Television Episodes:

Ask Harriet, Fox, 1998.

Television Theme Songs; Series:

The John Larroquette Show (also known as *Larroquette*), NBC, 1993.

Ask Harriet, Fox, 1998.

OTHER SOURCES

Electronic:

David Cassidy Website, http://www.davidcassidy.com, October 10, 2007.

CASTLE, Nick 1947–

PERSONAL

Full name, Nicholas Charles Castle, Jr.; born September 21, 1947, in Los Angeles, CA; son of Nick, Sr. (a choreographer and actor) and Millie Castle. *Education:* Attended Santa Monica College; University of Southern California, degree, filmmaking.

Addresses: *Agent*—Read, 8033 Sunset Blvd., Suite 937, Los Angeles, CA 90046. *Manager*—Todd Smith and Associates, 345 N. Maple Dr., Suite 393, Beverly Hills, CA 90210.

Career: Director and writer.

Member: Directors Guild of America, Writers Guild of America.

Awards, Honors: Grand Prize nomination, Avoriaz Fantastic Film Festival, 1985, for *The Last Starfighter;* Saturn Award nomination, best writing, Academy of Science Fiction, Fantasy, and Horror Films, 1987, for *The Boy Who Could Fly;* Silver Raven, Brussels International Festival of Fantasy Film, Bronze Gryphon, free to fly section, and Gold Medal of the Regional Council, Giffoni Film Festival, 2001, all for *Delivering Milo.*

CREDITS

Film Director:

TAG: The Assassination Game (also known as *Everybody Gets It in the End* and *Kiss Me, Kill Me*), New World, 1982.

The Last Starfighter, Universal, 1984.

The Boy Who Could Fly, Twentieth Century–Fox, 1986.

Tap, TriStar, 1989.

Dennis the Menace (also known as *Dennis*), Warner Bros., 1993.

Major Payne, Universal, 1995.

Mr. Wrong, Buena Vista, 1996.

Delivering Milo, IMMI Pictures/Lakeshore International, 2000.

The Seat Filler, The Momentum Experience, 2004.

Connors' War, Sony Pictures Video, 2006.

Film Work; Other:

Cinematographer, *The Resurrection of Bronco Billy* (short), 1970.

Assistant camera operator, *Dark Star,* 1974.

Film Appearances:

Artists and Models, Paramount, 1955.

Anything Goes, Paramount, 1956.

(Uncredited) Alien, *Dark Star,* 1974.

The shape, *Halloween* (also known as *John Carpenter's "Halloween"*), Falcon/Compass, 1978.

Member of "The Coupe DeVilles," *The Boy Who Could Fly,* Twentieth Century–Fox, 1986.

Himself, *"Halloween" Unmasked 2000* (documentary), Anchor Bay Entertainment, 1999.

Himself, *Return to "Escape from New York"* (documentary short), Metro–Goldwyn–Mayer Home Entertainment, 2003.

Himself, *"Halloween": 25 Years of Terror* (documentary), Anchor Bay Entertainment, 2006.

Television Work; Movies:

Director, *'Twas the Night,* 2001.

Television Work; Pilots:
Executive producer and director, *Shangri–La Plaza*, CBS, 1990.

Television Director; Episodic:
"The 21–Inch Sun," *Amazing Stories* (also known as *Steven Spielberg's "Amazing Stories"*), NBC, 1987.

Television Appearances; Specials:
Himself, *"Halloween": A Cut Above the Rest,* 2003.

Television Appearances; Episodic:
The Caterina Valente Show, 1971.

WRITINGS

Screenplays:
The Resurrection of Bronco Billy (short), 1970.
Skatetown U.S.A., Rastar/Columbia, 1979.
(With Dick Chudnow and Rick Friedberg) *K–GOD* (also known as *Pray TV*), 1980.
(With John Carpenter) *Escape from New York* (also known as *John Carpenter's "Escape from New York"*), Avco, 1981.
TAG: The Assassination Game (also known as *Everybody Gets It in the End, T.A.G.: The Assassination Game,* and *Kiss Me, Kill Me*), New World, 1982.
The Boy Who Could Fly, Twentieth Century–Fox, 1986.
Tap, TriStar, 1989.
August Rush, Warner Bros., 2007.

Screenplay Stories:
Skatetown U.S.A., Rastar/Columbia, 1979.
Hook, 1991.
August Rush, 2007.

Film Songs:
The Boy Who Could Fly, Twentieth Century–Fox, 1986.

Television Movies:
'Twas the Night, 2001.

Television Specials:
Perry Como's Hawaiian Holiday, 1975.
Perry Como's Hawaiian Holiday, NBC, 1976.

Television Pilots:
Shangri–La Plaza, CBS, 1990.

CHARBY, Jay
   See ELLISON, Harlan

CLARK, Jim 1931–
   (James Clark)

PERSONAL

Born May 24, 1931, in Boston, Lincolnshire, England; son of Vernon (a company director) and Florence (a homemaker; maiden name, Deal) Clark; married Laurence Mery (a film editor), July, 1963; children: David, Kate, Sybil.

Addresses: *Agent*—Tim Corrie, Peters Fraser and Dunlop, Drury House, 34–43 Russell St., London SC2B 5HA, England.

Career: Film editor, director, producer, and writer. Also worked as assistant editor, second unit director, and consultant.

Member: Directors Guild of America, Academy of Motion Picture Arts and Sciences, Association of Cinematography, Television, and Allied Technicians (Canada).

Awards, Honors: Film Award nomination, best film editing, British Academy of Film and Television Arts, 1977, for *Marathon Man;* Academy Award, best film editing, Film Award, best editing, British Academy of Film and Television Arts, and Eddie Award nomination, best edited feature film, American Cinema Editors, 1985, all for *The Killing Fields;* Academy Award nomination, best film editing, Film Award, best editing, British Academy of Film and Television Arts, and Eddie Award nomination, best edited feature film, 1987, for *The Mission;* film editing award from Guild of British Film Editors, c. 1999, for *Memphis Belle;* Career Achievement Award, American Cinema Editors, 2005; Film Award nomination, best film editing, British Academy of Film and Television Arts, 2005, for *Vera Drake.*

CREDITS

Film Editor; As James Clark:
One Wish Too Many (also known as *The Magic Marble*), Sterling Educational Films–Children's Film Foundation, 1956.
Surprise Package, Columbia, 1960.
The Grass Is Greener, Universal, 1960.
The Innocents, Twentieth Century–Fox, 1961.
Term of Trial, Warner Bros., 1962.
Charade, Universal, 1963.
The Pumpkin Eater, Columbia, 1964.
Darling, Embassy, 1965.

Film Editor; As Jim Clark:

X Y and Zee (also known as *Zee and Co.*), Columbia, 1972.

(And director) *Visions of Eight* (also known as *Olympic Visions, Muenchen 1972—8 beruehmte Regisseure sehen die Spiele der XX. Olympiade,* and *Olympiade Muenchen 1972*), 1973.

The Day of the Locust, Paramount, 1975.

The Adventure of Sherlock Holmes' Smarter Brother (also known as *Sherlock Holmes' Smarter Brother*), Twentieth Century–Fox, 1975.

Marathon Man, Paramount, 1976.

(With Arthur Schmidt) *The Last Remake of Beau Geste,* Universal, 1977.

Agatha, Warner Bros., 1979.

Yanks (also known as *Yanks—Gestern waren wir noch freunde*), Universal, 1979.

Honky Tonk Freeway, Universal, 1981.

Privates on Parade, HandMade Films, 1982, Orion Classics, 1984.

The Killing Fields, Warner Bros., 1984.

The Frog Prince, Warner Bros., 1985, released in the United States as *French Lesson,* Warner Bros., 1986.

The Mission, Warner Bros., 1986.

(With Bryan Oates) *Il giovane Toscanini* (also known as *Toscanini* and *Young Toscanini*), Italian International Films, 1988.

Spies Inc. (also known as *Code Name: Chaos, Spies, Lies and Alibis,* and *S.P.O.O.K.S.*), 1988.

Memphis Belle, Warner Bros., 1990.

Meeting Venus, Warner Bros., 1991.

This Boy's Life, Warner Bros., 1993.

A Good Man in Africa, Gramercy, 1994.

Nell, Twentieth Century–Fox, 1994.

Copycat, Warner Bros., 1995.

Marvin's Room, Miramax, 1996.

The Jackal (also known as *Le chacal* and *Der schakal*), Universal, 1998.

Onegin, Samuel Goldwyn Films, 1999.

The Trench (also known as *La tranchee*), Somme Productions, 1999.

The World Is Not Enough (also known as *Pressure Point* and *T.W.I.N.E.*), Metro–Goldwyn–Mayer/United Artists, 1999.

Kiss Kiss (Bang Bang), Offline Releasing, 2000.

City by the Sea (also known as *The Suspect*), Warner Bros., 2002.

Vera Drake, Fine Line, 2004.

Opal Dream (also known as *Opal Dream*), Strand Releasing, 2006.

Film Director:

Senghenydd: Portrait of a Mining Town, 1966.

(As James Clark) *The Christmas Tree,* CFF, 1966.

(As James Clark) *Think Dirty* (also known as *Every Home Should Have One*), British Lion, 1970.

Day of Rest, 1970.

Rentadick, Virgin, 1972.

Madhouse (also known as *Deathday, The Madhouse of Dr. Fear,* and *The Revenge of Dr. Death*), American International Pictures, 1974.

Film Appearances:

(Uncredited) Voice of narrator on television, *The Jackal* (also known as *Le chacal* and *Der schakal*), Universal, 1998.

Television Film Editor; Movies:

Radio Inside, Showtime, 1994.

The Gathering Storm, HBO, 2002.

WRITINGS

Screenplays:

(As James Clark; with Michael Barnes) *The Christmas Tree* (based on a story by Ed Harper), CFF, 1966.

CORMAN, Maddie 1969(?)–

PERSONAL

Full name, Madeleine Corman; born in 1969 (some source say 1970), in New York, NY; daughter of Michael (a lawyer) and Irene K. (a special education consultant) Corman; married Roger (divorced); married Jace Alexander (a director and actor), September 6, 1998; children: (second marriage) three. *Education:* Barnard College, Columbia University, New York City, B.A., English literature; studied acting with Carli Glynn at Circle Repertory Theatre School, New York City.

Addresses: *Agent*—Innovative Artists, 1505 10th St., Santa Monica, CA 90401. *Manager*—Barking Dog Entertainment, 9 Desbrosses St., 2nd Floor, New York, NY 10013.

Career: Actress. Appeared in television commercials.

CREDITS

Film Appearances:

Polly Franklin, *Seven Minutes in Heaven* (also known as *Deslices de joventud*), Warner Bros., 1985.

Laura Nelson, *Some Kind of Wonderful,* Paramount, 1987.

Zuzu Petals, *The Adventures of Ford Fairlane,* Twentieth Century–Fox, 1990.

Myra, *My New Gun,* IRS Media, 1992.

Womynist number two, *PCU* (also known as *PCU Pit Party*), Twentieth Century–Fox, 1994.

Missy, *Mr. Wrong,* Buena Vista, 1996.

Liz Curry, *Boys,* Buena Vista, 1996.

Peek–a–Boo girl, *Swingers,* Miramax, 1996.

Beth, *I Think I Do,* Strand Releasing, 1997.

Nina Manning, *Kissing Jake* (short), 1999.

Carol the photographer, *Mickey Blue Eyes,* Warner Bros., 1999.

Alan's mother, *For Caroline* (short), 2002.

Leezette, *Maid in Manhattan* (also known as *Made in New York*), Columbia, 2002.

Patty Mcpherson, *The Treatment,* New Yorker Films, 2006.

Lea, *Ira and Abby,* Magnolia Pictures, 2006.

Marilyn, *Beer League* (also known as *Arti Lange's "Beer League"*), Echo Bridge Entertainment, 2006.

Mousy, *Sunshine Cleaning,* 2008.

Television Appearances; Series:

Cynthia Tresch, *Mr. President,* Fox, 1987.

Ruthie Latham, *All–American Girl,* 1994–95.

Television Appearances; Movies:

Janine, *Extreme Close–Up* (also known as *Home Video*), NBC, 1990.

Julianne Hoffenberg, *Jenifer* (also known as *The Jenifer Estess Story*), CBS, 2001.

Television Appearances; Specials:

Mary Sanders, "I Want to Go Home," *ABC Afterschool Specials,* ABC, 1985.

Sheila Rosenthal, *Tracey Take On New York,* HBO, 1993.

Television Appearances; Episodic:

Haven Claven, "Allie Doesn't Live Here Anymore," *Kate & Allie,* CBS, 1988.

Haven Claven, "The Odd Couples," *Kate & Allie,* CBS, 1988.

Babs Bengal, "The Case of the Unnatural," *Mathnet,* PBS, 1991.

Babs Bengal, *Square One TV,* PBS, 1991.

Christie, "Kid Stuff," *Silk Stalkings,* USA Network, 1993.

Gail, "Death Becomes Him," *Diagnosis Murder,* CBS, 1994.

Receptionist, "Lunar Eclipse," *Central Park West* (also known as *C.P.W.*), CBS, 1995.

Mary Lou, "Cranked Up," *Pacific Blue,* USA Network, 1996.

Sheila Rosenthal, "Loss," *Tracey Takes On ...,* HBO, 1998.

Connie, "Dude Act Like a Lady," *House Rules,* NBC, 1998.

Melissa Slater, "Admissions," *Law & Order,* NBC, 1999.

Marjorie Whilden, "Tomorrow," *Law & Order: Criminal Intent* (also known as *Law & Order: CI*), NBC, 2002.

Andee Mae Haley, "Identity," *Law & Order,* NBC, 2003.

Tourist woman, "Opening Night," *Curb Your Enthusiasm,* HBO, 2004.

Bulimic meeting leader, *Rescue Me,* FX Channel, 2004.

Elaine Bowman, "Criminal Law," *Law & Order,* NBC, 2005.

Herself, "Beer League Special," *Howard Stern on Demand* (also known as *Howard TV on Demand*), 2006.

Helen Katz, "That Voodoo That You Do," *Queens Supreme,* 2007.

Stage Appearances:

(Stage debut) *Twelve Dreams,* Public Theatre, New York City, 1983.

Landscape of the Body, McGinn–Cazale Theatre, New York City, 1984.

CORT, Robert W. 1946–
(Robert Cort)

PERSONAL

Born July 2, 1946, in New York, NY; son of Mackie and Mildred Cort; married to Rosalie Swedlin (manager of writers and directors). *Education:* University of Pennsylvania, Philadelphia, PA, B.A. (magna cum laude), 1968, M.A., 1970; Wharton School, University of Pennsylvania, M.B.A.

Addresses: *Office*—Robert Cort Productions, 1041 North Formosa Ave., Administration Bldg., Suite 196, West Hollywood, CA 90046.

Career: Producer. McKinsey and Company, managing consultant in consumer marketing, 1974–76; Columbia Pictures, vice president of advertising, publicity, and promotion, 1976–80; Twentieth Century–Fox, executive vice president of marketing, 1980–81, senior vice president of production, 1981–83, executive vice president of production, 1983–85; Interscope Communications, partner and president, 1985; Cord/Madden Company, managing partner, 1996–2001; Robert Cort Productions, West Hollywood, CA, founder and producer, 2001—.

Awards, Honors: Emmy Award (with others), outstanding children's program, 1990, for *A Mother's Courage: The Mary Thomas Story*; Christopher Award (with others), motion picture, 1997, for *Mr. Holland's Opus*; Emmy Award (with others), outstanding made–for–

television movie, 2004, Christopher Award (with others), television and cable, 2005, both for *Something the Lord Made.*

CREDITS

Film Executive Producer:
Turk 182!, Twentieth Century–Fox, 1985.
Bill & Ted's Excellent Adventure, Orion, 1989.
Renegades, 1989.
Blind Fury, TriStar, 1989.
The First Power (also known as *Pentagram, Possessed, Possessed by Evil,* and *Transit*), Orion, 1990.
Bird on a Wire, Universal, 1990.
Eve of a Destruction, Orion, 1991.
Bill & Ted's Bogus Journey, Orion, 1991.
Paradise, Buena Vista, 1991.
The Hand That Rocks the Cradle, Buena Vista, 1992.
Jersey Girl, Triumph, 1992.
The Gun in Betty Lou's Handbag, Buena Vista, 1992.
Out on a Limb, Universal, 1992.
Holy Matrimony, Buena Vista, 1994.
Terminal Velocity, Buena Vista, 1994.
Imaginary Crimes, Warner Bros., 1994.
Operation Dumbo Drop (also known as *Dumbo Drop*), Buena Vista, 1995.
The Tie That Binds, Buena Vista, 1995.
Separate Lives, 1995.
Two Much (also known as *Loco de amor*), Buena Vista, 1995.
Jumanji, Columbia, 1995.
Boys, Buena Vista, 1996.
The Arrival (also known as *Shockwave*), Orion, 1996.
Kazaam, Buena Vista, 1996.
The Associate, Buena Vista, 1996.
Snow White: A Tale of Terror (also known as *Snow White, Snow White in the Black Forest, Snow White in the Dark Forest, Snow White: A Tale of Terror,* and *The Grimm Brothers' "Snow White"*), Gramercy Pictures, 1997.
Save the Last Dance 2, Paramount Home Video, 2006.

Film Co–Executive Producer:
Arachnophobia, Buena Vista, 1990.

Film Producer:
(As Robert Cort) *Critical Condition,* Paramount, 1987.
Outrageous Fortune, Buena Vista, 1987.
Revenge of the Nerds II: Nerds in Paradise (also known as *Revenge of the Nerds II*), Twentieth Century–Fox, 1987.
3 Men and a Baby (also known as *Three Men and a Baby*), Buena Vista, 1987.
The Seventh Sign, TriStar, 1988.
Cocktail, 1988.
Collision Course, President Home Entertainment, 1989.
An Innocent Man, Buena Vista, 1989.

A Gnome Named Gnorm (also known as *The Adventures of a Gnome Named Gnorm, Upworld,* and *Upworld, the Magic Little Alien*), Vestron Pictures, 1990.
3 Men and a Little Lady (also known as *Three Men and a Little Lady*), Buena Vista, 1990.
Class Action, Twentieth Century–Fox, 1991.
The Cutting Edge, Metro–Goldwyn–Mayer, 1992.
FernGully: The Last Rainforest (animated; also known as *FernGully 1*), Twentieth Century–Fox, 1992.
The Air Up There, Buena Vista, 1994.
Roommates, Buena Vista, 1995.
Mr. Holland's Opus, Buena Vista, 1995.
The Odd Couple II (also known as *Neil Simon's "The Odd Couple II"*), Paramount, 1998.
(As Robert Cort) *The Out–of–Towners,* Paramount, 1999.
Runaway Bride, Paramount, 1999.
Save the Last Dance, Paramount, 2001.
Against the Ropes (also known as *Die Promoterin* and *The Promoter*), Paramount, 2004.
Steppin' Up, 2006.

Television Executive Producer; Movies:
A Part of the Family, Lifetime, 1994.
Body Language, Showtime, 1995.
Harlan County War, Showtime, 2000.
The Rats (also known as *Killer Rats*), Fox, 2002.
Something the Lord Made, HBO, 2004.

Television Producer; Movies:
In the Company of Spies, Showtime, 1999.

Television Executive Producer; Specials:
A Mother's Courage: The Mary Thomas Story, NBC, 1989.

Television Appearances; Specials:
Appeared in *VH1 News Presents: Hollywood Secrets Revealed: Movie Screw Ups,* VH1.

WRITINGS

Novels:
Action!: A Novel, Random House, 2003.

OTHER SOURCES

Electronic:
Contemporary Authors Online, Thomson Gale, 2005.

COURTNEY, Robert
  See ELLISON, Harlan

CRAWFORD, Michael 1942–
(Dame Edith Shorthouse)

PERSONAL

Original name, Michael Patrick Dumble–Smith; born January 19, 1942, in Salisbury, Wiltshire, England; son of Arthur (a military pilot) and Doris (a homemaker; later surname, O'Keefe) Dumble–Smith; married Gabrielle Lewis (a radio music announcer), 1965 (divorced, 1975); children: Emma, Lucy. *Education:* Attended schools in Bexley and Dulwich, England.

Addresses: *Agent*—Steve Levine, International Creative Management, 10250 Constellation Way, 9th Floor, Los Angeles, CA 90067; (voice work and commercials) Tim Curtis, William Morris Agency, 1 William Morris Pl., Beverly Hills, CA 90212.

Career: Actor, singer, and writer. Began career as a boy soprano; sang in the choir of St. Paul's Cathedral; as a child made more than 500 television and radio appearances; also performed in radio plays for BBC–Radio, beginning c. 1957; performer on several tours of world cities. Once operated a foam–cushion business. Sick Children's Trust, president, 1987—; also affiliated with Lighthouse Foundation and National Society for the Prevention of Cruelty to Children.

Awards, Honors: Variety Club Award, most promising newcomer, 1965, and Film Award nomination, most promising newcomer to leading film roles, British Academy of Film and Television Arts, 1966, both for *The Knack ... and How to Get It;* Variety Club Awards, show business personality of the year and Silver Heart Award, 1974, for *Billy;* Television Award nominations, British Academy of Film and Television Arts, best actor, 1974, and best light entertainment performance, 1975, and *TV Times* Award, funniest man on television, 1974, all for *Some Mothers Do 'Ave "em;* Laurence Olivier Award, best actor in a musical, Society of West End Theatre, 1981, and Variety Club Award, show business personality of the year, both for *Barnum;* Laurence Olivier Award, best actor in a musical, 1986, Drama Desk Award, Antoinette Perry Award, and Outer Critics Circle Award, all best actor in a musical, and Drama League Award, all 1988, and Los Angeles DramaLogue Award, best actor in a leading role, 1989, all for *The Phantom of the Opera;* decorated officer, Order of the British Empire, 1987; Musical Achievement Award, Drama League of New York, 1988; Grammy Award nominations, best traditional pop vocal performance and best pop performance by a duo (with Barbra Streisand), National Academy of Recording Arts and Sciences, 1993, for *A Touch of Music in the Night;* Emmy

Award nomination, outstanding performance in a variety or musical program, 1998, for *Michael Crawford in Concert;* Variety Club Showbusiness Award, outstanding stage performance, 2004; Laurence Olivier Award, best supporting actor in a musical, 2005, for *The Woman in White;* certificate and badge, British Amateur Gymnastics Association.

CREDITS

Stage Appearances:
(West End debut) Buddy, *Come Blow Your Horn,* Prince of Wales Theatre, 1962.
Second citizen and second serving man, *Coriolanus,* Nottingham Playhouse, Nottingham, England, 1963.
Arnold Champion, *Travelling Light,* Prince of Wales Theatre, 1965.
Tom, *The Anniversary,* Duke of York's Theatre, London, 1966.
(Broadway debut) Tom, "White Lies," and Brindsley Miller, "Black Comedy," in *Black Comedy* (double bill), Ethel Barrymore Theatre, 1967.
Brian Runnicles, *No Sex Please, We're British,* Strand Theatre, London, 1971.
Bill Fisher (title role), *Billy* (musical), Drury Lane Theatre, London, 1974.
George, *Same Time, Next Year,* Prince of Wales Theatre, 1976.
Charlie Gordon, *Flowers for Algernon* (musical), Queen's Theatre, London, 1979.
Phineas Taylor "P. T." Barnum (title role), *Barnum* (musical), Palladium Theatre, London, 1981–83, then Manchester Opera House, Manchester, England, 1984–85, later Victoria Palace Theatre, London, 1985.
Erik (title role), *The Phantom of the Opera,* Her Majesty's Theatre, London, 1986–88, then Majestic Theatre, New York City, 1988–89.
EFX, MGM Grand, Las Vegas, NV, 1995.
My Favorite Broadway: The Love Songs, City Center Theatre, New York City, 2000.
Daryl Van Horne, *The Witches of Eastwick,* London production, 2000.
Count von Krolock and (as Dame Edith Shorthouse) Madam von Krolock, *Dance of the Vampires* (musical), Minskoff Theatre, New York City, 2002–2003.
Count Fosco, *The Woman in White* (musical), Palace Theatre, London, 2004–2005.

Appearances as child actor include role of Japeth, *Noye's Fiddle.*

Major Tours:
Sammy the little sweep, *Let's Make an Opera,* c. 1954.
Erik (title role), *The Phantom of the Opera,* international cities, beginning 1989.

The Music of Andrew Lloyd Webber, international cities, 1990–92.

Film Appearances:

Peter Toms, *Soapbox Derby,* Children's Film Foundation, 1958.

Jim Fenn, *Blow Your Own Trumpet,* Children's Film Foundation, 1958.

Kent, *A French Mistress,* 1960.

Nils Lindwall, *Two Living, One Dead* (also known as *Tvaa levande och en doed*), Emerson, 1961.

Staff Sergeant Junior Sailen, *The War Lover,* Columbia, 1962.

Alan Crabbe, *Two Left Feet,* British Lion, 1963.

Colin, *The Knack ... and How to Get It* (also known as *The Knack*), Lopert, 1965.

Hero, *A Funny Thing Happened on the Way to the Forum,* United Artists, 1966.

Michael Tremayne, *The Jokers,* Universal, 1966.

Lieutenant Ernest Goodbody, *How I Won the War,* United Artists, 1967.

Cornelius Hackl, *Hello, Dolly!,* Twentieth Century–Fox, 1969.

Harry Hayes, *The Games,* Twentieth Century–Fox, 1970.

Harry England, *Hello–Goodbye,* Twentieth Century–Fox, 1970.

White Rabbit, *Alice's Adventures in Wonderland,* American National, 1972.

Woody Wilkins, *Condorman,* Buena Vista, 1981.

Voice of Cornelius the badger, *Once upon a Forest* (animated), Twentieth Century–Fox, 1993.

Television Appearances; Series:

Billy Bunter of Greyfriars School, 1953.

John Drake, *The Adventures of Sir Francis Drake* (also known as *Sir Francis Drake*), ITV, 1961, then ABC, 1962.

Byron and other characters, *Not So Much a Programme, More a Way of Life* (also known as *Not So Much a Programme ...*), BBC, 1964.

Frank Spencer, *Some Mothers Do 'Ave 'Em,* BBC, 1973–79.

Dave Finn, *Chalk and Cheese,* 1979.

Dale's All Stars, BBC1, 2000.

Television Appearances; Specials:

Dermot Drage, "The Siege at Killyfaddy," *Armchair Theatre,* ABC (England), 1960.

Edward, "The Three Barrelled Shotgun," *Armchair Theatre,* ABC (England), 1966.

"Home Sweet Honeycombe," *Theatre 625,* BBC, 1968.

Constable, "The Policeman and the Cook," *ITV Saturday Night Theatre* (also known as *ITV Sunday Night Theatre*), ITV, 1970.

Himself and Frank Spencer, *To Be Perfectly Frank,* 1977.

Ferdinand Vanek, "Sorry," *Play for Today,* BBC1, 1978.

America's Tribute to Bob Hope (also known as *America at Its Finest: A Tribute to the Bob Hope Cultural Center*), NBC, 1988.

Bob Hope Lampoons Show Business, NBC, 1990.

The Andrew Lloyd Webber Story, Arts and Entertainment, 1992.

The Royal Variety Performance 1992, 1992.

David Foster's Christmas Album, NBC, 1993.

New Year's Eve in Vegas, Fox, 1995.

The 1996 Miss Universe Pageant, CBS, 1996.

The Fantastic World of Michael Crawford, Bravo, 1997.

Michael Crawford in Concert, PBS, 1998, broadcast in England as *An Evening with Michael Crawford in Concert,* 2001.

My Favorite Christmas Songs, PAX, 1998.

The Ghosts of Christmas Eve (also known as *TSO: The Ghosts of Christmas Eve*), Fox Family Channel, 1999.

Christmas Eve from the Crystal Cathedral, Fox Family Channel, 1999.

"My Favorite Broadway: The Love Songs," *Great Performances,* PBS, 2001.

I Love Christmas, BBC, 2001.

(Uncredited) Frank Spencer (in archive footage), *The 100 Greatest TV Characters,* Channel 4, 2001.

"30th Anniversary: A Celebration in Song," *Great Performances,* PBS, 2003.

Himself, *It Started with ... Swap Shop,* BBC, 2006.

Television Appearances; Movies:

Phineas Taylor "P. T." Barnum (title role), *Barnum!,* PBS, 1986.

Television Appearances; Awards Presentations:

The 42nd Annual Tony Awards, CBS, 1988.

Presenter, *The 44th Annual Tony Awards,* CBS, 1990.

The 45th Annual Tony Awards, CBS, 1991.

Presenter, *The 47th Annual Tony Awards,* CBS, 1993.

Variety Club Showbusiness Awards 2004, 2004.

Television Appearances; Episodic:

Howard Garland, "The Woman from Kimberley," *Dixon of Dock Green,* BBC, 1959.

Chris Kelly, "A Lead from Mother Kelly," *Dixon of Dock Green,* BBC, 1960.

Thief, "Easy Money," *Police Surgeon,* ITV, 1960.

Tony Hudson, "The Villa," *Alcoa Presents* (also known as *Alcoa Presents* and *One Step Beyond*), ABC, 1961.

Alan Murray, "Destiny Sixty-Three," *Suspense,* BBC, 1963.

BBC 3, BBC, 1966.

A Whole Scene Going, 1966.

Guest, "Alice in Wonderland," *Film Night,* 1972.

Parkinson, BBC, 1976, 1999, 2001.

The film director, "A Touch of Class," *To the Manor Born,* PBS, 1979.

The South Bank Show, 1997.

Bar patron, *Coronation Street* (also known as *Corrie*), ITV, 1998.

The Rosie O'Donnell Show, syndicated, 1998.

Richard & Judy, Channel 4, 2004.

Broadway Beat, 2006.

(Uncredited) Frank Spencer (in archive footage), "Bread," *Comedy Connections,* BBC, 2007.

Television Appearances; Other:

Also appeared in *Byron; Destiny; Move after Checkmate;* and *Still Life.*

RECORDINGS

Albums:

A Funny Thing Happened on the Way to the Forum (cast recording), United Artists, 1966.

Hello, Dolly! (cast recording), Twentieth Century–Fox, 1969.

Billy (original cast recording), CBS, 1974.

Flowers for Algernon (original cast recording), 1980.

Barnum (cast recording), 1981.

The Phantom of the Opera (cast recording), 1986.

Highlights from Phantom of the Opera, 1986.

Michael Crawford: Songs from the Stage and Screen, Columbia, 1988.

(Contributor) *The Premiere Collection of Andrew Lloyd Webber,* 1988.

Michael Crawford: With Love, 1989.

Michael Crawford Performs Andrew Lloyd Webber, 1991.

(Contributor) *Barry Manilow: Showstoppers,* 1991.

(Contributor) *The Premiere Collection of Andrew Lloyd Webber Encore,* 1992.

(Contributor) *A Christmas Spectacular of Carols and Songs,* 1992.

With Love/The Phantom Unmasked, 1992.

A Touch of Music in the Night, 1993.

(Contributor) *Barbra Streisand: Back to Broadway,* 1993.

(Contributor) *David Foster's Christmas Album,* 1993.

Once Upon a Forest (cast recording), 1993.

(Contributor) *London Symphony Orchestra Performs the Music of Tim Rice and Andrew Lloyd Webber,* 1994.

Favorite Love Songs, 1994.

EFX, 1995.

(Contributor) *The Very Best of Andrew Lloyd Webber,* 1996.

On Eagle's Wings, 1998.

Michael Crawford: In Concert, 1998.

(Contributor) *Ultimate Broadway,* 1998.

Michael Crawford: A Christmas Album, 1999.

(Contributor) *Sarah Brightman: The Andrew Lloyd Webber Collection,* 1999.

(Contributor) *Millennium Chorus,* 2000.

(Contributor) *Child of the Promise,* 2000.

Michael Crawford: The Disney Album, Walt Disney, 2001.

The Best of Michael Crawford, EMI, 2002.

The Woman in White (original London cast recording), 2004.

The Very Best of Michael Crawford, 2005.

Other albums include original soundtrack recordings of *Alice in Wonderland.*

Videos:

Andrew Lloyd Webber: The Premiere Collection Encore, 1992.

Michael Crawford: In Concert, 1998.

Audio Books:

Reader for the abridged audio–book version of his autobiography *Parcel Arrived Safely: Tied with String.*

WRITINGS

Books:

Parcel Arrived Safely: Tied with String (autobiography), Century Books, 1999.

ADAPTATIONS

Several 1978 episodes of the series *Some Mothers Do 'Ave 'Em* were based on stories by Crawford.

OTHER SOURCES

Books:

Contemporary Musicians, Volume 4, Gale, 1991.

Crawford, Michael, *Parcel Arrived Safely: Tied with String,* Century Books, 1999.

Newsmakers 1994, Issue 4, Gale, 1994.

Periodicals:

Chicago Tribune, August 21, 1988.

Hollywood Reporter, July 28, 1989, pp. 8–9.

Interview, February, 1988, p. 104.

New York, April 18, 1988, p. 51.

New York Times, February 1, 1988.

People Weekly, March 14, 1988, p. 95.

Playbill, November 30, 2002, p. 16.

CSOKAS, Marton 1966–

PERSONAL

Born June 30, 1966, in Invercargill, New Zealand; Hungarian citizen; son of Marton Csokas (an opera singer); mother, a nurse. *Education:* Canterbury University, Christchurch, New Zealand, B.A., art history; graduated from New Zealand Drama School, 1989.

Addresses: *Agent*—Sue Barnett & Associates, 1/96 Albion St., Surry Hills NSW 2010 Australia; William Morris Agency, One William Morris Pl., Beverly Hills, CA 90212.

Career: Actor. Stronghold Theatre, cofounder, presenter, producer, and actor, 1989–94; appeared in television commercials including Speights brewery.

Awards, Honors: Australian Film Awards nomination, best actor; Chapman Tripp Theatre Award, 1996; New Zealand Television and Film awards nomination, 1996, for *Broken English.*

CREDITS

Stage Appearances:
Ladies Night, Footbridge Theatre, Sydney, Australia, 1988.
Te Whanau a Tuanui Jones, Taki Rua Theatre, Wellington, New Zealand, 1990.
Septimus Hodge, *Arcadia,* 1997.
Closer, Circa Theatre, Wellington, New Zealand, 1998, then Auckland Theatre Company, Auckland, New Zealand, 1999.
Rafe Smith, *The Herbal Bed,* Melbourne Theatre Company, Melbourne, Australia, 1998.
Brutus, *Julius Caesar,* Auckland Theatre Company, 1998.
Clockwork Orange, Sydney, Australia, 1999.

Also appeared in *The Three Sisters,* New Zealand Drama School; *The Cherry Orchard,* New Zealand Drama School; *Happy End,* New Zealand Drama School; *Merry Wives of Windsor,* New Zealand Drama School; *Who's Afraid of Virginia Woolf,* New Zealand Drama School; *Icarus Mother,* Canterbury University, Christchurch, New Zealand; *As You Like It,* Christchurch Academy, Christchurch; *Today's Bay,* Christchurch Repertory, Christchurch; *Possibilities,* Stronghold Theatre; *Anglophiles,* Watershed Theatre; *Kevtch* and *Frontmen,* Maidment Theatre, Auckland, New Zealand; *Dancing in Lughnasa* and *Casement,* Court Theatre; *Amy's View,* Circa Theatre, Wellington, New Zealand; *Glorious Ruins,* Circa Theatre; *Angels in America,* Auckland Theatre Company, Auckland, New Zealand; *Peribanez Y El Comendador de Ocana;* as George, *Whose Afraid of Virginia Wolf,* Company B, Belvoir St. Theatre, Surry Hills, New South Wales.

Film Appearances:
Dennis, *Jack Brown Genius,* 1994.
Kane, *A Game with No Rules,* 1994.

Soldier, *Twilight of the Gods,* 1995.
Chicken, 1996.
Darko, *Broken English,* Sony Pictures Classics, 1996.
Soldier, "Twilight of the Gods," *Boy's Life 2,* First Run Features, 1997.
Raoul, *Hurrah* (also known as *Heaven Sent*), Spin Pictures, 1998.
Chug, *Accidents,* 1999.
Nick, *The Monkey's Mask* (also known as *Poetry, Sex, La maschera di scimmia,* and *Cercle intime*), Asmik Ace Entertainment, 2000.
Celeborn, *The Lord of the Rings: The Fellowship of the Ring* (also known as *The Fellowship of the Ring* and *The Lord of the Rings: The Fellowship of the Ring: The Motion Picture*), New Line Cinema, 2001.
Down and Under, Warner Bros., 2001.
Cady, *Rain,* Fireworks Pictures, 2001.
(Uncredited) Geonosian Archduke Poggle the Lesser, *Star War: Episode II—Attack of the Clones* (also known as *Attack of the Clones, Star Wars II,* and *Star Wars II: Attack of the Clones*), Twentieth Century–Fox, 2002.
Yorgi, *xXx* (also known as *Triple X*), Columbia, 2002.
Shad Kern, *Garage Days,* Fox Searchlight, 2002.
Mr. Smith, *Kangaroo Jack,* Warner Bros., 2003.
Sir William De Kere/William Decker, *Timeline,* Paramount, 2003.
Celeborn, *The Lord of the Rings: The Return of the King* (also known as *Der Herr der ringe: die ruckkehr des konigs* and *The Return of the King*), New Line Cinema, 2003.
Himself, *xXx: A Filmmaker's Diary* (documentary short), Columbia, 2003.
Vadim Timurouvic Lesiev, *Evilenko,* 21st Century Video, 2004.
Jarda, *The Bourne Supremacy* (also known as *Die Bourne Verschworung*), Universal, 2004.
Edgar Stark, *Asylum,* Paramount Classics, 2005.
Guy de Lusignan, *Kingdom of Heaven* (also known as *Konigreich der Himmel* and *El reino de los cielos*), Twentieth Century–Fox, 2005.
Captain Redding, *The Great Raid,* Miramax, 2005.
Trevor Goodchild, *Aeon Flux,* Paramount, 2005.
Himself, "*Kingdom of Heaven*": *Interactive Production Grid* (documentary), Twentieth Century Fox Home Entertainment, 2005.
Himself and Trevor Goodchild, *Creating a World: "Aeon Flux"* (short), Paramount Home Entertainment, 2006.
Himself, *The Path to Redemption* (documentary), Twentieth Century Fox Home Entertainment, 2006.
Himself, *Colors of the Crusade* (documentary short), Twentieth Century Fox Home Entertainment, 2006.
Hora, *Romulus, My Father,* Dendy Films, 2007.

Also appeared in *Casual Sex; Plain Tastes; Made Man; The Minute.*

Television Appearances; Series:
Dr. Leonard Rossi–Dodds, *Shortland Street,* TVNZ, 1994–96.
Various characters, *Xena: Warrior Princess,* syndicated, 1997–99, 2001.

Television Appearances; Miniseries:
Adrian Beckett, *The Farm,* ABC (Australia), 2001.

Television Appearances; Movies:
John Garth, *Swimming with Sharks* (also known as *Halifax f.p: Swimming with Sharks*), Nine Network, 1999.
Ted Healy, *The Three Stooges,* ABC, 2000.

Television Appearances; Specials:
Dr. Leonard Rossi–Dodds, *Happy Birthday 2 You,* TV2, 2000.

Television Appearances; Episodic:
"Same with No Rules," *Dark Tales,* 1990.
Sid, "By the Numbers," *The Ray Bradbury Theatre* (also known as *Le monde fantastique de Ray Bradbury, Mystery Theatre, Ray Bradbury presente, The Bradbury Trilogy,* and *The Ray Bradbury Theater*), USA Network, 1992.

Tarlus, "Promises," *Hercules: The Legendary Journeys,* syndicated, 1996.
Soldier, "Twilight of the Gods," *Boy's Life 2,* 1997.
Brother Thomas, "More Things in Heaven and Earth," *All Saints,* Seven Network, 1999.
Larry Lodans, *Wildside,* ABC (Australia), 1999.
Robert Tremain, "Shark Bait," *Water Rats,* Nine Network, 1999.
Cover Story, 1999–2000.
Br'ee, "Bone to Be Wild," *Farscape,* Sci–Fi Channel, 2000.
Qord, "The Golden Phoenix," *BeastMaster,* syndicated, 2000.
Qord, "Rescue," *BeastMaster,* syndicated, 2000.
Qord, "Revelations," *BeastMaster,* syndicated, 2000.
Kenner, "Tourist Season," *The Lost World* (also known as *Sir Arthur Conan Doyle's "The Lost World"*), DirecTV and syndicated, 2000.
Krider, "No Thanks for the Memories," *Cleopatra 2525,* syndicated, 2001.

Also appeared in *The Call Up; Shark in the Park.*

CURTIS, Price
    See ELLISON, Harlan

D

DANIELS, Jackson
See WOREN, Dan

DANIELS, Warren
See WOREN, Dan

DAVIDSON, Jack 1936–

PERSONAL

Born July 17, 1936, in Worcester, MA; son of Stanley Jack and Helen Mildred Davidson. *Education:* Boston University, B.F.A., 1963.

Career: Actor. Circle Repertory Company, New York City, member of company.

Awards, Honors: Best Actor Award, Columbia University Film Festival, 2003.

CREDITS

Film Appearances:
United Nations reporter, *The Next Man* (also known as *The Arab Conspiracy* and *Double Hit*), Allied Artists, 1976.
Congressman, *The Front,* Columbia, 1976.
Norman, *Shock Waves* (also known as *Almost Human* and *Death Corps*), Joseph Brenner Associates, 1977.
Husband, *Tattoo,* Twentieth Century–Fox, 1981.
Eric Clavel, *I, the Jury,* Twentieth Century–Fox, 1982.
Dr. Rosen, *Baby, It's You,* Paramount, 1983.
Third trader, *Trading Places,* Paramount, 1983.
George Spofford, *Reuben, Reuben,* Twentieth Century–Fox International Classics, 1983.
Boat man, *Harem,* 1985.
Davidson, *The Secret of My Succe$s,* Universal, 1987.
Lee Thomas, *Autumn Heart,* Arrow Releasing, 1999.

Stage Appearances:
A Fair Country, Lincoln Center Theatre, New York City, 1998.
Twelfth Night, Lincoln Center Theatre, 1998.
Salesman, *Ah, Wilderness!,* Vivian Beaumont Theatre, New York City, 1998.
The Little Foxes, Lincoln Center Theatre, 1998.
James, *Passion Play,* Actors Studio Free Theatre, New York City, 1999.
Chrysalle, *The Learned Ladies,* McCarter Theatre, 1999.
Enobarbus, *Antony and Cleopatra,* Berkeley Repertory Company, Berkeley, CA, 1999.
General Merrin, *Judgment at Nuremberg,* Longacre Theatre, New York City, 2001.

Appeared as Andrew Makepeace Ladd III, *Love Letters,* Alaska Theatre Festival; as standby, *A Moon for the Misbegotten,* Broadway production; and as understudy, *The Price,* Roundabout Theatre, New York City; appeared in *Cat on a Hot Tin Roof,* Virginia Stage Company; *The Clearing,* New York Stage and Film Theatre; *The Dybbuk,* Pittsburgh Public Theatre, Pittsburgh, PA; *Long Day's Journey into Night,* Intiman Theatre, Seattle, WA; *Minutes from the Blue Route,* New York Stage and Film Theatre; *Oedipus the King,* Wilma Theatre; *Picnic,* Long Wharf Theatre, New Haven, CT; *Romeo and Juliet,* Hartford Stage Company; *Shadowlands,* Pioneer Theatre Company; *The Tempest,* Virginia Stage Company; and *Three Hotels,* Circle Repertory Theatre, New York City; also appeared in Broadway productions of *Anna Christie* and *Captain Brassbound's Conversion,* and an off–Broadway production of *The Unexpected Man.*

Television Appearances; Series:
Hotel manager, *As the World Turns*, CBS, 1999.

Television Appearances; Episodic:
Judge Sorenson, "Substantial Justice," *Spenser: For Hire*, ABC, 1988.
Mr. Torrens, "Severance," *Law & Order*, NBC, 1992.
George Berman, "The Pursuit of Happiness," *Law & Order*, NBC, 1993.
Blumberg, "Pro Se," *Law & Order*, NBC, 1996.
Spense Carlyle, "Blood," *Law & Order*, NBC, 1997.
Bank manager, "Blood Money," *Law & Order*, NBC, 1999.
Duckman, "Home Is Where the Ducks Are," *Ed*, NBC, 2000.

Appeared in episodes of *Cagney & Lacey* and *The Equalizer*.

Other Television Appearances:
Judge Lawrence Hughes, *The Demon Murder Case* (also known as *The Rhode Island Murders*), NBC, 1983.
Priest, *Twelfth Night*, 1998.

Radio Appearances; Series:
Reader for the series *Symphony Space's Selected Shorts*, National Public Radio.

DELIA, Joe
(Joseph Delia)

PERSONAL

Born in Brooklyn, NY. *Education:* Studied composition, arranging, piano, and bass with Don Sebesky, Eddie Gomez, and Jimmy Garrison.

Addresses: *Agent*—Soundtrack Music Associates, 2229 Cloverfield Blvd., Santa Monica, CA 90405.

Career: Composer and musician. The Bruthers (music group), singer and keyboard player; composed jingles for major advertising campaigns; played keyboards, wrote arrangements, co–wrote songs, and toured with many musicians; scored industrial films; music director and piano player for the live Buster Poindexter Show, performed by David Johansen; record producer. Sarah Lawrence College, Bronxville, NY, composer in residence for two years.

CREDITS

Film Work:
Sound recording, *The Driller Killer*, Rochelle Films, 1979.

Music performer, *Ms. 45* (also known as *Angel of Vengeance* and *Rape Squad*), Rochelle Films, 1981.
Song arranger ("Sentimental Reasons"), *China Girl*, Vestron Pictures, 1987.
Piano player, *Drunks*, Shooting Gallery, 1995.
Musician at Chez Lounge, *The Funeral*, October Films, 1996.
Song performer and song arranger *The Blackout*, Trimark Pictures, 1997.
Orchestrator and piano, *No Looking Back*, Gramercy Pictures, 1998.
Keyboards, score arranger, and score producer, *The Tao of Steve*, Sony Pictures Classics, 2000.
Keyboards, bass, and guitar performer, music editing, music engineer, and song performer, *My Best Friend's Wife* (also known as *Grownups* and *Steve & Claire & Eric & Ami*), Curb Entertainment, 2001.
Sound mixing engineer, musician, and orchestrator, *Carlito's Way: Rise to Power*, Universal, 2005.

Film Appearances:
(Uncredited) Harlem ballroom band member, *King of New York*, Seven Arts Entertainment, 1990.
Himself, *A Short Film About the Long Career of Abel Ferrara* (documentary short), Artisan Entertainment, 2004.

Television Music Director; Specials:
Richard Belzer: Another Lone Nut, HBO, 1997.

Also worked as music director, *Richard Belzer Live*, Showtime.

Television Appearances; Episodic:
(Uncredited) Musician, "The Dutch Oven," *Miami Vice*, NBC, 1985.

WRITINGS

Film Scores:
(As Joseph Delia) *Nine Lives of a Wet Pussy* (also known as *9 Lives of a Wet Pussycat*), Navaron Films, 1976.
(As Joseph Delia) *The Driller Killer*, Rochelle Films, 1979.
Ms. 45 (also known as *Angel of Vengeance* and *Rape Squad*), Rochelle Films, 1981.
China Girl, Vestron Pictures, 1987.
Candy Mountain, International Film Exchange, 1987.
Freeway, New World Pictures, 1988.
Wolfpack, Braveworld, 1988.
Caged Fury, Columbia TriStar, 1989.
King of New York, Seven Arts Entertainment, 1990.
Body Trouble (also known as *Joker's Wild*), 1992.
Bad Lieutenant, Aries Films, 1992.
Body Snatchers, Warner Bros., 1993.

Dangerous Games (also known as *Snake Eyes*), Metro–Goldwyn–Mayer, 1993.

Drunks, Shooting Gallery, 1995.

The Addiction, October Films, 1995.

Twilight Highway, 1995.

The Funeral, October Films, 1996.

The Blackout, Trimark Pictures, 1997.

No Looking Back, Gramercy Pictures, 1998.

Fever, Lions Gate Films, 1999.

Ricky 6 (also known as *Say You Love Satan*), Shooting Gallery, 2000.

The Tao of Steve, Sony Pictures Classics, 2000.

My Best Friend's Wife (also known as *Grownups* and *Steve & Claire & Eric & Ami*), Curb Entertainment, 2001.

Bridget, 2002.

Bitter Jester (documentary), 2003.

Bought & Sold (also known as *A Jersey Tale*), Artisan Entertainment, 2003.

Incident at Blood Gorge, CustomFlix, 2005.

Carlito's Way: Rise to Power, Universal, 2005.

Television Scores; Movies:

The Substitute 2: School's Out (also known as *The Substitute II* and *The Substitute: Out of Siberia*), HBO, 1988.

The Enemy Within, HBO, 1994.

Time Served, 1999.

Television Scores; Specials:

Belzer on Broadway, Showtime, 1992.

Richard Belzer: Another Lone Nut, HBO, 1997.

The Heat: Inside the Inferno, The Learning Channel, 1999.

Satan in the Suburbs, Discovery Channel, 2000.

Also scored *Subways Stories,* HBO; *The Human Project,* Discovery Channel.

Television Scores; Pilots:

The Loner, ABC, 1988.

Television Scores; Episodic:

War of the Worlds (also known as *War of the Worlds: The Second Invasion*), syndicated, 1989–90.

Lost Civilizations (also known as *Time Life's "Lost Civilizations"*), NBC, 1994.

Dellaventura, CBS, 1997–98.

Digging for the Truth, History Channel, 2005–2007.

Also scored *Madison's Adventures,* BBC.

Television Additional Scores; Episodic:

"Brother's Keeper," *Miami Vice,* NBC, 1984.

Television Additional Music; Episodic:

Pee–wee's Playhouse, CBS, 1986.

"Partners of the Heart," *The American Experience,* PBS, 2003.

Video Game Scores:

Eternal Champions, Sega of America, 1993.

Stage Scores:

Co–wrote *Lollapalooza,* New York Shakespeare Festival.

OTHER SOURCES

Electronic:

Joe Delia Website, http://www.joedeliamusic.com, September 10, 2007.

DEVINE, Loretta 1949–

PERSONAL

Born August 21, 1949, in Houston, TX; daughter of James (a laborer) and Eunice (a beautician; maiden name, O'Neal) Devine. *Education:* University of Houston, B.A., speech and drama education, 1971; Brandeis University, M.F.A., theatre arts, 1976; studied acting with Ed Koven and improvisation with Gary Austin. *Politics:* Democrat. *Religion:* Baptist.

Addresses: *Agent*—Innovative Artists, 1505 Tenth St., Santa Monica, CA 90401. *Manager*—Essential Talent Management, 6565 Sunset Blvd., Suite 415, Los Angeles, CA 90028.

Career: Actress, singer, and director. Appeared in advertisements. Julia C. Hester House, youth program director and activity coordinator, 1971–72, founder of Hester House Players and Hester House Dancers, 1971; Black Arts Center, Houston, TX, director of theater department, 1972–74; Ethnic Arts Center Players, founder, 1972–74; Brandeis University, Waltham, MA, instructor in English, 1974–76; Texas Southern University, instructor, summer, 1974; Harvard University, instructor, summers, 1975–76.

Member: National Association for the Advancement of Colored People, Alpha Kappa Alpha.

Awards, Honors: Citizen Advocates for Justice Award, 1984; Image Award nomination, best actress, National Association for the Advancement of Colored People

(NAACP), 1988, Certificate of Recognition, Hollywood *DramaLogue,* 1988, and Hollywood *DramaLogue* Critics Award, best ensemble performance, 1989, all for *The Colored Museum;* Image Award, best actress, 1990, for *Woman from the Town;* San Diego Critics Circle Award nomination, best actress, 1990, for *Lady Day at Emerson's Bar and Grill; DramaLogue* Award, acting, and Los Angeles Drama Critics Circle Award, best featured performance, both 1991, for *The Rabbit Foot;* Image Award, outstanding supporting actress in a motion picture, 1996, for *Waiting to Exhale;* Image Award, outstanding supporting actress in a motion picture, 1997, for *The Preacher's Wife;* Image Award nomination, outstanding performance in a youth or children's series/special, 1999, for *One Day;* Black Reel Award nomination, network/cable—best supporting actress, 2000, for *Funny Valentines;* Image Award nomination, outstanding actress in a television movie, miniseries, or dramatic special, 2001, for *Freedom Song;* Image Award nominations, outstanding supporting actress in a drama series, 2001 and 2002, Image awards, outstanding supporting actress in a drama series, 2003 and 2004, and Golden Satellite Award nominations, best performance by an actress in a supporting role in a series, drama, International Press Academy, 2003 and 2004, all for *Boston Public;* Image Award nomination, outstanding supporting actress in a motion picture, 2002, for *Kingdom Come;* Independent Spirit Award nomination, best supporting female, Independent Feature Project/West, and Image Award nomination, outstanding supporting actress in a motion picture, both 2005, for *Woman Thou Art Loosed;* Black Movie Award nomination, outstanding performance by an actress in a supporting role, 2005, and Black Reel Award (with others), best ensemble, 2006, both for *Crash;* Image Award nomination, outstanding actress in a television movie, miniseries, or dramatic special, 2007, for *Life Is Not a Fairytale: The Fantasia Barrino Story.*

CREDITS

Stage Appearances:

Dionne, *Hair* (musical; also known as *Hair—Revival*), Biltmore Theatre, New York City, 1977.

Gloria, *Verandah,* New Dramatists, New York City, 1977.

Title role, *Karma,* Richard Allen Center, New York City, 1977.

Minister, *Godsong* (musical), La Mama Etc., New York City, 1977.

Soloist, *Langston Hughes,* AMAS Repertory Theatre, New York City, 1977.

Soloist, *Seasons Reasons,* Henry Street Settlement Playhouse, New York City, 1977.

Loretta, *Miss Truth,* Apollo Theatre, New York City, 1978.

Ms. Dabney, *Mahalia,* Henry Street Settlement Playhouse, 1978.

Stan's lady and ensemble member, *A Broadway Musical* (musical), Lunt–Fontanne Theatre, Theatre of the Riverside Church, New York City, 1978.

Virtue, *The Blacks,* Richard Allen Center, 1978.

Bones, Circle in the Square, New York City, 1978.

Young Mary, *Comin' Uptown* (musical), Winter Garden Theatre, New York City, 1979.

Jewel, *Lion and the Jewel,* Lincoln Center, New York City, 1980.

Precious, *Dementos,* City Center, New York City, 1980.

Lorell Robinson, *Dreamgirls* (musical), Imperial Theatre, New York City, beginning 1981.

The Casting of Kevin Christian, Shepherd Street Art Gallery, 1983.

Mermaid, *Gotta Getaway!,* Radio City Music Hall, New York City, 1984.

Janeen Earl–Taylor, *Long Time Since Yesterday,* Henry Street Settlement Playhouse, New Federal Theatre, New York City, 1985.

Lilly, *Big Deal* (musical), Broadway Theatre, New York City, 1986.

Lala, Wigs, and model, *The Colored Museum,* New York Shakespeare Festival, Public Theater, Susan Stein Shiva Theater, New York City, 1986–87, and produced elsewhere.

Cissy, *Woman from the Town,* 1990.

Delia, *Spunk,* Mark Taper Forum, Los Angeles, 1990.

Hot Mikado (musical), c. 1990.

Billie Holiday, *Lady Day at Emerson's Bar and Grill* (solo show), Old Globe, San Diego, CA, 1990, then Little Theatre, Phoenix, AZ, 1991.

Charlesetta, *East Texas Hot Links* (one–act), The Met, Los Angeles, 1991.

Holly Day, *The Rabbit Foot,* Los Angeles Theatre Center, Los Angeles, 1991.

Soloist, *Big Moments on Broadway,* John F. Kennedy Center for the Performing Arts Opera House, Washington, DC, 1991.

Soloist, *Rodgers, Hart, Hammerstein Tribute,* Embassy Theatre, 1991.

Charlesetta, *East Texas Hot Links* (one–act), New York Shakespeare Festival, Joseph Papp Public Theater, Anspacher Theater, New York City, 1994.

Also appeared in other productions, including *A Midsummer Night's Dream.*

Stage Director:

El Majj Malik, Black Arts Center, Houston, TX, 1972.

Who's Got His Own, Black Arts Center, 1972.

Black Cycle, Black Arts Center, 1973.

The Warning: A Theme for Linda, Black Arts Center, 1973.

Black Girl, Black Arts Center, 1974.

Nigger's Still Your First Name, Black Arts Center, 1974.

Shoes, Black Arts Center, 1974.

Film Appearances:

Will, 20 West, 1981.

Ms. Benson (a schoolteacher), *Anna to the Infinite Power* (also known as *Anna—voiman riivaama, Annas Geheimnis,* and *Salaperaeiset systerit*), 1983.

Verna McLaughlin, *Little Nikita* (also known as *The Sleepers, Espias sin identidad, Espios sem rosto, Kasvottomat vakoojat, Maly Nikita, Nikita, spie senza volto, O pequeno Nikita,* and *Spioner i familjen*), Columbia, 1987.

Bertha, *Stanley and Iris,* Metro–Goldwyn–Mayer/United Artists, 1988.

Diane, *Sticky Fingers,* Spectrafilm, 1988.

Blade's mother, *Class Act* (also known as *Dos caraduras y un plan, Koko koulun rap–pari,* and *Uma dupla de classe*), Warner Bros., 1991.

Nadine Biggs, *Livin' Large!* (also known as *The Tapes of Dexter Jackson*), Samuel Goldwyn, 1991.

Judy, *Caged Fear* (also known as *Hotel Oklahoma, Innocent Young People, Jail Force,* and *Oklahoma Hotel*), EAE, 1992.

Ula, *Amos & Andrew* (also known as *Amos & Andrew—Zwei fast perfekte Chaoten, Amos es Andrew bilincsben, Amos et Andrew, Atrapen al ladron. Al blanco o al negro?, Companheiros a forca, Filarakia gia desimo, Kaikkien kidnappausten kingi,* and *Nao chame a policia!*), Columbia, 1993.

Gloria Matthews, *Waiting to Exhale* (also known as *Az igazira varva, Bir oh desem, Czekajac na milosc, Donne, Esperando un respiro, Falando de amor, 4 mulheres apaixonadas, Haalla Andan, Haku paeaellae, Ou sont les hommes?, Venus dans la vierge,* and *Warten auf Mr. Right*), Twentieth Century–Fox, 1995.

Beverly, *The Preacher's Wife* (also known as *Ask melegi, Dragoste de inger, Espirito do desejo, La femme du pasteur, La femme du predicateur, La mujer del predicador, Rakastuin enkeliin, Rendezvous mit einem Engel,* and *Uno sguardo dal cielo*), Buena Vista, 1996.

Coco, *Lover Girl* (also known as *Lover Girls*), Bedford Entertainment, 1997.

Jackee, *The Price of Kissing,* Price of Kissing, 1997.

Pigfoot Mary, *Hoodlum* (also known as *Gangster, Harlem, N.Y.C., Hoods, Hampones (Hoodlum), Homens perigosos, Kvodo Shel Gangster, Les seigneurs de Harlem, Os reis do sub–mundo,* and *Truand*), Metro–Goldwyn–Mayer/United Artists, 1997.

Reese Wilson, *Urban Legend* (also known as *Mixed Culture, Rule, Urban Legends, Agada eronit, Duestere Legenden, Legende urbaine, Leggende metropolitane, Lenda urbana, Leyenda urbana, Leyendas urbanas, Mitos urbanos, Moerdande legender, Remsegek koenyve, Urban legend—kauhutarinoita,* and *Urbane legende*), TriStar, 1998.

Sylvia Finkelstein, *Love Kills* (also known as *Tappavat tunteet*), Trident Releasing, 1998.

Voice of Raul's mother, *Alyson's Closet* (short film), Trackster Pictures, 1998.

Zenia, *Down in the Delta* (also known as *Daroma La'Delta, Dem Laanga vaegen hem, Der Sommer,* *der alles veraenderte, Hem till Mississippi, Juuret Deltan sydaemessae, Juuret maalla, La reliquia, La vida en el sur, Loin d'ici,* and *Ressurreicao*), Miramax, 1998.

Floria, *The Breaks,* Artisan Entertainment, 1999.

Michelle, *Lillie,* Universal, 1999.

Principal, *Operation Splitsville,* Cineville, Inc., 1999.

Flo the doorwoman, *What Women Want* (also known as *Ce que femme veut, Ce que veulent les femmes, Ce-si doresc femeile?, Det kvinner vil ha, Do que as mulheres gostam, En que piensan las mujeres, Lo que ellas quieren, Mi kell a noenek?, Mitae nainen haluaa, O que as mulheres querem, Vad kvinnor vill ha,* and *Was Frauen wollen*), Paramount, 2000.

Health counselor, *Punks,* e2 Filmworks, 2000.

Marguerite Slocumb, *Kingdom Come* (also known as *El reino que se viene, Mejor en el cielo, Tjocka slaekten, Um ritual do barulho, Um ritual muito louco,* and *Venga il tuo regno*), Fox Searchlight Pictures, 2000.

Reese Wilson, *Urban Legends: Final Cut* (also known as *Rule 2, Urban Legend Final Cut, Urban Legends: Final Cut, Urban Legend 2, Urban Legend 2: The Final Cut, Duestere Legenden 2–Final Cut, Legendes urbaines: La suite, Legendes urbaines 2, Lendas urbanas 2, Lenda urbana 2, Leyendas urbanas: Corte final, Leyendas urbanas 2, Leyenda urbana 2, Mitos urbanos 2, Moerdande legender 2, Urban Legends—Kauhutarinoita 2,* and *Urban Legend 2: Coup de grace*), Columbia, 2000.

Delores, *Baby of the Family,* DownSouth Filmworks, 2001.

Margaret Calgrove, *I Am Sam* (also known as *A Nevem Sam, I Am Sam—A forca do amor, Ich bin Sam, Je suis Sam, Leccion de amor, Mi chiamo Sam, Mi nombre es Sam, Minae olen Sam, Sam je suis Sam, Uma licao de amor,* and *Yo soy Sam*), New Line Cinema, 2001.

Herself, *The Script* (short film), 2002.

Cassey Jordan, *Woman Thou Art Loosed,* Magnolia Pictures, 2004.

Miss Gladys, *King's Ransom,* New Line Cinema, 2005.

Shaniqua Johnson, *Crash* (also known as *Collision, L.A. Crash, Alto impacto, Crash—Alto impacto, Crash—Contatto fisico, Crash—No limite, Fatalna nesreca, Uetkoezesek,* and *Vidas cruzadas*), Lions Fate Films, 2005.

Jazz singer, *Dreamgirls* (musical; also known as *Drama, Devojke iz snova, Rueya kizlar, Sonadoras,* and *Sonadoras—Dreamgirls*), DreamWorks, 2006.

Dolly, *Cougar Club,* Open Sky Entertainment, 2007.

Evelyn, *Dirty Laundry,* Codeblack Entertainment, 2007.

Ma Dear, *This Christmas,* Screen Gems, 2007.

Dr. Racine Marguerite, *Spring Breakdown,* Warner Bros., 2008.

Herself, *Broadway: Beyond the Golden Age* (documentary; also known as *B.G.A. 2* and *Broadway: The Golden Age Two*), Second Act Productions, c. 2008.

First Sunday, Screen Gems, c. 2008.

Television Appearances; Series:
Stevie Rallen, *A Different World,* NBC, 1987–88.
Aunt Loretta Fontaine, *Sugar and Spice,* CBS, 1990.
Ellie, *Simple Folks,* CBS, beginning 1992.
Mo'Nique, UPN, 1999–2000.
Voice of Muriel Stubbs, *The PJs* (animated; also known as *PJs: The Projects, Hausmeister Stubbs,* and *Les Stubbs*), Fox, 1999–2000, The WB, 2000–2001.
Marla Hendricks, *Boston Public,* Fox, 2000–2005.
M. (Matilda) Pearl McGuire, *Wild Card* (also known as *Zoe Busiek: Wild Card*), Lifetime, 2004–2005.
Adele Webber, *Grey's Anatomy* (also known as *Complications, Procedure, Surgeons, Under the Knife,* and *Grey's Anatomy—Die jungen Aerzte*), ABC, 2005—.

Television Appearances; Miniseries:
Anne Maude Carter, *The Murder of Mary Phagan,* NBC, 1988.

Television Appearances; Movies:
Thelma, "Parent Trap III" (also known as "Ein Zwilling kommt selten allein," "Foeraeldrafaellan III," and "O novio das gemeas"), *The Magical World of Disney* (also known as *Disneyland, Disneylandia, The Disney Sunday Movie, Disney's Wonderful World, Walt Disney, Walt Disney Presents, Walt Disney's Wonderful World of Color,* and *The Wonderful World of Disney*), NBC, 1989.
Irene, "The American Clock" (also known as "Arthur Miller's 'The American Clock,'" "A maquina americana," "Die Stunde der Wahrheit," "El reloq americano," "Musta maanantai," and "O fim do sonho americano"), *TNT Screenworks,* TNT, 1993.
Nichols's secretary, *The Hard Truth* (also known as *Golpe final, The Hard Truth—Gnadenlose Enthuellung, Mortelle verite, Uno sporco affare,* and *Voie sans issue*), 1994.
Miss Mary, *Rebound: The Legend of Earl the Goat Manigault* (also known as *Rebound* and *L'etoile de Harlem*), HBO, 1996.
Connie Harper, *Don King: Only in America* (also known as *Don King: O dono dos ringues, Don King—O rei do boxe, Don King—Seulement en Amerique,* and *Don King—Una storia tutta americana*), HBO, 1997.
Everleen, *Clover,* 1997.
Dearie B., *Funny Valentines* (also known as *En compania de Daerit B.* and *Minha nova vida*), Black Entertainment Television, 1999.
Ruby Dandridge, *Introducing Dorothy Dandridge* (also known as *Face of an Angel*), HBO, 1999.
Snookie Tate, *Jackie's Back!* (also known as *Jackie's Back: Portrait of a Diva*), Lifetime, 1999.
Connie Travers, *Best Actress* (also known as *La mejor actriz*), E! Entertainment Television, 2000.
Evelyn Walker, *Freedom Song* (also known as *Freiheitsmarsch*), TNT, 2000.

Interviewer, *Book of Love* (also known as *Book of Love: The Definitive Reason Why Men Are Dogs*), Black Entertainment Television, c. 2002.
Addie Collins, *Life Is Not a Fairytale: The Fantasia Barrino Story* (also known as *La historia de Fantasia Barrino*), Lifetime, 2006.

Television Appearances; Specials:
Janine, "The Colored Museum," *Great Performances,* PBS, 1991.
One Day, 1998.
Judge, *Iron Chef USA: Showdown in Las Vegas,* UPN, 2001.
Herself, *The Fourth Annual Soul Train Christmas Starfest,* syndicated, 2001.
Presenter, *Women Rock!,* Lifetime, 2004.

Television Appearances; Awards Presentations:
Presenter, *The 39th Annual Tony Awards,* CBS, 1985.
Performer, *The 42nd Annual Tony Awards,* CBS, 1988.
The 27th Annual NAACP Image Awards, Fox, 1996.
Presenter, *The 28th Annual NAACP Image Awards,* Fox, 1997.
Presenter, *The 30th Annual NAACP Image Awards,* Fox, 1999.
The 2000 Essence Awards, Fox, 2000.
Presenter, *The 33rd NAACP Image Awards,* Fox, 2002.
Herself, *The 34th NAACP Image Awards,* Fox, 2003.
The 20th Annual IFP Independent Spirit Awards, Independent Film Channel and Bravo, 2005.
Cast presenter, *The 2006 Black Movie Awards—A Celebration of Black Cinema: Past, Present & Future,* TNT, 2006.
Presenter, *The 2007 Film Independent Spirit Awards,* Independent Film Channel, 2007.

Television Appearances; Episodic:
Lyndia Cummings, "Court of Love," *Amen,* NBC, 1988.
Juror, "Marital Blitz," *Cop Rock* (musical), ABC, 1990.
Nurse Hawking, "The Bitch's Back," *Murphy Brown,* CBS, 1990.
Nurse Tilda Barclay, "The Wilding," *Stat,* Disney Channel, 1991.
Valerie Hall, "Hard Bargains," *Reasonable Doubts,* NBC, 1991.
Cynthia, "Rock Throws Joey Out," *Roc* (also known as *Roc Live*), Fox, 1992.
Cynthia, "You Don't Send Me No Flowers," *Roc* (also known as *Roc Live*), Fox, 1993.
June, "Salon, Farewell, Auf Wiedersehn, Goodbye," *Family Album,* CBS, 1993.
Marla Melrose, "Close Encounters," *Picket Fences,* CBS, 1995.
Mrs. Duncan, "Reality Check," *Ned and Stacey,* Fox, 1995.
Voice of mother, "The Golden Goose," *Happily Ever After: Fairy Tales for Every Child* (animated), HBO, 1995.

Tonya Hawkins, "Amazing Grace" (crossover episode with *Touched by an Angel*), *Promised Land* (also known as *Home of the Brave*), CBS, 1997.
Tonya Hawkins, "Amazing Grace" (crossover episode with *Promised Land*), *Touched by an Angel,* CBS, 1997.
Sean's mother, "Graduation," *Clueless* (also known as *Clueless—Die wichtigen Dinge des Lebens, Clueless—Huolettomat,* and *Ni idea!*), UPN, 1999.
Steph, "It Takes Two," *Moesha,* UPN, 1999.
Gloria Rivers, "Playing God," *Family Law,* CBS, 2000.
Nora Mills, "I Will Survive," *Ally McBeal,* Fox, 2000.
Herself, *Intimate Portrait: Lela Rochon,* Lifetime, 2001.
Cherisse, "Positive," *Strong Medicine,* Lifetime, 2002.
Herself, *Headliners & Legends: Denzel Washington,* MSNBC, 2002.
Erika, "The Big Phat Mouth Episode: Parts 1 & 2," *Half & Half,* UPN, 2003.
Herself, *Pyramid,* syndicated, 2003.
Judge Vashti Jackson, "Trial and Errors," *Girlfriends,* UPN, 2005.
Missouri Moseley, "Home," *Supernatural* (also known as *Sobrenatural*), The WB, 2005.
Herself, *The Late Late Show with Craig Ferguson* (also known as *The Late Late Show*), CBS, 2005.
Annabelle Carruthers, "The Nutcrackers," *Boston Legal* (also known as *Fleet Street, The Practice: Fleet Street,* and *The Untitled Practice*), ABC, 2006.
Judge Vashti Jackson, "Ain't Nothing over There," *Girlfriends,* UPN, 2006.
Judge Vashti Jackson, "Party over Here," *Girlfriends,* UPN, 2006.
Herself, "The Making of 'Dreamgirls,'" *HBO First Look,* HBO, 2006.
Maxine (Chris's grandmother), "Everybody Hates Funerals," *Everybody Hates Chris* (also known as *Alle hassen Chris* and *Todo el mundo odia a Chris*), UPN, 2006.
Maxine (Chris's grandmother), "Everybody Hates Dirty Jokes," *Everybody Hates Chris* (also known as *Alle hassen Chris* and *Todo el mundo odia a Chris*), The CW, 2007.
Maxine (Chris's grandmother), "Everybody Hates Math," *Everybody Hates Chris* (also known as *Alle hassen Chris* and *Todo el mundo odia a Chris*), The CW, 2007.

Appeared in other programs, including an appearance as a cult leader in *Linc's,* Showtime; and an appearance as Crystal in *Out All Night,* NBC.

Television Appearances; Pilots:
Cheryl Kelly, "Sirens," *CBS Summer Playhouse,* CBS, 1987.
Stevie Rallen, *A Different World,* NBC, 1987.
Tonia Harris, *Heart and Soul,* ABC, 1989.
Aunt Charlotte, *In the House,* NBC, 1991.

Valerie Hall, *Reasonable Doubts,* NBC, 1991.
Patti, *Eli Stone,* ABC, 2007.

Appeared in other pilots, including an appearance as Rosie, *Cold Shoulder,* CBS; and in a pilot for The WB.

RECORDINGS

Albums; with Others:
Dreamgirls 1982 original Broadway cast recording), Decca, 1982.

Audiobooks:
Inspired by ... The Bible Experience, the New Testament, Zondervan, 2006.
Inspired by ... The Bible Experience, the Old Testament, Zondervan, 2007.
Inspired by ... The Bible Experience, the complete Bible, Zondervan, 2007.

Music Videos:
Ruben Studdard, "What If," c. 2004.

WRITINGS

Teleplays; Pilots:
Some sources state that Devine wrote the unsold television pilot *Managing the Hunks.*

OTHER SOURCES

Books:
Contemporary Black Biography, Volume 24, Gale Group, 2000.

Periodicals:
Essence, April, 2001, p. 75.

DICKNSON, Elizabeth Anne
   See PENA, Elizabeth

DRAKE, Bebe
   (Bebe Drake–Hooks, Bebe Drake–Massey, Bebe Drake Hoods, Bebe Drake Hooks)

PERSONAL

Addresses: *Agent*—Baron Entertainment, 5751 Wilshire Blvd., Suite 659, Los Angeles, CA 90036.

Career: Actress. Appeared in many television commercials.

CREDITS

Film Appearances:

(As Bebe Drake Hoods) Dorothy, *Report to the Commissioner* (also known as *Operation Undercover*), United Artists, 1975.

(As Bebe Drake Hooks) Neighbor, *Friday Foster,* Orion, 1975.

(As Bebe Drake–Hooks) Thelma, *Which Way Is Up?,* Universal, 1980.

(As Bebe Drake–Hooks) Policewoman, *The Last Married Couple in America,* Universal, 1980.

(As Bebe Drake–Massey) Female guard, *Xanadu,* Universal, 1980.

(As Bebe Drake–Massey) Dr. Young, school psychologist, *Oh, God! Book II,*. Warner Bros., 1980.

(As Bebe Drake–Massey) Nurse, *First Monday in October,* Paramount, 1981.

(As Bebe Drake–Massey) Female jail guard, *O'Hara's Wife,* PSO, 1982.

(As Bebe Drake–Massey) Angry prostitute, *Jo Jo Dancer, Your Life Is Calling,* Columbia, 1986.

(As Bebe Drake–Massey) Computer operator, *Alien Nation,* Twentieth Century–Fox, 1988.

(As Bebe Drake–Massey) Mrs. Strickland, *House Party,* New Line Cinema, 1990.

(As Bebe Drake–Massey) Mrs. Fischer, *Across the Tracks,* Desert, 1991.

(As Bebe Drake–Massey) Mrs. Jackson, *Boomerang,* Paramount, 1992.

(As Bebe Drake–Massey) Voice of barfly, *Bebe's Kids* (also known as *Robin Harris' "Bebe's Kids"*), 1992.

Ms. Murphy, *Jason's Lyrics,* Gramercy, 1994.

Jordan housekeeper, *Space Jam,* Warner Bros., 1996.

Mama Jackson, *How to Be a Player* (also known as *Def Jam's "How to Be a Player"*), Gramercy, 1997.

Mrs. Rush, *Anywhere But Here,* Twentieth Century–Fox, 1999.

Mrs. Pearly, *Friday After Next,* New Line Cinema, 2002.

Mrs. Brown, *Who Made the Potato Salad?,* Twentieth Century–Fox, 2006.

Mother–in–law, *Wild Hogs* (also known as *Blackberry*), Buena Vista, 2007.

Television Appearances; Series:

(As Bebe Drake–Hooks) Daffney, *Snip,* 1976.

Jeannie, *The Sanford Arms,* NBC, 1977.

(As Bebe Drake–Massey) Bebe, *New Attitude,* 1990.

Television Appearances; Episodic:

(As Bebe Drake–Hooks) Savannah Jones, "Sweet Daddy Williams," *Good Times,* CBS, 1976.

Ms. Jones, "X–rated Education," *Welcome Back, Kotter,* ABC, 1978.

Mrs. Cory, "Till Death Do Us Part, Maybe/Chubs/ Locked Away," *The Love Boat,* ABC, 1978.

(As Bebe Drake–Hooks) Mrs. Baker, "Florida's Favorite Passenger: Part 1 & 2," *Good Times,* CBS, 1979.

Mrs. Andrews, "Bradford vs. Bradford," *Eight Is Enough,* ABC, 1980.

Emma, "How Now Dow Jones," *The Jeffersons,* CBS, 1982.

Reba Williams, "Why Punish the Children," *Highway to Heaven,* NBC, 1987.

Freda, "The Fabulous Fortunes," *What's Happening Now!,* syndicated, 1988.

(As Bebe Drake–Massey) Emily Corbin, "Code 3," *Hunter,* NBC, 1989.

Velma Gaines, a recurring role, *A Different World,* NBC, 1989–1993.

Old lady, *Where I Live,* ABC, 1992.

Myra, "I've Got a Secret," *Martin,* 1992.

Myra, "Control," *Martin,* 1993.

(As Bebe Drake–Massey), "Bare Witness," *L.A. Law,* 1993.

(As Bebe Drake–Massey) Customer number one, "The Lacemakers," *Homefront,* 1993.

Myra, "I've Got Work to Do," *Martin,* 1994.

Neighbor, *High Incident,* ABC, 1996.

Braxton's mother, "And Bubba Makes Three," *The Jamie Foxx Show,* 1996.

Betty, "When the Funk Bites the Dust," *The Steve Harvey Show,* 1997.

Ms. James, "Marlon Joins a Cult," *The Wayan Bros.,* 1998.

Aunt Josephine, "Something About Queenie," *The Parent 'Hood',* 1999.

Geneva, "The Old Settler," *PBS Hollywood Presents,* 2001.

Darnell sister number one, "Forbidden Date," *The Proud Family,* Disney Channel, 2001.

Woman number one, "The Crawford Touch," *Dead Last,* YTV, 2001.

Doris Baynes, "Blind Eye," *The District,* 2003.

Voice of Thelma, *Fatherhood,* Nickelodeon, 2003.

Mama Lena, "Family Reunion," *The Bernie Mac Show,* 2004.

Television Appearances; Movies:

(As Bebe Drake Hooks) Gloria Townes, *The First Breeze of Summer,* 1976.

(As Bebe Drake–Hooks) Gloria, *The Cracker Factory,* 1979.

Jean Lewis, *Scared Straight! Another Story,* CBS, 1980.

(As Bebe Drake–Massey) Housekeeper, *Billionaire Boys Club,* 1987.

(As Bebe Drake–Massey) Postal clerk, *Moving Target,* 1988.

Winnie, *Heat Wave,* TNT, 1990.

(As Bebe Drake–Massey) Nurse, *Body Bags* (also known as *John Carpenter Presents "Body Bags"* and *John Carpenter Presents "Mind Games"*), Showtime, 1993.

Black kid's mother, *Riot,* Showtime, 1995.

Ruth Roswell, *Innocent Victims,* 1996.

Shampoo lady, *Norma Jean & Marilyn* (also known as *Norma Jean and Marilyn*), 1996.

Television Appearances; Miniseries:

Sevilla, *Backstairs at the White House,* 1979.

Cleo, *The Women of Brewster Place,* ABC, 1989.

Television Appearances; Pilots:

Gert, *The Boys,* ABC, 1992.

Carlotta, *Thea,* 1993.

Stage Appearances:

The Great Macdaddy, St. Mark's Playhouse, New York City, 1974.

Gloria Townes, *The First Breeze of Summer,* Palace Theatre, New York City, 1975, then St. Mark's Playhouse, 1975.

Viana, *Waiting for Mongo,* St. Mark's Playhouse, 1975.

DUKE, Bill 1943–

PERSONAL

Full name, William Henry Duke, Jr.; born February 26, 1943, in Poughkeepsie, NY; son of William Henry and Ethel Louise (maiden name, Douglas) Duke. *Education:* Boston University, School of Fine Arts, B.F.A., theatre, 1966; New York University, Tisch School of the Arts, M.F.A., fine arts, 1968; American Film Institute, M.F.A., 1971. *Avocational Interests:* Meditation, yoga, reading, music, martial arts.

Addresses: *Office*—Duke Media, 7510 Sunset Blvd., Suite 523, Hollywood, CA 90406; Yagya Productions, Inc., P.O. Box 609, Pacific Palisades, CA 90272. *Agent*—Agency for the Performing Arts, 405 South Beverly Dr., Beverly Hills, CA 90212. *Manager*—Rigberg Entertainment Group, 1180 South Beverly Dr., Suite 601, Los Angeles, CA 90035.

Career: Director, producer, actor, and writer. Weusi Kuumba Troupe, Brooklyn, New York City, former director; Sundance Film Festival, member of the dramatic jury, 1992; Howard University, Washington, DC, Time Warner professor and chair of the radio, television, and film department, beginning c. 2000; Yagya Productions, Inc., Pacific Palisades, CA, founder,

c. 2000, and chief executive officer, beginning c. 2000; Duke Media, Hollywood, CA, principal; Rosebud (film production company), founder. Mentor to young African American actors and directors. Teacher of transcendental meditation. Affiliated with organizations for the homeless, including the St. Joseph Center and the Willow Opportunity Center.

Member: Screen Directors Guild, Directors Guild of America, Writers Guild of America, Screen Actors Guild, American Film Institute (member of the board of trustees), Artists against Homelessness (founding member).

Awards, Honors: Winner of a national poetry contest as a student; Audelco Recognition Award, 1977, for *Unfinished Women …;* Best Young Director Award, American Film Institute, 1979, and Houston Film Festival Gold Award, both for *The Hero;* Special Jury Prize and nomination for the Grand Jury Prize, both in the dramatic category, both Sundance Film Festival, 1985, for "The Killing Floor," *American Playhouse;* New Vision Award, Black Filmmakers Hall of Fame, 1990; Image Award, special achievement—directing, National Association for the Advancement of Colored People (NAACP), 1991; Star Bright Award, Black American Society, 1991; Golden Palm Award nomination, Cannes International Film Festival, 1991, for *A Rage in Harlem;* the American Film Institute held "An Evening with Bill Duke" in 1992 to honor his achievement in film; CableACE Award, best directing, drama special or series, 1996, for *America's Dream;* Career Achievement Award, Acapulco Black Film Festival, 1997; Black Film Award nomination, best director, Acapulco Black Film Festival, 1998, for *Hoodlum;* Black Reel Award, television: best director, 2004, for *Deacons for Defense;* Black Reel Award nomination (with others), best director—television, 2006, for *Miracle's Boys.*

CREDITS

Film Director:

The Hero (short film), c. 1978.

Flag, 1986.

Maximum Security, 1987.

A Rage in Harlem (also known as *Harlem Action, A Rage in Harlem—La reine des pommes, Ei armoa Harlemissa, Harlem Action—Eine schwarze Komoedie, Ont blod i Harlem, Rabbia ad Harlem,* and *Redada en Harlem*), Miramax, 1991.

Deep Cover (also known as *Agent double, Az alvilag melyen, Cobertura total, Jenseits der weissen Linie, La cara sucia de la ley, Massima copertura, Melytengeri szoernyeteg,* and *Piilokyttae*), New Line Cinema, 1992.

The Cemetery Club (also known as *Looking for a Live One, A vivir que son dos dias, Aelska igen!, Die sieben besten Jahre, Efthymes monahikes gynaikes, Il club delle vedove, Kuolleiden aviomiesten seura,* and *Les veuves joyeuses*), Buena Vista, 1993.

Sister Act 2: Back in the Habit (also known as *Apaca-show 2., Cambio de habito 2, Cambio de habito 2: Mas locuras en el convento, Do cabare para o convento 2, En vaersting till syster II, En vaersting till syster 2—Redo att synda igen, Halloj i klosteret 2—Nonnernes hus, Mudanca de habito 2: Mais confusoes no convento, Mudanca de habito 2: Mais loucuras no convento, Nune pojejo 2, Nunnia ja konnia 2: Lisaeae saepinaeae, Rock 'n' nonne 2: De retour au couvent, Sister Act, acte 2, Sister Act 2: de vuelta al convento, Sister Act 2—In goettlicher Mission,* and *Sister act 2—piu svitata che mai*), Buena Vista, 1993.

Hoodlum (also known as *Gangster, Harlem, N.Y.C., Hoods, Hampones (Hoodlum), Homens perigosos, Kvodo Shel Gangster, Les seigneurs de Harlem, Os reis do sub-mundo,* and *Truand*), Metro-Goldwyn-Mayer/United Artists, 1997.

Angel: One More Road to Cross (also known as *Angel*), 2001.

Living in the Spirit Revue, 2001.

Cover (also known as *Invisible*), Twentieth Century-Fox, 2007.

Not Easily Broken, Sony Pictures Entertainment, 2007.

Some sources cite work on *Blacktime, Whitenoise,* c. 2002.

Film Executive Producer:

Sweet Potato Ride (short film), 1995.

Hoodlum (also known as *Gangster, Harlem, N.Y.C., Hoods, Hampones (Hoodlum), Homens perigosos, Kvodo Shel Gangster, Les seigneurs de Harlem, Os reis do sub-mundo,* and *Truand*), Metro-Goldwyn-Mayer/United Artists, 1997.

(With others) *Living in the Spirit Revue,* 2001.

The Pact (documentary), Spark Media/Duke Media, 2006.

Film Producer:

Cover (also known as *Invisible*), Twentieth Century-Fox, 2007.

Film Appearances:

Duane (Abdullah), *Car Wash,* Universal, 1976.

Leon James, *American Gigolo,* Paramount, 1980.

Cooke, *Commando,* Twentieth Century-Fox, 1985.

Malcolm, *No Man's Land,* Orion, 1987.

Sergeant Mac Eliot, *Predator,* Twentieth Century-Fox, 1987.

Captain Armbruster, *Action Jackson,* Lorimar, 1988.

Lieutenant Borel, *Street of No Return* (also known as *Sam Fuller's "Street of No Return," Rua sem regresso,* and *Sans espoir de retour*), Bac Films, 1988.

Albert Diggs, *Bird on a Wire,* Universal, 1990.

Detective, *Menace II Society* (also known as *Die Strassenkaempfer, Nella giungla di cemento, Perigo para a sociedade, Uehiskonna nuhtlus, Vakivallan kierre,* and *Veszelyes elemek*), New Line Cinema, 1993.

Mr. Johnson, *Sister Act 2: Back in the Habit* (also known as *Apaca-show 2., Cambio de habito 2, Cambio de habito 2: Mas locuras en el convento, Do cabare para o convento 2, En vaersting till syster II, En vaersting till syster 2—Redo att synda igen, Halloj I klosteret 2—Nonnernes hus, Mudanca de habito 2: Mais confusoes no convento, Mudanca de habito 2: Mais loucuras no convento, Nune pojejo 2, Nunnia ja konnia 2: Lisaeae saepinaeae, Rock 'n' nonne 2: De retour au couvent, Sister Act, acte 2, Sister Act 2: de vuelta al convento, Sister Act 2—In goettlicher Mission,* and *Sister act 2—piu svitata che mai*), Buena Vista, 1993.

World Beat (documentary), Western Sunrise Communications, 1993.

Detective Scott, *Susan's Plan* (also known as *Die Again, Dying to Get Rich, Delitto imperfetto, El pla de la Susan, El plan de Susan, Petollinen suunnitelma,* and *Susan a un plan*), Kusher-Locke, 1998.

(Uncredited) Head Drug Enforcement Administration (DEA) agent, *The Limey* (also known as *El halcon ingles, Englaenderen, L'anglais, L'inglese, Le limier, The Limey—Kostaja Lontoosta, Limey—Tasuja Londonist, O estranho, O falcao ingles,* and *Vengar la sangre*), Artisan Entertainment, 1999.

Studio producer, *Foolish,* Artisan Entertainment, 1999.

Detective Hicks, *Payback* (also known as *Porter, Arved klaariks, La revancha, Le reglement, Payback—La rivincita di Porter, Payback—Zahltag, Revancha,* and *Visszavago*), Warner Bros., 1999, director's cut released as *Payback: Straight Up—The Director's Cut.*

Detective Glass, *Fever* (also known as *Atrapado en la oscuridad, Febre a medo,* and *Instinto sombrio*), 1999, Lions Gate Films/Cowboy Book International, 2001.

Hinges, *Exit Wounds* (also known as *Blessures fatales, Dengeki, Exit Wounds—Die Copjaeger, Ferite mortali, Herida abierta, Hors limites, Izlazne rane, Kuulihaavad, Red de corrupcion,* and *Rede de corrupcao*), Warner Bros., 2001.

Mysterious voice on the telephone, *Love and a Bullet* (also known as *Love & Bullet, De profesion asesino, El ultimo disparo,* and *Rakkautta luotisateessa*), TriStar, 2002.

Police chief, *Red Dragon* (also known as *A Voeroes sarkany, Den rode drage, Dragao vermelho, Dragon rojo, Dragon rouge, El dragon rojo, Punainen lohikaeaerme, Roed drake,* and *Roter Drache*), Universal, 2002.

Earl, *Never Again,* USA Films, c. 2002.

Lieutenant Washington, *National Security* (also known as *National security—Sei in buone mani, Rahvuslik julgeolek, Securite nationale, Seguranca nacional,*

Seguridad nacional, and *Veijareita vai vartijoita?*), Columbia, 2003.

Levar, *Get Rich or Die Tryin'* (also known as *Hustler's Ambition, Locked and Loaded, Untitled 50 Cent Project,* and *Reussir ou mourir*), Paramount, 2005.

Trask, *X–Men: The Last Stand* (also known as *X–Men: Final Decision, X–Men 3, X3, X–mehed—viimane vastuhakk, X–men—Conflitto finale, X–Men—Der letzte Widerstand, X–men—I teliki anametrisi, X–men—L'affrontement final, X–men—L'engagement ultime, X–men—La batalla final, X–Men—O confronto final, X–men—Ostatni bastion, X–men—posledniyat sblasak, X–men—uppgoerelsen, X–men—viimeinen kohtaaminen, X–Men 3—Hamiflat Ha'acharon, X–men 3—La batalla final,* and *X–men 3—La decision final*), Twentieth Century–Fox, 2006.

Liquor supplier, *The Go–Getter,* Et Cetera Films/Two Roads Entertainment, 2007.

Miles Emory, *Yellow,* Sony Pictures Entertainment, 2007.

Henry Emboli, *We're Here to Help,* Crossroads Films, c. 2008.

Marble City, Twentieth Century–Fox, 2008.

Television Director; Miniseries:

"Miracle's Song," *Miracle's Boys,* The N (Noggin), 2005.

Television Director; Movies:

Johnnie Mae Gibson: FBI (also known as *Agent Gibson: Undercover FBI, Johnnie Gibson F.B.I., The Johnnie Gibson Story,* and *Tehtaevae Miamissa*), CBS, 1986.

(With others) *America's Dream* (also known as *Amerykanski sen*), HBO, 1996.

The Golden Spiders: A Nero Wolfe Mystery (also known as *Golden Spiders*), Arts and Entertainment, 2000.

Deacons for Defense (also known as *Em defesa dos nossos*), Showtime, 2003.

Television Director; Specials:

"The Meeting," *American Playhouse,* PBS, 1989.

"Raisin in the Sun," *American Playhouse,* PBS, 1989.

Television Director; Episodic:

"Double Trouble," *Flamingo Road,* NBC, 1982.

"To Catch a Thief," *Flamingo Road,* NBC, 1982.

Falcon Crest (also known as *The Vintage Years*), CBS, multiple episodes in 1982.

Knots Landing, CBS, episodes from 1982–87.

"Chop Shop," *Cagney & Lacey,* CBS, 1983.

"Crash of '83," *Dallas* (also known as *Oil*), CBS, 1983.

"Death by Kiki," *Hill Street Blues,* NBC, 1983.

"The Reckoning," *Dallas* (also known as *Oil*), CBS, 1983.

"Blues for Mr. Green," *Hill Street Blues,* NBC, 1984.

"The Bounty Hunter," *Cagney & Lacey,* CBS, 1984.

"Episode 4," *Emerald Point N.A.S.* (also known as *Navy*), CBS, 1984.

"The Hot Grounder," *Hunter,* NBC, 1984.

"Dangerous Ground," *Berrenger's,* NBC, 1985.

"I Will Abide," *Hell Town,* NBC, 1985.

MacGruder and Loud, ABC, episodes in 1985.

Me & Mom, ABC, episodes in 1985.

"Double Exposure," *Fame,* syndicated, 1986.

"Fever," *Starman,* ABC, 1986.

"The Professor," *Matlock,* NBC, 1986.

"Atomic Fallout," *Crime Story,* NBC, 1987.

"Frye for the Defense," *Amen,* NBC, 1987.

"The Junction," *The Twilight Zone,* CBS, 1987.

"The System," *Starman,* ABC, 1987.

"Baseballs of Death," *Miami Vice* (also known as *Gold Coast* and *Miami Unworthiness*), NBC, 1988.

"Fathers," *Blue Skies,* CBS, 1988.

"Short Timer," *Tour of Duty,* CBS, 1988.

"The Siege," *Spenser: For Hire,* ABC, 1988.

Heartbeat (also known as *HeartBeat, Private Practice,* and *Women's Medical*), ABC, episodes beginning c. 1988.

"The Divided Child," *A Man Called Hawk,* ABC, 1989.

"Kennonite," *Gideon Oliver* (also known as *By the Rivers of Babylon*), a segment of the *The ABC Mystery Movie* (also known as *The Mystery Movie, The ABC Monday Mystery Movie,* and *The ABC Saturday Mystery Movie*), ABC, 1989.

"Passing the Bar," *A Man Called Hawk,* ABC, 1989.

Brewster Place, ABC, episodes in 1990.

The Outsiders, Fox, episodes in 1990.

"Emma," *Legacy* (also known as *Loganin perhe*), UPN, 1998.

"The Search Party," *Legacy* (also known as *Loganin perhe*), UPN, 1998.

"Bride and Prejudice," *City of Angels* (also known as *Anglarnas stad, Englenes by, Enkelten kaupunki,* and *Orasul ingerilor*), CBS, 2000.

"Compassionate Release," *Strong Medicine,* Lifetime, 2002.

"Overkill," *Fastlane* (also known as *Fastlane: Brigada especial*), Fox, 2003.

"Partners of the Heart," *The American Experience,* PBS, 2003.

"Vamonos Chica," *Robbery Homicide Division* (also known as *Metro* and *R.H.D./LA: Robbery Homicide Division/Los Angeles*), CBS, 2003.

"Mr. Nobody," *Missing* (also known as *1–800–MISSING*), Lifetime, 2004.

"Prince among Slaves," *American Experience,* PBS, 2006.

Directed "Win or Lose," an episode of *Trauma Center,* ABC.

Television Work; Other; Episodic:

Developer, "You Must Remember This," *WonderWorks* (also known as *WonderWorks: You Must Remember This*), PBS, 1992.

Television Director; Pilots:

"The Killing Floor," *American Playhouse* (also known as *American Playhouse: The Killing Floor*), PBS, 1984.

New York Undercover (also known as *Uptown Undercover*), Fox, 1994.

Television Appearances; Series:

Luther Freeman, *Palmerstown, U.S.A.* (also known as *Kings of the Hill* and *Palmerstown*), CBS, 1980–81.

Himself, *Champlin on Film* (also known as *American Directors: The Next Wave* and *Champlin on Film: American Directors: The Next Wave*), Bravo, beginning c. 1989.

Amos Andrews, *Karen Sisco* (also known as *Ofiter Karen*), ABC, 2003, USA Network, 2004.

Television Appearances; Movies:

"Happy" Jordan, *Love Is Not Enough*, NBC, 1978.

Sergeant Matlovich vs. the U.S. Air Force, NBC, 1978.

Luther Seth Foster, *Dallas: The Early Years*, CBS, 1986.

Blackbird Wills, *Always Outnumbered* (also known as *Always Outnumbered, Always Outgunned*), HBO, 1998.

Jenga, *Who Killed Atlanta's Children?* (also known as *Echo of Murder*), Showtime, 2000.

Book of Love (also known as *Book of Love: The Definitive Reason Why Men Are Dogs*), Black Entertainment Television, c. 2002.

Television Appearances; Specials:

Mr. Sands, "Santiago's Ark," *ABC Afterschool Specials,* ABC, 1972.

Mr. Sands, "Santiago's America," *ABC Afterschool Specials,* ABC, 1975.

Second FBI agent, "The Meeting," *American Playhouse,* PBS, 1989.

Himself, *Frank Capra's American Dream*, 1997.

Himself, *Roots: Celebrating 25 Years* (also known as *Roots—Celebrating 25 Years: The Saga of an American Classic*), NBC, 2002.

Miracle's Boys: The Making of a Mini–Series, The N (Noggin), c. 2004.

Himself, *Ego Trip's Race–O–Rama,* VH1, 2005.

Television Appearances; Awards Presentations:

Presenter, *The Fourth Annual Trumpet Awards,* TBS, 1996.

Presenter, *The Fifth Annual Trumpet Awards,* TBS, 1997.

Television Appearances; Episodic:

Sylk, "Bad Dude," *Kojak,* CBS, 1976.

David Pearl, "Angels on the Run," *Charlie's Angels,* ABC, 1978.

Officer Dryden, "Hutchinson: Murder One (a.k.a. Hutchinson for Murder One)," *Starsky and Hutch,* ABC, 1978.

Mad Dog, "The Grass Ain't Greener," *Benson,* ABC, 1981.

Narrator, "Nat King Cole: Loved in Return," *Biography* (also known as *A&E Biography: Nat King Cole*), Arts and Entertainment, 1998.

Himself, "Good Times," *The E! True Hollywood Story* (also known as *Good Times: The E! True Hollywood Story* and *THS*), E! Entertainment Television, 2000.

Himself, "Redd Foxx: Say It Like It Is," *Biography* (also known as *A&E Biography: Redd Foxx*), Arts and Entertainment, 2000.

Himself, *Intimate Portrait: Robin Givens,* Lifetime, 2000.

Himself, "African Americans in Television," *Inside TV Land* (also known as *Inside TV Land: African Americans in Television*), TV Land, 2002.

Captain Bob Parish, "Get Your Mack On," *Fastlane* (also known as *Fastlane: Brigada especial*), Fox, 2002.

Captain Bob Parish, "Ryde or Die," *Fastlane* (also known as *Fastlane: Brigada especial*), Fox, 2002.

Voice of detective, "The Brave and the Bold: Part 1," *Justice League* (animated; also known as *JL, JLA, Justice League of America,* and *Justice League Unlimited*), Cartoon Network, 2002.

Captain Bob Parish, "Iced," *Fastlane* (also known as *Fastlane: Brigada especial*), Fox, 2003.

Captain Bob Parish, "Simone Says," *Fastlane* (also known as *Fastlane: Brigada especial*), Fox, 2003.

Himself, *Jimmy Kimmel Live,* ABC, 2005.

Phelan, "Black Market," *Battlestar Galactica* (also known as *Galactica, Galactica—Estrella de combate,* and *Taisteluplaneetta Galactica*), Sci–Fi Channel, 2006.

Warden Harris, "Every Man for Himself," *Lost,* ABC, 2006.

Also appeared in other programs, including *Maddox*.

Television Appearances; Pilots:

(Uncredited) Hit man, *New York Undercover* (also known as *Uptown Undercover*), Fox, 1994.

Ivor "Max" Maxwell, *Black Jaq,* ABC, 1998.

Police officer, *R.U.S./H.,* CBS, c. 2002.

Stage Director:

The Secret Place, Playwrights Horizons, New York City, 1972.

Unfinished Women ..., New York Shakespeare Festival, Public Theater, Mobile Theater, New York City, 1977.

Sonata, Theatre of the Arts, Los Angeles, 1985.

No Place to Be Somebody, Matrix Theatre, 1987.

Dutchman, Cherry Lane Theatre, New York City, 2007.

Directed other stage productions.

Stage Appearances:

Akano, *Slave Ship*, Brooklyn Academy of Music, Brooklyn, New York City, c. 1969–70.

First man, industrialist, and Rastus, *Day of Absence* (produced as part of a double–bill with *Brotherhood*), Negro Ensemble Company, St. Mark's Playhouse, New York City, 1970.

Ain't Supposed to Die a Natural Death, Ethel Barrymore Theatre, New York City, 1971, Ambassador Theatre, New York City, 1971–72.

Also appeared in other productions, including *Barefoot in the Park, The Emperor Jones, Look Back in Anger, Macbeth, Othello, Plaza Suite* (also known as *Neil Simon's "Plaza Suite"*), and *Richard III.*

RECORDINGS

Videos:

Himself, *If It Bleeds We Can Kill It: The Making of "Predator"* (short), Twentieth Century–Fox Home Entertainment, 2001.

Himself, *Predator: Character Design* (short), Twentieth Century–Fox Home Entertainment, 2001.

Himself, *Predator: Classified Action* (short), Twentieth Century–Fox Home Entertainment, 2001.

Himself, *Predator: The Life Inside* (short), Twentieth Century–Fox Home Entertainment, 2001.

Himself, *Predator: Old Painless* (short), Twentieth Century–Fox Home Entertainment, 2001.

Himself, *Predator: The Unseen Arnold* (short), Twentieth Century–Fox Home Entertainment, 2001.

Music Videos:

Busta Rhymes, "Dangerous," 1997.

Common, "Testify," 2005.

WRITINGS

Writings for the Stage:

An Adaptation: Dream (one–act), Negro Ensemble Company, New York City, 1971.

Sonata, Theatre Genesis, St. Mark's Playhouse, New York City, 1975, later at produced at Theatre of the Arts, Los Angeles, 1985.

Teleplays; Episodic:

"Cousin Raymond," *Good Times,* CBS, 1979.

Poetry:

Duke's poetry published in various books.

Nonfiction:

(With Danny Glover) *Black Light: The African American Hero,* Thunder's Mouth Press, 1993.

Writings; Other:

Author of *Heroes: A Black Family Picture Album,* Thunder's Mouth Press, 1991. Also wrote *Bill Duke's 24–Hours L.A.* Contributor of articles and poems to magazines and newspapers, including *Black Creation.*

OTHER SOURCES

Books:

Contemporary Black Biography, Volume 3, Gale, 1992.

Periodicals:

Ebony, January, 1991, p. 128.

Essence, February, 1994, p. 52; October, 2000, p. 78.

Jet, April 12, 1999, p. 24.

New York Times, April 10, 1980.

Premiere, April, 1991, pp. 40–42.

Shock Cinema, issue 27, 2005, pp. 3–6, 30.

US, October, 1991.

E

EBERT, Roger 1942–
(R. Hyde, Reinhold Timme)

PERSONAL

Full name, Roger Joseph Ebert; born June 18, 1942, in Urbana, IL; son of Walter H. and Annabel (maiden name, Stumm) Ebert; married Chaz Hammelsmith (an attorney), July 18, 1993. *Education:* University of Illinois, B.S., 1964; also attended University of Cape Town, South Africa, 1965; University of Chicago, 1966–67. *Avocational Interests:* Drawing, painting, art collecting, walking, reading, travel, cosmology, Darwinism.

Addresses: *Office*—c/o Chicago Sun–Times, 401 North Wabash, Chicago, IL 60611.

Career: Film critic, writer, and actor. *News Gazette,* Champaign–Urbana, IL, staff reporter, 1958–66; *Daily Illinois,* editor, 1963–64; U.S. Student Press Association, president, 1963–64; *Chicago Sun–Times,* Chicago, IL, film critic, 1967—; Chicago City College, instructor in English, 1967–68; Chicago Film Festival, juror, 1968—; University of Chicago, lecturer in film criticism, 1969—; National Endowment for the Arts and Humanities, consultant, 1972–77; Columbia College, lecturer, 1973–74, 1977–80; Art Institute of Chicago's Film Center, member of board of advisors, 1973—; University of Illinois Alumni Associate, member of board of directors, 1975–77; *US Magazine,* film critic, 1978–79; WMAQ–TV, Chicago, film critic, 1980–83; Ebert Company, Ltd., president, 1981—; WLS–TV, Chicago, IL, film critic, 1984—; *New York Post,* New York City, film critic, 1986—; CompuServe, film critic, 1991—; Microsoft Cinemania, worker, 1994–97; juror at film festivals.

Member: American Newspaper Guild, National Society of Film Critics, Writers Guild of America (West), Arts Club of Chicago, Cliff Dwellers Club of Chicago, University of Illinois Alumni Association (member of board of directors, 1975–77), Phi Delta Theta, Sigma Delta Chi.

Awards, Honors: Overseas Press Club Award, 1963; Chicago HeadlineClub Award, 1963; Rotary fellow, 1965; Stick o' Type Award, Chicago Newspaper Guild, 1973; Pulitzer Prize for distinguished criticism, 1975, for reviews and essays in *Chicago Sun–Times;* Chicago Emmy Award, 1979; man of the year (with Gene Siskel), Hollywood Radio and Television Society, 1993; honorary L.H.D., University of Colorado, 1993; Emmy Award nominations (with others), outstanding informational series, 1994, 1997, both for *Siskel & Ebert;* Kluge fellow in film studies, University of Virginia, 1995–96; inductee, Chicago Journalism Hall of Fame, 1997; Video Premiere Award, best audio commentary, DVD Exclusive Awards, 2001, for *Citizen Kane;* Special Achievement Award, American Society of Cinematographers, 2003; Lifetime Achievement Award, CINE Awards, 2005; star on Hollywood Walk of Fame, 2005.

CREDITS

Television Appearances; Series:
Host (with Gene Siskel), *Sneak Previews* (also known as *Opening Soon at a Theater Near You*), PBS, 1978–82.
Film critic, *NBC News,* NBC, 1980–83.
Host (with Siskel), *At the Movies* (also known as *Movie Views*), PBS, 1982–86.
Host (with Siskel), *Siskel & Ebert* (also known as *Siskel & Ebert & the Movies*), syndicated, 1986–99.
Host (with others), *Roger Ebert & the Movies,* 1999.
Host (with Richard Roeper), *Ebert & Roeper and the Movies,* 2000–2006.

Television Appearances; Specials:
Commentator, *1988 Summer Olympic Games,* 1988.

Host, *The Siskel & Ebert 500th Anniversary Special*, 1989.

Host, *Siskel & Ebert: The Future of the Movies* (also known as *Siskel & Ebert: The Future of the Movies with Steven Spielberg, George Lucas, and Martin Scorsese*), 1990.

Host, *The Siskel & Ebert Special*, 1990.

Siskel & Ebert: If We Picked the Winners, 1990.

A Comedy Salute to Michael Jordan, 1991.

Big Bird's Birthday or Let Me Eat Cake, 1991.

Narrator, *Doris Day: A Sentimental Journey*, 1991.

Living in America, VH1, 1991.

Host, *Siskel & Ebert: Actors on Acting*, 1991.

A Comedy Salute to Michael Jordan, 1991.

Bob Hope: The First Ninety Years, NBC, 1993.

Count on Me, PBS, 1993.

Host, *Hollywood Gets MADD*, syndicated, 1993.

Host, *Siskel & Ebert: If We Picked the Winners*, syndicated, 1993.

The Ten Best Films of 1992, syndicated, 1993.

The Worst Films of 1992, syndicated, 1993.

The 10th Annual Television Academy Hall of Fame, Disney Channel, 1994.

Presenter, *The 1994 CLIO Awards*, 1994.

Presenter, *The 17th Annual CableACE Awards*, 1995.

Ballyhoo: The Hollywood Sideshow!, AMC, 1996.

Host, *Siskel & Ebert: If We Picked the Winners*, syndicated, 1996.

Host, *The Siskel & Ebert Interviews*, CBS, 1996.

River Phoenix: The E! True Hollywood Story, E! Entertainment Television, 1997.

An African American Salute to the Academy Awards, syndicated, 1998.

Independent's Day, Sundance Channel, 1998.

Siskel & Ebert: If We Picked the Winners, syndicated, 1998.

The 29th NAACP Image Awards, 1998.

The Wild Ride of Outlaw Bikers, 1999.

The 15th Annual IFP/West Independent Spirit Awards, Independent Film Channel and Bravo, 2000.

Host, *IFP/West Independent Spirit Awards Pre–Show*, Independent Film Channel, 2000.

Host, *If We Picked the Winners*, syndicated, 2000.

It Conquered Hollywood! The Story of American International Pictures (documentary), AMC, 2001.

Host, *The 16th Annual IFP/West Independent Spirit Awards*, Independent Film Channel, 2001.

Host, *The 2002 IFP/West Independent Spirit Awards Nomination Show*, Independent Film Channel and Bravo, 2002.

(Uncredited) *Hollywood Rocks the Movies: The 1970s*, 2002.

Sam Peckinpah's West: Legacy of a Hollywood Renegade, Starz, 2004.

X–Rated, Channel 5, 2004.

Midnight Movies: From the Margin to the Mainstream, Starz, 2005.

Meg Ryan: The E! True Hollywood Story, E! Entertainment Television, 2005.

Service About Self, 2005.

The 20th IFP Independent Spirit Awards, Independent Film Channel and Bravo, 2005.

The 50 Greatest Documentaries, 2005.

Manufacturing Dissent, 2007.

Television Appearances; Episodic:

(Uncredited) Himself, *Saturday Night Live* (also known as *SNL*), NBC, 1982, 1983, 1985.

The Tonight Show Starring Johnny Carson, NBC, 1986.

"Russ Meyer," *The Incredibly Strange Film Show* (also known as *Son of the Incredibly Stranger Film Show*), 1988.

Late Night with David Letterman, NBC, 1990, 1991, 1992.

The Howard Stern Show, 1991.

The Arsenio Hall Show, syndicated, 1993.

Late Show with David Letterman (also known as *The Late Show*), CBS, 1993, 1994, 1995, 1996.

The Tonight Show with Jay Leno, NBC, multiple episodes, 1993–2005.

Howard Stern, E! Entertainment Television, 1994, 1995, 1997.

Voice of himself, "Siskel & Ebert & Jay & Alice," *The Critic* (animated), ABC, 1995.

The Late Late Show with Tom Snyder, CBS, 1996.

The Rodman World Tour, 1996.

(Uncredited) Himself, "The Cat," *Early Edition*, CBS, 1997.

"The Man Who Shows the Future," *The Works*, BBC, 1997.

"Chuck Jones: Extremes and In–Betweens—A Life in Animation," *Great Performances*, PBS, 2000.

Late Night with Conan O'Brien, NBC, 2000, 2005.

Independent View, PBS, 2002.

Jimmy Kimmel Live, ABC, 2004.

Hardball with Chris Matthews, CNBC, 2005.

Movies That Shook the World, AMC, 2005.

The Oprah Winfrey Show (also known as *Oprah*), syndicated, 2005.

The Tony Danza Show, syndicated, 2005, 2006.

The Daily Show (also known as *The Daily Show with Jon Stewart* and *The Daily Show with Jon Stewart Global Edition*), Comedy Central, 2006.

Live with Regis & Kelly, syndicated, 2006.

CBC News: The Hour (also known as *The Hour*), CBC, 2006.

Howard Stern on Demand (also known as *Howard TV on Demand*), 2006.

Also appeared as himself, *Sesame Street*, PBS.

Film Appearances:

Himself, *You Can't Do That! The Making of "A Hard Day's Night!"* (documentary; also known as *The Making of "A Hard Day's Night"*), 1995.

Himself, *Pitch* (documentary), Jane Balfour Films, Ltd., 1997.

Himself, *Welcome to Hollywood,* PM Entertainment Group, 1998.

Himself, *Chicago Filmmakers on the Chicago River* (documentary), 1998.

Himself, *Junket Whore,* 1998.

(Uncredited) Himself, *Book of Shadows: Blair Witch 2* (also known as *BW2, BWP2,* and *Book of Shadows: Blair Witch Project 2*), Artisan Entertainment, 2000.

Himself, *Welcome to Hollywood,* 2000.

Himself, *All the Love You Cannes!* (documentary), Troma Entertainment, 2002.

Himself, *Searching for Debra Winger* (documentary), 2002.

Himself, *Mysteries of Love,* Metro–Goldwyn–Mayer/United Artists Home Entertainment, 2002.

Himself, *Abby Singer* (also known as *Abby Singer 2007*), 2003.

Himself, *Sex at 24 Frames Per Second* (documentary; also known as *Playboy Presents "Sex at 24 Frames Per Second: The Ultimate Journey Through Sex in Cinema"*), Playboy Entertainment Group, 2003.

(Uncredited) Himself, *Jiminy Glick in Lalaland,* Metro–Goldwyn–Mayer, 2004.

Himself, *No Fighting in the War Room, or Dr. Strangelove and the Nuclear Threat* (documentary short), Columbia, 2004.

Himself, *The Outsider* (documentary), 2005.

Himself, *Midnight Movies: From the Margin to the Mainstream* (documentary), 2005.

Himself, *Dead Teenager Movie* (documentary short), New Line Home Video, 2006.

Manufacturing Dissent, 2007.

The Man Who Shot Chinatown: The Life and Work of John A. Alonzo, Films Transit International, 2007.

Himself, *Dead On: The Life and Cinema of George A. Romero* (documentary), New Eye Films, 2008.

Radio Appearances; Series:

Movie News, ABC, 1982–85.

Also contributor to *Critics at Large,* WBBM, Chicago.

WRITINGS

Screenplays:

Beyond the Valley of the Dolls (also known as *Hollywood Vixens*), Twentieth Century–Fox, 1970.

(As Reinhold Timme) *Up!* (also known as *Over, Under and Up!, Russ Meyer's "Up,"* and *Up! Smokey*), 1976.

(As R. Hyde; with Russ Meyer) *Beneath the Valley of the Ultra Vixens,* RM Films, 1979.

Television Specials:

The Siskel & Ebert Special, 1990.

Fiction:

Behind the Phantom's Mask: A Serial, Andrews and McMeel, 1993.

Nonfiction:

An Illini Century, University of Illinois Press, 1967.

Werner Herzog: Images at the Horizon, Baseline Books, 1980.

A Kiss Is Still a Kiss, Andrews and McMeel, 1984.

Roger Ebert's Movie Home Companion, Andrews and McMeel, 1985–93, published as *Roger Ebert's Video Companion,* 1994–98, and *Roger Ebert's Movie Yearbook,* 1998—.

(With Daniel Curley) *The Perfect London Walk,* Andrews and McMeel, 1986.

Two Weeks in the Midday Sun: A Cannes Notebook, Andrews and McMeel, 1987.

(With Gene Siskel) *The Future of the Movies: Interviews with Martin Scorsese, Steven Spielberg, and George Lucas,* Andrews and McMeel, 1991.

(Editor) *Ebert's Little Movie Glossary: A Compendium of Movie Cliches, Stereotypes, Obligatory Scenes, Hackneyed Formulas, Shopworn Conventions, and Outdated Archetypes,* Andrews and McMeel, 1994.

(With John Kratz) *The Computer Insectiary: A Field Guide to Viruses, Bugs, Worms, Trojan Horses, and Other Stuff That Will Eat Your Brain,* Andrews and McMeel, 1994.

Roger Ebert's Book of Film: From Tolstoy to Tarantino, the Finest Writing from a Century of Film, 1996.

Questions for the Movie Answer Man, 1997.

Roger Ebert's Movie Yearbook, Andrews and McMeel, 1998—.

(Editor) *Ebert's Bigger Little Movie Glossary: Greatly Expanded and Much Improved Compendium of Movie Cliches, Stereotypes, Obligatory Scenes, Hackneyed Formulas, Shopworn Conventions, and Outdated Archetypes,* Andrews and McMeel, 1999.

I Hated, Hated, HATED This Movie, Andrews and McMeel, 2000.

The Great Movies, Broadway, 2002.

The Great Movies II, Broadway, 2005.

Awake in the Dark: Forty Years of Reviews, Essays, and Interviews, University of Chicago, 2006.

Contributor to periodicals, including *Esquire, Oui, Film Comment, American Film, Critic,* and *Rolling Stone.*

OTHER SOURCES

Books:

Newsmakers 1998, Gale Group, 1998.

Periodicals:

Chicago Tribune, September 6, 1979.

Entertainment Weekly, May 17, 1996, p. 48; October 8, 1999, p. 84; September 22, 2000, p. 59.

Los Angeles Times, August 31, 1982.
New York Times Book Review, December 16, 1984.
People Weekly, August 20, 1984; November 1, 1999, p. 155; May 28, 2007, p. 87.
The Progressive, August, 2003, p. 33.
Variety, October 16, 2006, p. 6; February 5, 2007, p. 7.

EDER, Linda 1961–

PERSONAL

Born February 3, 1961, in Brainerd, MN; daughter of Georg (a pastry chef) and Leila Eder; married Frank Wildhorn (a composer), May, 1998 (divorced); children: Jake Ryan.

Career: Actress, singer, and recording artist. Performer in nightclubs in and around Minneapolis, MN, beginning 1980; headlined a solo show at Harrah's Casino, Atlantic City, NJ, c. 1908s.

Awards, Honors: *Theatre World* Award, Drama Desk Award nomination, best actress, and Outer Critics Circle Award nomination, best actress, 1997, all for *Jekyll & Hyde.*

CREDITS

Stage Appearances:
Lucy Harris, *Jekyll & Hyde* (musical), Plymouth Theatre, New York City, 1997–98.
An Evening with Linda Eder, Theatre at Carnegie Hall, New York City, 2000.
This Is Your Song: Broadway Sings Elton John (benefit performance), New Amsterdam Theatre, New York City, 2000.
My Favorite Broadway: The Love Songs, City Center Theatre, New York City, 2000.
Linda Eder at the Gershwin, George Gershwin Theatre, New York City, 2001.
Linda Eder: The Holiday Concert, Palace Theatre, New York City, 2004.

Also appeared as Trilby, *Svengali* (musical).

Major Tours:
Lucy Harris, *Jekyll & Hyde* (musical), U.S. cities, 1990–97.

Television Appearances; Movies:
Vocalist, *Running Mates,* 2000.

Television Appearances; Specials:
The Songwriter's Hall of Fame 20th Anniversary: The Magic of Music, 1989.
Goodwill Games Opening Celebration, 1998.
My Favorite Broadway: The Leading Ladies, PBS, 1999.
Linda Eder in Concert, 2000.
Pops Goes the Fourth 2000, 2000.
Linda Eder Christmas Special, 2001.
My Favorite Broadway: The Love Songs, PBS, 2001.
A Skating Tribute (The Legacy of the 1961 U.S. World Team), 2001.
Broadway's Best, Bravo, 2002.
"Linda Elder," *Bravo Profiles,* Bravo, 2002.

Television Appearances; Episodic:
Star Search, 1988.
The Rosie O'Donnell Show, syndicated, 1997, 2000, 2001, 2002.

Television Executive Producer; Specials:
Linda Eder, the Christmas Concert, 2001.
Host, *Trail Mix,* Animal Planet, 2006.

RECORDINGS

Albums:
Linda Eder, RCA, 1991.
The Scarlet Pimpernel (soundtrack), Angel, 1992.
And So Much More, Angel, 1994.
It's Time, Atlantic, 1997.
Jekyll & Hyde (original cast recording), Atlantic, 1997.
Civil War (soundtrack), Atlantic, 1998.
It's No Secret Anymore, Atlantic, 1999.
Christmas Stays the Same, Atlantic, 2000.
The Romantics Volume 1, Atlantic, 2001.
Gold, Atlantic, 2002.
Broadway My Way, Atlantic, 2003.
Storybook, Angel Records, 2003.
By Myself: The Songs of Judy Garland, Angel/EMI, 2005.
Leonard Bernstein's "Peter Pan," Koch Entertainment, 2005.
Greatest Hits, Rhino/WEA, 2007.

Also recorded the soundtrack album *Jekyll & Hyde Romantic Highlights,* RCA.

Singles:
"Something to Believe In," 1997.
"Never Dance," Atlantic, 1999.
"Christmas Song," Atlantic, 1999.
"Vienna," Atlantic, 2000.
"Until I Don't Love You Anymore," Atlantic, 2002.
"How in the World," Atlantic, 2002.
"I Am What I Am," Atlantic, 2003.

Videos:
Christmas Stays the Same, Rhino, 2004.

OTHER SOURCES

Books:
Contemporary Musicians, Volume 30, Gale, 2001.

Periodicals:
Billboard, November 20, 1999, p. 33.
People Weekly, November 10, 1997, p. 37.

Electronic:
Linda Eder Website, http://www.lindaeder.com, October 10, 2007.

EDMONDSON, Wallace
    See **ELLISON, Harlan**

ELLIS, Landon
    See **ELLISON, Harlan**

ELLISON, Harlan 1934–
   (Lee Archer, Phil "Cheech" Beldone, Cord Wainer **Bird, Cordwainer Bird, Jay Charby, Robert Courtney, Price Curtis, Wallace Edmondson, Landon Ellis, Sley Harson, Ellis Hart, Al Maddern, Alan Maddern, Paul Merchant, Nabrah Nosille, Bert Parker, Jay Solo, Derry Tiger)**

PERSONAL

Full name, Harlan Jay Ellison; born May 27, 1934, in Cleveland, OH; son of Louis Laverne (a dentist and jeweler) and Serita (maiden name, Rosenthal) Ellison; married Charlotte B. Stein, February 19, 1956 (divorced, 1960); married Billie Joyce Sanders, November 13, c. 1960 (divorced, c. 1963); married Lory Patrick, January 30, c. 1966 (divorced, c. 1966); married Lori Horwitz, June 5, c. 1976 (divorced, c. 1977); married Susan Anne Toth, 1986. *Education:* Attended Ohio State University, Columbus, OH, 1953–54 (some sources say 1953–55).

Addresses: *Agent*—Martin Shapiro, Shapiro–Lichtman, Inc., 8827 Beverly Blvd., Los Angeles, CA 90048. *Contact*—c/o The Harlan Ellison Recording Collection, PO Box 55548, Sherman Oaks, CA 91413–0548.

Career: Writer, 1954—. Cleveland Playhouse, Cleveland, OH, actor, 1944–49; *Rogue* (magazine), Chicago, IL, editor, 1959–60; Regency Books, Chicago, founder and editor, 1961–62; Canadian Broadcasting Co., editorial commentator, 1972–78; Kilimanjaro Corp., Sherman Oaks, CA, president, 1979—; Harlan Ellison Recording Collection, coproducer; *Dimensions* (magazine), publisher. Chevrolet GEO Imports, West Coast spokesperson, 1988–89; Great Expectations (video dating service), member of board of advisors. Michigan State University, East Lansing, MI, instructor at Clarion Workshops, 1969–77 and 1984; lecturer at colleges and universities, including Duke University, Durham, NC, Harvard University, Cambridge, MA, London School of Economics and Political Science, London, Massachusetts Institute of Technology, Cambridge, MA, Michigan State University, East Lansing, MI, New York University, New York City, Ohio State University, Columbus, OH, University of California, Los Angeles, and Yale University, New Haven, CT. *Military service:* U.S. Army, 1957–59.

Member: International PEN, Science Fiction Writers of America (cofounder; vice president, 1965–66), Writers Guild of America West (past member of board of directors), Screen Actors Guild, Lewis Carroll Society, Cleveland Science Fiction Society (cofounder).

Awards, Honors: Writers Guild of America Award, 1965, George Melies Fantasy Film Award, cinematic achievement, 1972, and ViRA Award of the videocassette recording industry, best vintage television, all for "Demon with a Glass Hand," *The Outer Limits;* Hugo Award, best short fiction, World Science Fiction Convention, and Nebula Award, best short story, Science Fiction Writers of America, both 1965, for "'Repent, Harlequin!' Said the Ticktockman"; Writers Guild of America Award and Hugo Award, best dramatic presentation, both 1967, and George Melies Fantasy Film Award, cinematic achievement, 1973, all for "The City on the Edge of Forever," *Star Trek;* Hugo Award, best short story, 1967, for "I Have No Mouth, and I Must Scream"; Hugo Award, best short story, 1968, for "The Beast That Shouted Love at the Heart of the World"; Special Plaque, World Science Fiction Convention, 1968, for *Dangerous Visions: 33 Original Stories;* Nova Award, most outstanding contribution to the field of science fiction, 1968; Nebula Award, best novella, 1969, for "A Boy and His Dog"; Locus Award, best short fiction, *Locus* magazine, 1970, for "The Region Between"; Certificate of Merit, Trieste Film Festival, 1970, and Locus Award, best short fiction, 1972, both for "Basilisk"; Special Plaque, World Science Fiction Convention, and Locus Award, best original anthology, both 1972, for *Again, Dangerous Visions: 46 Original Stories;* Writers Guild of America Award, 1973, for "Phoenix without Ashes," *Starlost;* Hugo Award, best novelette, Locus Award, best short fiction, and Jupiter Award, best novelette, Instructors of

Science Fiction in Higher Education, all 1973, for "The Deathbird"; Hugo Award and Locus Award, both best novelette, 1974, for "Adrift, Just off the Islets of Langerhans ... "; Edgar Allan Poe Award, Mystery Writers of America, 1974, for "The Whimper of Whipped Dogs"; Locus Award, best short fiction, 1975, for "Croatoan"; Hugo Award, best film, and Saturn Award, superior achievement and merit in fantasy film, Academy of Science Fiction, Fantasy, and Horror Films, both 1976, for *A Boy and His Dog;* Hugo Award, Nebula Award, Locus Award, and Jupiter Award, all 1977, and British Fantasy Award, 1979, all best short story, for "Jeffry Is Five"; Locus Award, best short fiction, 1978, for "Count the Clock That Tells the Time"; British Science Fiction Award, short fiction category, 1979, for *Deathbird Stories: A Pantheon of Modern Gods;* Locus Award, best novelette, 1982, for "Djinn, No Chaser"; Locus Award, best nonfiction, 1984, for *Sleepless Nights in the Procrustean Bed;* Locus Award, best novelette, 1985, for "Paladin of the Lost Hour"; Locus Award, best short fiction, 1985, for "With Virgil Oddum at the East Pole"; Writers Guild of America Award and Hugo Award, best dramatic presentation, both 1986, for "Paladin of the Lost Hour," *Twilight Zone;* Locus Award, best original anthology, 1986, for *Medea: Harlan's World;* Edgar Allan Poe Award, 1988, for "Soft Monkey"; Bram Stoker Award, superior achievement in a fiction collection, Horror Writers of America, 1988, for *The Essential Ellison: A Thirty–five Year Retrospective;* Locus Award, 1988, and World Fantasy Award and *Encyclopedia Americana* Annual Award, both 1989, all best short story collection, for *Angry Candy;* Locus Award, best short fiction, 1988, for "Eidolons"; Locus Award, best novelette, 1988, for "The Function of Dream Sleep"; Silver Pen Award for journalism, International PEN, 1988, for a column, "An Edge in My Voice"; Lifetime Achievement Award, Mystery Writers of America, 1988; Bram Stoker Award, superior achievement in nonfiction, 1990, for *Harlan Ellison's Watching;* award from International PEN, for continuing commitment to artistic freedom and the battle against censorship, 1990; World Fantasy Award, lifetime achievement, 1993; Nebula Award nomination, 1993, for "The Man Who Rowed Christopher Columbus to Freedom"; Locus Award, best novella, 1993, and Bram Stoker Award, superior achievement in a novella, and Nebula Award nomination, both 1994, all for "Mefisto in Onyx"; Living Legend Award, International Horror Critics, World Horror Convention, 1995; Deathrealm Award, best short fiction of 1995, and Bram Stoker Award, superior achievement in short fiction, 1996, both for "Chatting with Anubis"; Lifetime Achievement Award, Horror Writers Association, 1996; shared Spotlite Award, best adaptation of linear media, Computer Game Developers Association, 1997, for *I Have No Mouth, and I Must Scream;* Words, Wit, and Wisdom Award, National Women's Committee, Brandeis University, 1998; Audie Award, Audio Publishers Association, best male solo narration, 1999, for *City of Darkness;* Audie Award (with others), best multivoiced presentation, 1999, for *The Titanic Disaster Hearings: The Official Transcript of the 1912 Senatorial Investigation by Tom Kuntz;* Milford Award, for lifetime achievement in editing; Grammy Award nomination, best spoken word recording, National Academy of Recording Arts and Sciences, for *Harlan Ellison Reads Jeffry Is Five;* shared Top Ten Award (with Naren Shankar and A. E. van Vogt), Writers Guild of Canada, 2000, for "The Human Operators," *The Outer Limits.*

CREDITS

Television Work; Series:

Script supervisor, *The Sixth Sense,* ABC, c. 1972.

(As Cordwainer Bird) Creator, *The Starlost,* NBC, 1973.

(With Ben Bova) Creator, *Brillo,* ABC, 1974.

(With Larry Brody) Creator, *The Dark Forces,* NBC, 1986.

Conceptual consultant, *Babylon 5* (also known as *B5*), syndicated, 1994–98.

Television Work; Movies:

(As Cordwainer Bird) Creator, *The Starlost: Deception,* 1980.

(Uncredited) Consultant, *Babylon 5: The Gathering* (also known as *B5* and *Babylon 5*), TNT, 1993.

Conceptual consultant, *Babylon 5: In the Beginning* (also known as *In the Beginning*), TNT and syndicated, 1998.

Conceptual consultant, *Babylon 5: Thirdspace* (also known as *Thirdspace* and *Thirdspace: A Babylon 5 Adventure*), TNT, 1998.

Conceptual consultant, *Babylon 5: The River of Souls* (also known as *The River of Souls*), TNT, 1998.

Conceptual consultant, *Babylon 5: A Call to Arms* (also known as *A Call to Arms*), TNT, 1999.

Television Work; Episodic:

Story editor, "I Do Not Belong to the Human World," *The Sixth Sense,* ABC, 1972.

Story editor, "The Heart That Wouldn't Stay Buried," *The Sixth Sense,* ABC, 1972.

Director, *The Twilight Zone,* CBS, 1984–85.

Creative consultant, "Dead Women's Shoes/Wong's Lost and Found Emporium," *The Twilight Zone,* CBS, 1985.

Director, *Cutter's World,* 1987–88.

Television Appearances; Series:

Host, *Sci–Fi Buzz,* Sci–Fi Channel, 1993–98.

Television Appearances; Specials:

The History of the SF Film, 1982.

Stan Lee: The ComiX–MAN!, 1995.

Masters of Fantasy: Arthur C. Clarke, 1997.

Masters of Fantasy: Harlan Ellison, 1998.

Voyage to the Milky Way, 1999.
Truth About Science Fiction, 1999.

Television Appearances; Episodic:
The Barbour Report, 1986.
Himself, *Naked Hollywood,* 1991.
Additional voices, *The Pirates of Dark Water* (animated; also known as *Dark Water*), 1991–93.
Voice, *Mother Goose and Grimm* (animated), CBS, 1991.
Voice of Cordwainer Bird, "A Boy and His Cat," *Phantom 2040* (animated; also known as *Phantom 2040: The Ghost Who Walks*), syndicated, c. 1994.
Voice of Sparky the computer, "Ceremonies of Light and Dark," *Babylon 5* (also known as *B5*), syndicated, 1996.
Psi cop, "The Face of the Enemy," *Babylon 5* (also known as *B5*), syndicated, 1997.
Voice of Zooty, "Day of the Dead," *Babylon 5* (also known as *B5*), syndicated, 1998.
Grifter, "The Observer Effect," *Psi Factor: Chronicles of the Paranormal,* syndicated, 1999.

Also appeared as voice, *Space Cases.*

Film Appearances:
Man at orgy, *Godson,* Boxoffice International Pictures, 1971.
Narrator, *The Masters of Comic Book Art,* 1987.
Himself, *Shadows in the Dark: The Val Lewton Legacy* (documentary), Warner Bros. Pictures, 2005.
Himself, *Legends of the Dark Knight: The History of Batman* (documentary short), Warner Home Video, 2005.
Himself, *'Tis Autumn: The Search for Jackie Paris,* 2006.
Himself, *Dreams with Sharp Teeth* (documentary), 2007.
Himself, *Brother Theodore* (documentary), 2007.

Radio Appearances; Series:
Host, *Beyond 2000,* National Public Radio, 2000—.

RECORDINGS

Albums (Spoken Word/Short Story Collections):
Harlan! Harlan Ellison Reads Harlan Ellison, Alternate World Recordings, 1976.
Blood! The Life and Future Times of Jack the Ripper, Alternate World Recordings, 1977.
Harlan Ellison Reads Jeffry Is Five, Harlan Ellison Recording Collection, 1982.
Prince Myshkin, and Hold the Relish, Harlan Ellison Recording Collection, 1982.
Loving Reminiscences of the Dying Gasp of the Pulp Era, Harlan Ellison Recording Collection, 1982.

I'm Looking for Kadak, Harlan Ellison Recording Collection, 1982.
On the Road with Ellison, H. Ellison, 1983.
The Prowler in the City at the Edge of the World, Harlan Ellison Recording Collection, 1983.
On the Downhill Side, H. Ellison, 1984.
City of Darkness, c. 1999.

Other Spoken Word Recordings:
(Contributor) *The Titanic Disaster Hearings: The Official Transcript of the 1912 Senatorial Investigation by Tom Kuntz,* c. 1999.

Video Games (Appearances):
Voice of AM, *I Have No Mouth, and I Must Scream,* MGM Interactive, 1995.

Video Games (Work):
I Have No Mouth, and I Must Scream, MGM Interactive,1995.

WRITINGS

Screenplays:
(With Russell Rouse and Clarence Greene) *The Oscar* (based on the novel by Richard Sale), Embassy, 1966.
Harlan Ellison's Movie: An Original Screenplay, Twentieth Century–Fox, published by Mirage Press, 1990.

Also associated with the screenplays for *Best by Far; Blind Voices; Bug Jack Barron,* Universal, c. 1983; *The Dream Merchants,* Paramount; *Khadim,* Paramount; *Nick the Greek; None of the Above; Rumble,* American International Pictures; *Seven Worlds, Seven Warriors,* De Laurentiis Entertainment Group; *Stranglehold,* Twentieth Century–Fox; *Swing Low, Sweet Harriet,* Metro–Goldwyn–Mayer; *Would You Do It for a Penny?,* Playboy Productions.

Film Stories:
A Boy and His Dog (also known as *Psycho Boy and His Killer Dog*), 1975.
Jackpot, 1980.

Television Episodes:
"A Gift for a Warrior," *Route 66,* ABC, 1963.
"Who Killed Alex Debbs?," *Burke's Law* (also known as *Amos Burke—Secret Agent*), ABC, 1964.
"Who Killed Purity Mather?," *Burke's Law* (also known as *Amos Burke—Secret Agent*), ABC, 1964.
"Who Killed Andy Zygmunt?," *Burke's Law* (also known as *Amos Burke—Secret Agent*), ABC, 1964.

"Who Killed ½ of Glory Lee?," *Burke's Law* (also known as *Amos Burke—Secret Agent*), ABC, 1964.

(As Cord Wainer Bird) "The Price of Doom," *Voyage to the Bottom of the Sea*, 1964.

"Demon with a Glass Hand," *The Outer Limits*, Showtime and syndicated, 1964.

"Soldier," *The Outer Limits*, Showtime and syndicated, 1964.

"Memo from Purgatory," *Alfred Hitchcock Presents*, CBS, 1964.

"The Sort of Do–It–Yourself Dreadful Affair," *The Man from U.N.C.L.E.*, NBC, 1966.

"The Pieces of Fate Affair," *The Man from U.N.C.L.E.*, NBC, 1967.

"The City on the Edge of Forever," *Star Trek* (also known as *Star Trek: TOS* and *Star Trek: The Original Series*), 1967.

"Knife in the Darkness," *Cimarron Strip*, CBS, 1968.

(As Cordwainer Bird) "You Can't Get There from Here," *The Flying Nun*, 1968.

"The Whimper of Whipped Dogs," *The Young Lawyers*, 1971.

"Phoenix without Ashes," *The Starlost*, syndicated, 1973.

"Earth, Air, Fire and Water," *Ghost Story* (also known as *Circle of Fear*), 1973.

(As Cordwainer Bird) "Voyage of Discovery," *The Starlost*, 1973.

Brillo, ABC, 1974.

"The Crypt," *Logan's Run*, 1977.

The Twilight Zone, CBS, 1985–89.

The Dark Forces, NBC, 1986.

"Paladin of the Lost Hour," *The Twilight Zone*, CBS, 1986.

"The City on the Edge of Forever," *Star Trek*, NBC, 1994, published by Borderlands Press, 1995.

(As Cordwainer Bird) "The Face of Helene Bournouw," *The Hunger*, 1998.

"The Discarded," *Masters of Science Fiction*, ABC, 2007.

Also wrote "Where Do Elephants Go to Die?" *Ripcord*, syndicated; *Batman*; *Dark Room*; *Empire*; *The Great Adventure*; *Logan's Run*; *Manhunter*; *The Name of the Game*; *Rat Patrol*; *Letter to Loretta* (also known as *The Loretta Young Theatre*).

Television Stories; Episodic:

(As Cordwainer Bird) "Footsteps," *The Hunger*, 1998.

"A View from the Gallery," *Babylon 5* (also known as *B5*), 1998.

"Objects in Motion," *Babylon 5* (also known as *B5*), 1998.

"The Human Operators," *The Outer Limits* (also known as *The New Outer Limits*), Showtime and syndicated, 1999.

Television Movies:

(As Cordwainer Bird) *The Starlost: The Beginning*, 1980.

Television Specials:

The Tigers Are Loose, NBC, 1974.

Also wrote *Astra/Ella*; *Astral Man*; *Bring 'em Back Alive*; *The Contender*; *Cutter's World*; *Dark Destroyer*; *Heavy Metal*; *Man without Time*; *Mystery Show*; *The Other Place*; *Our Man Flint*; *Postmark: Jim Adam*; *Project 120*; *The Sniper*; *The Spirit*; *Tired Old Man*.

Television Pilots:

Masters of Science Fiction, ABC, 2007.

Plays:

The City on the Edge of Forever (based on his television script), published in *Six Science Fiction Plays*, edited by Roger Elwood, Pocket Books (New York City), 1976.

Video Game Dialog and Story:

I Have No Mouth, and I Must Scream, MGM Interactive, 1995.

Short Story Collections:

The Deadly Streets, Ace Books (New York City), 1958.

(Under pseudonym Paul Merchant) *Sex Gang*, Nightstand, 1959.

A Touch of Infinity, Ace Books, 1960, published as *Earthman, Go Home*, 1964.

Children of the Streets (also published as *The Juvies*), Ace Books, 1961.

Gentleman Junkie, and Other Stories of the Hung–up Generation, Regency Books (Chicago, IL), 1961.

Ellison Wonderland, Paperback Library, 1962.

Paingod, and Other Delusions (includes "'Repent, Harlequin!' Said the Ticktockman"), Pyramid Books, 1965.

I Have No Mouth, and I Must Scream, Pyramid Books, 1967.

From the Land of Fear, Belmont, 1967.

Love Ain't Nothing but Sex Misspelled, Trident, 1968.

The Beast That Shouted Love at the Heart of the World, Avon (New York City), 1969.

Over the Edge: Stories from Somewhere Else, Belmont, 1970.

Alone Against Tomorrow: Stories of Alienation in Speculative Fiction, Macmillan (New York City), 1971, abridged editions published as *All the Sounds of Fear*, Panther (England), 1973, and *The Time of the Eye*, Panther (England), 1974.

(Coauthor) *Partners in Wonder: Science Fiction Collaborations with Fourteen Other Wild Talents*, Walker and Co. (New York City), 1971.

De Helden van de Highway (published only in Dutch), 1973.

Approaching Oblivion: Road Signs on the Treadmill toward Tomorrow, Walker and Co., 1974.

Deathbird Stories: A Pantheon of Modern Gods (includes "The Whimper of Whipped Dogs"), Harper (New York City), 1975.

No Doors, No Windows, Pyramid Books, 1975.

Strange Wine: Fifteen New Stories from the Nightside of the World, Harper, 1978.

The Illustrated Harlan Ellison, edited by Byron Preiss, Baronet, 1978.

The Fantasies of Harlan Ellison, Gregg (Boston, MA), 1979.

Shatterday, Houghton (Boston), 1980.

Stalking the Nightmare, Phantasia Press (Huntington Woods, MI), 1982.

An Edge in My Voice, Donning (Norfolk, VA), 2nd edition, 1986.

The Essential Ellison: A Thirty–five Year Retrospective, edited by Terry Dowling, Richard Delap, and Gil Lamont, Nemo Press, 1986.

Angry Candy, Houghton, 1988.

Dreams with Sharp Teeth (includes revised versions of *I Have No Mouth, and I Must Scream, Deathbird Stories,* and *Shatterday*), Book–of–the–Month Club, 1991.

Spider Kiss, Armchair Detective Library, 1991.

Mind Fields: The Art of Jacek Yerka, the Fiction of Harlan Ellison, illustrated by Yerka, Morpheus International (Beverly Hills, CA), 1994.

Slippage, Houghton, 1994, published as *Slippage: Precariously Poised, Previously Uncollected Stories,* Mark V. Zeising Books, 1997.

(Author of preface and contributor of story) Mel Odom, *I Have No Mouth, and I Must Scream: The Official Strategy Guide,* Prima Publishing (Rocklin, CA), 1995.

Jokes Without Punchlines, 1995.

Rough Beasts, 1995.

Edgeworks: The Collected Ellison, White Wolf Publishing, Volumes 1–2, 1996, Volumes 3–4, 1997.

"Repent, Harlequin!" Said the Ticktockman: The Classic Story, illustrated by Rick Berry, Underwood Books, 1997.

(Coauthor) *The Outer Limits: Armageddon Dreams,* Quadrillion Media, 2000.

(For young adults) *Troublemakers: Stories by Harlan Ellison,* 2001.

Novels:

Rumble, Pyramid Books, 1958, published as *Web of the City,* 1975.

The Man with Nine Lives [and] *A Touch of Infinity* (stories), Ace Books, 1960.

The Sound of a Scythe (originally published as *The Man with Nine Lives*), Ace Books, 1960.

Spider Kiss (also published as *Rockabilly*), Fawcett (New York City), 1961.

Doomsman (bound with *Telepower* by Lee Hoffman), Belmont, 1967, published (bound with *The Thief of Thoth* by Lin Carter), 1972.

(With Edward Bryant) *The Starlost 1: Phoenix without Ashes,* Fawcett, 1975.

All the Lies That Are My Life, Underwood/Miller (San Francisco, CA), 1980.

Footsteps, illustrated by Ken Snyder, Footsteps (Hobbs, NM), 1989.

Run for the Stars (bound with *Echoes of Thunder* by Jack Dann and Jack C. Halderman II), Tor Books (New York City), 1991.

Mefisto in Onyx (novelette), Zeising Books, 1993.

Essay Collections:

Memos from Purgatory: Two Journeys of Our Times, Regency Books, 1961.

The Glass Teat: Essays of Opinion on the Subject of Television, Ace Books, 1970.

The Other Glass Teat: Further Essays of Opinion on Television, Pyramid Books, 1975.

The Book of Ellison, edited by Andrew Porter, Algol Press (New York City), 1978.

Sleepless Nights in the Procrustean Bed, edited by Marty Clark, Borgo, 1984.

An Edge in My Voice, Donning, 1985.

Harlan Ellison's Watching, Underwood/Miller, 1989.

The Harlan Ellison Hornbook (autobiographical essays), Penzler Books, 1990.

Editor:

Dangerous Visions: 33 Original Stories, Doubleday (New York City), 1967.

Nightshade and Damnations: The Finest Stories of Gerald Kersh, Fawcett, 1968.

Again, Dangerous Visions: 46 Original Stories, Doubleday, 1972.

Editor; "Discovery" Series of First Novels:

James Sutherland, *Stormtrack,* Pyramid Books, 1974.

Marta Randall, *Islands,* Pyramid Books, 1976.

Terry Carr, *The Light at the End of the Universe,* Pyramid Books, 1976.

Arthur Byron Cones, *Autumn Angels,* Pyramid Books, 1976.

Bruce Sterling, *Involution Ocean,* Pyramid Books, 1977.

Other:

Contributor, *Faster than Light,* edited by Jack Dann and George Zebrowski, Harper, 1976.

Coeditor and contributor, *Medea: Harlan's World* (includes "With Virgil Oddum at the East Pole"), Bantam (New York City), 1985.

Author, *Demon with a Glass Hand* (graphic novel), illustrated by Marshall Rogers, D.C. Comics, 1986.

Author, *Night and the Enemy* (graphic novel), illustrated by Ken Steacy, Comico, 1987.

Author, *Vic and Blood: The Chronicles of a Boy and His Dog* (graphic novel; based on his novella "A

Boy and His Dog"), illustrated by Richard Corben, St. Martin's (New York City), 1989.

(With Isaac Asimov) Coauthor, *I, Robot: The Illustrated Screenplay* (based on the story cycle by Asimov), Warner Books (New York City), 1994.

Author, *Harlan Ellison's Dream Corridor Special* (includes the story "Chatting with Anubis"), 1995.

Author (with Richard Corben), *Vic and Blood: The Continuing Adventures of a Boy and His Dog,* ibooks/Edgeworks Abbey, 2003.

Author, *Harlan Ellison's Dream Corridor Volume 2,* Dark Horse, 2007.

Author of books on juvenile delinquency. Past author of columns, including "The Glass Teat" and "Harlan Ellison Hornbook," both in *Los Angeles Free Press,* "An Edge in My Voice," in *Los Angeles Weekly,* and "Watching," a syndicated film review column; book critic, *Los Angeles Times,* 1969–82. Work represented in anthologies, including *The Best American Short Stories,* 1993. Contributor of more than 1,000 short stories, essays, and articles to periodicals, including *Analog, Ariel, Cosmopolitan, Datamation, Ellery Queen's Mystery, Galaxy, Heavy Metal, Magazine of Fantasy and Science Fiction, Omni,* and *Twilight Zone.* Some work appears under various pseudonyms, including Lee Archer, Phil "Cheech" Beldone, Cordwainer Bird, Jay Charby, Robert Courtney, Price Curtis, Wallace Edmondson, Landon Ellis, Sley Harson, Ellis Hart, Al Maddern, Alan Maddern, Paul Merchant, Nabrah Nosille, Bert Parker, Jay Solo, and Derry Tiger. Ellison's works have been translated into more than twenty–five languages, including French, German, Italian, Japanese, and Spanish.

ADAPTATIONS

The film *A Boy and His Dog,* released by Aquarius Releasing in 1975, is based on a novella by Ellison; the 1978 film *Jackpot* is based on one of his stories; the film *Mefisto in Onyx,* released by Miramax in 2001, is based on his novelette. Ellison's television episodes "Demon with a Glass Hand" and "Soldier," both broadcast on *The Outer Limits,* have been cited as the inspiration for the film *The Terminator,* released by Orion in 1984. Several of Ellison's short stories have been adapted for television, including "The Human Factor," an episode of *The Outer Limits.* The video game *I Have No Mouth, and I Must Scream* is based on Ellison's story of the same title.

OTHER SOURCES

Books:
Authors and Artists for Young Adults, Volume 29, Gale, 1999.

Porter, Andrew, editor, *The Book of Ellison,* Algol Press, 1978.
Slusser, George Edgar, *Harlan Ellison: Unrepentant Harlequin,* Borgo, 1977.
Swigart, Leslie Kay, *Harlan Ellison: A Bibliographical Checklist,* Williams Publishing (Dallas, TX), 1973.

Electronic:
Harlan Ellison Website, http://www.harlanellison.com, September 10, 2007.

EMMETT, Randall 1971–

PERSONAL

Born March 25, 1971, in Miami, FL. *Education:* School of Visual Arts, B.F.A., film and video producing, 1994; also attended Delphi University, Caysville, GA.

Addresses: *Office*—Family Room Entertainment and Emmett/Furla Films, 8530 Wilshire Blvd., Suite 420, Beverly Hills, CA 90211.

Career: Producer. Began career as an assistant to the producer at Simpson/Bruckheimer Pictures, 1994–?; assistant, Motion Picture Talent Division, International Creative Management; Family Room Entertainment, Beverly Hills, CA, founder and principal, 1998—; Emmett/Furla Films, Beverly Hills, CA, founder and partner, 1998—.

CREDITS

Film Producer:
Eyes Beyond Seeing, 1995.
April Fool (short), 1998.
Speedway Junky, Regent Releasing, 1999.
Escape to Grizzly Mountain, Metro–Goldwyn–Mayer Home Entertainment, 2000.
After Sex, 2000.
Held for Ransom, Cutting Edge Entertainment, 2000.
Ticker, Artisan Entertainment, 2001.
Good Advice, Family Room Entertainment, 2001.
Gentleman of the Hunt, 2002.
Run for the Money (also known as *Hard Cash*), Artisan Entertainment, 2002.
Shottas, Sony Pictures Home Entertainment, 2002.
Try Seventeen (also known as *All I Want*), Try Seventeen Productions, Inc., 2002.
Out for a Kill, Nu Image Films, 2003.
Blind Horizon, Lions Gate Films, 2003.
Belly of the Beast, Millennium Films, 2003.
Control, Lions Gate Films, 2004.

Today You Die, Nu Image Films, 2005.

Edison (also known as *Edison Force*), Sony Pictures Home Entertainment, 2005.

Before It Had a Name, First Look International, 2005.

The Tenants, Millennium Films, 2006.

16 Blocks, Warner Bros., 2006.

Mercenary for Justice (also known as *Mercenary*), Twentieth Century–Fox Home Entertainment, 2006.

The Wicker Man, Warner Bros., 2006.

The Contract, First Look International, 2006.

Home of the Brave, Metro–Goldwyn–Mayer, 2006.

King of California, First Look International, 2007.

Borderland, Lions Gate Films, 2007.

88 Minutes, TriStar, 2007.

Room Service (short), 2007.

Day of the Dead, Millennium Films, 2007.

Major Movie Star, 2008.

Film Coproducer:

Submerged, Nu Image Films, 2005.

Film Executive Producer:

Narc (also known as *Narco*), Lions Gate Films, 2002.

The Badge, Lions Gate Films, 2002.

Wonderland, Lions Gate Films, 2003.

A Love Song for Bobby Long, Lions Gate Films, 2004.

Unstoppable (also known as *9 Lives*), Columbia TriStar Home Entertainment, 2004.

Lonely Hearts (also known as *Lonely Hearts Killer*), Millennium Films, 2006.

White Air, Monarch Home Video, 2007.

Finding Rin Tin Tin, Haze Productions, 2007.

Film Co–Executive Producer:

Half Past Dead (also known as *Halbtot—Half Past Dead*), Screen Gems, 2002.

The Devil and Daniel Webster (also known as *Shortcut to Happiness*), Yari Film Group Releasing, 2004.

Loverboy, THINKFilm, 2005.

The Amityville Horror, Metro–Goldwyn–Mayer, 2005.

Film Associate Producer:

The Devil and Daniel Webster (also known as *Shortcut to Happiness*), Yari Film Group Releasing, 2004.

Film Production Assistant:

The Hard Way, 1991.

Film Appearances:

Himself, *Making "Mercenary for Justice"* (short), Twentieth Century–Fox, 2006.

Himself, *Absolute Power: The Making of "Edison Force"* (short), Sony, 2006.

Television Work; Movies:

Co–executive producer, *Cutaway,* USA Network, 2000.

Television Work; Specials:

Producer, *Andrew Dice Clay: I'm Over Here Now* (also known as *I'm Over Here Now*), pay per view, 2000.

Television Appearances; Specials:

Himself, *Rally for Relief,* 2005.

F

FANCY, Richard 1943–

PERSONAL

Born August 2, 1943, in Evanston, IL; father, in sales; mother, a radio performer; married; wife's name, Joanna; children. *Education:* Studied acting at the London Academy of Music and Dramatic Art.

Career: Actor. Appeared in advertisements.

Awards, Honors: *L.A. Weekly* Theatre Award nomination, leading male performance, 2000, for *The Master Builder.*

CREDITS

Television Appearances; Series:
Mr. Stravely, *It's Garry Shandling's Show,* Showtime, 1986–90, Fox, 1988–90.

Mr. Lippman, *Seinfeld,* NBC, 1991–98.

Bernie, *General Hospital* (also known as *Hopital central* and *Hospital general*), ABC, 1997–2003 (some sources cite beginning in 2006.

District attorney Bruce Logan, *The District,* CBS, 2000–2004.

Television Appearances; Miniseries:
Sam Adams, *George Washington,* CBS, 1984.

William Duer, *George Washington II: The Forging of a Nation,* CBS, 1986.

Dr. Breedlove, *From the Dead of the Night* (also known as *Nos bracos da morte* and *Schattenreich des Todes*), NBC, 1989.

Arthur Sackheim, *Murder One: Diary of a Serial Killer,* ABC, 1997.

Television Appearances; Movies:
Contract lawyer, *Call Me Anna* (also known as *Call Me Anna: The Patty Duke Story*), ABC, 1990.

Strathom, *Without Her Consent* (also known as *Bez jej zgody, Gegen ihren Willen, Raiskaus,* and *Un giorno da dimenticare*), NBC, 1990.

Justice Richard Marino, *Absolute Strangers* (also known as *Calkiem nieznajomi* and *Zwischen Leben und Tod*), CBS, 1991.

Marty, *Drive Like Lightning* (also known as *Der Stunt seines Lebens*), 1992.

Stephen Grant, *Afterburn* (also known as *Depois do fogo, F–16, autopsie d'un accident, F–16—Surmanloukku, Le crash du F16, Le triomphe de la verite, Przerwany lot F–16, Starfighter des Todes, Voo rasante,* and *Zuhanas utan*), HBO, 1992.

Dr. Michael Gottlieb, *And the Band Played On* (also known as *E a banda continua a tocar, E a vida continua, En el filo de la duda, Es a zenekar jatszik tovabb ..., Guerra al virus, Il grande gelo, Kai i zoi synehizetai, Les soldats de l'esperance, ... Und das Leben geht weiter,* and *Y la banda siguio tocando*), HBO, 1993.

Doctor, *Roswell* (also known as *Incident at Roswell* and *Roswell: The U.F.O. Cover–Up*), Showtime, 1994.

Harold Sherman, *Untamed Love* (also known as *La pequena rebelde*), Lifetime, 1994.

McClintock (a banker), *The Last Outlaw* (also known as *El ultimo forajido, El ultimo renegado, L'ultimo fuorilegge, O ultimo bandido, Os ultimos foras–da–lei,* and *Viimeinen lainsuojaton*), HBO, 1994.

Ed Ledbetter, *The O. J. Simpson Story* (also known as *A verdadeira historia de O. J. Simpson Story, Die O. J. Simpson Story,* and *O. J. Simpsonin tarina*), Fox, 1995.

Richard Tasman, *Innocent Victims* (also known as *Erreur judiciaire* and *Sijaiskaersijaet*), ABC, 1996.

Deutsch, *Primal Force* (also known as *Wild World* and *Agguato nell'isola della morte*), UPN, 1999.

Harold, *Come On, Get Happy: The Partridge Family Story* (also known as *C'Mon, Get Happy: The Partridge Family Story, Come on, get happy—Die Partridge Familie, Den sanna historien om familjen Partridge,* and *Partridge familyn tarina*), ABC, 1999.

George Prescott, *McBride: The Doctor Is Out … Really Out,* The Hallmark Channel, 2005.

Television Appearances; Episodic:

Minister, "There Goes the Bride," *Who's the Boss?,* ABC, 1987.

Norman Klein, "Pigmalion," *L.A. Law,* NBC, 1987.

Principal Kevin Altman, "The Test," *Starman,* ABC, 1987.

Elam Swope, "The Silence at Bethany," *The American Experience,* PBS, 1988.

Lieutenant, "Barbara Gets Shot," *Empty Nest,* NBC, 1988.

Man, "The Big Uneasy," *Newhart,* CBS, 1988.

Mr. Hauser, "A Funny Thing Happened on the Way to the Pageant," *227,* NBC, 1988.

Norman Klein, "Open Heart Perjury," *L.A. Law,* NBC, 1988.

Colonel Halsey, "Consider Me Gone," *ALF,* NBC, 1990.

Prosecuting attorney, "I'm Nobody," *Gabriel's Fire,* ABC, 1990.

Dr. Moss, "A Lesson in Life," *Nurses,* NBC, 1991.

Fred Epstein, "The Agony and the Agony," *Top of the Heap,* Fox, 1991.

Captain Satelk, "The First Duty," *Star Trek: The Next Generation* (also known as *The Next Generation* and *Star Trek: TNG*), syndicated, 1992.

Congressperson, "Cruel and Unusual Punishment," *Empty Nest,* NBC, 1992.

Dr. Chodash, "Chute Friends, Ask Questions Later," *Civil Wars,* ABC, 1992.

Dr. Chodash, "For Better or Perverse," *Civil Wars,* ABC, 1992.

Dr. Valenti, "Kodachrome," *The Wonder Years,* ABC, 1992.

Dr. Valenti, "Lunch Stories," *The Wonder Years,* ABC, 1992.

Senator Thatcher, "Send in the Clowns," *Murphy Brown,* CBS, 1992.

"Educating Janine," *Doogie Howser, M.D.,* ABC, 1992.

Dr. Saxon, "The Man of Steel Bars," *Lois & Clark: The New Adventures of Superman* (also known as *Lois & Clark* and *The New Adventures of Superman*), ABC, 1993.

"Foreign Co–Respondent," *L.A. Law,* NBC, 1993.

Wallace, "Booktopus," *All–American Girl* (also known as *All American Girl*), ABC, 1994.

Wayne Donnelly, "Killer Party," *Weird Science* (also known as *Ciencia loca, Code Lisa, Lisa—Der helle Wahnsinn, Lisa ja pojat,* and *Una chica explosiva*), USA Network, 1994.

Alien, "Tattoo," *Star Trek: Voyager* (also known as *Voyager*), UPN, 1995.

Allen Raffin, "What Ever Happened to Maria Rosa?," *Land's End,* syndicated, 1995.

Dr. Hayman, "Misery on 34th Street," *Bless This House,* CBS, 1995.

Dr. Mendelsohn, *Get Smart,* Fox, 1995.

Mr. Copeland, "Beam Me Up, Dr. Spock," *Dream On,* HBO, 1995, also broadcast on Fox.

Sam Arbogast, "Where There's Smoke," *Party of Five,* Fox, 1995.

E. Allen Wayne, " … Tell Our Moms We Done Our Best," *Space: Above and Beyond* (also known as *Above and Beyond, Space, Space 2063, Space: 2063, Avaruus 2063, Guerra dos mundos, Gwiezdna eskadra, Rummet aar 2063, Slaget om tellus,* and *Space: guerra estelar*), Fox, 1996.

James V. Forrestal, "Moving Targets," *Dark Skies* (also known as *Cielo negro, Dark Skies—l'impossible verite, Dark Skies—Oscure presenze,* and *Dark Skies—Toedliche Bedrohung*), NBC, 1996.

Martin Gutenhimmel, "In the Matter of: Acceptance," *Common Law,* ABC, 1996.

Martin Gutenhimmel, "In the Matter of: John's Fifteen Minutes," *Common Law,* ABC, 1996.

Stu Havlik, "Murder on the Run: Part 2," *Diagnosis Murder,* CBS, 1996.

Judge, "Harassed," *Union Square,* NBC, 1997.

Judge, "Veronica's Best Buddy, *Veronica's Closet,* NBC, 1997.

Judge Debelko, "Eleven Angry Men and One Dick," *3rd Rock from the Sun* (also known as *3rd Rock* and *Life as We Know It*), NBC, 1997.

Judge Debelko, "Romeo & Juliet & Dick," *3rd Rock from the Sun* (also known as *3rd Rock* and *Life as We Know It*), NBC, 1997.

Mr. Posner, "The One Where They're Going to Party!," *Friends* (also known as *Across the Hall, Friends Like Us, Insomnia Cafe,* and *Six of One*), NBC, 1997.

Mr. Thomas, "Tribes," *ER* (also known as *Emergency Room*), NBC, 1997.

Vincent Carraze, "Luther's Temptation," *Orleans* (also known as *New Orleans—Das Gesetz des Suedens*), CBS, 1997.

Vincent Carraze, "When the Saints Go Marching In," *Orleans* (also known as *New Orleans—Das Gesetz des Suedens*), CBS, 1997.

Chandler Evans, "Immaculate Conception," *The Nanny,* CBS, 1998.

Harold F. "Hal" Lomax, "First Do No Harm," *Diagnosis Murder,* CBS, 1998.

Mr. Broadman, "Norm, Crusading Social Worker," *Norm* (also known as *The Norm Show*), ABC, 1999.

Sector control, "Please Press One," *Sliders,* Fox, 1999.

Allen Prescott, "Forgiveness and Stuff," *Gilmore Girls* (also known as *Gilmore Girls: Beginnings* and *The Gilmore Way*), The WB, 2000.

Congressperson, "The White House Pro–Am," *The West Wing* (also known as *West Wing* and *El ala oeste de la Casablanca*), NBC, 2000.

Dr. Van Zandt, "Death Takes a Three Day Holiday," *The Hughleys*, UPN, 2000.

Judge, "Cry Me a Liver," *City of Angels* (also known as *Anglarnas stad, Englenes by, Enkelten kaupunki,* and *Orasul ingerilor*), CBS, 2000.

Rabbi Joseph Wolk, "Believers," *Crossing Jordan* (also known as *Untitled Tim Kring Project*), NBC, 2001.

Psychiatrist, "Insomnia," *Carnivale* (also known as *Circo, La caravane de l'etrange,* and *To tsirko tou mystiriou*), HBO, 2003.

Psychiatrist, "Lonnigan, Texas," *Carnivale* (also known as *Circo, La caravane de l'etrange,* and *To tsirko tou mystiriou*), HBO, 2003.

Senior partner, "Separation Anxiety," *The Lyon's Den* (also known as *I lovens hule* and *Lain luola*), NBC, 2003.

Howard Seigal, "You're Buggin' Me," *NYPD Blue*, ABC, 2004.

Palmer, "You Can't Take It With You," *Las Vegas* (also known as *Casino Eye*), NBC, 2004.

Father Michael Ryan, "Gone," *Boston Legal* (also known as *Fleet Street, The Practice: Fleet Street,* and *The Untitled Practice*), ABC, 2005.

Father Michael Ryan, "Legal Deficits," *Boston Legal* (also known as *Fleet Street, The Practice: Fleet Street,* and *The Untitled Practice*), ABC, 2005.

The judge, "Whereabouts," *Eyes*, ABC, 2005.

Thomas Galway, "Calculated Risk," *Numb3rs* (also known as *Numbers* and *Num3ers*), CBS, 2005.

Bob Lewis, "Dumb Luck," *The Closer* (also known as *L.A.: Enquetes prioritaires* and *Se apostasi anapnois*), TNT, 2007.

Doctor, "The Class Goes back to the Hospital," *The Class*, CBS, 2007.

Judge Dixon, "Shattered," *Crossing Jordan* (also known as *Untitled Tim Kring Project*), NBC, 2007.

Appeared in other programs, including appearances as Richard Pappas, *Moloney*, CBS; as Clarke Davenport, *Two Guys and a Girl* (also known as *Two Guys, a Girl and a Pizza Place*), ABC; and appearances in *Reasonable Doubts*, NBC; and *Strong Medicine*, Lifetime. Also appeared as Geoff Aull in "What the Past Will Bring," an unaired episode of *Bull* (also known as *Klippet* and *Wall Street porssihait*), TNT.

Television Appearances; Pilots:

First worker, "Once upon a Time in the City of New York," *Beauty and the Beast* (also known as *A Szepseg es a szoernyeteg, Die Schoene und das Biest, I pentamorfi kai to teras, La bella e la bestia, La bella y la bestia, La belle et la bete,* and *Skonheden og udyret*), CBS, 1987.

Captain Brunetti, "Nick Knight" (also known as "Midnight Cop"), *Forever Knight*, CBS, 1989.

Dr. Moss, "Son of a Pilot," *Nurses*, NBC, 1991.

Film Appearances:

Academy speaker, *Sunset* (also known as *Catalina, Asesinato en Beverly Hills, Assassinato em Hollywood, Intrigo a hollywood, Meurtre a Hollywood,* and *Sunset—Daemmerung in Hollywood*), TriStar, 1988.

Sergeant Barry, *Spellbinder* (also known as *Culto diabolico, Czarownica, La hora de los brujos, La trampa de la arana, Noiduttu,* and *Spellbinder—Ein teuflischer Plan*), Metro–Goldwyn–Mayer/United Artists, 1988.

Ballistics expert, *True Believer* (also known as *Fighting Justice, Coupable ressemblance, Das dreckige Spiel, Oikeutta vastaan, Solo ante la ley,* and *Verdetto finale*), Columbia, 1989.

Nolan, *Tango & Cash* (also known as *The Set Up, Duo de choc, Tango da Keshi, Tango e Cash—Os vingadores, Tango es Cash, Tango et Cash, Tango i kes,* and *Tango y Cash*), Warner Bros., 1989.

Yves Malmaison, *Identity Crisis*, 1989.

Intelligence captain, *Flight of the Intruder* (also known as *El vuelo del Intruder, Flug durch die Hoelle, Inkraektaren fraan skyn, Intruder: Missao de alto risco, Intruderek tamadasa, L'ultimo attacco, Le vol de l'intruder,* and *Paholaislentaejaet*), Paramount, 1990.

Minister, *What about Bob?* (also known as *Co jest z Bobem?, Comment ca va Bob?, Entaes Bob?, Hur maar Bob, Isten nem ver Bobbal, Ma kore im Bob?, Nosso querido Bob, Que pasa con Bob?, Quoi de neuf Bob?, Tutte le manie di Bob,* and *Was ist mit Bob?*), Buena Vista, 1991.

Detective, *Clifford* (also known as *Jurassic Boy, Clifford—Das kleine Scheusal,* and *Ma chi me l'ha fatto fare*), Orion, 1994.

Hospital doctor, *Species* (also known as *A experiencia, De vrouwelijke mutant, Especes, Especie mortal, Especies, La mutante, Peto, Specie mortal, Species: especie mortal, Species—hotet fraan rymden, Specii, Tehlikeli tuer,* and *Tuja vrsta*), Metro–Goldwyn–Mayer, 1995.

Mel Laird, *Nixon* (also known as *Gli intrighi del potere* and *Nixon—Der Untergang eines Praesidenten*), Buena Vista, 1995.

Senator Greenspan, *Lawnmower Man 2: Beyond Cyberspace* (also known as *Lawnmower Man 2: Jobe's War, Der Rasenmaehermann 2—Beyond Cyberspace, El cortador de cesped II: mas alla del ciberespacio, Graesklipparmannen 2, Il tagliaerbe 2:*

the cyberspace, *Kosiarz umyslow 2: Ponad cyber-przestrzenia, Le cobaye 2,* and *Le cobaye 2: Cyberspace*), New Line Cinema, 1996.

Judge, *Touch* (also known as *Les mains de Dieu, Milagres por encomenda, Tocat, Touch—Der Typ mit den magischen Haenden,* and *Touch—kosketus*), United Artists, 1997.

Mr. Haus, *Eat Your Heart Out* (also known as *American Shrimps*), First Look Pictures Releasing, 1997.

Murdstone, *'Til There Was You* (also known as *Ate tu apareceres ..., Ha–Dereh el Ha–Osher, Hasta que te encontre, Idoeszamitasom eloett, L'amour de ma vie, Si on s'aimait, Solo se ilm destino,* and *Zwei Singles in L.A.*), Paramount, 1997.

Father, *Ted,* Chronic Filmwerks, 1998.

Mr. Van Dough, *Richie Rich's Christmas Wish* (also known as *Richie Rich: A Christmas Story, Richi Richs jul,* and *Un souhait pour Noel*), Warner Home Video, 1998.

Johnson Heyward, *Being John Malkovich* (also known as *A John Malkovich menet, Como ser John Malkovich, Dans la peau de John Malkovich, Elaemaeni John Malkovichina, Essere John Malkovich, I huvudet paa John Malkovich, In mintea lui John Malkovich, Malkovich no ana, Queres ser John Malkovich?, Quero ser John Malkovich, Quieres ser John Malkovich?,* and *Sto myalo tou John Malkovich*), USA Films, 1999.

Captain, *3 Strikes* (also known as *Dreimal ist einmal zu viel, 3 vezes em apuros,* and *Tres delitos*), Metro–Goldwyn–Mayer, 2000.

Dr. Westworth and Dr. Edwards, *Psycho Beach Party* (also known as *Verano bizarro*), Strand Releasing/CinemaVault Releasing, 2000.

Mr. Meyerson, *Moonlight Mile* (also known as *Baby's in Black, Goodbye Hello, El compromiso, La vida continua, Moonlight mile—surun tie, Moonlight mile—Voglia di ricominciare,* and *Vida que segue*), Buena Vista, 2002.

Mr. Peterson, *The Girl next Door* (also known as *Girl next Door, La chica de al lado, La fille d'a cote, La ragazza della porta accanto, La vecina de al lado, Naabermaja pornostaar, Naegen neomu ajjilhan geunyeo, Sexbomba od vedle, Um show de vizinha,* and *Unelmien naapuri*), Twentieth Century–Fox, 2004.

Eli, *Shopgirl* (also known as *Chica de mostrador, Ena koritsi gia dyo,* and *Garota da vitrine*), Buena Vista, 2005.

Alford "Rip" Van Ronkel, *Hollywoodland* (also known as *Truth, Justice, and the American Way, Untitled George Reeves Project, Die Hollywood–Verschworueng, Hollywoodland—Bastidores da fama, Hollywoodland—Misterio y muerte detras de camas,* and *Sta adyta tou Hollywood*), Focus Features, 2006.

Pastor Mark, *Midnight Clear,* Jenkins Entertainment, c. 2007.

Dean Carpenter, *Halloween* (also known as *Hall9ween, Halloween 9, Halloween: Retribution, Trick or Treat,* and *Untitled Rob Zombie Halloween Project*), Metro–Goldwyn–Mayer, 2007.

Dick Houston, *Adventures of Power,* SpaceTime Films, 2007.

Stage Appearances:

Roscoe Dexter, *Singin' in the Rain* (musical), Gershwin Theatre, New York City, 1985.

Solness, *The Master Builder,* Pacific Resident Theatre, Venice, CA, beginning 1998.

Also appeared in other productions, including *Henry V, Kind Lady, Rites of Passage,* and *Sherlock Holmes,* all New York City productions.

FEENEY, Matthew 1968–

PERSONAL

Born July 12, 1968, in St. Paul, MN.

Career: Actor, comedian, casting director, and producer. Performed at Second City TV, Chicago, IL, New York Comedy Club, New York City, and the Comedy Store, Los Angeles; appeared in an American Red Cross Training Video; appeared in a print ad for Coca Cola "Red Zone" beverages; appeared in television commercials, including Minnesota Twins baseball, Best Buy electronics stores, and Old Dutch Restaurante Chips.

Awards, Honors: Gold Award, television and cable production, television special—comedy, WorldFest Houston, 2005, for *The WaZoo! Show.*

CREDITS

Film Appearances:

(Uncredited) Curious man, *Jingle All the Way,* Twentieth Century–Fox, 1996.

Spiro Coldreign, *Williams & Ree: The Movie II—Totem ReeCall,* TV Productions, 2000.

Man in cafe, *Herman U.S.A.* (also known as *Taking a Chance on Love*), Two Silks Releasing, 2001.

Sportsman juror, *Jurisprudence* (short), 2001.

Prosecutor, *Justice,* 2004.

Sheriff, *Almelund,* 2004.

Bruce, *Stealing Summer,* 2004.

Chief Engineer O'Malley, *The Final Frontier Revisited* (short), Paramount 2004.

Chief Engineer O'Malley, *Trekkies 2* (documentary), Paramount Home Video, 2004.

(Scenes deleted) Harry Berglund, *Factotum* (also known as *Factotum: A Man Who Performs Many Jobs*), IFC Films, 2005.

Voice of Frank, *Friction* (short), 48 Hour Film Project, 2005.

Farmer, *Sweet Land,* Libero, 2005.

Highball, *Not a King's Ransom* (short), 2005.

Michael, *Fall Into Me,* Westlake Entertainment Group, 2006.

Sheriff Zombie, *Doomed to Consume,* 2006.

Abraham, *For a List of Ways Technology Has Failed to Improve Daily Life Please Press Three* (short), 2006.

Reverend Buddy Baker, *Stimulus,* 2007.

Louis, *Memorizing Dates,* 2007.

Karaoke Canyon patron, *The Completely Remarkable, Utterly Fabulous Transformation of a Regular Joe,* 2007.

Sergeant Hoffman, *IceBreaker,* 2008.

Film Work:

Producer, casting director, and extras casting, *Stealing Summer,* 2004.

Extras casting associate, *Factotum* (also known as *Factotum: A Many Who Performs Many Jobs*), IFC Films, 2005.

Executive producer, casting director, and extras casting, *Fall Into Me,* Westlake Entertainment Group, 2006.

Executive producer and casting director, *Stimulus,* 2007.

Executive producer, casting director, and extras casting, *IceBreaker,* 2008.

Television Appearances; Series:

Officer Torgerson, *The Gale Whitman Show,* 2003–2004.

Television Appearances; Movies:

Rick Lansky, *Life Without Bail,* 2004.

Television Appearances; Pilots:

Various, *The WaZoo! Show,* 2002.

Television Appearances; Episodic:

(Uncredited) Cafe Nervosa patron, "Tales from the Crypt," *Frasier,* NBC, 2002.

Various characters, *The WaZoo! Show,* 2003.

Various characters, "Festival Cut," *The WaZoo! Show,* 2004.

Contestant, "Next Action Star," *Next Action Star,* NBC, 2004.

Gas station Matt, *Out 'N' About with R. J. Fritz,* 2006.

Mystery man, *Out 'N' About with R. J. Fritz,* 2006.

Elmer, *Out 'N' About with R. J. Fritz,* 2006.

Television Producer; Series:

The WaZoo! Show, 2002–2004.

Television Work; Pilots:

Executive director and casting director, *The WaZoo! Show,* 2002.

Television Work; Episodic:

Executive director and casting director, *The WaZoo! Show,* 2003.

Executive director and casting director, "Festival Cut," *The WaZoo! Show,* 2004.

FLYNN, Steven
  (Steve Flynn)

PERSONAL

Addresses: *Agent*—Mitchell K. Stubbs and Associates, 8675 West Washington Blvd., Suite 203, Culver City, CA 90232.

Career: Actor.

CREDITS

Television Appearances; Movies:

Scott, *Choices,* ABC, 1986.

Willie, *The High Price of Passion,* PBS, 1986.

P. F. "Floater" James, *Trenchcoat in Paradise,* CBS, 1989.

John W. Hinckley, Jr., *Without Warning: The James Brady Story,* HBO, 1991.

Noel Ferguson, *Matlock: The Witness Killings,* NBC, 1991.

Thomas King, *Lady Against the Odds,* NBC, 1992.

Jack (uncredited), *And Then There Was One,* Lifetime, 1994.

Henry "Lightening" Lytell, *Ed McBain's 87th Precinct: Lightning,* NBC, 1995.

(As Steve Flynn) Calaban, *Alien Nation: Millennium,* Fox, 1996.

James, *Brave New World,* NBC, 1998.

Bobby, *Scar City* (also known as *S.C.A.R.* and *Scarred City*), 1998.

John Dearman, *Roswell: The Aliens Attack,* UPN, 1999.

Television Appearances; Series:

Neil Delaney, *One Life to Live,* 1989.

Television Appearances; Episodic:

Ellis Agnes, "Urine Trouble Now," *L.A. Law,* NBC, 1989.

Eddie Oskowski, "The Devil and the Deep Blue Sea Mystery," *Father Dowling Mysteries* (also known as *Father Dowling Investigates*), 1990.

"Every Time We Say Goodbye," *Jake and the Fatman,* 1991.

Second editor, "Conversations with My Shrink," *Hearts Afire,* 1992.

The strangler, "Nightmoves," *Bodies of Evidence,* CBS, 1992.

The strangler, "The Cold Light of Day," *Bodies of Evidence,* CBS, 1992.

Brett Nelson, "Suspicious Minds," *Melrose Place,* Fox, 1993.

"Where There's a Will," *L.A. Law,* NBC, 1993.

Grant Gardner, *Home Free,* 1993.

Joe, "The Class Reunion," *Ellen* (also known as *These Friends of Mine*), ABC, 1994.

Donald Dixon, Jr./the ranger, "The Late Shift," *Renegade,* 1994.

Donald Dixon, Jr., "Sins of the Father," *Renegade,* 1995.

Donnie Dixon, "The Bad Seed," *Renegade,* 1995.

Grady, "One Strike and You're Out," *Courthouse,* CBS, 1995.

Ted, "Wingless: Part 3," *Wings,* NBC, 1996.

Chief Petty Officer Greg Connors, "Heroes," *JAG,* CBS, 1997.

"Why Can't Even a Couple of Us Get Along?," *Brooklyn South,* CBS, 1997.

"Touched by a Checkered Cab," *Brooklyn South,* CBS, 1997.

R. J. Roemer, "Indy Show," *The Pretender,* NBC, 1998.

Sam Little, "Once in a Lifetime," *Ally McBeal,* Fox, 1998.

Truman, "Prostrate before the Law," *NYPD Blue,* ABC, 1998.

Walker, "Too Cool for School," *Party of Five,* Fox, 2000.

"Simple Simon," *Hollywood Off-Ramp,* 2000.

Luke Lawson, "The Devil You Know," *The Invisible Man* (also known as *I–Man*), Sci–Fi Channel, 2000.

(Uncredited) Avery Chadsey, "The Fastest Year," *ER,* NBC, 2000.

Mark Brookline, "And It's Surely to Their Credit," *The West Wing,* NBC, 2000.

"The Fear Factor," *The Division* (also known as *Heart of the City*), Lifetime, 2001.

John Farren, "The River," *Cover Me: Based on the True Life of an FBI Family* (also known as *Cover Me*), USA Network, 2001.

Max, "Take Me Back," *The Chronicle* (also known as *Take Me Back*), Sci–Fi Channel, 2001.

District Attorney Martin Toomey, "Payback," *The Practice,* ABC, 2001.

District Attorney Martin Toomey, "The Thin Line," *The Practice,* ABC, 2001.

Ron Devine, "Blood Sugar Sex Magik," *10–8: Officers on Duty* (also known as *10–8* and *10–8: Police Patrol*), ABC, 2001.

Man on the street, "Trust No 1," *The X–Files,* Fox, 2002.

The killer, "The Truth Is Out There," *Crossing Jordan,* NBC, 2002.

Captain, "Out of Gas," *Firefly* (also known as *Firefly: The Series*), Fox, 2002.

Maklii, "Marauders," *Enterprise* (also known as *Star Trek: Enterprise*), UPN, 2002.

"The Eleventh Hour," *Providence,* NBC, 2002.

Mister Sterling, NBC, 2003.

District Attorney Martin Toomey, "Equal Justice," *The Practice,* ABC, 2003.

Chaplain Oliver Stephens, "Good Intentions," *JAG,* CBS, 2004.

Pete Tomello, "Without Consent," *The Guardian,* CBS, 2004.

Virgil Wilkins, "Abduction," *Dragnet* (also known as *L.A. Dragnet*), ABC, 2004.

Luke Sutton, "Three Generations Are Enough," *CSI: NY,* CBS, 2004.

Doug Windham, "The Running Man," *Numb3rs* (also known as *Num3ers*), CBS, 2006.

Russell Parks, "The Shot," *Close to Home,* CBS, 2006.

Craig Spengler, "To Protect & Serve," *The Closer,* TNT, 2006.

Appeared as Zack in an episode of *Empty Nest,* NBC.

Film Appearances:

Eddie Flowers, *Ulee's Gold,* Orion, 1997.

Michael, "Inside Out," *Boys Life 3,* 2000.

Romlet, *The Cutting Room* (short film), 2001.

Stage Appearances:

Shivaree, Long Wharf Theatre, New Haven, CT, 1984.

Dallas, *True to Life,* Young Playwrights Festival, Playwrights Horizons Theatre, New York City, 1985.

Understudy for Jake and Jake Too, *Sweet Sue,* Music Box Theatre, New York City, 1987.

David Appleton, *Another Antigone,* Playwrights Horizons Theatre, 1988.

FRAWLEY, James 1937–

PERSONAL

Born in 1937, in Houston, TX. *Education:* Studied acting at Carnegie Institute of Technology (now Carnegie–

Mellon University), Pittsburgh, PA, and at Actors Studio, New York City.

Addresses: *Agent*—International Creative Management, 10250 Constellation Way, Los Angeles, CA 90067.

Career: Director, producer, and actor. Teacher and operator of directors unit at Actors Studio, New York City; affiliated with Maya Films Ltd., Los Angeles.

Member: Directors Guild of America.

Awards, Honors: Emmy Award, outstanding directorial achievement, 1967, Emmy Award nomination, outstanding directorial achievement, 1968, both for *The Monkees;* Emmy Award nomination, outstanding directing for a comedy series, and Directors Guild of America Award nomination, outstanding directorial achievement in dramatic series—night, 1998, both for *Ally McBeal;* Emmy Award nomination, outstanding directing for a comedy series, 2001, for *Ed.*

CREDITS

Television Work; Series:
Supervising producer, *The Big Easy,* 1996.
Co–executive producer, *Vengeance Unlimited* (also known as *Mr. Chapel*), ABC, 1998.
Co–executive producer, *Thieves,* ABC, 2001.
Co–executive producer, *Book of Daniel,* NBC, 2005.
Co–executive producer, *Three Moons Over Milford,* ABC Family, 2006.

Television Director; Movies:
Columbo: Try and Catch Me, 1977.
Columbo: Make Me a Perfect Murder, 1978.
Columbo: How to Dial a Murder, 1978.
Gridlock (also known as *The Great American Traffic Jam*), NBC, 1980.
The Outlaws, ABC, 1984.
Assault and Matrimony, NBC, 1987.
Warm Hearts, Cold Feet (also known as *Babytalk*), CBS, 1987.
Spies, Lies, and Naked Thighs, CBS, 1988.
"Columbo: Murder, Smoke, and Shadows," *The ABC Mystery Movie,* ABC, 1989.
"Columbo: Murder—A Self–Portrait," *The ABC Mystery Movie,* ABC, 1989.
"Columbo: Sex and the Married Detective," *The ABC Mystery Movie,* ABC, 1989.
The Secret Life of Archie's Wife (also known as *Archie's Wife* and *Runaway Heart*), CBS, 1990.
Another Midnight Run, syndicated, 1994.

Cagney & Lacey: The Return, CBS, 1994.
The Shamrock Conspiracy, UPN, 1995.
Harrison: Cry of the City, UPN, 1995.
Sins of the Mind, USA Network, 1997.
On the Second Day of Christmas, Lifetime, 1997.
Mr. Headmistress, ABC, 1998.
The Three Stooges, ABC, 2000.
Nancy Drew, ABC, 2002.

Television Co–Executive Producer; Movies:
Nancy Drew, ABC, 2002.

Television Director; Pilots:
Delancey Street: The Crisis Within, NBC, 1975.
The Orphan and the Dude, ABC, 1975.
Bulba, ABC, 1981.
The Outlaws, ABC, 1983.
Wishman, ABC, 1983.
Steel Collar Man (also known as *D–5–B: Steel Collar Man*), CBS, 1985.
Adam's Apple, CBS, 1986.
The Big Easy, USA Network, 1996.
Ally McBeal, Fox, 1997.
Ed, NBC, 2000.
Three Moons Over Milford, ABC Family, 2006.
Side Order of Life, Lifetime, 2007.
Spellbound, The CW, 2007.

Television Director; Specials:
"The Saint" (also known as "The Saint in Manhattan" and "The Saint in New York"), *CBS Summer Playhouse,* CBS, 1987.
"Further Adventures" (also known as "Moving Targets"), *CBS Summer Playhouse,* CBS, 1988.

Television Director; Episodic:
The Monkees, NBC, 1966–68.
That Girl, 1967–68.
The Ugliest Girl in Town, ABC, 1968.
"Wailin' Wheeler Is Dead," *The Texas Wheelers,* 1974.
All That Glitters, syndicated, 1977.
The Eddie Capra Mysteries, NBC, 1978.
"The Eight Part of the Village," *Magnum, P.I.,* CBS, 1982.
"Romeo and Dreidelwood," *Mr. Merlin,* CBS, 1982.
"Alex Goes Popless," *Mr. Merlin,* CBS, 1982.
"The Lady on the Billboard," *The Devlin Connection,* NBC, 1982.
"Arsenic and Old Caviar," *The Devlin Connection,* NBC, 1982.
"Escape from Death Island," *Tales of the Gold Monkey* (also known as *Tales of the Golden Monkey*), 1982.
"High Stakes Lady," *Tales of the Gold Monkey* (also known as *Tales of the Golden Monkey*), 1982.

"Hansel and Gretel," *Faerie Tale Theatre* (also known as *Shelley Duvall's "Faerie Tale Theatre"*), 1983.

"The Arrow That Is Not Aimed," *Magnum, P.I.,* CBS, 1983.

Scarecrow and Mrs. King, CBS, 1983–85.

"The Rescue," *Wizards and Warriors,* 1983.

"Rembrandt's Girl," *Magnum, P.I.,* CBS, 1984.

Mickey Spillane's "Mike Hammer" (also known as *The New Mike Hammer*), CBS, 1984–85.

Tough Cookies, 1986.

"Trading Places," *Cagney & Lacey,* 1988.

"A Class Act," *Cagney & Lacey,* 1988.

Father Dowling Mysteries, 1990–91.

"I Could Write a Book," *Jake and the Fatman,* 1991.

"Rosie Gets the Blues," *The Trials of Rosie O'Neill,* 1991.

Law & Order, NBC, 1992–93.

"End Game," *Melrose Place,* Fox, 1993.

"Suspicious Minds," *Melrose Place,* Fox, 1993.

"Revenge," *Melrose Place,* Fox, 1993.

South Beach, NBC, 1993.

"Guns 'R' Us," *Picket Fences,* CBS, 1994.

"Enemy Lines," *Picket Fences,* CBS, 1994.

"With the Greatest of Ease," *Chicago Hope,* CBS, 1994.

"Full Moon," *Chicago Hope,* CBS, 1995.

"Every Day a Little Death," *Chicago Hope,* CBS, 1995.

"Without Mercy," *Picket Fences,* CBS, 1995.

"Reap the Whirlwind," *Picket Fences,* CBS, 1995.

"The Greatest Love Story Never Told," *Earth 2,* NBC, 1995.

"The Best, False Friend," *Central Park West* (also known as *C.P.W.*), CBS, 1995.

"The Burning of Atlanta," *The Client* (also known as *John Grisham's "The Client"*), CBS, 1995.

Courthouse, 1995.

"Julio Is My Dad," *Second Noah,* ABC, 1996.

"Triangle," *American Gothic,* CBS, 1996.

"Rebirth," *American Gothic,* CBS, 1996.

"A Time to Kill," *Chicago Hope,* CBS, 1996.

"Dead and Gone, Honey," *Spy Game,* ABC, 1997.

"Part IV," *The Practice,* ABC, 1997.

Vengeance Unlimited (also known as *Mr. Chapel*), ABC, 1998–99.

"They Are the Days," *Jack & Jill,* The WB, 1999.

"Part IV," *The Practice,* ABC, 1999.

Judging Amy, CBS, 1999–2005.

"The Screw Up," *That's Life,* ABC, 2000.

The Fugitive, CBS, 2000.

"There But for Fortune," *The Division* (also known as *Heart of the City*), Lifetime, 2001.

"Kate," *Kate Brasher,* 2001.

"X–Ray," *Smallville* (also known as *Smallville: Superman the Early Years*), The WB, 2001.

Thieves, ABC, 2001.

"Things to Do Today," *Ed,* NBC, 2002.

"1989," *Reunion,* Fox, 2005.

"Homecoming," *Ghost Whisperer,* CBS, 2005.

The Book of Daniel, NBC, 2005.

"Last Execution," *Ghost Whisperer,* CBS, 2006.

"Dead Man's Ridge," *Ghost Whisperer,* CBS, 2006.

"Brothers and Sisters," *In Justice,* ABC, 2006.

"Shoot the Moon," *Three Moons Over Milford,* ABC Family, 2006.

"Goodnight Moon," *Three Moons Over Milford,* ABC Family, 2006.

"Speed Demon," *Ghost Whisperer,* CBS, 2007.

"Scars and Souvenirs," *Grey's Anatomy,* ABC, 2007.

"Keeping Up Appearances," *Notes from the Underbelly,* ABC, 2007.

"Early Bird Catches the Word," *Side Order of Life,* Lifetime, 2007.

Shark, CBS, 2007.

Television Co–Executive Producer; Episodic:
"Roses and Truth," *Judging Amy,* CBS, 2002.

Television Executive Producer; Episodic:
"Catching It Early," *Judging Amy,* CBS, 2004.

"Dream a Little Dream," *Judging Amy,* CBS, 2005.

"The Paper War," *Judging Amy,* CBS, 2005.

"The New Normal," *Judging Amy,* CBS, 2005.

Television Appearances; Series:
Various characters, *The Monkees,* 1966–68.

Television Appearances; Movies:
Roark, *Columbo: Make Me a Perfect Murder,* 1978.

Man in airport, *Another Midnight Run,* 1994.

Television Appearances; Pilots:
Man on the beach, *Bulba,* ABC, 1981.

Television Appearances; Specials:
(Uncredited) Himself, *The Muppets Go Hollywood,* 1979.

Jail cellmate, "The Saint" (also known as "The Saint in Manhattan" and "The Saint in New York"), *CBS Summer Playhouse,* CBS, 1987.

Himself, *Hey, Hey We're the Monkees,* 1997.

Television Appearances; Episodic:
(Uncredited) Smiling Jack, "The Price of Doom," *Voyage to the Bottom of the Sea,* 1964.

Furnes, "Help Me, Kitty," *Gunsmoke* (also known as *Gun Law* and *Marshal Dillon*), 1964.

Lieutenant Manuera, "The Giuoco Piano Affair," *The Man from U.N.C.L.E.,* 1964.

Private Robert Renaldo, "The Inheritors: Parts 1 & 2," *The Outer Limits,* 1964.

Sergeant Gruenwald, "Faith Hope and Sergeant Aaronson," *Twelve O'Clock High,* 1965.

District Attorney Alvarez, "The Case of the Feather Cloak," *Perry Mason,* 1965.

Semenev, "The Exile," *Voyage to the Bottom of the Sea,* 1965.

Inspector Charles Jouet, "Grave Doubts," *The Rogues,* 1965.

Luther Hayes, "A Special Talent for Killing," *A Man Called Shenandoah,* 1965.

Joe Galardi, "Fifty–two Forty–five or Work," *The Dick Van Dyke Show,* 1965.

Lucien Garth, "The Weapon," *Burke's Law* (also known as *Amos Burke, Secret Agent*), 1965.

Luther Bernstein, "A Gift of Love," *Dr. Kildare,* 1965.

Luther Bernstein, "The Tent Dwellers," *Dr. Kildare,* 1965.

Luther Bernstein, "Going Home," *Dr. Kildare,* 1965.

German sergeant, "Who Was That German I Seen You With?," *McHale's Navy,* 1966.

Manolo, "Killers of the Deep," *Voyage to the Bottom of the Sea,* 1966.

Gestapo captain, "The Great Impersonation," *Hogan's Heroes,* 1966.

Pete, "Doralee," *The Fugitive,* 1966.

Max, "The Dippy Blonde Affair," *The Man from U.N.C.L.E.,* 1966.

(Uncredited) Yugoslavian guest, "Son of a Gypsy," *The Monkees,* 1966.

Bernard Frisby, "Doggone Martian," *My Favorite Martian,* 1966.

Kessler, "The Defector: Part 1," *The F.B.I.,* 1966.

Greenburg, "It's All Done with Mirrors," *I Spy,* 1966.

Ehrlich, "Field of Dishonor," *Blue Light,* 1966.

Waiter, "Miss Greta Regrets," *Occasional Wife,* 1966.

Bartender, "Triangle," *American Gothic,* 1996.

Himself, *The Footy Show,* Nine Network, 2007.

Film Director:

The Christian Licorice Store, National General, 1971.

Kid Blue, Twentieth Century–Fox, 1973.

The Big Bus, Paramount, 1976.

The Muppet Movie, Associated Film Distribution, 1979.

Fraternity Vacation, New World, 1985.

Film Work; Other:

Camera operator (wedding home movies), *Always (But Not Forever),* Samuel Goldwyn, 1985.

Film Appearances:

Truck driver, *Ladybug, Ladybug,* United Artists, 1963.

Sol Kelly, Sal Kelly, and Judge Kelly, *The Troublemaker,* Janus, 1964.

Stone, *Wild, Wild Winter,* Universal, 1966.

Tracks, 1976.

Waiter, *The Muppet Movie,* Associated Film Distribution, 1979.

WRITINGS

Television Episodes:

Thieves, ABC, 2001.

FRAZIER, John 1944–
(John R. Frazier)

PERSONAL

Born September 23, 1944, in Richmond, CA. *Education:* Attended Los Angeles Trade Technical School.

Career: Special effects artist. Haunted House (nightclub), Hollywood, CA, designer of special effects stage properties, 1963; National Broadcasting Co., special effects creator, until 1970.

Member: Local 44.

Awards, Honors: Academy Award nomination, and Film Award nomination, Film Award nomination (with others), best special effects, British Academy of Film and Television Arts, 1995, for *Speed;* Academy Award nomination, best special visual effects, Saturn Award nomination (with others), best special effects, Academy of Science Fiction, Fantasy, and Horror Films, Film Award (with others), best achievement in special visual effects, British Academy of Film and Television Arts, 1997, all for *Twister;* Academy Award nomination, best special visual effects, Saturn Award nomination (with others), best special effects, 1999, all for *Armageddon;* Academy Award nomination (with others), best effects—visual effects, Film Award (with others), best achievement in special visual effects, British Academy of Film and Television Arts, Saturn Award nomination (with others), best special effects, 2001, all for *The Perfect Storm;* Academy Award nomination (with others), best effects, visual effects, 2002, for *Pearl Harbor;* Academy Award nomination (with others), best visual effects, Online Film Critics Society Award nomination (with others), best visual effects, Film Award nomination (with others), best achievement in special visual effects, British Academy of Film and Television Arts, Saturn Award nomination (with others), best special effects, 2003, all for *Spider–Man;* Saturn Award nomination (with others), best special effects, 2003, for *xXx;* Academy Award (with others), best achievement in visual effects, Visual Effects Society Award nomination (with others), outstanding special effects in service to visual effects in a motion picture, Golden Satellite Award nomination (with others), best visual effects, International Press Academy, Film Award nomination (with others), best achievement in special visual effects, British Academy of Film and Television Arts, Saturn Award (with others), best special effects, 2005, all for *Spider–Man 2;* Academy Award nomination (with others), best achievement in visual effects, 2007, for *Poseidon;* two Clio Awards for television advertising campaigns for Honda and Lexus automobiles.

CREDITS

Film Special Effects:
The Hills Have Eyes (also known as *Wes Craven's "The Hills Have Eyes"*), Vestron Video, 1978.
Starhops (also known as *Curb Service*), 1978.
When You Comin' Back, Red Ryder?, 1979.
Roadie, United Artists, 1980.
Airplane! (also known as *Flying High* and *Flying High!*), Paramount, 1980.
Harry Tracy, 1981.
White Dog, Paramount, 1982.
Just One of the Guys, Columbia, 1985.
The Sure Thing, 1985.
Pretty in Pink, Paramount, 1986.
Like Father, Like Son, 1987.
The War of the Roses, Twentieth Century–Fox, 1989.
Pink Cadillac, 1989.
Mr. Baseball, 1992.
Father Hood, 1993.
Reality Bites, 1994.
National Treasure: Book of Secrets, Buena Vista, 2007.
The Pineapple Express, Sony, 2008.

Film Special Effects Supervisor:
Doctor Detroit, Universal, 1983.
Flashpoint, TriStar, 1984.
Gardens of Stone, TriStar, 1987.
Baby Boom, United Artists, 1987.
The Rookie, Warner Bros., 1990.
Outbreak, Warner Bros., 1995.
Twister, Warner Bros., 1996.
Hard Rain (also known as *Flood* and *Pluie d'enfer*), Paramount, 1998.
Armageddon, Buena Vista, 1998.
Forces of Nature, 1999.
Space Cowboys, Warner Bros., 2000.
The Perfect Storm, Warner Bros., 2000.
Almost Famous, DreamWorks Distribution, 2000.
Cast Away, Twentieth Century–Fox, 2000.
Pearl Harbor, Buena Vista, 2001.
Spider–Man, Columbia, 2002.

Windtalkers, Metro–Goldwyn–Mayer, 2002.
xXx (also known as *Triple X*), Columbia, 2002.
Tears of the Sun, Columbia, 2003.
Bad Boys II (also known as *Good Cops: Bad Boys II*), Columbia, 2003.
xXx: State of the Union (also known as *xXx 2: The Next Level, Cold Circle & Intersection,* and *xXx: The Next Level*), Sony, 2005.
Stealth, Columbia, 2005.
Domino, New Line Cinema, 2005.
(As John R. Frazier) *Poseidon,* Warner Bros., 2006.
Transformers, DreamWorks, 2007.

Film Special Effects Assistant:
Pee–wee's Big Adventure, Warner Bros., 1985.

Film Special Effects Coordinator:
Ferris Bueller's Day Off, 1986.
Ruthless People, Buena Vista, 1986.
Throw Momma from the Train, Orion, 1987.
The Great Outdoors, 1988.
Career Opportunities, 1991.
Child's Play 3, 1991.
V. I. Warshawski (also known as *V. I. Warshawski, Detective in High Heels*), Buena Vista, 1991.
Basic Instinct (also known as *Ice Cold Desire*), Columbia TriStar, 1992.
Unforgiven, Warner Bros., 1992.
Hoffa, 1992.
A Perfect World, Warner Bros., 1993.
Hot Shots! Part Deux (also known as *Hot Shots! 2*), 1993.
Speed, Twentieth Century–Fox, 1994.
The Stars Fell on Henrietta, Warner Bros., 1995.
(Second unit) *Waterworld,* Universal, 1995.
True Crime, Warner Bros., 1999.
The Haunting (also known as *La maldicion*), DreamWorks Distribution, 1999.
The Perfect Storm, Warner Bros., 2000.
Prison Life, Incarcerated Entertainment Productions, 2000.
Pearl Harbor, Buena Vista, 2001.
Windtalkers, Metro–Goldwyn–Mayer, 2001.
The Island, DreamWorks, 2005.

Film Special Effects Consultant:
The Bridges of Madison County, Warner Bros., 1995.
Absolute Power, Columbia, 1997.
Midnight in the Garden of Good and Evil, Warner Bros., 1997.

Film Special Effects Director:
Spider–Man 2, Columbia, 2004.
Domino, New Line Cinema, 2005.
Deja vu (also known as *Feline*), Buena Vista, 2006.

(As John R. Frazier) *Spider–Man 3,* Columbia, 2007.
Pirates of the Caribbean: At World's End (also known as *P.O.T.C. 3* and *Pirates 3*), Buena Vista, 2007.
The Kingdom, Universal, 2007.

Film Appearances:
Priest, *Armageddon,* Buena Vista, 1998.
Truck driver, *What Women Want,* Paramount, 2000.
Himself, *The Future in Action* (short), DreamWorks Home Entertainment, 2005.
Himself, *"Poseidon": A Ship on a Soundstage* (short), Warner Home Video, 2006.

Television Work; Series:
Special effects, *Space Academy,* 1977.
Special effects coordinator, *Sunset Beat,* 1990.

Also worked as special effects coordinator, *The F.B.I.,* NBC.

Television Special Effects; Movies:
Stranger in our House, 1978.
A Vacation in Hell, 1979.
Cry for the Strangers, 1982.
Happy, 1983.
It Came Upon a Midnight Clear, 1984.
Generation, 1985.
Blind Justice, CBS, 1986.

Television Work; Miniseries:
Special effects, *Alcatraz: The Whole Shocking Story,* 1980.

Special effects coordinator, *George Washington,* NBC, 1984.

Also worked as special effects coordinator, *Roots,* NBC.

Television Work; Specials:
The Magic of David Copperfield: The Niagara Falls Challenge, 1990.

Television Work; Episodic:
Special effects, "Working," *American Playhouse,* 1982.
Special effects, "Panic at Malibu Pier," *Baywatch,* 1989.

Television Appearances; Specials:
Journey to the Screen: The Making of "Pearl Harbor," 2001.
The 77th Annual Academy Awards, ABC, 2005.

Television Appearances; Episodic:
"Physical Effects: Causes and Effects," *Movie Magic,* 1994.
"Atmospheric Effects: Eye of the Storm," *Movie Magic,* 1994.
"The Haunting," *HBO First Look,* HBO, 1999.
"Bad Boys II," *HBO First Look,* HBO, 2003.
(As John R. Frazier) "The Making of 'Poseidon'," *HBO First Look,* HBO, 2006.
"'Transformers': Their War, Our World," *HBO First Look,* HBO, 2007.

G

G, Melanie
    See **BROWN, Melanie**

GAGHAN, Stephen 1965–

PERSONAL

Full name, Stephen Wharton Gaghan; born May 6, 1965, in Louisville, KY; married Marian "Minnie" Mortimer, May 19, 2007; children: (with Michael McCraine, an actress, model, and photographer) Gardner, Betsy. *Education:* Attended business college in Massachusetts and the University of Kentucky, Lexington, Kentucky.

Addresses: *Agent*—William Morris Agency, One William Morris Pl., Beverly Hills, CA 90212.

Career: Screenwriter, story editor, and director. Unnamed Stephen Gaghan Company, principal; directed a television commercial for Wii video game system, 2006, and MasterCard, 2007. Previously founded a catalog company, Fallen Empire, Inc.; worked for *The Paris Review;* also worked as a receptionist, graphic designer, photographer's assistant, and political fundraiser.

Awards, Honors: Emmy Award nomination (with others), outstanding writing for a drama series, 1997, for *NYPD Blue;* Edgar Allan Poe Award nomination (with others), best television episode, Mystery Writers of America, 1998, for *The Practice;* Sierra Award nomination, best screenplay—original, Las Vegas Film Critics Society, 2000, Academy Award, best writing, screenplay based on material previously produced or published, Film Award, best screenplay—adapted, British Academy of Film and Television Arts, Golden Globe Award, best screenplay—motion picture, Writers Guild of America Screen Award, best screenplay based on material previously produced or published, Southeastern Film Critics Association Award, best screenplay—adapted, Golden Satellite Award nomination, best screenplay—adapted, International Press Academy, Online Film Critics Association Award nomination, best screenplay, Edgar Allan Poe Award (with Simon Moore), best motion picture, Chicago Film Critics Association Award nomination, best screenplay, Critics Choice Award, Broadcast Film Critics Association, best screenplay—adapted, 2001, all for *Traffic;* Best Film Award nomination, Sitges—Catalonian International Film Festival, 2003, for *Abandon;* National Board of Review Award, best screenplay—adapted, 2005, Academy Award nomination, best writing—original screenplay, Writers Guild of America Screen Award nomination, best adapted screenplay, University of Southern California Scripter Award nomination (with Robert Baer), Edgar Allan Poe Award (with Baer), best motion picture screenplay, 2006, Robert Festival Award nomination, best American film, 2007, all for *Syriana.*

CREDITS

Film Director:
Abandon, Paramount, 2002.
Syriana, Warner Bros., 2005.

Film Appearances:
Adam, *Alfie,* Paramount, 2004.

Television Work; Series:
Story editor, *American Gothic,* CBS, 1995.
Coproducer, *Sleepwalkers,* NBC, 1997.
Executive story editor, *The Practice,* ABC, 1997–98.

Television Appearances; Specials:
Inside "Traffic": The Making of "Traffic," 2000.
The 73rd Annual Academy Awards, ABC, 2001.

The 58th Annual Golden Globe Awards, NBC, 2001.
Hollywood High, AMC, 2003.

Television Appearances; Episodic:
"Syriana," *HBO First Look,* HBO, 2005.
The Big Story, 2005.
The Charlie Rose Show, PBS, 2005.
"Inside the Academy Awards," *Sunday Morning Shoot-out,* AMC, 2006.
The Film Programme (also known as *Film 2006*), BBC, 2006.
"Stephen Gaghan/Ani DiFranco," *The Henry Rollins Show,* Independent Film Channel, 2006.
Entourage, HBO, 2007.

WRITINGS

Screenplays:
I Still Know What You Did Last Summer, Sony, 1998.
Rules of Engagement (also known as *Les regeles d'engagement, Rules—Sekunden der entscheidung,* and *Rules of Engagement—Die Regein des krieges*), Paramount, 2000.
Traffic (also known as *Traffic—Die Macht des kartells*), USA Films, 2000.
(Uncredited rewrite) *Black Hawk Down,* Sony, 2001.
(Uncredited) *Phone Booth,* Twentieth Century–Fox, 2002.
Abandon, Paramount, 2002.
The Alamo (also known as *Bowie*), Buena Vista, 2004.
Havoc, New Line Home Video, 2005.
Syriana, Warner Bros., 2005.

Television Episodes:
New York Undercover (also known as *Uptown Undercover*), Fox, 1994.
"Damned If You Don't," *American Gothic,* CBS, 1995.
"Where's 'Swaldo," *NYPD Blue,* ABC, 1996.
"First Degree," *The Practice,* ABC, 1997.
"Sex, Lies and Monkeys," *The Practice,* ABC, 1997.
Sleepwalkers, 1997.

Published short fiction in *The Iowa Review.*

GARANT, Ben 1970–
(R. Ben Garant, Robert Ben Garant)

PERSONAL

Born September 14, 1970, in Cookeville, TN; married Jennifer.

Addresses: *Agent*—Creative Artists Agency, 2000 Avenue of the Stars, Los Angeles, CA 90067. *Manager*—Principato/Young Management, 9465 Wilshire Blvd., Suite 880, Beverly Hills, CA 90212.

Career: Actor, writer, director, and producer. Writing partner of Thomas Lennon; The State (comedy troupe), member; once toured as a Teenage Mutant Ninja Turtle.

Awards, Honors: Emmy Award nomination (with Glen Roven), outstanding main title theme music, 1999, for *Viva Variety.*

CREDITS

Film Appearances:
Party attendee with Mohawk, *I'm Your Man,* 1992.
(As Robert Ben Garant) Commercial director, *Herbie Fully Loaded,* 2005.
Campus rent–a–cop, *Bickford Shmeckler's Cool Ideas,* 2006.
(As Robert Ben Garant) Deputy Travis Junior, *Reno 911!: Miami* (also known as *"Reno 911!: Miami": The Movie*), Twentieth Century–Fox, 2007.
Himself, *The Ten,* THINKFilm, 2007.
Himself, *Living with Lew* (documentary), 2007.

Film Work:
Director, producer, and executive producer, *Reno 911!: Miami* (also known as *"Reno 911!: Miami": The Movie*), Twentieth Century–Fox, 2007.
Director and producer, *Balls of Fury,* Rogue Pictures, 2007.

Television Appearances; Series:
Various characters, *You Wrote It, You Watch It,* MTV, 1992.
Various, *The State,* MTV, 1994–95.
Various characters, *Viva Variety,* Comedy Central, 1997.
(As Robert Ben Garant) Deputy Travis Junior, *Reno 911!,* Comedy Central, 2003—.

Television Appearances; Specials:
Various, *The State's 43rd Annual All–Star Halloween Special,* CBS, 1995.
(As R. Ben Garant) Host, *Reel Comedy: "Taxi,"* Comedy Central, 2004.
Comedy Central's Bar Mitzvah Bash!, Comedy Central, 2004.
Spike TV's Video Game Awards 2006, Spike TV, 2006.
Reel Comedy: "Reno 911!: Miami," Comedy Central, 2007.

Television Appearances; Episodic:
Deputy Travis Junior, *Last Call with Carson Daly,* NBC, 2007.
"Reno 911!: Miami," *Making a Scene,* 2007.

Television Work; Series:
Creator, *The State,* MTV, 1994.
Producer and supervising producer, *Viva Variety,* Comedy Central, 1997.
Executive producer, showrunner, and (uncredited) creator, *Reno 911!,* Comedy Central, 2003—.

Television Work; Specials:
Creator and producer, *The State's 43rd Annual All–Star Halloween Special,* CBS, 1995.

Television Work; Episodic:
Director, *Reno 911!,* Comedy Central, 2005.

WRITINGS

Screenplays:
I'm Your Man, Interfilm Technologies, 1992.
(As Robert Ben Garant) *Taxi* (also known as *New York Taxi* and *Taxi 2004*), Twentieth Century–Fox, 2004.
(As Robert Ben Garant; with Thomas Lennon) *The Pacifier* (also known as *Gnome* and *Le pacificateur*), Buena Vista, 2005.
(As Robert Ben Garant; with Lennon; and story) *Herbie Fully Loaded,* Buena Vista, 2005.
(As Robert Ben Garant) *Let's Go to Prison,* Universal, 2006.
(As Robert Ben Garant; and screen story) *Night at the Museum,* Twentieth Century–Fox, 2006.
(As Robert Ben Garant; with Lennon) *Reno 911!: Miami* (also known as *"Reno 911!: Miami": The Movie*), Twentieth Century–Fox, 2007.
(As Robert Ben Garant) *Balls of Fury,* Rogue Pictures, 2007.

Television Specials:
The State's 43rd Annual All–Star Halloween Special, CBS, 1995.

Television Episodes:
You Wrote It, You Watch It, MTV, 1992.
The State, MTV, 1994.
Viva Variety, Comedy Central, 1997.
Strangers with Candy, Comedy Central, 1999.
Reno 911!, Comedy Central, 2003—.

GARRETT, Beau 1982–

PERSONAL

Full name, Beau Jesse Garrett; born December 28, 1982, in Beverly Hills, CA.

Addresses: *Agent*—International Creative Management, 10250 Constellation Way, 9th Floor, Los Angeles, CA 90067. *Manager*—Sean Fay, 1 Management, 9000 Sunset Blvd., Suite 1550, Los Angeles, CA 90069.

Career: Actress.

CREDITS

Film Appearances:
Amy Harrington, *Turistas* (also known as *Paradise Lost*), Fox Atomic, 2006.
Caya, *Unearthed,* Ardight Films, 2006.
Krista, *Live!,* Atlas Entertainment/Mosaic Media Group, 2007.
Captain Frankie Raye, *Fantastic Four: Rise of the Silver Surfer,* Twentieth Century–Fox, 2007.

Television Appearances; Episodic:
Natalia, "Meteor Shower," *North Shore,* Fox, 2004.
Fiona, "The Script and the Sherpa," *Entourage,* HBO, 2004.
Lynnet, "Moving On," *Wildfire,* ABC Family Channel, 2007.

Television Appearances; Other:
Fiona, *Head Cases* (pilot), Fox, 2005.
Backstage: Hollywood Fashion (special), 2007.

GARRISON, Miranda 1950–

PERSONAL

Born 1950.

Career: Choreographer and actress.

CREDITS

Film Choreographer:
Sunset (also known as *Catalina*), TriStar, 1988.
Chances Are, TriStar, 1989.
(Uncredited) *Uncle Buck,* Universal, 1989.
The Forbidden Dance (also known as *Lambada, the Forbidden Dance*), Columbia, 1990.
The Rocketeer, Buena Vista/Walt Disney Pictures, 1991.
The Naked Gun 2 ½: The Smell of Fear, Paramount, 1991.
Ambition, 1991.
Straight Talk, Buena Vista, 1992.
A River Runs Through It, Columbia, 1992.

Son in Law, Buena Vista, 1993.

Born Yesterday, Buena Vista, 1993.

When a Man Loves a Woman (also known as *To Have and To Hold*), 1994.

Naked Gun 33 1/3: The Final Insult, Paramount, 1994.

Mulholland Falls, Metro–Goldwyn–Mayer, 1996.

(Uncredited) *Multiplicity,* Columbia, 1996.

Manhattan Merengue!, BMG Video, 1996.

Selena, Warner Bros., 1997.

Looking for Lola, 1998.

Macarena, Dow Knut Productions, 1998.

The Wonderful Ice Cream Suit, Buena Vista/Walt Disney Pictures, 1998.

BASEketball, Universal, 1998.

Go, TriStar, 1999.

The Adventures of Elmo in Grouchland, Columbia, 1999.

Pumpkin, Metro–Goldwyn–Mayer/United Artists, 2002.

First Daughter, Twentieth Century–Fox, 2004.

The Skeleton Key, Universal, 2005.

Poseidon, Warner Bros., 2006.

Moe, 2008.

Film Work; Other:

Assistant choreographer, *Dirty Dancing,* Vestron, 1987.

Associate choreographer, *Salsa,* Cannon Group, 1988.

Tango choreographer, *Vibes* (also known as *Vibes: The Secret of the Golden Pyramids*), Columbia, 1988.

Assistant choreographer, *Life Stinks* (also known as *Life Sucks*), 1991.

Assistant choreographer, *Evita,* 1996.

Film Appearances:

Barmaid, *Breaker! Breaker!* (also known as *Breaker, Breaker* and *Cindy Jo and the Texas Turnaround*), American International Pictures, 1977.

Xanadu dancer, *Xanadu,* Universal, 1980.

Vivian Pressman, *Dirty Dancing,* Vestron, 1987.

Luna, *Salsa,* Cannon Group, 1988.

Spanish dancer, *Sunset* (also known as *Catalina*), TriStar, 1988.

Esmeralda, *Mack the Knife* (also known as *The Threepenny Opera*), 21st Century Film Corp., 1990.

Mickey, *The Forbidden Dance* (also known as *Lambada, the Forbidden Dance*), Columbia, 1990.

Apache dancer, *Mr. Saturday Night,* Columbia, 1992.

Show choreographer, *Macarena,* Dow Knut Productions, 1998.

Show choreographer, *Looking for Lola,* 1998.

Wife, *The Wonderful Ice Cream Suit,* 1998.

Dancer, *Dirty Dancing: Havana Nights* (also known as *Dirty Dancing 2*), Lions Gate Films, 2004.

Television Choreographer; Miniseries:

Life with Judy Garland: Me and My Shadows (also known as *Judy Garland: L'ombre d'une etoile*), 2001.

Television Choreographer; Movies:

My Boyfriend's Back, NBC, 1989.

Barbarians at the Gate, HBO, 1993.

Winchell, HBO, 1998.

And the Beat Goes On: The Sonny and Cher Story, ABC, 1999.

Come On, Get Happy: The Partridge Family Story, 1999.

Television Associate Choreographer; Movies:

The Way She Movies, VH1, 2001.

Television Choreographer; Episodic:

Caroline in the City (also known as *Caroline*), NBC, 1995.

"Who's the Boss," *Fired Up,* NBC, 1997.

According to Jim, ABC, 2004.

Television Appearances; Movies:

Nicole the choreographer, *Growing Up Brady,* NBC, 2000.

Anna, *The Way She Movies,* VH1, 2001.

Television Appearances; Specials:

Dancer, *The 4th Annual Desi Awards,* syndicated, 1992.

"*Dirty Dancing*": *The E! True Hollywood Story,* E! Entertainment Television, 2000.

Television Appearances; Episodic:

Dancer, "Another Woman's Lipstick," *Red Shoe Diaries,* Showtime, 1992.

Dance instructor, "Deliverance," *Chicago Hope,* CBS, 1998.

Evelyn Manning, "Under the Gun," *Blind Justice,* 2005.

Stage Work:

Director and choreographer, *Selena: A Musical Celebration of Life,* Doolittle Theatre, Hollywood, CA, 2001.

RECORDINGS

Videos:

How to Salsa, Movies Unlimited, 1988.

GELBART, Larry 1928–
(Francis Burns)

PERSONAL

Full name, Larry Simon Gelbart; born February 25, 1928, in Chicago, IL; son of Harry (a barber and barbershop owner) and Frieda (a seamstress; maiden name, Sturner) Gelbart; married Patricia "Pat" Marshall (a singer and actress), November 25, 1956; children: Adam, Becky; (stepchildren) Cathy (a writer; deceased), Gary, Paul. *Education:* Attended John Marshall High School, Chicago, IL, and Fairfax High School, Los Angeles.

Addresses: *Agent*—Creative Artists Agency, 2000 Avenue of the Stars, Los Angeles, CA 90067.

Career: Writer, producer, and director. Northwestern University, Evanston, IL, artist–in–residence, 1984–85. Basin Street West (restaurant), co–owner. *Military service:* U.S. Army, 1946–47.

Member: Writers Guild of America, West, Dramatists Guild, Authors League, PEN Center USA West, Writers Guild of Great Britain, International PEN, American Society of Composers, Authors and Publishers, Directors Guild of America, Motion Picture Academy of Arts and Sciences (member of board of governors).

Awards, Honors: Emmy Award nominations (with others), best comedy writing, 1956, 1957, and 1958, all for *Caesar's Hour;* Emmy Award nomination, best writing of a single musical or variety program, 1958, for *Sid Caesar's "Chevy Show";* Sylvania Award, c. 1959, and Emmy Award, outstanding program achievement in the field of humor, 1960, both for *The Art Carney Show;* Antoinette Perry awards (with Burt Shevelove), best author of a musical and best musical, both 1963, for *A Funny Thing Happened on the Way to the Forum;* Emmy Award nomination, outstanding writing achievement in a comedy or variety show, 1963, for *The Danny Kaye Show;* Writers Guild of America Screen Award nomination (with Blake Edwards), best written American comedy, 1963, for *The Notorious Landlady;* Emmy Award nomination, best writing in comedy–variety, variety, or music, 1973, for *Barbra Streisand ... and Other Musical Instruments;* Emmy Award nomination, outstanding writing achievement in comedy, Writers Guild of America Award, best writing in an episodic comedy, 1973, Writers Guild of America awards, 1974, Emmy Award (with Gene Reynolds), outstanding comedy series, 1974, HUMANITAS Prize, 1974, George Foster Peabody Broadcasting Award (with others), Henry W. Grady School of Journalism and Mass Communications, University of Georgia, 1975, Emmy Award nominations (with Reynolds), outstanding comedy series, 1975 and 1976, and HUMANITAS Prize, 30 minute category, 1976, all for *M*A*S*H;* Emmy Award nominations (with others), outstanding writing achievement in comedy, 1976, for "Hawkeye" and "The More I See You," both episodes of *M*A*S*H;* Writers Guild of America Screen Award, best comedy adapted from another medium, Academy Award

nomination, best writing, screenplay based on material from another medium, and Saturn Award nomination, best writing, Academy of Science Fiction, Fantasy, and Horror Films, all 1978, all for *Oh, God!;* Writers Guild of America Screen Award (with Sheldon Keller), best comedy written directly for the screen, 1979, and Christopher Award, both for *Movie, Movie;* Laurel Award for Television Writing Achievement, Writers Guild of America, 1981; New York Film Critics Circle Award and Los Angeles Film Critics Award, both best screenplay, both with Murray Schisgal, 1982, Writers Guild of America Screen Award, best comedy written directly for the screen, National Society of Film Critics Award, best screenplay, and Golden Globe Award nomination, best screenplay—motion picture, all with Schisgal, all 1983, Academy Award nomination (with Schisgal and Don McGuire), best writing, screenplay written directly for the screen, 1983, and Film Award nomination (with Schisgal), best adapted screenplay, British Academy of Film and Television Arts, 1984, all for *Tootsie;* Emmy Award nomination, outstanding directing in a comedy series, 1983, for "Fallout," an episode of *AfterM*A*S*H;* granted an honorary doctor of letters, Union College, 1986; Pacific Broadcasting Pioneers Award, 1987; Lee Strasberg Award for Lifetime Achievement in the Arts and Sciences, 1990; special Outer Critics Circle citation for contribution to comedy, 1990, for *City of Angels* and *Mastergate;* Antoinette Perry Award, best book of a musical, Drama Desk Award, best book of a musical, New York Drama Critics Circle Award, best musical, Outer Critics Circle Award, outstanding Broadway musical, and Edgar Allan Poe Award, best mystery play, Mystery Writers of America, all 1990, London Critics Circle Award, best new musical, 1993, and Laurence Olivier Award, best musical, Society of West End Theatre, 1994, all for *City of Angels;* Beverly Hills Theater Guild Spotlight Award, 1991; Emmy Award, outstanding individual achievement in writing in a miniseries or special, and American Television Award, best made–for–television motion picture, both 1993, TV Critics Association Award, program of the year, c. 1993, Writers Guild of America Award (television), adapted long form, and CableACE Award, best writing, movie or miniseries, both 1994, all for *Barbarians at the Gate;* Writers Guild of America Lifetime Achievement Award, 1997; Emmy Award nomination, outstanding writing for a miniseries or a special, 1997, and PEN Center USA West Literary Award, best teleplay, 1998, both for *Weapons of Mass Distraction;* Distinguished Citizens Award (with Pat Gelbart), Maple Counseling Center, 1999; granted an honorary doctorate of humane letters, Hofstra University, 1999; William S. Paley Award for excellence in television, Anti–Defamation League, 2001; citation for distinguished service, American Medical Association (AMA), 2001; Writers Guild of America Award (television), original long form, Emmy Award nomination, outstanding writing for a miniseries, movie, or a dramatic special, Emmy Award nomination (with others), outstanding made for television movie, and nomination for Television Producer of the Year Award in Longform (with others), Golden Laurel awards, Producers Guild of America, all 2004, all for *And Starring Pancho Villa as Himself;* Valentine Davies Award, Writers Guild of America, 2007; Kieser Award, HUMANITAS Prize, 2007.

CREDITS

Television Work; Series:
Producer, *The Marty Feldman Comedy Machine,* Associated Television, 1971–72, ABC, 1972.
Developer, executive producer (with Gene Reynolds), and executive script consultant, *M*A*S*H* (also known as *MASH*), CBS, 1972–76.
(With Reynolds) Producer, *Roll Out!,* CBS, 1973–74.
(With Reynolds) Executive producer, *Karen,* ABC, 1975.
Creator and producer, *United States,* NBC, 1980, also broadcast on Arts and Entertainment.
Developer, executive creative consultant, and producer, *AfterM*A*S*H* (also known as *AfterMASH*), CBS, 1983–84.
Executive producer, *Fast Track,* Showtime, 1997–98.

Television Executive Producer; Movies:
Barbarians at the Gate (also known as *Barbarzyncy u bram, Der Konzern, Kaos paa Wall Street, Les requins de la finance, Panico en Wall Street, Selvagens em Wall Street,* and *Sota poerssikadulla*), HBO, 1993.
Weapons of Mass Distraction (also known as *Dirty Game, Armados de poder, Im Sog der Gier,* and *O quarto poder*), HBO, 1997.
And Starring Pancho Villa as Himself (also known as *Pancho Villa* and *Pancho Villa dans son propre role*), HBO, 2003.

Television Creative Consultant; Specials:
To Life! America Celebrates Israel's 50th, 1998.

Television Producer; Awards Presentations:
The 57th Annual Academy Awards, ABC, 1985.

Television Director; Episodic:
M*A*S*H (also known as *MASH*), CBS, episodes c. 1974–76.
"Fallout," *AfterM*A*S*H* (also known as *AfterMASH*), CBS, 1983.
"It Had to Be You," *AfterM*A*S*H* (also known as *AfterMASH*), CBS, 1984.

Television Producer; Pilots:
(With Gene Reynolds) *If I Love You, Am I Trapped Forever?,* CBS, 1974.

Corsairs (also known as *The Corsairs, Rosebud, Rosebud, My Ass,* and *Untitled Larry Gelbart Project*), ABC, 2002.

Television Appearances; Specials:
Himself, *Making "M*A*S*H,"* PBS, 1981.
Himself, *Memories of "M*A*S*H,"* CBS, 1991.
Bob Hope: The First Ninety Years (also known as *Bob Hope: The First 90 Years* and *Bob Hope: A 90th Birthday Celebration*), NBC, 1993.
Himself, *Caesar's Writers,* PBS, 1996.
Himself, *AFI's 100 Years ... 100 Movies,* CBS, 1998.
Himself, *M*A*S*H, Tootsie, & God: A Tribute to Larry Gelbart,* 1998.
Himself, *NYTV: By the People Who Made It* (also known as *NYTV: By the People Who Made It: Part I & II*), WNET (PBS affiliate), 1998.
Norman Jewison on Comedy in the 20th Century: Funny Is Money, 1999.
Himself, *AFI's 100 Years, 100 Laughs: America's Funniest Movies,* CBS, 2000.
The '70s: The Decade That Changed Television, ABC, 2000.
Himself, *Hail Sid Caesar!: The Golden Age of Comedy,* Showtime, 2001.
Himself, *Brilliant but Cancelled,* Trio, 2002.
Himself, *"M*A*S*H": 30th Anniversary Reunion,* Fox, 2002.
Himself, *The Perfect Pitch* (also known as *Brilliant but Cancelled: The Perfect Pitch*), Trio, 2002.
Himself, *TV's Most Censored Moments,* TRIO and USA Network, 2002.
Himself, *Bob Hope: The Road to Laughter,* PBS, 2003.
Himself, *Funny Already: A History of Jewish Comedy* (also known as *Funny Already* and *Funny Already: How Jewish Comedy Made America Laugh*), Channel 4 (England), 2004.

Television Appearances; Awards Presentations:
Presenter, *The 58th Annual Academy Awards Presentation,* ABC, 1986.
The 44th Annual Tony Awards, CBS, 1990.
The American Television Awards, ABC, 1993.

Television Appearances; Episodic:
Himself, *The College of Comedy with Alan King,* broadcast on *Great Performances,* PBS, c. 1997.
"Neil Simon: The People's Playwright," *Biography* (also known as *A&E Biography: Neil Simon*), Arts and Entertainment, 1999.
Himself, *The Martin Short Show* (also known as *El show de Martin Short*), syndicated, 1999.
Himself, "The Dick Van Dyke Show," *Inside TV Land* (also known as *Inside TV Land: The Dick Van Dyke Show*), TV Land, 2000.

The Museum of Television and Radio: Influences, Bravo, 2000.

Joe, "The Two Hundredth," *Frasier* (also known as *Dr. Frasier Crane*), NBC, 2001.

Himself, "M*A*S*H: Comedy under Fire," *History vs. Hollywood* (also known as *History through the Lens*), History Channel, 2001.

The College of Comedy III with Alan King (also known as *The College of Comedy 3 with Alan King*), broadcast on *Great Performances,* PBS, c. 2001.

Himself, *Intimate Portrait: Angie Dickinson,* Lifetime, 2003.

Himself, *Real Time with Bill Maher,* HBO, 2004.

Himself, "Changing Times and Trends," *TV Land Confidential* (also known as *TV Land Confidential: The Untold Stories*), TV Land, 2005.

Himself, "Writing, Rehearsing & Recording," *TV Land Confidential* (also known as *TV Land Confidential: The Untold Stories*), TV Land, 2005.

Film Producer:

Associate producer, *The Wrong Box,* Columbia, 1966.

Executive producer, *Blame It on Rio,* Twentieth Century–Fox, 1984.

Involved with other projects, including serving as the executive producer of *Power Failure.*

Film Appearances; Documentaries:

Himself, *Jackie Mason: An Equal Opportunity Offender,* Kultur International Films, 1995.

Himself, *Patriot Act: A Jeffrey Ross Home Movie,* c. 2005.

Himself, *Olhar estrangeiro,* Riofilmes, 2006.

Stage Work; Director:

A Funny Thing Happened on the Way to the Forum, London, 1986.

RECORDINGS

Videos:

Himself, *Academy of Television Arts and Sciences 50th Anniversary Celebration Tribute to Bob Hope,* 1996.

Himself, *The Sid Caesar Collection: Creating the Comedy,* 2000.

Himself, *The Sid Caesar Collection: The Fan Favorites— The Dream Team of Comedy,* Creative Light Worldwide, 2000.

Himself, *The Sid Caesar Collection: The Fan Favorites— The Professor and Other Clowns,* Creative Light Worldwide, 2000.

Himself, *The Sid Caesar Collection: Inside the Writer's Room,* 2000.

Himself, *The Sid Caesar Collection: The Magic of Live TV,* 2000.

Himself, *The Sid Caesar Collection: The Fan Favorites— Love and Laughter,* Creative Light Worldwide, 2001.

Himself, *Sid Caesar Collection: Buried Treasures—The Impact of Sid Caesar,* Creative Light Entertainment, 2003.

Himself, *Sid Caesar Collection: Buried Treasures—The Legend of Sid Caesar,* Creative Light Entertainment, 2003.

Himself, *Sid Caesar Collection: Buried Treasures— Shining Stars,* Creative Light Worldwide, 2003.

Himself, *On Your Marx, Get Set, Go!* (short), Warner Home Video, 2004.

Himself, *Remarks on Marx: A Night at the Opera* (short), Warner Home Video, 2004.

WRITINGS

Teleplays; Movies:

Barbarians at the Gate (also known as *Barbarzyncy u bram, Der Konzern, Kaos paa Wall Street, Les requins de la finance, Panico en Wall Street, Selvagens em Wall Street,* and *Sota poerssikadulla*), HBO, 1993.

Weapons of Mass Distraction (also known as *Dirty Game, Armados de poder, Im Sog der Gier,* and *O quarto poder*), HBO, 1997.

And Starring Pancho Villa as Himself (also known as *Pancho Villa* and *Pancho Villa dans son propre role*), HBO, 2003.

Teleplays; Specials:

(With Woody Allen) *The Sid Caesar Show,* NBC, 1958.

Sid Caesar's "Chevy Show," NBC, c. 1958.

(With Sheldon Keller) *The Art Carney Show* (also known as *The Art Carney Special*), NBC, 1959.

The Rosalind Russell Show, NBC, 1959.

(With Keller) *The Best of Anything,* NBC, 1960.

Four for Tonight (also known as *Star Parade*), NBC, 1960.

(With Allen) *Hooray for Love,* CBS, 1960.

(With Gary Belkin) *The Chevrolet Golden Anniversary Show,* CBS, 1961.

Opening Tonight, CBS, 1962.

Judy Garland and Her Guests, Phil Silvers and Robert Goulet (also known as *Judy and Her Guests, Phil Silvers and Robert Goulet*), CBS, 1963.

Barbra Streisand ... and Other Musical Instruments, CBS, 1973.

Mastergate (based on his play), Showtime, 1992.

Teleplays; Often with Others; Episodic:

Four Star Revue (also known as *The All–Star Revue*), NBC, episodes from c. 1950–53.

Your Show of Shows (also known as *Sid Caesar's "Show of Shows"*), NBC, episodes from c. 1950–54.

The Red Buttons Show, CBS, episodes from c. 1952–54, and NBC, episodes c. 1954–55.

"The Face Is Familiar," *General Electric Theater* (also known as *G.E. Theater*), CBS, 1954.

(With Hal Collins) *Honestly, Celeste!,* CBS, episodes in 1954.

The Patrice Munsel Show, ABC, episodes from c. 1954–62 (some sources cite from c. 1957–58.

(With Neil Simon, Woody Allen, Mel Brooks, and Mel Tolkin) *Caesar's Hour,* NBC, episodes from c. 1955–57.

The Pat Boone Chevy Showroom (also known as *The Pat Boone Show*), ABC, episodes from c. 1957–60.

The Danny Kaye Show, CBS, episodes from c. 1963–67.

Comedy Playhouse, episodes beginning c. 1971.

The Marty Feldman Comedy Machine, Associated Television, episodes in 1971–72, broadcast on ABC, 1972.

M*A*S*H (also known as *MASH;* based on the novel and film), CBS, episodes from 1972–83.

Roll Out!, CBS, episodes in 1973–74.

Karen, ABC, episodes in 1975.

United States, NBC, 1980, also broadcast on Arts and Entertainment.

AfterM*A*S*H (also known as *AfterMASH*), CBS, episodes in 1983–84.

Wrote material that has appeared in other television programs.

Teleplays; Pilots:

Perils of Pauline, c. 1960.

Eddie (also known as *Bel Air Patrol*), CBS, 1971.

My Wives Jane, CBS, 1971.

M*A*S*H (also known as *MASH;* based on the novel and film), CBS, 1972.

If I Love You, Am I Trapped Forever?, CBS, 1974.

Riding High, NBC, 1977.

Wrote other pilots, including *Network,* CBS. Wrote an unaired pilot for *Three's Company* (also known as *Herzbube mit zwei Damen, Tre cuori in affitto,* and *Un hombre en casa*), ABC.

Screenplays:

(With Blake Edwards) *The Notorious Landlady* (based on a story by Margery Sharp), Columbia, 1962.

(With Carl Reiner; and story with Reiner) *The Thrill of It All,* Universal, 1963.

(With Norman Panama and Peter Barnes) *Not with My Wife, You Don't!* (based on a story by Panama and Melvin Frank), Warner Bros., 1966.

(With Burt Shevelove) *The Wrong Box* (based on a novel by Robert Louis Stevenson and Lloyd Osbourne), Columbia, 1966.

(With Luigi Magni) *La cintura di castita* (also known as *The Chastity Belt* and *On My Way to the Crusades, I Met a Girl Who …;* based on a story by Ugo Liberatore), Warner Bros./Seven Arts, 1968.

(Uncredited; with Francesco Maselli, Luisa Montagnana, and Virgil C. Leone) *Ruba al prossimo tuo* (also known as *A Fine Pair;* based on a story by Montagnana), National General, 1969.

Oh, God! (based on a novel by Avery Corman), Warner Bros., 1977, also served as the basis for other screenplays.

(With Sheldon Keller) *Movie, Movie,* Warner Bros., 1978.

(As Francis Burns) *Rough Cut* (also known as *Roughcut*), Paramount, 1980.

Neighbors (also known as *Neighbours;* based on a novel by Thomas Berger), Columbia, 1981.

(With Murray Schisgal; and story with Don McGuire) *Tootsie* (also known as *Would I Lie to You?* and *Tootsie—lyoemaetoen lyyli*), Columbia, 1982.

(With Charlie Peters) *Blame It on Rio* (based on the screenplay by Claude Berri), Twentieth Century–Fox, 1984.

(With others) *The Nutty Professor* (also known as *Boelcsek koevere, Catlak profesoer, Den galna professorn, Der verrueckte Professor, El profesor chiflado, Gruby i chudszy, Il professore matto, Le professeur foldingue, Luckasti profesor, Nigaud de professeur, The nutty professor: el profesor chiflado, O professor aloprado, O professor chanfrado, Paehkaehullu professori,* and *Trceni profesor;* based on the earlier film of the same name), Universal, 1996.

Bedazzled (also known as *Teuflisch*), Twentieth Century–Fox, 2000.

C–Scam, Landscape Films, 2000.

(Uncredited; with others) *Chicago* (also known as *Chicago: The Musical;* based on the musical), Miramax, 2002.

Author of other screenplays, including *John Deere, Nothing Sacred, Power Failure* (based on his play), and (with others) *Frank.*

Film Music; Songs:

Song lyrics, *Movie, Movie,* Warner Bros., 1978.

"Christmas Song," *The Girl next Door* (also known as *Girl next Door, La chica de al lado, La fille d'a cote, La ragazza della porta accanto, La vecina de al lado, Naabermaja pornostaar, Naegen neomu ajjil-*

han geunyeo, Sexbomba od vedle, Um show de vizinha, and *Unelmien naapuri*), Twentieth Century–Fox, 2004.

Writings for the Stage:

(With Bill Manhoff and Laurence Marks) *My L.A.,* Forum Theatre, Los Angeles, 1948, also produced in 1950.

Author of book, *The Conquering Hero* (musical), American National Theatre and Academy (ANTA), New York City, 1961.

(With Burt Shevelove) Composer, lyricist, and author of book, *A Funny Thing Happened on the Way to the Forum* (musical; based on the work of Plautus), Alvin Theatre, New York City, 1962–64, Mark Hellinger Theatre, New York City, 1964, Majestic Theatre, New York City, 1964, then Lunt–Fontanne Theatre, New York City, 1972, later toured U.S. cities, 1974 and 1980–87, and produced in other productions, also produced as a feature film and released by United Artists, 1966, published by Dutton, 1963.

Jump, produced in London, 1972.

Sly Fox (based on the play *Volpone* by Ben Jonson), Broadhurst Theatre, New York City, 1976–78, then toured U.S. cities, 1978–81, also produced in other productions, published by Samuel French, 1978.

Author of book, *Ballroom* (musical), Majestic Theatre, 1978–79.

Author of book, *One, Two, Three, Four, Five* (musical; also known as *History Loves Company*), workshop production at Manhattan Theatre Club, New York City, 1987 and 1988–89.

(With others) *Jerome Robbins' "Broadway"* (musical revue), Imperial Theatre, New York City, 1989.

Mastergate, American Repertory Theatre, Cambridge, MA, then Criterion Center Theatre, New York City, 1989, published by Samuel French, 1990.

Author of book, *City of Angels* (musical), Virginia Theatre, New York City, 1989–92, published by Applause, 1990.

(Narration for ballet) *Peter and the Wolf* (symphonic piece), produced in New York City, 1991.

Power Failure, produced in Cambridge, MA, 1991.

Author of book, *Lysistrata* (musical; based on the play by Aristophanes), c. 2002.

Author of book, *Like Jazz* (musical), Mark Taper Forum, Los Angeles, 2003.

Wrote material for Bob Hope's USO (United Service Organizations) tours to visit military personnel. Worked on other projects for the stage.

Writings for the Radio; with Others:

Duffy's Tavern, NBC, beginning c. 1946.

The Eddie Cantor Show (also known as *The Chase and Sanborn Hour* and *Time to Smile*), beginning c. 1946.

Maxwell House Coffee Time with Danny Thomas (also known as *Maxwell House Coffee Time*), CBS, beginning c. 1946.

Command Performance, Armed Forces Radio Service, 1946–47.

Jack Carson, 1947–48.

The Jack Paar Show, CBS, beginning c. 1949.

The Joan Davis Show (also known as *Leave It to Joan*), CBS, beginning c. 1949.

The Bob Hope Show, NBC, 1949–52.

Writings for the Internet; Series:

Wrote episodes for an Internet series, c. 2000.

Songs:

Wrote songs, including "Let's Go Steady" and "Wallflower."

Nonfiction:

(With others) *Stand–Up Comedians on Television,* New York Museum of Television and Radio, Harry N. Abrams, 1996.

Laughing Matters: On Writing M*A*S*H, Tootsie, Oh, God!, and a Few Other Funny Things (autobiography; also known as *Laughing Matters*), Random House, 1998.

OTHER SOURCES

Books:

Contemporary Dramatists, sixth edition, St. James Press, 1999.

Contemporary Literary Criticism, Gale, Volume 21, 1982, Volume 61, 1990.

Laufe, Abe, *Broadway's Greatest Musicals,* Funk & Wagnalls, 1970.

Malarcher, Jay, *The Classically American Comedy of Larry Gelbart,* Scarecrow Press, 2003.

Periodicals:

Entertainment Weekly, March 6, 1998, p. 72.

New York Times, January 5, 1977; December 10, 1989, p. H5; May 15, 1997.

New York Times Magazine, October 8, 1989, pp. 53–56, 89–91.

People Weekly, April 13, 1998, p. 135.

Reader's Digest, August, 1998, pp. 154–55.

Theatre Week, December 18, 1989, p. 14.

Time, June 30, 2003, p. G5.

TV Guide, March 15, 2003, pp. 26–29.

U.S. News & World Report, February 28, 1983, p. 53.

Electronic:
Contemporary Authors Online, Gale, 2001.

GIERASCH, Stefan 1926–
(Steven Gierasch)

PERSONAL

Born February 5, 1926, in New York, NY.

Career: Actor. Milwaukee Repertory Theatre, Milwaukee, WI, member of company, 1965–66; Trinity Square Repertory Company, Providence, RI, member of company, 1966–67; APA–Phoenix Repertory Company, member of company, 1967–68; Studio Arena Theatre, Buffalo, NY, member of company, 1967–68; Long Wharf Theatre, New Haven, CT, member of company, 1971–72; Los Angeles Theatre Center, Los Angeles, member of company, 1987–91.

Member: Actors' Equity Association, Screen Actors Guild, Actors Studio.

CREDITS

Film Appearances:
Billy, *The Young Don't Cry,* Columbia, 1957.
Stage Struck (also known as *Eine Tages oeffnet sich die Tuer, Fascino del palcoscenico, Foedd till stjaerna, Lagrimas da ribalta, Les feux du theatre,* and *Viattomuuden kukka*), Buena Vista, c. 1958.
(Uncredited) Soldier, *That Kind of Woman* (also known as *Esa clase de mujer, Mulher daquela especie, Quel tipo di donna, So etwas von Frau!, Sortin nainen, Uma certa mulher,* and *Une espece de garce*), Paramount, 1959.
Preacher, *The Hustler* (also known as *Robert Rossen's "The Hustler"*), Twentieth Century–Fox, 1961.
Willy Herzallerliebst, *The Traveling Executioner,* Metro–Goldwyn–Mayer, 1970.
Del Gue, *Jeremiah Johnson,* Warner Bros., 1972.
Fritz, *What's Up, Doc?* (also known as *Aska vakit yok, Essa pequena e uma parada, Go'dag yxskaft?, Is' was, Doc?, Ma papa ti manda sola?, Mi van, doki?, No i co, doktorku, On s'fait la valise, Doc?, Ottaaks' paeaehaen?, Que me pasa, doctor?, Que pasa, doctor?,* and *Que se passa doutor?*), Warner Bros., 1972.
Landlord, *The New Centurions* (also known as *Precinct 45: Los Angeles Police*), Columbia, 1972.
Himself, *The Saga of Jeremiah Johnson* (short documentary), 1972.

Mayor Jason Hobart, *High Plains Drifter,* Universal, 1973.
Sanitation foreman, *Claudine,* Twentieth Century–Fox, 1974.
Sergeant Danaher, *Cornbread, Earl and Me* (also known as *Hit the Open Man*), American International Pictures, 1975.
Hotel clerk, *The Great Texas Dynamite Chase* (also known as *Dynamite Women*), New World Pictures, 1976.
Johnson and Professor Schreiner, *Silver Streak* (also known as *Transamerica Express, Chicago-expressen, El expreso de Chicago, Hopeanuoli, O expresso de Chicago, Trans–Amerika–Express,* and *Wagons lits con omicidi*), Twentieth Century–Fox, 1976.
Principal Morton, *Carrie* (also known as *Carrie, a estranha, Carrie au bal du diable, Carrie—Des Satans juengste Tochter, Carrie: Extrano presentimiento, Carrie, lo sguardo di Satana, Ekrixis orgis, Keri,* and *Kiusaajat*), United Artists, 1976.
Mr. Bowtie, *Looking for Mr. Goodbar* (also known as *A la recherche de M. Goodbar, A la recherche de Mister Goodbar, A procura de Mr. Goodbar, Auf der Suche nach Mr. Goodbar, Buscando al senor Goodbar, Etsin sinua Mr. Goodbar, Hvor er Mr. Goodbar?, In cerca di mr. Goodbar,* and *Var finns Mr. Goodbar?*), Paramount, 1977.
Lieutenant Jennings, *Blue Sunshine* (also known as *Adistaktoi dolofonoi, Falakroi dolofonoi, Helvetestrippen, Helvetinmakta, Le rayon bleu,* and *Sindrome del terrore*), Cinema Shares, 1978.
Charlie Goodman, *The Champ* (also known as *Campeon, Der Champ, Il campione, Le champion, Mestari, Mistrz, O campeo, O champ, Sampiyon, Sippuro Shel Alooff,* and *Utmaningen*), Metro–Goldwyn–Mayer/United Artists, 1979.
Dr. Dimitrios, *Blood Beach* (also known as *Blodiga sandens offer, Blood Beach—Horror am Strand, Den blodiga stranden, Playa sangrienta, Spiaggia di sangue, To beach party tou aimatos,* and *Verisen hiekan uhrit*), Jerry Gross Organization, 1981.
Charlie, *Perfect* (also known as *Byc doskonalym, Perfect—taehtaeimenae taeydellisyys,* and *Perfeicao*), Columbia, 1985.
Trupiano, *The Rosary Murders* (also known as *Confession criminelle, Den sjaette doedssynden, Der Moerder mit dem Rosenkranz, I delitti del rosario, Los crimenes del rosario, O misterio do rosario negro,* and *Rukousnauhamurhaaja*), New Line Cinema, 1987.
Edgar De Witt, *Spellbinder* (also known as *Culto diabolico, Czarownica, La hora de los brujos, La trampa de la arana, Noiduttu,* and *Spellbinder—Ein teuflischer Plan*), Metro–Goldwyn–Mayer/United Artists, 1988.
Dr. Vogel, *Megaville,* Amazing Movies, 1990.

Stuart Stratland, Sr., *Mistress* (also known as *Hollywood Mistress*), Rainbow Film Company, 1992.

Grandpa Glickes, *Jack the Bear* (also known as *Isaeni, ystaevaeni, Jack der Baer, Jack, el oso, Jack, o urso, Mein Vater—Mein Freund, My Dad—Ein ganz unglaublicher Vater,* and *Un eroe piccolo piccolo*), Twentieth Century–Fox, 1993.

House majority leader, *Dave* (also known as *Dave, president d'un jour, Dave, presidente por un dia, Dave—Presidente per un giorno, Dave—Presidente por um dia, President d'un jour,* and *Presidente por um dia*), Warner Bros., 1993.

Edward Sawyer, *Junior* (also known as *Ufaklik*), Universal, 1994.

Warden James Humson, *Murder in the First* (also known as *Alcatraz—kohtaloni, Assassinato em primeiro grau, Homicidio en primer grado, L'isola dell'ingiustizia—Alcatraz, Lebenslang in Alcatraz, Meurtre a Alcatraz, Meurtre avec premeditation, Morderstwo pierwszego stopnia, O condenado de Alcatraz,* and *Overlagt mord*), Warner Bros., 1995.

Professor Beckmore, *Starry Night* (also known as *Noite estrelada*), Universal Studios Home Video, 1999.

Nathan, *Legend of the Phantom Rider* (also known as *Pelgidium Granger* and *Trigon: The Legend of Pelgidium*), A–Mark Entertainment, c. 2002.

Sam, *Off Track Betting* (short film), 2003.

Dr. Greenson, *Cover–Up '62,* Golden Girl Productions, 2004.

Television Appearances; Series:

J. Powell Karbo, *A.E.S. Hudson Street,* ABC, 1978.

Professor Michael Woodard and Joshua Collins, *Dark Shadows* (also known as *Dark Shadows Revival*), NBC, 1991.

Television Appearances; Miniseries:

Gannon, *Captains and the Kings* (also known as *Capitanes y los reyes, Capitanes y reyes, Des Preis der Macht,* and *Koningen en paupers*), NBC, 1976.

Niendorf, *Beggarman, Thief,* NBC, 1979.

Real estate agent, *The Winds of War* (also known as *Der Feuersturm, Krigets vindar, Le souffle de la guerre, Soden tuulet,* and *Vientos de guerra*), ABC, 1983.

Trenor Park, *Dream West* (also known as *Das Abenteuerliche Leben des John Charles Fremont* and *Der Grosse Traum*), CBS, 1986.

Judge Watts, *Cruel Doubt,* NBC, 1992.

Television Appearances; Movies:

Carmedly, *This Is the West That Was,* NBC, 1974.

Al Davis, *Return to Earth,* ABC, 1976.

General Mordecai Gur, *Victory at Entebbe* (also known as *La lunga notte di Entebbe, Segern vid Entebbe, Unternehmen Entebbe, Victoire a Entebbe, Victoria en Entebbe,* and *Voitto Entebbessae*), ABC, 1976.

Michael Curtiz, *My Wicked, Wicked Ways ... The Legend of Errol Flynn* (also known as *Die Errol–Flynn–Legende, Errol Flynn—Hollywoodin paha poika, Hela mitt syndiga liv,* and *Mes 400 coups: la legende d'Errol Flynn*), CBS, 1985.

Otto Wilshke, *Incident at Dark River* (also known as *Dark River—A Father's Revenge* and *The Smell of Money*), TNT, 1989.

Mr. Spizey, *Empty Cradle* (also known as *Le berceau vide, Madre a cualquier precio, Obsessao maternal, Tyhjae kehto,* and *Wiegenlied des Schreckens*), ABC, 1993.

Albert Osborn, Sr., *Crime of the Century* (also known as *Le crime du siecle*), HBO, 1996.

Zuckerman, *The Rockford Files: Friends and Foul Play,* NBC, 1996.

Television Appearances; Specials:

Third Hassidim, "The Dybbuk," *The Play of the Week,* syndicated, 1960.

"Particular Men," *Playhouse New York,* WNET (PBS affiliate), 1972.

Mikhail Skrobotov, "Enemies," *Great Performances,* PBS, 1974.

Orgon, *Tartuffe,* PBS, 1978.

Television Appearances; Episodic:

"October Story," *Goodyear Playhouse* (also known as *Goodyear Television Playhouse*), NBC, 1951.

"The Dusty Drawer," *Goodyear Playhouse* (also known as *Goodyear Television Playhouse*), NBC, 1952.

Attendant, *Mister Peepers,* NBC, c. 1952.

"Adapt or Die," *The Philco Television Playhouse* (also known as *Arena Theatre, The Philco–Goodyear Television Playhouse,* and *Repertory Theatre*), NBC, 1954.

Julien, "The Liberation of Paris (August 25, 1944)," *You Are There,* CBS, 1955.

Goldstein, "Walk down the Hill," *Studio One* (also known as *Studio One Summer Theatre, Studio One in Hollywood, Summer Theatre, Westinghouse Studio One,* and *Westinghouse Summer Theatre*), CBS, 1957.

"Small Take," *Brenner,* CBS, 1959.

"Jimmy Hines," *The Witness,* CBS, 1960.

Dolan, "The Best Defense," *The Defenders,* CBS, 1961.

Cooker, "The Pea," *The Untouchables,* ABC, 1962.

Sheriff, "Just Married," *The Lloyd Bridges Show,* CBS, 1962.

Gil Kellerman, "The Charlie Argos Story," *The Untouchables,* ABC, 1963.

Graff Erlich, "Point of Entry," *Stoney Burke,* ABC, 1963.

Jack Morgan, "End of an Image," *Empire* (also known as *Big G* and *Redigo*), NBC, 1963.

Sergeant Boyles, "Diagnosis: Danger," *The Alfred Hitchcock Hour,* CBS, 1963.

Willie Kovar, "Ship's Doctor," *Dr. Kildare,* NBC, 1963.

"Run, Little Man, Run," *Arrest and Trial,* ABC, 1963.

Mark Douglas, "Gunfighter, R.I.P.," *Gunsmoke* (also known as *Gun Law* and *Marshal Dillon*), CBS, 1966.

Orville Winters, "The Witness: Part I," *Bonanza* (also known as *Ponderosa*), NBC, 1969.

Grady, "The Iron Butterfly," *Bonanza* (also known as *Ponderosa*), NBC, 1971.

"The Siege," *Nichols* (also known as *James Garner* and *James Garner as Nichols*), NBC, 1971.

Muller, "Shadow Soldiers," *Ironside* (also known as *The Raymond Burr Show*), NBC, 1972.

"Run, Lincoln, Run," *The Mod Squad,* ABC, 1973.

McBurney and Kai Tong, "The Cenotaph: Parts 1 & 2," *Kung Fu,* ABC, 1974.

Herr Mueller, "The Old Diamond Games," *Switch,* CBS, 1975.

Arthur Fingal Solkin, "Vendetta," *Starsky and Hutch,* ABC, 1976.

Hart, "The Hundred Thousand Ruble Rumble," *Switch,* CBS, 1976.

Keller, "Power Failure," *Barney Miller,* ABC, 1976.

Mitchell, "The Parting Shot," *City of Angels,* NBC, 1976.

Monty Logan, "The Last Phantom," *Holmes and Yo–Yo* (also known as *Holmes and Yoyo*), ABC, 1976.

Nagel, "The Serbian Connection," *Serpico,* NBC, 1976.

"Homicide Is a Fine Art," *Jigsaw John,* NBC, 1976.

"Open Season," *Baretta,* ABC, 1977.

Sawyer, "Creature from beyond the Door," *Lucan,* ABC, 1978.

"Kidnapping: Part 1," *Barney Miller,* ABC, 1978.

Ben Masters, "The Dove Hunt," *Dallas* (also known as *Oil*), CBS, 1979.

Dr. Joseph Burlson, "The DNA Story," *Barney Miller,* ABC, 1979.

Maximillian, "The Inventor/On the Other Side," *Fantasy Island,* ABC, 1979.

Mr. Buchanan, "Deep Shock," *The Incredible Hulk,* CBS, 1980.

Colonel Ditka, "Give 'Em Hell, Hawkeye," *M*A*S*H* (also known as *MASH*), CBS, 1981.

Colonel Ditka, "Identity Crisis," *M*A*S*H* (also known as *MASH*), CBS, 1981.

Lupton, "Paternity," *Barney Miller,* ABC, 1981.

Charlie Wilson and Otto Rottermeyer, "Stolen Tears," *Quincy M.E.* (also known as *Quincy*), NBC, 1982.

Karpov, "It's All Downhill from Here," *The Greatest American Hero,* ABC, 1982.

Allan West, "Mission: Incredible: Parts 1, 2 & 3," *The Jeffersons,* CBS, 1983.

Elijah Croon, "The Ape Boy," *Tales of the Gold Monkey* (also known as *Tales of the Golden Monkey*), ABC, 1983.

Felix Schneiderman, "A Steele at Any Price," *Remington Steele,* NBC, 1983.

Heinrich von Schlauser, "Raiders of the Lost Sub," *Riptide,* NBC, 1984.

Monty, "On the Run," *Matt Houston,* ABC, 1984.

Sam Giannini, "Lord of the Valley," *Falcon Crest* (also known as *The Vintage Years*), CBS, 1984.

Carl, "Breakdown," *Alfred Hitchcock Presents* (also known as *Alfred Hitchcock esittaeae, Alfred Hitchcock presenta, Alfred Hitchcock presente,* and *Alfred Hitchcock zeigt*), NBC, 1985.

Koulermous, "The Reckoning," *The Colbys* (also known as *Dynasty II: The Colbys*), ABC, 1986.

Russian diplomat, "Monsters!/A Small Talent for War/A Matter of Minutes," *The Twilight Zone,* CBS, 1986.

Dr. Cornwall, "Witness for the Defense," *Murder, She Wrote,* CBS, 1987.

"The Black Ship," *Werewolf* (also known as *La malediction du loup–garou*), Fox, 1987.

Dr. Leo Krebs, "Victims of Circumstance," *Miami Vice* (also known as *Gold Coast* and *Miami Unworthiness*), NBC, 1989.

Mr. Anawalt, "Don't Paint Your Chickens," *Cheers,* NBC, 1989.

Otto Freik, "The Confidence Mystery," *Father Dowling Mysteries* (also known as *Father Dowling Investigates*), ABC, 1990.

Sideshow owner, "Lower Berth," *Tales from the Crypt* (also known as *HBO's "Tales from the Crypt"*), HBO, 1990.

Dr. Hal Moseley, "A Matter of Time," *Star Trek: The Next Generation* (also known as *The Next Generation* and *Star Trek: TNG*), syndicated, 1991.

Professor Truwald, "And the Walls Came Tumbling Down," *Knots Landing,* CBS, 1992.

Judge Brudister (some sources cite role as Judge Brewster), "Save the Mule," *The Practice,* ABC, 1997.

Congressperson Leon Beckwith, "Collateral Damage," *The Pretender,* NBC, 1998.

Daniel, "Of Past Regret and Future Fear," *ER* (also known as *Emergency Room*), NBC, 1998.

(As Steven Gierasch) Charles Reed, "Faces," *Brimstone* (also known as *Brimstone: el pacto* and *Le damne*), Fox, 1999.

Television Appearances; Pilots:

Dr. Nate Tishman, *Kate McShane,* CBS, 1975.

Robert F. Powell (district attorney), *Hazard's People,* CBS, 1976.

Axel Kalb, *Stunts Unlimited,* ABC, 1980.

Chef, *Gabe and Walker,* ABC, 1981.

Dr. Sidney Gelson, *The Million Dollar Face,* NBC, 1981.

Sam Purdy, *Big Bend Country,* CBS, 1981.

Klaus, *Shannon's Deal,* NBC, 1989.

Professor Michael Woodard, *Dark Shadows* (also known as *Dark Shadows Revival*), NBC, 1990.

Stage Appearances:

Dexter and understudy, *Kiss and Tell,* Biltmore Theatre, New York City, 1943.

Get Away, Old Man, Cort Theatre, New York City, 1943.

Third legionnaire, *Snafu,* Hudson Theatre, New York City, 1944, Biltmore Theatre, 1945.

Newsboy, *Billion Dollar Baby* (musical), Alvin Theatre, New York City, 1945–46.

Soldier, *Montserrat,* Fulton Theatre, New York City, 1949.

Marty, *Night Music,* American National Theatre and Academy (ANTA) Playhouse, New York City, 1951.

Micah, *The Scarecrow,* Theatre de Lys, New York City, 1953.

Sanathanaka, *The Little Clay Cart,* Theatre de Lys, 1953.

Valentin and Sidi, *Maya,* Theatre de Lys, 1953.

The drunk, *Mardi Gras,* Locust Theatre, Philadelphia, PA, 1954.

Smith, *The Threepenny Opera* (musical theatre), Theatre de Lys, 1955.

Matvai, *A Month in the Country,* Phoenix Theatre, New York City, 1956.

Postmaster, *Purple Dust,* Cherry Lane Theatre, New York City, beginning 1956.

Max Steiner, *Compulsion,* Ambassador Theatre, New York City, 1957–58.

The guard, *Deathwatch,* Theatre East, New York City, 1958.

Tommy Owens, *The Shadow of a Gunman,* Bijou Theatre, New York City, 1958–59.

Herr Zeller, *The Sound of Music* (musical), Lunt–Fontanne Theatre, New York City, 1959–62, Mark Hellinger Theatre, New York City, 1962–63.

Patch Keegan, *Little Moon of Alban,* Longacre Theatre, New York City, 1960.

Jimmy Beales, *Roots,* Mayfair Theatre, New York City, beginning 1961.

Gus, *The Collection* (produced as part of a double–bill with *The Dumbwaiter*), Cherry Lane Theatre, 1962.

Leon Hallett, *Isle of Children,* Cort Theatre, 1962.

Kenneth O'Keefe, *The Ginger Man,* Orpheum Theatre, New York City, beginning 1963.

Jacobson, *The Deputy,* Brooks Atkinson Theatre, New York City, 1964.

Pantagleize, Milwaukee Repertory Theatre, Milwaukee, WI, 1965.

Saint Joan, Milwaukee Repertory Theatre, 1965.

The Tempest, Milwaukee Repertory Theatre, 1965.

The Time of Your Life, Milwaukee Repertory Theatre, 1965.

Under Milk Wood, Milwaukee Repertory Theatre, 1965.

The Glass Menagerie, Milwaukee Repertory Theatre, 1966.

Henry IV, Part I, Milwaukee Repertory Theatre, 1966.

Mother Courage, Milwaukee Repertory Theatre, 1966.

Saint Joan, Trinity Square Playhouse, Providence, RI, 1966.

Pierre, *War and Peace,* APA–Phoenix Repertory Company, Lyceum Theatre, New York City, 1967.

Ah! Wilderness, Trinity Square Playhouse, 1967, then Circle in the Square, Ford's Theatre, Washington, DC, 1969–70.

Duke of York, *Richard II,* American Shakespeare Festival Theatre, Stratford, CT, 1968.

Holofernes, *Love's Labour's Lost,* American Shakespeare Festival Theatre, 1968.

Jacques, *As You Like It,* American Shakespeare Festival Theatre, 1968.

Enrico IV, Studio Arena Theatre, Buffalo, NY, 1968.

Zelo Shimansky (Pa), *Seven Days of Mourning,* Circle in the Square, New York City, 1969–70.

Perowne, *AC/DC,* Chelsea Theatre Center, Brooklyn, New York City, 1971.

Arsenic and Old Lace, Circle in the Square, Ford's Theatre, 1971.

Hamlet, Long Wharf Theatre, New Haven, CT, 1972.

Clegg, *Owners,* Mercer–Shaw Theatre, New York City, 1973.

Moke, *Nellie Toole & Co.,* Theatre Four, New York City, 1973.

Harry Hope, *The Iceman Cometh,* Circle in the Square, Joseph E. Levine Theatre, New York City, 1973–74.

Candy, *Of Mice and Men,* Brooks Atkinson Theatre, 1974–75.

Orgon, *Tartuffe,* Circle in the Square Theatre, New York City, 1977.

Semmelweiss, John F. Kennedy Center for the Performing Arts, Eisenhower Theater, Washington, DC, 1978.

The Man with the Flower in His Mouth, produced as part of a double–bill in *A Special Evening,* Ensemble Studio Theatre, New York City, 1979.

Park Your Car in Harvard Yard, Los Angeles Actors Theatre, Los Angeles, 1981–82.

Jack Jerome, *Brighton Beach Memoirs,* Alvin Theatre, 1983–85, 46th Street Theatre, New York City, 1985–86.

Big Daddy, *Cat on a Hot Tin Roof,* Long Wharf Theatre, 1984–85.

Akbar, *Nanawatai,* Los Angeles Theatre Center, Los Angeles, 1985–86.

Mr. Crampton, *You Never Can Tell,* Circle in the Square Theatre, 1986–87.

Earl of Gloucester, *King Lear,* Los Angeles Theatre Center, 1987–88.

Sand and Stone, Sundays at the Itchey Foot, Center Theatre Group, Mark Taper Forum, Los Angeles, 1988–89.

The Marriage of Bette and Boo, Los Angeles Theatre Center, 1989–90.

Jacob Stern, *Unexpected Tenderness,* Lee Strasberg Theatre Institute, Marilyn Monroe Theatre, Los Angeles, 1998.

Also appeared in other productions, including *Bella Figura, A Hatful of Rain,* and *Old Tune.*

Major Tours:
Phil Hogan, *A Moon for the Misbegotten,* 1969.

GILBORN, Steven 1936–
(Stephen Gilborn, Steve Gilborn)

PERSONAL

Born 1936, in Los Angeles, CA. *Education:* Graduated from Swarthmore College, 1958.

Addresses: *Agent*—Don Buchwald & Associates, 6500 Wilshire Blvd., Suite 2200, Los Angeles, CA 90048. *Manager*—Sweeney Management, 8755 Lookout Mountain Ave., Los Angeles, CA 90046.

Career: Actor. Massachusetts Institute of Technology, Cambridge, MA, humanities professor, 1960s; instructor at various other institutions, including the University of California, Berkeley, and Columbia University. Also known as Stephen Gilborn.

CREDITS

Television Appearances; Series:
Headmaster Alfred W. Litton, *Teech,* CBS, 1991.
Ed Woolly, *Angel Falls,* CBS, 1993.
Harold Morgan, *Ellen* (also known as *These Friends of Mine*), ABC, 1994–99.
Assistant district attorney Gavin Bullock, *The Practice,* ABC, 1998–2001.
Dr. Chris Carlisle, *Get Real* (also known as *Asuntos de familia, Helt aerligt!, Irti arjesta, La famille Green, Realitatile vietii,* and *Sechs unter einem Dach*), Fox, 1999.
Voice of old man, *The Big O* (anime; also known as *Big O* and *The Big O II*), WoWow and Cartoon Network, beginning c. 2000.

Television Appearances; Miniseries:
Maitre d', *Doubletake* (also known as *Doubletake–O crime perfeito, Im Dschungel des Boesen, Jaeaekylmae murha, Kill Hero,* and *Meprise*), CBS, 1985.
Judge Cavanaugh, *Love, Lies and Murder* (also known as *Labyrinth der Luegen* and *Rakkautta, valheita ja murhia*), NBC, 1991.
Family Album (also known as *Danielle Steel's "Family Album"*), NBC, 1994.

Television Appearances; Movies:
Phillip, *Enormous Changes at the Last Minute* (also known as *Enormous Changes, Trumps,* and *Drei Frauen in New York*), ABC, 1983.
Dr. George Johnson (medical examiner), *Columbo: Columbo Goes to College,* broadcast as part of *The ABC Mystery Movie* (also known as *The Mystery Movie, The ABC Monday Mystery Movie,* and *The ABC Saturday Mystery Movie*), ABC, 1990.

Dr. George Johnson (medical examiner), *Columbo: Uneasy Lies the Crown,* broadcast as part of *The ABC Mystery Movie* (also known as *The Mystery Movie, The ABC Monday Mystery Movie,* and *The ABC Saturday Mystery Movie*), ABC, 1990.
George M. Hill, *The Dreamer of Oz* (also known as *The Dreamer of Oz: The L. Frank Baum Story*), CBS, 1990.
Dr. Dalton, *Absolute Strangers* (also known as *Calkiem nieznajomi* and *Zwischen Leben und Tod*), CBS, 1991.
Dr. George Johnson (medical examiner), *Columbo: Caution! Murder Can Be Hazardous to Your Health,* broadcast as part of *The ABC Mystery Movie* (also known as *The Mystery Movie, The ABC Monday Mystery Movie,* and *The ABC Saturday Mystery Movie*), ABC, 1991.
Dr. George Johnson (medical examiner), *Columbo: Columbo and the Murder of a Rock Star* (also known as *Murder of a Rock Star*), broadcast as part of *The ABC Mystery Movie* (also known as *The Mystery Movie, The ABC Monday Mystery Movie,* and *The ABC Saturday Mystery Movie*), ABC, 1991.
Doctor, *Grand Tour: Disaster in Time* (also known as *Disaster in Time, The Grand Tour,* and *Timescape*), Showtime, 1992.
Dr. Andrews, *Desperate Choices: To Save My Child* (also known as *The Final Choice* and *Solomon's Choice*), NBC, 1992.
Harvey, *A Private Matter* (also known as *Miss Sherri*), HBO, 1992.
Desperate Rescue: The Cathy Mahone Story (also known as *Ich will mein Kind!, La veritable histoire de Cathy Mahone, Nicht ohne mein Kind,* and *Tahdon lapseni takaisin*), NBC, 1992.
Dr. Green, *Heartbeat* (also known as *Danielle Steel's "Heartbeat"*), NBC, 1993.
Victim of Love: The Shannon Mohr Story (also known as *Crimes of Passion: Victim of Love*), NBC, 1993.
Steve, *Saved by the Bell: Wedding in Las Vegas* (also known as *California College—Hochzeit in Las Vegas, Casamento atribulado,* and *Salvado por la campana: Boda en Las Vegas*), NBC, 1994.
Dr. Sorenson, *Her Costly Affair* (also known as *Consensual Relations*), NBC, 1996.
Peter Lassally, *The Late Shift* (also known as *Changement de decors, Die Jay Leno–Story,* and *Los reyes de la noche*), HBO, 1996.
Lew Roth, *About Sarah* (also known as *Des fleurs pour Sarah, Promessa,* and *Zycie Sary*), CBS, 1998.

Television Appearances; Specials:
Tartuffe, PBS, 1978.
The Dave Thomas Comedy Show (also known as *Dave Thomas*), CBS, 1990.
Judge Donato, "The Writing on the Wall," *CBS Schoolbreak Special,* CBS, 1994.
Mr. Pritchard, "Boys Will Be Boys," *ABC Afterschool Specials,* ABC, 1994.
William Braimen, *Grandpa's Funeral,* Showtime, 1994.

Television Appearances; Episodic:

Dr. Purcell, "To Tony, with Love," *Who's the Boss?,* ABC, 1989.

Howard, "Ebb Tide," *The Golden Girls* (also known as *Golden Girls, Miami Nice, Bnot Zahav, Cuori senza eta, Las chicas de oro, Les craquantes, Los anos dorados, Oereglanyok, Pantertanter,* and *Tyttoekullat*), NBC, 1989.

Mr. Arthur A. Collins, "Math Class," *The Wonder Years,* ABC, 1989.

Mr. Arthur A. Collins, "Math Class Squared," *The Wonder Years,* ABC, 1989.

"Trojan War," *Kate & Allie,* CBS, 1989.

Axel Roark, "The Descent," *Gabriel's Fire,* ABC, 1990.

Axel Roark, "The Wind Rancher," *Gabriel's Fire,* ABC, 1990.

Herb, "The Men Who Knew Too Much: Parts 1 & 2," *Perfect Strangers,* ABC, 1990.

Judge Greenbaum, "The Reaper's Helper," *Law & Order* (also known as *Law & Order Prime*), NBC, 1990.

Judge Marton, "Happily Ever After," *Law & Order* (also known as *Law & Order Prime*), NBC, 1990.

Lawyer Robert Richards, "On Your Honor," *L.A. Law,* NBC, 1990.

Martin, "The Chimes at Midnight," *Beauty and the Beast* (also known as *A Szepseg es a szoernyeteg, Die Schoene und das Biest, I pentamorfi kai to teras, La bella e la bestia, La bella y la bestia, La belle et la bete,* and *Skonheden og udyret*), CBS, 1990.

Mr. Arthur A. Collins, "Math Class," *The Wonder Years,* ABC, 1990.

Professor Kratzman, "Children of a Legal Mom," *Brand New Life,* NBC, 1990.

Jedidiah, "Roots," *Get a Life* (also known as *Buscate la vida*), Fox, 1991.

Leo Casabian, "The Strangler," *Matlock,* NBC, 1991.

Mr. Arthur A. Collins, "The Wonder Years," *The Wonder Years,* ABC, 1991.

Mr. Leland, "A Horse Is a Horse," *Knots Landing,* CBS, 1991.

Mr. Leland, "Where There's a Will, There's a Way," *Knots Landing,* CBS, 1991.

Priest, "The Pope's Ring," *The Golden Girls* (also known as *Golden Girls, Miami Nice, Bnot Zahav, Cuori senza eta, Las chicas de oro, Les craquantes, Los anos dorados, Oereglanyok, Pantertanter,* and *Tyttoekullat*), NBC, 1991.

Raymond Lurie, "One Woman's Word," *Reasonable Doubts,* NBC, 1991.

Dr. Armstrong, "Heartfelt," *Murphy Brown,* CBS, 1992.

Dr. Euless, "Aunt Poison," *The Torkelsons* (also known as *Almost Home*), NBC, 1992.

Dr. Norman Gorman, "The Commitment," *Baby Talk,* ABC, 1992.

Lawyer Robert Richards, "Wine Knot," *L.A. Law,* NBC, 1992.

John O'Donnell, "Our Denial," *Crime & Punishment,* NBC, 1993.

Lawyer Robert Richards, "Vindaloo in the Villows," *L.A. Law,* NBC, 1993.

Lucas Addler, "Different," *Sisters,* NBC, 1993.

Mr. Pipper, "The Last Laugh," *Blossom,* NBC, 1993.

Rabbi Meltzer, "The Wild Pitch," *Brooklyn Bridge,* CBS, 1993.

Bill Jennings, "Working Girl," *Coach,* ABC, 1994.

Dr. Brennan, "Abominable Snowman," *Picket Fences* (also known as *Smalltown USA, High Secret City—La ville du grand secret, La famiglia Brock, Picket Fences—Tatort Gartenzaun, Rome—Stadt im Zwielicht, Rooman sheriffi, Sheriffen, Smaastadsliv,* and *Un drole de sherif*), CBS, 1994.

Dr. Brennan, "Guns 'R' Us," *Picket Fences* (also known as *Smalltown USA, High Secret City—La ville du grand secret, La famiglia Brock, Picket Fences—Tatort Gartenzaun, Rome—Stadt im Zwielicht, Rooman sheriffi, Sheriffen, Smaastadsliv,* and *Un drole de sherif*), CBS, 1994.

Dr. Brennan, "Paging Doctor God," *Picket Fences* (also known as *Smalltown USA, High Secret City—La ville du grand secret, La famiglia Brock, Picket Fences—Tatort Gartenzaun, Rome—Stadt im Zwielicht, Rooman sheriffi, Sheriffen, Smaastadsliv,* and *Un drole de sherif*), CBS, 1994.

Fred Hoblit, "Hack Like Me," *Dream On,* HBO, 1994, also broadcast on Fox.

Fred Hoblit, "Where There's Smoke, You're Fired," *Dream On,* HBO, 1994, also broadcast on Fox.

Jeffrey Higgins, "A Hair-Razing Experience," *Living Single* (also known as *My Girls*), Fox, 1994.

Mr. Einhorn (some sources cite role as Mr. Finhorn), "Last Tango," *Blossom,* NBC, 1994.

Silhouette police officer, "Church of Metropolis," *Lois & Clark: The New Adventures of Superman* (also known as *Lois & Clark* and *The New Adventures of Superman*), ABC, 1994.

Doctor, "The Bigger They Are, the Harder They Fall," *Unhappily Ever After* (also known as *Unhappily ...*), The WB, 1995.

Doctor, "Gift of the Magnovox," *Unhappily Ever After* (also known as *Unhappily ...*), The WB, 1995.

Funeral director, "Goodbye Charley," *Empty Nest,* NBC, 1995.

Jeffrey Higgins, "He Works Hard for the Money," *Living Single* (also known as *My Girls*), Fox, 1995.

Nelson Clifford, "Contempt," *Hudson Street,* CBS, 1995.

Dr. Fisher, *The Wright Verdicts,* CBS, 1995.

(As Steve Gilborn) Dr. Randall, "A Shift in the Night," *ER* (also known as *Emergency Room*), NBC, 1996.

Jeffrey Higgins, "Glass Ceiling," *Living Single* (also known as *My Girls*), Fox, 1996.

Marty Jackson, "Awards Show," *NewsRadio* (also known as *News Radio, The Station, Dias de radio,* and *Dies de radio*), NBC, 1996.

Professor Simon Adler, "Chapter Eleven," *Murder One,* ABC, 1996.

Arthur Kandib, Ph.D., "Quiz Show," *Boy Meets World,* ABC, 1997.

Clyde Tannen, "Positive I.D." (also known as "Positive I.D.s"), *Chicago Hope,* CBS, 1997.

Jeffrey Higgins, "Swing Out Sisters," *Living Single* (also known as *My Girls*), Fox, 1997.

Professor Tomassi, "Astrology," *Mad about You* (also known as *Loved by You*), NBC, 1997.

Mr. Undercoffler, "And Those Who Can't," *Maggie Winters,* CBS, 1998.

Saul Verna, "Honor Thy Jack," *The Closer* (also known as *Tom Selleck Show*), CBS, 1998.

Victor Lewis, "Where the Hookers Grow," *Melrose Place,* Fox, 1998.

Irwin Klein, "Mr. Dragon Goes to Washington," *Action* (also known as *Dragon*), Fox, 1999.

Abe Hollenback, "Stealing Home," *Family Law,* CBS, 2000.

Dr. Solomon, "Weenis between Us," *City of Angels* (also known as *Anglarnas stad, Englenes by, Enkelten kaupunki,* and *Orasul ingerilor*), CBS, 2000.

James Posey, "The Witches of Gulfport," *JAG,* CBS, 2000.

Simon, "Monica's Bad Day," *Touched by an Angel,* CBS, 2000.

Congressperson Paul Dearborn, "Bartlet for America," *The West Wing* (also known as *West Wing* and *El ala oeste de la Casablanca*), NBC, 2001.

Dr. Harrison, "Surgery," *Malcolm in the Middle* (also known as *Fighting in Underpants*), Fox, 2001.

"An Eye for a Finger," *Two Guys and a Girl* (also known as *Two Guys, a Girl and a Pizza Place*), ABC, 2001.

Arthur, "Little Andy in Charge," *Andy Richter Controls the Universe* (also known as *Anything Can Happen, Andy Richter und die Welt, Andy Richter, universumi direktor,* and *Le monde merveilleux d'Andy Richter*), Fox, 2002.

Clerk, "Wall of Shame," *8 Simple Rules ... for Dating My Teenage Daughter* (also known as *8 Simple Rules, A Few Simple Rules, 8 lihtsat reeglit minu teismelise tuetrega kohtumiseks, 8 semplici regole ... per uscire con mia figlia, Fingrene vaek fra min teenagedatter, Meine wilden Toechter, No con mis hijas, Papa ni ha hi mi tsu, Teinitytoen kasvatusopas,* and *Touche pas a mes filles*), ABC, 2002.

Dr. Corey Barrish (some sources cite role as Dr. Buerge), "Healthy McDowell Movement," *NYPD Blue,* ABC, 2002.

Gene Michaels, "Still Thankful," *Still Standing,* CBS, 2002.

Judge James Kenudson, "The Tick vs. Justice," *The Tick* (also known as *Superpunkki*), Fox, 2002.

Mr. Dretler, "Every Stranger's Face I See," *Judging Amy,* CBS, 2002.

Uncle Rory and Krelvin, "Hell's Bells," *Buffy the Vampire Slayer* (also known as *BtVS, Buffy, Buffy the Vampire Slayer: The Series, Nightfall, Bafi, ubica vampira, Buffy, a vampirok reme, Buffy, cacadora de vampiros, Buffy contre les vampires, Buffy i vampirofonissa, Buffy—Im Bann der Daemonen, Buffy, l'ammazzavampiri, Buffy, la cazavampiros, Buffy och vampyrerna, Buffy—Vampyrdaeberen, Buffy vampyrdoedaren, Buffy—*

Vampyrenes skrekk, Buffy—Vampyrernes skraek, and *Buffy, vampyyrintappaja*), UPN, 2002.

Gene Michaels, "Still Responsible," *Still Standing,* CBS, 2004.

Mr. Malvert, "The Old Mac Magic," *The Bernie Mac Show* (also known as *Bernie Mac Show*), Fox, 2004.

Ethan's father, *Significant Others,* Bravo, 2004.

Bertram Osgood, "Take My Wife, Please," *According to Jim* (also known as *The Dad, Immer wieder Jim, Jim hat immer recht, Jims vaerld, La vita secondo Jim,* and *Perheen kalleudet*), ABC, 2005.

Member of town council, "Teen Things I Hate about You," *Complete Savages* (also known as *Savages, Kuusi miestae ja kaaos, La familia salvaje,* and *Les sauvages*), ABC, 2005.

Abe Golde, "The Road Home," *Without a Trace* (also known as *Vanished* and *W.A.T.*), CBS, 2006.

Amos Derringer, "Tastes Like a Ho Ho," *Damages* (also known as *Glenn Close TV Project*), fX Channel, 2007.

Appeared in other programs, including appearances as Robert Cutler, *Civil Wars,* ABC; as Sam Fletcher, *Loving* (also known as *The City*), ABC; and as Judge Elfinbine, *Sweet Justice* (also known as *Alles schoen und Recht, Dulce justicia,* and *La loi de la Nouvelle–Orleans*), NBC. Appeared as Stratton in "The Outsider," an unaired episode of *Hearts Afire* (also known as *Al senador, ni caso* and *Kuess' mich, John*), CBS; appeared as Dr. Wagner in "Mini–pause," an unaired episode of *The Tony Danza Show* (also known as *Ein Vater zum Kuessen*), NBC; and appeared in "A Man for Half a Season," an unaired episode of *Total Security* (also known as *Os vigilantes* and *Taeyttae turvaa*), ABC.

Television Appearances; Pilots:

Carl Stalling (some sources cite role as Mr. Weidner), *The Danger Team* (also known as *Danger Team*), ABC, 1991.

Richard, *Common Law,* ABC, 1996.

Freddy Fontaine, *The Brian Benben Show* (also known as *Benben, The Benben Show,* and *Uutispuuroa*), CBS, 1998.

Irv, *Out of Practice* (also known as *Hoidon tarpeessa, Out of practice—Doktor, single sucht ...,* and *Terapia en familia*), CBS, 2005.

Appeared in other pilots, including *The Kirk Franklin Show,* ABC.

Film Appearances:

Jimmy, *Vamping* (also known as *La casa vuota dopo il funerale* and *Seducao perversa*), Atlantic Releasing, 1984.

Tonda, *Anna* (also known as *Anna—Exil in New York, Anna y Cristina,* and *Ola gin tin Anna*), Vestron Pictures, 1987.

Ed, *He Said, She Said* (also known as *A guerra dos sexos, Dice lui, dice lei, El dijo, ella dijo, Elle et lui, Minun, sinun,* and *Na typisch!*), Paramount, 1991.

Dr. Hubbard, *Safe* (also known as *Chemical Syndrome* and *Seguro*), Sony Pictures Classics, 1995.

Mr. Phillips, *The Brady Bunch Movie* (also known as *A familia sol, la, si, do, Bradyjeva klapa, Bradys klarar sivan!, Die Brady Family, La tribu de los Brady,* and *Rokkava Bradyn perhe*), Paramount, 1995.

Arthur, *Joyride* (also known as *Die Fahrt in Nirgendwo* and *Robo inocente*), Live Entertainment, 1996.

Artie, *Dunston Checks In* (also known as *Drole de singe, Dunston checkar in, Dunston—Allein im Hotel, Dunston—licenza di ridere, Dunston—Otelde tek basina, Dunston—Panique au palace, Dunston—vallaton varas, Ek Bandar Hotel Ke Andar, Macaco a solta, panico no hotel, Majomparade, Malpa w hotelu, Mi colega Dunston, Mon ami Dunston,* and *Orangutan v hotelu Majestic*), Twentieth Century–Fox, 1996.

The father, *Gasp* (short film), 1996.

Gil Reeves, *Final Vendetta* (also known as *Surrogate Mother, Sweet Evil, Adoravel assassina, Engel mit blutigen Haenden, Les griffes de la cigogne,* and *Mas alla del odio*), A–Pix Entertainment, 1996.

Mr. Phillips, *A Very Brady Sequel* (also known as *A volta de familia sol, la, si, do, Bradys faar tilloekning, Die Brady Family 2, El retorno de los Brady, Les nouvelles aventures de la famille Brady,* and *Les nouvelles aventures de la tribu Brady*), Paramount, 1996.

Samuel Levine (Micki's father), *Wedding Bell Blues* (also known as *Die Stunde der Teufelinnen, In fuga a Las Vegas,* and *Maridos Precisam–se*), BMG Independents, 1996.

Howard's agent, *Private Parts* (also known as *Howard Stern's "Private Parts," Private Parts—Dirty Radio, Czesci intymne, Howard Sternin intiimit osat, Intim reszek, Naga resnica, Partes privadas, Parties intimes, Private Parts—Howard Sterns liv och under, O rei da baixaria,* and *O rei da radio*), Paramount, 1997.

Voice of father, *Alien: Resurrection* (also known as *Alien 4, Alien—A ressurreicao, Alien—Aateruppstaar, Alien—Die Wiedergeburt, Alien—genopstandelsen, Alien—I anagennisi, Alien—yloesnousemus, Alien: Dirilis, Alien: La clonazione, Alien: La resurrection, Alien: O regresso, Alien 4 feltamad a halal, Alien, la resurrection, Alien resurreccion, Obcy: Przebudzenie, Osmi potnik—Ponovno vstajenje, Vetrelec: Vzkriseni,* and *Yaratik: Dirilis*), Twentieth Century–Fox, 1997.

Dr. Sam Litvack, *Doctor Dolittle* (also known as *Dr. Dolittle, Docteur Dolittle, Elaeintohtori,* and *Il dottor Dolittle*), Twentieth Century–Fox, 1998.

Blake, *Nurse Betty* (also known as *Betty, Betty Love, Betty Sizemore, A enfermeira Betty, Betty noever, Betty tur och retur, Garde Betty, Ha–Ahot Betty, Nurse Betty—Gefaehrliche Traeume, Persiguiendo a Betty,* and *Poetaja Betty*), USA Films, 2000.

George, *Reunion* (also known as *Dogme #17—Reunion*), FilmMates Entertainment, 2001, recut version known as *American Reunion.*

Judge Guilder, *Evolution* (also known as *Evolucao, Evolucio, Evolucion,* and *Evoluutio*), DreamWorks, 2001.

Doctor, *Coastlines* (also known as *No limite da razao*), Curb Entertainment, 2002, IFC First Take, 2006.

Mumford, *The Kiss,* MTI Home Video, c. 2004.

Sid Silver, *Formosa,* KOAN Inc., 2005.

Stage Appearances:

Peter Mortensgaard, *Rosmersholm,* Roundabout Stage II, New York City, 1974.

Friar Thomas and understudy for the role of Vincentio, *Measure for Measure,* New York Shakespeare Festival, Joseph Papp Public Theater, Delacorte Theater, New York City, 1976.

Le Fer and understudy for the roles of Williams and a constable, *Henry V,* New York Shakespeare Festival, Joseph Papp Public Theater, Delacorte Theater, 1976.

Deputy and understudy for the roles of M. Loyal, Orgon, and police officer, *Tartuffe,* Circle in the Square Theatre, New York City, 1977.

Understudy for the roles of Colin and others, *Ashes,* New York Shakespeare Festival, Joseph Papp Public Theater, Anspacher Theater, New York City, 1977.

Understudy for the role of Rabbi Azriel, *The Dybbuk,* New York Shakespeare Festival, Joseph Papp Public Theater, Newman Theater, New York City, 1977–78.

Mr. Salt, first guard, and elderly man, *Museum,* New York Shakespeare Festival, Joseph Papp Public Theater, LuEsther Hall, New York City, 1978.

Alchonon, *Teibele and Her Demon,* Brooks Atkinson Theatre, New York City, 1979–80.

Simon Blumberg, *Isn't It Romantic,* Playwrights Horizons Theatre, New York City, 1983–84, Lucille Lortel Theatre, New York City, 1984–85.

Norton Quinn, *Principia Scriptoriae,* Manhattan Theatre Club Stage I, New York City, 1986.

Member of the Interact Theatre Company; appeared in other stage productions.

Radio Appearances:

Reader, "The Unfound Pig," *Selected Shorts,* 2003.

RECORDINGS

Video Games:

Voice of father, *Alien: Resurrection,* Fox Interactive, 2000.

GILMOUR, Ian 1955–

PERSONAL

Born 1955 in New Zealand. *Education:* Earned diploma in screen direction at the Australian Film, Television, and Radio School.

Addresses: *Agent*—Cameron's, 61 Marlborough St., 7th Floor, Surry Hills, New South Wales 2010 Australia.

Career: Actor and director.

Awards, Honors: Australian Film Institute Award nomination, best direction in television, 2003, for *Bootleg.*

CREDITS

Television Producer; Series:
The Adventures of Skippy, 1992.

Television Director; Miniseries:
The New Adventures of Black Beauty, Seven Network, 1992.
Bordertown, ABC (Australia), 1995.
Bootleg, BBC, 2002.

Television Work; Movies:
Director, *Code Red* (also known as *Code Red: The Rubicon Conspiracy*), UPN, 2001.
Locusts: The 8th Plague, Sci–Fi Channel, 2005.
Magma: Volcanic Disaster, Sci–Fi Channel, 2006.

Television Director; Episodic:
The Flying Doctors, Nine Network, 1986.
Skirts, 1990.
"A Bunch of Big Girls," *Phoenix,* ABC (Australia), 1992.
"Old Rules, New Games," *Phoenix,* ABC (Australia), 1992.
"Hair of the Dog," *Phoenix,* ABC (Australia), 1992.
Snowy, Nine Network, 1993.
Newlyweds, Seven Network, 1993.
Heartbreak High, Ten Network, 1994–95, ABC (Australia), 1997.
Flipper (also known as *The New Adventures of Flipper*), 1995.
"Dancing Partners," *Twisted Tales* (also known as *Twisted*), Nine Network, 1996.
"The Price of Success," *State Coroner,* 1997.
"Shortcut to Death," *State Coroner,* 1997.
Tales of the South Seas, 1998.

"Double Blind," *Water Rats,* Nine Network, 1999.
"Cut–off Point," *Water Rats,* Nine Network,1999.
The Lost World (also known as *Sir Arthur Conan Doyle's "The Lost World"*), DirecTV and syndicated, 1999.
BeastMaster, syndicated, 1999.
McLeod's Daughters, Nine Network, 2001.
Flatland, 2002.
"Waltzing Sakamoto," *The Cooks,* Ten Network, 2004.
"Heart of Marshmallow," *The Cooks,* Ten Network, 2004.
Headland, Seven Network, 2005.
Monarch Cove, Lifetime, 2006.
"Taylor's Self Portrait," *Mortified,* Nine Network, 2007.
"Girl Power," *Mortified,* Nine Network, 2007.

Television Appearances; Series:
Wayne Hopkins, *The Box,* Ten Network, 1974.
Freddie, *Ride On Stranger,* ABC (Australia), 1979.
Kevin Burns, *Prisoner* (also known as *Caged Women* and *Prisoner: Cell Block H*), Ten Network and syndicated, 1980.
Waterloo Station, Nine Network, 1983.

Television Appearances; Miniseries:
Scotty McAllister, *The Challenge,* 1986.
A Place in the World, ABC (Australia), 1989.

Television Appearances; Movies:
Rusty Bugles, ABC (Australia), 1981.
Second policeman, *Room to Move,* 1987.
Dr. Frank Harrison, *Malpractice,* 1989.

Television Appearances; Episodic:
Jeff, "Cliff Hanger," *Chopper Squad,* Ten, 1978.
"The Slammer," *Spring & Fall,* ABC (Australia), 1980.
"Sons and Datsuns," *Kingswood Country,* Seven Network, 1982.
Spike, "The Push: Parts 1 & 2," *A Country Practice,* Seven Network, 1982.
Donald Cook, "Good Intentions: Parts 1 & 2," *A Country Practice,* Seven Network, 1984.
Second policeman, "Room to Move," *Winners,* PBS, 1985.
Colin Neilson, "The Hometown Hero," *The Flying Doctors,* Nine Network, 1987.

Film Director:
Double Sculls, 1986.
Still Twisted, 1997.
Joe Wilkinson, Minotaur International, 1999.

Film Appearances:
Eddie, *The Chant of Jimmie Blacksmith,* 1978.
Tim, *Mouth to Mouth,* Vega Film Productions, 1978.
Scott, *The Odd Angry Shot,* Vestron Video, 1979.

Steve, *Just Out of Reach,* Portrait Films, 1979.

Garry, *Now and Then,* 1979.

Eddie, *The Chant of Jimmie Blacksmith,* New Yorker Films, 1980.

Steve Adams, *A Dangerous Summer* (also known as *Burning Man* and *Flash Fire*), Samuel Goldwyn Company, 1981.

Simmo, *Undercover,* 1983.

Shadow, *Going Down,* X Productions, 1983.

Sharon's ex–boyfriend, *One Night Stand,* Sultan Video/TransWorld Entertainment, 1984.

Barman, *Silver City,* Samuel Goldwyn Company, 1984.

Jock Pollock, *The Boy Who Had Everything* (also known as *Winner Takes All*), Alfred Road Films/Multi Films Investments, 1984.

"Marjorie," *The Coca–Cola Kid,* Cinecom International/Film Gallery, 1985.

John Buckland, *A Cry in the Dark* (also known as *Evil Angels*), Warner Bros., 1988.

Steamship official, *The First Kangaroos,* 1988.

GLADSTEIN, Richard N.
(Richard Gladstein)

PERSONAL

Married Lauri (a musician); children: Milo. *Education:* Attended Boston University, College of Communications, Boston, MA.

Addresses: *Office*—FilmColony, 465 South Sycamore Ave., Los Angeles, CA 90036.

Career: Producer. Began career working freelance on film and television productions in New York City; Angelika Films, New York City, director of acquisitions and distribution; Live Entertainment, vice president of production and acquisitions, 1987–93; Miramax Films, head of production, 1993–95; FilmColony, Los Angeles, CA, founder and president, 1995——.

Awards, Honors: Academy Award nomination, best picture, Motion Picture Producer of the Year Award nomination, Producers Guild of America Golden Laurel Awards, 2000, both for *The Cider House Rules;* Motion Picture Producer of the Year Award nomination (with Nellie Bellflower), Producers Guild of America Golden Laurel Awards, Film Award nomination (with Nellie Bellflower), best film, British Academy of Film and Television Arts, Academy Award nomination (with Bellflower), best motion picture of the year, 2005, all for *Finding Neverland.*

CREDITS

Film Executive Producer:

Silent Night, Deadly Night 3: Better Watch Out! (also known as *Blind Terror*), International Video Entertainment, 1989.

Lonely Hearts, Gibraltar Entertainment, 1991.

Age Isn't Everything, 1991.

Beyond the Law (also known as *Fixing the Shadow*), Live, 1992.

Reservoir Dogs, Miramax, 1992.

Only You, 1992.

Lonely Hearts, Live Entertainment, 1992.

Dark Horse, Live Video, 1992.

A House in the Hills, Live Video, 1993.

The Young Americans, Gramercy, 1993.

The Crossing Guard, Miramax, 1995.

The Journey of August King, Miramax, 1995.

Jackie Brown, Miramax, 1997.

Duplex (also known as *Der Appartement–Schreck* and *Our House*), Miramax, 2003.

Film Producer:

Initiation: Silent Night, Deadly Night 4 (also known as *Bugs* and *Silent Night, Deadly Night 4: Initiation*), Live Video, 1990.

Silent Night, Deadly Night 5: The Toy Maker, International Video Entertainment, 1991.

54 (also known as *Fifty–Four*), Miramax, 1998.

Hurlyburly, Fine Line Features, 1998.

She's All That, Miramax, 1999.

The Cider House Rules, Miramax, 1999.

The Bourne Identity (also known as *Die Bourne Identitat*), Universal, 2002.

Levity, Sony, 2003.

Finding Neverland, Miramax, 2004.

Journey to the End of the Night, Nu Image Films, 2006.

The Nanny Diaries, Weinstein Company, 2007.

Killshot, Metro–Goldwyn–Mayer, 2007.

Mr. Magorium's Wonder Emporium, Twentieth Century–Fox, 2007.

Film Co–Executive Producer:

Pulp Fiction, Miramax, 1994.

Film Appearances:

Silent Night, Deadly Night 3: Better Watch Out! (also known as *Blind Terror*), International Video Entertainment, 1989.

Woody, *Initiation: Silent Night, Deadly Night 4* (also known as *Bugs* and *Silent Night, Deadly Night 4: Initiation*), Live Video, 1990.

Driver dad, *Silent Night, Deadly Night 5: The Toy Maker,* International Video Entertainment, 1991.

Quentin Tarantino: Hollywood's Boy Wonder, BBC, 1994.

Himself, *"The Cider House Rules": The Making of an American Classic* (documentary short), Miramax, 1999.

(As Richard Gladstein) Himself, *The Magic of "Finding Neverland"* (short), Buena Vista Home Entertainment, 2005.

(As Richard Gladstein) Himself, *"Finding Neverland": On the Red Carpet* (short), 2005.

Television Producer; Movies:
Since You've Been Gone, ABC, 1998.

Television Appearances; Specials:
(As Richard Gladstein) *The Blockbuster Imperative,* Trio, 2003.

"Reservoir Dogs" Revisited, 2005.

WRITINGS

Screenplays:
Silent Night, Deadly Night 3: Better Watch Out! (also known as *Blind Terror*), 1989.

GOINES, Siena

PERSONAL

Born March 28, in Washington, DC.

Addresses: *Manager*—Lena Roklin, Nine Yards/Roklin Management, 8530 Wilshire Blvd., 5th Floor, Beverly Hills, CA 90211.

Career: Actress.

Awards, Honors: Image Award nomination, outstanding actress in a daytime drama series, National Association for the Advancement of Colored People, 2000, for *The Young and the Restless.*

CREDITS

Film Appearances:
Carol, *Restaurant,* Ardustry Home Entertainment, 1998.
Katie, *In the Weeds,* Moonstone Entertainment, 2000.
Tammy, *The Sweetest Thing,* Columbia TriStar, 2002.

Studio executive, *My Short Film* (short film), American Express, 2004.

Angela Morris, *Rancid,* Lightning Home Entertainment, 2004.

Woman at speed dating place, *The 40 Year Old Virgin,* Universal, 2005.

Tanya, *Only in Miami* (short film), Brownhornet Productions, 2006.

Anna, *Flight of the Living Dead: Outbreak on a Plane* (also known as *Flight of the Living Dead* and *Plane Dead*), New Line Home Video, 2007.

Christy, *Jekyll,* Creative Light Entertainment, 2007.

Karla, *Hunter's Moon,* Stouffer Entertainment, 2007.

Nadine, *The Mannsfield 12,* Asiatic Associates/Henna, 2007.

Lynn Hutto, *Throwing Stars,* Not Yet Rated Films/Grass Roots Films/TigerLily Media, 2007.

Television Appearances; Series:
Callie Rogers, *The Young and the Restless* (also known as *Y&R*), CBS, 1998–2000.

Mia, a recurring role, *Judging Amy,* CBS, between 2000 and 2004.

Valerie Davis, a recurring role, *Passions* (also known as *Harmony's Passions* and *The Passions Storm*), NBC, 2007.

Sarah Mason, a recurring role, *Jericho,* CBS, 2007.

Television Appearances; Movies:
Jody, *Co–ed Call Girl,* CBS, 1996.
Candace Clark, *The Rockford Files: Friends and Foul Play,* CBS, 1996.
Marva, *Joe and Max* (also known as *Joe and Max— Rivalen im ring*), Starz, 2002.

Television Appearances; Pilots:
Windfall, NBC, 2006.

Television Appearances; Episodic:
Janice, "Dog Catchers," *In the House,* UPN, 1995.
Cindy, *Moloney,* CBS, 1996.
Arli$$, HBO, 1996.
Maya, "Grip till It Hurts," *Women: Stories of Passion,* Showtime, 1997.
Maya, "Get a Grip," *Women: Stories of Passion,* Showtime, 1997.
Tanya Worrell, "Bridge over Troubled Watters," *Chicago Hope,* CBS, 1998.
Rain, "Ghosts of the Confederacy," *The Magnificent Seven,* CBS, 1998.
Rain, "Penance," *The Magnificent Seven,* CBS, 2000.
(Uncredited) Inspirational muse, "Muse to My Ears," *Charmed,* The WB, 2001.
Willa, "The Box," *The Division* (also known as *Heart of the City*), Lifetime, 2004.

Willa, "Zero Tolerance: Part 1," *The Division* (also known as *Heart of the City*), Lifetime, 2004.

GOMEZ, Rick 1972–

PERSONAL

Full name, Richard Harper Gomez; born June 1, 1972, in Bayonne, NJ; son of Rick Gomez, Sr.; married Jenifer Wymore (an actress), September 15, 2001; children: two.

Addresses: *Agent*—Agency for the Performing Arts, 405 South Beverly Dr., Beverly Hills, CA 90212. *Manager*—Sam Maydew, The Collective, 9100 Wilshire Blvd., Suite 700 W., Beverly Hills, CA 90212.

Career: Actor and voice performer. Appeared in commercials for Pizza Hut restaurants, 1996, and automaker Volkswagen, 2002.

CREDITS

Film Appearances:
(Uncredited) Thug, *Teenage Mutant Ninja Turtles* (also known as *Teenage Mutant Ninja Turtles: The Movie*), New Line Cinema, 1990.
Peter, *Mercy,* Unapix Entertainment, 1995.
Kevin, *Enough Already,* Wolfeboro Films, 1998.
Second punk, *Shark in a Bottle,* Atmosphere Films, 1998.
Rick, *Three to Tango,* Warner Bros., 1999.
David, *Blue Shark Hash,* 2000.
Pilot, *Final Flight of the Osiris* (animated short film; also known as *The Animatrix* and *The Animatrix: Final Flight of the Osiris*), Warner Bros., 2003.
Kevin, *11:14,* 2003, New Line Cinema, 2005.
Mr. Vidal, *Delusion* (short film), Pop Art Films, 2003.
Spin Doctor Fred, *Fronterz,* 2004.
Tom Dowd, *Ray,* Universal, 2004.
Voice of lead mercenary, *The Chronicles of Riddick: Dark Fury* (animated short film), Universal, 2004.
Klump, *Sin City* (also known as *Frank Miller's "Sin City"*), Dimension Films, 2005.
Voice of Zack for English version, *Final Fantasy VII: Advent Children,* Destination Films, 2005.
Voice, *Magnificent Desolation: Walking on the Moon 3D* (animated short film), IMAX, 2005.
Sheriff, *Transformers,* DreamWorks, 2007.

Film Work:
Co–executive producer, *A Waiter Tomorrow* (short film), Kang Is Man, 1998.

Television Appearances; Series:
Sully, *Bob and Sully,* Comedy Central, 1995.
Robert Moore, *Hitz,* UPN, 1997.
Bud and other roles, *Gary the Rat,* Spike, 2003.
Voices of Slips, Windsor, Frankie Lion, and others, *My Gym Partner's a Monkey* (animated), Cartoon Network, 2005.
Dave Greco, *What About Brian,* ABC, 2006–2007.

Television Appearances; Movies:
Video editor, *Mary and Rhoda,* ABC, 2000.
Milio, *Helter Skelter,* CBS, 2004.
Detective Rodriguez, *Detective* (also known as *Arthur Hailey's "Detective"*), Lifetime, 2005.

Television Appearances; Miniseries:
Sergeant George Luz, *Band of Brothers,* HBO, 2001.

Television Appearances; Episodic:
Endless Mike Hellstrom, "Yellow Fever," *The Adventures of Pete & Pete* (also known as *Pete and Pete*), Nickelodeon, 1994.
Ticket taker, "Atonement," *Law & Order,* NBC, 1996.
Lonnie, "Circles: The Vegie Stash–o–Matic," *The Eddie Files,* 1997.
Ricky, "Love Thy Neighbor," *In–Laws,* NBC, 2002.
Detective Daniel Ramos, "Home Invasion," *Boomtown,* NBC, 2003.
Detective Daniel Ramos, "Execution," *Boomtown,* NBC, 2003.
Detective Daniel Ramos, "Storm Watch," *Boomtown,* NBC, 2003.

Television Appearances; Other:
Todd, *Clerks* (pilot), 1995.
Himself, *The Making of "Band of Brothers"* (special), HBO, 2001.

RECORDINGS

Videos Games:
Voice of Gippal for English version, *Final Fantasy X–2* (also known as *Fainaru fantajii X–2*), Square Enix, 2003.
Voices, *Call of Duty 2,* Activision, 2005.
Voices, *Call of Duty 2: Big Red One,* Activision, 2005.
Voice of Zack, *Crisis Core: Final Fantasy VII,* Square Enix, 2007.

GOODWIN, Robbie
See GREENBERG, Robbie

GORDON, Stuart 1947–

PERSONAL

Born August 11, 1947, in Chicago, IL; son of Bernard Leo (a cosmetics executive) and Rosalie (a social worker and English teacher; maiden name, Sabbath) Gordon; married Carolyn Purdy (an actress and writer), December 20, 1968; children: Suzanna Katherine, Jillian Bess, Margaret Berni. *Education:* Attended University of Wisconsin, Madison, WI, 1965–69. *Religion:* Jewish.

Addresses: *Office*—Red Hen Productions, 3607 West Magnolia, Suite L, Burbank, CA 91505. *Agent*—Dean A. Schramm, Jim Preminger Agency, 11111 Santa Monica Blvd., Suite 530, Los Angeles, CA 90025. *Manager*—Industry Entertainment, 955 South Carrillo Dr., 3rd Floor, Los Angeles, CA 90048.

Career: Director, producer, writer, and actor. Broom Street Theatre, Madison, WI, founder, 1968; Screw Theatre, former affiliate; Organic Theatre Company, Madison, then Chicago, IL, founder and producing director, 1969–85; Red Hen Productions, Burbank, CA, principal. Worked as a commercial artist, c. 1965. Past member of board of directors, Illinois Arts Council and League of Chicago Theatres.

Member: Writers Guild of America West, Theatre Communications Group (past member of board of directors).

Awards, Honors: Golden Hugo Award, Chicago International Film Festival, c. 1977, and Drama Desk Award nomination, unique theatrical experience, and local Emmy Award, best direction, 1979, all for *Bleacher Bums;* grant, National Endowment for the Arts, c. 1978; Critics Prize, Cannes Film Festival, and Caixa de Catalunya, best film, Sitges–Catalonian International Film Festival, both 1985, Fantafestival Award, best film, and Avoriaz Fantastic Film Festival Award, both 1986, all for *Re–Animator;* International Fantasy Film Award nomination, best film, Fantasporto, 1990, for *Robot Jox;* International Fantasy Film Award nomination, best film, 1991, for *The Pit and the Pendulum;* nomination for Grand Prize, Avoriaz Fantastic Film Festival, 1993, for *Fortress;* Sitges–Catalonian International Film Festival Award nomination, best film, 1996, for *Space Truckers;* International Fantasy Film Award nomination, best film, and Fantafestival Award, best direction, both 1998, for *The Wonderful Ice Cream Suit;* Sitges–Catalonian International Film Festival Award nomination, 2001, and International Fantasy Film Award nomination, 2002, both best film, for *Dagon;* nomination for grand special prize, Deauville

Film Festival, 2005, New Visions Award, Sitges–Catalonian International Film Festival, 2006, and Mar del Plata Film Festival Award nomination, best film, 2006, all for *Edmond;* Joseph Jefferson Awards for writing and directing in Chicago.

CREDITS

Stage Director:

Candide, Organic Theatre Company, Body Politic Theatre, Chicago, IL, then Public Theatre, New York City, 1971.

Warp, Organic Theatre Company, Body Politic Theatre, then Ambassador Theatre, New York City, 1973.

The Wonderful Ice Cream Suit, Organic Theatre Company, Uptown Center Theatre, Chicago, IL, 1973.

Bloody Bess, Organic Theatre Company, Uptown Center Theatre, 1974.

The Adventures of Huckleberry Finn, Organic Theatre Company, Uptown Center Theatre, 1974.

Sexual Perversity in Chicago, Organic Theatre Company, Uptown Center Theatre, 1974.

Chemin de Fer, Goodman Theatre, Chicago, IL, 1975.

Cops, Organic Theatre Company, Uptown Center Theatre, 1976.

Bleacher Bums, Organic Theatre Company, Uptown Center Theatre, 1977, then Performing Garage, later (also producer) American Place Theatre, both New York City, 1978.

Fornicopia, Organic Theatre Company, Uptown Center Theatre, 1980.

The Little Sister, Organic Theatre Company, Uptown Center Theatre, 1980.

The King Must Die, Organic Theatre Company, Buckingham Theatre, 1981.

E/R, Organic Theatre Company, 1982.

The Adventures of Huckleberry Finn, Goodman Theatre, 1985.

Ghost Man, c. 1995.

Kabbalah, Lex Theatre, Los Angeles, 2000.

Also directed other Organic Theatre Company productions, including *Animal Farm, The Beckoning Fair One, Dr. Rat, The Great Switcheroo, Mrs. Bixby and the Colonels Coat, Odyssey, Poe, Richard III, The Sirens of Titan,* and *The Visitor.*

Stage Director; Major Tours:

Bloody Bess, Organic Theatre Company, European cities, 1974.

The Wonderful Ice Cream Suit, Organic Theatre Company, European cities, 1974.

The Adventures of Huckleberry Finn, Organic Theatre Company, European cities, 1975, and U.S. cities, 1976.

The Sirens of Titan, Organic Theatre Company, West Coast cities, 1977.

The Wonderful Ice Cream Suit, Organic Theatre Company, West Coast cities, 1977.

Stage Appearances:

Appeared in a production of *Marat/Sade.*

Film Director:

Re–Animator, Empire, 1985.

From Beyond (also known as *H. P. Lovecraft's "From Beyond"*), Empire, 1986.

Dolls, Empire, 1987.

Robot Jox (also known as *Robojox*), Triumph, 1990.

The Pit and the Pendulum (also known as *The Inquisitor*), Paramount, 1991.

Fortress, Dimension Films, 1993.

Castle Freak (also known as *Stuart Gordon's "Castle Freak"*), Full Moon Enterprises, 1995.

(And producer) *Space Truckers* (also known as *Star Truckers*), Pachyderm Productions, 1997.

(And producer) *The Wonderful Ice Cream Suit,* Buena Vista/Walt Disney, 1998.

Dagon (also known as *Dagon: Sect of the Sea, H. P. Lovecraft's "Dagon," The Lost Island,* and *Dagon—La secta del mar*), Lions Gate Films, 2001.

(And coproducer) *King of the Ants,* Asylum, 2003.

(And producer) *Edmond,* First Independent Pictures, 2006.

Stuck, Rigel Entertainment, 2007.

Film Executive Producer:

Honey, I Blew Up the Kid, Buena Vista, 1992.

The Progeny, Fries Film Group, 1999.

Snail Boy, 2000.

Deathbed (also known as *Stuart Gordon's "Deathbed"*), Film 2000/Full Moon Pictures/Shadow Entertainment, 2002.

Film Appearances:

(Uncredited) Bartender, *Robot Jox* (also known as *Robojox*), Triumph, 1990.

Biker, *The Arrival* (also known as *The Unwelcomed*), 1990.

Second doctor, *Susan's Plan* (also known as *Dying to Get Rich*), Kushner–Locke Productions, 1998.

Chicago Filmmakers on the Chicago River (documentary), Film Foetus, 1998.

(Uncredited) Party guest, *Bread and Roses* (also known as *Pan y rosas*), Lions Gate Films, 2000.

Clint's biker relative, *Snail Boy,* 2000.

The Eldritch Influence: The Life, Vision, and Phenomenon of H. P. Lovecraft (documentary), 2003.

Television Work; Movies:

Director, *Daughter of Darkness,* CBS, 1990.

Co–executive producer, *Bleacher Bums* (also known as *The Cheap Seats*), Showtime, 2002.

Television Director; Specials:

(With Pat Denny) *Bleacher Bums,* PBS, 1979.

Television Director; Episodic:

"Honey, Let's Trick–or–Treat," *Honey, I Shrunk the Kids: The TV Show,* 1998.

Television Appearances; Episodic:

"Dark Desires: Sexuality in the Horror Film," *SexTV,* 2003.

Television Appearances; Other:

Boogeymen II: Masters of Horror (special), Sci–Fi Channel, 2004.

The 100 Scariest Movie Moments (miniseries), Bravo, 2004.

Hitchcocked! (special), Starz, 2006.

RECORDINGS

Video Appearances:

King of the Ants: Behind the Scenes, Asylum Home Entertainment, 2003.

Cinemaker, Full Moon, 2004.

Dreams, Darkness, and Damnation: An Interview with Stuart Gordon, Anchor Bay Entertainment, 2006.

The Fearmakers Collection, Elite Entertainment, 2007.

Video Director:

Kid Safe: The Video, 1988.

WRITINGS

Stage Plays:

(With Bury St. Edmund) *Warp,* Organic Theatre Company, Body Politic Theatre, Chicago, IL, 1971–72, then Ambassador Theatre, New York City, 1973.

(With William J. Norris and John Ostrander) *Bloody Bess,* Organic Theatre Company, Uptown Center Theatre, Chicago, IL, 1974.

(With Joe Mantagna and others) *Bleacher Bums,* Organic Theatre Company, Uptown Center Theatre, 1977, then Performing Garage, later American Place Theatre, both New York City, 1978.

(With wife Carolyn Purdy–Gordon) *The Little Sister* (based on novel by Raymond Chandler), Organic Theatre Company, 1980.

(With Ronald Berman and others) *E/R,* Organic Theatre Company, 1982.

Screenplays:
(With William J. Norris and Dennis Paoli) *Re–Animator* (based on H. P. Lovecraft's story "Herbert West: The Re–Animator"), Empire, 1985.
(With Paoli and Brian Yuzna) *From Beyond* (also known as *H. P. Lovecraft's "From Beyond*;" based on Lovecraft's story of the same title), Empire, 1986.
(With Paoli and Nicholas St. John) *Body Snatchers,* Warner Bros., 1993.
The Dentist, Trimark Pictures, 1996.
Space Truckers (also known as *Star Truckers;* also based on story by Gordon), Pachyderm Productions, 1997.
Dagon (also known as *Dagon: Sect of the Sea, H. P. Lovecraft's "Dagon," The Lost Island,* and *Dagon—La secta del mar*), Lions Gate Films, 2001.

Television Episodes:
"H. P. Lovecraft's 'Dreams in the Witch–House,'" *Masters of Horror,* Showtime, 2005.
"The Black Cat," *Masters of Horror,* Showtime, 2007.

Videos:
Kid Safe: The Video, 1988.

ADAPTATIONS

The 1979 television special and 2002 television movie *Bleacher Bums* were based on Gordon's stage play of the same title. The stage play *Warp* inspired a comic-book series, published by First Comics in 1982; the play *E/R* was adapted as a television series aired on CBS, 1984–85; the play *Sexual Perversity in Chicago* was adapted as the film *About Last Night,* released by TriStar in 1986. The film *Honey, I Shrunk the Kids* was based on a story by Gordon and released by Buena Vista in 1989; sequels were based on characters created by Gordon. The film *Robot Jox* was based on a story by Gordon; the 1996 film *Robo Warriors* was based on characters created by Gordon. The film *Re-Animator* inspired a comic–book series, published by Pacific Comics, 1990. Other films based on stories by Gordon include *Castle Freak* (also known as *Stuart Gordon's "Castle Freak"*), Full Moon Enterprises, 1995; *The Progeny,* Fries Film Group, 1999; and *Stuck,* Rigel Entertainment, 2007. The 1998 television movie *The Dentist 2* (also known as *The Dentist 2: Brace Yourself*) was based on characters created by Gordon.

OTHER SOURCES

Periodicals:
Dark Side, April, 2004, pp. 6–9.
Fangoria, July, 1993, pp. 52–56.
Femme Fatales, November 12, 1999, p. 4.
Film Comment, February, 1987, p. 68.

Rolling Stone, November 20, 1986, p. 109.
Rue Morgue, May, 2006, pp. 16–18, 20.
Shivers, January, 2004, pp. 26–30.
Starlog, August, 1989, pp. 20–22, 34; August, 1992; August, 1997.

GRAF, Allan
(Alan Graf, Allan L. Graf, Allan Lee Graf, Allen Graf, Alan Graff)

PERSONAL

Education: Graduated from the University of Southern California, Los Angeles, 1973.

Addresses: *Agent*—Paradigm, 360 North Crescent Dr., North Bldg., Beverly Hills, CA 90210.

Career: Actor, stunt coordinator, stunts, second unit director, and football coordinator. Played professional football with the Portland Storm of the World Football League, 1974–76, and the Los Angeles Rams.

Awards, Honors: Taurus Award nomination, best stunt coordinator and/or second unit director—feature, World Stunt Awards, 2003, *We Were Soldiers.*

CREDITS

Film Work:
(Uncredited) Stunt double for Dick Butkus, *Gus,* Buena Vista, 1976.
(Uncredited) Stunts, *The Cannonball Run,* Twentieth Century–Fox, 1981.
Stunts, *Fighting Back* (also known as *Death Vengeance*), Paramount, 1982.
Stunts, *Star Trek: The Wrath of Khan* (also known as *Star Trek II: The Wrath of Khan*), Paramount, 1982.
Stunts, *D.C. Cab* (also known as *Mr. T and Company* and *Street Fleet*), Universal, 1983.
Stunts, *Code Name: Zebra,* Transcontinental, 1984.
Stunts, *City Heat,* Warner Bros., 1984.
Stunts, *Surf II,* Aquarius Releasing, 1984.
Stunts, *Real Genius,* TriStar, 1985.
Stunts, *Gung Ho* (also known as *Working Class Man*), Paramount, 1986.
Stunts, *Back to School,* Orion, 1986.
Stunts, *Raising Arizona,* Twentieth Century–Fox, 1987.
Stunts, *Extreme Prejudice,* TriStar, 1987.
Stunts, *Dragnet,* Universal, 1987.
(Uncredited) Stunts, *RoboCop,* Orion, 1987.
Stunts, *Real Men,* 1987.

(As Allen Graf) Stunts, *Action Jackson,* Lorimar Film Entertainment, 1988.

Stunts, *Sunset* (also known as *Catalina*), TriStar, 1988.

Stunts, *Red Heat,* Artisan Entertainment, 1988.

Stunts, *License to Drive,* Twentieth Century–Fox, 1988.

Stunts, *They Live* (also known as *John Carpenter's "They Live"* and *They Live!*), MCA/Universal, 1988.

Stunts, *K–9,* Universal, 1989.

Stunt coordinator and second unit director, *Johnny Handsome,* Columbia TriStar, 1989.

(As Allan L. Graf) Second unit director and stunt coordinator, *Another 48 Hrs.,* Paramount, 1990.

(Uncredited) Stunts and stunt coordinator, *The Fourth War,* Cannon, 1990.

Stunts, *Total Recall,* TriStar, 1990.

Football coordinator, stunt coordinator, and second unit director, *Necessary Roughness,* Paramount, 1991.

Stunts, *Dutch* (also known as *Driving Me Crazy*), Twentieth Century–Fox, 1991.

Stunts, *The Butcher's Wife,* Paramount, 1991.

Second unit director and stunt coordinator, *Wayne's World,* Paramount, 1992.

Second unit director and stunt coordinator, *Trespass* (also known as *Looters*), Universal, 1992.

Stunt coordinator, *Wild Orchid II: Two Shades of Blue* (also known as *Wild Orchard 2: Blue Movie Blue*), Triumph, 1992.

(As Allan L. Graf) Second unit director, stunt coordinator, and head football coach, *The Program,* Buena Vista, 1993.

Second unit director and stunt coordinator, *Geronimo: An American Legend,* Columbia, 1993.

Second unit director and stunt coordinator, *The Specialist* (also known as *El especilista*), Warner Bros., 1994.

Stunts, *F.T.W.* (also known as *F.T.W.: Fuck the World* and *Last Ride*), 1994.

Second unit director and stunt coordinator, *Wild Bill,* Metro–Goldwyn–Mayer, 1995.

Stunts, *Chameleon,* Samuel Goldwyn Company, 1995.

Second unit director and (uncredited) stunts and stunt coordinator, *Last Man Standing,* New Line Cinema, 1996.

(As Alan Graf) Stunt coordinator, *Broken Arrow,* Twentieth Century–Fox, 1996.

Stunts, *Independence Day* (also known as *ID4*), Twentieth Century–Fox, 1996.

Second unit director, football sequences, stunt coordinator, and (uncredited) football coordinator, *Jerry Maguire,* TriStar, 1996.

Second unit director and stunt coordinator, *Vegas Vacation* (also known as *National Lampoon's "Vegas Vacation"*), Warner Bros., 1997.

Second unit director, *Double Team* (also known as *The Colony*), Columbia, 1997.

Stunts, *Steel,* Warner Bros., 1997.

Stunts, *A Life Less Ordinary,* Twentieth Century–Fox, 1997.

Second unit director and stunt coordinator, *The Replacement Killers,* Columbia, 1998.

Second unit director and stunt coordinator, *The Waterboy,* Buena Vista, 1998.

Stunts, *The Odd Couple II* (also known as *Neil Simon's "The Odd Couple II"*), Paramount, 1998.

Stunt coordinator, *The Deep End of the Ocean,* Columbia, 1999.

Stunts, *Magnolia* (also known as *mag–no'il–a*), New Line Cinema, 1999.

Second unit director, stunt coordinator, and football coordinator, *Any Given Sunday,* Warner Bros., 1999.

Second unit director and stunt coordinator, *Supernova,* Metro–Goldwyn–Mayer, 2000.

Football coordinator, *Boys and Girls,* Dimension, 2000.

Second unit director, stunt coordinator, and football coordinator, *The Replacements,* Warner Bros., 2000.

(As Allan L. Graf) Second unit director and stunt coordinator, *A Knight's Tale,* Columbia, 2001.

Second unit director and stunt coordinator, *Domestic Disturbance,* Paramount, 2001.

Stunts, *Megiddo: The Omega Code 2* (also known as *Megiddo*), Gener8Xion Entertainment, 2001.

Second unit director and stunt coordinator, *We Were Soldiers* (also known as *Wir waren Heiden*), Paramount, 2002.

Stunt coordinator, *Punch–Drunk Love,* Columbia, 2002.

Stunts, *Pirates of the Caribbean: The Curse of the Black Pearl* (also known as *P.O.T.C.*), Buena Vista, 2003.

Stunts, *S.W.A.T.,* Columbia, 2003.

Second unit director and stunt coordinator, *Timeline,* Paramount, 2003.

Stunt performer, *Bad Santa* (also known as *Badder Santa*), Dimension Films, 2003.

Stunts, *Starsky & Hutch,* Warner Bros., 2004.

(As Allan L. Graf) Football coordinator, *The Ladykillers,* Buena Vista, 2004.

Second unit director, stunt coordinator, and football coordinator, *Friday Night Lights,* Universal, 2004.

Stunts, *Herbie: Fully Loaded,* Buena Vista, 2005.

Second unit director and stunt coordinator, *Man of the House,* Columbia, 2005.

Second unit director, stunt coordinator, and football coordinator, *Two for the Money,* Universal, 2005.

Stunts, *Bad News Bears,* Paramount, 2005.

Stunt coordinator and football coordinator, *Gridiron Gang,* Columbia, 2006.

Stunt player, *The Fast and Furious: Tokyo Drift,* Universal, 2006.

Second unit director, stunt coordinator, and football coordinator, *The Comebacks,* Twentieth Century–Fox, 2007.

Second unit director, stunt coordinator, and football coordinator, *The Express,* Universal, 2008.

Film Appearances:

Uniformed cop, *The Driver,* Twentieth Century–Fox, 1978.

Bank customer, *The Long Riders,* United Artists, 1980.

Tiny, *Roadie,* United Starts, 1980.

Hunter, *Southern Comfort,* Twentieth Century–Fox, 1981.

Baseball fan, *I Ought to Be in Pictures,* Twentieth Century–Fox, 1982.

Sam, *Poltergeist,* Metro–Goldwyn–Mayer/United Artists, 1982.

Deputy, *Impulse,* Twentieth Century–Fox, 1984.

Tiny, *Space Rage* (also known as *A Dollar a Day, Space Rage: Breakout on Prison Planet,* and *Trackers*), Vestron Pictures, 1985.

Camden Brave, *Brewster's Millions,* Universal, 1985.

Alvin, *Crossroads,* Columbia, 1986.

Graf, *Blue City,* Paramount, 1986.

Biker, *Out of Bounds,* Columbia, 1986.

Collins, *Over the Top* (also known as *Meet Me Half Way*), Warner Bros., 1987.

(Uncredited) Sal's bodyguard, *RoboCop,* Orion, 1987.

(Uncredited) Hartman (clown), *Real Men,* United Artists, 1987.

Workman, *The Presidio* (also known as *The Presidio: The Scene of the Crime*), Paramount, 1988.

Joliet prison guard, *Red Heat,* Artisan Entertainment, 1988.

Bob Lemoyne, *Johnny Handsome,* Columbia TriStar, 1989.

Bookman's guard, *The Wizard of Speed and Time,* Shapiro–Glickenhaus, 1989.

Studie, *Flashback,* Paramount, 1990.

Bus driver, *Another 48 Hrs.,* Paramount, 1990.

Theatre man number two, *Come See the Paradise,* Twentieth Century–Fox, 1990.

Miami cop, *The Doors,* TriStar, 1991.

Billy Bob's bartender, *Necessary Roughness,* Paramount, 1991.

Hank the cook, *Universal Soldier,* TriStar, 1992.

Bus driver, *Nowhere to Run,* Columbia, 1993.

Bus driver, *The Specialist* (also known as *El Especialista*), Warner Bros., 1994.

Convoy driver, *Last Man Standing,* New Line Cinema, 1996.

Wife beater, *L.A. Confidential,* Warner Bros., 1997.

Man with gun, *Boogie Nights,* New Line Cinema, 1997.

Lenny, *Trojan War* (also known as *Rescue Me*), Warner Bros., 1997.

Gordon, Valentine's head bodyguard, *The Limey,* Artisan Entertainment, 1999.

Firefighter, *Magnolia* (also known as *mag–no'li–a*), New Line Cinema, 1999.

Referee, *Any Give Sunday,* Warner Bros., 1999.

(Uncredited) Dallas head coach, *The Replacements,* Warner Bros., 2000.

(As Alan Graf) Football referee, *Thirteen Days,* New Line Cinema, 2000.

Himself, *School of Hard Knocks* (documentary short), Columbia TriStar, 2001.

Interrogator, *Looney Tunes: Back in Action* (also known as *"Looney Tunes Back in Action": The Movie*), Warner Bros., 2003.

Himself, *Journey Through "Timeline"* (documentary), Paramount Home Entertainment, 2004.

Himself, *Broken Trail: The Making of a Legendary Western,* 2006.

Soup waiter, *Beerfest,* Warner Bros., 2006.

Referee, *Gridiron Gang,* Columbia, 2006.

Television Work; Series:

Stunt coordinator, *Bring 'Em Back Alive,* CBS, 1982.

Stunts, *The A–Team,* NBC, 1983.

Television Work; Miniseries:

Second unit director, *Broken Trail,* AMC, 2006.

Television Work; Movies:

Second unit director and stunt coordinator, *Rise and Walk: The Dennis Byrd Story,* Fox, 1994.

Stunts, *Revenge of the Nerds IV: Nerds in Love,* Fox, 1994.

Second unit director, *The Law and Mrs. Lee,* 2003.

Television Work; Pilots:

Second unit director, stunt coordinator, and football coordinator, *Friday Night Lights,* NBC, 2006.

Television Work; Episodic:

Stunt coordinator, *Love & War,* CBS, 1993–94.

Stunt coordinator, "Juarez," *Red Shoe Diaries,* Showtime, 1996.

Stunt coordinator, "Reconnoitering the Rim," *Deadwood,* HBO, 2004.

Second unit director and football coordinator, "Eyes Wide Open," *Friday Night Lights,* NBC, 2006.

Second unit director and football coordinator, "Wind Sprints," *Friday Night Lights,* NBC, 2006.

Second unit director and football coordinator, "Homecoming," *Friday Night Lights,* NBC, 2006.

Television Appearances; Series:

Captain Turner, *Deadwood,* HBO, 2005–2006.

Television Appearances; Movies:

For the Love of It, ABC, 1980.

Johnson, *White Water Rebels,* CBS, 1983.

Jason, *Braker,* ABC, 1985.

Wheeler, *Assassin,* CBS, 1986.

(As Alan Graff) *Blood Vows: The Story of a Mafia Wife,* NBC, 1987.

Ox, *The Cover Girl and the Cop,* NBC, 1989.

Elmo, *Fever,* HBO, 1991.

Rugged man, *Kiss of a Killer,* ABC, 1993.

Irene's father, *Lake Consequence,* Showtime, 1993.

Jets assistant coach, *Rise and Walk: The Dennis Byrd Story,* Fox, 1994.

Television Appearances; Specials:
Starz Special: "Gridiron Gang," Starz, 2006.

Television Appearances; Episodic:
Heavy number one, "Does She or Doesn't She?," *Hart to Hart,* ABC, 1980.

Carl, "Mr. Galaxy," *Charlie's Angels,* ABC, 1981.

Thug, "Something Fishy," *Riptide,* NBC, 1984.

Handley, "HX–1," *Airwolf* (also known as *Lobo del aire*), CBS, 1984.

(As Alan Graff) Highway patrolman, "Mouth of the Snake: Part 1," *Knight Rider,* NBC, 1984.

Gunman at the Tee Mar office, "Professor Jonathan Higgins," *Magnum, P.I.,* CBS, 1985.

Construction worker, "Lost Link," *Misfits of Science,* NBC, 1985.

"Collision Course," *Falcon Crest,* CBS, 1986.

Jarrett, "Voo Doo Knight," *Knight Rider,* NBC, 1986.

Other man, "The Grey Team," *The A–Team,* NBC, 1986.

(As Allen Graf) Richard, "First Date," *Perfect Strangers,* ABC, 1986.

Al, "Get a Job," *Perfect Strangers,* ABC, 1987.

Lou, "Close Encounters," *Valerie* (also known as *The Hogan Family, The Hogans,* and *Valerie's Family*), NBC, 1988.

(As Allen Graf) Richard, "College Bound," *Perfect Strangers,* ABC, 1988.

Deputy sheriff, "Charley," *Falcon Crest,* CBS, 1989.

Driver, "Cutting Cards," *Tales from the Crypt* (also known as *HBO's "Tales from the Crypt"*), HBO, 1990.

Dick, *L.A. Law,* NBC, 1990.

John, "The Game," *Red Shoe Diaries,* Showtime, 1994.

Man hitting window, "It's Miller Time," *Murphy Brown,* CBS, 1995.

(Uncredited) Thug number two, "Cowboy," *Walker, Texas Ranger* (also known as *Walker*), CBS, 1995.

Kevin Richards, "Everyday Heroes," *Walker, Texas Ranger* (also known as *Walker*), CBS, 1998.

Himself, "Full Contact: The Making of 'Any Given Sunday,'" *HBO First Look,* HBO, 1999.

Guy at bar, *Love Boat: The Next Wave,* UPN, 1999.

Big man, "Justice Delayed," *Walker, Texas Ranger* (also known as *Walker*), CBS, 2000.

Cab driver, "Love Is All Around: Part 2," *Ally McBeal,* Fox, 2002.

Santa, "Chris–Mess," *Becker,* CBS, 2002.

Inmate number one, "My Heart Belongs to Daddy," *Desperate Housewives,* ABC, 2005.

Panthers defensive coach, "Wind Sprints," *Friday Night Lights,* NBC, 2006.

Coach Graf, "Who's Your Daddy," *Friday Night Lights,* NBC, 2006.

Also appeared as man in restaurant, "The Thrill of Agony, the Victory of Defeat," *My Sister Sam,* CBS; in *Deadwood,* HBO.

GREENBERG, Robbie
(Robbie Goodwin)

PERSONAL

Addresses: *Agent*—The Gersh Agency, 232 North Canon Dr., Beverly Hills, CA 90210.

Career: Cinematographer. Worked as a cinematographer and director on commercials.

Member: American Society of Cinematographers.

Awards, Honors: Emmy Award nomination, outstanding cinematography for a miniseries or a movie, American Society of Cinematographers Award, outstanding achievement in cinematography in movies of the week or miniseries, 1999, both for *Winchell;* Emmy Award, outstanding cinematography for a miniseries, movie, or special, American Society of Cinematographers Award, outstanding achievement in cinematography in movies of the week or miniseries, 2000, both for *Introducing Dorothy Dandridge;* Emmy Award nomination, outstanding cinematography for a miniseries or a movie, 2002, for *James Dean;* Emmy Award nomination, outstanding cinematography for a miniseries or movie, American Society of Cinematographers Award, outstanding achievement in cinematography in movies of the week, miniseries, or pilot for basic or pay television, 2004, both for *Iron Jawed Angels;* Emmy Award nomination, outstanding cinematography for a miniseries or movie, 2005, American Society of Cinematographers Award, outstanding achievement in cinematography in movies of the week, miniseries, or pilot, 2006, both for *Warm Springs.*

CREDITS

Film Cinematographer:
A Rainy Day (short), Direct Cinema Ltd., 1978.

Doctor Dracula (also known as *Svengali*), Independent International Pictures, 1978.

Youngblood, American International Pictures, 1978.

Rust Never Sleeps (documentary), International Harmony, 1979.

(As Robin Goodwin) *Swamp Thing,* Embassy Pictures, 1982.

Time Walker (also known as *Being From Another Planet*), New World Pictures, 1982.

Night Warning (also known as *Butcher, Baker, Nightmare Maker, Momma's Boy, Nightmare Maker, The Evil Protege,* and *Thrilled to Death*), Comworld, 1983.

Movers and Shakers, Metro–Goldwyn–Mayer/United Artists Entertainment Company, 1985.
Creator (also known as *The Big Picture*), Universal, 1985.
Sweet Dreams, TriStar, 1985.
The Milagro Beanfield War, Universal, 1988.
Far North, Alive Films, 1988.
All I Want for Christmas, Paramount, 1991.
Free Willy (also known as *Sauvez Willy*), Warner Bros., 1993.
Squanto: A Warrior's Tale (also known as *The Last Great Warrior*), Buena Vista, 1994.
Under Siege 2: Dark Territory (also known as *Under Siege 2*), Warner Bros., 1995.
Sunset Park, TriStar, 1996.
Fools Rush In, Columbia, 1997.
Snow Day, 2000.
Save the Last Dance, Paramount, 2001.
A Guy Thing, Metro–Goldwyn–Mayer, 2003.
Marci X, Paramount, 2003.
Even Money, 2006.
The Santa Clause 3: The Escape Clause (also known as *Pretender*), Yari Film Group Releasing, 2006.
Wild Hogs (also known as *Blackberry*), Buena Vista, 2007.

Film Work; Other:
Camera operator, *Night Warning* (also known as *Butcher, Baker, Nightmare Maker, Momma's Boy, Nightmare Maker, The Evil Protege,* and *Thrilled to Death*), Comworld, 1983.
Industry mentor, *Riding Shotgun* (short), 2004.

Film Appearances:
Cinematographer Style, 2006.

Television Cinematographer; Movies:
The Lathe of Heaven, PBS, 1980.
The Winter of Our Discontent (also known as *John Steinbeck's "The Winter of Our Discontent"*), CBS, 1983.
My Mother's Secret Life, ABC, 1984.
Second Serve (also known as *I Change My Life*), CBS, 1986.
Winchell, HBO, 1998.
Introducing Dorothy Dandridge (also known as *Face of an Angel*), 1999.
"1972," *If These Walls Could Talk 2,* HBO, 2000.
James Dean, TNT, 2001.
Iron Jawed Angels, HBO, 2004.
Warm Springs, HBO, 2005.

Television Cinematographer; Pilots:
This Girl for Hire (movie), CBS, 1983.
South of Sunset, VH1, 1993.

Television Cinematographer; Episodic:
"Cell Test," *Prison Break,* Fox, 2005.

GRILLO, Frank 1963–
(Frank J. Grillo)

PERSONAL

Born June 8, 1963, in New York, NY; married, wife's name Kathy, 1991 (divorced, 1998); married Wendy Moniz (an actress), October 28, 2000; children: (first marriage) Remy (son); (second marriage) Liam. *Education:* New York University, graduated.

Addresses: *Agent*—Steven Muller, Innovative Artists Talent and Literary Agency, 1505 10th St., Santa Monica, CA 90401. *Manager*—Andrea Pett–Joseph, Brillstein Entertainment Partners, 9150 Wilshire Blvd., Suite 350, Beverly Hills, CA 90212.

Career: Actor. Appeared in commercials.

CREDITS

Television Appearances; Series:
Hart Jessup, *The Guiding Light,* CBS, 1996–99.
Detective Marty Russo, *Blind Justice,* ABC, 2005.
Nick Savrinn, *Prison Break* (also known as *Prison Break: Manhunt* and *Prison Break: On the Run*), Fox, 2005–2006.
Pig, *The Kill Point,* Spike, 2007.

Television Appearances; Pilots:
Anthony Stigliano, *Battery Park,* NBC, 2000.
Detective Marty Russo, *Blind Justice,* ABC, 2005.
Detective Henry Callaway, *Hollis & Rae,* ABC, 2006.
Pig, *The Kill Point,* Spike, 2007.

Appeared in pilots for *Fiona* and *Legacy.*

Television Appearances; Movies:
Detective Terence Gillette, *Hunter: Return to Justice,* NBC, 2002.
Detective Terence Gillette, *Hunter: Back in Force,* NBC, 2003.

Television Appearances; Episodic:
Franco LaPuma, "Ladies Night Out," *Silk Stalkings,* USA Network, 1993.
(As Frank J. Grillo) Jerry Tate, "Ghost in the Road," *Poltergeist: The Legacy,* Showtime, 1996.

Cliff Dobbs, "Truth or Consequences," *Wasteland,* ABC, 1999.

Cliff Dobbs, "The Object of My Affection," *Wasteland,* ABC, 1999.

Cliff Dobbs, "Great Expectations," *Wasteland,* ABC, 1999.

Anthony Stigliano, "Rabbit Punch," *Battery Park,* NBC, 2000.

Anthony Stigliano, "How Do You Solve a Problem like Maria?," *Battery Park,* NBC, 2000.

Anthony Stigliano, "You Give Law a Bad Name," *Battery Park,* NBC, 2000.

Detective Hunter, "Textbook Perfect," *For the People* (also known as *Para la gente*), Lifetime, 2002.

Frank Barbarossa, "Deception," *Law & Order: Special Victims Unit* (also known as *Law & Order: SVU* and *Special Victims Unit*), NBC, 2002.

Officer Paul Jackson, "Our Gang," *The Shield,* FX Network, 2002.

Officer Paul Jackson, "Dragonchasers," *The Shield,* FX Network, 2002.

Officer Paul Jackson, "Breakpoint," *The Shield,* FX Network, 2003.

Officer Paul Jackson, "Dominoes Falling," *The Shield,* FX Network, 2003.

Garrison Kick, "Nostalgia," *Karen Sisco,* ABC, 2003.

Vince Dymecki, "Breath of Life," *The District,* CBS, 2004.

Gary Sinclair, "Happenstance," *CSI: Crime Scene Investigation* (also known as *C.S.I., CSI: Las Vegas, CSI Weekends,* and *Les experts*), CBS, 2006.

Neil Rawlings, "Tail Spin," *Without a Trace* (also known as *W.A.T.*), CBS, 2007.

Jeremy Shapiro, "The Burning Beduoin," *Las Vegas,* NBC, 2007.

Television Appearances; Other:

Presenter, *Soap Opera Update Awards* (special), Lifetime, 1997.

Dr. Oliver Cornbluth, *The Madness of Jane,* 2007.

Film Appearances:

(As Frank J. Grillo) FBI agent, *Deadly Rivals,* MCA/ Universal Home Video, 1993.

Vince Carlucci, *Deadly Charades,* Mystique Films, 1996.

General, *Simplicity* (short film), Compression Films, 2002.

Andy, *The Sweetest Thing,* Columbia TriStar, 2002.

Pre–crime cop, *Minority Report,* Twentieth Century– Fox, 2002.

Rocco, *April's Shower,* Regent Releasing, 2004.

Ben Chaffin, *Raw Footage* (short film), Iona Pictures, 2007.

RECORDINGS

Videos:

Autonomy: Power Abs (exercise video), 1994.

GRUNER, Olivier 1960–

PERSONAL

Born August 2, 1960, in Paris, France; father, a surgeon. *Avocational Interests:* Skiing.

Addresses: *Agent*—Ray Cavaleri, Cavaleri and Associates Talent Agency, 178 South Victory Blvd., Suite 205, Burbank, CA 91502.

Career: Actor, producer, and martial arts choreographer. Former world kickboxing champion. Also worked as a model. *Military service:* French Army, c. 1978–82; served in Senegal.

CREDITS

Film Appearances:

Jacques, *Angel Town,* Imperial Entertainment, 1990.

Alex Rain, *Nemesis,* Imperial Entertainment, 1993.

Raymond Stokes, *Velocity Trap,* New City Releasing, 1997.

Lieutenant Shaun Lambert, *Interceptors* (also known as *Interceptor Force, The Last Line of Defence,* and *Predator 3: Intercepters*), United Film Organization, 1999.

Michael Rogers, *Kumite,* 2000.

Adrian Kaminski, *G.O.D.* (also known as *Guaranteed on Delivery* and *Guaranteed Overnight Delivery*), Amsell Entertainment, 2000.

Marcus Clay, *Crackerjack 3,* North American Releasing, 2000.

Cody, *Extreme Honor* (also known as *Last Line of Defence 2*), Dreamfactory/Hollywood Feature Entertainment, 2001.

Captain, *Power Elite,* Cine Excel Entertainment, 2002.

Dirk Longstreet, *The Circuit 2: The Final Punch* (also known as *The Circuit 2*), Twentieth Century–Fox Home Entertainment, 2002.

Paul Gerard, *Deadly Engagement* (also known as *Omega Force*), Third Millennium, 2003.

Phil Yordan, *Soft Target* (also known as *Crooked*), Gorilla Pictures, 2005.

Luc Remy, *SWAT: Warhead One,* 2005.

Dirk Longstreet, *The Circuit 3* (also known as *The Circuit 3: Street Monk* and *Street Monk*), Film One, 2006.

Blizhniy Boy: The Ultimate Fighter, Universal Vision Productions, 2007.

Anton, *Brother's War,* Almighty Dog Productions, 2007.

Nash, *Lost Warrior: Left Behind,* Gorilla Pictures, 2007.

Film Work:

Producer, *Interceptors* (also known as *Interceptor Force, The Last Line of Defence,* and *Predator 3: Intercepters*), United Film Organization, 1999.

Executive producer, *The Circuit,* Amsell Entertainment, 2002.

Executive producer, *The Circuit 2: The Final Punch* (also known as *The Circuit 2*), Twentieth Century–Fox Home Entertainment, 2002.

Television Appearances; Movies:

Joseph Charlegrand, *Savate* (also known as *The Fighter*), 1994.

"J269," *Automatic,* 1994.

Alex (title role), *Savage,* 1995.

Caution Templer, *Mars,* 1996.

Captain Carl Hawk May, *Mercenary,* HBO and Cinemax, 1997.

Captain Carl Hawk May, *Mercenary II: Thick and Thin* (also known as *Thick and Thin*), 1997.

Alex, *T.N.T.,* 1998.

Jacques, *The White Pony,* 1999.

Lieutenant Sean Lambert, *Interceptor Force 2* (also known as *Alpha Force* and *They Have Returned*), Sci–Fi Channel, 2002.

Television Appearances; Episodic:

Dieter Vanderval, "Wild Life," *Martial Law,* CBS, 1999.

Tawrens, "Tawrens," *Code Name: Eternity* (also known as *Code: Eternity*), Sci–Fi Channel, 2000.

Tawrens, "Thief," *Code Name: Eternity* (also known as *Code: Eternity*), Sci–Fi Channel, 2000.

Tawrens, "Fatal Error," *Code Name: Eternity* (also known as *Code: Eternity*), Sci–Fi Channel, 2000.

Television Work; Movies:

Fight choreographer, *Savate* (also known as *The Fighter*), 1994.

Fight choreographer, *Automatic,* 1994.

Associate producer, *Savage,* 1995.

Associate producer and fight choreographer, *Mercenary,* HBO and Cinemax, 1997.

ADAPTATIONS

The 2007 film *Lost Warrior: Left Behind* was based on a story by Gruner.

GUGLIELMI, Noel 1970–
(Noel Albert Guglielmi, Noel Gugliemi)

PERSONAL

Surname is pronounced "Gool–yel–mee"; born 1970, in Santa Monica, CA.

Addresses: *Agent*—Nancy Chaidez, Nancy Chaidez and Associates, 1555 Vine St., Suite 223, Hollywood, CA 90028; Tracy Christian, Don Buchwald and Associates, 6500 Wilshire Blvd., Suite 2200, Los Angeles, CA 90048.

Career: Actor. Appeared in commercial for Pep Boys auto parts store. Sometimes sources credit him as Noel Gugliemi.

CREDITS

Film Appearances:

(Uncredited) *Road Dogz,* Shooting Star Partners, 2000.

Angel, *Price of Glory,* New Line Cinema, 2000.

(Uncredited) Mexican Mafia soldier, *Brother,* Sony Pictures Classics, 2001.

Johnny, *The Barrio Murders,* 2001.

Gang leader, *The Animal,* Columbia, 2001.

Hector, *The Fast and the Furious,* Universal, 2001.

Moreno, *Training Day,* Warner Bros., 2001.

Ghetto Rhapsody, Asylum, 2001.

Latino convict, *National Security,* Columbia, 2003.

First inmate, *Masked and Anonymous,* Sony Pictures Classics, 2003.

First student, *Old School,* DreamWorks, 2003.

Snuffy, *Malibu's Most Wanted,* Warner Bros., 2003.

Hood, *Bruce Almighty,* Universal, 2003.

Joker, *Double Blade* (short film), Magenta Pictures, 2003.

Latino thug, *S.W.A.T.,* Columbia, 2003.

Capone, *Wasabi Tuna,* Cafe Entertainment Studios, 2003.

Second bar thug, *El Matador,* Madacy Entertainment, 2003.

Manuel, *Wrong Turn* (short film), 2003.

Robert, *Party Animalz,* Artisan Entertainment, 2004.

Paco, *Candy Paint* (short film), School of Cinema and Television, University of Southern California, 2005.

J. C., *Duck,* 2005, Right Brained Releasing, 2007.

Flaco, *Harsh Times,* Metro–Goldwyn–Mayer, 2005.

Noel, *Hallowed,* Lifeline Entertainment, 2006.

Santos, *Seven Mummies,* American World Pictures, 2006.

Rubin, *Platinum Illusions,* Urban Dynasty/Fantasy World Entertainment, 2006.

Gio, *The Virgin of Juarez,* First Look International, 2006.

Diablo, *Jack's Law,* 11 Pictures/Dr. October, 2006.

Fatcap, *Hood of Horror* (also known as *Snoop Dogg's "Hood of Horror"*), Freestyle Releasing/Xenon Pictures, 2006.

Dusty, *Splinter,* Image Entertainment, 2006.

Warehouse rooftop hood, *Crank,* Lions Gate Films, 2006.

First subway guy, *School for Scoundrels,* Metro–Goldwyn–Mayer, 2006.

Big Lucky, *Six Thugs,* After Tha Fact Films, 2006.

Caesar, *Last Rites* (also known as *Gangs of the Dead*), Screen Media Ventures, 2006.

Big Dino, *Get Pony Boy,* Voila Productions, 2007.

Lalo, *Gordon Glass,* Big Easy Productions, 2007.

Random, *Evilution,* Black Gate Entertainment/Island Gateway Films, 2007.

Vinnie, *Loaded,* Arsenal Pictures, 2007.

Second cholo, *Ode,* Kiran Entertainment/Mega Bollywood, 2007.

Army Ranger Ignacio Garza, *Black Mountain,* Black Mountain Films, 2007.

Jesus, *2001 Maniacs: Beverly Hellbillys,* Darclight Films, 2007.

Television Appearances; Pilots:

Frank Ortiz, *Get Real,* Fox, 1999.

Chico, *Without a Trace* (also known as *W.A.T.*), CBS, 2002.

Television Appearances; Movies:

(Uncredited) Street thug, *The Dukes of Hazzard: Hazzard in Hollywood,* NBC, 2000.

Chicken, *Employee of the Month,* Showtime, 2004.

Television Appearances; Series:

Host, *Cruzin TV,* 2004.

Television Appearances; Episodic:

Lalo, "El Baile," *Resurrection Blvd.,* Showtime, 2000.

First gangbanger, "Surekill," *The X–Files,* Fox, 2001.

(As Noel Albert Guglielmi) Vince, "Life Serial," *Buffy the Vampire Slayer* (also known as *BtVS, Buffy,* and *Buffy the Vampire Slayer: The Series*), UPN, 2001.

David Ramirez, "Alter Boys," *CSI: Crime Scene Investigation* (also known as *C.S.I., CSI: Las Vegas, CSI Weekends,* and *Les experts*), CBS, 2001.

Craig, "6:00 p.m.–7:00 p.m.," *24,* Fox, 2002.

Driver vamp, "Deep Down," *Angel* (also known as *Angel: The Series*), The WB, 2002.

Paco, "City of Strivers," *Robbery Homicide Division* (also known as *R.H.D./LA: Robbery Homicide Division/Los Angeles*), CBS, 2002.

Marco, "A Claude Casey Production," *Less than Perfect,* ABC, 2002.

Jose Rincon, "Laughlin All the Way to the Clink," *NYPD Blue,* ABC, 2003.

Prophets gang leader, "Slipknot," *The Shield,* FX Network, 2003.

Jose, "Street Boss," *The Handler,* CBS, 2003.

(Uncredited0 Man, "Mr. Monk and the Paperboy," *Monk,* USA Network, 2004.

Satchel, *The Young and the Restless* (also known as *Y&R*), CBS, 2004.

Rico Dominguez, "Shootout," *CSI: Miami,* CBS, 2005.

Cesar, "Soldier," *Sleeper Cell* (also known as *Sleeper Cell: American Terror*), Showtime, 2005.

Felix, "Judas," *Wanted,* TNT, 2005.

Victor Castillo, "Bait and Switch," *Las Vegas,* NBC, 2006.

Appeared as Dante in an episode of *The District,* CBS.

RECORDINGS

Videos:

Voice of gangster, *Grand Theft Auto: San Andreas* (video game; also known as *GTA: San Andreas* and *San Andreas*), Rockstar Games, 2004.

The Making of "Seven Mummies," American World Pictures, 2005.

Voice of Cortez, *187 Ride or Die* (video game), Ubi Soft France, 2005.

GUILLAUME, Robert 1927–

PERSONAL

Original name, Robert Peter Williams; born November 30, 1927, in St. Louis, MO; married Marlene, 1955 (divorced); married Fay Hauser, 1978 (divorced); married Donna Brown (a television producer), 1985; children: (first marriage) Kevin (an actor), Jacques (a singer; deceased); (second marriage) Rachel Jeanette; (with others) Patricia, Melissa. *Education:* Attended St. Louis University and Washington University, St. Louis, MO; studied opera and musical theatre in Cleveland, OH.

Addresses: *Agent*—Agency for the Performing Arts, 405 South Beverly Dr., Beverly Hills, CA 90212; Cunningham, Escott, Slevin and Doherty Talent Agency, 10635 Santa Monica Blvd. Suite 140, Los Angeles, CA 90025. *Manager*—Alan David Management, 8840 Wilshire Blvd., Beverly Hills, CA 90211.

Career: Actor, producer, director, and song performer. Founded Guillaume/Margo Productions and Confetti Entertainment; appeared in television commercials for Bounce fabric softener, 1970s, Black History Month, 2000, Swiffer Dusters, 2004, and Philip's Milk of Magnesia. Also worked as a dishwasher, sales clerk, postal clerk, and streetcar driver. *Military service:* U.S. Army, 1945–46.

Member: American Federation of Television and Radio Artists, Screen Actors Guild.

Awards, Honors: Antoinette Perry Award nomination, best actor in a musical, Drama Desk Award, outstanding actor in a musical, 1977, both for *Guys and Dolls;*

Emmy Award, outstanding supporting actor in a comedy or comedy–variety series, 1979, TV Land Award nomination, best broadcast butler, 2004, both for *Soap;* Emmy Awards, outstanding supporting actor in a comedy or comedy–variety series, 1979, and outstanding lead actor in a comedy series, 1985, Emmy Award nominations, outstanding lead actor in a comedy series, 1980, 1982, 1983, 1984, Golden Globe Award nomination, best performance by an actor in a television series–comedy/musical, 1983, 1984, 1985, Emmy Award, all for *Benson;* Daytime Emmy Award nomination, outstanding performer in an animated program, 2000, for *Happily Ever After: Fairy Tales for Every Child;* Image Award nominations, outstanding lead actor in a comedy series, 1999, 2001, and outstanding supporting actor in a comedy series, 2000, National Association for the Advancement of Colored People, Screen Actors Guild Award nomination (with others), outstanding performance by an ensemble in a comedy series, 2000, Golden Satellite Award nomination, best performance by an actor in a series, comedy, or musical, International Press Academy, 2001, all for *Sports Night;* Golden Nymph, Monte–Carlo TV Festival, outstanding male actor, 2001; Video Premiere Award nomination (with others), best animated character performance, 2001, for *The Land Before Times VIII: The Big Freeze;* Interactive Achievement Award, outstanding achievement in character performance—male, Academy of Interactive Arts and Sciences, 2005, for *Half–Life 2;* Received Star on Hollywood Walk of Fame.

CREDITS

Stage Appearances:
Second geologist and singer, *Finian's Rainbow,* 46th Street Theatre, New York City, 1960.
(Broadway debut) Ako, *Kwamina,* Fifty–Fourth Street Theatre, New York City, 1961.
Carl, *Fly Blackbird,* Mayfair Theatre, New York City, 1962.
C. J. Moore, *Tambourines to Glory,* New York City, 1963.
Ensemble, *Jacques Brel Is Alive and Well and Living in Paris,* Village Gate Theatre, New York City, 1968, then Charles Playhouse, Boston, MA, 1969–70.
Frankie, *No Place to Be Somebody,* Arena Stage, Washington, DC, 1969–70.
Karl, *The Life and Times of J. Walter Smintheus,* Theatre de Lys, New York City, 1970.
Fire in the Mindhouse, Center Stage, Baltimore, MD, 1970–71.
Allan, *Charlie Was Here and Now He's Gone,* Eastside Playhouse, New York City, 1971.
Title role, *Purlie,* Shubert Theatre, Philadelphia, PA, 1971, then Billy Rose Theatre, New York City, 1972.
Jacques Brel Is Alive and Well Living in Paris, Royal Theatre, New York City, 1972.

Benito Cereno, Goodman Theatre, Chicago, IL, 1975–76.
Marshall, *Apple Pie,* New York Shakespeare Festival, Anspacher Theatre, Public Theatre, New York City, 1976.
Nathan Detroit, *Guys and Dolls,* Broadway Theatre, New York City, 1976.
Don Juan, Goodman Theatre, 1977.
Night of 100 Stars, Radio City Music Hall, New York City, 1982.
Cabaret, Riverside Resort, Las Vegas, NV, 1987.
Title role, *Phantom of the Opera,* Los Angeles, CA, 1990.
Title role, *Cyrano—The Musical,* Neil Simon Theatre, New York City, 1993–94.

Made stage debut as Billy Bigelow, *Carousel;* also appeared in *Golden Boy,* New York City; *Music! Music!,* New York City; *Othello,* New York City; *Porgy and Bess,* New York City; *Miracle Play,* New York City.

Film Appearances:
Jordan Gaines, *Super Fly T.N.T.,* Paramount, 1973.
Fred, *Seems Like Old Times* (also known as *Neil Simon's "Seems Like Old Times"*), Columbia, 1980.
Martin Luther King, *Prince Jack,* Castle Hill, 1985.
V.A. Officer, *They Still Call Me Bruce,* Shapiro/Jihee Productions, 1987.
Philmore Walker, *Wanted: Dead or Alive,* New World Pictures, 1987.
Dr. Frank Napier, *Lean on Me,* Warner Bros., 1989.
Hawkins, *Death Warrant,* 1990.
Ted Reed, Jeff's father, *The Meteor Man,* 1993.
Voice of Rafiki, *The Lion King* (animated; also known as *El rey leon*), 1994.
Agent Steve Bishop, *Spy Hard,* Buena Vista, 1996.
Wilkes, *First Kid,* Buena Vista, 1996.
Voice of Rafiki, *The Lion King II: Simba's Pride* (animated), Buena Vista Home Video, 1998.
Singing voice, *The Easter Story Keepers,* 1998.
Detective Green, *Silicon Towers,* 1999.
Voice of Mr. Thicknose, *The Land Before Time VIII: The Big Freeze* (animated; also known as *The Land Before Time 8: The Big Freeze* and *The Land Before Time: The Big Freeze*), Universal Studios Home Video, 2001.
Voice of Ben, *The Adventures of Tom Thumb & Thumbelina* (animated), Buena Vista, 2002.
Riley, *13th Child* (also known as *The 13th Child, Legend of the Jersey Devil*), MTI Home Video, 2002.
Older Dr. Bennett, *Big Fish,* 2003.
Reader, *Unchained Memories: Readings from the Slave Narratives* (documentary), 2003.
TV in Black: The First Fifty Years, Koch Vision, 2004.
Voice of Rafiki, *The Lion King 1 ½* (also known as *The Lion King 3;* animated), Buena Vista, 2004.
Doc, *Jack Satin,* 2005.

Broadway: Beyond the Golden Age (also known as *B.G.A. 2* and *Broadway: The Golden Age 2*), 2008.

Television Appearances; Series:
Benson Dubois, *Soap*, ABC, 1977–80.
Benson Dubois, *Benson*, ABC, 1979–86.
3-2-1 Contact, 1980.
Dr. Edward Sawyer, *The Robert Guillaume Show*, ABC, 1989.
Voice of Citizen, *Captain Planet and the Planeteers* (animated; also known as *The New Adventures of Captain Planet*), 1990.
Detective Bob Ballard, *Pacific Station*, 1991.
Voice of Detective Catfish, *Fish Police* (animated), 1992.
Voice of Rafiki, *The Lion King: Timon & Pumbaa* (animated; also known as *Timon and Pumbaa*), Disney Channel, 1995.
Isaac Jaffe, *Sports Night*, ABC, 1998–2000.

Television Appearances; Miniseries:
Frederick Douglass, *North and South*, ABC, 1985.
Jolson Mossburger, *A Good Day to Die* (also known as *Children of the Dust*), CBS, 1995.
Ambassador Lee Lancaster, *Pandora's Clock* (also known as *Doomsday Virus*), NBC, 1996.

Television Appearances; Movies:
Larry Cooper, *The Kid from Left Field*, NBC, 1979.
Blake, *The Kid with the Broken Halo*, NBC, 1982.
Professor Mills, *The Kid with the 200 I.Q.*, NBC, 1983.
Harlan Wade, *Perry Mason: The Case of the Scandalous Scoundrel*, NBC, 1987.
Carter Guthrie, *Fire and Rain*, USA Network, 1989.
Eugene St. Clair, *The Penthouse*, ABC, 1989.
Uncle Buddy/W. B. Jackson, *You Must Remember This* (also known as *Wonderworks: "You Must Remember This"*), 1992.
Congressman Sydley Sellers, *Mastergate*, 1992.
(Uncredited) Police commissioner, *Murder Without Motive: The Edmund Perry Story* (also known as *Best Intentions*), 1992.
Robert "Maximum Bob" Smith, *Greyhounds*, CBS, 1994.
Reverend Devers, *Run for the Dream: The Gail Devers Story*, Showtime, 1996.
Rob Barnes, *Panic in the Skies!*, Family Channel, 1996.
Merlin, *Crystal Cave* (also known as *The Crystal Cave: Lessons from the Teachings of Merlin*), 1996.
Merlin, *Alchemy*, 1996.
Voice, *Snow White*, 1996.
Mr. Gower and Mr. Martini, *Merry Christmas, George Bailey*, PBS, 1997.
Garrett, *His Bodyguard* (also known as *Silent Echoes*), USA Network, 1998.
Narrator, *The Happy Prince*, 1999.

Television Appearances; Specials:
Porgy in Wien, 1966.
Jack Lemmon in 'S Wonderful, 'S Marvelous, 'S Gershwin, NBC, 1972.
ABC's Silver Anniversary Celebration—25 and Still the One, ABC, 1978.
Dean Martin Celebrity Roast: Jack Klugman, NBC, 1978.
Rich Little's Washington Follies, ABC, 1978.
Benson, *Soap Retrospective II*, ABC, 1978.
Presenter, *The 32nd Annual Tony Awards*, CBS, 1978.
The Singer, *Bob Hope Special: Bob Hope in the Star–Makers*, NBC, 1980.
The Donna Summer Special, ABC, 1980.
Hal Linden's Big Apple, ABC, 1980.
Title role, *Purlie*, PBS, 1981.
Host, *Magic with the Stars*, NBC, 1982.
Texaco Star Theater: Opening Night, NBC, 1982.
Night of 100 Stars, 1982.
Performer, *The 37th Annual Tony Awards*, CBS, 1983.
Host, *The World's Funniest Commercial Goofs*, ABC, 1983.
Host, *The 5th Annual Black Achievement Awards*, 1984.
The 38th Annual Tony Awards, CBS, 1985.
Life's Most Embarrassing Moments, 1985.
The 37th Annual Primetime Emmy Awards, ABC, 1985.
Host, *The World's Funniest Commercial Goofs*, ABC, 1985.
Host, *Passion and Memory*, PBS, 1986.
Title role, *John Grin's "Christmas"* (also known as *Christmas*), ABC, 1986.
The 7th Annual Black Achievement Awards, 1986.
We the People 200: The Constitutional Gala, CBS, 1987.
"The Music Makers: An ASCAP Celebration of American Music at Wolf Trap," *Great Performances*, PBS, 1987.
Host, *Living the Dream: A Tribute to Dr. Martin Luther King*, syndicated, 1988.
The Debbie Allen Special, ABC, 1989.
The 15th Annual People's Choice Awards, CBS, 1989.
Host, *SST: Screen, Stage, Television*, ABC, 1989.
The 22nd Annual NAACP Image Awards, NBC, 1990.
Motown 30: What's Goin On!, 1990.
Host, *Disney's "Great American Celebration"* (also known as *Great American Celebration*), 1991.
Story of a People: Expressions in Black, 1991.
The Dream Is Alive: The 20th Anniversary Celebration of Walt Disney World, 1991.
Hoke Coleburn, *Driving Miss Daisy*, 1992.
Co–host, *In a New Light: A Call to Action in the War Against AIDS* (also known as *In a New Light*), 1992.
Gleason Golightly, "Space Traders," *Cosmic Slop*, HBO, 1994.
Host, *The Making of "The Lion King"*, Disney Channel, 1994.
Host, *Disney's Young Musicians Symphony Orchestra*, Disney Channel, 1994.

Cincinnati Pops Holiday: Erich Kunzel's Halloween Spooktacular, PBS, 1996.

Narrator, *Mother Goose: A Rappin and Rhymin Special,* HBO, 1997.

Robert, *Shari's Passover Surprise* (also known as *Lamb Chop's Passover Special*), PBS, 1997.

Host, *The Sixth Annual Trumpet Awards,* TBS, 1998.

Presenter, *The 51st Annual Primetime Emmy Awards,* Fox, 1999.

Narrator, *Ali Baba and the Forty Thieves: An Animated Special from the "Happily Ever After: Fairy Tales for Every Child" Series* (animated), HBO, 1999.

Narrator, *Bremen Town Musicians: An Animated Special from the "Happily Ever After: Fairy Tales for Every Child" Series* (animated), HBO, 1999.

Narrator, *Empress Nightingale: An Animated Special from the "Happily Ever After: Fairy Tales for Every Child" Series* (animated), HBO, 1999.

Narrator, *Happy Prince: An Animated Special from the "Happily Ever After: Fairy Tales for Every Child" Series* (animated), HBO, 1999.

Narrator, *Henny Penny: An Animated Special from the "Happily Ever After: Fairy Tales for Every Child" Series* (animated), HBO, 1999.

Presenter, *Thirteenth Annual Genesis Awards,* Animal Planet, 1999.

Narrator, *Three Little Pigs: From the "Happily Ever After: Fairy Tales for Every Child" Series* (animated), HBO, 1999.

The 31st Annual NAACP Image Awards, Fox, 2000.

Narrator, *Aesop's Fables: A Whodunit Musical: An Animated Special from the "Happily Ever After: Fairy Tales for Every Child" Series* (animated), HBO, 2000.

Presenter, *Essence Awards 2000,* Fox, 2000.

Narrator, *Frog Princess: An Animated Special from the "Happily Ever After: Fairy Tales for Every Child" Series* (animated), HBO, 2000.

Narrator, *The Princess and the Pauper: An Animated Special from the "Happily Ever After: Fairy Tales for Every Child" Series* (animated), HBO, 2000.

Narrator, *Rip Van Winkle: An Animated Special from the "Happily Ever After: Fairy Tales for Every Child" Series* (animated), HBO, 2000.

Narrator, *The Robinita Hood: An Animated Special from the "Happily Ever After: Fairy Tales for Every Child" Series* (animated), HBO, 2000.

Narrator, *Snow Queen: An Animated Special from the "Happily Ever After: Fairy Tales for Every Child" Series* (animated), HBO, 2000.

Narrator, *Steadfast Tin Soldier: An Animated Special from the "Happily Ever After: Fairy Tales for Every Child" Series* (animated), HBO, 2000.

Narrator, *The Valiant Little Tailor: An Animated Special from the "Happily Ever After: Fairy Tales for Every Child" Series* (animated), HBO, 2001.

Inside TV Land: African Americans in Television, TV Land, 2002.

TV Land Moguls, TV Land, 2004.

Inside TV Land: Primetime Politics, TV Land, 2004.

Also appeared in *Mel and Susan Together;* himself, *"Superfly: Ron O'Neal Story": E! True Hollywood Story,* E! Entertainment Television.

Television Appearances; Pilots:
Host, *It Hurts Only When You Laugh,* NBC, 1983.

Television Appearances; Episodic:
The Leslie Uggams Show, 1969.

Robert Barron, "The Wheel Deal," *Julia,* 1969.

Carothers, "The Soft Phase of Peace," *Marcus Welby, M.D.* (also known as *Robert Young, Family Doctor*), 1970.

Dr. Franklin, "Chain Letter," *All in the Family,* CBS, 1975.

Fred's lawyer, "Steinberg and Son," *Sanford & Son,* 1975.

Dr. Franklin, "Chain Letter," *All in the Family,* 1975.

Charles Thompson, "George Won't Talk," *The Jeffersons,* 1975.

Fishbone, "Requiem for a Wino," *Good Times,* 1977.

The Tonight Show Starring Johnny Carson, NBC, 1979.

Frank Belloque, "The Kinfolk/Sis and the Slicker/Moonlight and Moonshine: Parts 1 & 2," *The Love Boat,* ABC, 1980.

Allan Curtis, "Two Grapes on the Vine/Aunt Sylvia/Deductible Divorce," *The Love Boat,* ABC, 1981.

Barbara Mandrell and the Mandrell Sisters, 1981.

Host, *Saturday Night Live* (also known as *SNL*), 1983.

Frank Stoner, "Shadow Play," *Hotel* (also known as *Arthur Hailey's "Hotel"*), ABC, 1986.

The Bob Monkhouse Show, 1986.

Leon, *Sister Kate,* ABC, 1989.

Sam, *Carol & Company,* NBC, 1990.

Dean Winston, "To Be Continued," *A Different World,* NBC, 1991.

Dean Winston, "Never Can Say Goodbye," *A Different World,* NBC, 1991.

Kenneth Rollins, "Diet, Diet My Darling," *L.A. Law,* 1992.

Professor Murphy, "Really Gross Anatomy," *A Different World,* NBC, 1992.

Ted Sill, *Jack's Place,* 1992.

Father Morrissey, "Miracle Cure," *Diagnosis Murder,* CBS, 1993.

Dr. Arthur Hemmings, "A Question of Ethics," *Saved by the Bell: The College Years,* NBC, 1993.

Eugene Sayers, "Who Killed the Fashion King?," *Burke's Law,* CBS, 1994.

Storytime, PBS, 1994.

Mr. Pete Fletcher, "You'd Better Shop Around," *The Fresh Prince of Bel-Air,* NBC, 1994.

Voice of himself, "My Shadow," *Reading Rainbow,* PBS, 1994.

Professor Bernard Slater, "Porky's Revenge," *Sparks,* UPN, 1996.

Martin Woolridge, "Christmas," *Promised Land* (also known as *Home of the Brave*), CBS, 1996.

Dr. Baxter, "Goode Day," *Goode Behavior,* 1997.

Judge Dawes, "Jones vs. God," *Touched by an Angel,* CBS, 1997.

Mr. Brown, "Monster," *The Outer Limits* (also known as *The New Outer Limits*), 1998.

Arthur, Dee's father, "All This and Turkey, Too," *Moesha,* UPN, 2000.

Cody Grant, "Every Pictures Tells a Story," *8 Simple Rules … for Dating My Teenage Daughter* (also known as *8 Simple Rules*), ABC, 2003.

Judge Barnett, "To Know Her," *Century City,* CBS, 2004.

Larry King Live, CNN, 2005.

"Network Notes," *TV Land Confidential,* TV Land, 2005.

"When Real Life and Screen Life Collide," *TV Land Confidential,* TV Land, 2005.

"Top 10 TV Spinoffs," *TV Land's Top Ten,* TV Land, 2006.

Gylne tider, 2006, 2007.

Also appeared in *Dinah; Jim Nabors' Show.*

Television Executive Producer; Series:

Executive producer, *The Robert Guillaume Show,* ABC, 1989.

Television Executive Producer; Movies:

(With Phil Margo) *The Kid with the 200 I.Q.,* NBC, 1983.

The Fantastic World of D. C. Collins, 1984.

Television Work; Specials:

Producer and director, *John Grin's "Christmas"* (also known as *Christmas*), ABC, 1986.

Co–executive producer, *SST: Screen, Stage, Television,* 1989.

RECORDINGS

Taped Readings:

(With Christopher Noth) *Kiss the Girls,* Time Warner AudioBook, 1995.

Video Games:

Voice of Rafiki, *The Lion King,* 1994.

Voice, *Extreme Skate Adventure* (also known as *Disney's "Extreme Skate Adventure"*), 2003.

Voice of Dr. Eli Vance, *Half–Life 2,* Sierra Studios, 2004.

(English version) Voice of Raifiki, *Kingdom Hearts II* (also known as *Kingudamu hatsu*), Square Enix, 2005.

Voice of Dr. Eli Vance, *Half–Life 2: Episode One,* Electronic Arts, 2006.

Voice of Dr. Eli Vance, *Half–Life 3: Episode Two,* Electronic Arts, 2007.

Music Videos:

Appeared in P. Diddy's "Diddy."

WRITINGS

Autobiography:

(With David Ritz) *Guillaume: A Life,* University of Missouri Press, 2002.

OTHER SOURCES

Books:

Contemporary Black Biography, Vol. 48, Thomson Gale, 2005.

Periodicals:

Jet, October 11, 1999, p. 32; December 11, 2000, p. 30.

People Weekly, October 11, 1999, p. 77.

TV Guide, March 27, 1999.

GULZAR, Melanie
   See BROWN, Melanie

GUY, Jasmine 1964–

PERSONAL

Born March 10, 1964, in Boston, MA; daughter of William (a Baptist minister and college instructor in religion and philosophy) and Jaye (a high school English teacher; maiden name, Rudolph) Guy; married Terrence Duckette (an investment broker), August 22, 1998; children: Imani. *Education:* Studied at Alvin Ailey Dance Theatre, New York, NY.

Addresses: *Agent*—Stone Manners Talent and Literary, 900 Broadway, Suite 803, New York, NY 10003. *Manager*—Kass and Stokes Management, 9229 Sunset Blvd., Suite 504, Los Angeles, CA 90069.

Career: Actress, dancer, singer, songwriter, writer, and director. American Dance Theatre, artist with second and third companies, c. 1981–83; also performed with Atlanta Ballet Junior Company and Alvin Ailey Dance Theatre. Taught dance to underprivileged children.

Awards, Honors: Image Awards, outstanding lead actress in a comedy series, National Association for the Advancement of Colored People, 1990, 1991, 1992, 1993, 1994, 1995, all for *A Different World;* Image Award nomination, outstanding supporting actress in a drama series, 1996, for *Melrose Place;* Image Award nomination, outstanding lead actress in a television movie, miniseries, or drama special, 1997, for *America's Dream;* Imagination Award nomination, outstanding supporting actress in a drama series, 2005, for *Dead Like Me.*

CREDITS

Film Appearances:
Dina, *School Daze,* Columbia, 1988.
Biao cheng (also known as *Runaway, Runaway Blues,* and *Slake's Limbo*), 1989.
Dominique LaRue, *Harlem Nights,* Paramount, 1989.
Herself, *Time Out: The Truth About HIV, AIDS, and You* (short), Paramount, 1992.
Lena, *Boy Meets Girl,* 1993.
Blossom, *Kla$h* (also known as *Klash*), 1995.
Voice of Sawyer (speaking), *Cats Don't Dance,* Warner Bros., 1997.
Madeline, Columbia TriStar, 1998.
Linda, *Guinevere,* Miramax, 1999.
Sylvia, *Lillie,* Universal, 1999.
Tina, *Diamond Men,* 2000.
The Law of Enclosures, 2000.
Nikki, *Dying on the Edge,* 2001.
Reader, *Unchained Memories: Readings from the Slave Narratives* (documentary), 2002.
Herself, *Tupac: Resurrection* (documentary), Paramount, 2003.
Herself, *TV in Black: The First Fifty Years* (documentary), 2004.
Herself, *College Daze* (documentary short), Columbia TriStar Home Entertainment, 2005.
Herself, *Birth of a Nation: The Making of "School Daze"* (documentary short), Columbia TriStar Home Entertainment, 2005.
Herself, *Dead Like Me ... Again* (documentary short), Metro–Goldwyn–Mayer Home Entertainment, 2005.
Voice of Ephigenie Mukanyandwi, *Rwanda Rising,* 2007.
Herself, *Angels Can't Help But Laugh* (documentary), 2007.
Cynthia, *Tru Loved,* 2007.

Also appeared in *The Altoona Riding Club.*

Television Appearances; Series:
Dancer, *Fame,* 1982.

Whitley Marion Gilbert Wayne *A Different World,* NBC, 1987–93.
Roxy Harris, *Dead Like Me,* Showtime, 2003–2004.

Television Appearances; Miniseries:
Bank teller, *At Mother's Request,* CBS, 1987.
Easter, *Queen* (also known as *Alex Haley's "Queen"*), CBS, 1993.
Family member, *A Century of Women,* CNN, 1994.
Juliet Mercier, *Feast of All Saints* (also known as *Anne Rice's "The Feast of All Saints"*), Showtime, 2001.

Television Appearances; Movies:
Teresa Hopkins, *A Killer Among Us,* NBC, 1990.
Alice Nichols, *Stompin at the Savoy,* CBS, 1992.
Elna Du Vaul, "The Boy Who Painted Christ Black," *America's Dream,* HBO, 1996.
Darnell Russell, *Perfect Crime,* USA Network, 1997.
Ruby Moore, *Carrie,* NBC, 2002.

Television Appearances; Specials:
(Uncredited) Herself, *Uptown Comedy Express,* 1987.
Charlie, "Runaway," *WonderWorks,* PBS, 1989.
Best Catches, CBS, 1989.
Funny Women of Television: A Museum of Television & Radio Tribute (also known as *The Funny Women of Television*), NBC, 1991.
Gladys Knight's Holiday Family Reunion Concert, 1991.
Host, *Six Comics in Search of a Generation,* 1992.
Addicted to Fame, NBC, 1994.
Voice, *Going, Going, Almost Gone! Animals in Danger* (also known as *The World Wildlife Fund Presents: "Going, Going, Almost Gone! Animals in Danger"*), HBO, 1994.
Great American Music: A Salute to Fast Cars, Family Channel, 1994.
Growing Up Funny, Lifetime, 1994.
The Soul Train 25th Anniversary Hall of Fame Special, CBS, 1995.
Intimate Portrait: Queen Latifah, Lifetime, 1996.
Live Broadway USA, syndicated, 1998.
Bob Fosse: The E! True Hollywood Story, E! Entertainment Television, 1999.
Host, *An Evening of Stars: A Celebration of Educational Excellence Benefiting the United Negro College Fund,* Black Entertainment Television and syndicated, 1999.
Voice of Frog Princess Lylah, *Frog Princess: An Animated Special from the "Happily Ever After: Fairy Tales for Every Child"* Series (animated), HBO, 2000.
It's Black Entertainment, Showtime, 2000.
Broadway on Broadway, NBC, 2000.
Just Cause, Oxygen, 2001.
Intimate Portrait: Jasmine Guy, Lifetime, 2001.
Inside TV Land: Taboo TV, TV Land, 2002.

Intimate Portrait: Tisha Campbell–Martin, Lifetime, 2002.
Intimate Portrait: Isabel Sanford, Lifetime, 2003.
Dorothy Dandridge: An American Beauty, 2003.
TV's Most Memorable Weddings, NBC, 2003.
50 Most Wicked Women of Primetime, E! Entertainment Television, 2004.
I Was a Network Star, 2006.

Television Appearances; Awards Presentations:
16th Annual Black Filmmakers Hall of Fame, syndicated, 1989.
The 21st Annual NAACP Image Awards, NBC, 1989.
The 3rd Annual Soul Train Music Awards, syndicated, 1989.
The 41st Annual Emmy Awards, Fox, 1989.
The 3rd Annual American Comedy Awards, ABC, 1989.
The 22nd Annual NAACP Image Awards, NBC, 1990.
The Fifth Annual Stellar Gospel Music Awards, syndicated, 1990.
The 63rd Annual Academy Awards Presentation, ABC, 1991.
Presenter, *The 3rd Annual International Rock Awards,* 1991.
Soul Train Comedy Awards, 1992.
Presenter, *The 14th Annual CableACE Awards,* 1993.
Presenter, *The 25th NAACP Image Awards,* NBC, 1993.
The 26th Annual NAACP Image Awards, NBC, 1994.
Presenter, *The Fourth Annual Trumpet Awards,* 1996.
The 56th Annual Primetime Emmy Awards, ABC, 2004.
The 2005 Trumpet Awards, TBS, 2005.
The 2007 Trumpet Awards, TBS, 2007.

Television Appearances; Pilots:
Fame, 1982.
Lena, *Boy Meets Girl,* NBC, 1993.

Television Appearances; Episodic:
Gloria, "Out of the Past, *The Equalizer,* CBS, 1986.
Kayla Samuels, "Love at First Fight," *The Fresh Prince of Bel–Air,* NBC, 1991.
Caitlin Mills, "Bye, Bye, Baby," *Melrose Place,* Fox, 1995.
Caitlin Mills, "They Shoot Mothers, Don't They? Parts 1 & 2," *Melrose Place,* Fox, 1995.
Kathleen, "Sympathy for the Devil," *Touched by an Angel,* CBS, 1995.
LaVonna Runnels, "Leavin' Can Wait," *NYPD Blue,* ABC, 1995.
Voice, "Rumpelstiltskin," *Happily Ever After: Fairy Tales for Every Child* (animated), HBO, 1995.
Attorney Angela Winters, "The People vs. Lois Lane: Parts 1 & 2," *Lois & Clark: The New Adventures of Superman,* ABC, 1996.
Dr. Jessica Bryce, "Shrink to Fit," *Living Single* (also known as *My Girls*), Fox, 1996.
Kathleen, "Lost and Found," *Touched by an Angel,* CBS, 1996.

Washington, "The Heist," *The Outer Limits* (also known as *The New Outer Limits*), syndicated and Showtime, 1996.
Kathleen, "Clipped Wings," *Touched by an Angel,* CBS, 1997.
The Rosie O'Donnell Show, syndicated, 1997.
Paige, "Two Men and a Baby," *Malcolm & Eddie,* UPN, 1998.
Blue, *Any Day Now,* 1999.
Allegra, "Boys Can't Help It," *Ladies Man,* CBS, 1999.
Allegra, "Jimmy's Song," *Ladies Man,* CBS, 1999.
Allegra, "Neutered Jimmy," *Ladies Man,* CBS, 1999.
Amanda, "A Beautiful Day," *Partners,* 1999.
Courtney Goode, estranged wife of Johnnie B. Goode, "The Music in Me," *Linc,* Showtime, 2000.
Herself, "Humph! Humph! Humph!," *Between the Lions,* PBS, 2001.
Voice of Ava, Queen of Symmetria, "Secrets of Symmetria," *Cyberchase* (animated), PBS, 2002.
Delilah, "Lights, Camera, Action," *The Parkers,* UPN, 2002.
The Wayne Brady Show, syndicated, 2004.
Tavis Smiley, PBS, 2004.
Dennis Miller, CNBC, 2005.
"Network Notes," *TV Land Confidential,* TV Land, 2005.
"Being Bad Behind the Scenes," *TV Land Confidential,* TV Land, 2005.
In the Mix (also known as *In the Cutz*), Urban America, 2006.
Pistache, "Checkin' Out," *That's So Raven* (also known as *That's So Raven!*), Disney Channel, 2006.

Also appeared in *Loving,* ABC; *Ryan's Hope,* ABC; *Hollywood Squares; Win, Lose, or Draw;* as herself, "Diahann Carroll," *Celebrity Profile,* E! Entertainment Television.

Television Director; Episodic:
A Different World, NBC, 1992.

Stage Appearances:
A crow, a Kalidah, and a citizen of the Emerald City, *The Wiz,* Majestic Theatre, New York City, 1975, later Lunt–Fontanne Theatre, New York City, 1984.
Mickey, waitress, and Annie (understudy), *Leader of the Pack,* Ambassador Theatre, New York City, 1985.
Diana Ross, Tina Turner, and Annette Funicello, *Beehive,* Village Gate Upstairs, New York City, 1986.
Betty Rizzo, *Grease,* Eugene O'Neill Theatre, New York City, 1997.
Velma Kelly, *Chicago,* Las Vegas, NV, 1999.
Velma Kelly, *Chicago,* Shubert Theatre, New York City, 2000.
Jessie Brewster, *The Violet Hour,* Biltmore Theatre, New York City, 2003.
Agnes, *The Fourposter,* Wilmington, DE, 2005.

Also appeared in *Dancin' in the Street,* Boston, MA.

Major Tours:
Betty Rizzo, *Grease,* 1996–97.
Velma Kelly, *Chicago,* U.S. cities, 1997.

Also toured as in *The Wiz,* United States and Japan; and *Bubbling Brown Sugar,* Europe.

RECORDINGS

Albums:
Jasmine Guy, Warner Bros., 1990.

Also recorded *Leader of the Pack* (original cast recording), Elektra.

Music Videos:
"Liberian Girl," *Michael Jackson: HIStory on Film— Volume II,* Sony Music, 1997.

Also appeared in Melba Moore's "Lift Every Voice."

WRITINGS

Television Episodes:
"The Power of the Pen," *A Different World,* NBC, 1990.
"War and Peace," *A Different World,* NBC, 1991.
"Baby, It's Cold Outside," *A Different World,* NBC, 1992.

Film Songs:
Gremlins 2: The New Batch, 1990.

Books:
Afeni Shakur: Evolution of a Revolutionary, Pocket, 2004.

Also writer of short stories and poems.

OTHER SOURCES

Books:
Contemporary Black Biography, Volume 2, Gale Research, 1992.
Notable Black American Women, Book 3, Gale Group, 2002.

Periodicals:
Ebony, June, 1988.
Ebony Man, May, 1989.
Essence, March, 1997, p. 71; October, 2003, p. 152.
Faces International, Fall, 1991.
Gavin Report, April 26, 1991.
Jet, August 23, 1999, p. 45.
Today's Black Woman, June, 1995.

Electronic:
Jasmine Guy Website, http://www.jasmineguy.org, September 10, 2007.

H

HAIDUK, Stacy 1968–

PERSONAL

Born April 24, 1968, in Grand Rapids, MI; daughter of two teachers; married Bradford Tatum (an actor, director, and writer). *Education:* Studied with the Joffrey Ballet, New York, NY; studied acting in New York City. *Avocational Interests:* Dance, reading poetry, writing, and painting.

Addresses: *Manager*—Brad Warshaw Management, Los Angeles, CA.

Career: Actress. Appeared in television commercials; previously worked as a dancer in music videos, bartender, and restaurant hostess.

CREDITS

Film Appearances:
Laundromat lady, *Magic Sticks,* 1987.
Alison, *Steel and Lace,* Fries Entertainment, 1990.
Beth, *Luther the Geek,* 1990.
Julia, *Little City,* Miramax, 1998.
Ally "Al" Malone, *Desert Thunder,* 1998.
Anna McAffery, *Standing on Fishes,* 1999.
(Scenes deleted) Soap opera nurse, *Nurse Betty* (also known as *Nurse Betty—Gefahrliche traume*), 2000.
Ilona, *Gabriela,* Power Point Films, 2001.
West, *Salt,* 2006.
Lela, *The Mansfield 12,* 2007.
Janet, *Victim,* 2007.
Bernice Lowe, *Within,* Power Point Films, 2008.

Film Work:
Producer, *Salt,* 2006.

Television Appearances; Series:
Lana Lang, *Superboy* (also known as *The Adventures of Superboy*), syndicated 1988–92.
Rhea McPherson, *The Round Table,* NBC, 1992.
Lieutenant Commander Katie Hitchcock, *SeaQuest DSV* (also known as *SeaQuest 2032*), NBC, 1993–94.
Lillie Langtry, *Kindred: The Embraced,* Fox, 1996.
Colleen Patterson, *Melrose Place,* Fox, 1997.
Hannah Nichols, *All My Children,* ABC, 2007.

Television Appearances; Miniseries:
Alexa Windom, *Final Approach,* Hallmark Channel, 2008.

Television Appearances; Movies:
Claire (Jane Olsen in German version), *Sketch Artist,* Showtime, 1992.
Lieutenant Commander Katie Hitchcock, *SeaQuest DSV,* NBC, 1993.
Raphaella Phillips, *A Perfect Stranger* (also known as *Danielle Steele's "A Perfect Stranger,"* NBC, 1994.
Jessica, *Yesterday's Target,* 1996.
Lena Girard, *The Beneficiary,* HBO, 1997.
Jennifer Carter, *The Darwin Conspiracy,* UPN, 1999.
Monica Angelini, *Jane Doe: Til Death Do Us Part,* Hallmark Channel, 2005.
Savannah, *Attack of the Sabertooth,* Sci–Fi Channel, 2005.
Shawna, *The Sitter,* 2007.

Television Appearances; Pilots:
Stephanie Ridgeway, *Bouncers,* UPN, 1997.

Television Appearances; Episodic:
Claire David, "Stormy Mikey," *Parker Lewis Can't Lose* (also known as *Parker Lewis*), Fox, 1991.
Lilly, "Dream Lover," *Route 66,* NBC, 1993.
Janice Deluca, "Chicago Holiday: Parts 1 & 2," *Due South* (also known as *Direction: Sud*), CTV and CBS, 1994.

Sandy Maddox, "The Sandman," *C–16: FBI* (also known as *C–16*), ABC, 1997.
Pamela Smith, "Danger Zone," *Nash Bridges* (also known as *Bridges*), CBS, 1998.
Rosalyn Stone, "Encore," *Brimstone,* Fox, 1998.
Andrea, "Do the Right Thing," *Profiler,* NBC, 1998.
Guardian of the Urn, "Feats of Clay," *Charmed,* The WB, 1999.
Rosalyn Smith, "It's a Helluva Life," *Brimstone,* Fox, 1999.
Rosalyn Smith, "The Mourning After," *Brimstone,* Fox, 1999.
Veronica Archer, "Dead End on Blank Street," *The Sentinel,* UPN, 1999.
Margaret "Maggie" Waterston, "All Things," *The X–Files,* Fox, 2000.
Mrs. Evans, "Mother's Day," *The Division* (also known as *Heart of the City*), 2001.
Impaled mom, "The Crossing," *ER,* NBC, 2001.
Dawn Kaye, "Body Count," *CSI: Miami,* CBS, 2003.
Melissa Dorn, "My Other Left Foot," *Navy NCIS: Naval Criminal Investigative Service* (also known as *NCIS* and *NCIS: Naval Criminal Investigative Service*), CBS, 2004.
Barb Furillo, "Mothers," *Wildfire,* ABC Family, 2005.
Mrs. Cartland, "The Elephant in the Room," *Crossing Jordan,* NBC, 2006.
Anne Bowen in 1984, "The River," *Cold Case,* CBS, 2006.
Debra Archerson, "Sweet 16," *CSI: NY* (also known as *CSI: New York*), CBS, 2006.
FBI agent, "Don't Look Back," *Heroes,* NBC, 2006.
FBI agent, "Seven Minutes to Midnight," *Heroes,* NBC, 2006.
FBI agent, "Godsend," *Heroes,* NBC, 2006.

Also appeared in *Another World,* NBC.

RECORDINGS

Music Videos:
Appeared in music videos for Sawyer Brown, Herb Alpert, and Laura Branigan.

HAMMER, Ben 1925–

PERSONAL

Full name, Benjamin Hammer; born December 8, 1925, in Brooklyn, New York, NY; son of Morris and Mollie (maiden name, Nadler) Hammer; married Dorothea (a potter), December 21, 1958; children: Marlayna, Paula. *Education:* Brooklyn College, B.A., 1948. *Avocational Interests:* Motorcycles, airplanes, travel.

Career: Actor. *Military service:* U.S. Army, staff sergeant, 1945–46.

Member: Actors' Equity Association, Screen Actors Guild, American Federation of Television and Radio Artists, Academy of Motion Picture Arts and Sciences, Academy of Television Arts and Sciences.

CREDITS

Stage Appearances:
Mr. Otto Frank, *The Diary of Anne Frank,* Cort Theatre, New York City, 1955–57, Ambassador Theatre, New York City, 1957.
Pavlat, *The Great Sebastians,* American National Theatre and Academy (ANTA) Playhouse, New York City, 1956, Coronet Theatre, New York City, 1956.
Understudy, *The Tenth Man,* Booth Theatre, New York City, 1959–61, Ambassador Theatre, 1961.
Old soldier and ordinance officer, *Mother Courage and Her Children* (also known as *Mother Courage*), Martin Beck Theatre, New York City, 1963.
Prisoner, *The Deputy,* Brooks Atkinson Theatre, New York City, 1964.
Fray Vincente de Valverde, *The Royal Hunt of the Sun,* American National Theatre and Academy (ANTA) Playhouse, 1965–66.
Thomas A. Morgan and understudy for the roles of Edward Teller and John Lansdale, *In the Matter of J. Robert Oppenheimer,* Lincoln Center, Vivian Beaumont Theater, New York City, 1969.
Ambassador of the Soviet Union, *Murderous Angels,* Phoenix Theatre, Playhouse Theatre, New York City, 1971–72.
Thomas Putnam, *The Crucible,* Lincoln Center, Vivian Beaumont Theater, 1972.
Henry IV, Part I, Mark Taper Forum, Los Angeles, 1972.
D. P. and Moshe Dayan, *Golda,* Morosco Theatre, New York City, 1977–78.
Earl of Derby, *The Tragedy of Richard III,* New York Shakespeare Festival, Joseph Papp Public Theater, Delacorte Theater, New York City, 1990.
Elihu, *Invention for Fathers and Sons,* American Jewish Theatre, New York City, 1992.
Vassily Vorolilch Smukov, *Slavs!,* New York Theatre Workshop, 1994–95.
Ferapont, *Three Sisters,* Criterion Theatre Center Stage Right, New York City, 1997.
More Stately Mansions, New York Theatre Workshop, beginning 1997.
Gabe, *The Gathering,* Cort Theatre, 2001.
Sewerman, *The Madwoman of Chaillot,* the Colleagues Theatre Company, Neighborhood Playhouse, New York City, 2001.
Enoch Cryder, *A Last Dance for Sybil,* New Federal Theatre, New York City, 2002.

Reb Bassevi and Elijah the prophet, *The Golem,* Culture Project, Manhattan Ensemble Theatre, New York City, 2002.

Max Aberdam, *Meshugah* (also known as *Meshugga*), Naked Angels at the Kirk at Theatre Row, New York City, 2003.

Mr. Green, *Visiting Mr. Green,* Two River Theater Company, Red Bank, NJ, 2005, English Theatre, Frankfurt, Germany, c. 2006.

Appeared in other productions, including *Tamara,* Los Angeles production; as well as *Broadway Bound* and *Camping with Henry and Tom.*

Major Tours:
Come Back, Little Sheba, 1950–51.
The Diary of Anne Frank, Theatre Guild tour, 1957–58.

Film Appearances:
Zabriskie Point, Metro–Goldwyn–Mayer, 1970.
Second doctor, *Johnny Got His Gun* (also known as *Dalton Trumbo's "Johnny Got His Gun," E deram-ihe uma espingarda, E Johnny prese il fucile, Johnny cogio su fusil, Johnny poszedl na wojne, Johnny s'en va–t–en guerre, Johnny vai a guerra, Johnny zieht in den Krieg,* and *Sotilaspoika*), Cinemation Industries, 1971.
Herb Kline, *Invasion of the Bee Girls* (also known as *Graveyard Tramps*), Centaur, 1973.
Vicar, *Haunts* (also known as *The Veil*), Intercontinental Releasing Corporation, 1977.
Nichols, *The Competition* (also known as *A competicao, Das grosse Finale, El concurso, Kilpailu, Konkurs, La competicion,* and *Un amor em competicao*), Columbia, 1980.
The First Family, Warner Bros., 1980.
Young Dar's father, *The Beastmaster* (also known as *Beastmaster—Der Befreier, Dar l'invincible, El senor de las bestias, Kaan principe guerriero, Kungasonen, O guerreiro sagrado, Varvos mahitis, Voittamaton kostaja,* and *Wladca zwierzat*), Metro–Goldwyn–Mayer, 1982.
Danny's father, *Running Hot* (also known as *Highway to Hell*), New Line Cinema, 1984.
Dr. Goldman, *Jagged Edge* (also known as *A double tranchant, Al filo de la sospecha, Das Messer, Doppio taglio, I akri tou nimatos, Kniven aer enda vittnet, Lahav Meshunan, Noz,* and *Viiltaevae terae*), Columbia, 1985.
Hans (the maitre d'), *Mannequin* (also known as *Ikkunaprinsessa, Manekin, Manequim, Maniqui,* and *Skyltdockan*), Twentieth Century–Fox, 1987.
Reunion, 1988.
Histoires d'Amerique (also known as *American Stories, Food, Family and Philosophy, Family and Philosophy, Geschichten aus Amerika,* and *Histoires d'Amerique: Family and Philosophy*), 1988, Metro Pictures, 1990.

Hal, *Survival Quest* (also known as *Camp der verlorenen Teufel*), Metro–Goldwyn–Mayer, 1989.
Dr. Koch, *Crazy People* (also known as *Crazy People—hulluja ihmisiae, Gente loca, Gente louca, Les fous de la pub, Loco, loco, pero no tanto, Nichts ist irrer als die Wahrheit, Pubblifollia,* and *Szalency*), Paramount, 1990.
Cristina's father, *Miliardi* (also known as *Billions, Millions, Milhoes,* and *Miliardi/Millions*), Cecchi Gori Group/Penta Films, 1991.
Chaim Pearlman, *Nick and Rachel,* 1996.
Judge Weisman, *Sleepers* (also known as *Kardes gibiydiler, Katuvarpuset, La correction, Los hijos de la calle, Pokoli lecke, Sentimento de revolta,* and *Sleepers—A vinganca adormecida*), Warner Bros., 1996.
Moses Weiss, *The Last New Yorker,* Brink Films, 1996.
Vladimire Tiomkin, *Subterfuge* (also known as *Into Deep—Jagd in der Tiefe*), Avalanche Home Entertainment, 1996.

Television Appearances; Series:
Oakley Reynolds, *The Edge of Night,* CBS, 1962.
Hal Conrad, *Search for Tomorrow,* CBS, 1974.
Chief Dwight Buchanan, *Holmes and Yo–Yo* (also known as *Holmes and Yoyo*), ABC, 1976.
Max Chapman, *Guiding Light,* CBS, 1977–78.
Striker Bellman, *Another World* (also known as *Another World: Bay City*), NBC, 1979.
Captain Alex Morgan, *The Young and the Restless* (also known as *Y&R, The Innocent Years, Atithasa niata, Les feux de l'amour, Schatten der Leidenschaft,* and *Tunteita ja tuoksuja*), CBS, c. 1982–83.
Judge Herman Mooney and Judge Cornell, *Law & Order* (also known as *Law & Order Prime*), NBC, 1991–2002.

Television Appearances; Miniseries:
The Law, NBC, 1975.
Dr. Palmer, *The Amazing Howard Hughes* (also known as *Der Legendaere Howard Hughes, Howard Hughes—Eine Legende, Zadziwiajacy Howard Hughes,* and *Zwariowany Howard Hughes*), CBS, 1977.
Beggarman, Thief, NBC, 1979.
Sumner Welles, *The Winds of War* (also known as *Der Feuersturm, Krigets vindar, Le souffle de la guerre, Soden tuulet,* and *Vientos de guerra*), ABC, 1983.

Television Appearances; Movies:
Lieutenant colonel Leacock, *The Execution of Private Slovik* (also known as *The Execution of Private Eddie Slovik, Arkebuseringen av menige Slovik, Execute pour desertion, L'execution du soldat Slovik, La ejecucion del soldado Slovik,* and *Teloitusjoukon edessae*), broadcast on *NBC Wednesday Night at the Movies,* NBC, 1974.

Inchon admiral, *Collision Course: Truman vs. Mac-Arthur* (also known as *Collision Course*), ABC, 1975.

Dr. Feinberg, *Griffin and Phoenix: A Love Story* (also known as *Griffin and Phoenix, Today Is Forever, Jaeljet hiekassa, Kort lycka, Quando passi da queste parti ...,* and *Siempre hay tiempo para amar*), ABC, 1976.

Yaakobi, *Victory at Entebbe* (also known as *La lunga notte di Entebbe, Segern vid Entebbe, Unternehmen Entebbe, Victoire a Entebbe, Victoria en Entebbe,* and *Voitto Entebbessae*), ABC, 1976.

Oglethorpe, *Confessions of a Married Man* (also known as *Bekenntnisse eines Ehemanns*), ABC, 1983.

Also appeared in *An Affair to Forget.*

Television Appearances; Episodic:

"Jetfighter," *ABC Album* (also known as *The Plymouth Playhouse*), ABC, 1953.

"Wings over Barriers," *Goodyear Playhouse* (also known as *Goodyear Television Playhouse*), NBC, 1953.

Doctor, "The Return," *Johnny Staccato* (also known as *Staccato*), NBC, 1959.

Talaferio, "The Ivy League Bank Robbers," *M Squad* (also known as *Dezernat "M"*), NBC, 1959.

Dr. John Harvey, "Call from Tomorrow," *Alcoa Presents: One Step Beyond* (also known as *Alcoa Presents* and *One Step Beyond*), ABC, 1960.

Professor John Wyler, "Spell of Murder," *Peter Gunn*, NBC, 1960.

Brecht, "Line of Duty," *87th Precinct*, NBC, 1961.

Dan Gordon, "Dialogues with Death," *Thriller* (also known as *Boris Karloff's "Thriller"* and *Boris Karloff presenta*), NBC, 1961.

Mr. Packer, "I before E Except after C," *East Side/West Side*, CBS, 1963.

Spragg, "A Messenger to Everyone," *The Nurses* (also known as *The Doctors and the Nurses*), CBS, 1964.

Bill Simpson, *Another World* (also known as *Another World: Bay City*), NBC, 1964.

Callao, "Elena," *Mission: Impossible*, CBS, 1966.

Flagg, "An Inside Job," *Ironside* (also known as *The Raymond Burr Show*), NBC, 1967.

Mr. Mitchell, "The Honeymooners: Hair to a Fortune," *The Jackie Gleason Show* (also known as *The Color Honeymooners*), CBS, 1967.

Paul G. Fremont, "The Phony Police Racket," *Dragnet '67* (also known as *Dragnet*), NBC, 1967.

Quincey King, "Vengeance Trail," *The Virginian* (also known as *The Men from Shiloh*), NBC, 1967.

Fleming, "Robert Phillips vs. the Man," *Ironside* (also known as *The Raymond Burr Show*), NBC, 1968.

Tom Campbell, "The Land of the Fox," *The Outsider*, NBC, 1968.

Mr. Farris, *Days of Our Lives* (also known as *Cruise of Deception: Days of Our Lives, Days, DOOL, Des jours et des vies, Horton–sagaen, I gode og onde dager, Los dias de nuestras vidas, Meres agapis, Paeivien viemaeae, Vaara baesta aar, Zeit der Sehnsucht,* and *Zile din viata noastra*), NBC, 1968.

Quinn, "My Friend, My Enemy," *Bonanza* (also known as *Ponderosa*), NBC, 1969.

Bryan Fox, "At the Edge of the Night," *The Young Lawyers*, ABC, 1970.

Plainclothes man, "The Ambassador's Daughter," *Monty Nash*, syndicated, 1971.

Ron Hentzel, "Voice from a Nightmare," *Owen Marshall: Counselor at Law*, ABC, 1971.

Henry Cole, "The Loose Connection," *Barnaby Jones*, CBS, 1973.

Prosecutor, "Murder in Movieland," *Hawkins*, CBS, 1973.

Sergeant Glaser, "The Ten Year Honeymoon," *Police Story*, NBC, 1973.

"Girl on the Run," *Jigsaw*, ABC, 1973.

"Love and Carmen Lopez/Love and the Cover/Love and the Cryin' Cowboy," *Love, American Style*, ABC, 1973.

Hank Pritchard, "Race against Time: Parts 1 & 2," *Mannix*, CBS, 1974.

Shaeffer, "A Small Favor for an Old Friend," *Mannix*, CBS, 1974.

Walter Miller, "Smack," *Police Woman*, NBC, 1974.

Arthur Handler, "A Fallen Idol," *Petrocelli*, NBC, 1975.

Bo Willis, "The White Lightning War," *The Six Million Dollar Man* (also known as *Cyborg, De Man van zes miljoen, Der sechs Millionen Dollar Mann, El hombre de los seis millones de dolares, Kuuden miljoonan dollarin mies, L'homme qui valait 3 milliards,* and *L'uomo da sei milioni di dollari*), ABC, 1975.

General Stacey, "Return of the Robot Maker," *The Six Million Dollar Man* (also known as *Cyborg, De Man van zes miljoen, Der sechs Millionen Dollar Mann, El hombre de los seis millones de dolares, Kuuden miljoonan dollarin mies, L'homme qui valait 3 milliards,* and *L'uomo da sei milioni di dollari*), ABC, 1975.

Gus, "From Baltimore to Eternity," *Movin' On*, NBC, 1975.

Mr. Daly, "Labyrinth," *The Streets of San Francisco*, ABC, 1975.

Nick Vane, "Close Cover before Killing," *Kojak*, CBS, 1975.

Sergeant Irv Berman, "The Man in the Shadows," *Police Story*, NBC, 1975.

Alex Kadescho, "Suspect Your Local Police," *Gemini Man*, NBC, 1976.

Alex Ross, "Both Sides of the Law," *Kojak*, CBS, 1976.

Gerald Gardner, "Most Likely to Succeed," *The Streets of San Francisco*, ABC, 1976.

Hendricks, "Mary Had More Than a Little," *Barbary Coast*, ABC, 1976.

George Faylon, "Angel on High," *Charlie's Angels*, ABC, 1978.

"Life on the Line," *The Hardy Boys/Nancy Drew Mysteries* (also known as *The Nancy Drew Mysteries*), ABC, 1978.

Judge Henry Becker, "Nowhere to Run," *Quincy, M.E.* (also known as *Quincy*), NBC, 1979.

State senator Kane, "Last Rights," *Quincy, M.E.* (also known as *Quincy*), NBC, 1980.

"The Millionaire's Life," *Tenspeed and Brown Shoe,* NBC, 1980.

Attorney Ted Marshall, "The Golden Hour," *Quincy, M.E.* (also known as *Quincy*), NBC, 1981.

Mr. Kelleher, "Wax Museum," *The Incredible Hulk,* CBS, 1981.

"A Simple Operation," *CHiPs* (also known as *Chips* and *CHiPs Patrol*), NBC, 1981.

"Old Love," *Barney Miller,* ABC, 1982.

"Jennifer: The Movie," *Jennifer Slept Here,* NBC, 1983.

Army general, "Showdown!," *The A Team,* NBC, 1984.

Bill Drake, "Spontaneous Combustion," *Fame,* syndicated, 1984.

Gregory Paulson, "Double Play," *Simon & Simon,* CBS, 1984.

Porson, "Harts on the Run," *Hart to Hart* (also known as *Hart & Hart, Detectivii Hart, Hart aber herzlich, Par i hjaerter, Par i hjerter,* and *Pour l'amour du risque*), ABC, 1984.

Dr. Francis Watkins, "Where Have All the Children Gone?," *Airwolf* (also known as *Lobo del aire*), CBS, 1985.

Admiral Tucker, "Summit," *Highway to Heaven,* NBC, 1986.

Dr. Perry, "Nightmare," *T. J. Hooker,* ABC, 1986.

Ron Jeffries, "The Whole Truth," *Ed* (also known as *Stuckeyville*), NBC, 2000.

Also appeared in other programs, including *One Life to Live* (also known as *Between Heaven and Hell*), ABC.

Television Appearances; Pilots:
Judge DeKana, "The Marcus–Nelson Murders," *Kojak* (also known as *Kojak: The Marcus–Nelson Murders*), CBS, 1973.

Daniel Bronstein, *Street Killing,* ABC, 1976.

Dr. Bronson, *Freebie and the Bean,* CBS, 1980.

Schrimer, *Cagney & Lacey,* CBS, 1981.

Matthew Cutter, *Advice to the Lovelorn* (also known as *Hymne a l'amour, Lemmenkoukerot,* and *Was dich bewegt*), NBC, 1989.

RECORDINGS

Videos:
Austin Buhler, *MysteryDisc: Murder, Anyone?,* Ghost Dance, 1982.

HARDIN, Jerry 1929–
(Jerry Harden)

PERSONAL

Born November 20, 1929, in Dallas, TX; children: Melora (an actress), Shawn (a producer). *Education:* Southwestern University, B.A., Georgetown, TX; studied at the Royal Academy of Dramatic Art, London, as a Fulbright scholar.

Addresses: *Agent*—Mitchell K. Stubbs and Associates, 8675 West Washington Blvd., Suite 203, Culver City, CA 90232.

Career: Actor.

CREDITS

Film Appearances:
(Uncredited) Niles Penland, *Thunder Road,* United Artists, 1958.

Keats, *Our Time* (also known as *Death of Her Innocence*), 1974.

(Uncredited) Man number two, *Earthquake,* 1974.

Desk sergeant, *Mitchell,* Allied Artists, 1975.

Pastor James Clayton Hewlitt, *Born of Water,* 1976.

General Mason, *Foes,* 1977.

Wilbur, *Wolf Lake* (also known as *The Honor Guard*), 1978.

Map man, *1941,* Universal, 1979.

Patterson, *Head over Heels* (also known as *Chilly Scenes of Winter*), United Artists, 1979.

Cattle buyer, *Heartland,* Levitt–Pickman, 1980.

Harry, *Reds,* Paramount, 1981.

Governor, *Honky Tonk Freeway,* Universal, 1981.

Colonel Sean Patrick, *Missing,* Universal, 1982.

Harry Gondorf, *Tempest,* Columbia, 1982.

Snuffy, *Honkytonk Man,* Warner Bros., 1982.

Masen, *Cujo,* Warner Bros., 1983.

Mr. Dolson, *Mass Appeal,* Universal, 1984.

Warren Williams, *Heartbreakers,* Orion, 1984.

Tony Owens, *The Falcon and the Snowman,* Orion, 1985.

Vic Flint, *Warning Sign,* Twentieth Century–Fox, 1985.

Pinstripe lawyer, *Big Trouble in Little China* (also known as *John Carpenter's "Big Trouble in Little China"*), Twentieth Century–Fox, 1986.

John Lipton, *Wanted: Dead or Alive,* New World Pictures, 1986.

Dean Reilly, *Let's Get Harry* (also known as *The Rescue*), TriStar, 1987.

Reverend Ray Horner, *Valentino Returns,* 1988.

Emerson Capps, *The Milagro Beanfield War,* Universal, 1988.

Brewer, *Little Nikita* (also known as *The Sleepers*), 1988.

The sheriff, *War Party* (also known as *War Game*), 1988.

Thibodeaux, *Blaze,* 1989.

Bennett Fidlow, *Pacific Heights,* 1990.

George Harshaw, *The Hot Spot,* 1990.

Royce McKnight, *The Firm,* Paramount, 1993.

Harley Mason, *The Associate,* Buena Vista, 1996.

Barney DeLaughter, *Ghosts of Mississippi* (also known as *Ghosts from the Past*), Sony Pictures Entertainment, 1996.

Deep Throat, *"The X–Files": The Unopened File,* 1996.

Papa Joe Kiley, *Black Dawn* (also known as *Good Cop, Bad Cop*), Brimstone Entertainment, 1997.

Mr. Sherman, *Certain Guys,* 2000.

Sam Hayes, *Island Prey,* York Entertainment, 2001.

Mr. Sally, *Burl's* (short), 2003.

Jake, *Extreme Dating,* Warner Home Video, 2004.

Nate Salisbury, *Hidalgo* (also known as *Dash*), Buena Vista, 2004.

Pharmacist/clown, *Are We There Yet?,* Columbia, 2005.

Michael Stevens, *Outside a Dream* (short), 2005.

Martin Lennox, *The Last Lullaby,* 2007.

Rex, *You,* 2007.

Also appeared as Pastor James Clayton Hewlitt, *Born of Water.*

Television Appearances; Series:

Wild Bill Weschester, *Filthy Rich,* CBS, 1982–83.

District Attorney Malcolm Gold, *L.A. Law,* NBC, 1986–92.

Deep Throat, *The X–Files,* Fox, 1993–95.

Dr. Cassidy, *Dr. Quinn, Medicine Woman,* CBS, 1993–98.

Dennis Carter, *Melrose Place,* Fox, 1994–95.

Leon Gillenwater, *Orleans,* CBS, 1997.

Television Appearances; Miniseries:

Jonah Comyns, *The Chisholms,* CBS, 1979.

Roots: The Next Generations, ABC, 1979.

General Philip Olafson, *World War III,* NBC, 1982.

Jonah Job, *Celebrity* (also known as *Tommy Thompson's "Celebrity"*), NBC, 1984.

Brock Walters, *Bluegrass,* CBS, 1988.

Reverend Garson Wilson, *Pandora's Clock* (also known as *Doomsday Virus*), NBC, 1996.

Ben Taylor, *From the Earth to the Moon,* HBO, 1998.

Television Appearances; Movies:

Neill, *Hurricane* (also known as *Hurricane Hunters*), ABC, 1974.

Chief Ed Kern, *Guilty or Innocent: The Sam Sheppard Murder Case,* NBC, 1975.

Macklin, *The Oregon Trail,* PBS, 1976.

Manager, *The 3,000 Mile Chase,* NBC, 1977.

Bud Dozier, *Kate Bliss and the Ticker Tape Kid,* ABC, 1978.

Friendly Fire, ABC, 1979.

Sheriff Mel Cobb, *Gideon's Trumpet,* CBS, 1980.

Angel Dusted (also known as *Angel Dust*), NBC, 1981.

Dr. Watson, *The Children Nobody Wanted,* CBS, 1981.

Thou Shalt Not Kill, NBC, 1982.

The Mysterious Two, NBC, 1982.

In Love with an Older Woman, 1982.

Sheriff Bergus, *Attack on Fear,* CBS, 1984.

Dave McDonough, *Do You Remember Love,* CBS, 1985.

District Attorney Malcolm Gold, *L.A. Law,* NBC, 1986.

Earl, *LBJ: The Early Years,* NBC, 1987.

Mayor Artie Lyons, *The Town Bully* (also known as *A Friendly, Quiet Little Town*), ABC, 1988.

Reynolds, *Roots: The Gift,* ABC, 1988.

Roe vs. Wade, NBC, 1989.

Cal, *Hi Honey, I'm Dead,* Fox, 1991.

Lowell, *Plymouth,* ABC, 1991.

Mort Webber, *Murder of Innocence,* CBS, 1993.

T. K. Macready, *Where Are My Children?,* ABC, 1994.

(As Jerry Harden) The doctor, *A Streetcar Named Desire,* 1995.

Slick, *Bermuda Triangle,* ABC, 1996.

Happy Chandler, *Soul of the Game* (also known as *Field of Honour*), HBO, 1996.

Colonel McNally, *The Second Civil War,* HBO, 1997.

Television Appearances; Specials:

Mayor Bob, *Hometown Boy Makes Good,* HBO, 1990.

Inside "The X Files," Fox, 1998.

Television Appearances; Pilots:

District Attorney Malcolm Gold, *L.A. Law,* NBC, 1986.

Television Appearances; Episodic:

Stark, "The Best Laid Plans," *Ironside* (also known as *The Raymond Burr Show*), 1973.

Bob Ranger, "The Foundling," *Gunsmoke* (also known as *Gun Law* and *Marshall Dillon*), 1974.

Doorman, "Accounts Balanced," *Harry O,* 1974.

Rancher Frank Dixon, *Sara,* CBS, 1976.

George Dillard, "Forbidden City," *Harry O,* 1976.

Lewis, "Prisoners of War," *Baa Baa Black Sheep* (also known as *Black Sheep Squadron*), 1976.

Jury foreman, "Jury Duty: Parts 1 & 2," *Family,* 1976.

"Two–Star Killer," *The Feather and Father Gang,* 1976.

Walter Link, "Coulter City Wildcat," *The Rockford Files* (also known as *Jim Rockford, Private Investigator*), 1976.

McEvoy, "The Gardener's Son," *Visions,* 1977.

Psychiatrist, "The Set–Up: Part 2," *Starsky and Hutch,* 1977.

Will Dane, "The Wild Child," *Rafferty,* 1977.

Lieutenant Carson, "Time Out," *The Streets of San Francisco,* 1977.

Knute Jacobs, "The Mayor's Committee from Deer Lick Falls," *The Rockford Files* (also known as *Jim Rockford, Private Investigator*), 1977.

Marton, "The Appointment," *Baretta*, 1978.

Hank Slade, "Mortal Mission," *Little House on the Prairie*, 1979.

Officer Plyler, "Fish Story," *WKRP in Cincinnati*, 1979.

Charlie Wade, "Sliding By," *The White Shadow*, 1979.

"Half Past Noon," *Young Maverick*, 1980.

Mayor Sindell, "Deadlock in Parma," *The Rockford Files* (also known as *Jim Rockford, Private Investigator*), 1980.

Bartender, "Bottom of the Bottle: Part 1," *Knots Landing*, 1980.

Elroy Askew, "Making of a President," *Dallas*, CBS, 1981.

Sheriff Dean, "Sanctuary," *The Incredible Hulk*, 1981.

Mr. Wilson, "Tip Off the Old Block," *Bosom Buddies*, 1982.

Ray Walker, "The First Miracle: Parts 1 & 2," *Father Murphy*, 1982.

Crandall, "Sudden Death," *Scarecrow and Mrs. King*, 1983.

Tim Higgins, "Song of the Wild West," *Highway to Heaven*, 1984.

Orville Kincaid, "What Goes Around Comes Around," *Simon and Simon*, 1984.

Lowell McKenzie, "A Pocketful of Steele," *Remington Steele*, 1984.

Hardin, "Bushido," *Miami Vice*, 1985.

Warden, "Final Escape," *Alfred Hitchcock Presents*, 1985.

Nevada Bob, "Benson the Hero," *Benson*, 1985.

Nevada Bob, "$1,000,000 an Hour," *Benson*, 1985.

Professor Cooper, "Adult Education," *The Golden Girls*, CBS, 1986.

Lyndon B. Johnson, "Profile in Silver," *The Twilight Zone*, 1986.

Gus, "The Test," *Starman*, 1987.

Radue, "When the Bough Breaks," *Star Trek: The Next Generation* (also known as *Star Trek: TNG*), 1988.

Gary, "Little Sister," *The Golden Girls*, CBS, 1989.

Avery Campbell, "The Broker," *Matlock*, CBS, 1990.

"The Gates of Paradise," *Paradise* (also known as *Guns of Paradise*), 1990.

"City of Lost Souls: Parts 1 & 2," *Midnight Caller*, 1991.

Billy, *Evening Shade*, CBS, 1991.

"All God's Children," *I'll Fly Away*, NBC, 1991.

Ed Saxton, "Roberto!—January 27, 1982," *Quantum Leap*, NBC, 1992.

Samuel Clemens/Mark Twain, "Time's Arrow: Parts 1 & 2," *Star Trek: The Next Generation* (also known as *Star Trek: TNG*), 1992.

Billy Reed, "The Torrents of Winter," *Knots Landing*, 1992.

Dr. Graham, "Savor the Veal: Parts 1, 2 & 3," *Who's the Boss?*, 1992.

Dave Tooey, "Frank the Potato Man," *Picket Fences*, CBS, 1992.

Al, "Togetherness," *Mad About You*, NBC, 1993.

Judge Benedict Choate, "To Kill a Billionaire," *Time Trax*, 1993.

Wayne Irig, "The Green, Green Glow of Home," *Lois and Clark: The New Adventures of Superman* (also known as *Lois & Clark* and *The New Adventures of Superman*), ABC, 1993.

Hamish McPherson, "Northern Explosion," *Murder, She Wrote*, CBS, 1994.

Norman Gilford, "A Nest of Vipers," *Murder, She Wrote*, CBS, 1994.

Dennis Carter, "In–Laws and Outlaws," *Melrose Place*, Fox, 1994.

Dennis Carter, "Grand Delusions," *Melrose Place*, Fox, 1994.

Dennis Carter, "And Justice for None," *Melrose Place*, Fox, 1994.

Dennis Carter, "They Shoot Mothers, Don't They?: Part 2," *Melrose Place*, Fox, 1994.

Dr. Neria, "Emanations," *Star Trek: Voyager* (also known as *Voyager*), UPN, 1995.

Bigoted man, *Sisters*, NBC, 1995.

Colonel Sherwood, "All in the Family," *Murphy Brown*, CBS, 1996.

Tom Sampson, "What You Don't Know Can Kill You," *Murder, She Wrote*, CBS, 1996.

Deep Throat, "Musings of a Cigarette Smoking Man," *The X–Files*, Fox, 1996.

Mr. Scrumbus, "Guess Who's Coming to Seder," *Sisters*, NBC, 1996.

"Baby–Sitting," *Orleans*, 1997.

Johnny, the mechanic, "Full Engagement," *JAG*, CBS, 1997.

Minister, "The Affair," *Ally McBeal*, Fox, 1997.

Senator Leason, "Impact," *JAG*, CBS, 1997.

Mr. Conklin, "One Day Out West," *The Magnificent Seven*, CBS, 1998.

Sheriff Dohdig, "Caroline and the Fright before Christmas," *Caroline in the City* (also known as *Caroline*), NBC, 1998.

Thurston Driscoll, "Faces," *Brimstone*, Fox, 1999.

Isaac Clark, "Revelations," *Sliders*, Sci–Fi Channel, 1999.

Judge Kevin Donati, *Family Law*, CBS, 1999.

Deep Throat, "The Sixth Extinction II: Amor Fati," *The X–Files*, Fox, 1999.

(Uncredited) Deep Throat, "The Truth," *The X–Files*, Fox, 2002.

"Age of Consent," *First Monday*, CBS, 2002.

Judge Samuel Prescott, "Lies of Minelli," *Philly*, ABC, 2002.

Sam Hansen, "Oh Mother, Who Art Thou?," *The Division* (also known as *Heart of the City*), Lifetime, 2003.

Sumner Charles, "Adelle Coffin," *Nip/Tuck*, FX Channel, 2003.

Grinds, "Still Bill's Dad," *Still Standing*, CBS, 2004.

Vernon Abbott, "Necessary Risks," *Crossing Jordan*, NBC, 2004.

Also appeared as Reverend Horace Blake, *Dark Justice;* Rex Fuller, "Food," *Strange World;* in "Layin' Track," *Young Maverick.*

Stage Appearances:

H. C. Curry, *The Rainmaker,* Brooks Atkinson Theatre, New York City, 1999.

HARDING, Jeff

PERSONAL

Education: B.A., studio art. *Avocational Interests:* Carpentry and golf.

Career: Actor. Worked behind the scenes in summer stock at Brunswick Music Theatre; taught in Morocco; Palace Theatre, London, England, master carpenter.

CREDITS

Film Appearances:

Policeman number thirteen, *Ragtime* (also known as *Love and Glory*), Paramount, 1981.

Mike Lockwood, *Space Riders,* Lumiere Pictures, 1984.

Scream for Help, Lorimar, 1984.

Brian Ryan, *The Razor's Edge,* Columbia, 1984.

John, *Blood Tracks* (also known as *Heavy Metal*), 1985.

Carson, *The Aviator,* Metro–Goldwyn–Mayer/United Artists Entertainment Company, 1985.

Fitz–Hume's associate, *Spies Like Us,* Warner Bros., 1985.

Doug, *Riders of the Storm* (also known as *The American Way*), Miramax, 1986.

Gerald, *Love Potion* (also known as *Shock Treatment*), 1987.

Sergeant, *A Time of Destiny,* Columbia Pictures, 1988.

Larry DeLeo, *Murder Story,* Academy Entertainment, 1989.

Agent Merrow, *Bullseye!,* 21st Century Pictures Corp., 1990.

Radio announcer, *The Runner* (also known as *Escape from Survival Zone* and *Survival Island*), 1992.

Vice–president number two, *Hackers,* Metro–Goldwyn–Mayer, 1995.

(English version) Voice of Kusangi, *X* (animated; also known as *X/1999* and *X: Their Destiny Was Foreordained 1999*), Manga Video, 1996.

(Uncredited) Newsreader, *Tomorrow Never Dies,* United Artists, 1997.

Tim Ryan, *RPM,* New City Releasing, 1998.

Man at party, *The Misadventures of Margaret* (also known as *Les folies de Margaret*), Metro–Goldwyn–Mayer, 1998.

(English version) Lloyd, *Makyu senjo* (animated), Manga Entertainment, 1998.

Cody, *De–Lovely,* Metro–Goldwyn–Mayer, 2004.

Phil, *Alfie,* Paramount, 2004.

Company director, *The White Countess,* Sony Pictures Classics, 2005.

CIA agent, *Alien Autopsy,* Warner Bros., 2006.

Television Appearances; Series:

Greg, *Timeslip,* YTV, 1985.

Orrin Hudson, *Howard's Way,* BBC, 1989–90.

(English version) Voice, *Moomin* (animated; also known as *I mumindalen* and *Tanoshii Moomin ikka*), 1990.

Tales from the Poop Deck, 1992.

Trainer, BBC, 1992.

General Bill Damon, *The Tomorrow People,* ITV, 1992–95.

Ed Winchester, *The Fast Show* (also known as *Brilliant!*), BBC, 1994.

Television Appearances; Miniseries:

United States consul, *The First Olympics: Athens 1896* (also known as *The First Modern Olympics*), NBC, 1984.

Young reporter, *Ellis Island,* CBS, 1984.

John, *Strong Medicine* (also known as *Arthur Hailey's "Strong Medicine"*), syndicated, 1986.

Television Appearances; Movies:

Peter Fagan, *Helen Keller: The Miracle Continues,* syndicated, 1984.

Sanders, *The Dirty Dozen: Next Mission,* NBC, 1985.

Earl, *The Canterville Ghost,* syndicated, 1986.

Milo Radulovich, *Murrow,* HBO, 1986.

Epping, *The Fifth Missile* (also known as *Operation Fire*), NBC, 1986.

West Point professor, *The Last Days of Patton,* CBS, 1986.

Joe Wright, *The Ted Kennedy Jr. Story,* NBC, 1986.

Officer number one, *The Forgotten,* USA Network, 1989.

Michael Hunter, *The Little Riders,* Disney Channel, 1996.

Captain Farragut, *20,000 Leagues Under the Sea,* CBS, 1997.

Lieutenant Colonel number one, *Something in April,* HBO, 2005.

Television Appearances; Episodic:

"The Great Motor Race," *Q.E.D.* (also known as *Mastermind*), CBS, 1982.

Freddie, *Nancy Astor,* PBS, 1984.

Trainer, BBC, 1992.

Reporter, "Out of the Hive," *Bugs,* BBC, 1995.

Dr. Eastman, "Hate Street," *Space Precinct,* syndicated, 1995.

Father Buzz Cagney, "Going to America," *Father Ted,* Channel 4 and BBC America, 1998.

"Neighbours," *The Armando Iannucci Shows,* Channel 4, 2001.

"Imagination," *The Armando Iannucci Shows,* Channel 4, 2001.

John Stevens, "The Panama Canal," *Seven Wonders of the Industrial World,* BBC, 2003.

Healthy Harry, "Fit for Nothing," *The Basil Brush Show,* 2003.

HAREWOOD, David 1965–

PERSONAL

Born December 8, 1965, in Birmingham, England; son of Romeo (a truck driver) and Malene (a caterer) Harewood. *Education:* Trained with National Youth Theatre, London; Royal Academy of Dramatic Art, graduated.

Addresses: *Agent*—Cornerstone Talent Agency, 37 West 20th St., Suite 1108, New York, NY 10011; Marmont Management, Langham House, 308 Regent St., London W1B 3AT, England.

Career: Actor. Royal Academy of Dramatic Art, associate member; director of a children's theatre group in London.

CREDITS

Film Appearances:
Sergeant Streete, *The Hawk,* Castle Hill, 1993.

Jessop, *Mad Dogs and Englishman* (also known as *Shameless*), Columbia, 1995.

Moses, *I Wonder Who's Kissing You Now,* Zentropa Entertainments, 1998.

Prince of Morocco, *The Merchant of Venice* (also known as *William Shakespeare's "The Merchant of Venice"* and *Il mercante di Venezia*), Metro–Goldwyn–Mayer/Sony Pictures Classics, 2004.

Inspector Marshall, *Separate Lies,* Fox Searchlight, 2005.

(English version) Voice of Erito, *Strings,* Wellspring Media, 2005.

Captain Poison, *Blood Diamond,* Warner Bros., 2006.

Television Appearances; Series:
Daniel, *Agony Again,* BBC, 1995.

Joe Robinson, a recurring role, *The Vice,* BBC America, between 1999 and 2003.

Augustus "Gus" Pottinger, *Babyfather* (also known as *Babyfather 2*), BBC, 2001–2002.

Max Robertson, *Fat Friends,* BBC America, 2004–2005.

Television Appearances; Movies:
Terry, *Harnessing Peacocks,* Arts and Entertainment, 1992.

Steward, *Great Moments in Aviation* (also known as *Shades of Fear*), BBC, 1993.

Stevie Johnson, *Anna Lee: Headcase,* ITV, 1993.

Macduff, *Macbeth on the Estate,* BBC, 1997.

Matthew Bedwell and Reverend Nicholas Bedwell, *The Ruby in the Smoke,* PBS, 2006.

Television Appearances; Miniseries:
David West, *For the Greater Good,* BBC, 1991.

Trevor, *Hearts and Minds,* Channel 4, 1995.

Television Appearances; Pilots:
Trevor Watkins, *Bermuda Grace,* NBC, 1994.

Police sergeant, *Cold Feet,* 1997.

Television Appearances; Specials:
Narrator, *Rappin' at the Royal,* 2005.

Out of Africa: Heroes and Icons, BBC, 2005.

Television Appearances; Episodic:
Paul Grant, "A Will to Die," *Casualty,* BBC1, 1990.

Williams, "Eye–Witness," *The Bill,* ITV1, 1990.

Jonathon, "Murder at Tea Time," *Murder Most Horrid,* BBC1, 1991.

Derek Puley, "Takeover," *Spatz,* ITV, 1991.

Derek Puley, "Driving Miss Wesley," *Spatz,* ITV, 1992.

Derek Puley, *Spatz,* ITV, 1993.

Doctor, "Friendly Fire," *Press Gang,* ITV, 1993.

Nick, *Medics,* ITV, 1993.

Paul Johnson, "Big Wednesday," *Game–On,* BBC, 1995.

Robbie Coker, "True to Life Player," *The Bill,* ITV1, 1997.

David Adams, "Mute of Malice," *Kavanagh QC,* ITV, 1997.

Henry, "As Stars Look Down," *Ballykissangel,* BBC1, 1998.

Deputy Inspector Peterson, "Playing God," *An Unsuitable Job for a Woman,* PBS, 1999.

Dr. Mike Gregson, *Always and Everyone* (also known as *A&E* and *St. Saviours*), Granada, 2000.

Angus Stuart, "Death by Water: Part 1," *Silent Witness,* BBC, 2004.

From Bard to Verse, 2004.

The Terry and Gaby Show, Channel 5, 2004.

Deputy Inspector Branston, *New Street Law,* BBC, 2006.

Martin Viner, "Ducking and Diving," *New Tricks,* PBS, 2007.

Television Appearances; Other:
Jean–Baptiste, *Pirate Prince,* 1991.

Stage Appearances:
Badnuff, London, 2004.
Lord Asriel, *His Dark Materials,* National Theatre, Olivier Theatre, London, 2004–2005.
Henry Percy (Hotspur), *Henry IV, Parts 1 & 2,* National Theatre, London, 2005.

Major Tours:
Antony, *Anthony and Cleopatra,* New York Shakespeare Company, Anspacher Theatre, Public Theatre, New York City, 1995–97.
Title role, *Othello,* National Theatre, London, 1997–98.

OTHER SOURCES

Books:
Contemporary Black Biography, Volume 52, Gale, 2006.

HARSON, Sley
        See ELLISON, Harlan

HART, Ellis
        See ELLISON, Harlan

HEWLETT, David 1968–
        (David Hewlitt)

PERSONAL

Full name, David Ian Hewlett; born April 18, 1968, in Redhill, Surrey, England; brother of Kate Hewlett (an actress); married Soo Garay (an actress), November 5, 2000 (divorced, February 2004); engaged to Jane Loughman (a producer), December 25, 2006.

Career: Actor. Previously ran Darkyl (an Internet company) with Kate Hewlett, his sister.

Awards, Honors: Golden Sheaf Award, best performance, Yorkton Short Film and Video Festival, 1997, for *Elevated;* Gemini Award nominations, best perfor-

mance by an actor in a featured supporting role in a dramatic series, Academy of Canadian Cinema and Television, 1997, 1998, both *Traders.*

CREDITS

Film Appearances:
Chuckie, *The Darkside* (also known as *The Dark Side*), 1987.
Leon, *Pin ...* (also known as *Pin: A Plastic Nightmare*), 1988.
Dead Meat, 1989.
Jimmy, *Where the Heart Is,* Buena Vista, 1990.
Terry McBride, *Deep Sleep,* Deep Sleep Productions, 1990.
David Kellum, *Scanners II: The New Order,* Triton Pictures, 1991.
Deadpan Winchester, *Desire and Hell at Sunset Motel,* Two Moon Releasing, 1992.
Detective Trayne, *Blood Brothers* (also known as *Native Strangers*), USA Pictures, 1993.
Steven Lunny at age twenty–five, *The Boys of St. Vincent: 15 Years Later* (also known as *Les garcons de Saint–Vincent: quinze ans plus tard*), 1993.
Worth, *Cube,* Trimark Pictures, 1997.
Hank, *Elevated* (short), Canadian Film Centre, 1997.
Andrew, *Bad Day on the Block* (also known as *The Fireman* and *Under Pressure*), New City Releasing, 1997.
Martyn, *Clutch,* Cineplex Odeon, 1998.
Martin and voice of soldier, *Milkman,* 1998.
Rob Fitzgerald, *Joe's Wedding,* Astral, 1998.
Nick, *The Life Before This,* First Look Pictures Releasing, 1999.
Gord, *Autoerotica,* 1999.
The victim, *Blind,* 1999.
D. J., *Amateur Night,* Naughty Bones Productions/Chemical Pictures, 1999.
Bryan, *Ice Men,* Black Walk Films/Black Walk Productions/First Frame Films, 2001.
Bud, *Chasing Cain,* Muse Distribution International, 2001.
Michael, *Century Hotel,* TVA International, 2001.
Murray, *Treed Murray* (also known as *Entre l'arbe et l'ecorce* and *Get Down*), Alliance Atlantis Communications, 2001.
Virgil C. Dunn, *Cypher,* Miramax, 2002.
Himself, *Made in Canada, Volume 1: Best of the CFC,* The Asylum, 2002.
Roger, *Friday Night* (short), 2003.
Dave, *Nothing,* Alliance Atlantis Motion Picture Distribution, 2003.
Lawrence Yeager, *Foolproof* (also known as *A toute epreuve*), DEJ Productions, 2003.
Bryan, *Ice Men,* Wolfe Releasing, 2004.
Emmett, *Boa vs. Python,* Columbia TriStar, 2004.
Patrick, *A Dog's Breakfast,* Metro–Goldwyn–Mayer, 2007.

Film Work:
Art director, *The Wake,* 1987.
Director, *A Dog's Breakfast,* Metro–Goldwyn–Mayer, 2007.

Television Appearances; Series:
Dr. Nicholas "Nickie" Elder, *Kung Fu: The Legend Continues,* syndicated, 1993–96.
Monster Force, syndicated, 1994.
Grant Jansky, *Traders,* Lifetime and Global, 1996–2000.
Dr. Rodney McKay, *Stargate SG–1,* Showtime, 2001, then Sci–Fi Channel, 2002–2007.
Dr. Rodney McKay, *Stargate: Atlantis* (also known as *La porte d'Atlantis*), Sci–Fi Channel, 2004–2008.

Television Appearances; Miniseries:
"Ruska" Rostislav, *The First Circle,* CBC, 1991.
Gerry Capano, *And Never Let Her Go,* CBS, 2001.

Television Appearances; Movies:
Joe Dobson, *The Penthouse,* ABC, 1989.
Myles Chapman, *Quiet Killer* (also known as *Black Death* and *New York, alerte a la peste*), CTV and CBS, 1992.
Gary Hammond, *Split Images,* syndicated, 1992.
Mel, *On the Second Day of Christmas,* Lifetime, 1997.
Andrew, *Under Pressure,* 1999.
Le medecin, *Survivor,* UPN, 1999.
Gus Gruber, *The Triangle,* TBS, 2001.
Anders Raeborne, *Darklight,* Sci–Fi Channel, 2004.

Television Appearances; Specials:
Walter Jenkins, *A Savage Christmas: The Fall of Hong Kong* (also known as *La bataille de Hong Kong, La bravoure et le mepris, partie 1, Savage Christmas: Hong Kong 1941,* and *The Valour and the Horror, Part 1*), CBC, 1992.
Himself and Rodney McKay, *Preview to "Atlantis,"* Sci–Fi Channel, 2004.
Himself and Rodney McKay, *From "Stargate" to "Atlantis": Sci Fi Lowdown,* Sci–Fi Channel, 2004.
Himself and Rodney McKay, *Sci Fi Lowdown: Behind the "Stargate"—Secrets Revealed* (also known as *Beyond the Stargate: Secrets Revealed*), Sci–Fi Channel, 2005.
Himself and Rodney McKay, *Sci Fi Inside: Sci Fi Friday,* Sci–Fi Channel, 2005.
06 Spaceys, Space Channel, 2006.
Sci Fi Inside: "Stargate SG–1" 200th Episode, Sci–Fi Channel, 2006.
07 Spaceys, Space Channel, 2007.

Television Appearances; Episodic:
(As David Hewlitt) "Simon Says," *Night Heat,* 1987.
Cal, "Tales of the Undead," *Friday the 13th* (also known as *Friday's Curse* and *Friday the 13th: The Series*), syndicated, 1988.
"A Walk on the Wild Side," *My Secret Identity,* syndicated, 1988.
Dave Lister, "Murder by Video," *Street Legal,* CBC, 1988.
"Relatively Speaking," *Katts and Dog,* CTV and Family Channel, 1991.
"Killing Ground," *Katts and Dog,* CTV and Family Channel, 1992.
Matthew Reed, "Dead Air," *Forever Knight,* CBS, 1992.
Tom, "A Kiss Is Just a Psi," *Beyond Reality,* Fox, 1992.
Tom, "The Loving Cup," *Beyond Reality,* Fox, 1993.
Tim Woolrich, "Persons Living or Dead," *Street Legal,* CBC, 1994.
"O'er the Ramparts We Watched," *Twice in a Lifetime,* CTV and PAX, 1999.
Mr. Schudy, "Never Say Never," *ER,* NBC, 2001.
Hector Freimark, "The Taking of Crows," *Mutant X,* syndicated, 2003.
Fred Watkins, "Hawks and Handsaws," *Without a Trace* (also known as *W.A.T.*), CBS, 2004.
Frederick, "Family Values," *The District,* CBS, 2004.
Larry Tolso, *Sanctuary,* 2007.

Also appeared in (as David Hewlitt) "Live by the Sword," *The Campbells,* syndicated.

Television Work; Series:
Executive producer, *Starcrossed,* Sci–Fi Channel, 2007.

WRITINGS

Screenplays:
(Story only) *Nothing,* Alliance Atlantis Motion Picture Distribution, 2003.
A Dog's Breakfast, Metro–Goldwyn–Mayer, 2007.

Television Episodes:
Starcrossed, Sci–Fi Channel, 2007.

HIPP, Paul 1963(?)–

PERSONAL

Born July 17, 1963 (some sources cite July 9, 1964), in Philadelphia, PA; son of Jack and Nancy Hipp. *Education:* Trained for the stage with William Hickey and Mira Rostova in New York City.

Addresses: *Agent*—Stone Manners Talent and Literary Agency, 6500 Wilshire Blvd., Suite 550, Los Angeles, CA 90048.

Career: Actor, singer, composer and songwriter, director, producer, and film editor. Paul Hipp and the Heroes, band leader; worked as a street singer and guitarist in New York City; performed at clubs in Greenwich Village; appeared in commercials.

Member: Screen Actors Guild, Actors' Equity Association, American Federation of Television and Radio Artists.

Awards, Honors: Antoinette Perry Award nomination and Laurence Olivier Award nomination, Society of West End Theatre, both best performance by an actor in a musical, 1991, *Theater World* Award, best Broadway debut performance, Outer Critics Circle Award, Drama Desk nomination, and Dora Mavor Moore Award nomination, Toronto Theatre Alliance, all for *Buddy: The Buddy Holly Story.*

CREDITS

Film Appearances:
Nino Villache, *China Girl,* Vestron, 1987.
Michael, *Sticky Fingers,* Spectrafilm, 1988.
Doogie, *Fathers & Sons,* Columbia, 1991.
Dr. Shorts, *Lethal Weapon 3,* Warner Bros., 1992.
Jesus, *Bad Lieutenant,* Aries Film Releasing, 1992.
Dan O'Dare, *Bad Channels,* 1992.
Boy Meets Girl, 1993.
Ghouly, *The Funeral,* October Films, 1996.
Fitch, *Face/Off* (also known as *Face Off*), Paramount, 1997.
Joe Odom, *Midnight in the Garden of Good and Evil,* Warner Bros., 1997.
Dylan, *Vicious Circles,* Trimark Pictures, 1997.
Robert Marrs, *Cleopatra's Second Husband,* Indican Pictures, 1998.
Richard Johnson, *Another Day in Paradise,* Trimark Pictures, 1998.
Danny Pierce, *Waking the Dead,* USA Films, 1999.
Quinn, *More Dogs than Bones,* Dream Entertainment, Inc., 2000.
Dick, *Death of a Dog,* Groovy Fish Productions, 2000.
Alexander, *Sunset Tuxedo* (short film), 2004.
Vice president, *Bye Bye Benjamin* (short film), American Film Institute, 2006.
Jason Klein, *Dirt Nap* (also known as *Two Tickets to Paradise*), Scrudge, 2006.
Frank, *Hide & Seek* (short film), DaDoo Productions, 2006.
Comma, *South of Pico,* Snails Pace Productions/Vent Productions, 2007.

Film Work:
Song performer, "I Want You Back," and song producer, *Body Snatchers,* Warner Bros., 1993.

Producer, director, and film editor, *Death of a Dog,* Groovy Fish Productions, 2000.

Television Appearances; Series:
Elliot Quinn, *Three Sisters,* NBC, 2001–2002.

Television Appearances; Movies:
Elvis Presley, *Liberace: Behind the Music,* CBS, 1988.
Nicholas "Nick" De Noia, *The Chippendales Murder,* USA Network, 2000.
Shaman, *Teenage Caveman,* Cinemax, 2002.

Television Appearances; Specials:
Macy's Thanksgiving Day Parade, NBC, 1990.
Peter Tullis, *The Last Shot,* Showtime, 1993.

Television Appearances; Pilots:
Richard/Ricky, *Fantasy Island,* 1998.
Manchild, Showtime, 2007.

Television Appearances; Episodic:
Andrew McCauley, *The Hat Squad,* 1992.
Nick Bosch, "On a Dead Man's Chest," *Tales from the Crypt* (also known as *HBO's "Tales from the Crypt"*), HBO, 1992.
Harry, "Love Is Hell," *Parker Lewis Can't Lose* (also known as *Parker Lewis*), 1992.
Charlie Nevers, "Dial 'H' for Murder," *The Cosby Mysteries,* 1995.
Aaron Crow, "Vanishing Act," *Nash Bridges* (also known as *Bridges*), CBS, 1996.
Simon, "Testing, Testing," *Men Behaving Badly* (also known as *It's a Man's World*), NBC, 1997.
Lewis Abernathy, "Black Pearl," *Pacific Blue,* 1997.
Lon Colomby, "Vegas Mother's Day: Parts 1 & 2," *Cover Me: Based on the True Life of an FBI Family* (also known as *Cover Me*), USA Network, 2001.
Craig Turner, "Lockdown," *ER,* NBC, 2002.
Craig Turner, "Chaos Theory," *ER,* NBC, 2002.
Vince Fisher, "Game Over," *CSI: Miami,* CBS, 2005.
Bert, "The Road to Damascus," *Carnivale,* HBO, 2005.
Bert, "Outskirts, Damascus, NE," *Carnivale,* HBO, 2005.
Bert/Bertha Hagenback, "New Canaan, CA," *Carnivale,* HBO, 2005.
Marc Coleman, "My Chopped Liver," *Scrubs,* NBC, 2006.
William Mamet, "Stealing Home," *CSI: NY,* CBS, 2006.
Dr. Woods, "Heroic Measures," *The Closer,* TNT, 2006.
Detective Chris Pappas, "The Damage Done," *Without a Trace* (also known as *W.A.T.*), CBS, 2006.

Also appeared in episodes of *Entertainment Tonight,* syndicated, *Good Morning America,* ABC, and *Today,* NBC.

Television Appearances; Other:
Buddy Holly, *Nothing like a Royal Show,* London Weekend Television), 1990.

Stage Appearances:
Title role, *Buddy: The Buddy Holly Story* (musical), West End production, c. 1989, then Shubert Theatre, New York City, 1990–91.
Berger, *Hair* (musical), Old Vic Theatre, London, 1993.

Appeared as Gene Vincent, *Be Bop a Lulu,* Theatre–Theatre, Los Angeles; in *A Minor Incident,* Theatre Row Theatre, New York City, and Royal Albert Hall, London; and *Rockabilly Road,* New York City.

RECORDINGS

Albums:
Recorded main theme for the film *China Girl;* recorded an album of original material with band Paul Hipp and the Heroes.

WRITINGS

Film Scripts:
(And music composer) *Sunset Tuxedo* (short film), 2004.

Songs Featured in Films:
China Girl, Vestron, 1987.
Body Snatchers, 1993.

Songs; Other:
(With Carole King) "I Can't Stop Thinking about You" and "Time Heals All Wounds," *City Streets,* 1990.

OTHER SOURCES

Periodicals:
Interview, September, 1990, p. 64.

HOFFMAN, Rick 1970–

PERSONAL

Born June 12, 1970, in New York, NY. *Education:* Studied drama at the University of Arizona.

Addresses: *Agent*—The Gersh Agency, 232 North Canon Dr., Beverly Hills, CA 90210. *Manager*—Raw Talent Management, 9615 Brighton Way, Suite 300, Beverly Hills, CA 90210.

Career: Actor. Appeared as himself on *Tom Green Live,* an internet series, 2007. Previously worked as a waiter.

CREDITS

Film Appearances:
Night security at federal building, *Conspiracy Theory,* Warner Bros., 1997.
Protestor, *The Fanatics* (also known as *Fumbleheads*), 1997.
Police officer at port, *Lethal Weapon 4* (also known as *Lethal 4*), Warner Bros., 1998.
Clerk, *Border to Border,* Independent Artists, 1998.
Bartender, *Johnny Skidmarks* (also known as *The Killer Inside*), 1998.
Doctor, *What Planet Are You From?,* Columbia/Sony Pictures Entertainment, 2000.
Regis, *A Better Way to Die,* 2000.
Richard, *Looking for Bobby D,* 2001.
Rich Green, *The Agent Who Stole Christmas,* 2001.
James Lockridge, *Blood Work,* Warner Bros., 2002.
Rick, *Farm Sluts* (short), 2003.
Louis, *I Love Your Work,* THINKFilm, 2003.
(Uncredited) New York businessman on bus, *The Day After Tomorrow,* Twentieth Century–Fox, 2004.
Lawyer, *Cellular* (also known as *Final Call—Wenn er auflegtm muss sie sterben*), New Line Cinema, 2004.
Gay man, *Our Time Is Up* (short), 2004.
The American client, *Hostel,* Lions Gate Films, 2005.
Angry face, *Smiley Face,* First Look International, 2007.
Goldman, *The Condemned,* Lionsgate, 2007.
Blither, *Postal,* Freestyle Releasing, 2007.

Television Appearances; Series:
Freddie Sacker, *The $treet,* Fox, 2000–2001.
Terry Loomis, *Philly,* ABC, 2001–2002.
Jerry Best, *The Bernie Mac Show,* Fox, 2002–2005.
Patrick Van Dorn, *Jake In Progress,* ABC, 2005–2006.

Television Appearances; Movies:
Mugger, *Just Perfect,* 1990.
Clark Cavanaugh, *Paradise,* 2004.

Television Appearances; Specials:
Fuse Fangoria Chainsaw Awards, Fuse Network, 2006.
30 Even Scarier Movie Moments, Bravo, 2006.

Television Appearances; Pilots:
Arnich, *Andy Richter Controls the Universe,* Fox, 2002.
Consultant at the bar, *Miss Match,* NBC, 2003.

Television Appearances; Episodic:

Pizza man, "Ferbus' Day Out," *Masked Rider* (also known as *Saban's "Masked Rider"*), 1996.

Photographer, "Exposed," *The Pretender*, NBC, 1997.

Robber, "Again with the Porno Video," *Alright Already*, 1997.

Tino Scarlatti, "Big Top Val," *V.I.P.* (also known as *V.I.P.—Die Bodyguards*), syndicated, 1999.

Benji Brickman, "Sail Away," *Providence*, NBC, 1999.

Phil Berman, "As If By Fate," *Crossing Jordan*, NBC, 2002.

Bruno Gomez, "Bait," *CSI: Miami*, CBS, 2003.

Gary Moscovitz, "Life Rules," *Without a Trace* (also known as *W.A.T.*), CBS, 2004.

District Attorney Harvey Clarke, "Coming Home," *The Practice*, ABC, 2004.

District Attorney Harvey Clarke, "Pre–Trial Blues," *The Practice*, ABC, 2004.

District Attorney Harvey Clarke, "Mr. Shore Goes to Town," *The Practice*, ABC, 2004.

Agent Colmes, "Mr. Monk Meets the Godfather," *Monk*, USA Network, 2004.

Dr. Miles Feldstein, "Manhattan Manhunt," *CSI: NY* (also known as *CSI: New York*), CBS, 2005.

Lance Addison, "The Price You Pay," *Commander in Chief*, ABC, 2006.

Lance Addison, "Happy Birthday, Madam President," *Commander in Chief*, ABC, 2006.

Voice of Caroler number one and John Hinkley, "The Best Christmas Story Never," *American Dad!* (animated), Fox, 2006.

Sam Harris, "Here Comes the Judge," *Shark*, CBS, 2007.

Also appeared as Kate's auction date, "The Price of Love," *Miss Match*, NBC.

HOFHEIMER, Charlie 1981–

PERSONAL

Born April 17, 1981, in Brooklyn, NY. *Education:* Attended New York City Lab School. *Avocational Interests:* Baseball, soccer, piano, horseback riding, and hockey.

Addresses: *Agent*—Innovative Artists, 1505 10th St., Santa Monica, CA 90401.

Career: Actor.

CREDITS

Film Appearances:

Jim Garland, *Lassie*, Paramount, 1994.

John Cooke, *Boys*, Buena Vista, 1996.

Scott Andrews, *Fathers Day*, Warner Bros., 1997.

James, *Edge City*, 1997.

Nick at age seventeen, *Music of the Heart*, Miramax, 1999.

Jim, *Last Ball*, 2000.

Smith, *Black Hawk Down*, Columbia, 2001.

James Powell, *The Ghost of F. Scott Fitzgerald* (short), 2002.

Kevin the security guard, *The Village* (also known as *Grey* and *M. Night Shayamalan's "The Village"*), Buena Vista, 2004.

Raymond, *Blur*, 2007.

Television Appearances; Movies:

T. J. Medieros, *Blue Moon*, CBS, 1999.

Television Appearances; Episodic:

Dean Wilson, "The Tale of the Water Demons," *Are You Afraid of the Dark?*, Nickelodeon, 1994.

"A Question of Truth," *New York News*, CBS, 1995.

Andrew Jameson, "Wannabe," *Law and Order*, NBC, 1995.

Ben Karmel, "Homesick," *Law and Order*, NBC, 1996.

Jeff, "The Tale of the Unexpected Visitor, *Are You Afraid of the Dark?*, Nickelodeon, 1996.

"Breaking In, Breaking Out, Breaking Up, Breaking Down," *Trinity*, NBC, 1999.

Nick, "A Girl's Life," *Now and Again*, CBS, 1999.

Jerry Dupree, "Tortured," *Law & Order: Special Victims Unit* (also known as *Law & Order: SVU* and *Special Victims Unit*), NBC, 2003.

Kevin McCallum, "A Night at the Movies," *CSI: Crime Scene Investigation* (also known as *C.S.I.*, *CSI: Weekends*, *CSI: Las Vegas*, and *Les Experts*), CBS, 2003.

Petty Officer First Class Bobby Wilkes, "High Seas," *Naval NCIS: Naval Criminal Investigative Service* (also known as *NCIS* and *NCIS: Naval Criminal Investigative Service*), CBS, 2003.

Private Scott Strickland, *American Dreams*, NBC, 2003.

Ron Allen, "The Running Man," *Numb3rs* (also known as *Num3ers*), CBS, 2006.

David Channing, "Second Opinion," *Medium*, NBC, 2007.

Stage Appearances:

Kenny Simmonds, *Minor Demons*, Currican Theatre, New York City, 1996, then Century Theater, New York City, 1997.

Ovid Bernstein and Tobias Pfeiffer II, *Old Money*, Mitzi E. Newhouse Theatre, New York City, 2000.

Made Broadway debut as Jimmy, *On the Waterfront*; also appeared as Matt, *Spittin Image*, Forum Theatre; Hart, *Ruler of My Destiny*, Long Wharf Theatre, New Haven, CT; Matty, *Opelika*, Third Eye Repertory Company, New York City; Jim Hawkins, *Treasure Island*, Blue Light Theatre Company, New York City.

HOODS, Bebe Drake
See DRAKE, Bebe

HOOKS, Bebe Drake
See DRAKE, Bebe

HUFF, Brent 1961–

PERSONAL

Born in 1961; married Shawn. *Education:* Attended the University of Missouri.

Career: Actor, director, and screenwriter.

Awards, Honors: Keltonborn Foundation Award, best short film, for *Defiance.*

CREDITS

Film Appearances:
(Uncredited) Extra, *King Kong,* 1976.
Keith, *Coach,* Crown International Pictures, 1978.
Willard, *The Perils of Gwendoline in the Land of the Yik Yak* (also known as *Gwendoline* and *The Perils of Gwendoline*), Samuel Goldwyn Company, 1984.
Steve Gordon, *Nine Deaths of the Ninja* (also known as *9 Deaths of the Ninja*), Cannon Films, 1985.
Sam Black, *Deadly Passion,* 1985.
Tommy Roth, *Armed Response* (also known as *Jade Jungle*), Cintel Films, 1986.
Zar, *Stormquest* (also known as *El ojo de la tormenta*), 1987.
Morgan, *Cop Game* (also known as *Giochi di poliziotto*), 1988.
Michael Ransom, *Strike Commando 2* (also known as *Trappola diabolica*), 1989.
Sam Wood, *Born to Fight* (also known as *Nato per combattere*), 1989.
Steve, *Sulle tracce del condor* (also known as *Condor* and *After the Condor*), 1990.
Parker Parks, *Falling from Grace,* Columbia, 1992.
Red, *We the People* (also known as *Final Justice*), 1994.
Tinkercrank, *Tinkercrank,* 1995.
Long John, *Oblivion 2: Backlash* (also known as *Backlash: Oblivion 2*), Full Moon, 1996.
Final Justice, 1996.
Agent Adams, *Dead Tides,* Live Entertainment, 1997.
Till, *Scorpio One,* 1997.
Bobby Joe, *Girls Night,* 1998.
Defiance (short), 1998.
Callin, *The Bad Pack,* Avalanche Home Entertainment, 1998.
Randall Garrett, *Hitman's Run,* Avalanche Home Entertainment, 1999.
Officer Mack, *Hot Boyz* (also known as *Gang Law*), Artisan Entertainment, 1999.
David Anderson, *Hijack* (also known as *The Last Siege*), Hallmark Entertainment, 1999.
Miss Illinois local pageant host, *Beautiful,* Destination Films, 2000.
Agent Mack Taylor, *Submerged* (also known as *Destination: Impact*), New City Releasing, 2000.
Pete Springer, *More Mercy* (also known as *Bad Bizness*), Royal Oaks Entertainment, 2003.
Shane Newman, *Final Examination,* Artisan Entertainment, 2003.
Temptation, 2004.
Dennis, *Glass Trap,* Marla's Gardens Company, 2005.
Evan, *Serbian Scars,* 2007.
Second seater, *Fast Glass,* 2008.

Film Director:
We the People (also known as *Final Justice*), 1994.
Final Justice, 1996.
Defiance (short), 1998.
The Bad Pack, Avalanche Home Entertainment, 1998.
100 Mile Rule, Velocity Home Entertainment, 2002.
Lap Dancing (short), 2003.
Treasure Raiders, 2007.
Welcome to Paradise, First Look International, 2007.
Serbian Scars, 2007.

Film Supervising Producer:
Serbian Scars, 2007.

Television Appearances; Series:
Adam Burns and Inferno, *Black Scorpion* (also known as *Roger Corman Presents "Black Scorpion"*), 1998.
Steve "Psycho" Kessick, *Pensacola: Wings of Gold,* syndicated, 1998–99.

Television Appearances; Movies:
Samuels, *Summer Fantasy,* NBC, 1984.
Georg, *Tierarztin Christine,* 1993.
Werner Sternbach–Stolze, *Das Paradies am ende der berge,* 1993.
Birnbaum, *Der blaue diamant* (also known as *Hunt for the Blue Diamond*), 1993.
Tilden, *I Spy Returns,* CBS, 1994.
Der schwarze fluch odliche leidenschaften, 1994.
Lawrence Brent, *Hollywood Confidential,* UPN, 1997.
Officer Raimi, *Dead & Deader,* Sci–Fi Channel, 2006.

Television Appearances; Specials:
Challenger, *Star Search,* syndicated, 1983.

Television Appearances; Episodic:
Unicorn of Death, *Wizards and Warriors,* CBS, 1983.
Cowboy, *In Living Color,* Fox, 1991.
Tony, "The Plague," *Diagnosis Murder,* CBS, 1994.
Officer Doug Vogel, "Murder by Friendly Fire," *Diagnosis Murder,* CBS, 1996.
Clint Hill, "Moving Targets," *Dark Skies,* NBC, 1996.
Colonel Howard Pegament, "Surface Warfare," *JAG,* CBS, 2000.
Kevin, "Calling Dr. Con," *Lucky,* FX Channel, 2003.
Meade, "Sherry Darlin'," *Cold Case,* CBS, 2003.
Agent Broder, "No Exit," *The West Wing,* NBC, 2004.

WRITINGS

Screenplays:
We the People (also known as *Final Justice*), 1994.
Final Justice, 1996.
Defiance (short), 1998.
The Bad Pack, Avalanche Home Entertainment, 1998.
Power Play, First Look International, 2002.
Face of Terror, Sony Pictures Home Entertainment, 2003.
Welcome to Paradise, First Look International, 2007.

HUTMAN, Jon
(John Hutman)

PERSONAL

Education: Earned degree in architecture from Yale University, New Haven, CT; also studied scenic design, painting, and lighting at Yale University School of Drama.

Addresses: *Agent*—The Gersh Agency, 232 N. Canon Dr., Beverly Hills, CA 90210.

Career: Production designer, visual consultant, set dresser, art director, director, and producer.

Member: Art Directors Guild.

Awards, Honors: Excellence in Production Design Award nomination (with Tony Fanning), television series, Society of Motion Picture and Television Art Directors, Emmy Award (with others), outstanding art director for a single–camera series, 2000, both for *The West Wing;* Excellence in Production Design Award nomination (with others), feature film—contemporary film, 2004, for *Something's Gotta Give.*

CREDITS

Film Art Department Assistant:
The Hotel New Hampshire, 1984.

Film Set Dresser:
To Live and Die in L.A., 1985.

Film Art Department Visual Consultant:
Ruthless People, Buena Vista, 1986.
(As John Hutman; Los Angeles art department) *Boxing Helena,* Orion Classics, 1993.

Film Assistant:
(To Lilly Kilvert) *Ruthless People,* Buena Vista, 1986.

Film Art Director:
Wanted: Dead or Alive, New World Pictures, 1987.
Siesta, 1987.
Surrender, 1987.
Shag (also known as *Shag: The Movie*), Hemdale Film, 1989.
Worth Winning, 1989.
I Love You to Death, TriStar Pictures, 1990.

Film Production Designer:
Heathers, New World Pictures, 1989.
Meet the Applegates (also known as *The Applegates*), Triton Pictures, 1990.
Taking Care of Business (also known as *Filofax*), Buena Vista, 1991.
Little Man Tate, Columbia TriStar, 1991.
A River Runs Through It, Columbia Pictures, 1992.
Trespass (also known as *Looters*), 1992.
Flesh and Bone, Paramount, 1993.
Nell, Twentieth Century–Fox, 1994.
Quiz Show, Buena Vista, 1994.
French Kiss (also known as *Paris Match*), Twentieth Century–Fox, 1995.
Lolita, Samuel Goldwyn, 1997.
The Horse Whisperer, Buena Vista, 1998.
Mumford, Buena Vista, 1999.
Coyote Ugly, Buena Vista, 2000.
What Women Want, Paramount, 2000.
Dreamcatcher (also known as *L'attrapeur de reves*), Warner Bros., 2003.
Something's Gotta Give, Columbia, 2003.
The Interpreter (also known as *L'Inteprete*), Universal, 2005.
The Holiday, Universal, 2006.

Film Head Decorator:
I Love You to Death, 1990.

Film Coproducer:
Mumford, 1999.
Dreamcatcher (also known as *L'attrapeur de reves*), 2003.

Film Appearances:
Reporter number one, *The Hotel New Hampshire,* Orion, 1984.

Television Work; Series:
Design consultant and producer, *Gideon's Crossing,* ABC, 2000–2001.
Visual consultant, *The Evidence,* ABC, 2005.

Television Assistant Set Decorator; Movies:
A Different Affair, CBS, 1987.

Television Work; Pilots:
Art director, *The West Wing,* NBC, 1999.
Visual consultant, *The Evidence,* ABC, 2006.

Television Director; Episodic:
Gideon's Crossing, ABC, 2000.
"Gone Quiet," *The West Wing,* NBC, 2001.
Cold Case, CBS, 2005.

Television Appearances; Episodic:
"Jodie Foster," *Biography,* Art and Entertainment, 2005.
"The Interpreter," *HBO First Look,* HBO, 2005.

HYDE, R.
    See **EBERT, Roger**

I–J

ISSYANOV, Ravil
(Ravil Isyanov)

PERSONAL

Surname is sometimes transliterated as "Isyanov."

Career: Actor.

CREDITS

Film Appearances:
Georgi, *Back in the U.S.S.R.,* Twentieth Century–Fox, 1992.
Russian hacker, *Hackers,* Metro–Goldwyn–Mayer, 1995.
MiG pilot, *GoldenEye,* Metro–Goldwyn–Mayer, 1995.
Lieutenant, *Two Deaths,* Castle Hill, 1996.
Cornelius, *Hamlet* (also known as *William Shakespeare's "Hamlet"*), Columbia, 1996.
Tretiak guard, *The Saint,* Paramount, 1997.
Ghazzi Murad, *The Jackal* (also known as *Le chacal* and *Der Schakal*), Universal, 1997.
Rykoff, *The Omega Code,* Providence Entertainment, 1999.
(Uncredited) Viktor Dorestoy, *Doomsdayer* (also known as *Il giorno del giudizio*), ABS–CBN Entertainment/Quantum Entertainment, 1999.
Sergei, *The Adventures of Young Indiana Jones: Adventures in the Secret Service,* 1999.
Lermontov, *Along Came a Spider* (also known as *Im Netz der spinne* and *Le masque de l'araignee*), Paramount, 2001.
Henry Capri, *Arachnid* (also known as *Amazon*), Lions Gate Films, 2001.
Igor Suslov, *K–19: The Widowmaker* (also known as *K*19: The Widowmaker, K–19—Showdown in der Tiefe,* and *K–19: Terreur sous la mer*), Paramount, 2002.

Morris Menke, *Holes,* Buena Vista, 2003.
Curtis, *Mr. & Mrs. Smith,* Twentieth Century–Fox, 2005.
General Sikorsky, *The Good German,* Warner Bros., 2006.

Television Appearances; Movies:
Yakov, *Stalin* (also known as *Sztalin*), 1992.
Mikhael, *Deadly Voyage,* 1996.
Kot, *Circles of Deceit: Kalon,* 1996.
Greek supervisor, *Under Pressure* (also known as *The Cruel Deep* and *Escape under Pressure*), HBO, 2000.
Casper, *Octopus,* USA Network, 2000.

Television Appearances; Miniseries:
Boris Levitsky, *The Man Who Made Husbands Jealous,* 1997.

Television Appearances; Episodic:
Student, "Moldavian Rhapsody," *The Good Guys,* 1993.
Sergei, "Petrograd, July 1917," *The Young Indiana Jones Chronicles,* 1993.
Misha, "UN1407," *The Lifeboat,* 1994.
Vlad, "From Russia with Love," *Bad Boys,* 1996.
Joseph Vukavitch, "As Time Goes By," *Seven Days* (also known as *Seven Days: The Series*), UPN, 1998.
Political Officer Kuriyov, "Last Breath," *Seven Days* (also known as *Seven Days: The Series*), UPN, 1999.
Monk, "No Place like Home," *Buffy the Vampire Slayer* (also known as *BtVS, Buffy,* and *Buffy the Vampire Slayer: The Series*), The WB, 2000.
"The Iron Coffin," *JAG,* CBS, 2001.
Luri Karpachev, "So It Begins," *Alias,* ABC, 2001.
Stavro/Dorchak, "Thanksgiving," *The Agency,* CBS, 2002.
Luri Karpachev, "A Dark Turn," *Alias,* ABC, 2003.
"Prodigy," *Without a Trace* (also known as *W.A.T.*), CBS, 2003.

Russian aide, "First Dance," *Commander in Chief,* ABC, 2005.

Glushko, "Race for Rockets," *Space Race,* BBC, 2005.

Glushko, "Race to the Moon," *Space Race,* BBC, 2006.

Bierko's henchman, "Day 5: 4:00 a.m.–5:00 a.m.," *24,* Fox, 2006.

Bierko's henchman, "Day 5: 5:00 a.m.–6:00 a.m.," *24,* Fox, 2006.

Nikolai Puchenko, "Faking It," *Navy NCIS: Naval Criminal Investigative Service* (also known as *NCIS* and *NCIS: Naval Criminal Investigative Service*), CBS, 2006.

Maslin, Bedfellows," *The Unit,* CBS, 2007.

Stage Appearances:

Fleance and young Seyward, *Macbeth,* English Shakespeare Company, Royalty Theatre, London, 1992.

Caliban, *The Tempest,* English Shakespeare Company, Royalty Theatre, 1992.

Christensen, *Casement,* Theatre at Riverside Studios, London, 1995.

RECORDINGS

Video Games:

Voice of Ivan Verov, *Star Trek: Away Team,* Activision, 2001.

JEROME, Timothy 1943–
(Tim Jerome)

PERSONAL

Born December 29, 1943, in Los Angeles, CA; children: Emma. *Education:* Graduate of Ithaca College.

Career: Actor. McCarter Repertory Company, Princeton University, member, 1967–68; Arena Stage, Washington, DC, member of company, 1978–79 and 1979–80; National Music Theater Network, Inc., founder.

Awards, Honors: Antoinette Perry Award nomination, featured actor in a musical, and Drama Desk Award nomination, 1987, both for *Me and My Girl.*

CREDITS

Stage Appearances:

(Broadway debut) Dr. Carrasco, *Man of La Mancha,* American National Theatre and Academy (ANTA), Washington Square Theatre, New York City, 1965, then Martin Beck Theatre, New York City, 1968, later Mark Hellinger Theatre, New York City, 1971.

Nathan Rothschild, *The Rothschilds,* Lunt–Fontanne Theatre, New York City, 1970.

Macheath, *The Beggars Opera,* Brooklyn Academy of Music, Brooklyn, NY, 1972.

Understudy for the roles of Lucifer and God, *The Creation of the World and Other Business,* Shubert Theatre, New York City, 1972.

Reader, *The Winter Calligraphy of Ustad Selim,* American Musical and Dramatic Academy (AMDA) Theatre, New York City, 1974.

Pretzels, Theatre Four, New York City, 1974.

Feldman, *The Magic Show,* Cort Theatre, New York City, 1974.

St. Joan, Long Wharf Theatre, New Haven, CT, 1976.

Himself, Moony Shapiro, Mr. Woo, cop, Fat German, USO entertainer, and Senator "Beanpole" Pickles, *The Mooney Shapiro Songbook,* Morosco Theatre, New York City, 1981.

Bustopher Jones, Asparagus, Growltiger, *Cats,* Winter Garden Theatre, New York City, 1982–86.

Willy, *Colette Collage,* York Theatre Company, Church of the Heavenly Rest, New York City, 1983.

Dr. Glass and Senator Blake, *Room Service,* Roundabout Theatre, New York City, 1986.

Herbert Parchester, *Me and My Girl,* Marquis Theatre, New York City, 1986–89.

Monsieur Firmin, *The Phantom of the Opera,* Majestic Theatre, New York City, 1988.

General Director Preysing, Saxonia Mills, *Grand Hotel,* Martin Beck Theatre, 1989.

Romance in Hard Times, New York Shakespeare Festival, Anspacher Theatre, New York City, 1989.

Lost in Yonkers, Richard Rogers Theatre, New York City, 1991–93.

Cardinal Pointy, *The Petrified Prince,* Public Theatre, New York City, 1994–95.

John Hemings, *Swansong,* White Barn Theatre, Westport, CT, 2002.

Benoit and Alcindoro, *La Boheme,* Broadway Theatre, New York City, 2002–2003.

Professor Porter, *Tarzan* (also known as *Disney's "Tarzan"*) Richard Rogers Theatre, 2006–2007.

Also appeared in *Civilization and Its Discontents,* off–Broadway production; *The Little Prince,* off–Broadway production; *1940s's Radio Hour; Tintypes; Tomfoolery; Plenty; Joseph;* as Maurice, *Beauty and the Beast,* Broadway production.

Major Tours:

Dr. Carrasco, *Man of La Mancha,* U.S. cities, 1969.

The teacher, *The Baker's Wife,* U.S. cities, 1976.

Film Appearances:

Mr. Graham, *Getting Wasted,* 1980.

Rabbi, *Compromising Positions,* Paramount, 1985.

Jud/bartender, *Betrayed* (also known as *Summer Lightning Sundown*), Metro–Goldwyn–Mayer, 1988.

(As Tim Jerome) Dixie Davis, *Billy Bathgate,* 1991.

Paul, *Husbands and Wives,* 1992.

Academic, *I.Q.,* 1994.

X–ray room doctor, *Everyone Says I Love You,* Miramax, 1996.

Director/Harry's character, *Deconstructing Harry,* 1997.

(As Tim Jerome) Dr. Bauer, *A Price Above Rubies,* Miramax, 1998.

(As Tim Jerome) Harvey, *Mixing Nia,* Xenon Entertainment Group, 1998.

Hotel clerk, *Celebrity,* Miramax, 1998.

Bert Weston, *Cradle Will Rock,* Buena Vista, 1999.

Journalist, *Thirteen Days,* New Line Cinema, 2000.

(As Tim Jerome) Dr. Lance, *Sidewalks of New York,* 2001.

(As Tim Jerome) Injured scientist, *Spider–Man 2,* Columbia, 2004.

Television Appearances; Episodic:

Harold Sanders, "Good–bye, Mr. Fish: Part 2," *Barney Miller,* 1977.

Murray, "Fudge," *Lou Grant,* 1977.

Carlson Jr., "Wyatt Loves Bonnie," *The Tony Randall Show,* 1978.

(As Tim Jerome) "Playing the Roxy," *Laverne & Shirley* (also known as *Laverne & Shirley & Company* and *Laverne & Shirley & Friends*), 1978.

Extra, "Nightmare," *Lucan,* 1978.

(As Tim Jerome) Voice, *Heritage: Civilization and the Jews,* 1984.

(As Tim Jerome) Sam Laval, "All in the Family," *Law & Order,* NBC, 2004.

(As Tim Jerome) Peter Lynch, "Revelations," *Third Watch,* NBC, 2005.

JOHNSON, Kenneth 1942–
(Ken Johnson, Lillian Weezer)

PERSONAL

Born October 26, 1942, in Pine Bluff, AR; son of Helene (maiden name, Brown) Johnson; married Bonnie Hollaway, February 2, 1963 (divorced, 1975); married Susan Appling, June 19, 1977; children: (first marriage) David, Juliet, Michael; (second marriage) Katharine, Olivia. *Education:* Carnegie Institute of Technology (now Carnegie–Mellon University), Pittsburgh, PA, B.F.A., 1964.

Addresses: Office—Kenneth Johnson Productions, 4461 Vista Del Monte Ave., Suite 1, Sherman Oaks, CA 91403–2948.

Career: Director, producer, and writer. Kenneth Johnson Productions, Sherman Oaks, CA, executive producer and developer of television series and movies; also worked as a stage manager in New York City. University of California, Los Angeles, instructor in film and television; also taught at University of Southern California and at England's national film and television school.

Awards, Honors: Television Award nomination, best original or adapted multi–part long–form series, Writers Guild of America, 1984, for *V;* Founder's Award, Viewers for Quality Television, 1990, for *Alien Nation;* Edgar Allan Poe Award nomination, best television feature or miniseries, Mystery Writers of America, 1994, for *Sherlock Holmes Returns;* Lifetime Achievement Award, *Sci–Fi Universe,* 1996.

CREDITS

Television Work; Series:

Producer, *The Reel Game* (game show), ABC, 1971.

Producer and director, *Hollywood's Talking* (game show), CBS, 1973.

Producer (with others), *The Six Million Dollar Man,* ABC, 1973–78.

Creator, producer, and supervising producer, *The Bionic Woman,* ABC, 1976–77, NBC, 1977–78.

Creator and executive producer, *The Incredible Hulk,* CBS, 1978–82.

Creator and executive producer, *The Curse of Dracula* (also known as *Cliffhangers: The Curse of Dracula, Dracula '79, The Loves of Dracula,* and *The World of Dracula*), NBC, 1979.

Creator and executive producer, *Stop Susan Williams,* NBC, 1979.

Creator and executive producer, *The Secret Empire* (also known as *Cliffhangers: The Secret Empire*), NBC, 1979.

Executive producer (with others) *Hot Pursuit,* NBC, 1984.

Creator and executive producer, *Shadow Chasers,* ABC, 1985.

Creator and executive producer, *Alien Nation,* Fox, 1989–90.

Director, *JAG,* CBS, multiple episodes, between 2002 and 2004.

Began as associate producer, became producer, *The Mike Douglas Show,* syndicated, c. 1964–66; also producer of *Juvenile Jury.*

Television Work; Miniseries:

Creator, executive producer, and director, *V* (also known as *V: The Original Mini Series*), NBC, 1983.

Creator and executive producer, *V: The Final Battle,* NBC, 1984.

Executive producer and director, *Venus Rising,* PAX, 2002.

Television Executive Producer and Director; Movies:

The Incredible Hulk: Married (also known as *Bride of the Incredible Hulk*), CBS, 1978.
Senior Trip!, CBS, 1981.
The Liberators, ABC, 1987.
Sherlock Holmes Returns (also known as *1994 Baker Street: Sherlock Holmes Returns*), CBS, 1993.
Alien Nation: Dark Horizon, Fox, 1994.
Alien Nation: Body and Soul, Fox, 1995.
Alien Nation: Millennium, Fox, 1996.
Alien Nation: The Enemy Within, Fox, 1996.
Alien Nation: The Udara Legacy, Fox, 1997.
The Master Race, 2001.

Television Director; Movies:

Zenon: Girl of the 21st Century, Disney Channel, 1999.
Don't Look Under the Bed, Disney Channel, 1999.
The Valley of Secrets, TBS, 2002.

Television Work; Pilots:

Executive producer and director, *The Incredible Hulk,* CBS, 1977.
Producer and director, *The Return of the Incredible Hulk* (also known as *The Incredible Hulk: Death in the Family*), CBS, 1977.
Executive producer and director, *Hot Pursuit,* NBC, 1984.
Executive producer and director, *Shadow Chasers,* ABC, 1985.
Executive producer and director, *Alien Nation,* Fox, 1989.

Television Work; Specials:

Director, *The Alan King Special,* ABC, 1969.
Director, *Alan King Looks Back in Anger—A Review of 1972,* ABC, 1973.
Producer, with Don Kibbee, and director, *Alan King in Las Vegas, Part I,* ABC, 1973.
Producer, with Kibbee; and director, *Alan King in Las Vegas, Part II,* ABC, 1973.
Producer, *The Secret of Bigfoot* (also known as *The Six Million Dollar Man: The Secret of Bigfoot*), 1975.
Executive producer and director, *The Girl Who Saved the World,* 1979.

Television Director; Episodic:

Hollywood's Talking (game show), CBS, 1973.
"The Framing of Billy the Kid," *Griff,* ABC, 1973.
"The Ghost Hunter," *The Bionic Woman,* ABC, 1976.
"Doomsday Is Tomorrow: Parts 1 & 2," *The Bionic Woman,* ABC, 1977.
"Married: Parts 1 & 2," *The Incredible Hulk,* CBS, 1978.
Stop Susan Williams, NBC, 1979.

The Secret Empire (also known as *Cliffhangers: The Secret Empire*), NBC, 1979.
The Curse of Dracula (also known as *Cliffhangers: The Curse of Dracula, Dracula '79, The Loves of Dracula,* and *The World of Dracula*), NBC, 1979.
"Prometheus: Parts 1 & 2," *The Incredible Hulk,* CBS, 1980.
Shadow Chasers, ABC, 1985.
Premiere episode, *Alien Nation,* Fox, 1989.

Also directed episodes of *Adam–12,* NBC; and *Seven Days* (also known as *Seven Days: The Series*), UPN.

Television Appearances; Pilots:

(Uncredited) Voice of Scotty, *The Incredible Hulk,* CBS, 1977.

Television Appearances; Episodic:

"Pedro Arrupe: A Man for Others," *For Our Times,* CBS, 1987.

Film Director:

(And producer, as Ken Johnson) *An Evening with Edgar Allan Poe,* 1972.
Short Circuit 2, TriStar, 1988.
Steel, Warner Bros., 1997.

WRITINGS

Television Series:

Griff, ABC, 1973.
The Bionic Woman, ABC, 1976–77.
(And composer of theme music) *Alien Nation,* Fox, 1989.

Also writer for *The Six Million Dollar Man,* ABC.

Television Pilots:

The Bionic Woman (also known as *The Six Million Dollar Man: The Bionic Woman*), CBS, 1975.
The Incredible Hulk (based on characters created by Stan Lee and Marvel Comics), CBS, 1977.
The Return of the Incredible Hulk (also known as *The Incredible Hulk: Death in the Family*), CBS, 1977.
Hot Pursuit, NBC, 1984.
Shadow Chasers, ABC, 1985.
Alien Nation, Fox, 1989.

Television Movies:

The Incredible Hulk: Married (also known as *The Bride of the Incredible Hulk*), CBS, 1978.
(And music composer) *Senior Trip!,* CBS, 1981.
The Liberators, ABC, 1987.

Sherlock Holmes Returns (also known as *1994 Baker Street: Sherlock Holmes Returns*), CBS, 1993.
Alien Nation: Millennium, Fox, 1996.
The Master Race, 2001.
The Valley of Secrets, TBS, 2002.

Television Miniseries:
V (also known as *V: The Original Mini Series*), NBC, 1983.
(As Lillian Weezer) *V: The Final Battle,* NBC, 1984.
Venus Rising, PAX, 2002.

Television Specials:
The Secret of Bigfoot (also known as *The Six Million Dollar Man: The Secret of Bigfoot*), 1975.

Television Episodes:
"The Final Round," *The Incredible Hulk,* CBS, 1978.
"Never Give a Trucker an Even Break," *The Incredible Hulk,* CBS, 1978.
"Married: Parts 1 & 2," *The Incredible Hulk,* CBS, 1978.
"Prometheus: Parts 1 & 2," *The Incredible Hulk,* CBS, 1980.

Screenplays:
An Evening with Edgar Allan Poe, 1972.
(And song "Steel Yourself") *Steel,* Warner Bros., 1997.

Novels:
V: The Second Generation, TOR, 2007.

ADAPTATIONS

The 1979 special *The Girl Who Saved the World* was based on characters created by Johnson. The film *D3: The Mighty Ducks,* released by Buena Vista in 1996, was based on a story by Johnson.

OTHER SOURCES

Electronic:
Kenneth Johnson Official Site, http://www.kennethjohnson.us, August 10, 2007.

JONES, Cherry 1956–

PERSONAL

Born November 21, 1956, in Paris, TN; father, a flower shop owner; mother, a high school teacher; companion of Mary O'Connor (an architect). *Education:* Carnegie–Mellon University, B.F.A., drama.

Addresses: *Agent*—William Morris Agency, One William Morris Pl., Beverly Hills, CA 90212.

Career: Actress. American Repertory Theatre, Cambridge, MA, founding member and member of company, 1980–?; Arena Stage, Washington, DC, guest artist, 1983–84. Previously worked as a waitress.

Member: Actors Equity.

Awards, Honors: Antoinette Perry Award nomination, best performance by a leading actress in a play, 1991, for *Our Country's Good;* Obie Award, *Village Voice,* 1992, for *The Baltimore Waltz;* Antoinette Perry Award, best actress, Drama Desk Award, outstanding lead actress in a play, Outer Critics' Circle Award, outstanding lead actress in a play, Drama League Award, 1995, Los Angeles Drama Critics Circle Award, outstanding lead performance, 1997, all for *The Heiress;* Elliot Norton Award, sustained excellence, 1995; Madge Evans and Sidney Kingsley Award, excellence in theater, 1998; Drama Desk Award, outstanding lead actress in a play, Outer Critics Circle Award, outstanding lead actress in a play, Lucille Lortel Award, outstanding actress, 1998, all for *Pride's Crossing;* Antoinette Perry Award nomination, best actress in a play, 2000, for *A Moon for the Misbegotten;* Chlotrudis Award nomination, best supporting actress, 2000, for *Cradle Will Rock;* Vito Russo Award, Gay and Lesbian Alliance Against Defamation (GLAAD), 2004; Antoinette Perry Award, best performance by a leading actress in a play, Lucille Lortel Award, outstanding lead actress, Drama Desk Award, outstanding actress in a play, Obie Award, performance, 2005, all for *Doubt;* Antoinette Perry Award, best actress in a play, Drama Desk Award, outstanding actress in a play, Drama Desk Award nomination, outstanding actress in a play, 2006, all for *Faith Healer;* Joseph Jefferson Award, for *The Good Person of Setzuan;* Joseph Jefferson Award, for *The Night of the Iguana.*

CREDITS

Stage Appearances:
Rosalind, *As You Like It,* American Repertory Theatre, Cambridge, MA, 1980.
Dorcas, *The Winter's Tale,* Helen Owen Carey Playhouse, Brooklyn, NY, 1980.
Millicent, *He and She,* Brooklyn Academy of Music Theatre, Brooklyn, 1980.
A Midsummer Night's Dream, American Repertory Theatre, 1981.
Irina, *Three Sisters,* American Repertory Theatre, 1983.

The Boys from Syracuse, American Repertory Theatre, 1983.

Liz, *The Philanthropist,* Manhattan Theatre Club, New York City, 1983.

Kitty Chase, *The Ballad of Soapy Smith,* New York Shakespeare Festival, Public Theatre, New York City, 1984.

Love's Labour's Lost, American Repertory Theatre, 1984.

Sally Bowles, *I Am a Camera,* American Jewish Theatre, New York City, 1984.

Cecily Cardew, *The Importance of Being Earnest,* Samuel Beckett Theatre, New York City, 1985.

Lynne, *Steppin' Out,* John Golden Theatre, New York City, 1987.

Sara Littlefield, *Claptrap,* Manhattan Theatre Club, 1987.

Dorine, *Tartuffe,* Portland Stage Company, Portland, ME, 1987.

Fran, *Big Time: Scenes from a Service Economy,* American Theatre Exchange, Joyce Theatre, New York City, 1988.

Lady Macbeth, *Macbeth,* Mark Hellinger Theatre, New York City, 1988.

Light Shining in Buckinghamshire, Perry Street Theatre, New York City, 1991.

Reverend Johnson, Liz Morden, *Our Country's Good,* Nederlander Theatre, New York City, 1991.

Anna, the sister, *The Baltimore Waltz,* Circle Repertory Theatre, New York City, 1992.

Constance Ledbelly, *Goodnight Desdemona (Good Morning Juliet),* East 13th Street Theatre, New York City, 1992.

Angel, Emily, Mormon mother, *Angels in America: Perestroika,* Walter Kerr Theatre, New York City, 1993–94.

Ella Chapter, Emily, The Angel, and woman in the South Bronx, *Angels in America: Millennium Approaches,* Walter Kerr Theatre, New York City, 1993–94.

Bianca, *Desdemona,* Circle Repertory Theatre, 1993.

Anna, *And Baby Makes Seven,* Lucille Lortel Theatre, New York City, 1993.

Catherine Sloper, *The Heiress,* Lincoln Center, New York City, 1995, Ahmanson Theatre, Los Angeles, c. 1997.

Hannah Jelkes, *The Night of the Iguana,* Roundabout Theatre, New York City, 1996.

Necessary Targets, Helen Hayes Theatre, New York City, 1996.

Mabel Tidings Bigelow, *Pride's Crossing,* Old Globe Theatre, then Mitzi E. Newhouse Theatre, New York City, 1997–98.

Psyche, New York Philharmonic, Lincoln Center, 1998.

Maxine, *Tongue of a Bird,* Joseph Papp Public Theatre, New York City, 1999.

Josie Hogan, *A Moon for the Misbegotten,* Goodman Theatre, Chicago, IL, then Walter Kerr Theatre, 2000.

Barbara Undershaft, *Major Barbara,* American Airlines Theatre, New York City, 2001.

Title role, *Lysistrata,* Loeb Drama Center, Cambridge, MA, 2002.

Mary McCarthy, *Imaginary Friends,* Old Globe Theatre, San Diego, CA, 2002, then Ethel Barrymore Theatre, New York City, 2002–2003.

Mary Stassos, *Flesh and Blood,* New York Theatre Workshop, New York City, 2003.

Sister Aloysius, *Doubt,* Walter Kerr Theatre, 2005–2006, then Ahmanson Theatre, 2006.

Grace Hardy, *Faith Healer,* Booth Theatre, New York City, 2006.

Also appeared as Viola, *Twelfth Night,* American Repertory Theatre, Cambridge, MA; title role, *Major Barbara,* American Repertory Theatre; *Sganarelle,* American Repertory Theatre; *The Journey of the Fifth Horse,* American Repertory Theatre; *Ghosts,* American Repertory Theatre; *The School for Scandal,* American Repertory Theatre; *Baby with the Bath Water,* American Repertory Theatre; *The Caucasian Chalk Circle,* American Repertory Theatre; *The Good Person of Setzuan; The Seagull; Mastergate,* American Repertory Theatre.

Film Appearances:
Ginger McDonald, *The Big Town* (also known as *The Arm*), Columbia, 1987.

Cindy Montgomery, *Light of Day* (also known as *Born in the U.S.A.*), TriStar, 1987.

Patty, *HouseSitter,* 1992.

Virginia, *Polio Water,* 1995.

Lucy, the maid, *Julian Po* (also known as *The Tears of Julian Po*), Fine Line Features, 1997.

Voice of Annie Adams Fields, *Out of the Past,* Unapix Entertainment, 1998.

Liz Hammond, *The Horse Whisperer,* Buena Vista, 1998.

Hallie Flanagan, *Cradle Will Rock,* Buena Vista, 1999.

Pamela Duncan, *Erin Brockovich,* Universal, 2000.

Edie Bailey, *The Perfect Storm* (also known as *Der Sturm*), Warner Bros., 2000.

Grandma "Buggy" Abbott, *Divine Secrets of the Ya–Ya Sisterhood,* Warner Bros., 2002.

Officer Paski, *Signs* (also known as *M. Night Shyamalan's "Signs"*), Buena Vista, 2002.

Herself, *Making "Signs"* (documentary), Buena Vista Home Entertainment, 2003.

Mrs. Clack, *The Village* (also known as *Grey* and *M. Night Shyamalan's "The Village"*), Buena Vista, 2004.

Molly Star/Mrs. Caldwell, *Ocean's Twelve,* Warner Bros., 2004.

Julia Tyler, *Swimmers,* Skouras Pictures, 2005.

Herself, *RSC Meets USA: Working Shakespeare,* 2005.

Voice of herself, *Chaos and Order: Making American Theater,* Films for the Humanities, 2005.

Broadway: Beyond the Golden Age (documentary; also known as *B.G.A. 2* and *Broadway: The Golden Age 2*), 2008.

Television Appearances; Series:
Frankie, *Loving,* 1992.
President Allison Taylor, *24,* Fox, 2008.

Television Appearances; Miniseries:
Voice, *The West,* 1996.
Voices, *Jazz,* PBS, 2001.

Television Appearances; Movies:
Tina Crawford, *Alex: The Life of a Child,* ABC, 1986.
Mimi Barnes, *Murder in a Small Town,* Arts and Entertainment, 1999.
Mimi Barnes, *The Lady in Question,* Arts and Entertainment, 1999.
Lizbeth Studevant, *Cora Unashamed,* PBS, 2000.
Sandy Cataldi, *What Makes a Family,* Lifetime, 2000.

Television Appearances; Specials:
Voice, *Margaret Sanger,* PBS, 1998.
Presenter, *The 55th Annual Tony Awards,* CBS, 2001.
Narrator, *Miss America,* PBS, 2002.
The 50th Annual Drama Desk Awards, 2005.
The 59th Annual Tony Awards, CBS, 2005.

Television Appearances; Pilots:
Secretary, *O'Malley,* NBC, 1983.
Janice Eaton, *Adam's Apple,* CBS, 1986.
Sister Marie, *Clubhouse,* CBS, 2004.

Television Appearances; Episodic:
Tracy Kincaid, "Sleepless Dream," *Spenser: For Hire,* 1987.
Voice, "Innocence Lost: The Plea," *Frontline,* PBS, 1997.
The Rosie O'Donnell Show, syndicated, 1999, 2000.
In the Life, 2001.
Janet, *Frasier,* NBC, 2001.
Narrator, "Miss America," *The American Experience,* PBS, 2002.
"ODB on Parole," *Inside Out,* MTV, 2003.
Barbara Layton, "Eppur Si Muove," *The West Wing,* NBC, 2004.
Sister Marie, "Breaking a Slump," *Clubhouse,* CBS, 2004.

Radio Appearances:
Read stories on *Selected Shorts,* National Public Radio.

RECORDINGS

Taped Readings:
Secrecy, Random House Audio, 1997.
The Grilling Season: A Culinary Mystery, Random House Audio, 1997.
Prime Cut, Random House Audio, 1998.

Practical Magic, Audioworks, 1998.
Tough Cookie, Random House Audio, 2000.
Sticks & Stones, Random House Audio, 2001.
Body of Lies, Random House Audio, 2002.
Little House in the Big Woods, HarperAudio, 2003.
On the Banks of Plum Creek, HarperChildren's Audio, 2003.
Little House on the Prairie, HarperChildren's Audio, 2003.
Bulfinch's Mythology: Gods and Heroes, Caedmon, 2003.
Farmer Boy, Harper Children's Audio, 2004.
So B. It, Harper Children's Audio, 2004.
By the Shores of the Silver Lake, Harper's Children Audio, 2004.
The Heart Is a Lonely Hunter, Harper, 2004.
The Long Winter, Harper Children's Audio, 2005.
Children Playing Before a Statue of Hercules, Simon & Schuster Audio, 2005.
Little Town on the Prairie, Harper Children's Audio, 2005.
Those Happy Golden Years, Harper Children's Audio, 2006.
The First Four Years, Harper Children's Audio, 2006.
Little House in the Big Woods (unabridged), Harper Children's Audio, 2007.

OTHER SOURCES

Books:
Newsmakers 1999, Issue 3, Gale Group, 1999.

Periodicals:
New York Times, May 26, 1991, p. H5.

JONES, Simon 1950–

PERSONAL

Born July 27, 1950, in Charlton Park, Wiltshire, England; married Nancy Lewis, December 3, 1983; children: Timothy. *Education:* Attended Cambridge University.

Addresses: *Agent*—Innovative Artists, 1505 10th St., Santa Monica, CA 90401.

Career: Actor. The Actors Company Theatre (TACT), New York, NY, co–artistic director; voice for commercials, including voice for Frosted Mini Wheats character, 2001–02.

Awards, Honors: Outer Critics Circle Award nomination, outstanding featured actor in a play, 2000, for *Waiting in the Wings;* Drama Desk Award nomination, for *Privates on Parade.*

CREDITS

Film Appearances:
Joachim, *Sir Henry at Rawlinson End,* Charisma Films, 1980.
Sergeant Eric Young–Love, *Privates on Parade,* 1982, Orion, 1984.
Henderson, *Giro City* (also known as *And Nothing but the Truth*), Castle Hill, 1982.
Jeremy Portland–Smythe, *The Meaning of Live* (also known as *Monty Python's "The Meaning of Life"*), Universal, 1983.
Arrest official, *Brazil,* Universal, 1985.
Toby Prooth, *Club Paradise,* Warner Bros., 1986.
Party guest, *Green Card,* Buena Vista, 1990.
Anderson, *American Friends,* Castle Hill, 1991.
Albert, *For Love or Money* (also known as *The Concierge*), Universal, 1993.
Donald Shellhammer, *Miracle on 34th Street,* Twentieth Century–Fox, 1994.
Zoologist, *Twelve Monkeys,* Universal, 1995.
Harry Sloan, *The Devil's Own,* Columbia, 1997.
(Uncredited) The accountant, *The Thomas Crown Affair,* 1999.
Himself, *Broadway: The Golden Age, by the Legends Who Were There* (also known as *Broadway, Broadway: The Golden Age,* and *Broadway: The Movie*), Dada Films, 2004.
Ghostly image, *The Hitchhiker's Guide to the Galaxy,* Buena Vista/Touchstone, 2005.
The Duck, *Spectropia,* Bustlelamp Productions, 2006.

Some sources cite role of removal man in a film titled *Guru in Seven,* 1998.

Television Appearances; Series:
Basil Bastedes, *Muck and Brass,* 1982.
Newscaster, *The News Is the News,* NBC, 1983.
Eric, *Sunday Premiere: Claws,* BBC, 1987.
Norman Asher, *Tattingers* (also known as *Nick & Hillary*), NBC, 1989.
Guy Armitage, *One Life to Live,* ABC, 1997.

Television Appearances; Miniseries:
Arthur Dent, *The Hitchhiker's Guide to the Galaxy,* BBC, 1981.
"Bridey," Lord Brideshead, *Brideshead Revisited,* PBS, 1982.
Andrew, *The Price,* 1985.
Ambrose Serle, *Liberty! The American Revolution,* PBS, 1997.
Paramour, AMC, 1999.

Thomas Penn, *Benjamin Franklin,* PBS, 2002.
Sir Michael Boal, *Cambridge Spies,* BBC, 2003.

Television Appearances; Specials:
"The Kindness of Mrs. Radcliffe," *BBC2 Playhouse,* BBC, 1981.
"No Visible Scar," *Play for Today,* BBC, 1981.
C. S. Lewis, *The Question of God: Sigmund Freud & C. S. Lewis,* 2004.
Voice of Plato, *Quest for Atlantis: Starting New Secrets,* Sci–Fo Channel, 2006.
Himself, *What the Pythons Did Next,* 2007.

Television Appearances; Movies:
Professor Anysley, *Griffin & Phoenix,* Lifetime, 2006.

Television Appearances; Pilots:
Jamison, "King of the Building," *CBS Summer Playhouse,* CBS, 1987.

Television Appearances; Episodic:
Juan, "The Blitz," *Rock Follies,* ITV, 1976.
Juan, "The Pounds Sterling," *Rock Follies,* ITV, 1976.
Mr. Thornbury, "Hannah," *Victorian Scandals,* Granada, 1976.
Calvin, "Two Harts Are Better Than One," *Hart to Hart,* ABC, 1983.
Sir Walter Raleigh, "Potato," *Blackadder II,* BBC, 1986.
Barnaby Friar, "Witness for the Defense," *Murder, She Wrote,* CBS, 1987.
Dr. Miles Rangel, "Dr. Jekyll and Mr. Loudon," *Newhart,* CBS, 1987.
Arthur Dent, "Douglas Adams," *The South Bank Show,* ITV, 1992.
Geoffrey Butler, *Loving,* 1992.
Winston Murdoch, "The Fine Art of Murder," *The Cosby Mysteries,* NBC, 1994.
Ted E. Peck, "Valentino Speaks!" *Remember WENN,* AMC, 1996.
Dr. Eckert, *As the World Turns,* 1999.
Judge Mason Kessler, "The Bill of Wrongs," *Oz,* HBO, 2000.
Darien Marshall, "Folly," *Law & Order: Special Victims Unit* (also known as *Law & Order: SVU*), NBC, 2001.
Interviewee, "Douglas Adams: The Man Who Blew Up the World," *Omnibus,* BBC, 2001.
Judge Mason Kessler, "Exeunt Omnes," *Oz,* HBO, 2003.

Television Appearances; Other:
Out of the Trees, 1976.
Jack Cavendish, *Shrinks,* 1990.

Stage Appearances:
Zachariah, *Wild Oats, or "The Strolling Gentleman,"* Aldwych Theatre, London, 1976.

Wilson, *Terra Nova,* American Place Theatre, New York City, 1984.

Max, *The Real Thing,* Plymouth Theatre, New York City, c. 1985.

Colin, *Benefactors,* Brooks Atkinson Theatre, New York City, 1985–86.

Bill, *Woman in Mind,* Manhattan Theatre Club Stage I, New York City, 1988.

Giles Flack, *Privates on Parade,* Roundabout Theatre Company, Union Square Theatre, New York City, 1989.

Reginald Bridgenorth, *Getting Married,* Circle in the Square, New York City, 1991.

Henry Higgins, *My Fair Lady* (musical), Michigan Opera Theatre, Detroit, MI, then Paper Mill Playhouse, Millburn, NJ, 1991.

Moon, *The Real Inspector Hound,* and Hamlet, *The Fifteen Minute Hamlet* (double–bill), Roundabout Theatre Club, Criterion Center Stage Right Theatre, New York City, 1992.

Elyot Chase, *Private Lives,* Broadhurst Theatre, New York City, 1992.

Joseph Surface, *The School for Scandal,* Lyceum Theatre, New York City, 1995.

Sebastian Sebastian, *Call Me Madam,* City Center Theatre, New York City, 1995.

The Cocktail Party, Edinburgh Festival, Edinburgh, Scotland, 1997.

Barnabas Goche, Vicar General, *The Herbal Bed,* Eugene O'Neill Theatre, New York City, 1998.

Crampton, *You Never Can Tell,* Roundabout Theatre Company, Laura Pels Theatre, New York City, 1998.

Romainville, *Ring 'round the Moon,* Belasco Theatre, New York City, 1999.

Perry Lascoe, *Waiting in the Wings,* Eugene O'Neill Theatre, 1999–2000, then Walter Kerr Theatre, New York City, 2000.

First Lady (staged reading), The Actors Company Theatre (TACT), New York City, 2000.

Sherlock Holmes, *Baker Street,* York Theatre Company, Theatre at St. Peter's, New York City, 2001.

James, *Passion Play,* Minetta Lane Theatre, New York City, 2001.

Sir Francis Chesney, *Where's Charley?* (musical), Adams Memorial Theatre, Williamstown, MA, 2002.

Mr. Micawber, *David Copperfield,* Westport Country Playhouse, Westport, CT, 2005.

Robert, *Betrayal,* Singapore Repertory Theatre, Singapore, 2005.

Reginald Paget, *Quartet,* Bay Street Theatre, Sag Harbor, NY, 2006.

Jack, *Home,* TACT, Becket Theatre, New York City, 2006.

Phallacy, Cherry Lane Theatre, New York City, 2007.

Appeared in *The Gay Divorce,* Theatre at Carnegie Hall, New York City; *Hapgood,* Los Angeles production; and *The Quick–Change Room,* off–Broadway production; appeared in benefit and concert performances, including *Anything Goes,* Manchester, England; *Betting on Bertie,* Promenade Theatre, New York City; "Call Me Madam," *City Center Encores!,* City Center Theatre, New York City; and *Darling of the Day,* York Theatre, New York City.

Radio Appearances; Series:
Arthur Dent, *The Hitchhiker's Guide to the Galaxy,* 1978, 2004, 2005.

Host of *Talk of New York,* BBC–4.

Radio Appearances; Pilots:
Sexton Blake, *The Adventures of Sexton Blake,* 2006.

Radio Appearances; Episodic:
Panelist, *Quote/Unquote,* BBC4, 2006.
28 Acts in 28 Minutes, BBC4, 2007.

Internet Appearances:
Participated in the Internet presentations "Alice in Wonderland" and "The History of the Devil," both *Seeing Ear Theatre.*

RECORDINGS

Audio Books; Reader:
Billy Budd, by Herman Melville, DH Audio, 1986.
Long Dark Tea–Time of the Soul, by Douglas Adams, Simon & Schuster Audio, 1989.
Rat Race, by Dick Francis, Harper Audio, 1990.
Curtain, by Michael Korda, 1991.
Comeback, by Dick Francis, Harper, 1991.
Driving Force, by Dick Francis, HarperAudio, 1992.
The Hitch Hiker's Guide to the Galaxy, by Douglas Adams, BBC Audiobooks, 1993.
The Way through the Woods, by Durkin Hayes, 1993.
A Bad Heart, by Ruth Rendell, DH Audio, 1993.
Decider, 1994.
Fist of God, by Frederick Forsyth, Random House Audio, 1994.
Free to Trade: An Unprecedented Financial Thriller of International Proportions, by Michael Ridpath, HarperAudio, 1994.
Wild Horses, 1995.
The Return of Merlin: A Novel, by Deepak Chopra, Random House Audio, 1995.
The Fall of the Coin, by Ruth Rendell, DH Audio, 1998.
The Professor and the Madman, by Simon Winchester, Harper, 1998.
AccessWalks London, by Nan Lyons, HarperAudio, 1999.
Leading Ladies of Mystery, by Ellis Peters and Ruth Rendell, Thomas T. Beeler, 1999.

PSV Come to Grief, by Dick Francis, Simon & Schuster Audio, 1999.

The Twisted Root, by Anne Perry, Random House Audio, 1999.

The Cloud Sketcher, by Richard Rayner, Landmark Audiobooks, 2000.

Slaves of Obsession, by Anne Perry, Random House Audio, 2000.

French Lessons: Adventures with Knife, Fork, and Corkscrew, by Peter Mayle, Random House Audio, 2001.

The Hitchhiker's Guide to the Galaxy: The Primary Phase, by Douglas Adams, BBC Audiobooks, 2001.

A Traitor to Memory, by Elizabeth George, Random House Audio, 2001.

The Fifth Sorceress, by Robert Newcomb, Random House Audio, 2002.

The Salmon of Doubt: Hitchhiking the Galaxy One Last Time, by Douglas Adams, New Millennium Audio, 2002.

The Thief Lord, by Cornelia Funke, Listening Library, 2002.

Throwing the Elephant/What Would Machiavelli Do?, by Stanley Bing, HarperAudio, 2002.

The Gates of Dawn, by Robert Newcomb, Random House Audio, 2003.

Into Africa: The Epic Adventures of Stanley and Livingstone, by Martin Dugard, Random House Audio, 2003.

Lionboy, by Zizou Corder, Highbridge Audio, 2003.

A Place of Hiding, by Elizabeth George, Hodder & Stoughton Audio Books, 2003.

The Bartimaeus Trilogy: The Golem's Eye Book Two, by Jonathan Stroud, Listening Library, 2004.

Millions, by Frank Cottrell Boyce, HarperChildren's Audio, 2004.

The Hitchhiker's Guide to the Galaxy Quandary Phase, by Douglas Adams, Sound Library, 2005.

The Bartimaeus Trilogy: Ptolemy's Gate, by Jonathan Stroud, Listening Library, 2005.

The Last Voyage of Columbus: Being the Epic Tale of the Great Captain's Fourth Expedition, Including Accounts of Swordfight, Mutiny, Shipwreck, Gold, War, Hurricane, and Discovery, by Martin Dugard, Hachette Audio, 2005.

The Noel Coward CD Audio Collection Selections, by Noel Coward, Caedmon, 2005.

The Bartimaeus Trilogy: The Amulet of Samarkand, by Jonathan Stroud, Listening Library, 2006.

The Kindness of Mrs. Radcliffe Written by Noel Coward, HarperCollins, 2006.

Cheap Excursion Written by Noel Coward, HarperCollins, 2006.

The Secret Supper: A Novel, by Javier Sierra, Simon & Schuster Audio, 2006.

The Selected Poetry of Noel Coward, HarperCollins, 2006.

In Secret Service; A Novel, by Mitch Silver, Simon & Schuster Audio, 2007.

Also narrator for *Brief Encounter: A Complete Adaptation Written by Noel Coward.*

Videos:

Himself and Arthur Dent, *The Making of "The Hitchhiker's Guide to the Galaxy,"* BBC, 1993.

Himself, *Life, the Universe, and Douglas Adams,* Greater Talent Network/Greengrass Communications/PointBreak Productions, 2002.

OTHER SOURCES

Periodicals:
Dreamwatch, October, 2004, pp. 42–43.

K

PERSONAL

Son of Jeannette Kerner (an actress); married Nicola O'Shea (an executive); children: Haley Lelean O'Shea Kerner. *Education:* Stanford University, undergraduate degree with distinction; University of California, Berkeley, M.B.A.; University of California, San Francisco, J.D.

Addresses: *Agent*—Creative Artists Agency, 2000 Avenue of the Stars, Los Angeles, CA 90067. *Office*—Kerner Entertainment Group, 469 Saint Pierre Rd., Los Angeles, CA 90077.

Career: Producer and studio executive. Worked for CBS–TV affiliate, San Francisco, CA, during college; Ball, Hunt, Brown and Baerwitz, Beverly Hills, CA, worked in motion picture department; CBS–TV, Los Angeles, CA, worked as talent and program negotiator in Business Affairs department through 1978; joined Universal/NBC as director of program development, 1978–80; worked in development at QM Productions, 1980; joined ABC Entertainment as director of dramatic series development, 1981–83, then vice president of dramatic development, 1983–86; Avnet/Kerner Co. (production company), founder (with Jon Avnet), 1986; Kerner Entertainment Company, Los Angeles, CA, producer. Community College Industry Partnership, member of new media advisory committee; Starbright Foundation, member of board of directors; Minnesota Film Board, member of advisory board; President's Advisory Council to the City, member; Media Office, Inc., member of board of directors; Committee of the Arts of the Beverly Hills Bar Association, founder and former chairperson.

Awards, Honors: CableACE Award (with others), movie or miniseries, National Cable Television Association,

1991, for *Heat Wave;* Wise Owl Award (with others), best television and theatrical film fiction, Retirement Research Foundation, 1992, for *Fried Green Tomatoes.*

CREDITS

Film Producer:
(With Jon Avnet) *Less Than Zero,* Twentieth Century–Fox, 1987.
Funny About Love, Paramount, 1990.
(With Avnet) *Fried Green Tomatoes* (also known as *Fried Green Tomatoes at the Whistle Stop Cafe*), Universal, 1991.
(With Avnet) *The Mighty Ducks* (also known as *Champions* and *The Mighty Ducks Are Champions*), Buena Vista, 1992.
(With Avnet) *D2: The Mighty Ducks* (also known as *The Mighty Ducks 2*), Buena Vista, 1994.
(With Avnet) *The War,* Universal, 1994.
(With Avnet) *When a Man Loves a Woman* (also known as *To Have and To Hold*), 1994.
(With Avnet) *Up Close and Personal,* Buena Vista, 1996.
(With Avnet) *D3: The Mighty Ducks,* Buena Vista, 1996.
(With Avnet) *George of the Jungle,* Buena Vista, 1997.
(With Avnet) *Red Corner,* Metro–Goldwyn–Mayer, 1997.
Inspector Gadget, Buena Vista/Walt Disney Pictures, 1999.
Winterdance, Buena Vista, 2001.
Snow Dogs (also known as *Chiens des neiges*), 2002.
George of the Jungle 2, 2003.
Charlotte's Web (also known as *Schweinchen Wilbur und seine freunde*), 2006.
Summer School, 2008.

Film Executive Producer:
(With Jon Avnet) *The Three Musketeers,* Buena Vista, 1993.
(With Avnet) *Miami Rhapsody,* Buena Vista, 1995.
Inspector Gadget 2 (also known as *IG2*), 2003.

Also worked as executive producer (with Avnet), *Men Don't Leave.*

Film Appearances:
Himself, *"Fried Green Tomatoes": The Moments of Discovery,* 1998.
Airline passenger, *George of the Jungle 2,* 2003.
Himself, *"Charlotte's Web": What Makes a Classic,* 2007.
Himself, *"Charlotte's Web": Some Voices,* 2007.
Himself, *"Charlotte's Web": Making Some Movie,* 2007.
Himself, *"Charlotte's Web": How Do They Do That?,* 2007.

Television Work; Series:
Producer, *Dogs,* 1997.

Television Work; Miniseries:
Executive producer, *Naomi & Wynonna: Love Can Build a Bridge* (also known as *Love Can Build a Bridge*), NBC, 1995.
(With Jon Avnet and Carol Schreder) Executive producer, *"Mama Flora's Family," Hallmark Hall of Fame,* CBS, 1998.
(With Avnet) Producer, *Uprising,* NBC, 2001.

Television Producer; Movies:
(With Jon Avnet) *Breaking Point,* ABC, 1989.
(With Avnet) *Heat Wave,* TNT, 1990.
(With Avnet) *The Switch,* CBS, 1993.

Television Executive Producer; Movies:
(With Jon Avnet) *Side by Side,* 1988.
(With Avnet) *My First Love,* 1988.
(With Jon) *Do You Know the Muffin Man?,* CBS, 1989.
(With Avnet) *Backfield in Motion,* ABC, 1991.
(With Avnet) *The Nightman* (also known as *The Watchman*), NBC, 1992.
(With Avnet) *For Their Own Good,* ABC, 1993.
Poodle Springs, HBO, 1998.
(With Avnet) *My Last Love* (also known as *To Live For*), ABC, 1999.
A House Divided, Showtime, 2000.
Red Skies, 2002.
A Wrinkle in Time (also kwon as *Un raccourci dans le temps*), 2003.

KERSHNER, Irvin 1923–
   (Irv Kershner)

PERSONAL

Born April 29, 1923, in Philadelphia, PA. *Education:* Attended Temple University, 1946, Drexel Institute of Technology (now Drexel University), and Cambridge University; graduated from University of Southern California.

Career: Director, actor, and producer. U.S. Information Services, documentary filmmaker in the Middle East, 1950–52; Ophite Productions, former affiliate.

Member: Directors Guild of America.

Awards, Honors: OCIC Award of International Catholic Organization for Cinema and Audiovisual and nomination for Golden Palm, both Cannes Film Festival, 1961, for *Hoodlum Priest;* Emmy Award nomination, outstanding directing in a special dramatic program, 1977, for *Raid on Entebbe;* Saturn Award, best director, Academy of Science Fiction, Horror, and Fantasy Films, 1981, for *The Empire Strikes Back;* President Award, director of distinction, Fort Lauderdale International Film Festival, 2002.

CREDITS

Film Director:
Stakeout on Dope Street, Warner Bros., 1958.
The Young Captives, Paramount, 1959.
Hoodlum Priest, United Artists, 1961.
A Face in the Rain, Embassy, 1963.
The Luck of Ginger Coffey, Continental Distributing, 1964.
A Fine Madness, Warner Bros., 1966.
The Flim–Flam Man (released in England as *One Born Every Minute*), Twentieth Century–Fox, 1967.
Loving, Columbia, 1970.
Up the Sandbox, National General, 1972.
S*P*Y*S, Twentieth Century–Fox, 1974.
The Return of a Man Called Horse, United Artists, 1976.
Eyes of Laura Mars, Columbia, 1978.
The Empire Strikes Back (also known as *Star Wars: Episode V—The Empire Strikes Back* and *Star Wars V: The Empire Strikes Back*), Twentieth Century–Fox, 1980.
Never Say Never Again, Warner Bros., 1983.
Robocop 2, Orion, 1990.

Film Work; Other:
Executive producer, *Wildfire,* Zupnik Enterprises, 1988.
Producer, *American Perfekt,* American Perfekt Productions, 1997.

Film Appearances:
Zebedee, *The Last Temptation of Christ,* Universal, 1988.
Walters, *On Deadly Ground,* Warner Bros., 1994.
Mr. Stoff, *Angus* (also known as *Angus–Voll Cool*), 1996.
Himself, *Tell Them Who You Are* (documentary), Think-Film, 2004.
Himself, *Geeks* (documentary), Post No Bills Films, 2004.

(As Irv Kershner) Statistics professor, *Berkeley,* Jeffrey White Productions/Jung N Restless Productions, 2005.

Television Work; Series:
Director, *Confidential File* (also known as *Paul Coates's "Confidential File"*), syndicated, 1953–55.

Television Director; Movies:
Raid on Entebbe, NBC, 1977.
Traveling Man, HBO, 1989.

Television Director; Episodic:
"Land," *The Rebel,* ABC, 1960.
"Degrees of Guilt," *Cain's Hundred,* 1961.
"My Good Friend Krikor," *Ben Casey,* ABC, 1961.
"And by the Sweat of Thy Brow," *Naked City,* ABC, 1962.
"The End of the World, Baby," *Kraft Suspense Theatre,* 1963.
"Hell Toupee," *Amazing Stories,* (also known as *Steven Spielberg's "Amazing Stories"*), 1986.
"To Be or Not to Be," *SeaQuest DSV* (also known as *SeaQuest 2032*), 1993.

Television Appearances; Movies:
(As Irv Kershner) Gentleman, *Manhood,* Showtime, 2003.

Television Appearances; Specials:
SPFX: The Empire Strikes Back, CBS, 1980.
From "Star Wars" to "Jedi:" The Making of a Saga, PBS, 1983.
Star Wars: The Magic and the Mystery, 1997.
Hans Hofmann: Artist/Teacher, Teacher/Artist, 2003.
Empire of Dreams: The Story of the "Star Wars" Trilogy, Arts and Entertainment, 2004.
When Star Wars Ruled the World, VH1, 2004.
"Star Wars:" Feel the Force, 2005.
Shooting the Police: Cops on Film, Starz, 2006.

Television Appearances; Episodic:
Showbiz Today, Cable News Network, 1991.

RECORDINGS

Videos:
Ray Harryhausen: The Early Years Collection, Sparkhill Productions, 2005.
Ben–Hur: The Epic that Changed Cinema, Warner Bros. Entertainment, 2005.

WRITINGS

Screenplays:
Coauthor, *Stakeout on Dope Street* (also based on story by Kershner), Warner Bros., 1958.

(Uncredited) Coauthor, *A Man Called Horse,* National General, 1970.

OTHER SOURCES

Periodicals:
American Film, January–February, 1981, pp. 45–51.
Shock Cinema, Issue 24, 2004, pp. 34–36.

KIRSCHNER, David 1955–
(David M. Kirschner)

PERSONAL

Born in 1955 in Van Nuys, CA. *Education:* Attended the University of Southern California, School of Film, Los Angeles, through 1976.

Addresses: *Agent*—William Morris Agency, One William Morris Place, Beverly Hills, CA 90212.

Career: Producer and writer. Began career as an illustrator for Jim Henson's Muppet and *Sesame Street* characters; designed album covers for Neil Diamond and Olivia Newton–John; Hanna–Barbera, Los Angeles, CA, president and chief executive officer, 1989—, and chairman, 1992—.

Awards, Honors: Emmy Award nomination (with others), outstanding animated program (for programming one hour to less), 1994, for *The Town That Santa Forgot;* Annie Award nomination (with Paul Gertz), best individual achievement—producing in a feature production, 1997, Golden Crown Award, Annecy International Animated Film Festival, Annie Award (with Gertz), best individual achievement—producing in a feature production, 1997, all for *Cats Don't Dance;* Children's Book of the Year Award, American Library Association, for *The Pagemaster.*

CREDITS

Film Work:
Executive producer, *An American Tail,* 1986.
Producer and creator: Chucky doll, *Child's Play,* Metro–Goldwyn–Mayer, 1988.
Producer and creator: Chucky doll, *Child's Play 2* (also known as *Child's Play 2: Chucky's Back*), Universal, 1990.
Executive producer and creator: Chucky doll, *Child's Play 3* (also known as *Child's Play 3: Look Who's Stalking* and *Child's Play III*), Universal, 1991.

Executive producer and creator, *An American Tail: Fievel Goes West* (animated), 1991.

Executive producer, *Monster in My Pocket: The Big Scream* (animated), Kidmark, 1992.

Producer, *Hocus Pocus*, Buena Vista, 1993.

Producer, *Once Upon a Forest,* Twentieth Century–Fox, 1993.

Executive producer, *The Halloween Tree*, 1993.

Producer, *The Pagemaster*, Lauren Film, 1994.

Executive producer, *The Flintstones*, Universal, 1994.

Producer, *Cats Don't Dance* (animated), Warner Bros., 1997.

Producer and Chucky and Tiffany dolls creator, *Bride of Chucky*, Universal, 1998.

Producer, *Titan A.E.* (also known as *Titan: After Earth*), Twentieth Century–Fox, 2000.

Producer, *Immortals,* Universal, 2001.

Producer, *Frailty* (also known as *Damonisch* and *Frailty—Nessuno e al sicuro*), Lions Gate Films, 2001.

Producer, *Secondhand Lions,* New Line Cinema, 2003.

Producer and Chucky, Tiffany, and Glen dolls creator, *Seeds of Chucky* (also known as *Childs Play 5*), Rogue Pictures, 2004.

Producer, *Thru the Moebius Strip* (animated), Fantastic Films International, 2005.

Producer, *Curious George* (animated), Universal, 2006.

Producer, *Miss Potter,* Weinstein Company, 2006.

Producer, *Martian Child,* New Line Cinema, 2007.

Film Appearances:

Himself, *The Making of "Frailty"* (documentary), Live Home Video, 2002.

Himself, *"Secondhand Lions": One Screenplay's Wild Ride in Hollywood* (documentary short), New Line Home Video, 2004.

Himself, *Conceiving the "Seed of Chucky"* (documentary short), Rogue Pictures, 2005.

Television Work; Series:

Executive producer and creator, *Wake, Rattle & Roll* (also known as *Jump, Rattle & Roll*), syndicated, 1990.

Executive producer and creator, *Gravedale High* (also known as *Rick Moranis in "Gravedale High"*), NBC, 1990.

Executive producer, *Bill & Ted's Excellent Adventure,* 1990.

Executive producer and creator, *The Pirates of Dark Water* (also known as *Dark Water*), 1991–93.

Creator, *Fievel's American Tails,* 1992.

Executive producer, *The Addams Family,* 1992.

Executive producer and coproducer, *Monster in My Pocket*, ABC, 1992.

Executive producer, *Fish Police,* 1992.

Co–executive producer, *Capitol Critters,* 1992.

Executive producer, *Earth: Final Conflict* (also known as *Gene Roddenberry's "Battleground Earth," Gene*

Roddenberry's "Earth: Final Conflict," EFC, and *Mission Erde: Sie sind unter uns*), syndicated, 1997.

Executive producer, *Curious George,* 2006.

Television Work; Miniseries:

Executive producer, *5ive Days to Midnight* (also known as *Five Days to Midnight*), Sci–Fi Channel, 2004.

Television Work; Movies:

Executive producer, *The Dreamer of Oz* (also known as *The Dreamer of Oz: The L. Frank Baum Story*), CBS, 1990.

Television Work; Specials:

Producer, *Rose Petal Place: Real Friends* (also known as *Rose–Petal Place*), syndicated, 1985.

Executive producer, *The Town That Santa Forgot,* NBC, 1993.

Executive producer, *The Halloween Tree,* syndicated, 1993.

Television Work; Pilots:

Poochinski, NBC, 1990.

The Last Halloween, CBS, 1991.

Television Appearances; Specials:

The 100 Scariest Movie Moments, Bravo, 2004.

WRITINGS

Screenplays:

Hocus Pocus, Buena Vista, 1993.

The Pagemaster (animated), Twentieth Century–Fox, 1994.

Screenplay Stories:

An American Tail (animated), Universal, 1986.

Hocus Pocus, Buena Vista, 1993.

The Pagemaster (animated), Twentieth Century–Fox, 1994.

Television Movie Stories:

The Dreamer of Oz (also known as *The Dreamer of Oz: The L. Frank Baum Story*), CBS, 1990.

Television Pilot Stories:

Poochinski, NBC, 1990.

Television Episodes:

"Law & Order," *Earth: Final Conflict* (also known as *Gene Roddenberry's "Battleground Earth," Gene Roddenberry's "Earth: Final Conflict," EFC,* and *Mission Erde: Sie sind unter uns*), syndicated, 1998.

Children's Books:

Rose Petal Place, 1979.

An American Tony and Fievel, Amblin Entertainment, 1986.

(Illustrator only) *Fievel's Friends,* Amblin, 1986.

(Illustrator only) *An American Tail,* Hutchinson Children's Books, Ltd., 1987.

(With Ernie Contreras) *The Pagemaster,* Turner, 1993.

KROEKER, Allan
(Alan Kroeker)

PERSONAL

Born in Winnipeg, Manitoba, Canada.

Addresses: *Agent*—Diverse Talent Group, 1875 Century Park East, Suite 2250, Los Angeles, CA 90067.

Career: Director, cinematographer, and writer.

Awards, Honors: Gemini Award nominations, best direction in a dramatic program or series, Academy of Canadian Cinema and Television, 1986, for *Tramp at the Door,* 1987, for *Heaven on Earth,* and 1993, for *Forever Knight.*

CREDITS

Television Director; with Others; Miniseries:

Frontiers, [Canada], 1985.

Les aventuriers du Nouveau–Monde, [France], 1986.

Television Director; Movies:

The Prodigal, CanWest Global Television, 1983.

Tramp at the Door, CanWest Global Television, 1985.

Director, *Heaven on Earth,* CBC and BBC, 1987, broadcast on *Masterpiece Theatre* (also known as *ExxonMobil Masterpiece Theatre* and *Mobil Masterpiece Theatre*), PBS, c. 1988.

Age–Old Friends (also known as *A Month of Sundays*), HBO, 1989.

Hostile Advances: The Kerry Ellison Story (also known as *Bedrohliche Leidenschaft, Historia de un acoso sexual, Seule contre tous,* and *Vivendo em perigo*), Lifetime, 1996.

Once a Thief: Brother against Brother (episodes "Endgame" and "Family Reunion" re–edited as a movie; also known as *John Woo's "Once a Thief: Brother against Brother"*), The Movie Channel, c. 1998.

Television Director; Episodic:

"Judgment Call," *Street Legal,* CBC, 1987.

"Star Struck," *Street Legal,* CBC, 1987.

(As Alan Kroeker) "Hail and Farewell," *The Ray Bradbury Theater* (also known as *The Bradbury Trilogy, Mystery Theatre, Ray Bradbury Theater, Le monde fantastique de Ray Bradbury,* and *Ray Bradbury presente*), HBO, 1989.

"Something in the Walls," *The Twilight Zone,* CBS, 1989.

"Epitaph for a Lonely Soul," *Friday the 13th* (also known as *Friday's Curse, Friday the 13th: The Series, The 13th Hour, Aaveita ja kummituksia, Erben des Fluchs, Kauhun kammio, L'entrepot du diable, Misterio para tres, Pentek 13, Perjantain kirous,* and *Vendredi 13*), syndicated, 1990.

"The Long Road Home," *Friday the 13th* (also known as *Friday's Curse, Friday the 13th: The Series, The 13th Hour, Aaveita ja kummituksia, Erben des Fluchs, Kauhun kammio, L'entrepot du diable, Misterio para tres, Pentek 13, Perjantain kirous,* and *Vendredi 13*), syndicated, 1990.

"Enemy in Our Midst," *Beyond Reality* (also known as *Mas alla de la realidad*), USA Network, 1991.

"I Love Lucard," *Dracula: The Series,* syndicated, 1991.

"Klaus Encounters of the Interred Kind," *Dracula: The Series,* syndicated, 1991.

"Mirror, Mirror," *Beyond Reality* (also known as *Mas alla de la realidad*), USA Network, 1991.

"Return Visit," *Beyond Reality* (also known as *Mas alla de la realidad*), USA Network, 1991.

(Sometimes as Alan Kroeker) *Forever Knight,* multiple episodes, CBS, 1992, syndicated, 1994–95, USA and syndicated, 1995.

"Disciple," *Kung Fu: The Legend Continues,* syndicated, 1993.

"Redemption," *Kung Fu: The Legend Continues,* syndicated, 1993.

"Shadow Assassin," *Kung Fu: The Legend Continues,* syndicated, 1993.

"Sunday at the Hotel with George," *Kung Fu: The Legend Continues,* syndicated, 1993.

(As Alan Kroeker) "A Friend in Need," *Road to Avonlea* (also known as *Avonlea* and *Tales from Avonlea*), CBC and Disney Channel, 1994.

"Strictly Melodrama," *Road to Avonlea* (also known as *Avonlea* and *Tales from Avonlea*), CBC and Disney Channel, 1994.

TekWar (also known as *TekWar: The Series*), syndicated, multiple episodes, 1994–95.

Lonesome Dove: The Outlaw Years, CTV (Canada), multiple episodes, 1995–96.

"Echo of Murder," *Viper,* syndicated, 1996.

PSI Factor: Chronicles of the Paranormal (also known as *PSI Factor*), CanWest Global Television and syndicated, multiple episodes, 1996.

Star Trek: Deep Space Nine (also known as *Deep Space Nine, DS9,* and *Star Trek: DS9*), syndicated, multiple episodes, 1996–99.

Star Trek: Voyager (also known as *Voyager*), syndicated, multiple episodes, 1997–2001.

"Family Reunion," *Once a Thief* (also known as *John Woo's "Once a Thief," John Woo's "The Thief," John Woo's Violent Tradition, Kerran varas, aina varas?, Ladrao que rouba ladrao, Les repentis,* and *Matar a un ladron*), CTV (Canada) and syndicated, 1998.

"The First of Its Kind," *Earth: Final Conflict* (also known as *EFC, Gene Roddenberry's "Battleground Earth," Gene Roddenberry's "Earth: Final Conflict," Invasion planete Terre,* and *Mission Erde: Sie sind unter uns*), syndicated, 1998.

"Crackdown," *Earth: Final Conflict* (also known as *EFC, Gene Roddenberry's "Battleground Earth," Gene Roddenberry's "Earth: Final Conflict," Invasion planete Terre,* and *Mission Erde: Sie sind unter uns*), syndicated, 1999.

"A Fine Mess," *Beverly Hills 90210,* Fox, 1999.

"The Painting," *Poltergeist: The Legacy* (also known as *Poltergeist, El legado, Poltergeist—Die unheimliche Macht, Poltergeist: El legado,* and *Poltergeist, les aventuriers du surnaturel*), Showtime and syndicated, 1999.

"The Vanished," *Earth: Final Conflict* (also known as *EFC, Gene Roddenberry's "Battleground Earth," Gene Roddenberry's "Earth: Final Conflict," Invasion planete Terre,* and *Mission Erde: Sie sind unter uns*), syndicated, 1999.

"And Don't Forget to Give Me Back My Black T–Shirt," *Beverly Hills 90210,* Fox, 2000.

"Demons," *Mysterious Ways* (also known as *One Clear Moment, Anexegeta phainomena, Les chemins de l'etrange, Mysterious ways—les chemins de l'etrange, Rajatapaus,* and *Senderos misteriosos*), NBC and PAX TV, 2000.

"Under the Night," *Andromeda* (also known as *Gene Roddenberry's "Andromeda"*), Sci–Fi Channel, 2000.

"Busted," *Roswell* (also known as *Roswell High*), UPN, 2001.

"Cry Your Name," *Roswell* (also known as *Roswell High*), The WB, 2001.

"Music of a Distant Drum," *Andromeda* (also known as *Gene Roddenberry's "Andromeda"*), Sci–Fi Channel, 2001.

"Two," *Dark Angel* (also known as *James Cameron's "Dark Angel"*), Fox, 2001.

"Una Salus Victus," *Andromeda* (also known as *Gene Roddenberry's "Andromeda"*), Sci–Fi Channel, 2001.

"We All Scream for Ice Cream," *Charmed,* The WB, 2001.

Enterprise (also known as *Star Trek: Enterprise, Star Trek: Series V,* and *Star Trek: Untitled Fifth Series*), UPN, multiple episodes, 2001–2005.

"Ariel," *Firefly* (also known as *Firefly: The Series* and *Firefly—Der Aufbruch der Serenity*), Fox, 2002.

"Evergreen," *The Twilight Zone,* UPN, 2002.

"Gabe's Story," *The Twilight Zone,* UPN, 2002.

"Good Deeds," *Street Time,* Showtime, 2002.

"She Ain't Heavy," *Dark Angel* (also known as *James Cameron's "Dark Angel"*), Fox, 2002.

"The Sins of Sonny Walker," *UC: Undercover* (also known as *Undercover*), NBC, 2002.

"A Tale of Two Parts," *Roswell* (also known as *Roswell High*), UPN, 2002.

"It's Still a Good Life," *The Twilight Zone,* UPN, 2003.

"Right to Life," *Street Time,* Showtime, 2003.

"Whiskey–Tango–Foxtrot," *Jake 2.0,* UPN, 2003.

"Bastille Day," *Battlestar Galactica* (also known as *Galactica, Galactica—Estrella de combate,* and *Taisteluplaneetta Galactica*), Sci–Fi Channel, 2004.

"Crime Dog," *Wonderfalls* (also known as *Maid of the Mist* and *Touched by a Crazy Person*), Fox, 2004.

"Reunion," *Tru Calling* (also known as *Heroine, Tru,* and *True Calling*), Fox, 2004.

"Everything Nice," *The Inside* (also known as *The inside—Dans la tete des tueurs*), Fox, 2005.

"The Man in the Bear," *Bones* (also known as *Brennan, Bones—Die Knochenjaegerin, Dr. Csont,* and *Kondid*), Fox, 2005.

"The Man in the SUV," *Bones* (also known as *Brennan, Bones—Die Knochenjaegerin, Dr. Csont,* and *Kondid*), Fox, 2005.

"Resistance," *Battlestar Galactica* (also known as *Galactica, Galactica—Estrella de combate,* and *Taisteluplaneetta Galactica*), Sci–Fi Channel, 2005.

"Thief of Hearts," *The Inside* (also known as *The inside—Dans la tete des tueurs*), Fox, 2005.

Threshold (also known as *A Kueszoeb, Aporrito shedio Threshold, Kynnys tuntemattomaan, Nemesis—Der Angriff, Operacion Threshold,* and *Threshold—Premier contact*), CBS, 2005.

"Faith," *Supernatural* (also known as *Sobrenatural*), The WB, 2006.

"Two Bodies in the Lab," *Bones* (also known as *Brennan, Bones—Die Knochenjaegerin, Dr. Csont,* and *Kondid*), Fox, 2006.

"The Girl in the Gator," *Bones* (also known as *Brennan, Bones—Die Knochenjaegerin, Dr. Csont,* and *Kondid*), Fox, 2007.

"Love Hurts," *Blood Ties,* Lifetime, 2007.

Directed "Mirrors of the Soul," "See No Evil," and "Stand and Deliver," all episodes of *The Campbells,* CTV (Canada) and syndicated; directed "The Last Hurrah," "Warts and All," and "Where Do I Belong," all episodes of *Ready or Not* (also known as *Les premieres fois*), CanWest Global Television, Showtime Movie Channel, and Disney Channel; and directed episodes of other programs, including *Destiny Ridge* (also known as *The New Destiny Ridge*), CanWest Global Television and syndicated.

Television Director; Pilots:
"Blood Price," *Blood Ties,* Lifetime, 2007.

Film Work:
Cinematographer, *A House on the Prairie* (short documentary), National Film Board of Canada, 1978.

Cinematographer, *The System: Out of Sight, Out of Mind* (short film), National Film Board of Canada, 1978.

Cinematographer, *Going the Distance* (documentary; also known as *Commonwealth Games* and *Edmonton et comment s'y rendre*), National Film Board of Canada, 1979.

Cinematographer, *The Top Few Inches* (short documentary), National Film Board of Canada, 1979.

Director, editor, and cinematographer, *Tudor King* (short film), National Film Board of Canada, 1979.

Cinematographer, *Darts in the Dark: An Introduction to W. O. Mitchell* (short documentary), National Film Board of Canada, 1980.

Cinematographer, *The Strongest Man in the World*, 1980.

Cinematographer, *W. O. Mitchell: Novelist in Hiding* (documentary), National Film Board of Canada, 1980.

Director, *God Is Not a Fish Inspector*, 1980.

Director, *The Pedlar*, 1982.

Cinematographer, *Laughter in My Soul* (short documentary), National Film Board of Canada, 1983.

Director, *In the Fall* (short film), 1984.

Producer, *Reunion* (short film), National Film Board of Canada, 1984.

Director, *Red Shoes* (short film), Atlantis Films, 1986.

Director, *Showdown at Williams Creek* (also known as *Kootenai Brown, The Legend of Kootenai Brown,* and *Wer erschoss Jim Blessing?*), National Film Board of Canada/Festival Films, 1991.

Director (live action), *L5: First City in Space* (short live action and animated film), IMAX Corporation, 1996.

WRITINGS

Teleplays; Movies:

Tramp at the Door, CanWest Global Television, 1985.

Teleplays; Episodic:

"The Return," *Lonesome Dove: The Outlaw Years,* CTV (Canada), 1995.

Screenplays:

Tudor King (short film), National Film Board of Canada, 1979.

The Pedlar, 1982.

In the Fall (short film), 1984.

Reunion (short film), National Film Board of Canada, 1984.

Red Shoes (short film), Atlantis Films, 1986.

OTHER SOURCES

Periodicals:

Winnipeg Sun, September 29, 2000.

L

PERSONAL

Surname is sometimes spelled as Lamarche, La Marche, or La'Marche; born March 30, 1958, in Toronto, Ontario, Canada; married Robin G. Eisenman (an actress), May 19, 1991 (separated); children: Jonathan.

Addresses: *Agent*—International Creative Management, 10250 Constellation Way, 9th Floor, Los Angeles, CA 90067; (voice work) Danis Panaro Nist, 9201 West Olympic Blvd., Beverly Hills, CA 90212.

Career: Actor and voice artist. Appeared in television commercials, including voice of Toucan Sam for Froot Loops breakfast cereal; previously worked as a standup comedian opening for performers such as Rodney Dangerfield, George Carlin, the Temptations, and the Four Tops.

Awards, Honors: Emmy Award nomination (with others), outstanding individual performance in a variety or music program, 1989, for *D.C. Follies;* Daytime Emmy Award nomination, outstanding performer in an animated program, and Annie Award, outstanding male voice actor in an animated television production, International Animated Film Society, both 1998, for *Pinky & the Brain;* Annie Award nomination, outstanding male voice actor in an animated feature production, 2000, for *Wakko's Wish.*

CREDITS

Television Appearances; Animated Series:
Voice of Chief Quimby, *Inspector Gadget* (also known as *Inspecteur Gadget*), syndicated, 1985–86.

Voice of Puzzle, *Popples* (also known as *Poporuzu*), syndicated, 1986.

Voice of Egon Spengler, *The Real Ghostbusters,* ABC, 1986–91.

Voice of George Wilson and Henry Mitchell, *Dennis the Menace* (also known as *Denis la malice*), CBS, 1987.

Voice of Popeye, *Popeye and Son,* 1987.

Puppet voice, *D.C. Follies,* PBS, 1987.

Voice of Egon Spengler, *Slimer! and the Real Ghostbusters,* syndicated, 1988.

Voices of General Patton and other characters, *Tale Spin,* syndicated, 1990.

Voice of Sid, *Gravedale High* (also known as *Rick Moranis in "Gravedale High"*), NBC, 1990.

Voices of Low–Light and Destro, *G.I. Joe,* 1990.

Voices of Dizzy Devil and Plucky Duck, *Tiny Toon Adventures* (also known as *Steven Spielberg Presents … "Tiny Toon Adventures"*), Fox, 1990–93.

Voice of Hugh Tasmanian Devil and Timothy Platypus, *Taz–Mania,* Fox, 1991.

Voices of Dizzy Devil, Tim Burton, and other characters, *The Plucky Duck Show,* 1992.

Voices of Brain, Squit pigeon, and others, *Animaniacs* (also known as *Steven Spielberg Presents "Animaniacs"*), Fox, 1993–94.

Voices of Jeremy Hawke and Orson Welles, *The Critic,* ABC, 1994.

Multiple voices, *The Tick,* Fox, between 1994 and 1996.

Multiple voices, *Gadget Boy and Heather* (also known as *Gadget Boy*), syndicated, 1995.

Voices of Kidd Chaos and Comptroller, *The Adventures of Hyperman,* CBS, 1995.

Voices of Longhorn and other characters, *Freakazoid!,* The WB, between 1995 and 1996.

Miscellaneous voices, *Duckman,* USA Network, between 1995 and 1997.

Voice of the Brain, *Pinky & the Brain,* The WB, 1995–98.

Miscellaneous voices, *The Simpsons,* Fox, between 1995 and 2007.

Voice of radio announcer, *Road Rovers,* The WB, 1996.

Voices of Dr. Splitz, Splitzy, and other characters, *Captain Simian and the Space Monkeys,* syndicated, 1996.

Voices of Etno Polino and other characters, *Space Goofs* (also known as *Home to Rent, Stupid Invaders,* and *Les zinzins de l'espace*), Fox, 1997.

Voices of Mooch and Mr. Squad, *The Wacky World of Tex Avery,* syndicated, 1997.

Voices of Chief Strombolli, Myren Dabble, Doris, Humus, Mulch, and others, *Gadget Boy's Adventures in History,* History Channel, 1997.

Voice of Egon Spengler, *Extreme Ghostbusters,* syndicated, 1997.

Voice, *Channel Umptee-3,* The WB, 1997.

Miscellaneous voices, *King of the Hill,* Fox, between 1997 and 1999.

Voices of George Washington, Abraham Lincoln, and other characters, *Histeria!,* 1998.

Voices of space slugs, *The Secret Files of the SpyDogs,* Fox, 1998.

Voice of the Brain, *Pinky, Elmyra & the Brain,* The WB, 1998–99.

Voices of Oscar Wildcat, Mr. Duckstein, and other characters, *Queer Duck,* 1999.

Voice of Sleet, *Sonic Underground,* syndicated, 1999.

Voice of Mortimer Mouse, *Mickey Mouse Works,* 1999.

Voices of the garbage man and other characters, *Dilbert,* UPN, 1999–2000.

Narrator, voices of Jacques Morbo and others, *Futurama,* Fox, 1999–2003.

Voice of Dirt, *Poochini's Yard* (also known as *Poochini*), 2000.

Voices of Mortimer Mouse, Scuttle, Basil of Baker Street, Ratigan, March Hare, and other characters, *House of Mouse,* ABC, 2001–2002.

Voices of Fred Flintstone, Quick Draw McGraw, and other characters, *Harvey Birdman, Attorney at Law,* Cartoon Network, between 2001 and 2007.

Voice of robot dad, *Whatever Happened to Robot Jones?,* Cartoon Network, 2002.

Voice of Baron Blitz, *Disney's "Teamo Supremo,"* ABC, 2002.

Multiple voices, *Kim Possible* (also known as *Disney's "Kim Possible"*), Disney Channel, between 2002 and 2005.

Multiple voices, *Stripperella* (also known as *Stan Lee's "Stripperella"*), Spike, 2003.

Voice of Salem, *Sabrina's Secret Life,* 2003.

Voices of Yosemite Sam as K'chutha Sa'am and other characters, *Duck Dodgers* (also known as *Duck Dodgers in the 24 1/2th Century*), Cartoon Network, between 2003 and 2006.

Voices of Elite ice cream man, Mr. Frybingle, train conductor, and other characters, *Codename: Kids Next Door,* Cartoon Network, 2004.

Voice of Gus, *Tripping the Rift,* Sci-Fi Channel, 2004–2005.

Voices of Hovis, Kraken, Luther, Old Stinky, and other characters, *Catscratch,* Nickelodeon, between 2004 and 2006.

Voice of Chief, *Tak & the Power of Juju,* Nickelodeon, 2007.

Television Appearances; Live–Action Series:

Lips by Maurice, *The All–Night Show,* 1980.

Principal Crawford, announcer, film narrator, and others, *Teen Angel,* ABC, multiple episodes, between 1997 and 1998.

Announcer, *The Howie Mandel Show,* syndicated, 1998–99.

Voices of Harry Waller and Bernard the Sarcastic Cockatoo, *The Chimp Channel,* TBS, 1999.

Television Appearances; Animated Movies:

Voice of Cyclops, *Scooby Doo in Arabian Nights* (also known as *Arabian Nights* and *Scooby Doo's "Arabian Nights"*), syndicated, 1994.

Voice of Dizzy Devil, *Tiny Toon Adventures: Night Ghoulery,* 1995.

Voice of Inspector Gadget, *Inspector Gadget's Last Case: Claw's Revenge* (also known as *Inspector Gadget in Claw's Revenge*), Nickelodeon, 2002.

Voice of Henry Mitchell, *Dennis the Menace in Cruise Control* (also known as *Dennis the Menace: Cruise Control*), Nickelodeon, 2002.

Voices of Bumpy Snits, first ferryman, and first cowpoke, *Party Wagon,* Cartoon Network, 2004.

Voice of "Big Daddy" Brotherson, *Kim Possible: So the Drama* (also known as *Disney's "Kim Possible" Movie: So the Drama*), Disney Channel, 2005.

Voices of pirate and Thurdigree Burns, *Casper's Scare School,* 2006.

Voice of father, *Codename: Kids Next Door—Operation Z.E.R.O.* (also known as *Operation: Z.E.R.O.*), Cartoon Network, 2006.

Television Appearances; Specials:

Voices of Don Rattles, Steed Martin, and Peter Easter Bat, *Easter Fever* (animated), 1980.

Voice of George Wilson, *Dennis the Menace in Mayday for Mother* (animated), 1981.

The 9th Annual Young Comedians Special (also known as *Rodney Dangerfield Hosts the 9th Annual Young Comedians Special*), HBO, 1984.

Voice of Sid, *The Roquefort Gang,* 1985.

DTV "Doggone" Valentine, 1987.

Spitting Image: The 1987 Movie Awards, NBC, 1987.

Voice, *Sid & Marty Krofft's Redeye Express,* 1988.

Voice, *The Halloween Door,* 1989.

Voice, *Tiny Toon Adventures: The Looney Beginning* (animated), 1990.

Announcer, *Howie,* 1992.

Voice of Parum–Pum, *It's a Wonderful Tiny Toons Christmas Special* (animated), 1992.

Voice of Chief Quimby, *Inspector Gadget Saves Christmas* (animated), 1992.

Voice of Dizzy Devil, *Tiny Toons Spring Break* (animated), 1994.

Voice of the Brain, *A Pinky & the Brain Christmas Special* (animated), The WB, 1995.

Voices, *Siegfried and Roy: Masters of the Impossible,* Fox, 1996.

Voice of the Brain, *Kids' WB! Sneak Peek* (animated), The WB, 1996.

Narrator, *The Puppies Present Incredible Animal Tales,* ABC, 1998.

Voice of Bo, *The Life & Adventures of Santa Claus* (animated), 2000.

Voices, *A Baby Blues Christmas Special* (animated), Cartoon network, 2002.

Television Appearances; Animated Pilots:

Voice of Mr. Mcmcmc, bus driver, and principal, *Whatever Happened to Robot Jones?,* Cartoon Network, 2000.

Voice of Bigguy N De Skye, *Imp, Inc.,* Cartoon Network, 2001.

Voices of Principal Pixiefrog, Mr. Hornbill, and other characters, *My Gym Partner's a Monkey,* Cartoon Network, 2006.

Television Appearances; Animated Episodes:

Voice of Six Gun, "Thief in the Night," *Transformers* (also known as *Super God Robot Force, Transformers: Generation, Transformers: 2010,* and *Tatakae! Cho robot seimeitai Transformer*), syndicated, 1986.

Voice of Count Roy, "The Duck in the Iron Mask," *DuckTales* (also known as *Disney's DuckTales*), 1987.

Voice of Dishonest John, "Framed Threep," *Beany and Cecil,* 1988.

Voice of Dishonest John, "The Bad Guy Flu!/D. J.'s Disappearing Act," *Beany and Cecil,* 1988.

Voice of Inspector Gadget, "Defective Gadgetry," *The Super Mario Bros. Super Show!* (also known as *Club Mario*), 1989.

Voice of Inspector Gadget, "Treasure of the Sierra Brooklyn," *The Super Mario Bros. Super Show!* (also known as *Club Mario*), syndicated, 1989.

Voice of Zoltan, "Give a Little Whistle," *Attack of the Killer Tomatoes,* Fox, 1990.

Voice of Duke Nukem, "Deadly Ransom," *Captain Planet and the Planeteers* (also known as *The New Adventures of Captain Planet*), TBS and syndicated, 1990.

Voice of Verminous Skumm, "Mind Pollution," *Captain Planet and the Planeteers* (also known as *The New Adventures of Captain Planet*), TBS and syndicated, 1993.

Voices of Tuttle Turtle, Mr. Blackenblue, and Smarts, "The Stork Exchange," *Bonkers* (also known as *Disney's "Bonkers"*), syndicated, 1993.

Voice of Murphy, "The Man Who Killed Batman," *Batman* (also known as *The Adventures of Batman & Robin* and *Batman: The Animated Series*), Fox, 1993.

Voice of the guardian, "Super Sonic," *Sonic the Hedgehog,* 1993.

Voice of Scuttle, "Scuttle," *The Little Mermaid* (also known as *Disney's "The Little Mermaid"*), 1994.

Voice of Scuttle, "Island of Fear," *The Little Mermaid* (also known as *Disney's "The Little Mermaid"*), 1994.

Voice of Pasha, Arun, and Deepuk, "Bloodlines," *The Real Adventures of Jonny Quest* (also known as *Jonny Quest: The Real Adventures*) Cartoon Network and syndicated, 1996.

Voice of Conglomo Lizard, "Ed Good, Rocko Bad/Teed Off," *Rocko's Modern Life,* 1996.

Voices of "Big" Bob Pataki and others, "Arnold's Christmas," *Hey Arnold!,* Nickelodeon, 1996.

Voices of "Big" Bob Pataki and Douglas Cain, "Arnold's Halloween," *Hey Arnold!,* Nickelodeon, 1997.

Voices of Dr. Strange and Dr. Stephen Strange, "Mind over Anti–Matter," *The Incredible Hulk,* 1997.

Voice of Chuck Pearson, "One of the Guys," *Pepper Ann* (also known as *Disney's "Pepper Ann"*), ABC, 1997.

Voice of Pasha the Peddler and the Keeper, "The Bangalore Falcon," *The Real Adventures of Jonny Quest* (also known as *Jonny Quest: The Real Adventures*), Cartoon Network and syndicated, 1997.

Voice of Dick McMan, Ratman, Simion, and Washington, "Rushmore Rumble/A Boy and His Bug/You Vegetabelieve It," *Dexter's Laboratory* (also known as *Dexter's Lab* and *Dexter de Shiyanshi*), Cartoon Network, 1998.

Voice of Ambassador, "Speed Trap," *Buzz Lightyear of Star Command,* ABC, 2000.

Voice, "Tarzan and the Rough Rider," *The Legend of Tarzan* (also known as *Disney's "The Legend of Tarzan"*), 2001.

Voice of Tommy Vinegar, "Bucketheads," *The Oblongs ...,* 2001.

Voice, "Heroine Addict," *The Oblongs ...,* 2001.

Voice, "The Golden Child," *The Oblongs ...,* 2001.

Voice, "Father of the Bribe," *The Oblongs ...,* 2001.

Voice of Babe Ruth, "Orb of Aten," *The Mummy: The Animated Series* (also known as *The Mummy: Secrets of the Medjai*), 2001.

Voice of Tso Lan, "The Stronger Evil," *Jackie Chan Adventures,* The WB, 2001.

Voices of ship captain and prisoner, "Tarzan and the Prison Break," *The Legend of Tarzan* (also known as *Disney's "The Legend of Tarzan"*), 2001.

Voice of WHOOP vulcanologist, "The Get Away," *Totally Spies!* (also known as *Totally Spies Undercover!*), ABC Family Channel, 2001.

Voice of Tso Lan, "The Eighth Door," *Jackie Chan Adventures,* The WB, 2002.

Voice of Cardiff Zendo, "Enter the Cat," *Jackie Chan Adventures,* The WB, 2002.

Voice of Chewbaccastan ambassador, "Abductions," *Totally Spies!* (also known as *Totally Spies Undercover!*), ABC Family Channel, 2002.

Voice of Estroy, "Grim or Gregory/Search and Estroy/Something Stupid This Way Comes," *Grim & Evil* (also known as *The Grim Adventures of Billy & Mandy*), Cartoon Network, 2002.

Voice of Tubbimura, "Shen Yi Bu," *Xiaolin Showdown*, The WB, 2003.

Voice of Zia, "A Beautiful Mine," *The Adventure of Jimmy Neutron: Boy Genius*, Nickelodeon, 2003.

Voice, "Totally Switched," *Totally Spies!* (also known as *Totally Spies Undercover!*), Cartoon Network, 2004.

Voice of Tubbimura, "Royal Rumble," *Xiaolin Showdown*, The WB, 2004.

Voices of Zia and Tee, "Men at Work," *The Adventure of Jimmy Neutron: Boy Genius*, Nickelodeon, 2004.

Voices of first pigeon, elk boss, second cowman, and other characters "Wilderness Protection Program," *Johnny Bravo*, Cartoon Network, 2004.

Voices of Estroy, second dude, and clerk, "Gridlocked and Loaded/Fool's Paradise," *Evil Con Carne*, Cartoon Network, 2004.

Voice of male chicken, "Ocean," *Wonder Showzen*, MTV, 2005.

Voices of Master Fung and others, "Finding Omi," *Xiaolin Showdown*, The WB, 2005.

Voice of Zia, "The League of Villains," *The Adventure of Jimmy Neutron: Boy Genius*, Nickelodeon, 2005.

Voices of Dimitri the Terrible and Scotty, "Magic Takes a Holiday," *The Life and Times of Juniper Lee*, Cartoon Network, 2005.

Voices of Master Fung and others, "Time after Time: Part 2," *Xiaolin Showdown*, The WB, 2006.

Voice of guy in jerky suit, "The Jerky Girls," *The Replacements*, Disney Channel, 2006.

Voices of Zix and ticket vendor, "Incredible Shrinking Town," *The Adventure of Jimmy Neutron: Boy Genius*, Nickelodeon, 2006.

Voice of Bruiser, "A Matter of Family," *The Batman*, CW Network, 2006.

Voice of George Georgiopolis, "Freaks & Greeks," *Drawn Together*, Comedy Central, 2006.

Voices of ice cream vendor and Ophiuchus Sam, "Secret of the Guardian Strike Sword," *Loonatics Unleashed*, CW Network, 2006.

Voice of Pierre Le Pew, "I Am Slamacus," *Loonatics Unleashed*, CW Network, 2006.

Voice of Mr. Beale, Southern Gentleman, "Peanuts! Get Yer Peanuts!," *Class of 3000*, Cartoon Network, 2006.

Voice of Birdsdorf, "Hornswiggle," *Random! Cartoons*, Nickelodeon, 2006.

Voice of Klemp, "Solomon Fix," *Random! Cartoons*, Nickelodeon, 2007.

Voices of Bjorn and first working troll, "Ivan the Unbearable," *Random! Cartoons*, Nickelodeon, 2007.

Also voice for episodes of *Beethoven*, CBS, *Family Guy*, Fox, *Jumanji*, UPN, *Kid Notorious*, Comedy Central, *Teenage Mutant Ninja Turtles*, and *Tom and Jerry Kids Show*.

Television Appearances; Live–Action Episodes:
Young man on street, *Sidestreet*, 1975.

Mockingbird Maurice, "The Princess Who Had Never Laughed," *Faerie Tale Theatre* (also known as *Shelley Duvall's "Faerie Tale Theatre"*), 1986.

Rod Sperling, "Seven Little Indians," *The Facts of Life*, NBC, 1987.

Voice, "Oy to the World!" *The Nanny*, CBS, 1995.

Narrator and voice of radio announcer, "No Guts, No Cory," *Boy Meets World*, ABC, 1997.

(Uncredited) Voice of Sylar, "Don't Look Back," *Heroes*, NBC, 2006.

"Supermodels," *Sexiest …*, E! Entertainment Television, 2006.

"Action Heroes," *Sexiest …*, E! Entertainment Television, 2006.

Narrator for *Sex and the Silver Screen*, Showtime; also performed for episodes of *An Evening at the Improv*.

Television Appearances; Other:
Celebrity voices, *The Wrong Coast* (animated miniseries), AMC, 2004.

Television Work; Additional Voices; Series:
Where's Waldo? (also known as *Where's Wally?*), CBS, 1991–92.

Problem Child, USA Network, 1993.

Mighty Max, 1993.

Where on Earth Is Carmen Sandiego?, PBS, 1994.

Beethoven, CBS, 1994.

The Twisted Adventures of Felix the Cat (also known as *The Twisted Tales of Felix the Cat*), CBS, 1995.

Animated Film Appearances:
Voice of sailor, *Rock & Rule* (also known as *Ring of Power* and *Rock 'n' Rule*), Metro–Goldwyn–Mayer, 1983.

Voice of Chief Quimby, *The Amazing Adventures of Inspector Gadget*, 1986.

Voice of Dizzy Devil, *Tiny Toon Adventures: How I Spent My Vacation* (also known as *How I Spent My Vacation*), Warner Bros. Home Video, 1992.

Narrator of English version, *Heisei tanuki gassen pompoko* (also known as *Pom poko* and *The Raccoon War*), 1994.

Voice of Yosemite Sam as General Pandemonium, *Carrotblanca* (animated short film), Warner Bros., 1995.

Voice of Lost and Found officer, *All Dogs Go to Heaven 2*, Metro–Goldwyn–Mayer, 1996.

Voice, *Bugs Bunny's Funky Monkeys*, 1997.

Voice of Dr. Quizzical, *The Wacky Adventures of Ronald McDonald: Scared Silly,* 1998.

Voices of the Brain mouse and Squit pigeon, *Wakko's Wish* (animated; also known as *Steven Spielberg Presents "Animaniacs: Wakko's Wish"*), 1999.

Voice of Mr. Lawrence Talbot, *Alvin and the Chipmunks Meet the Wolfman,* 2000.

Voices of Mogorb, King of the Awgwas, and other characters *The Life & Adventures of Santa Claus,* Universal Pictures Home Video, 2000.

Voice, *Mickey's Magical Christmas: Snowed In at the House of Mouse,* Buena Vista Home Video/Walt Disney Home Video, 2001.

Voice of Balto, *Balto: Wolf Quest,* Universal Studios, 2002.

Voices of Spike and Alley Cat, *Tom and Jerry: The Magic Ring,* Warner Home Video, 2002.

Voices of "Big Bob" Pataki and head of security, *Hey Arnold! The Movie,* Paramount, 2002.

Voice of Horace, *101 Dalmatians II: Patch's London Adventure,* Walt Disney Home Video, 2003.

Voices of Yosemite Sam and Wile E. Coyote, *Looney Tunes: Reality Check,* Warner Bros., 2003.

Voices of Yosemite Sam, ghost of William Shakespeare, Dr. Moron, and Pepe Le Pew, *Looney Tunes: Stranger than Fiction,* Warner Bros., 2003.

Voices of Beagle Boys, *Mickey, Donald, Goofy: The Three Musketeers,* Buena Vista, 2004.

Voice, *Hare and Loathing in Las Vegas* (short film), Warner Bros., Animation, 2004.

Voice of Alex Baldwin, *Team America: World Police,* Paramount, 2004.

Voice of Balto, *Balto III: Wings of Change,* Universal Studios, 2004.

Voice of Inspector Gadget, *Inspector's Gadget's Biggest Caper Ever,* Lions Gate Films Home Entertainment, 2005.

Voice of Igg the cow, *Barnyard* (also known as *Barnyard: The Original Party Animals* and *Der Tierisch verrueckte Bauernhof*), Paramount, 2006.

Voices of Oscar Wildcat, Martin Duckstein, and other characters, *Queer Duck: The Movie,* Paramount Home Entertainment, 2006.

Voice of second judge, *Holly Hobbie and Friends: Christmas Wishes,* Paramount, 2006.

Voice of Yosemite Sam, *Bah Humduck! A Looney Tunes Christmas,* Warner Home Video, 2006.

Host, *The Writers Flipped: They Have No Script* (short film), Warner Home Video, 2006.

Voices of Morbo, Donbot, Clamps, and other characters, *Futurama: Bender's Big Score!,* Twentieth Century–Fox, 2007.

Film Appearances; Other:

Dickie, *The Funny Farm,* New World, 1983.

Voices of Dr. Vincent "Vegas Vinnie"/"Doc" Whiskers, Super Jack, and other characters, *Cool World* (live–action and animated), Paramount, 1992.

Voices of snake, frill–necked lizard, and turtle, *Napoleon,* 1994.

(Uncredited) Voice of Orson Welles, *Ed Wood,* Buena Vista, 1994.

Voice of Pepe le Pew, *Space Jam* (live–action and animated), Warner Bros., 1996.

(Uncredited) Phone voice of Fred Bishop, *As Good as It Gets,* Sony Pictures Entertainment, 1997.

RECORDINGS

Videos:

Voice, *Tamagotchi Video Adventures,* 1997.

Voices of Inspector Gadget and Chief Quimby, *Inspector Gadget: Gadget's Greatest Gadgets,* 1999.

Himself, *Futurama Featurette,* Twentieth Century–Fox, 2002.

Himself, *Comic Book: The Movie,* Miramax Home Entertainment, 2004.

Himself, *Are You Pondering, What I'm Pondering?,* Warner Home Video, 2006.

Himself, *Animaniacs Live!,* Warner Home Video, 2006.

Video Games:

Voice, *Monty Python's Complete Waste of Time,* 7th Level, 1994.

Voices of Nestor, Gas Guard Gunner, "Rottwheeler" Sizeable Bill, and other characters, *Full Throttle,* LucasArts, 1995.

Voice of Yosemite San, *The Junkyard Run,* 1998.

Voices, *Descent 3* (also known as *D3*), Interplay Productions, 1999.

Voices of Yoshim, Renal Bloodscalp, Chief Inspector Brega, Lloyd Avatar of Rillifane, and Hendak, *Forgotten Realms: Baldur's Gate II: Shadows of Amn,* 2000.

Voice of Yosemite Sam, *Bugs Bunny & Taz: Time Busters,* 2000.

Voice of Yosemite Sam, *Looney Tunes Racing,* 2000.

Voice of Yosemite Sam, *Looney Tunes: Space Race,* 2000.

Voice of Etno Polino, *Stupid Invaders,* 2001.

Voice, *Star Trek: Starfleet Command; Orion Pirates,* 2001.

Voice of Yosemite Sam, *Sheep Raider* (also known as *Looney Tunes: Sheep Raider*), 2001.

Voice of Yosemite Sam, *Taz Wanted,* Infogrames, 2002.

Voice, *Freelancer,* Microsoft, 2003.

Voices of Morbo, Salt, sun god, Destructor, and other characters, *Futurama,* 2003.

Voice, *Looney Tunes: Back in Action,* 2003.

Voice of Jack O'Lantern, *The Grim Adventures of Billy & Mandy,* Midway, 2006.

Voice of Master Fung, *Xiaolin Showdown,* Konami Digital Entertainment America, 2006.

OTHER SOURCES

Periodicals:

TV Guide, September 27, 2003, p. 20.

LAMBERT, Robert K.
(Robert Lambert)

PERSONAL

Avocational interests: Auto racing, building race cars.
Avocational Interests: Auto racing, building race cars.

Addresses: *Agent*—United Talent Agency, 9560 Wilshire Blvd., Suite 500, Beverly Hills, CA 90212.

Career: Film editor and producer. Began career as assistant film editor for a commercial and animation company; David L. Wolper Productions, editor, beginning in 1986; also worked as second unit director, production executive, post–production supervisor, and editorial supervisor.

Member: American Cinema Editors.

Awards, Honors: Emmy Award nomination, outstanding achievement in film editing for entertainment programming for a special, 1976, for *I Will Fight No More Forever;* Emmy Award nomination (with Peter C. Johnson), outstanding individual achievement, and Eddie Award (with Johnson), best edited documentary, American Cinema Editors, both 1977, for *Life Goes to the Movies;* Eddie Award nomination (with others), best edited documentary, 1979, for *The Secret Life of Plants;* Emmy Award nomination, outstanding editing for a single–camera production of a miniseries or special, 1989, for *The Hijacking of the Achille Lauro;* Eddie Award nomination (with others), best edited episode from a television miniseries, 1989, for *Shadow on the Sun;* Eddie Award nomination, best edited episode from a television miniseries, 1991, for *Women and Men: Stories of Seduction;* Online Film Critics Society Award nomination, best film editing, 2000, for *Three Kings.*

CREDITS

Film Editor:
Wattstax (documentary), Columbia, 1973.
Visions of Eight, 1973.
(And associate producer) *Up from the Ape* (also known as *The Animal Within*), 1974.
(With Peter C. Johnson) *Life Goes to the Movies* (documentary), 1976.
The Mysterious Monsters (also known as *Bigfoot the Mysterious Monster*), Schick Sunn Classic, 1976.
(And music editor) *Sorcerer* (also known as *Wages of Fear*), Paramount/Universal, 1977.
The Driver, Twentieth Century–Fox, 1978.

The Secret Life of Plants (documentary), Paramount, 1978.
The Brink's Job (also known as *Big Stickup at Brink's*), Universal, 1978.
(With others) *The Final Countdown* (documentary; also known as *U.S.S. Nimitz: Lost in the Pacific*), United Artists, 1980.
The Border, Universal, 1982.
The Hotel New Hampshire, Orion, 1984.
Heavenly Bodies, Metro–Goldwyn–Mayer, 1984.
(And associate producer) *Bring On the Night* (documentary; also known as *Sting: Bring On the Night*), Samuel Goldwyn Company, 1985.
Critical Condition, Paramount, 1987.
Final Cut, Forward Pictures, 1988.
(As Robert Lambert) Additional editing, *Above the Law* (also known as *Nico* and *Nico: Above the Law*), Warner Bros., 1988.
Additional editing, *Last Action Hero,* Sony Pictures Releasing, 1993.
Blue Sky, Orion, 1994.
Blue Chips, Paramount, 1994.
Ed, Universal, 1996.
Picture of Priority (also known as *Angel on Fire*), 1998.
Without Limits, Warner Bros., 1998.
Three Kings, Warner Bros., 1999.
Red Planet, Warner Bros., 2000.
Rush Hour 2, 2001.
Rollerball, Metro–Goldwyn–Mayer, 2002.
(And associate producer) *House of 1000 Corpses,* Lions Gate Films, 2003.
(And associate producer) *Bulletproof Monk,* Metro–Goldwyn–Mayer, 2003.
Suspect Zero (also known as *Suspect 0*), Paramount, 2004.
I Heart Huckabees (also known as *I Love Huckabees*), Twentieth Century–Fox, 2004.
Ask the Dust, Paramount, 2006.
Pulse, Dimension Films, 2006.
The Nativity Story, New Line Cinema, 2006.

Film Work; Other:
Producer, *Casa Hollywood,* Casa Hollywood, 1996.

Film Appearances:
(As Robert Lambert) Daryl, *I Heart Huckabees* (also known as *I Love Huckabees*), Twentieth Century–Fox, 2004.

Television Film Editor; Miniseries:
(With others) *Shadow on the Sun* (also known as *Beryl Markham: A Shadow on the Sun*), CBS, 1988.
The Phantom of the Opera, NBC, 1990.

Television Film Editor; Movies:
(And associate producer) *Cowboy,* 1983.
The Hijacking of the Achille Lauro, 1989.

Women and Men: Stories of Seduction, 1990.
(And associate producer) *In the Arms of a Killer,* NBC, 1992.
The Angel of Pennsylvania Avenue (also known as *L'ange de Noel*), 1996.

Television Film Editor; Other:
Making of the President 1968, 1969.
(And associate producer) *Plimpton!* (occasional series of documentary specials), 1970, 1971, 1972.
I Will Fight No More Forever (special), 1975.
Area 57 (pilot), NBC, 2007.

LAWRENCE, Steve 1935–

PERSONAL

Original name, Sidney Leibowitz; born July 8, 1935, in Brooklyn, NY; son of Max (a cantor and house painter) and Anna (maiden name, Gelb) Leibowitz; married Eydie Gorme (an entertainer), December 29, 1957; children: David Nessim (a composer), Michael (died, 1986). *Education:* Studied singing with Fred Steele.

Addresses: *Agent*—Cunningham/Escott/Slevin and Doherty Talent Agency, 10635 Santa Monica Blvd., Suite 140, Los Angeles, CA 90025.

Career: Singer, actor, and producer. Performed as an accompanist with brother, Bernie Leibowitz, at bars and clubs in New York City; worked as a singer at venues in New York City in the 1950s, including appearance at the Copacabana nightclub, 1957; performed with wife Eydie Gorme in Las Vegas, NV, for several years, often in support of Frank Sinatra; GL Music, founder, 1989; GLG Productions, Inc., co–owner. Brooksdale Hospital, member of board of governors. *Military service:* U.S. Army, official vocalist of the U.S. Army Band, 1958–60; received Commendation Medal.

Member: Actor's Equity Association, American Federation of Television and Radio Artists, American Guild of Variety Artists, Screen Actors Guild, Friars Club (member of board of governors).

Awards, Honors: First prize from *Arthur Godfrey's Talent Scouts,* 1950; Grammy Award (with Eydie Gorme), best pop vocalist duo, National Academy of Recording Arts and Sciences, 1960, for *We Got Us;* Grammy Award nomination, best performance by a male vocalist, 1961, for *Portrait of My Love;* Institute of High Fidelity Award (with Gorme), 1963, for outstanding contributions to the musical arts; *Variety*/New York Drama

Critics Poll Award, best male performer in a musical, and Antoinette Perry Award nomination, best actor in a musical, both 1964, for *What Makes Sammy Run?;* Emmy Award nomination (with Gorme and others), outstanding comedy, variety, or music special, 1976, for *Steve and Eydie: Our Love Is Here to Stay;* Television Critics Circle Award, achievement in music, 1976; Film Advisory Board Award of Excellence (with Gorme), 1977, for *Steve Lawrence and Eydie Gorme: From This Moment On ... Cole Porter;* Emmy Award (with Gorme and others), outstanding comedy, variety, or music program, 1978, for *Steve & Eydie Celebrate Irving Berlin.*

CREDITS

Television Appearances; Series:
The Steve Allen Show (also known as *The Steve Allen Plymouth Show*), multiple appearances, between 1956 and 1960.
Cohost, *The Steve Lawrence and Eydie Gorme Show,* NBC, 1958.
Guest panelist, *What's My Line?,* multiple appearances, between 1958 and 1966.
The Steve Lawrence Show, CBS, 1965.
The Carol Burnett Show (also known as *Carol Burnett and Friends*), 1977.
Cohost, *Foul–ups, Bleeps, and Blunders,* ABC, 1984.

Television Appearances; Specials:
The General Motors 50th Anniversary Show, NBC, 1957.
The Jane Powell Show, NBC, 1961.
Ghost of Christmas Past, *Carol for Another Christmas,* ABC, 1964.
The Best on Record, NBC, 1965.
Host, *NBC Follies of 1965,* NBC, 1966.
The Bob Hope Show, NBC, 1967.
The Bob Hope Show, NBC, 1969.
What It Was, Was Love, NBC, 1969.
Steve and Eydie ... on Stage, NBC, 1973.
Lights, Camera, Monty!, ABC, 1975.
Steve and Eydie: Our Love Is Here to Stay, CBS, 1975.
Jubilee! (also known as *The Bell Telephone Jubilee*), NBC, 1976.
Steve Lawrence and Eydie Gorme: From This Moment On ... Cole Porter, ABC, 1977.
Bob Hope Special: Bob Hope's All–Star Tribute to the Palace Theatre, NBC, 1978.
Steve & Eydie Celebrate Irving Berlin, NBC, 1978.
Bert Convey Special—There's A Meeting Here Tonight, syndicated, 1981.
Bob Hope Special: Bob Hope's 30th Anniversary Television Special (also known as *The Bob Hope Anniversary Show*), NBC, 1981.
100 Years of America's Popular Music (also known as *Live from Studio 8H: 100 Years of America's Popular Music*), NBC, 1981.

(In archive footage) *TV's Funniest Game Show Moments,* 1984.

All Star Party for "Dutch" Reagan, CBS, 1985.

All Star Party for Clint Eastwood, CBS, 1986.

This Is Your Life, NBC, 1987.

The Fifth Annual Television Academy Hall of Fame, Fox, 1989.

Sinatra 75: The Best Is Yet to Come (also known as *Frank Sinatra: Seventy–fifth Birthday Celebration*), CBS, 1990.

The Sixth Annual Television Academy Hall of Fame, Fox, 1990.

Interviewee, *Steve Allen,* 1994.

Sinatra Duets, 1994.

Sinatra: 80 Years My Way, 1995.

Marvin Hamlisch & the Pittsburgh Pops, 1996.

Steve Allen's 75th Birthday Celebration, 1997.

"Sammy Davis, Jr.: Mr. Entertainment," *Biography,* Arts and Entertainment, 1999.

Hitmakers: The Teens Who Stole Pop Music, Arts and Entertainment, 2001.

"Burt Bacharach," *Biography,* Arts and Entertainment, 2001.

"Judy Garland: By Myself," *American Masters,* PBS, 2004.

Host (with Eydie Gorme) of Greater New York United Cerebral Palsy telethons, WOR (New York City), 1960–69.

Television Appearances; Miniseries:

Tweedledum, *Alice in Wonderland* (also known as *Alice through the Looking Glass*), CBS, 1985.

Television Appearances; Episodic:

Arthur Godfrey's Talent Scouts, CBS, 1950.

The Steve Allen Show, WNBC (New York City), 1953.

Tonight! (also known as *The Knickerbocker Beer Presents the Steve Allen Show, Knickerbocker Beer Show,* and *The Tonight Show*), NBC, 1957.

Person to Person, 1958.

The Dinah Shore Show (also known as *The Dinah Shore Chevy Show*), NBC, 1958, 1959.

The Garry Moore Show, CBS, c. 1959.

Toast of the Town (also known as *The Ed Sullivan Show*), several appearances, between 1959 and 1970.

The Perry Como Show (also known as *The Chesterfield Supper Club* and *Perry Como's Kraft Music Hall*), 1960.

Here's Hollywood, 1961.

"USO—Wherever They Go!," *The DuPont Show of the Week,* 1961.

The Bell Telephone Hour, NBC, 1962, 1963.

The Judy Garland Show, 1963.

Contestant, *Password* (also known as *Password All–Stars*), 1963, 1964.

Host, *On Parade,* NBC, 1964.

Guest host, *The Hollywood Palace,* 1965.

The Hollywood Palace, 1967, 1969, 1970.

The Andy Williams Show, 1967.

Cohost, *The Kraft Music Hall,* 1970.

This Is Tom Jones, 1970.

The Merv Griffin Show, 1970.

Dr. Sam Havers, "The Corrupted," *Medical Center,* CBS, 1971.

Danny Turner, "The Replacement," *The New Dick Van Dyke Show,* 1971.

Mark Bannett/Radha Ramadi, "The Dear Departed," *Night Gallery* (also known as *Rod Serling's "Night Gallery"*), NBC, 1971.

The Pearl Bailey Show, 1971.

The Flip Wilson Show, 1971, 1974.

Rowan & Martin's Laugh–In (also known as *Laugh–In*), 1972.

The Dean Martin Show (also known as *The Dean Martin Comedy Hour*), 1972, 1973.

Himself, "Lucy, the Peacemaker," *Here's Lucy,* 1973.

Aide–de–camp, "Celebrity Roast: George Washington," *The Dean Martin Show* (also known as *The Dean Martin Comedy Hour*), 1974.

"Celebrity Roast: Dan Rowan and Dick Martin," *The Dean Martin Show* (also known as *The Dean Martin Comedy Hour*), 1974.

Himself, "Earthquake II," *Sanford and Son,* 1975.

Duke, "Two Frogs on a Mongoose," *Police Story,* 1976.

The Sonny and Cher Show, 1976.

The Tonight Show Starring Johnny Carson, NBC, 1977, 1982.

"The Broken Badge," *Police Story,* 1978.

Michael Post, "Express to Terror," *Supertrain,* 1979.

Guest host, *The Big Show,* NBC, 1980.

Sonny Daye, "Ties My Father Sold Me," *Hardcastle and McCormick,* ABC, 1984.

Sonny Daye, "McCormick's Bar and Grill," *Hardcastle and McCormick,* ABC, 1986.

Mack Howard, "No Laughing Murder," *Murder, She Wrote,* CBS, 1987.

Don Palermo, "A Streetcar Named Congress Douglas," *Bob,* CBS, 1992.

Sonny Baxter, "Half That Jazz," *Empty Nest,* NBC, 1994.

Danny Bernard, "Who Killed Skippy's Master?" *Burke's Law,* CBS, 1994.

Voice of Howard, "Frasier Crane's Day Off," *Frasier,* NBC, 1994.

Himself, "Canasta Masta," *The Nanny,* CBS, 1995.

The Rosie O'Donnell Show, syndicated, 1997, 1998.

Morty Fine, "Ma'ternal Affairs," *The Nanny,* CBS, 1999.

Morty Fine, "The Finale: Part 1," *The Nanny,* CBS, 1999.

Mike Rodzinski, "All Dressed Up and Nowhere to Die," *Diagnosis Murder,* CBS, 2000.

Steve the bartender, "There's the Rub," *Gilmore Girls* (also known as *Gilmore Girls: Beginnings*), The WB, 2002.

Mitch Urbana, "Big Middle," *CSI: Crime Scene Investigation* (also known as *C.S.I., CSI: Las Vegas,* and *Les experts*), CBS, 2005.

Also appeared as guest, *The Steve Allen Comedy Hour,* early 1980s.

Television Appearances; Awards Presentations:
The 48th Annual Academy Awards, ABC, 1976.
The Television Critics Circle Awards, CBS, 1977.
The 51st Annual Academy Awards, ABC, 1979.

Television Executive Producer; Specials:
Steve and Eydie … on Stage, NBC, 1973.
Steve & Eydie Celebrate Irving Berlin, NBC, 1978.

Television Work; Other:
Theme song performer, *The Facts of Life* (series), 1960.
Producer, *The Long Way Home,* Granada, 1989.

Film Appearances:
Gary McBride, *Stand Up and Be Counted,* Columbia, 1972.
Maury Sline, *The Blues Brothers,* Universal, 1980.
Jack Fenwick, *The Lonely Guy,* Universal, 1984.
Maury Sline, *Blues Brothers 2000,* Universal, 1998.
Himself, *Play It to the Bone* (also known as *Play It*), Buena Vista, 1999.
The Contract, Atilla Pictures/Lavetta Entertainment, 1999.
Arthur Mydanick, *The Yards,* Miramax, 2000.
Boxing spectator, *Ocean's Eleven* (also known as *11* and *O11*), Warner Bros., 2001.

Film Work; Song Performer:
"You Had to Be There," *Falling in Love Again* (also known as *In Love*), 1980.
"The Best Is Yet to Come," *Mr. 3000,* Buena Vista, 2004.
Title song, *Bewitched,* Sony Pictures Releasing, 2005.
"Volare," *Maxed Out: Hard Times, Easy Credit, and the Era of Predatory Lenders* (documentary; also known as *Maxed Out: Our Credit*), Red Envelope Entertainment, 2007.

Stage Appearances:
Joey, *Pal Joey,* Carousel Theatre, Framingham, MA, 1962.
(Broadway debut) Sammy Glick, *What Makes Sammy Run?* (musical), Fifty–Fourth Street Theatre, 1964–65.
Larry Davis, *Golden Rainbow* (musical), Shubert Theatre, New York City, 1968, then George Abbott Theatre, New York City, 1968–69.

Major Tours:
An Evening with Steve Lawrence and Eydie Gorme, U.S. cities, 1963.

Also toured with Eydie Gorme in U.S. cities, 1960–61.

Radio Appearances:
Appeared on Arthur Godfrey's radio show in New York City, c. 1951.

RECORDINGS

Albums:
Steve Lawrence, King Records, 1953.
About That Girl, Coral Records, 1956.
Songs by Steve Lawrence, Coral, 1956.
Here's Steve Lawrence, 1958.
Swing Softly with Me, ABC–Paramount, 1959.
We Got Us, ABC–Paramount, c. 1960.
Eydie Gorme and Steve Lawrence Sing the Golden Hits, Universal Special Products, 1960.
Portrait of My Love, United Artists, 1961.
The Very Best of Eydie & Steve, 1962.
Steve & Eydie at the Movies, Columbia, 1963.
Winners!, 1963.
Two on the Aisle, 1963.
Our Best to You, 1964.
That Holiday Feeling!, GL, 1964.
Everybody Knows, 1964.
Academy Award Losers, GL, 1964.
The Steve Lawrence Show, Columbia, 1965.
What Makes Sammy Run? (original soundtrack recording), GL, 1965.
Together on Broadway, 1967.
Golden Rainbow (original soundtrack recording), GL, 1968.
Real True Lovin', 1969.
What It Was, Was Love (soundtrack recording), RCA, 1969.
The Best of Steve & Eydie, Curb, 1977.
Steve & Eydie & Friends Celebrate Gershwin, 1979.
Take It on Home, 1981.
Pretty Blue Eyes, Universal Special Products, 1985.
All About Love, Universal, 1987.
The Best of Steve Lawrence, Paramount, 1987.
Greatest Hits, Columbia, 1987.
Come Waltz with Me, 1987.
People Will Say We're in Love, 1987.
Swinging West, GL, 1989.
Alone Together, 1989.
The Steve Lawrence Sound, 1991.
Songs Everybody Knows, 1991.
Songs by Steve Lawrence, Taragon, 1995.
Sing More Golden Hits, Universal Special Markets, 1995.
We'll Take Romance: The Best of Steve Lawrence & Eydie Gorme, 1954–1960, Music Club, 1995.
Steve Lawrence Sings Sinatra: A Musical Tribute to the Man and His Music, GL, 2003.
New York, New York, Bluemountain Records, 2003.
Greatest Hits, Vol 1, GL, 2004.
Greatest Hits, Vol. 2, GL, 2004.
Love Songs from the Movies, GL, 2005.
All My Love Belongs to You, Varese Sarabande, 2005.

It's Us Again, GL, 2007.
Long before I Knew You, Jasmine, 2007.

Also recorded *Come Waltz with Me; Lawrence Goes Latin; On a Clear Day: Steve Lawrence Sings Up a Storm; Portrait of Steve; Steve Lawrence Sings of Love & Sad Young Men; Through the Years;* and *Together Forever.* Singles include "Poinciana," King Records, 1951; "Pretty Blue Eyes," ABC–Paramount, 1959; "Footsteps," ABC–Paramount, 1960; "All about Love," Coral; "Don't Be Afraid Little Darlin'," and "Go Away Little Girl;" singles with Gorme include "Make Yourself Comfortable"/"I've Gotta Crow," Coral, 1954.

WRITINGS

Film Composer:
Title song, *The Man from the Diner's Club,* 1963.
Nickelodeon Days, 1962.

OTHER SOURCES

Electronic:
Steve and Eydie Official Site, http://www.steveandeydie. com, September 2, 2007.

LEE, Joie 1962–
(Joie Susannah Lee, Joy Lee)

PERSONAL

First name pronounced "Jwah"; original name, Joy Lee; born June 22, 1962, in Brooklyn, NY; daughter of William "Bill" James Edwards (a jazz bassist, composer, and actor) and Jacquelyn (a teacher of arts and black literature; maiden name, Shelton) Lee; sister of Spike Lee (an actor, producer, director, and writer), Cinque Lee (an actor), and David Lee (a photographer). *Education:* Attended Sarah Lawrence College, Bronxville, NY, for two years.

Addresses: *Agent*—Don Buchwald and Associates, 6500 Wilshire Blvd., Suite 2200, Los Angeles, CA 90048.

Career: Actress. Child Hoods Productions, cofounder, 1992. Member of faculty at New School, School of Visual Arts, and Black Nexxus; Actors Studio, member.

Member: Actors' Equity Association.

CREDITS

Film Appearances:
Clorinda Bradford, *She's Gotta Have It,* Island, 1986.
Lizzie Life, *School Daze,* Columbia, 1988.
First customer, *Coffee and Cigarettes II* (short film; also known as *Coffee and Cigarettes: Memphis Version*), 1988.
Jade, *Do the Right Thing,* Universal, 1989.
Athena, *Bail Jumper,* Angelika, 1990.
Indigo Downes, *Mo' Better Blues,* Universal, 1990.
(As Joy Lee) Cathy, *A Kiss Before Dying,* Universal, 1991.
Lois, *Fathers and Sons,* Pacific Pictures, 1992.
(As Joie Susannah Lee) Aunt Maxine, *Crooklyn,* Universal, 1994.
(As Joie Susannah Lee) Marie, *Losing Isaiah,* Paramount, 1995.
(As Joie Susannah Lee) Switchboard operator, *Girl 6,* Fox Searchlight Pictures, 1996.
Jindal, *Get on the Bus,* Columbia, 1996.
Joie, *Nowhere Fast,* 1997.
(As Joie Susannah Lee) Poet woman, *Personals* (also known as *Hook'd Up*), Unapix Entertainment, 1998.
"Bed Stuy" woman interviewee, *Summer of Sam,* Buena Vista, 1999.
Good twin, "Twins," *Coffee and Cigarettes,* United Artists, 2003.
Gloria Reid, *She Hate Me,* Sony Pictures Classics, 2004.
Annie, *Full Grown Men,* 2006.

Also appeared in *What Goes Around Comes Around* (short).

Film Work:
Associate producer, *Crooklyn,* Universal, 1994.
Producer, *Nowhere Fast,* 1997.
(As Joie Susannah Lee) Director and producer, *Snapped* (short), 2000.
Executive producer, "Jesus Children of America" (short), *All the Invisible Children* (also known as *Les enfants invisibles*), 2005.

Television Appearances; Episodic:
"The Lost Weekend," *The Cosby Show,* NBC, 1989.
Angela Balding, "Zero Tolerance," *100 Centre Street,* Arts and Entertainment, 2002.
Prison nurse, "Rotten," *Law & Order: Special Victims Unit* (also known as *Law & Order: SVU* and *Special Victims Unit*), 2003.

Television Appearances; Specials:
Making "Do the Right Thing," 1989.
The 19th Annual Black Filmmakers Hall of Fame, syndicated, 1992.

Television Work; Movies:
Coach for Zelda Harris, *Clover,* 1997.

Stage Appearances:
Zora Neale Hurston and Teets, *Mulebone,* Ethel Barrymore Theatre, New York City, 1991.
(As Joie Susannah Lee) *The Hologram Theory,* Off-Broadway production, 2000.

RECORDINGS

Music Videos:
Appeared in the Neville Brothers' "Sister Rosa."

WRITINGS

Screenplays:
(With Cinque Lee and Spike Lee) *Crooklyn,* Universal, 1994.
Snapped (short), 2000.
"Jesus Children of America" (short), *All the Invisible Children* (also known as *Les enfants invisibles*), 2005.

Television Movies:
Wrote (with Spike Lee) *Flight 770* (short), BBC.

Television Pilots:
Cowrote *Accidentally on Purpose,* Nickelodeon.

OTHER SOURCES

Books:
Contemporary Authors Online, Thomson Gale, 2007.
Contemporary Black Biography, Volume 1, Gale, 1992.

LITTLETON, Carol 1942(?)–

PERSONAL

Born 1942 (some source cite 1948), in Oklahoma; married John Bailey (a cinematographer, camera operator, and director), March 11, 1972. *Education:* University of Oklahoma, B.A., 1965, M.A., 1969; also attended University of Mexico, University of Mainz, and University of Paris.

Addresses: *Agent*—United Talent Agency, 9560 Wilshire Blvd., Suite 500, Beverly Hills, CA 90212–2427.

Career: Film editor. Former owner of a company that made commercial spot advertisements, 1972–77, and of Galloping Tintypes (commercial editing firm); worked as a film editor at American Film Institute and with Jerry Sims Productions; also worked as assistant film editor.

Member: Society of Motion Picture Film Editors (local president, 1988–92), Academy of Motion Picture Arts and Sciences (member of board of governors, 1995—).

Awards, Honors: Fulbright scholar in France, 1960s; Academy Award nomination, Film Award nomination, British Academy of Film and Television Arts, and Eddie Award nomination, American Cinema Editors, all best film editing, 1983, for *E.T.: The Extra–Terrestrial;* Golden Satellite Award nomination (with Andy Keir), best motion picture film editing, International Press Academy, 1999, for *Beloved;* Emmy Award, outstanding single–camera picture editing for a miniseries, movie, or special, 2000, for *Oprah Winfrey Presents: "Tuesdays with Morrie."*

CREDITS

Film Editor:
Legacy, 1976.
The Mafu Cage (also known as *The Cage, Deviation, Don't Ring the Doorbell,* and *My Sister, My Love,*), Clouds, 1978.
French Postcards (also known as *Wer geht denn noch zur uni?*), Paramount, 1979.
Body Heat, Warner Bros., 1981.
E.T.: The Extra–Terrestrial (also known as *E.T.;* also released as *E.T. the Extra–Terrestrial: The 20th Anniversary*), Universal, 1982.
The Big Chill, Columbia, 1983.
Places in the Heart, TriStar, 1984.
Silverado, Sony Pictures Releasing, 1985.
Brighton Beach Memoirs (also known as *Neil Simon's "Brighton Beach Memoirs"*), Universal, 1986.
Swimming to Cambodia (also known as *Spalding Gray's "Swimming to Cambodia"*), Cinecom International 1987.
Vibes (also known as *Vibes: The Secret of the Golden Pyramids*), Columbia, 1988.
The Accidental Tourist, Warner Bros., 1988.
White Palace, Universal, 1990.
The Search for Signs of Intelligent Life in the Universe, Orion, 1991.
Grand Canyon, Twentieth Century–Fox, 1991.
Benny & Joon, Metro–Goldwyn–Mayer, 1993.
China Moon, Orion, 1994.
Wyatt Earp, Warner Bros., 1994.
Diabolique, Warner Bros., 1996.
Twilight, Paramount, 1998.
Beloved, Buena Vista, 1998.

Mumford, Buena Vista, 1999.
The Anniversary Party, Fine Line, 2001.
The Truth about Charlie (also known as *Die wahrheit ueber Charlie*), Universal, 2002.
Dreamcatcher (also known as *L'attrapeur de reves*), Warner Bros., 2003.
The Manchurian Candidate, Paramount, 2004.
In the Land of Women, Warner Bros., 2007.
Margot at the Wedding, Paramount, 2007.

Film Work; Other:
Supervising editor, *Roadie,* United Artists, 1980.
Additional editing, *What Women Want,* 2000.

Television Film Editor; Movies:
Battered, 1978.
Tuesdays with Morrie (also known as *Oprah Winfrey Presents: "Tuesdays with Morrie"*), ABC, 1999.

Television appearances; Specials:
Wyatt Earp: Walk with a Legend, 1994.

Television Appearances; Episodic:
"The Anniversary Party," *Anatomy of a Scene,* Sundance Channel, 2001.

RECORDINGS

Videos:
The Making of "E.T. the Extra–Terrestrial" (also known as *E.T.: The Extra–Terrestrial—A Look Back*), 1996.
The Making of "Silverado," Columbia TriStar Home Entertainment, 1999.
The Cutting Edge: The Magic of Movie Editing, Warner Home Video, 2005.
The Maltese Falcon: One Magnificent Bird, Warner Home Video, 2006.

OTHER SOURCES

Books:
International Dictionary of Films and Filmmakers, Volume 4: *Writers and Production Artists,* St. James Press, 1996.
Women Filmmakers and Their Films, St. James Press, 1998.

LONDON, Jerry 1937–

PERSONAL

Full name, Jerome R. London; born January 21, 1937, in Los Angeles, CA; son of Micky and Ann (maiden name, Rae) London; married Marilynn Landau, June 15, 1958; children: Lisa Monet, Todd Mitchell (an actor and producer). *Education:* Attended University of California, Los Angeles.

Addresses: *Manager*—Don Klein, Don Klein Management Group, 8840 Wilshire Blvd., Suite 207, Beverly Hills, CA 90211.

Career: Director, producer, and film editor. Desilu Productions, Los Angeles, apprentice film editor, 1955, film editor, 1955–65; Bing Crosby Productions, associate producer, 1965–71; Jerry London Productions, founder, 1984.

Awards, Honors: Emmy Award nomination, outstanding directing in a limited series or special, and Directors Guild of America Award (with others), outstanding directorial achievement in specials, both 1981, for *Shogun;* Emmy Award nominations (with others), outstanding limited series, 1984, for *Chiefs,* and 1985, for *Ellis Island.*

CREDITS

Television Director; Movies:
Killdozer, 1974.
McNaughton's Daughter (also known as *Try to Catch a Saint*), 1976.
Cover Girls, 1977.
Swan Song, 1980.
Father Figure, 1980.
(And producer) *The Ordeal of Bill Carney,* CBS, 1981.
(And executive producer) *Manhunt for Claude Dallas,* CBS, 1986.
(And executive producer) *Kiss Shot,* CBS, 1989.
(And executive producer) *The Haunting of Sarah Hardy,* USA Network, 1989.
Vestige of Honor, CBS, 1990.
Victim of Love (also known as *Raw Heat*), CBS, 1991.
(And producer) *Calendar Girl, Cop Killer: The Bambi Bembenek Story* (also known as *The Heart of the Lie*), ABC, 1992.
Labor of Love: The Arlette Schweitzer Story, CBS, 1993.
A Twist of the Knife, CBS, 1993.
The Return of I Spy (also known as *I Spy Returns*), CBS, 1993.
A Mother's Gift (also known as *A Lantern in Her Hand*), CBS, 1995.
A Promise to Carolyn, CBS, 1996.
A Holiday for Love (also known as *Christmas in My Hometown*), CBS, 1996.
Get to the Heart: The Barbara Mandrell Story, CBS, 1997.
I'll Be Home for Christmas, CBS, 1997.
Stolen Women, Captured Hearts (also known as *Stolen Women*), CBS, 1997.
Beauty, CBS, 1998.

As Time Runs Out (also known as *Course contre le temps*), CBS, 1999.

Take Me Home: The John Denver Story, CBS, 2000.

(And producer) *Dr. Quinn, Medicine Woman: The Heart Within,* CBS, 2001.

Counterstrike, TBS, 2003.

Television Executive Producer; Movies:

With Intent to Kill (movie; also known as *Urge to Kill*), CBS, 1984.

Family Sins (movie), CBS, 1987.

Television Director; Miniseries:

Wheels (also known as *Arthur Hailey's "Wheels"*), 1977.

Evening in Byzantium, 1978.

Women in White, 1979.

Shogun (also known as *James Clavell's "Shogun"*), NBC, 1980.

The Scarlet and the Black (also known as *The Vatican Pimpernel* and *Scarlatto e nero*), 1982.

(And supervising producer) *Chiefs* (also known as *Once Upon a Murder*), CBS, 1983.

(And supervising producer) *Ellis Island,* CBS, 1984.

(And supervising producer) *If Tomorrow Comes,* CBS, 1985.

(And producer) *Dadah Is Death* (also known as *Barlow and Chambers: A Long Way from Home* and *Deadly Decision*), CBS, 1988.

A Season of Giants (also known as *Michelangelo: The Last Giant*), TNT, 1991.

Grass Roots, NBC, 1992.

Television Director; Series:

The Bob Newhart Show, CBS, multiple episodes, 1973.

The Rockford Files (also known as *Jim Rockford, Private Investigator*), NBC, multiple episodes, between 1974 and 1977.

Television Series Work; Other:

Editor, *Hogan's Heroes,* CBS, 1965–66.

Editorial supervisor, *Hogan's Heroes,* CBS, 1965–69.

Producer, *Hotel* (also known as *Arthur Hailey's "Hotel"*), ABC, 1983.

Producer, *Hollywood Beat,* ABC, 1985.

Associate producer of *The Doris Day Show.*

Television Director; Episodic:

"Home Is Where the Heart Is," *The Partridge Family,* 1972.

"Waiting for Bolero," *The Partridge Family,* 1972.

"My Heart Belongs to a Two Car Garage," *The Partridge Family,* 1972.

"The Partridge Papers," *The Partridge Family,* 1972.

"Career Fever," *The Brady Bunch,* 1972.

"Fright Night," *The Brady Bunch,* 1972.

"Ellen's Flip Side," *Temperatures Rising* (also known as *The New Temperatures Rising Show*), 1972.

"Good Luck, Leftkowitz," *Temperatures Rising* (also known as *The New Temperatures Rising Show*), 1972.

"Love and the Return of Raymond," *Love, American Style,* ABC, 1972.

"Love and the Old Lover," *Love, American Style,* ABC, 1973.

"Love and the Model Apartment," *Love, American Style,* ABC, 1973.

"Adios Johnny Bravo," *The Brady Bunch,* 1973.

"The Elopement," *The Brady Bunch,* 1973.

"Lou's Second Date," *Mary Tyler Moore* (also known as *The Mary Tyler Moore Show*), CBS, 1974.

"Burning Bright," *The Six Million Dollar Man,* ABC, 1974.

"Nuclear Alert," *The Six Million Dollar Man,* ABC, 1974.

"You Go to My Head," *Happy Days* (also known as *Happy Days Again*), ABC, 1974.

"Mayday," *Harry O,* ABC, 1975.

"Hostage," *Harry O,* ABC, 1976.

"Canyon of Death," *The Bionic Woman,* 1976.

"Say Goodbye to Yesterday," *City of Angels,* 1976.

"Sarah Who?," *Police Woman,* 1976.

"Tour de Force—Killer Aboard," *Hawaii Five-0* (also known as *McGarrett*), 1976.

"Pressure Point," *Police Story,* NBC, 1977.

Premiere episode, *Hollywood Beat,* ABC, 1985.

"My Darlin' Clementine," *Tall Tales and Legends* (also known as *Shelley Duvall's "Tall Tales and Legends"*), Showtime, 1987.

California, 1997.

"Hostage," *100 Centre Street,* Arts and Entertainment, 2001.

"And Justice for Some," *100 Centre Street,* Arts and Entertainment, 2001.

"No Good Deed Goes Unpunished," *100 Centre Street,* Arts and Entertainment, 2001.

"Killer Instinct," *JAG,* CBS, 2001.

"Dog Robber: Part 2," *JAG,* CBS, 2001.

"What It Means to You," *The Guardian,* CBS, 2003.

"Maternal Mirrors," *Strong Medicine,* Lifetime, 2003.

"Life in the Balance," *Strong Medicine,* Lifetime, 2004.

"What About What Was Supposed to Be ...," *What About Brian,* ABC, 2006.

Also directed episodes of *Chicago Hope,* CBS; *Delvecchio,* CBS; *Diagnosis Murder,* CBS; *Dream On,* HBO; *Dr. Quinn, Medicine Woman; The Feather and Father Gang,* ABC; *The Flying Nun; Here We Go Again,* ABC; *Hogan's Heroes,* CBS; *Joe Forrester,* NBC; *Kojak,* CBS; *Lucas Tanner,* NBC; *Marcus Welby, M.D.* (also known as *Robert Young, Family Doctor*), ABC; *The Paul Lynde Show; Petrocelli,* NBC.

Television Director; Pilots:
The Chicago Story, NBC, 1981.
(And producer) *Hotel* (also known as *Arthur Hailey's "Hotel"*), ABC, 1983.
(And producer) *MacGruder and Loud,* ABC, 1984.
(And producer) *Dark Mansions,* ABC, 1986.
(And producer) *Harry's Hong Kong* (also known as *China Hand),* ABC, 1987.
The Cosby Mysteries (also known as *Guy Hanks I),* NBC, 1994.

Television Producer; Pilots:
Bridget Loves Bernie, 1972.

Television Director; Specials:
Ma and Pa, 1974.
The World of Darkness, CBS, 1977.
Escapade, CBS, 1978.
(And producer) *The Gift of Life,* CBS, 1982.

Television Associate Producer; Episodic:
"Bombsight," *Hogan's Heroes,* CBS, 1969.

Film Director:
(And executive producer) *Games Guys Play,* 1975.
Rent–a–Cop, Kings Road Productions, 1988.

LONG, Jodi 1954–

PERSONAL

Original name, Jodi Leung; born January 7 (some sources cite January 1), 1954, in New York, NY; daughter of Lawrence K. (a vaudevillian and golf professional) and Kimiye (a vaudevillian; maiden name, Tsunemitsu) Leung. *Education:* State University of New York, Purchase, B.F.A., 1976; trained for the stage with Joseph Anthony, Robert Lewis, Norman Ayrton, Alan Schneider, Valerie Bettis, and Shelley Winters.

Career: Actress.

Member: Actors' Equity Association, Screen Actors Guild, American Federation of Television and Radio Artists.

Awards, Honors: Maverick Award, career achievement, Los Angeles Women's Theatre, 2000.

CREDITS

Stage Appearances:
(Broadway debut) Hop daughter, *Nowhere to Go but Up,* Winter Garden Theatre, 1962.

Rossignol, *Marat/Sade,* Changing Space Theatre, New York City, 1976.
Blue, *Strippers,* Everyman Theatre, New York City, 1977.
Monica Chin Lee, *The Verandah,* Gene Frankel Theatre Workshop, then New Dramatists Theatre, both New York City, 1978.
Ophelia, *Hamlet,* Everyman Theatre, 1978.
Blossom Springfield, *Fathers and Sons,* New York Shakespeare Festival, Public Theatre, New York City, 1978.
Company, Arena Stage, Washington, DC, 1978–79.
Selina, *Loose Ends,* Arena Stage, then Circle in the Square, New York City, 1979–80.
Sumi, *Monkey Music,* Pan Asian Repertory Theatre, New York City, 1980.
Bacchae woman, *The Bacchae,* Circle in the Square, 1980.
Joanne, *Family Devotions,* New York Shakespeare Festival, Estelle R. Newman Theatre, Public Theatre, New York City, 1981.
Commentator, *Rowher,* Pan Asian Repertory Theatre, 1982.
Titania, *A Midsummer Night's Dream,* Pittsburgh Public Theatre, Pittsburgh, PA, 1982.
Becky Lou, *The Tooth of Crime,* Syracuse Stage, Syracuse, NY, then La Mama Experimental Theatre Club, New York City, 1983.
Hippolyta and Titania, *A Midsummer Night's Dream,* Pan Asian Repertory Theatre, 1983.
Alice, *I'm Getting My Act Together And ...,* Cincinnati Playhouse in the Park, Cincinnati, OH, 1983.
Cherie, *Bus Stop,* Byrdcliff Theatre, Woodstock, NY, 1983.
Company, Actors Theatre of Louisville, Louisville, KY, 1984–85.
Helena, *A Midsummer Night's Dream,* New York City, 1984–85.
Zuma, *The Dream of Kitamura,* Theater of the Open Eye, New York City, 1985.
The Painful Adventures of Pericles, Prince of Tyre, Hartford Stage Company, Hartford, CT, 1986–87.
Anna, *Nothing Sacred,* Hartford Stage Company, 1988–89.
Judy Adams, *The Wash,* Manhattan Theatre Club, New York City, then City Theatre Group, Mark Taper Forum, Los Angeles, 1990.
Nam–Jun Vuong, *Getting Away with Murder,* Broadhurst Theatre, New York City, 1996.
Eng Luan, *Golden Child,* New York Shakespeare Festival, Estelle R. Newman Theatre, Public Theatre, 1996.
Sonja, *Red,* Manhattan Theatre Club Stage II, 1999.
Penny Nercessian/Betina Brevoort, *Old Money,* Mitzi E. Newhouse Theatre, New York City, 2000–2001.
Madame Liang, *Flower Drum Song* (musical), workshop production, 2000, then Virginia Theatre, New York City, 2002–2003.
Katya, *McReele,* Roundabout Theatre Company, Laura Pels Theatre, New York City, 2005.

Appeared as Billie Dawn, *Born Yesterday;* Helena, *Midsummer Night's Dream,* Apple Corps Theatre; Montgomery, *Mirrors Remembered,* New York Stage and Film Theatre, New York City; and Marina, *Pericles,* Hartford Stage, Hartford, CT; also appeared in *Dear Kenneth Blake,* Ensemble Studio Theatre, New York City.

Major Tours:
1000 Airlines on the Roof (solo show), U.S., European, and Australian cities, 1988.

Also toured as Suzy Q in a production of *Flower Drum Song.*

Television Appearances; Series:
Katherine Kim, *All–American Girl,* ABC, 1994–95.
Claire, a recurring role, *Miss Match,* NBC, between 2003 and 2005.

Also voice for *American Dad.*

Television Appearances; Movies:
Jade Precious Stone, *Jade Snow,* 1976.
Gail, "Nurse," *CBS Movie of the Week,* CBS, 1980.
Mrs. Yamata, "How to Be a Perfect Person in Just Three Days," *WonderWorks,* PBS, 1983.
Sangreaves, *Vestige of Honor,* CBS, 1990.
Bank teller, *How to Murder a Millionaire,* CBS, 1990.
Linda Chong, *Firestorm: 72 Hours in Oakland,* ABC, 1993.
Helen, *Murder in Mind,* HBO, 1997.

Television Appearances; Episodic:
Mrs. Lin, "China Rain," *The Equalizer,* 1985.
"Three Little Spies," *Scarecrow and Mrs. King,* 1986.
JoAnn, "Trust Me," *The Cosby Show,* 1988.
JoAnn, "Getting the Story," *The Cosby Show,* 1990.
Woman in line, "April Fool's Day," *Roseanne,* ABC, 1990.
"Speak, Lawyers, for Me," *L.A. Law,* 1991.
Eileen Arata, "Trial and Error," *Designing Women,* CBS, 1992.
Madame Ybarra, "Home Alone," *Cafe Americain,* NBC, 1993.
Madame Ybarra, "Love the One You're With," *Cafe Americain,* NBC, 1994.
Angelique, "Blood Is Thicker than Watercolor," *The Wayans Bros.,* 1995.
Joan, "Retribution," *Michael Hayes,* CBS, 1997.
Joan, "Mob Mentality," *Michael Hayes,* CBS, 1998.
Joan, "Devotion," *Michael Hayes,* CBS, 1998.
Herself, *Judge Judy,* Court TV, 1998.
Patty Aston, "The Cheating Curve," *Sex and the City,* HBO, 1999.
Tracy, "Decisions," *Family Law,* CBS, 1999.

Rhonda, "Destiny in a Bottle," *Chicken Soup for the Soul,* PAX, 2000.
"Manuelo in the Middle: Part 2," *So Little Time,* 2001.
Polly Seager, "Unfamiliar Territory," *The Division* (also known as *Heart of the City*), Lifetime, 2002.
Center director, "Tortured," *Law & Order: Special Victims Unit* (also known as *Law & Order: SVU* and *Special Victims Unit*), NBC, 2003.
Mrs. Kim, "Honor Bound," *Without a Trace* (also known as *W.A.T.*), CBS, 2005.
Judge, "Finding Judas," *House M.D.* (also known as *House*), Fox, 2006.

Film Appearances:
Betsy Okamoto, *Rollover,* Warner Bros., 1981.
Shanghai Rose, *Ringers,* 1982.
Reporter, *Splash,* Buena Vista, 1984.
Cocktail waitress, *The Bedroom Window,* De Laurentiis Entertainment Group, 1987.
Wendy Yoshimura, *Patty Hearst* (also known as *Patty*), Atlantic Releasing, 1988.
Mui, *Soursweet,* Skouras, 1988.
First reporter at Democratic convention, *Born on the Fourth of July,* Universal, 1989.
Television reporter, "Oedipus Wrecks," *New York Stories,* Buena Vista, 1989.
First dream woman, *The Exorcist III* (also known as *The Exorcist III: Legion* and *William Peter Blatty's "The Exorcist III"*), Twentieth Century–Fox, 1990.
Half of a Park Avenue couple, *Alice,* Paramount, 1990.
Yakimoto Yakimura, *The Pickle* (also known as *The Adventures of the Flying Pickle*), Sony Pictures Releasing, 1993.
Wendy Wong, *Amos & Andrew,* Sony Pictures Releasing, 1993.
Nikko's mom, *Robocop 3,* Orion, 1993.
Officer Kim Lee, *Striking Distance,* Sony Pictures Releasing, 1993.
Corey Chang, *His and Hers,* Alliance Independent Films, 1997.
Father Gladden's fan, *Celebrity,* Miramax, 1998.
Keecia's mom, *The Hot Chick,* Buena Vista, 2002.
Feng shui woman, *New Suit,* Trillion Entertainment, 2003.
Mrs. Wong, *Red Thread* (short film), Pathfinder Pictures, 2004.

Some sources also credit appearance in a film titled *Special Delivery.*

RECORDINGS

Videos:
Appeared in the music video "Bizarre Love Triangle" by New Order.

OTHER SOURCES

Periodicals:
Interview, December, 1988, p. 31.

LOVEJOY, Deirdre 1962–

PERSONAL

Born June 30, 1962, in Abilene, TX; mother's name, Marcia. *Education:* University of Evansville, graduated; New York University, M.F.A.

Addresses: *Manager*—Amy Guenther, Gateway Management Partners, 5225 Wilshire Blvd., Los Angeles, CA 90036.

Career: Actress.

Awards, Honors: Helen Hayes Award nomination, Washington Theatre Awards Society, for *How I Learned to Drive.*

CREDITS

Television Appearances; Series:
Attorney Rhonda Pearlman, *The Wire,* HBO, 2002–2006.

Television Appearances; Miniseries:
Rosemary Kennedy, *The Kennedys of Massachusetts,* ABC, 1990.
Detective Linda Arndt, *Perfect Murder, Perfect Town* (also known as *Perfect Murder, Perfect Town: Jon Benet and the City of Boulder*), CBS, 2000.
Laura's lawyer, *Kingpin,* NBC, 2003.

Television Appearances; Episodic:
Judith Crockit, "Virtue," *Law & Order,* NBC, 1994.
Crime scene unit technician, "Thrill," *Law & Order,* NBC, 1997.
Karen Sealey, "Breaking In, Breaking Out, Breaking Up, Breaking Down," *Trinity,* 1999.
Third reporter, "Politically Incorrect," *Spin City,* ABC, 1999.
Nancy, "Patterns," *Third Watch,* NBC, 1999.
First reporter, "How to Bury a Millionaire," *Spin City,* ABC, 1999.
Reporter, "Airplane!" *Spin City,* ABC, 2000.
Hernandez, "Slaves," *Law & Order: Special Victims Unit* (also known as *Law & Order: SVU* and *Special Victims Unit*), NBC, 2000.

Hernandez, "Secrets," *Law & Order: Special Victims Unit* (also known as *Law & Order: SVU* and *Special Victims Unit*), NBC, 2001.
Ms. Diamond, "Closure," *Ed,* NBC, 2001.
Penny Halliwell, "Malignant," *Law & Order: Criminal Intent* (also known as *Law & Order: CI*), NBC, 2002.
Mrs. Peterson, "In Extremis," *Without a Trace* (also known as *W.A.T.*), CBS, 2002.
Taylor, "Orders," *Strong Medicine,* Lifetime, 2003.
Courtney, "A Time for Every Purpose," *Touched by an Angel,* CBS, 2003.
State's attorney, "The Long Goodbye," *Judging Amy,* CBS, 2003.
Michelle Foster, "Chatty Chatty Bang Bang," *NYPD Blue,* ABC, 2004.
Lisa Wolfe, "Eppur Si Muove," *The West Wing,* NBC, 2004.
Lisa Wolfe, "The Supremes," *The West Wing,* NBC, 2004.
Allie Tedesco, "Hannah Tedesco," *Nip/Tuck,* FX Network, 2005.
Melissa Langner, "Heroic Measures," *The Closer,* TNT, 2006.
Daria Samson, "Waste Not," *Numb3rs* (also known as *Num3ers*), CBS, 2006.
Ellen Porter, "Prodigal Son," *Close to Home,* CBS, 2006.
Ellen Porter, "Barren," *Close to Home,* CBS, 2007.
Shannon, "Aunt Myra Doesn't Pee a Lot," *Two and a Half Men,* CBS, 2007.

Television Appearances; Specials:
The devil, *Punch and Judy Get Divorced,* 1992.

Film Appearances:
Nurse Wells, *Sour Grapes,* Columbia, 1998.
Jean, *Number One* (short film), 1998.
Officer Isabel, *Random Hearts,* Columbia, 1999.
Fighting neighbor, *The Talented Mr. Ripley* (also known as *The Mysterious Yearning Secretive Sad Lonely Troubled Confused Loving Musical Gifted Intelligent Beautiful Tender Sensitive Haunted Passionate Talented Mr. Ripley*), Paramount, 1999.
(Uncredited) Police officer, *Shaft* (also known as *Shaft—Noch Fragen?*), Paramount, 2000.
Beverly Modina, *My Sister's Wedding,* 2001.
Student teacher, *Thirteen Conversations about One Thing* (also known as *13 Conversations*), Sony Pictures Classics, 2002.
Nora's mom/Katherine Clark, *Step Up,* Buena Vista, 2006.

Stage Appearances:
Elizabeth Panelli, *Getting & Spending,* Helen Hayes Theatre, New York City, 1998.
imPerfect Chemistry, Minetta Lane Theatre, New York City, 2000.

Diane, *The Gathering,* Cort Theatre, New York City, 2000–2001.

Lady Macbeth, *Macbeth,* Old Globe Theatre, San Diego, CA, 2005.

The Sisters Rosensweig, Old Globe Theatre, 2006.

Adriana, *The Comedy of Errors,* Old Globe Theatre, 2006.

Appeared in *Church of the Soul Survivor,* Actors Theatre of Louisville, Louisville, KY; as Julia, *Dark Rapture,* American Conservatory Theatre, San Francisco, CA; as Lady Utterwood, *Heartbreak House,* regional production; in *Henry IV, Part 1,* New York Shakespeare Festival, New York City; as Li'l Bit, *How I Learned to Drive,* Century Theatre and Arena Stage, Washington, DC; as Ms. McCracken, *The Lively Lad,* regional production; as telephone girl, *Machinal,* New York Shakespeare Festival, Delacorte Theatre, Public Theatre, New York City; as Helena, *A Midsummer Night's Dream,* New York Shakespeare Festival; as Brooke, *Noises Off,* Actors Theatre of Louisville; in *Once Around the City,* New York Stage and Film Theatre, New York City; as Lewis, *The Preservation Society,* Primary Stages, New York City; as Clarissa Churhcill, *Red Memories,* New York Stage and Film Theatre; as Lydia Languish, *The Rivals,* Williamstown Theatre Festival, Williamstown, MA; as Elizabeth, *Six Degrees of Separation,* Vivian Beaumont Theatre, Lincoln Center, New York City; and as Liz, *The Water Children,* Playwrights Horizons Theatre, New York City; also appeared in *Church of the Soul Survivor;* also performed at Center Stage, Baltimore, MD; Goodman Theatre, Chicago, IL; Indiana Repertory Theatre; Philadelphia Festival Theatre, Philadelphia, PA; and Vineyard Theatre.

OTHER SOURCES

Electronic:

Deirdre Lovejoy Official Site, http://www. deirdrelovejoy.com, July 31, 2007.

LOWRY, Sam
   See SODERBERGH, Steven

LURIE, Evan 1954–

PERSONAL

Born September 28, 1954, in Worcester, MA. *Education:* Studied music.

Addresses: *Agent*—Soundtrack Music Associates, 2229 Cloverfield Blvd., Santa Monica, CA 90405.

Career: Composer, musician, singer, recording artist, orchestrator, music conductor, and song arranger. Lounge Lizards (music group), performer.

CREDITS

Film Work:

Pianist, *The Kill–Off,* Cabriolet Films, 1990.

Orchestrator, score conductor, and pianist, *Joe Gould's Secret* (also known as *Cronica de uma certa New York, El secreto de Joe Gould, El secreto de un poeta, Joe Goulds Geheimnis, Joe Goulds hemlighet,* and *Le secret de Joe Gould*), USA Films, 2000.

Song arranger and performer, *Famous* (also known as *Lisa Picard Is Famous*), First Look International, 2000.

Music performer, "The Spinster's Waltz," *Just a Kiss,* Paramount, 2002.

Film Appearances:

The Kitchen Presents Two Moon July (music documentary; also known as *Two Moon July*), Kitchen, 1986.

Force of Circumstance, Ad Hoc, 1990.

Television Work; Series:

Vocalist and keyboard performer, *Fishing with John,* Bravo and Independent Film Channel, c. 1991–92.

Music performer, *Oswald* (animated), Nickelodeon, 2001–2004.

RECORDINGS

Albums:

Happy? Here? Now?, 1985.

Pieces for Bandoneon, Crepuscule, 1989.

Selling Water by the Side of the River, Antilles, 1990.

How I Spent My Vacation, Tzadik, 1998.

WRITINGS

Film Music:

Song "Coffee House Blues," *The Loveless* (also known as *Breakdown*), 1982, Atlantic Releasing, 1984.

Doomed Love, 1983.

Chochin (also known as *Paper Lantern*), Toei, Inc., 1987.

Il piccolo diavolo (also known as *The Little Devil*), Cecchi Gori Group, 1988.

Kizu, Toei, Inc., 1988.

The Kill–Off, Cabriolet Films, 1990.

Johnny Stecchino (also known as *Johnny Toothpick, Dzoni cackalica, Hammastikku–Johnny, Johnny Palillo, Johnny Palito, Johnny Tandestoker, Johnny tandpetaren,* and *Zahnstocher Johnny*), 1991, subtitled version released by New Line Cinema, 1992.

Under Cover of Darkness, Blue Moon Pictures/Wellington Lippert, 1992.

The Night We Never Met (also known as *Die Nacht mit meinem Traummann, Ha–Lyla sh'Lo Nifgashnu, Ilta on meidaen?, Kaerlekstrassel i New York, La noche que nunca tuvimos, La notte che non c'incontrammo,* and *Mesma casa, outras noites*), Miramax, 1993.

Il mostro (also known as *The Monster* and *Le monstre*), Lions Gate Films, 1994, subtitled version released by Cinepix Film Properties, 1996.

The Salesman and Other Adventures (short film), 1995.

Layin' Low, Shooting Gallery, 1996.

Phinehas (short film), 1996.

Trees Lounge (also known as *Bizim kafe, Mosche da bar, O bar da esquina, Ponto de encontro, Trees Lounge—Die Bar, in der sich alles dreht,* and *Trees Lounge. Una ultima copa*), Orion, 1996.

Office Killer (also known as *La asesina de la oficina, Mente paranoica,* and *Office Killer—L'impiegata modello*), Miramax/Strand Releasing, 1997.

Homo Heights (also known as *Happy Heights*), Lehmann–Moore Productions, 1998.

O.K. Garage (also known as *All Revved Up*), New City Releasing, 1998.

Side Streets, Cargo Films, 1998.

(Including song "Tate's Song") *Famous* (also known as *Lisa Picard Is Famous*), First Look International, 2000.

Fear of Fiction, 3DD Entertainment, 2000.

(Including song "Tenor Bop") *Joe Gould's Secret* (also known as *Cronica de uma certa New York, El secreto de Joe Gould, El secreto de un poeta, Joe Goulds Geheimnis, Joe Goulds hemlighet,* and *Le secret de Joe Gould*), USA Films, 2000.

Happy Accidents (also known as *Feliz acidente, Feliz coincidencia,* and *Lyckliga tillfaelligheter*), IFC Films, 2001.

The Whole Shebang (also known as *Feuerwerk auf italienisch* and *Koko hoito*), Lions Gate Films, 2001.

Face Addict (documentary), Funny Balloons, 2005.

Lonesome Jim, IFC Films, 2006.

Interview (also known as *Untitled Steve Buscemi Project* and *Alitheies kai psemata*), Sony Pictures Classics, 2007.

Lurie's music and songs have appeared in films, television productions, and other media.

Television Music; Series:
Oswald (animated), Nickelodeon, 2001–2004.
The Backyardigans (animated), Nickelodeon, 2004—.

Television Music; Episodic:
"Before You Go: A Daughter's Diary," *Family Video Diaries,* HBO, 1996.
Songs, "A Hard Straight," *Independent Lens,* PBS, 2004.

Albums:
Happy? Here? Now?, 1985.
Pieces for Bandoneon, Crepuscule, 1989.
Selling Water by the Side of the River, Antilles, 1990.
How I Spent My Vacation, Tzadik, 1998.

Albums; Soundtracks:
Il mostro, Cam, 1999.
Il piccolo diavolo, Cinevox, 1999.
Chochin, Absor, 2001.

LUTTER, Ellen

PERSONAL

Education: State University of New York at New Paltz, fine arts degree; also attended the Fashion Institute of Technology, New York, NY.

Addresses: *Agent*—The Gersh Agency, 232 North Canon Dr., Beverly Hills, CA 90210.

Career: Costume designer and wardrobe supervisor.

CREDITS

Film Costume Designer:
Mother's Day, Troma Entertainment, 1980.
He Knows You're Alone, United Artists, 1980.
Friday the 13th Part 2, Paramount, 1981.
When Nature Calls (also known as *The Outdoorsters*), Troma Entertainment, 1985.
Homeboy, 1988.
Jakarta, 1989.
Thunder Born, 1990.
Thank You and Good Night, Aries, 1991.
(Mississippi) *Mississippi Masala,* Samuel Goldwyn Company, 1991.
The Night We Never Met, Miramax, 1992.
Fresh, Miramax, 1994.
The Dutch Master (short; also known as *Der flamische meister*), Ziegler Films, 1994.
Scene Six, Take One, 1994.
Living in Oblivion, Sony Pictures Classics, 1995.
New Jersey Drive, Gramercy Pictures, 1995.
(Live action sequences) *Balto,* Universal, 1995.
Flirting with Disaster, Miramax, 1996.

Box of Moon Light, Lions Gate Films, 1996.
Cop Land, Miramax, 1997.
Le zombi de Cap–Rouge, United International Pictures, 1997.
The Repair Shop, 1998.
A Price Above Rubies, Miramax, 1998.
54, Miramax, 1998.
Big Daddy, Columbia, 1999.
28 Days, Columbia, 2000.
Little Nicky, New Line Cinema, 2000.
Mr. Deeds, Columbia, 2002.
Anger Management, Columbia, 2003.
50 First Dates, Columbia, 2004.
House of D, Lions Gate Films, 2004.
The Longest Yard, Paramount, 2005.
Click, Sony, 2006.
White Pants (short), 2007.
I Now Pronounce You Chuck and Larry, Universal, 2007.
You Don't Mess with the Zohan, 2008.

Film Wardrobe Supervisor:
Nocturna (also known as *Granddaughter of Dracula*), Compass International Pictures, 1979.
Squeeze Play, Troma Entertainment, 1980.
He Knows You're Alone (also known as *Blood Wedding*), Metro–Goldwyn–Mayer, 1980.
Mississippi Burning, Orion, 1988.
(Second unit) *Friday the 13th Part VIII—Jason Takes Manhattan,* Paramount, 1989.

Film Work; Other:
Production coordinator, *Nocturna* (also known as *Granddaughter of Dracula*), Compass International Pictures, 1979.
Production secretary, *Something Short of Paradise* (also known as *Perfect Love*), American International Pictures, 1979.
Production office coordinator, *Squeeze Play,* Troma Entertainment, 1980.
Wardrobe and hair stylist, *Rent Control,* Group S, 1984.

Wardrobe assistant, *Fear City* (also known as *Border* and *Ripper*), Aquarius Releasing, 1984.
Wardrobe for Mr. Lundgren, *The Shooter* (also known as *Desafio final, Hidden Assassin,* and *Strelec*), Miramax, 1995.

Film Appearances:
Stand–in for Jason Voorhees feet, *Friday the 13th Part 2,* Paramount, 1981.
"Raging Bullshit" trailer, *When Nature Calls* (also known as *The Outdoorsters*), Troma Entertainment, 1985.
Herself, *Adam Sandler Goes to Hell* (documentary short), New Line Home Video, 2001.
Herself, *Skull Session: The Making of "Anger Management"* (documentary short; also known as *The Making of "Anger Management"*), Columbia, 2003.

Television Costume Designer; Series:
The Job, ABC, 2001.
Six Degrees, ABC, 2006.

Television Work; Movies:
Wardrobe assistant, *Sessions,* ABC, 1983.
Wardrobe supervisor, *Broken Vows,* CBS, 1987.
Costume designer, *Path to Paradise: The Untold Story of the World Trade Center Bombing* (also known as *Path to Paradise*), HBO, 1997.
Costume designer, *Remembering Charlie,* Lifetime, 2003.

Television Work; Specials:
Costume designer assistant, *The Wide Net,* PBS, 1987.
Costume designer, *The Secret Life of Mary–Margaret: Portrait of a Bulimic,* HBO, 1992.

Television Costume Designer; Episodic:
"Blood Brothers: The Joey DiPaolo Story," *Lifestories: Families in Crisis,* HBO, 1992.
"Sex and the City," *Sex and the City,* HBO, 1998.

M

MA, Raymond

PERSONAL

Career: Actor.

CREDITS

Film Appearances:
Cab driver in Okinawa, *The Karate Kid, Part II*, Columbia, 1986.
Camp commander, *White Ghost*, Gibraltar Entertainment, 1988.
Mr. Chin, *Fatal Choice*, 1995.
Billy Tan, *Midnight Man* (also known as *Blood for Blood*), Artisan Entertainment, 1995.
Li Chen, *Street Corner Justice*, New City Releasing, 1996.
Paradise Hotel clerk, *City of Industry*, Orion, 1997.
Dr. Cheng, *Lethal Weapon 4* (also known as *Lethal 4*), Warner Bros., 1998.
Mr. Tam, *The Animal*, Columbia, 2001.
Chef, *Stuart Little 2*, Columbia, 2002.
Mr. Ma, *Old School*, DreamWorks, 2003.
First massage parlor manager, *Paris*, DEJ Productions, 2003.
Marks, *Starsky & Hutch*, Warner Bros., 2004.
Abraham Mao, *Ethan Mao*, Margin Films, 2004.
Factory owner, *American Zombie*, iHQ, 2007.
Mr. Li, "American Boyfriend," *A Good Day to Be Black and Sexy*, 2007.
Motel owner, *Two: Thirteen*, 2008.

Film Work:
Stunts, *The Hanoi Hilton*, 1987.
Foley artist, *The Vineyard*, New World Pictures, 1989.

Television Appearances; Series:
Ling, *Crisis Center*, NBC, 1997.

Television Appearances; Movies:
Pig Eye, *In Love and War*, NBC, 1987.
Justice Woo, *Supreme Courtships*, 2007.
Guy, *The Rich Inner Life of Penelope Cloud*, 2007.

Television Appearances; Specials:
Reenactment actor, "*The Twilight Zone Trial*": *The E! True Hollywood Story*, E! Entertainment Television, 2000.

Television Appearances; Pilots:
Mr. Astin, *Conrad Bloom*, NBC, 1998.
Larry Ming, *Payne*, CBS, 1999.
Ambassador Reng–Lang Lin, *H.U.D.*, NBC, 2000.

Television Appearances; Episodic:
Duc Lo, "Two Birds of a Feather," *Magnum, P.I.*, CBS, 1983.
Yamamoto, "All Shook Up," *Sledge Hammer!* (also known as *Sledge Hammer: The Early Years*), 1986.
Mr. Chan, "Fathers and Guns," *Hill Street Blues*, NBC, 1986.
Jimmy Ito, "The Annihilator," *Matlock*, NBC, 1987.
Cook, "Turning Point," *Hunter*, NBC, 1987.
David Addison Wannabe, "Cool Hand Dave: Part 2," *Moonlighting*, ABC, 1987.
Mr. Tsung, "I Wish It Would Rain," *Tour of Duty*, CBS, 1989.
Cheng Tze Duck, "Hit the Road, Jack," *Civil Wars*, ABC, 1993.
Mr. Li, "A Death in Hong Kong," *Murder, She Wrote*, CBS, 1993.
"Foreign Correspondent," *L.A. Law*, NBC, 1993.
Mr. Fong, "Vanishing Act," *One West Waikiki*, CBS, 1994.
Chinese food guy, "Tess Makes the Man," *Pig Sty*, UPN, 1995.

Tou, "Pal Joey," *Picket Fences,* CBS, 1995.

Mr. Chow, "Sorry, Wong Suspect," *NYPD Blue,* ABC, 1996.

"Friends," *Vengeance Unlimited* (also known as *Mr. Chapel*), ABC, 1999.

Kuang, "Silicon Sting," *L.A. Heat,* syndicated, 1999.

Jimmy Ming, "What Ever Happened to Baby Payne?," *Payne,* CBS, 1999.

Jimmy Ming, "Pacific Ocean Duck," *Payne,* CBS, 1999.

Mr. Li, "Aloha Christmas," *Ladies Man,* CBS, 1999.

Chinese diplomat, "The Field Trip Episode," *Opposite Sex,* Fox, 2000.

Voice of Mongolian man, "Horse Sense," *The Wild Thornberrys* (animated), Nickelodeon, 2000.

Professor Wong, "The Best Laid Plans," *Dharma & Greg,* ABC, 2000.

Mr. Wong, "The End of Innocence: Part 2," *Dharma & Greg,* ABC, 2001.

Taiwanese businessman, "Truth Be Told," *Alias,* ABC, 2001.

Camera man, "Not the Best Man," *The Steve Harvey Show,* The WB, 2001.

Wang, "The Invisible Woman," *The Invisible Man* (also known as *The I–Man*), 2002.

Mr. Tasaki, "A Father's Footsteps," *Power Rangers Wild Force,* Fox, 2002.

Convenience store manager, "The Big Ruckus," *Dragnet* (also known as *L.A. Dragnet*), ABC, 2003.

Rufus, "23," *Will & Grace,* NBC, 2003.

Jon Su Jin, "Let It Bleed," *10–8: Officers on Duty* (also known as *10–8* and *10–8: Police Patrol*), ABC, 2003.

Chinese President Lian, "Impact Winter," *The West Wing,* NBC, 2004.

Tailor, "Damascus, NE," *Carnivale,* HBO, 2005.

Sammy, "4x4," *CSI: Crime Scene Investigation* (also known as *C.S.I., CSI: Las Vegas,* and *Les Experts*), CBS, 2005.

Scott's ex–boss, "Stole Beer from a Golfer," *My Name Is Earl,* NBC, 2005.

Mr. Park, "Arguments for the Quickie," *Two and a Half Men,* CBS, 2006.

Zhang Tao, "Nevada Day: Parts 1 & 2," *Studio 60 on the Sunset Strip* (also known as *Studio 60*), NBC, 2006.

Zhang Tao, "Monday," *Studio 60 on the Sunset Strip* (also known as *Studio 60*), NBC, 2007.

Zhang Tao, "The Harriet Dinner: Part II," *Studio 60 on the Sunset Strip* (also known as *Studio 60*), NBC, 2007.

Minister, "Your Goose Is Cooked," *In Case of Emergency,* ABC, 2007.

Also appeared as Dr. Lee, "Love Sucks," *Action,* syndicated.

MADDERN, Alan
    See ELLISON, Harlan

MALONEY, Peter

PERSONAL

Married Ellen Sandler (an actress and playwright; marriage ended); married Kristin Griffith (an actress); children: one son. *Education:* Graduated from Syracuse University; studied acting with Uta Hagen.

Addresses: *Office*—Paradigm&360 North Crescent Dr., North Bldg., Beverly Hills, CA 90210.

Career: Actor, director, and playwright. Open Theatre, New York City, member of company, 1966–70; New Dramatists, Inc., past member. Ford's Theatre, Washington, DC, choreographer at Circle in the Square, 1971; Asolo State Theatre, Sarasota, FL, actor, 1976–77; Syracuse Stage, Syracuse, NY, director, 1977–78 and 1980–81; Actors Theatre of Louisville, Louisville, KY, director, 1979–80; member of Ensemble Studio Theatre and Actors' Studio, both New York City. Also worked as professional magician and encyclopedia salesman.

Awards, Honors: Burns Mantle Theatre Yearbook Award, best actor of the year, 1970, for *The Serpent.*

CREDITS

Stage Appearances:

Peter Mitchell, *The Fisherman,* and Goodfellow Pincher, *The Fourth Pig* (double–bill), Maidman Playhouse, New York City, 1965.

Sailor, *Hotel Passionato,* East 74th Street Theatre, New York City, 1965.

Nicholas Tyler, *The Experiment,* Orpheum Theatre, New York City, 1967.

Forensic, *Forensic and the Navigators,* Astor Place Theatre, New York City, 1970.

The sheep, *The Serpent: A Ceremony,* Open Theatre, Washington Square Methodist Church, New York City, 1970.

Clov, *Endgame,* Open Theatre, Washington Square Methodist Church, 1970.

Terminal, Open Theatre, Washington Square Methodist Church, 1970.

Jury member, *Twelve Angry Men,* Queens Playhouse, New York, 1972.

Katar, *And They Put Handcuffs on the Flowers,* Mercer–O'Casey Theatre, New York City, 1972.

Pylades and family member, *The Orphan,* New York Shakespeare Festival, Public Theatre, New York City, 1973.

Charlie Hughes, *Hughie,* John Golden Theatre, New York City, 1975.

Fourth actor, cashier, newspaper vendor, conductor, gypsy, Francisco, and Polonius II, *Poor Murderer,* Ethel Barrymore Theatre, New York City, 1976.

Candida, Massachusetts Center Repertory Company Theatre, Boston, MA, 1977.

Soren, Bernard, and Alf, *Big and Little,* Phoenix Theatre Company, Marymount Manhattan Theatre, New York City, 1979.

Mr. Webb, *Our Town,* Lincoln Center Theatre Company, Lyceum Theatre, New York City, 1988.

Richard Noakes, *Arcadia,* Lincoln Center Theatre Company, 1995.

John Frick, *The Last Yankee* (in double–bill with *I Can't Remember Anything*), Signature Theatre, New York City, 1998.

Dr. McSharry, *The Cripple of Inishmaan,* New York Shakespeare Festival, Estelle R. Newman Theatre, Joseph Papp Public Theatre, New York City, 1998.

The Water Engine and *Mr. Happiness,* Atlantic Theatre Company, New York City, 1999.

George, *Sexual Perversity in Chicago* and *The Duck Variations* (double–bill), Atlantic Theatre Company, 2000.

"Madmen," *Marathon 2000,* Series A, Ensemble Studio Theatre, New York City, 2000.

Joe Stengel, *Dinner at Eight,* Vivian Beaumont Theatre, New York City, 2002.

Saunders, *Lend Me a Tenor,* George Street Playhouse, New Brunswick, NJ, 2005.

Boris Semyonov–Pishchik, *The Cherry Orchard,* Atlantic Theatre Company, 2005.

Mr. Kidd, *Celebration & The Room,* Atlantic Theatre Company, 2005.

Also appeared in *The Dadshuttle, Down the Shore,* and *Stanley,* all Broadway productions; *Abe Lincoln in Illinois, Carousel,* and *Six Degrees of Separation,* all Lincoln Center Theatre, New York City; *Hunger and Thirst, The Merchant of Venice,* and *The Skin of Our Teeth,* all Berkshire Theatre Festival, Stockbridge, MA; *The Chalk Garden; No Time for Comedy;* as Dr. Mac-Farlane, *Hobson's Choice,* Atlantic Theatre, New York City; Signor Sirelli, *Right You Are,* National Actors Theatre, The Michael Schimmel Center for the Arts at Pace University, New York City; Daly, old lady, Palmer, pantaloon, and stage crew, *Mr. Fox: A Rumination,* Peter Norton Space, New York City; George Booth, *The Voysey Inheritance,* Atlantic Theatre, New York City.

Major Tours:

Appeared as Charlie Hughes, *Hughie,* U.S. cities.

Stage Director:

Time Trial, New York Shakespeare Festival, Public Theatre, New York City, 1975.

The Elusive Angel, New Dramatists, New York City, 1975.

The Slab Boys, Hudson Guild Theatre, New York City, 1980.

The New Yorkers, Morse Center Trinity Theatre, New York City, 1984.

"The Frog Prince," *Marathon '85,* Ensemble Studio Theatre, New York City, 1985.

Mandragola, Folger Shakespeare Theatre, Washington, DC, 1986.

"Goodbye Oscar," *Marathon '99,* Ensemble Studio Theatre, 1999.

Also directed *No Time Flat.*

Stage Work; Other:

Stage manager, *Doubletalk,* Theatre De Lys, New York City, 1964.

Magic consultant, *Feathertop,* Workshop of the Performing Arts Theatre, New York City, 1984.

Film Appearances:

Earl Roberts, *Greetings,* Sigma III, 1968.

Putney's chauffeur, *Putney Swope,* Cinema V, 1969.

Pharmacist, *Hi, Mom!* (also known as *Blue Manhattan, Confessions of a Peeping Tom,* and *Son of Greetings*), Sigma III, 1970.

Jake Guzik, *Capone,* Twentieth Century–Fox, 1975.

Deadly Hero, 1976.

Doctor, *Breaking Away,* Twentieth Century–Fox, 1979.

Newspaper clerk, *The Amityville Horror,* American International Pictures, 1979.

Martin, *A Little Romance* (also known as *I love you, je t'aime*), Orion, 1979.

Lee McHugh, *Hide in Plain Sight,* Metro–Goldwyn–Mayer/United Artists, 1980.

Frank, *The Children* (also known as *The Children of Ravensback*), 1980.

Bennings, *The Thing* (also known as *John Carpenter's "The Thing"*), Universal, 1982.

Der Zauberberg (also known as *Le montagne magique* and *The Magic Mountain*), 1982.

Ian, *Desperately Seeking Susan,* Orion, 1985.

Dr. Dominick Princi, *Manhunter* (also known as *Red Dragon: The Pursuit of Hannibal Lecter* and *Red Dragon: The Curse of Hannibal Lecter*), De Laurentiis Entertainment Group, 1986.

Waiter, *Bright Lights, Big City,* Metro–Goldwyn–Mayer/United Artists, 1988.

Dr. Wilson, *The Appointments of Dennis Jennings,* 1988.

Dr. Peter Ames, *Lost Angels* (also known as *The Road Home*), Orion/Vestron, 1989.

Luther Aslinger, *Tune In Tomorrow ...* (also known as *Aunt Julia and the Scriptwriter*), 1990.

Colonel Finck, *JFK* (also known as *JFK—Affaire non classee*), 1991.

Federal watchman, *The Public Eye,* 1992.

Dr. Playhand, *Robot in the Family,* 1994.

Dad, *Jeffrey,* 1995.

Mr. Randall, *Extreme Measures,* Warner Bros., 1996.

Biff Quigley, *Thinner* (also known as *Stephen King's "Thinner"*), Paramount, 1996.

Dr. Griggs, *The Crucible,* Twentieth Century–Fox, 1996.

Senior, *The Dadshuttle,* 1996.

Researcher, *Private Parts* (also known as *Howard Stern's "Private Parts"*), Paramount, 1997.

Jacob Webber, *Washington Square,* Buena Vista, 1997.

Desk clerk, *The Object of My Affection,* Twentieth Century–Fox, 1998.

Detective Timothy Dowd, *Summer of Sam,* Buena Vista, 1999.

Maurice, *Curtain Call,* Curtain Call LP, 1999.

Dr. Jacobs, *Boiler Room,* New Line Cinema, 2000.

Dr. Pill, *Requiem for a Dream* (also known as *Delusion Over Addiction*), 2000.

Duncan Flynn, *K–PAX* (also known as *K–PAX—Alles is moglich*), MCA/Universal, 2001.

Cliff Mendelson, *Standard Time* (also known as *Anything But Love*), Samuel Goldwyn Films, 2002.

Television Appearances; Series:
Red, *Rescue Me,* FX Channel, 2005.

Television Appearances; Miniseries:
John Steinbeck's "East of Eden" (also known as *East of Eden*), ABC, 1981.

Mr. Perkins, *Queen* (also known as *Alex Haley's "Queen"*), CBS, 1993.

Television Appearances; Movies:
Band leader Artie Podell, *Columbo: Troubled Waters,* NBC, 1975.

Veterinarian, *My Old Man,* CBS, 1979.

Eli Clay, *Sanctuary of Fear,* 1979.

Darryl F. Zanuck, *Moviola: This Year's Blonde* (also known as *This Year's Blonde* and *The Secret Love of Marilyn Monroe*), NBC, 1980.

Henry, the druggist, *Revenge of the Stepford Wives,* NBC, 1980.

Charles Davidson, *Money, Power, Murder,* CBS, 1989.

Ray Kaplan, *Citizen Cohn,* HBO, 1992.

William Michie, *Assault at West Point: The Court–Martial of Johnson Whittaker* (also known as *Assault at West Point*), Showtime, 1994.

Mitch James, *Thicker than Blood,* TNT, 1998.

Television Appearances; Pilots:
Mr. Hardy, Julie's boss, *The Four of Us,* ABC, 1977.

Eli Clay, *Sanctuary of Fear* (also known as *Father Brown, Detective, Girl in the Park,* and *Sanctuary of Death*), NBC, 1979.

Mustaf, *Callahan,* ABC, 1982.

The Fixer, *The Saint* (broadcast as an episode of *CBS Summer Playhouse*), CBS, 1987.

Plaintiff's lawyer, *Queens Supreme,* CBS, 2003.

Television Appearances; Specials:
Dr. Wilson, *The Appointments of Dennis Jennings* (also known as *Steven Wright in The Appointments of Dennis Jennings*), HBO, 1989.

Mr. Webb, *Our Town,* WNET (New York City), 1989.

Second Sidney, *Vaclav Havel's "Largo Desolato,"* PBS, 1990.

Arthur Rowe, *Love Off Limits,* CBS, 1993.

Voice, *Crucible of Empire: The Spanish American War,* PBS, 1999.

Television Appearances; Episodic:
Alex Conrad, "Ghosts," *Lou Grant,* 1982.

Dr. Burgess, "Bypass," *St. Elsewhere,* 1982.

Red Donnelly, "Home Is the Hero," *Spenser: For Hire,* 1986.

Narrator, *Voices and Visions,* PBS, 1988.

Lab technician, "Animal Instinct," *Law and Order,* NBC, 1993.

Mr. Gianetti, "On the Air," *Remember WENN,* AMC, 1996.

McClancy, *Dellaventura,* CBS, 1997.

Mr. Stansley, "Your Life Is Now," *Ed,* NBC, 2000.

"Enemy Within," *Law & Order: Criminal Intent* (also known as *Law & Order: CI*), NBC, 2001.

"The Collar," *Law & Order,* NBC, 2002.

Voice, "Electric Nation," *Great Projects: The Building of America,* PBS, 2002.

Voice, "Bridging New York," *Great Projects: The Building of America,* PBS, 2002.

Voice, "A Tale of Two Rivers," *Great Projects: The Building of America,* PBS, 2002.

Geoffrey Downs, "Charisma," *Law & Order: Special Victims Unit* (also known as *Law & Order: SVU* and *Special Victims Unit*), NBC, 2004.

"The Healer," *Law & Order: Criminal Intent* (also known as *Law & Order: CI*), NBC, 2006.

Also appeared in *N.Y.P.D.,* ABC.

WRITINGS

Stage Plays:
Amazing Grace, New Dramatists, New York City, 1977.

Bicycle Boys, Ensemble Studio Theatre, New York City, 1978.

(Adapter) *Mandragola,* Folger Shakespeare Theatre, Washington, DC, 1986.

"Accident," *Marathon 2000,* Series B, Ensemble Studio Theatre, 2000.

Also wrote *American Garage; Bad Blood; In the Devil's Bathtub* (published in *Kenyon Review*); *Lost and Found; Pastorale.*

MANCUSO, Frank, Jr. 1958–

PERSONAL

Born October 9, 1958, in Buffalo, NY; son of Frank G. Mancuso, Sr. (a film executive). *Education:* Upsala College, B.A.

Addresses: *Office*—360 Pictures, 301 North Canon Dr., Suite 207, Beverly Hills, CA 90210.

Career: Producer and screenwriter. Paramount Pictures–Canada, film booker of short subjects, c. 1972; FGM Entertainment, president, 1985–?; Delcath, director, 1998–?; 360 Pictures, Beverly Hills, CA, partner.

CREDITS

Film Associate Producer:
Friday the 13th Part 2, Paramount, 1981.

Film Producer:
Off the Wall, 1982.
Friday the 13th Part 3: 3D (also known as *Friday the 13th Part III* and *Friday the 13th Part 3*), Paramount, 1983.
The Man Who Wasn't There, Paramount, 1983.
Friday the 13th: The Final Chapter (also known as *Friday the 13th Part 4* and *Friday the 13th: Last Chapter*), Paramount, 1984.
April Fool's Day, Paramount, 1986.
Back to the Beach (also known as *Malibu Beach Girls*), Paramount, 1987.
Permanent Record, 1988.
Internal Affairs, Paramount, 1990.
He Said, She Said, 1991.
Body Parts, Paramount, 1991.
Cool World, Paramount, 1992.
Species, Metro–Goldwyn–Mayer, 1995.
Fled (also known as *Perseguidos*), Metro–Goldwyn–Mayer, 1996.
Hoodlum, Metro–Goldwyn–Mayer/United Artists, 1997.
Species II, Metro–Goldwyn–Mayer, 1998.
Ronin, Metro–Goldwyn–Mayer/United Artists, 1998.
Stigmata, Metro–Goldwyn–Mayer, 1999.
Mary Jane's Last Dance, Metro–Goldwyn–Mayer, 2000.
Next Best Friend, TriStar, 2002.
Species III, Metro–Goldwyn–Mayer Home Entertainment, 2004.
The Lost City, Magnolia Pictures, 2005.
Crossover, TriStar, 2006.
I Know Who Killed Me, TriStar, 2007.

Film Executive Producer:
Friday the 13th Part V: A New Beginning (also known as *Friday the 13th: A New Beginning*), Paramount, 1985.
(Uncredited) *Friday the 13th Part VII: The New Blood,* Paramount, 1988.
Crossover, 2006.
Species: The Awakening, Twentieth Century Fox Home Entertainment, 2007.

Film Work; Other:
Location assistant, *Urban Cowboy,* 1980.

Film Appearances:
Radio cop, *Internal Affairs,* Paramount, 1990.

Television Producer; Series:
Friday the 13th (also known as *Friday the 13th: The Series* and *Friday Curse*), syndicated, 1987–90.
War of the Worlds (also known as *War of the Worlds: The Second Invasion*), syndicated, 1989–90.

Television Executive Producer; Movies:
The Limbic Region, Showtime, 1996.
The Escape, TMC, 1997.

Television Creator; Episodic:
"The Inheritance," *Friday the 13th* (also known as *Friday the 13th: The Series* and *Friday's Curse*), 1987.

Television Appearances; Specials:
Divine Rites: The Story of Stigmata, 1999.

WRITINGS

Television Episodes:
"The Inheritance," *Friday the 13th* (also known as *Friday the 13th: The Series* and *Friday's Curse*), 1987.

MANDEL, Howie 1955–

PERSONAL

Full name, Howie Michael Mandel II; born November 29, 1955, in Toronto, Ontario, Canada; father, a lighting manufacturer and realtor; married Terry Soil, March, 1980; children: Jackie, Riley Paige, Alex.

Addresses: *Agent*—International Creative Management, 10250 Constellation Way, 9th Floor, Los Angeles, CA

90067. *Manager*—3 Arts Entertainment, 9460 Wilshire Blvd., 7th Floor, Beverly Hills, CA 90212.

Career: Comedian, actor, producer, director, and writer. Worked as door–to–door carpet salesman and later as owner of carpet stores, c. 1975–79; also owner of a novelty business. Performed at Comedy Store, Los Angeles, CA, and at nightclubs in Atlantic City, Las Vegas, New York City, and Los Angeles.

Awards, Honors: Golden Apple, male discovery of the year, 1998; Gemini Award nomination, best performance by an actor in a guest role in a dramatic series, Academy of Canadian Cinema and Television, 1998, for *The Outer Limits.*

CREDITS

Film Appearances:
Matt Lloyd, *Gas,* Paramount, 1981.
Larry Pound, *Funny Farm,* Mutual, 1982.
Voice of Gizmo, *Gremlins,* 1984.
Himself, *Where Did I Come From?,* 1985.
Dennis Powell, *A Fine Mess* (also known as *Blake Edwards' "A Fine Mess"*), Columbia, 1986.
The Canadian Conspiracy, Shtick Productions, 1986.
Himself, *Paramount Comedy Theatre, Vol. 1: Well Developed,* 1986.
Host, *Paramount Comedy Theatre, Vol. 2: Decent Exposures,* 1987.
Bobo Shand, *Walk Like a Man* (also known as *Bobo the Dog Boy*), Metro–Goldwyn–Mayer/United Artists, 1987.
Maurice, *Little Monsters* (also known as *Little Ghost Figures*), Metro–Goldwyn–Mayer/United Artists, 1989.
Voice of Gizmo, *Gremlins II: The New Batch* (also known as *Gremlins 2: The New Batch*), Warner Bros., 1990.
Moe, *Magic Kid II,* 1994.
Jason Quincy, *Tribulation,* Artist View Entertainment, 2000.
Voice of Jack, *The Tangerine Bear,* Artisan Entertainment, 2000.
Cody, *Spin Cycle,* 2000.
The Sandman, *Hansel & Gretel,* Innovation Film Group, 2002.
Voice of Spencer, *Pinocchio 3000* (animated; also known as *P3K: Pinocho 3000* and *Pinocchio le robot*), 2004.
Himself, *The Aristocrats* (documentary; also known as *The @r!$t*(r@t$*), THINKFilm, 2005.
Himself, *Heckler,* 2007.
Himself, *Certifiably Jonathan* (documentary), 2007.
Joe Burns, *Room Service,* 2007.

Also voice of Omni, *Once Upon a Star.*

Film Work:
Executive producer, *The Legend of Willie Brown,* 1998.

Television Appearances; Series:
The Shape of Things, NBC, 1982.
Various, *Laugh Trax,* syndicated, 1982.
Dr. Wayne Fiscus, *St. Elsewhere,* NBC, 1982–88.
Voices of Animal, Skeeter, and Bunson Honeydew, *Muppets Babies* (animated; also known as *Muppets, Babies, and Monsters* and *Jim Henson's "Muppet Babies"*), CBS, 1984–86.
Himself and voices of Bobby Generic and Mr. Generic, *Bobby's World,* Fox, 1990–98.
Ernie Lapidus, *Good Grief,* Fox, 1990.
Howie, 1992.
Professor, *The Amazing Live Sea–Monkeys,* 1992.
Howie Mandel's Sunny Skies, Showtime, 1994–96.
Host, *The Howie Mandel Show,* syndicated, 1997–99.
Hidden Howie (also known as *Hidden Howie: The Private Life of a Public Nuisance*), Bravo, 2003–2005.
Host, *Deal or No Deal* (game show), NBC, 2005—.

Television Appearances; Movies:
Humpty Dumpty, *Mother Goose Rock 'n' Rhyme,* Disney Channel, 1990.
Voice of Mealy, *David Copperfield* (also known as *Charles Dickens' "David Copperfield"*), PBS, 1993.
Danny Klay, *Shake, Rattle, and Rock!,* Showtime, 1994.
Voice of Sam–I–Am, *In Search of Dr. Seuss,* TNT, 1994.
Charlie, the TV show host, *Harrison Bergeron* (also known as *Kurt Vonnegut's "Harrison Bergeron"*), Showtime, 1995.
Himself, *Jackie's Back!* (also known as *Jackie's Back: Portrait of a Diva*), Lifetime, 1999.
Marty, *Spinning out of Control,* E! Entertainment Television, 2001.
Rabbi, *Crown Heights,* 2004.
Voice of Pupa, *The Great Polar Bear Adventure,* Animal Planet, 2006.
Narrator, *The Great American Christmas,* USA Network, 2006.

Television Appearances; Specials:
The 6th Annual Young Comedians (also known as *HBO Presents "The 6th Annual Young Comedians"*), HBO, 1981.
Cinemax Comedy Experiment, Cinemax, 1985.
Joan Rivers and Friends Salute Heidi Abromowitz, 1985.
The 37th Annual Emmy Awards, ABC, 1985.
Presenter, *American Video Awards,* ABC, 1985.
The 38th Annual Emmy Awards, NBC, 1986.
On Location: Howie Mandel, HBO, 1986.
The Young Comedians All–Star Reunion, HBO, 1986.
Comic Relief, 1986.
The 39th Annual Emmy Awards, Fox, 1987.
Host, *Juno Music Awards,* 1987.

"Howie from Maui—Live!," *HBO Comedy Hour,* HBO, 1987.

Live! from London, 1988.

The Comedy Store 15th Year Class Reunion (also known as *Comedy Store Reunion*), NBC, 1988.

Comic Relief III, HBO, 1989.

Howie Mandel: Hooray for Howiewould!, Showtime, 1990.

Jerry, *Between Cars,* HA! TV Comedy Network, 1990.

The Walt Disney World Happy Easter Parade, 1990.

The 4th Annual American Comedy Awards, ABC, 1990.

Howie Newman, *Howie and Rose,* 1990.

The All–Star Salute to Our Troops, 1991.

Howie Mandel: Howie Spent Our Summer, 1992.

Free to Laugh: A Comedy and Music Special for Amnesty International, 1992.

Birth of the Team, Disney Channel, 1992.

Class Clowns, 1992.

Martin & Lewis: Their Golden Age of Comedy, 1992.

Who Makes You Laugh?, ABC, 1995.

Howie Morgan, *Grownups,* ABC, 1995.

Celebrity First Loves, Fox, 1995.

Comic Relief's 10th Anniversary, HBO, 1996.

Caesar's Palace 30th Anniversary Celebration, ABC, 1996.

Presenter, *Walt Disney Company and McDonald's Present the American Teacher Awards,* 1996.

Howie Mandel on Ice, HBO, 1997.

Canned Ham: Deconstructing Harry, Comedy Central, 1997.

50 Years of Television: A Celebration of the Academy of Television Arts and Sciences Golden Anniversary, 1997.

Sex with Cindy Crawford, ABC, 1998.

Comedy Central Presents Behind–the–Scenes at the American Comedy Awards, Comedy Network, 1999.

It's Only Talk: The Real Story of America's Talk Shows, Arts and Entertainment, 1999.

MTV's New Year's Eve Uncensored, MTV, 2000.

The Tonight Show with Jay Leno (also known as *Jay Leno*), NBC, 2001, 2003, 2005, 2006, 2007.

(Uncredited) *Added Attractions: The Hollywood Shorts Story,* TCM, 2002.

TV Guide 50 Best Shows of All Time: A 50th Anniversary Celebration, ABC, 2002.

Hidden Howie, NBC, 2003.

VH1 Goes Inside Live with Regis and Kelly, VH1, 2004.

Comedy Gold, CBC, 2005.

The 58th Annual Primetime Emmy Awards, NBC, 2006.

Comic Relief 2006, TNT and HBO, 2006.

The 2006 Billboard Music Awards, Fox, 2006.

Narrator, *The Great American Christmas,* USA Network, 2006.

Presenter, *The 58th Annual Primetime Emmy Awards,* NBC, 2006.

Himself, *Studio 60 on the Sunset Strip* (also known as *Studio 60*), NBC, 2006.

The Big Idea with Donny Deutsch, CNBC, 2006, 2007.

Also appeared as presenter, *The Watusi Tour,* HBO.

Television Appearances; Pilots:

Rock Comedy (pilot for *Laugh Trax*), syndicated, 1982.

Welcome to the Fun Zone, NBC, 1984.

Television Appearances; Episodic:

Make Me Laugh, syndicated, 1979–80.

The Shape of Things, 1982.

Waldo, "The Princess Who Had Never Laughed," *Faerie Tale Theatre* (also known as *Shelley Duvall's "Faerie Tale Theatre"*), Showtime, 1984.

The Tonight Show Starring Johnny Carson, NBC, 1985.

Alan King: Inside the Comedy Mind, 1991.

Comics Only, 1991.

(Uncredited) Himself, "ZooTV at Night," *The Ben Stiller Show,* 1993.

The Arsenio Hall Show, syndicated, 1994.

Interior decorator Larry, "Every Mother's Son," *Homicide: Life on the Street* (also known as *Homicide*), NBC, 1995.

Stuart Wyler, *Bless This House,* CBS, 1995.

Politically Incorrect (also known as *P.I.*), ABC, 1995, 2002.

Live with Regis and Kathie Lee, 1995.

Late Night with Conan O'Brien, NBC, 1995, 2000, 2005, 2006, 2007.

Mr. Mxyzptlk, "Twas the Night before Mxymas," *Lois and Clark: The New Adventures of Superman* (also known as *Lois & Clark* and *The New Adventures of Superman*), ABC, 1996.

Carl, "Second Thoughts," *The Outer Limits* (also known as *The New Outer Limits*), Showtime and syndicated, 1997.

The Rosie O'Donnell Show, syndicated, 1997, 1998, 2000.

Himself, "Making Whoppi," *The Nanny,* CBS, 1998.

Howard Stern, syndicated, 1998, 1999.

(Uncredited) Himself, "Sisters," *Providence,* NBC, 1999.

Jerry show announcer, *Sunset Beach,* 1999.

The Howard Stern Radio Show, syndicated, 1999.

Live with Regis and Kelly, 2004, 2005, 2006, 2007.

Celebrity Poker Showdown, Bravo, 2005.

Weekends at the DL, Comedy Central, 2005.

The Tony Danza Show, syndicated, 2005.

Jimmy Kimmel Live, ABC, 2005, 2006.

Last Call with Carson Daly, NBC, 2006.

Square Off, TV Guide Channel, 2006.

"Top 10 TV Spinoffs," *TV Land's Top Ten,* TV Land, 2006.

Mad TV, Fox, 2006.

Ellen: The Ellen DeGeneres Show, syndicated, 2006.

The Late Late Show with Craig Ferguson, CBS, 2006.

Entertainment Tonight (also known as *E.T.*), syndicated, 2006.

Howard Stern on Demand (also known as *Howard TV on Demand*), 2006.

The Megan Mullally Show, syndicated, 2006.

Larry King Live, CNN, 2007.

Himself, "Heads Will Roll," *Medium,* NBC, 2007.

The Bronx Bunny Show, Starz, 2007.

Also appeared in *Bizarre; An Evening at the Improv; The Max Headroom Show; The Merv Griffin Show; Norm Crosby Comedy Show.*

Television Work; Series:
Executive producer, *Bobby's World,* Fox, 1990–98.
Executive producer and creator, *The Amazing Live Sea–Monkeys,* 1992.
Executive producer, *Howie Mandel's Sunny Skies,* Showtime, 1994–96.
Executive producer, *The Howie Mandel Show,* syndicated, 1998.
Executive producer, *Hidden Howie* (also known as *Hidden Howie: The Private Life of a Public Nuisance*), Bravo, 2003–2005.

Television Work; Specials:
Executive producer, *On Location: Howie Mandel,* HBO, 1986.
Executive producer, *Howie Mandel: Hooray for Howiewould!,* Showtime, 1990.
Executive producer and writing supervisor, *Howie,* 1992.
Executive producer and director, *Howie Mandel: Howie Spent Our Summer,* 1992.
Executive producer, *Howie Mandel on Ice,* HBO, 1997.

Television Work; Pilots:
Co–executive producer, *Grownups,* ABC, 1995.
Producer, *Hidden Howie* (also known as *Hidden Howie: The Private Life of a Public Nuisance*), 2003.

Television Director; Episodic:
Howie Mandel's Sunny Skies, Showtime, 1994–96.

RECORDINGS

Albums:
Howie Mandel Fits like a Glove, Warner Bros., 1986.

Also recorded *The Watusi Tour.*

Videos:
Howie Mandel's North American Watusi Tour, Paramount, 1987.

Video Games:
Narrator, *The Great Word Adventure,* 1995.
Host, *Deal or No Deal* (also known as *Imagination DVD TV Games: "Deal or No Deal"*), Imagination Games, 2006.

WRITINGS

Television Specials:
On Location: Howie Mandel, HBO, 1986.

(Uncredited) *The Young Comedians All–Star Reunion,* 1986.
Howie, 1992.
Howie Mandel on Ice, HBO, 1997.

Television Pilots:
Welcome to the Fun Zone, NBC, 1984.

Television Episodes:
Bobby's World (also based on character created by Mandel), Fox, 1990–98.
The Amazing Live Sea–Monkeys, 1992.
Howie Mandel's Sunny Skies, Showtime, 1994–96.
The Howie Mandel Show, syndicated, 1998.
Hidden Howie (also known as *Hidden Howie: The Private Life of a Public Nuisance*), Bravo, 2003–2005.

OTHER SOURCES

Books:
Newsmakers 1989, Issue 4, Gale, 1989.

Periodicals:
Broadcasting and Cable, June 15, 1998, p. 34.
Entertainment Weekly, November 10, 1995, p. 70.
Hollywood Reporter, October, 1987.
Newsweek, February 27, 2006, p. 66.
Parade, October 4, 1998, p. 30.
People Weekly, March 13, 2006, p. 78.

Electronic:
Howie Mandel Website, http://www.howiemandel.com, October 1, 2007.

MATTHEWS, Dakin 1933–

PERSONAL

Born November 7, 1933, in Oakland, CA; married Anne McNaughton (an actress and director); children: four. *Education:* Earned a degree in theology; attended Gregorian Pontifical University, Rome.

Career: Actor and writer. City Center Acting Company, New York City, founding member; Antaeus Company, founding member and artistic director, 1991–2003; Andak Stage Company, founder, after 2003; former artistic director of California Actors Theatre and Berkeley Shakespeare Festival. California State University, Hayward, professor of English, now professor emeritus; Juilliard School, New York City, former drama instructor.

Awards, Honors: Robby Award, 2003, for *Major Barbara*; St. Clair Bayfield Award, best New York performance in a Shakespearean play, Actors' Equity Foundation, 2003, and Special Drama Desk Award, 2004, both for *Henry IV.*

CREDITS

Television Appearances; Series:

Herb Kelcher, a recurring role, *My Two Dads,* between 1987 and 1989.
Walt McCrorey, *Down Home,* CBS, 1990.
Roscoe Davis, *Drexell's Class,* Fox, 1991–92.
Harry Polachek, *Cutters,* CBS, 1993.
Elliot, *The Jeff Foxworthy Show* (also known as *Somewhere in America*), NBC, 1995–96.
Frank Gerard, *The Office,* CBS, 1995.
Bishop Peter Jerome, *Soul Man,* ABC, 1997.
Headmaster Hanlin Charleston, a recurring role, *Gilmore Girls* (also known as *Gilmore Girls: Beginnings*), The WB, between 2000 and 2004, then CW Network, 2007.
Joe Heffernan, a recurring role, *The King of Queens,* CBS, between 2001 and 2007.
Merle Horstradt, a recurring role, *Jack & Bobby,* The WB, 2004–2005.

Television Appearances; Miniseries:

Prosecutor, *Fresno,* CBS, 1986.
Judge Harvey R. Sorkow, *Baby M,* 1988.
Hiram Evans, *Cross of Fire,* NBC, 1989.
(Uncredited) Attorney General Edwin Meese, *Guts and Glory: The Rise and Fall of Oliver North,* 1989.
Uncle Gene, *Blind Faith,* NBC, 1990.
Dean Barrow, *Menendez: A Killing in Beverly Hills,* CBS, 1994.
Ben's father, *Nothing Lasts Forever* (also known as *Sidney Sheldon's "Nothing Lasts Forever"*), CBS, 1995.
Wadsworth, Sr., *Rough Riders,* 1997.
Dr. Floyd Thompson, *From the Earth to the Moon,* HBO, 1998.

Television Appearances; Movies:

Sam Mitgang, *The Silence at Bethany,* 1988.
Catlett, *Terrorist on Trial: The United States vs. Salim Ajami* (also known as *Hostile Witness* and *In the Hands of the Enemy*), 1988.
Adam Berger, *Naked Lie,* CBS, 1989.
Dr. Cutler, *Out on the Edge,* CBS, 1989.
Charles Rusher, *My Brother's Wife,* 1989.
Carter Dickson III, *Easy Come, Easy Go,* 1989.
Judge Aaron S. Mitofsky, *Fine Things* (also known as *Danielle Steel's "Fine Things"*), NBC, 1990.
Cox, *The Whereabouts of Jenny,* ABC, 1991.
Dr. Thomas, *The Perfect Tribute,* ABC, 1991.
District Attorney Buron Fitts, *White Hot: The Mysterious Murder of Thelma Todd,* NBC, 1991.

Sheriff Dobbs, *Jailbirds,* CBS, 1991.
Francis Haynes, *... And Then She Was Gone* (also known as *In a Stranger's Hand*), NBC, 1991.
Deputy Director Waugh, *Under Cover* (also known as *The Company*), Fox, 1991.
Howards, *Murder without Motive: The Edmund Perry Story* (also known as *Best Intentions*), NBC, 1992.
Larry, *For Richer, for Poorer* (also known as *Father, Son, and the Mistress*), HBO, 1992.
Roland Strom, *Grave Secrets: The Legacy of Hilltop Drive* (also known as *Grave Secrets*), CBS, 1992.
Tom (some sources cite name as Jim) McCall, *Revolver,* NBC, 1992.
Albee Ferguson, *Criminal Behavior,* ABC, 1992.
George Durrard, *Rio Shannon,* ABC, 1993.
Congressman Phil Burton, *And the Band Played On,* HBO, 1993.
Hart to Hart Returns, NBC, 1993.
Henry Ashley, *Staying Afloat,* 1993.
Vice President Walter Kelly, *The Enemy Within,* HBO, 1994.
Andy Thornell, *White Mile,* HBO, 1994.
Dr. Cyrill Dubcheck, *Virus* (also known as *Formula for Death, Robin Cook's "Formula for Death," Robin Cook's "Outbreak,"* and *Robin Cook's "Virus"*), NBC, 1995.
Fred Burnham, *Best Friends for Life,* CBS, 1998.
R. T. Sloan, Sr., *The Big Time,* TNT, 2002.

Television Appearances; Episodic:

Michael Fleming, "Gourmet Steele," *Remington Steele,* NBC, 1985.
"Where There's Hope, There's Crosby," *St. Elsewhere,* NBC, 1986.
Stanley Kunin, "December Bribe," *L.A. Law,* NBC, 1987.
Prosecutor, "People vs. Matlock," *Matlock,* NBC, 1987.
Jim, "Newsstruck," *Newhart,* 1988.
Wyler, "The Men Will Cheer and the Boys Will Shout," *Aaron's Way,* 1988.
Agent Simon, "Don't Look Back," *Something Is Out There,* 1988.
Detective Kane, "Carousel," *Dallas,* 1988.
David, "The Younger Girl," *Dear John* (also known as *Dear John USA*), 1988.
Tanner, "Home," *TV 101,* 1988.
Dr. Harold Stratford, "Patients Are a Virtue," *Doctor Doctor,* CBS, 1989.
Dr. Harold Stratford, "Pediatricks," *Doctor Doctor,* CBS, 1989.
"Easy Come, Easy Go," *Christine Cromwell,* 1989.
Judge, "Tony and Angela Get Divorced," *Who's the Boss?,* 1991.
Neal Gillen, "The Wind around the Tower," *Murder, She Wrote,* CBS, 1992.
Stephen Hygate, "Love in Bloom," *L.A. Law,* NBC, 1992.
Stephen Hygate, "Helter Shelter," *L.A. Law,* NBC, 1992.

Stephen Hygate, "Christmas Stalking," *L.A. Law,* NBC, 1992.

Henry Marshall, "Cross Examination," *Picket Fences,* 1993.

Mr. Brooks, "Cat's in the Cradle," *Herman's Head,* Fox, 1993.

Stephen Hygate, "Leap of Faith," *L.A. Law,* NBC, 1993.

Dennis Moylan, "A Killing in Cork," *Murder, She Wrote,* CBS, 1993.

William Thornton, "Pros & Cons," *Coach,* ABC, 1994.

Elton Malone, "A Very Fatal Funeral," *Diagnosis Murder,* CBS, 1994.

Buford Hazlitt, "The Scent of Murder," *Murder, She Wrote,* CBS, 1995.

"Zodiac," *Nash Bridges* (also known as *Bridges*), CBS, 1996.

Ben Braxton, "High Noon," *Ink,* 1996.

EZ Streets, CBS, 1996.

Governor Luke McElroy, "Ambition," *Vengeance Unlimited* (also known as *Mr. Chapel*), 1998.

The colonel, "Seek and Ye Shall Find," *Touched by an Angel,* CBS, 1998.

Leo Cornell, Sr., *Buddy Faro,* 1998.

Dick Johnson, "Sisters," *Providence,* NBC, 1999.

Admiral Patterson, "Relativity," *Star Trek: Voyager* (also known as *Voyager*), UPN, 1999.

Judge Langdon, "Decisions," *Family Law,* CBS, 1999.

Dean Sterrett, "The Yummy Mummy," *The Nanny,* 1999.

Dick Johnson, "Sisters," *Providence,* NBC, 1999.

Dick, "Tying the Not," *Providence,* NBC, 1999.

Mr. Stark, "Tis the Season," *Ally McBeal,* Fox, 2000.

Mr. Harrison, "Charma Loves Greb," *Dharma & Greg,* ABC, 2000.

Simon Blye, "Take Out the Trash Day," *The West Wing,* NBC, 2000.

Max Sheppard, "Cry Me a Liver," *City of Angels,* CBS, 2000.

Les, "When Nina Met Her Parents," *Just Shoot Me,* NBC, 2000.

Reverend Meadows, "Motherly Advice," *The Geena Davis Show,* ABC, 2000.

Steve, "Discrimination," *The Michael Richards Show,* NBC, 2000.

Judge William Aldrich, "Summary Judgments," *The Practice,* ABC, 2000.

Judge William Aldrich, "Germ Warfare," *The Practice,* ABC, 2000.

Judge William Aldrich, "Officers of the Court," *The Practice,* ABC, 2000.

Monsignor D'Amico, "Confession," *Diagnosis Murder,* CBS, 2001.

Hal Lainson, "Lost and Found," *Citizen Baines,* CBS, 2001.

Jameson Bishop, " ... And Then You Die," *First Years,* NBC, 2001.

Uncle Marble, "The Balls Game," *Leap fo Faith,* NBC, 2002.

Angel of Destiny, "Witch Way Now?," *Charmed,* The WB, 2002.

Mr. Chandler, "The Frozen Zone," *Judging Amy,* CBS, 2002.

Reverend Steinflash, "The Wedding Planner," *Providence,* NBC, 2002.

Judge Lander, "The Making of a Trial Attorney," *The Practice,* ABC, 2003.

Judge, "Trick or Treat," *The Lyon's Den,* NBC, 2003.

Simon Clifton, "The Brothers Grim," *NYPD Blue,* ABC, 2004.

Simon Clifton, "Peeler? I Hardley Knew Her," *NYPD Blue,* ABC, 2004.

Simon Clifton, "Traylor Trash," *NYPD Blue,* ABC, 2004.

Marvin/Santa Claus, "Damned if You Do," *House M.D.* (also known as *House*), Fox, 2004.

Evander Geddes, "Creed, OK," *Carnivale,* HBO, 2005.

Mr. Mitchell, "Standards and Practices," *The Closer,* TNT, 2005.

Jim Sullivan, "Christmas Is Ruined," *Huff,* Showtime, 2005.

Reverend Sikes, "Live Alone and Like It," *Desperate Housewives,* ABC, 2005.

Reverend Sikes, "Next," *Desperate Housewives,* ABC, 2005.

Reverend Sikes, "All the Juicy Details," *Desperate Housewives,* ABC, 2006.

Reverend Sikes, "It Takes Two," *Desperate Housewives,* ABC, 2006.

Maz'rai, "Stronghold," *Stargate SG–1* (also known as *La porte des etoiles*), Sci-Fi Channel, 2006.

Jim Sullivan, "Maps Don't Talk 2," *Huff,* Showtime, 2006.

Jim Sullivan, "Whipped Doggie," *Huff,* Showtime, 2006.

Governor Reynolds, "Eyebrow Girl vs. Smirkface," *Jake in Progress,* ABC, 2006.

Dr. Pittman, "Father Knows Best," *Dexter,* Showtime, 2006.

Judge Harvey Fletcher, "Angel of Death," *Boston Legal,* ABC, 2007.

Judge Arthur Brock, "Head Games," *Medium,* NBC, 2007.

Some sources cite appearance as Fletch Porter in an episode of *Love & War.*

Television Appearances; Pilots:
Businessman, *Family Affair,* The WB, 2002.
Merle Horstradt, *Jack & Bobby,* The WB, 2004.

Television Appearances; Specials:
Field reporter, *The Legend of the Beverly Hillbillies,* 1993.

Film Appearances:
Judge Lawrence Box, *Nuts,* Warner Bros., 1987.
Old Man Morrison, *Like Father, Like Son,* TriStar, 1987.
Sam Mitgang, *The Silence at Bethany,* 1987.
Marion Corey, Jr., *Funny Farm,* Warner Bros., 1988.

William Singer, *Sunset* (also known as *Catalina*), TriStar, 1988.

Mr. McBain, *Permanent Record,* Paramount, 1988.

Bob, *Clean & Sober,* Warner Bros., 1988.

Mission commander, *Body Wars,* 1989.

Washington Post editor, *Wired,* Taurus Entertainment, 1989.

Charlie, *The Fabulous Baker Boys,* Twentieth Century–Fox, 1990.

Mr. Seymour, *Ghost Dad,* Universal, 1990.

Singleton, *Eve of Destruction,* Orion, 1991.

Colonel Cochrane, *Child's Play 3* (also known as *Child's Play 3: Look Who's Stalking*), Universal, 1991.

Police captain, *Undercover Blues,* Metro–Goldwyn–Mayer, 1993.

Dr. Feldman, *The Temp,* Paramount, 1993.

Voice of King William, *The Swan Princess* (animated), New Line Cinema, 1994.

Intervention counselor, *Stuart Saves His Family* (also known as *Stuart Stupid—Eine familie zum kotzen*), Paramount, 1995.

Passenger Tucker, *Bean* (also known as *Bean: The Movie* and *Bean: The Ultimate Disaster Movie*), Gramercy, 1997.

Minister, *Flubber* (also known as *Disney's "Flubber: The Absent Minded Professor"*), Buena Vista, 1997.

Senator Wright, *The Siege,* Twentieth Century–Fox, 1998.

Voice, *The Swan Princess: Sing Along* (animated), 1998.

Dr. Jacobson, *The Muse,* October Films, 1999.

(Uncredited) Voice of race judge, *An Extremely Goofy Movie* (animated), Buena Vista, 2000.

Arthur Lundhal, *Thirteen Days,* New Line Cinema, 2000.

Mr. Fairchild, *The Fighting Temptations,* Paramount, 2003.

Film Work:
Additional voices, *Gen 13,* 1999.

Stage Appearances:
Sir Oliver Surface and a gentleman, *The School for Scandal,* City Center Acting Company, Theatre of Good Shepherd–Faith Church, New York City, 1972.

Pat, *The Hostage,* City Center Acting Company, Theatre of Good Shepherd–Faith Church, 1972.

Fabritio and member of ensemble, *Women Beware Women,* City Center Acting Company, Theatre of Good Shepherd–Faith Church, 1972.

Bubnov, *The Lower Depths,* City Center Acting Company, Theatre of Good Shepherd–Faith Church, 1972.

Coriolanus, 1988.

Mrs. Warren's Profession by George Bernard Shaw (staged reading; also recorded for future radio broadcasts), L.A. Theatre Works, Los Angeles, 1996.

State of the Union (staged reading; also recorded for future radio broadcasts), L.A. Theatre Works, 1996.

Noah, *Freedomland,* Playwrights Horizons Theatre, New York City, 1998–99, and South Coast Repertory Theatre, Costa Mesa, CA.

Falstaff, *The Merry Wives of Windsor,* Old Globe Theatre, San Diego, CA, 1999.

Augie Belfast, *Man Who Had All the Luck,* Ivy Substation Theatre, Culver City, CA, 2000.

Capulet and member of chorus, *Romeo and Juliet,* Center Theatre Group, Ahmanson Theatre, Los Angeles, 2001.

Mercadet the Napoleon of Finance, Ivy Substation Theatre, 2001.

Arnolphe, *The School for Wives,* South Coast Repertory Theatre, 2002.

Andrew Undershaft, *Major Barbara,* South Coast Repertory Theatre, 2002.

The Proof of the Promise, Antaeus Theatre Company, El Paso, TX, 2002.

Henry IV, Lincoln Center Theatre, New York City, 2003.

The Prince of L.A., Old Globe Theatre, San Diego, CA, 2005.

Dick Cheney, *Stuff Happens,* Mark Taper Forum, Los Angeles, 2005.

The fixer, *Water & Power,* Mark Taper Forum, 2006.

Also appeared in *Legal Briefs* and as C. S. Lewis, *Shadowlands,* both South Coast Repertory Theatre, Costa Mesa, CA.

Stage Director:
Henry V, Old Globe Theatre, San Diego, CA, 1998.

(With John Achorn) *Mercadet the Napoleon of Finance,* Antaeus Company, Ivy Substation Theatre, Culver City, CA, 2001.

RECORDINGS

Audio Books; Reader:
Ravelstein by Saul Bellow, Highbridge, 2000.

WRITINGS

Translator:
Agustin Moreto, *Spite for Spite,* Smith & Kraus, 1995.

Juan Ruiz de Alarcon, *The Truth Can't Be Trusted; or, The Liar,* University Press of the South, 1997.

Juan Ruiz de Alarcon, *The Walls Have Ears,* University Press of the South, 1998.

Also translated the Ruiz de Alarcon play *The Proof of the Promise.*

Other:
Contributor to scholarly journals.

MAXWELL REID, Daphne 1948–
    (Daphne Maxwell, Daphne Maxwell Reed, Daphne Reid, Daphne Maxell Reid, Daphne Maxwell Reid)

PERSONAL

Full name, Daphne Etta Maxwell–Reid; born July 13, 1948, in New York, NY; daughter of Green and Rosalee Maxwell; married second husband, Timothy L. Reid (an actor, producer, director, and writer), December 4, 1982; children: (first marriage) Christopher Tubbs; (second marriage; stepchildren) Timothy L., Jr. (an actor), Tori LeAnn (an actress). *Education:* Northwestern University, B.A., 1970; studied acting with Robert Hooks.

Addresses: *Office*—New Millennium Studios, 1 New Millennium Dr., Petersburg, VA 23805.

Career: Actress, executive, and writer. Timalove Enterprises, Inc., Encino, CA, vice president; New Millennium Studios, Petersburg, VA, cofounder; president of Daphne Maxwell, Inc. and Reidmont Productions. Clothing and costume designer, pattern maker, and seamstress. Governor's Alliance for a Drug–Free Virginia, chair of board of directors; Virginia Museum of Fine Arts, member of board of directors. Worked as a fashion model in New York City; appeared in television commercials.

Member: Screen Actors Guild (member of board of directors, 1974–76).

Awards, Honors: Best New Product Award, Home Sewing and Crafts Association, 1993; Image Award nomination, outstanding supporting actress in a comedy series, National Association for the Advancement of Colored People, 1996, for *The Fresh Prince of Bel–Air;* honorary degrees, Norfolk State University, 1996, and Virginia Commonwealth University, 1999.

CREDITS

Television Appearances; Series:
(As Daphne Maxwell) Temple Hill, a recurring role, *Simon & Simon,* CBS, between 1983 and 1987.
Cohost, *CBS Summer Playhouse,* CBS, 1987.
Micki Dennis, *Snoops,* CBS, 1989.

(As Daphne Maxwell Reid) Vivian Banks, *The Fresh Prince of Bel Air* (also known as *The Fresh Prince Show*), NBC, 1993–96.
Frances Hunter, a recurring role, *Eve,* UPN, between 2003 and 2006.

Television Appearances; Movies:
Joan Haines, *The Long Journey Home,* CBS, 1987.
Coach Dawson, "You Must Remember This" (also known as "The Family Business"), *WonderWorks Family Movie,* PBS, 1992.
(As Daphne Maxwell Reid) Cathy McLemore, *Alley Cats Strike!,* Disney Channel, 2000.
Judge Landers, *Polly and Marie,* 2007.

Television Appearances; Miniseries:
Harriet Jacobs, "Seeds of Destruction," *Slavery and the Making of America,* PBS, 2005.
Herself, *State of the Black Union: Jamestown—The First 400 Years,* 2007.

Television Appearances; Specials:
Host, *The CBS All–American Thanksgiving Day Parade,* CBS, 1987.
The 57th Annual Hollywood Christmas Parade, syndicated, 1988.
Host, *The 4th Annual CBS Easter Parade,* CBS, 1988.
Host, *The CBS Tournament of Roses Parade,* CBS, 1988.
CBS team member, *Battle of the Network Stars XIX,* ABC, 1988.
Living the Dream: A Tribute to Dr. Martin Luther King Jr., 1988.
Judith Daniels, "The Cheats" (also known as "Lost Honor"), *ABC Afterschool Specials,* ABC, 1989.
US Magazine—Live at the Emmys!, Fox, 1989.
CBS Premiere Preview Spectacular, CBS, 1989.
Host, *The CBS All–American Thanksgiving Day Parade,* CBS, 1989.
The American Red Cross Emergency Test, ABC, 1990.
Host, *Martin Luther King, Jr. Parade,* TBS, 1990.
The All New Circus of the Stars & Side Show, CBS, 1991.
Will You Marry Me?, ABC, 1992.
Inside TV Land: African Americans in Television, TV Land, 2002.

Television Appearances; Episodic:
(As Daphne Maxwell) Premiere episode, *The Duke,* NBC, 1979.
(As Maxwell) "Long and Thin, Lorna Lynch," *The Duke,* NBC, 1979.
(As Maxwell) Dr. Karla Meredith, "The Shangri–La Syndrome," *A Man Called Sloane,* NBC, 1979.
(As Maxwell) Elaine Parker, "Real Families," *WKRP in Cincinnati,* CBS, 1980.
Sheila Roberts, "Chipped Beef," *Hill Street Blues,* 1981.

(As Maxwell) Jessica Langtree, "Circumstantial Evidence," *WKRP in Cincinnati,* CBS, 1982.

"Pal–I–Money–o–Mine/Does Father Know Best?/An 'A' for Gopher," *The Love Boat,* 1982.

(As Maxwell) "Once Again with Vigorish," *Hardcastle and McCormick,* ABC, 1983.

(As Maxwell) Nurse Lewis, "There's Always a Catch," *The A–Team,* NBC, 1983.

Saleswoman, "Filling Buddy's Shoes," *The Duck Factory,* 1984.

Mrs. Richards, "Stolen," *Matt Houston,* 1984.

(As Maxwell) Nancy, *Paper Dolls,* 1984.

(As Maxwell) Noreen Adler, "The Clinic," *Cagney & Lacey,* 1985.

(As Maxwell) Kamora Kaboko, "Skins," *The A–Team,* NBC, 1985.

"Another Fine Mess," *The Insiders,* ABC, 1985.

News anchor, "Blues in the Night," *Hill Street Blues,* 1985.

Hanna Griffin, "Food Fight," *Frank's Place,* CBS, 1987.

Super Password, 1987.

(As Daphne Maxwell Reid) Nan Wynn, "The Body Politic," *Murder, She Wrote,* CBS, 1988.

(As Maxwell Reid) Panelist, *The New Hollywood Squares,* 1988.

Guest host, *The Home Show,* ABC, 1988.

Body by Jake, syndicated, 1988.

"The Myth about George Washington," *American Treasury,* CBS, 1989.

"The Circus," *American Treasury,* CBS, 1989.

"Famous Abolitionists," *American Treasury,* CBS, 1989.

"Foreign Lands," *American Treasury,* CBS, 1989.

Millicent, "Clair's Reunion," *The Cosby Show,* 1992.

"Shooting in Rome," *Murder, She Wrote,* CBS, 1995.

(As Maxwell Reid) Herself, "I, Whoops, There It Is," *The Fresh Prince of Bel–Air,* 1996.

(As Maxwell Reid) Charmagne, "Double Exposure," *Sister, Sister,* ABC, 1996.

(As Maxwell Reid) Cleo Stanton, "My Pest Friend's Wedding," *In the House,* UPN, 1998.

(As Maxwell Reid) Eartha, "Lovers and Other Traitors," *Linc's,* Showtime, 1998.

Eartha, "What I Did for Love," *Linc's,* Showtime, 1998.

Mrs. Avery, "Justice Delayed," *Crossing Jordan,* NBC, 2004.

(As Daphne Maxell Reid) Herself, "Changing Times and Trends," *TV Land Confidential* (also known as *TV Land Confidential: The Untold Stories*), TV Land, 2005.

Television Appearances; Awards Presentations:

The 9th Annual American Black Achievement Awards, ABC, 1988.

Presenter, *The 21st NAACP Image Awards,* NBC, 1989.

The 10th Annual American Black Achievement Awards, syndicated, 1989.

The 10th Annual ACE Awards (also known as *The Golden ACE Awards*), syndicated, 1989.

(As Daphne Reid) *The 22nd Annual NAACP Image Awards,* NBC, 1990.

Host, *The Fourth Annual Trumpet Awards,* TBS, 1996.

Television Appearances; Other:

(As Daphne Maxwell) Merissa Lane, *Coach of the Year* (pilot), NBC, 1980.

Memories Then and Now, 1988.

Film Appearances:

(As Daphne Maxwell) Helene, *Protocol,* Warner Bros., 1984.

(As Daphne Reid) *Color Adjustment,* 1991.

(As Daphne Maxwell Reid) Miss Maxey, *Once upon a Time … When We Were Colored,* Republic, 1996.

(As Daphne Maxwell Reid) Marty's wife, *Asunder,* New Millennium Releasing, 1998.

Film Work:

(As Daphne Maxwell Reid) Co–executive producer, *Asunder,* New Millennium Releasing, 1998.

(As Maxwell Reid) Executive producer, *For Real,* Obsidian Home Entertainment, 2003.

Radio Appearances; Series:

Cohost, *The Tim and Daphne Show,* syndicated, 1990–91.

Stage Appearances:

Appeared in an off–Broadway production of *The Skin of Our Teeth.*

RECORDINGS

Videos:

(As Daphne Maxwell Reid) Co–executive producer, *Paul Mooney: Analyzing White America* (also known as *Paul Mooney Live! Analyzing White America* and *Paul Mooney's "Analyzing White America"*), New Millennium Releasing, 2002.

(In archive footage), *TV in Black: The First Fifty Years,* Koch Vision, 2004.

Host, *14th Annual Inner City Destiny Awards,* 2006.

Creator and producer of the video series *Suddenly You're Sewing,* McCall Pattern Co.

WRITINGS

Books:

Author (with husband Timothy L. Reid) of *In the Spirit of Food: Tim and Daphne's Cookin' Book.*

OTHER SOURCES

Periodicals:
Ebony, February, 1992, p. 90.
People Weekly, June 26, 2000, p. 87.

Electronic:
New Millennium Studios, http://www.nmstudios.com, August 23, 2007.

McARTHUR, Alex 1957–

PERSONAL

Born March 6, 1957, in Telford, PA (some sources cite Sellersville, PA); son of Bruce (a contractor) and Dolores McArthur; married Tammi Krevi; children: Roxann, three sons, including Jacob Bruce. *Education:* Attended DeAnza College and San Jose State University; Trained at Herbert Berkoff School of Acting. *Avocational Interests:* Music.

Addresses: *Agent*—Geneva Bray, GVA Talent Agency, 9229 Sunset Blvd., Suite 320, Hollywood, CA 90069. *Manager*—Christopher Black, Opus Entertainment, 5225 Wilshire Blvd., Suite 905, Los Angeles, CA 90036.

Career: Actor. Previously worked as a model, a bartender at Studio 54, and a carpenter.

Awards, Honors: Gemini Award nomination, best supporting actor, Academy of Canadian Cinema and Television, 1994, for *Woman on the Run: The Lawrencia Bembenek Story.*

CREDITS

Television Appearances; Series:
Ken Forest, a recurring role, *Knots Landing,* 1985–86.
Richard Braun, *The Fifth Corner,* NBC, 1992.
Dickie Baineaux, *The Road Home,* CBS, 1994.

Television Appearances; Movies:
Bo Reinecker, *With Intent to Kill* (also known as *Urge to Kill*), 1984.
Deputy Sam, *Command 5,* ABC, 1984.
Joey Caputo, *Silent Witness,* 1985.
Cory Yeager, *Crime of Innocence,* 1985.
Duell McCall, *Desperado,* 1987.
Duell McCall, *The Return of Desperado,* 1988.

Duell McCall, *Desperado: Avalanche at Devil's Ridge,* NBC, 1988.
Patrick McClaren, *L.A. Takedown* (also known as *Crimewave, L.A. Crimewave,* and *Made in L.A.*), NBC, 1989.
Duell McCall, *Desperado: Badlands Justice,* NBC, 1989.
Duell McCall, *Desperado: The Outlaw Wars,* NBC, 1989.
Stephen Smith, *Shoot First: A Cop's Vengeance* (also known as *Vigilante Cop*), ITC, 1991.
Nick Gugliatto, *Woman on the Run: The Lawrencia Bembenek Story* (also known as *Woman on Trial: The Lawrencia Bembenek Story*), NBC, 1993.
Frank Bodin, *Sharon's Secret,* 1995.
Detective Bert Kling, *Ed McBain's 87th Precinct: Lightning,* NBC, 1995.
Steven Warren, *The Spiral Staircase* (also known as *Le secret du manoir*), Fox Family Channel, 2000.
Jake Vincent, *Out for Blood,* Sci–Fi Channel, 2004.
John White, *Lost Colony,* Sci–Fi Channel, 2007.

Television Appearances; Episodic:
Tony DeVito, "Where the Girls Are," *Riptide,* 1984.
Antov, "Waiting for Godorsky," *Scarecrow and Mrs. King,* CBS, 1984.
Brent, "Oh, You Kid," *Hill Street Blues,* NBC, 1985.
Ed Bingham, "Full Moon," *Touched by an Angel,* CBS, 1997.
Josh Butler, "Josh," *The Outer Limits* (also known as *The New Outer Limits*), 1998.
Johnny Coburn, "Sleepwalker," *Dead Man's Gun,* Showtime, 1999.
Gabriel, "Which Prue Is It, Anyway?," *Charmed,* The WB, 1999.
Dwayne Haskell, "Kiss of Death," *Chicago Hope,* CBS, 1999.
Alex Tanner, "Untouchable," *Hunter,* NBC, 2003.
"Baby, the Rain Must Fall," *The Division* (also known as *Heart of the City*), Lifetime, 2004.

Television Appearances; Other:
Tom Vaughan, *Drug Wars: The Cocaine Cartel* (miniseries), NBC, 1992.
Studio 54: The E! True Hollywood Story (special), E! Entertainment Television, 1998.

Film Appearances:
(Uncredited) Bellboy at Plaza Hotel, *They All Laughed,* Twentieth Century–Fox, 1981.
Walter Parker, *Desert Hearts,* Samuel Goldwyn Company, 1985.
Charlie Reece, *Rampage,* Miramax, 1988.
Cody Gifford, *Race for Glory,* New Century Vista, 1989.
Keith Bauers, *Perfect Alibi* (also known as *Where's Mommy Now*), Rysher Entertainment, 1995.
Richard Darling, *Ladykiller* (also known as *Scene of the Crime*), Concorde, 1996.

Cynic, *Conspiracy Theory,* Warner Bros., 1997.
Detective Davey Sikes, *Kiss the Girls,* Paramount, 1997.
Peter Rinaldi, *Devil in the Flesh* (also known as *Dearly Devoted*), 1998.
Jack, *Running Home,* 1999.
(Uncredited) Dr. John Sims, *Teacher's Pet* (also known as *Dearly Devoted II, Devil in the Flesh 2,* and *La chair et le diable*), Unapix Films, 2000.
Recording studio executive, *Dischord,* Artistic License, 2001.
Nick, *Route 666,* Trimark Pictures, 2001.
Tom Kempton, *Suspended Animation* (also known as *Mayhem*), First Run Features, 2001.
Fred Dowd, *Stealing Candy* (also known as *Internet Queen*), Lions Gate Films Home Entertainment, 2002.
Roger Craig, *The Commission,* 2003.

RECORDINGS

Videos:
Madonna: The Immaculate Collection, 1990.

Appeared as boyfriend in the music video "Papa Don't Preach" by Madonna, 1986.

OTHER SOURCES

Periodicals:
IN Fashion, November–December, 1987; May–June, 1988.
Interview, May, 1987.
Los Angeles Times, April 11, 1992.
TV Host Weekly, December 16, 1989.

McCANN, Sean 1935–
(Sean McCaan)

PERSONAL

Born September 24, 1935, in Windsor, Ontario, Canada. *Education:* Studied at St. Peter Seminary, London, Ontario, Canada. *Avocational Interests:* History, politics, baseball (Toronto Blue Jays), and poetry.

Career: Actor. Also worked as an associate baseball scout for the Toronto Blue Jays and as a public speaker. Member of board of directors, Canadian Baseball Hall of Fame.

Member: Alliance of Canadian Cinema, Television, and Radio Artists, Toronto Performers Council.

Awards, Honors: Gemini Award nomination, best supporting actor, Academy of Canadian Cinema and Television, 1987, for *Night Heat;* Earl Grey Award, Gemini Awards, 1989; Genie Award nomination, performance by an actor in a supporting role, Academy of Canadian Cinema and Television, 1996, for *Swann;* Gemini Award, best guest actor in a series, 1999, for *Power Play;* Gemini Award nominations, best performance in a pre–school program or series, 1999, 2000, both for *Noddy.*

CREDITS

Film Appearances:
Peter O'Lurgan, *A Quiet Day in Belfast,* Ambassador Film Distributors, 1974.
Polanski, *Sudden Fury,* Ambassador Film Distributors, 1975.
Cluny, *The Far Shore* (also known as *The Art of Lust* and *L utre rive*), Astral Films, 1976.
Inspector, *The Uncanny,* Astral Films, 1977.
Carl, *Starship Invasions* (also known as *Alien Nation, Project Genocide,* and *War of the Aliens*), Warner Bros., 1977.
Car salesman, *Three Card Monte,* Ambassador Film Distributors, 1978.
Lieutenant Grace, *Title Shot,* Ambassador Film Distributors, 1979.
Jake, *Nothing Personal,* Orion, 1980.
Detective, *Atlantic City* (also known as *Atlantic City, U.S.A.*), Paramount, 1980.
Colonel Warner, *Hog Wild* (also known as *Les focus de la moto*), 1980.
Man in soup line, *Silence of the North,* Universal, 1981.
News reporter, *Death Hunt,* Twentieth Century–Fox, 1981.
Roger, *Tulips,* 1981.
Jack, *Hank Williams: The Show He Never Gave,* 1982.
Canada's Sweetheart: The Saga of Hal C. Banks, National Film Board of Canada, 1985.
One Step Away, 1985.
Jack Crew, *Flying* (also known as *Dream to Believe* and *Teenage Dream*), Cinema Group, 1986.
Anne's father, *Crazy Moon* (also known as *Huggers* and *D'amour et d'eau fraiche*), Miramax, 1986.
Roy McMullin, *The Big Town,* Columbia, 1987.
Ed, *Taking Care,* 1987.
The King Chronicle, Part 1: Mackenzie King and the Unseen Hand, National Film Board of Canada, 1988.
The King Chronicle, Part 2: Mackenzie King and the Great Beyond, National Film Board of Canada, 1988.
The King Chronicle, Part 3: Mackenzie King and the Zombie Army, National Film Board of Canada, 1988.

Jacob Fisher, *Criminal Law,* Hemdale Film Corporation, 1988.

Rudy, *Mindfield,* Allegro Films Distribution, 1989.

Marv, *Run,* Buena Vista, 1991.

O'Brien, *Naked Lunch* (also known as *Le festin nu*), Twentieth Century–Fox, 1991.

Jim, *Bordertown Cafe,* 1991.

Mackenzie King, *Mackenzie King and the Conscription Crisis,* 1991.

John O'Doyle, *I'll Never Get to Heaven,* 1992.

Nolan, *Guilty As Sin,* Buena Vista, 1993.

Lieutenant Crow, *The Neighbor,* 1993.

Ray Fox, *The Air Up There,* Buena Vista, 1994.

Chief Burnell, *Trapped in Paradise,* 1994.

Mr. Rittenhauer, *Tommy Boy,* Paramount, 1995.

Wilcox, *Iron Eagle IV* (also known as *Aigle de fer IV*), Trimark Pictures, 1995.

(Archive footage) Mackenzie King, *Donald Brittain: Filmmaker,* 1995.

Homer, *Swann,* Norstar Releasing, 1996.

Clute Mirkovich, *Gang in Blue,* 1996.

Evan Twombley, *Affliction,* Lions Gate Films, Inc., 1997.

Chief Al Cork, *Simon Birch* (also known as *Angels and Armadillos*), Buena Vista, 1998.

Kevin, *Woman Wanted,* 2000.

Inspector Berkley, *Possible Worlds* (also known as *Mondes possibles*), Alliance Atlantis Communications, 2000.

Hank, *The Law of Enclosures,* 2000.

Judge, *Chicago,* Miramax, 2002.

Walter Bush, *Miracle,* Buena Vista, 2004.

Moss Coogan, *Moss* (short), 2004.

Ernest Grey, *The River King,* Momentum Pictures, 2005.

Television Appearances; Series:

Inspector Alec Woodward, *Sidestreet,* CTV and CBS, 1975.

Jim Baxter, *The Baxters,* syndicated, 1980–81.

Lieutenant Jim Hogan, *Night Heat,* CBS, 1985–89.

The Campbells, CTV and syndicated, 1986.

Marlowe, *Jim Lee's Wild C.A.T.s: Covert Action Teams,* CBS, 1994.

Noah, *Noddy,* PBS, 1999.

Dr. W. S. Finch, *Naturally, Sadie* (also known as *The Complete Freaks of Nature*), Family Channel Canada, 2005–2006.

Television Appearances; Miniseries:

Dr. O'Reilly, *Anne of Green Gables,* CBC and PBS, 1985.

I'll Take Manhattan, CBS, 1987.

William Lyon Mackenzie King, *The King Chronicle,* 1988.

Captain Ed Melchen, *Passion and Paradise,* ABC, 1989.

Diane's father, *Small Sacrifices,* ABC, 1989.

Power, *Common Ground,* CBS, 1990.

Defense attorney, *Deadly Matrimony* (also known as *Shattered Promises*), NBC, 1992.

Premier Mitch Hepburn, *Million Dollar Babies* (also known as *Les jurnelles Dionne*), CBS, 1994.

Television Appearances; Movies:

Dr. Farris, *Torn Between Two Lovers,* CBS, 1979.

Lou Carmen, *Off Your Rocker,* 1982.

Lieutenant Yaeger, *The Guardian,* HBO, 1984.

Hockey Night, CBC, 1984.

When We First Met, 1984.

Harold Stern, *Reckless Disregard,* 1985.

Dr. Ralph Stanwyck, *Alex: The Life of a Child,* ABC, 1986.

Unnatural Causes, NBC, 1986.

John Benedict, *The High Price of Passion,* PBS, 1986.

Many Happy Returns, 1986.

Paul Worthy, *Easy Prey,* ABC, 1986.

Shields, *Ghost of a Chance,* 1987.

Ed, *Prescription for Murder,* 1987.

Captain Ed Melchen, *Passion and Paradise* (also known as *Murder in Paradise*), 1989.

Victor Morgan, *Murder Times Seven* (also known as *Murder X 7*), CBS, 1990.

Defense attorney, *Deadly Matrimony* (also kwon as *Shattered Promises*), 1992.

Albert Grant, *Trial and Error,* USA Network, 1993.

Detective Shapiro, *Fatal Vows: The Alexandra O'Hara Story,* CBS, 1994.

Almost Golden: The Jessica Savitch Story (also known as *Almost Golden*), Lifetime, 1995.

Nancy's father, *Fight for Justice: The Nancy Conn Story,* NBC, 1995.

Lee Keating, *Sins of Silence,* CBS, 1996.

Mr. Ellison, *Hostile Advances: The Kerry Ellison Story,* Lifetime, 1996.

Clute Mirkovich, *Gang in Blue,* Showtime, 1996.

What Happened to Bobby Earl?, (also known as *Murder in a College Town*), CBS, 1997.

... First Do No Harm, ABC, 1997.

Hal, *The Absolute Truth,* CBS, 1997.

Albert Grant, *Trial & Error,* 1997.

Mike McConnell, *Every 9 Seconds* (also known as *A Call for Help*), NBC, 1997.

John Broderick, *The Defenders: Payback,* Showtime, 1997.

Pappy, *Dogboys* (also known as *Tracked* and *Dresses pour tuer*), TMC, 1998.

Theodore Warfield, *Evidence of Blood,* TMC, 1998.

Jim Grkowski, *Family of Cops III: Under Suspicion,* CBS, 1999.

Colonel Woodburn, *Roswell: The Aliens Attack,* UPN, 1999.

Justice, 1999.

Melton, *Who Killed Atlanta's Children?* (also known as *Echo of Murder*), Showtime, 2000.

Rutherford, *A House Divided,* Showtime, 2000.

Judge Black, *What Makes a Family,* Lifetime, 2000.

Donald Regan, *The Day Reagan Was Shot,* Showtime, 2001.

John McCormack, *Keep the Faith, Baby,* Showtime, 2002.

Scared Silent, 2002.

John Mitchell, *The Pentagon Papers,* FX Channel, 2003.

George Schultz, *The Reagans,* Showtime, 2003.

Dr. Stanpole, *A Separate Peace,* 2004.

Mel Bernstein, *The Winning Season,* TNT, 2004.

Ambulance Girl, Lifetime, 2005.

Mayor, *The Wives He Forgot,* Lifetime, 2006.

Judge, *Me and Luke* (also known as *A Dad for Christmas*), Lifetime, 2006.

Verne Grandy, *Wedding Wars,* Arts and Entertainment, 2006.

Television Appearances; Specials:

Joe Dunne, *In This Corner,* CBC, 1985.

Television Appearances; Pilots:

Matty Barker, *The World of Darkness,* CBS, 1977.

Lieutenant O'Leary, *Police File,* ABC, 1994.

Brackett, *Leap Years,* 2001.

Television Appearances; Episodic:

Larson, "Mary Theresa Is Missing," *The King of Kensington,* CBC, 1977.

Chuck, "Cementhead," *For the Record,* CBC, 1978.

Sheriff Johnson, "Double Trouble," *The Littlest Hobo,* CTV and syndicated, 1979.

Joe, "Photo Finish," *The Littlest Hobo,* CTV and syndicated, 1981.

Jack Petaski, "Trooper," *The Littlest Hobo,* CTV and syndicated, 1982.

"Family Business," *Diamonds,* CBC, 1988.

"Doctor, Lawyer, Liar, Thief," *Diamonds,* CBC, 1988.

Jim Briggs, "Second Growth," *The Beachcombers,* CBC, 1989.

Vince Ventura, "The Prisoner," *Friday the 13th* (also known as *Friday the 13th: The Series* and *Friday's Curse*), syndicated, 1989.

Vince Ventura, "Bad Penny," *Friday the 13th* (also known as *Friday the 13th: The Series* and *Friday's Curse*), syndicated, 1989.

Captain Briggs, "The Cool Katt," *Hardball,* NBC, 1990.

Captain Briggs, "Sex, Cops, and Videotape," *Hardball,* NBC, 1990.

Sid Novak, Sr., "Sing for Me, Olivia," *Street Legal,* CBC, 1991.

Captain Murphy, "Fire in the Streets," *Counterstrike* (also known as *Force de frappe*), 1991.

Taylor, "Final Cut," *E.N.G.,* Lifetime and CTV, 1992.

Wylie, "The First Battle," *The Hidden Room,* 1993.

Voice, *Little Bear* (also known as *Maurice Sendak's "Little Bear"*), 1995.

Noah, "The Magic Key," *Noddy,* 1998.

Ray Malone, "Perambulate Me Back to My Habitual Abode," *Power Play,* CTV and UPN, 1998.

Ray Malone, "Changing the Luck," *Power Play,* CTV and UPN, 1998.

Ray Malone, "All for One," *Power Play,* CTV and UPN, 1998.

"Paying the Piper," *Falcone,* CBS, 2000.

Edgar Brackett, *Leap Years,* 2001.

Also appeared as Henry Sterling, "Pledge of Allegiance," *Traders.*

McCARTHY, Andrew 1962–

PERSONAL

Full name, Andrew T. McCarthy; born November 29, 1962, in New York, NY (some sources say Westfield, NJ); father, a stock broker; brother of Justin McCarthy (a writer and director); married Carol Schneider (an actress), October 9, 1999; children: Sam. *Education:* Studied theatre at New York University; studied acting at the Circle in the Square Theatre School. *Religion:* Roman Catholic. *Avocational Interests:* Playing pool, traveling, and kayaking.

Addresses: *Agent*—Innovative Artists, 1505 Tenth St., Santa Monica, CA 90401; Creative Film Management International, 440 Park Ave. South, New York, NY 10016. *Manager*—One Entertainment, 12 West 57th St., Penthouse, New York, NY 10019.

Career: Actor. Hartford Stage Company, Hartford, CT, associate artist; member of Ensemble Studio Theatre and Actors' Studio, New York, NY.

Member: Actors' Equity Association, Screen Actors Guild.

Awards, Honors: Fantafestival Award, best actor, 1987, for *Mannequin;* Audience Award, best short film, Sedona International Film Festival, 2005, for *News for the Church.*

CREDITS

Film Appearances:

Jonathan Ogner, *Class,* Orion, 1983.

Michael Dunn, *Heaven Help Us* (also known as *Catholic Boys*), TriStar, 1985.

Kevin Dolenz, *St. Elmo's Fire,* Columbia, 1985.

Blane McDonough, *Pretty in Pink,* Paramount, 1986.

Henry Hopper, *Waiting for the Moon* (also known as *Warten auf den mond*), Skouras, 1987.

Jonathan Switcher, *Mannequin,* Twentieth Century–Fox, 1987.

Clay Easton, *Less Than Zero,* Twentieth Century–Fox, 1987.

Boys (also known as *Boy's Life*), TriStar, 1988.

Wade Corey, *Kansas,* Transworld, 1988.

Matt Larkin, *Fresh Horses,* Columbia, 1988.

Larry Wilson, *Weekend at Bernie's* (also known as *Hot and Cold*), Twentieth Century–Fox, 1989.

Henry Miller, *Jours tranquiles a Clichy* (also known as *Quiet Days in Clichy, Giorni felici a Clichy,* and *Stille tage in Clichy*), 1990.

The assassin, *Club Extinction* (also known as *Dr. M* and *Docteur M*), Prism Entertainment, 1991.

David Raybourne, *Year of the Gun,* Triumph Releasing, 1991.

Clifford Godfrey, *Only You* (also known as *Love Stinks*), Live Home Video, 1992.

Ted Jordan, *The Joy Luck Club,* Buena Vista, 1993.

Larry Wilson, *Weekend at Bernie's II,* TriStar, 1993.

Reggie Barker, *Dead Funny,* 1994.

Eddie Parker, *Mrs. Parker and the Vicious Circle* (also known as *Mrs. Parker and the Round Table*), Fine Line, 1994.

Jerry Logan, *Night of the Running Man,* Trimark Pictures, 1994.

Rupert Grimm, *Getting In* (also known as *Student Body*), Foxboro Entertainment/Lindemann Entertainment Group, 1994.

David Mander, *Dream Man,* Republic Pictures, 1995.

Jimmy Fields, *Mulholland Falls,* Metro–Goldwyn–Mayer, 1996.

Howard, *Everything Relative,* Tara Releasing, 1996.

Don Henderson, *Cosas que nunca te dije* (also known as *Coses que no et vaig dir mai* and *Things I Never Told You*), Ocean Films, 1996.

Richard Ramsay, *Escape Clause,* Metro–Goldwyn–Mayer, 1996.

Frank, *Bela Donna* (also known as *White Dunes*), Araba Films, 1998.

Cop, *I Woke Up Early the Day I Died* (also known as *Ed Wood's "I Woke Up Early the Day I Died"* and *I Awoke Early the Day I Died*), 1998, Cinequanon Pictures International, 1999.

Bertie Krohn, *I'm Losing You,* Lions Gate Films, 1998.

Fool's Errand, Platonic Films, 1998.

Detective Henry Smith, *A Twist of Faith* (also known as *Au–dela du mal* and *Beyond Redemption*), Avalanche Home Entertainment, 1999.

Cecil Sweeney, *New Waterford Girl* (also known as *La fille de New Waterford*), 1999, Alliance Atlantis Communications, 2000.

Kurt Bishop, *New World Disorder,* Promark Entertainment Group/York Entertainment, 1999.

A clown, *Jump,* Arrow Releasing, 1999.

Eric Shelton, *Nowhere in Sight,* Saban Pictures International, 2000.

Standard Time, Intrinsic Value Films/Jubilee Productions, 2001.

Raymond Cane, *Diggity: Home at Last* (also known as *Diggity's Treasure* and *Heaven Must Wait*), Mackinac Media, 2001.

Elliot Shephard, *Standard Time* (also known as *Anything But Love*), Samuel Goldwyn Films, 2002.

Josh, *2BPerfectly Honest,* Monarch Home Video, 2004.

Charles King, *The Orphan King,* 2005.

The Spiderwick Chronicles, Paramount, 2008.

Michael, *Camp Hope,* 2008.

Film Work:

Producer and director, *News for the Church* (short), 2004.

Television Appearances; Series:

Aaron Gerrity, *E–Ring,* NBC, 2005.

Television Appearances; Miniseries:

Bobby Kennedy, *Jackie Bouvier Kennedy Onassis,* 2000.

Television Appearances; Movies:

Arthur Beniker, *The Beniker Gang* (also known as *Dear Lola* and *Dear Lola, or How to Start Your Own Family*), 1985.

Jonathan, *The Courtyard,* Showtime, 1995.

Richard, *The Christmas Tree,* ABC, 1996.

Rabbit (Mike), *Hostile Force* (also known as *The Heist* and *Alarm fuer Security 13*), 1996.

Pete Weber, *Stag,* HBO, 1997.

Keith Lussier, *A Father for Brittany* (also known as *A Change of Heart*), CBS, 1998.

Ben Carroway, *Perfect Assassins* (also known as *A Breed Apart*), HBO, 1998.

Stanley Banner, *A Storm in Summer,* Showtime, 2000.

Mike Harper, *The Secret Life of Zoey,* Lifetime, 2002.

Tyler Ross, *Straight from the Heart,* Hallmark Channel, 2003.

Kit Freers, *The Hollywood Mom's Mystery,* 2004.

Hank Robinson, *Crusader,* 2004.

Television Appearances; Specials:

The Making of "Class," 1983.

Martin, "The Common Pursuit," *Great Performances,* PBS, 1992.

The Brat Pack: The E! True Hollywood Story, E! Entertainment Television, 1999.

Narrator, *Intimate Portrait: Park Overall,* Lifetime, 2000.

Retrosexual: The 80's, VH1, 2004.

100 Greatest Teen Stars, VH1, 2006.

Television Appearances; Pilots:

Michael Lewis, *The Sight,* FX Channel, 2000.

Joe Bennett, *Lipstick Jungle,* NBC, 2007.

Television Appearances; Episodic:

Edwin, "Grandpa's Ghost," *Amazing Stories* (also known as *Steven Spielberg's "Amazing Stores"*), 1986.

Arthur, "Loved to Death," *Tales from the Crypt* (also known as *HBO's "Tales from the Crypt"*), HBO, 1991.

The Rosie O'Donnell Show, syndicated, 1997.

Randolph Morrow, "Slaves," *Law & Order: Special Victims Unit* (also known as *Law & Order: SVU* and *Special Victims Unit*), NBC, 2000.

The Late, Late Show with Craig Kilborn (also known as *The Late, Late Show*), CBS, 2003.

Attorney Finnerty, "Absentia," *Law & Order,* NBC, 2003.

Marshall, "The Monsters Are on Maple Street," *The Twilight Zone,* UPN, 2003.

Derek Philby, "Mr. Monk Goes Back to School," *Monk,* USA Network, 2003.

Dr. Hook, "The Young and the Headless," *Kingdom Hospital* (also known as *Stephen King's "Kingdom Hospital"*), ABC, 2004.

The O'Reilly Factor, Fox News, 2005.

Gylne tider, 2006.

Stage Appearances:

Flem, *The Boys of Winter,* Biltmore Theatre, New York City, 1985.

Franz, "Mariens Kammer," and Kip, "Life Under Water," both in *Marathon '85,* Ensemble Studio Theatre, New York City, 1985.

Sid, *Bodies, Rest and Motion,* Mitzi E. Newhouse Theatre, New York City, 1986–87.

Marathon '88, Ensemble Studio Theatre, 1988.

Arthur, *Psychopathia Sexualis,* Stage 1, Manhattan Theatre Club, New York City, 1997.

Clifford, *Side Man,* Roundabout Theatre, New York City, 1998, then John Golden Theatre, New York City, 1998–99.

The Death of Papa, Hartford Stage Theatre, Hartford, CT, 1999.

Jamie Tyrone, *Long Day's Journey into Night,* Hartford Stage Theatre, 1999.

The Glass Menagerie, Hartford Stage Theatre, 2001.

The Exonerated, 45 Bleecker Theatre, New York City, 2002–2004.

Carter, *Fat Pig,* Lucille Lortel Theatre, New York City, 2004–2005.

Jack, *The 24 Hour Plays 2005,* American Airlines Theatre, New York City, 2005.

Also appeared in *Neptune's Hips,* Ensemble Studio Theatre, New York City; *Been Taken,* Off–Broadway production; *Herself As Lust,* Off–Broadway production; *Ah, Wilderness!,* New York City; *A Midsummer Night's Dream,* New York City; *Waiting for the Moon,* French production; *A Moon for the Misbegotten; Mr. Morton Waits for His Bus; Trumbo,* Bay Street Theatre, Sag Harbor, NY; *A Distant Country Called Youth,* Williams-town Theatre Festival, Williamstown, CT, and Hartford Stage, Hartford, CT; *Hate Mail,* Penguin Repertory Theatre, Stony Point, NY.

Stage Work:

Director, *The 24 Hour Plays 2006,* American Airlines Theatre, New York City, 2006.

RECORDINGS

Music Videos:

Appeared in John Parr's "St. Elmo's Fire (Man in Motion)."

WRITINGS

Screenplays:

News for the Church (short), 2004.

OTHER SOURCES

Periodicals:

People Weekly, April 19, 1999, p. 118.

TV Guide, March 14, 1998, p. 7.

Electronic:

Andrew McCarthy Website, http://www.andrewmccarthy.com, October 1, 2007.

McGRATH, Debra 1954–
(Deb McGrath)

PERSONAL

Born July 5, 1954, in Canada; married Colin Mochrie (an actor and comedian), 1989; children: Luke. *Education:* Studied with The Second City, Toronto, Ontario, Canada, 1983.

Addresses: *Office*—Canadian Accents, Inc., 26 Yarmouth Rd., Toronto, Ontario M4K 1V3, Canada.

Career: Actress, comedienne, writer, and producer. Women Fully Clothed (comedy group), member. Canadian Accents, Inc. (production company), co-founder, 2003. Participated in conferences of the Alliance of Canadian Cinema, Television and Radio Artists (ACTRA).

Member: Alliance of Canadian Cinema, Television and Radio Artists (ACTRA).

Awards, Honors: Canadian Comedy Award nomination, pretty funny female performance, 2003, for *The Gavin Crawford Show;* Canadian Comedy Award, pretty funny female performance in a film, and Canadian Comedy Award nomination, pretty funny film writing, both 2004, for *Expecting.*

CREDITS

Television Appearances; Series:
Member of ensemble, *Bizarre,* Showtime and syndicated, 1980–85.
Anne Marie Snelling, *My Talk Show,* syndicated, 1990–91.
Voice of Valerie Chuckles, *George and Martha* (animated), HBO, HBO Family, and YTV (Canada), 1999–2000.
(As Deb McGrath) Voice of Mama, *Seven Little Monsters* (animated; also known as *Ta mikra teratakia*), YTV (Canada) and PBS, 2000–2003.
Shirley Armstrong, *Paradise Falls* (also known as *Bienvenue a Paradise Falls* and *Ongelmia paratiisissa*), Showcase Network, beginning 2001.
The Joe Blow Show, The Comedy Network (Canada), beginning 2003.
Ruby Kendall, *Getting Along Famously,* CBC, 2006.
Mayor Ann Popowicz, *Little Mosque on the Prairie* (also known as *La petite mosquee dans la prairie*), CBC, 2007—.

Television Appearances; Movies:
Rosemary Hudson, *Partners 'n Love* (also known as *Socios enamorados*), Family Channel, 1992.
Dawn, "Mr. Headmistress" (also known as "Herr eller fru rektor?," "La senorita director," and "Uma directora quase perfeita"), *The Wonderful World of Disney,* ABC, 1998.
Cornelia, "Eloise at the Plaza," *The Wonderful World of Disney,* ABC, 2003.
Cornelia, "Eloise at Christmastime" (also known as "Eloise fete Noel"), *The Wonderful World of Disney,* ABC, 2003.
Mary Matalin, *DC 9/11: Time of Crisis* (also known as *The Big Dance, DC 9/11: I ora tis krisis,* and *11 de setembro–Tempo de crise*), Showtime, 2003.

Television Appearances; Specials:
Out of Our Minds, syndicated, 1984.
Mother, "I'll Die Loving," *Really Weird Tales,* HBO, 1987.
Ursula, *Burnt Toast* (collection of operatic vignettes), broadcast on *Bravo!FACT Presents,* Bravo! (Canada), c. 2005.

Television Appearances; Awards Presentations:
(With Women Fully Clothed) *The Sixth Annual Canadian Comedy Awards,* Comedy Network (Canada), 2005.

Television Appearances; Episodic:
McConnachie, "Maudlin o' the Night," SCTV Channel, Cinemax, 1983.
Real estate agent, "World–Class City," *Street Legal,* CBC, 1989.
Voice of Nurse Peck, "Stress Test!," *The Raccoons* (animated; also known as *Les amis ratons* and *Les aventures de raccoons*), Disney Channel, 1990.
Julia McCrindle, "Sex and Death," *Street Legal,* CBC, 1993.
Bambi Taker, "Prime Suspect," *Robocop* (also known as *RoboCop: The Series*), syndicated, 1994.
Bambi Taker, "Trouble in Delta City," *Robocop* (also known as *RoboCop: The Series*), syndicated, 1994.
Tammy Markles, "Pizzas and Promises," *Due South* (also known as *Due South: The Series* and *Direction: Sud*), CTV (Canada) and CBS, 1994.
Reenie Bigelow, "Train to Nowhere," *Wind at My Back,* CBC, 1997.
Premiere episode, *Supertown Challenge,* The Comedy Network (Canada), 1998.
Reenie Bigelow, "The Crystal Skull," *Wind at My Back,* CBC, 1999.
(As Deb McGrath) Hilda Banks, "Culture Club," *The Gavin Crawford Show,* The Comedy Network (Canada), 2000.
Nurse, "Ethaniel's Story," *Code Name: Eternity* (also known as *Code: Eternity, Code Name: Eternity—Gefahr aus dem All,* and *Koodinimi: Ikuisuus*), Sci–Fi Channel, 2000.
The Gavin Crawford Show, The Comedy Network (Canada), c. 2003.
Marty Klein, *This Is Wonderland* (also known as *Wonderland* and *La corte di Alice*), CBC, 2006.

Television Appearances; Pilots:
Ruby Kendall, *Getting Along Famously,* CBC, 2005.
Mayor Ann Popowicz, "Little Mosque," *Little Mosque on the Prairie* (also known as *La petite mosquee dans la prairie*), CBC, 2007.

Television Work; Series:
Cocreator and coproducer, *My Talk Show,* syndicated, 1990–91.
Executive producer, *Getting Along Famously,* CBC, 2006.

Television Work; Pilots:
Co–executive producer, *Getting Along Famously,* CBC, 2005.

Film Appearances:
Mrs. Noonan, *One Magic Christmas* (also known as *Disney's "One Magic Christmas," Father Christmas,*

Czarodziejskie Boze Narodzenie, En foertrollad jul, Joulukuun kaksi paeivaeae, O natal magico, Un drole de Noel, Un magico natale, and *Wenn Traeume wahr waeren*), Buena Vista, 1985.

Liz Dunshane, *Termini Station* (also known as *Paeaeteasema*), 1989, Northern Arts Entertainment, 1991.

Cis, *The Real Blonde,* Paramount, 1998.

Anita, *Expecting* (also known as *Party surprise!*), Corus Entertainment/Perch Lake Pictures/Steel City Productions, 2002.

Herself, *Women Fully Clothed: All Dressed Up and Places to Go* (documentary), c. 2007.

WRITINGS

Teleplays; with Others; Series:

My Talk Show, syndicated, 1990–91.

Go Girl!, Women's Television Network (Canada), beginning 1998.

Getting Along Famously, CBC, 2006.

Teleplays; Pilots:

Getting Along Famously, CBC, 2005.

With Pat Profit, wrote the pilot *The Cameleon,* HBO.

Screenplays:

Expecting (also known as *Party surprise!*), Corus Entertainment/Perch Lake Pictures/Steel City Productions, 2002.

Writings for the Stage:

I've Got a Sequel Part II, The Second City Mainstage, Toronto, Ontario, Canada, 1983.

No Man Is a Centre Island, The Second City Mainstage, 1983.

Andy Warhol: Your 15 Minutes Are Up, The Second City Mainstage, 1985.

Bob Has Seen the Wind, The Second City Mainstage, 1987.

Wrote material for Women Fully Clothed.

MENDELSOHN, Ben 1969–

PERSONAL

Full name, Paul Benjamin Mendelsohn; born April 3, 1969 in Melbourne, Victoria, Australia. *Education:* Attended a boarding school in Pennsylvania; trained for the stage at St. Martin's Theatre, London.

Addresses: *Agent*—RGM Associates, 64–76 Kippax St., Suite 202, Level 2, Surry Hills, New South Wales 2010, Australia; International Creative Management, 10250 Constellation Way, 9th Floor, Los Angeles, CA 90067. *Manager*—Untitled Entertainment, 331 North Maple Dr., 3rd Floor, Beverly Hills, CA 90210.

Career: Actor. Appeared in television commercials.

Awards, Honors: Australian Film Institute Award, best supporting actor, 1987, for *The Year My Voice Broke;* Australian Film Institute Award nomination, best actor, 1990, for *The Big Steal;* Australian Film Institute Award nomination, best actor, 1991, for *Spotswood;* Australian Film Institute Award nomination, best actor, 1995, for *Metal Skin;* Camerio Award, best actor, Carrousel International du Film, 2000, for *Amy;* Australian Film Institute Award nomination, best actor in a leading role, 2001, Film Critics Circle of Australia Award nomination, best actor—male, 2002, both for *Mullet;* Silver Logie Award nomination, most outstanding actor, 2007, for *Love My Way.*

CREDITS

Film Appearances:

Peter, *The Still Point,* Colosimo Film Productions, 1985.

Trevor, *The Year My Voice Broke,* 1987, Avenue Pictures, 1988.

Gazza, *Lover Boy,* Seon Films Australia, 1988.

Gary Wilson, *Return Home,* Musical Films, 1990.

Luke O'Hagan, *Nirvana Street Murder,* 1990.

Danny Clark, *The Big Steal,* Cascade Films, 1990.

O'Flynn, *Quigley Down Under* (also known as *Quigley*), Metro–Goldwyn–Mayer, 1990.

Carey, *Spotswood* (also known as *The Efficiency Expert*), Miramax, 1992.

Farmboy, *Map of the Human Heart,* Miramax, 1993.

Nursery manager, *Say a Little Prayer,* Beyond Films/Flying Films Productions, 1993.

Dazey, *Metal Skin* (also known as *Speed*), Phaedra Cinema, 1994.

Lewis, *Sirens,* Miramax, 1994.

Lewis, *Cosi,* 1996, Miramax, 1997.

Kev, *Idiot Box,* Central Park Films, 1996.

Jerry, *True Love and Chaos,* Westside Films, 1997.

Lee Gordon, *The Singer and the Swinger,* 1999.

John, *Sample People,* 2000.

Malcolm Bench, *Vertical Limit,* Columbia, 2000.

Robert Buchanan, *Amy,* World Wide Motion Pictures, 2001.

Eddie "Mullet" Maloney, *Mullet,* 2001.

Rupert Murdoch, *Black and White,* New Vision Films, 2002.

Ben, *The New World,* 2005.

Rupert Kathner, *Hunt Angels,* Palace Films, 2006.

Kyle Sorenson, *The Adventures of Beatle Boyin,* 2007.

The Floating World, 2007.
Australia, New Line Cinema, 2008.

Television Appearances; Series:
Ted Morgan, *The Henderson Kids,* Ten Network, 1985.
Bartholomew "Bart" Jones, *Prime Time,* Nine Network, 1986.
Fame and Misfortune, 1986.
Warren Murphy, *Neighbours,* Ten Network, 1987.
Biz, *Close Ups,* ABC (Australia), 1996.
Rob, *The Secret Life of Us,* Ten Network, 2005.
Lewis, *Love My Way,* 2006–2007.

Television Appearances; Miniseries:
Lindsay, *All the Way,* 1988.
Matthew, *This Man … This Woman,* ABC (Australia), 1989.
Vince McCaffery, *Queen Kat, Carmel, & St. Jude,* 1998.
Alexander Hall, *Child Star: The Shirley Temple Story,* ABC, 2001.

Television Appearances; Movies:
Peter Donaldson, *Halifax f.p: My Lovely Girl,* 1995.
Doug Petersen, *Secret Men's Business,* 1999.
Dr. Larry Stewart, *Second Chance,* Ten Network, 2005.

Also appeared in *The Henderson Kids; Security.*

Television Appearances; Specials:
Sellebrity Sellection, 1999.

Television Appearances; Episodic:
"Slow Attack," *Special Squad,* 1984.
Luke Dawson, "A Little Knowledge: Parts 1 & 2," *A Country Practice,* Seven Network, 1985.
Brian, "Realms of Gold," *The Flying Doctors,* Nine Network, 1987.
Brad Harris, "Blues for Judy," *The Flying Doctors,* Nine Network, 1989.
Dean Forman, "Wild Card," *Police Rescue,* 1995.
Dale Banks, "High Country Justice," *Snowy River: The McGregor Saga* (also known as *Banjo Paterson's "The Man from Snowy River"*), Family Channel and Nine Network, 1995.
Ben, *G.P.,* 1996.
Brian O'Malley, "Unfinished Business," *Good Guys Bad Guys,* Nine Network, 1997.
Guest presenter, "The Prodigal Son: Jason Donovan," *Australian Story,* ABC (Australia), 2001.
Himself, "Faff," *Love Is a Four–Letter Word,* ABC (Australia), 2001.
Sko, "I–Yensche, You–Yensch," *Farscape,* Sci–Fi Channel, 2002.
Himself, Lewis, and Danny Clark, "On Thin Ice/The Memory Pill/Love Her Way," *60 Minutes,* CBS, 2007.

Also appeared in *The Flying Doctors.*

Television Work; Specials:
Executive producer, *Sellebrity Sellection,* 1999.

Stage Appearances:
Appeared in *Cosi,* Belvoir Street Theatre, Sydney, Australia; *The Selection,* Melbourne Theatre Company, Melbourne, Australia.

RECORDINGS

Videos:
INXS's "Full Moon Dirty Hearts," 1993.

MENDELSON, Lee 1933–

PERSONAL

Born March 24, 1933, in San Francisco, CA; son of Palmer C. (a grower) and Jeanette D. (maiden name, Wise) Mendelson; married Debbie; children: Glenn, Linda, Jason, Sean. *Education:* Stanford University, B.A., 1954.

Addresses: *Office*—Lee Mendelson Film Productions Inc., 330 Primrose Rd., Suite 310, Burlingame, CA 94010–4028.

Career: Producer, director, and writer. Worked for KPIX–TV, 1961–63; Lee Mendelson Film Productions, Inc., Los Angeles and Burlingame, CA, chairman of the board and president, 1963—. Stanford University, guest instructor in communications; KQED (educational station), member of board of directors. *Military service:* U.S. Air Force, 1954–57, served as navigator; became first lieutenant; received Commendation Ribbon.

Member: Writers Guild of America, Directors Guild of America.

Awards, Honors: Emmy Award (with Bill Melendez), outstanding children's program, and George Foster Peabody Broadcasting Award, Henry W. Grady School of Journalism and Mass Communications, University of Georgia, both 1965, for *A Charlie Brown Christmas;* Emmy Award nomination (with Melendez), outstanding children's program, 1966, for *It's the Great Pumpkin, Charlie Brown;* Emmy Award, achievement in cultural documentaries, 1967, for *John Steinbeck's "America and Americans";* Emmy Award nominations (with Melendez), achievement in children's programming, 1967, for *He's Your Dog, Charlie Brown* and *You're in Love, Charlie Brown;* Emmy Award nomination (with Walt

DeFaria and Sheldon Fay, Jr.), achievement in cultural documentary programming, 1969, for *Charlie Brown and Charles Schulz;* Emmy Award nomination (with Melendez), outstanding children's special, 1973, for *A Charlie Brown Thanksgiving;* Emmy Award nomination (with Melendez), outstanding children's special, 1974, for *Be My Valentine, Charlie Brown;* Emmy Award (with Warren Lockhart), outstanding children's informational special, 1975, for *Happy Anniversary, Charlie Brown;* Emmy Award (with Melendez), outstanding children's special, 1976, for *You're a Good Sport, Charlie Brown;* Emmy Award nomination (with Melendez), outstanding children's special, 1976, for *It's Arbor Day, Charlie Brown;* Emmy Award nomination (with Melendez), outstanding animated program, 1978, for *You're the Greatest, Charlie Brown;* Emmy Award nomination (with Melendez), outstanding animated program, 1979, for *She's a Good Skate, Charlie Brown;* Grammy Award nomination (with Jymn Magon), outstanding recording for children, 1979, for *You're in Love, Charlie Brown;* Emmy Award (with Melendez), outstanding animated program, 1980, for *Life Is a Circus, Charlie Brown;* Emmy Award nomination (with Melendez), outstanding animated program, 1980, for *It's Magic, Charlie Brown;* Emmy Award nominations (with Melendez), outstanding animated program, 1981, for *Charlie Brown Celebration* and *Someday You'll Find Her, Charlie Brown;* Emmy Award nominations (with Melendez), outstanding animated program, 1982, for *Here Comes Garfield, Is This Goodbye, Charlie Brown?,* and *What Have We Learned, Charlie Brown?;* Emmy Award (with Melendez and Jay Poyner), outstanding animated program, for *Garfield on the Town,* and Emmy Award nomination (with Melendez), outstanding animated program, 1983, for *It's Flashbeagle, Charlie Brown;* Peabody Award (with Melendez and CBS), 1983, for *What Have We Learned, Charlie Brown?;* Emmy Award nomination (with Melendez), outstanding animated program, 1984, for *Snoopy's Getting Married, Charlie Brown;* Grammy Award nomination (with Magon, Ed Bogas, and Desiree Goyette), outstanding recording for children, 1984, for *Flashbeagle;* Emmy Award nomination (with Melendez), outstanding animated program, 1985, for *The Charlie Brown and Snoopy Show;* Emmy Award (with others), outstanding animated program, 1986, for *Cathy;* Young Artist Award nomination, best family animation production, 1996, for *This Is America, Charlie Brown;* Emmy Award nomination (with Walter C. Miller), outstanding children's program, 2000, for *Here's to You, Charlie Brown: 50 Great Years;* Emmy Award nomination (with Jason Mendelson), outstanding children's program, 2002, for *The Making of "A Charlie Brown Christmas."*

CREDITS

Television Executive Producer; Animated Specials:

A Charlie Brown Christmas, CBS, 1965.
Be My Valentine, Charlie Brown, CBS, 1974.

She's a Good Skate, Charlie Brown, CBS, 1979.
Life Is a Circus, Charlie Brown (also known as *Life's a Circus, Charlie Brown*), CBS, 1980.
Someday You'll Find Her, Charlie Brown, CBS, 1981.
It's Your 20th Television Anniversary, Charlie Brown, CBS, 1985.
Cathy, CBS, 1986.
Cathy's Last Resort, CBS, 1988.
Snoopy: The Musical, CBS, 1988.
Cathy's Valentine, CBS, 1989.
Snoopy's Reunion (also known as *Toon Night*), CBS, 1991.
It's Christmas Time Again, Charlie Brown, CBS, 1992.
You're in the Super Bowl, Charlie Brown, 1993.

Television Producer (with Bill Melendez); Animated Specials:

Charlie Brown's All–Stars, CBS, 1966.
It's the Great Pumpkin, Charlie Brown, CBS, 1966.
You're in Love, Charlie Brown, CBS, 1967.
He's Your Dog, Charlie Brown, CBS, 1967.
It Was a Short Summer, Charlie Brown, CBS, 1969.
Play It Again, Charlie Brown, CBS, 1971.
You're Not Elected, Charlie Brown, CBS, 1972.
A Charlie Brown Thanksgiving, CBS, 1972.
There's No Time for Love, Charlie Brown, CBS, 1973.
It's the Easter Beagle, Charlie Brown, CBS, 1974.
It's a Mystery, Charlie Brown, CBS, 1974.
You're a Good Sport, Charlie Brown, CBS, 1975.
It's Arbor Day, Charlie Brown, CBS, 1976.
It's Your First Kiss, Charlie Brown, CBS, 1977.
What a Nightmare, Charlie Brown!, CBS, 1977.
You're the Greatest, Charlie Brown, CBS, 1979.
It's an Adventure, Charlie Brown, 1980.
Charlie Brown Celebration, CBS, 1981.
It's Magic, Charlie Brown, CBS, 1981.
Here Comes Garfield, CBS, 1982.
Is This Goodbye, Charlie Brown?, CBS, 1983.
What Have We Learned, Charlie Brown?, CBS, 1983.
Garfield on the Town, CBS, 1983.
It's Flashbeagle, Charlie Brown, CBS, 1984.
Snoopy's Getting Married, Charlie Brown, CBS, 1984.
You're a Good Man, CBS, 1985.
The Romance of Betty Boop, CBS, 1985.
Happy New Year, Charlie Brown!, CBS, 1985.
It's the Girl in the Red Truck, Charlie Brown (also known as *The Girl in the Red Truck*), CBS, 1988.
You Don't Look 40, Charlie Brown (also known as *Celebrating 40 Years in the Comics and 25 Years on Television*), CBS, 1990.

Television Executive Producer; Animated Specials:

It's the Pied Piper, Charlie Brown, 2000.
A Charlie Brown Valentine (also known as *Charlie Brown's Valentine's Day Special*), ABC, 2002.
I Want a Dog for Christmas, Charlie Brown, ABC, 2003.

Television Producer; Animated Specials:
Why, Charlie Brown, Why?, CBS, 1990.
It Was My Best Birthday Ever, Charlie Brown, 1997.
Lucy Must Be Traded, Charlie Brown, ABC, 2003.

Television Director; Animated Specials:
It's Your 20th Television Anniversary, Charlie Brown, CBS, 1985.
(With Bill Melendez) *You Don't Look 40, Charlie Brown* (also known as *Celebrating 40 Years in the Comics and 25 Years on Television*), CBS, 1990.
He's a Bully, Charlie Brown, ABC, 2006.

Television Executive Producer; Specials:
Travels with Charley, NBC, 1968.
The Fabulous Funnies, NBC, 1968.
(With Walt DeFaria) *Charlie Brown and Charles Schulz*, CBS, 1969.
Sunday Funnies, NBC, 1983.
Good Grief, Charlie Brown: A Tribute to Charles Schulz, 2000.
Here's to You, Charlie Brown: 50 Great Years, 2000.
The Making of "A Charlie Brown Christmas," ABC, 2001.

Television Producer; Specials:
John Steinbeck's "America and Americans," NBC, 1967.
The Rod McKuen Special, NBC, 1969.
(With Walt DeFaria) *The Wonderful World of Pizzazz*, NBC, 1969.
(With Warren L. Lockhart) *"You're a Good Man, Charlie Brown,"* Hallmark Hall of Fame, NBC, 1973.
(With Lockhart) *Happy Anniversary, Charlie Brown*, CBS, 1975.
(With Karen Crommie) *The Fantastic Funnies*, CBS, 1980.

Television Director; Specials:
The Fantastic Funnies, CBS, 1980.
The Making of "A Charlie Brown Christmas," ABC, 2001.

Television Executive Producer; Series:
Hot Dog, NBC, 1970–1971.
(With Lee Rich and Philip Capice) *Eight Is Enough*, ABC, 1977–81.
(With Robert Guenette and Chris Pye) *You Asked For It*, syndicated, 1981–83.
The Charlie Brown and Snoopy Show (animated) CBS, 1983—.
Mother Goose & Grimm (animated; also known as *Grimmy*), 1992.
Garfield and Friends (animated), CBS, 1994.

Television Producer; Series:
(With Bill Melendez) *The Charlie Brown and Snoopy Show*, CBS, 1983—.

Television Executive Producer; Miniseries:
This is America, Charlie Brown! (also known as *Charlie Brown and Snoopy's History of America*, *You're on Nickelodeon Charlie Brown*, and *Charlie Brown's History of the U.S.*), CBS, 1988.

Television Producer; Movies:
The Unexplained, 1970.

Television Appearances; Specials:
The Making of "A Charlie Brown Christmas," ABC, 2001.

Film Executive Producer:
Come to Your Senses, 1971.
It's the Pied Piper, Charlie Brown (animated), Paramount, 2000.

Film Producer (with Bill Melendez); Animated Features:
A Boy Named Charlie Brown (also known as *A Boy Called Charlie Brown*), National General, 1969.
Snoopy, Come Home, National General, 1972.
Race for Your Life, Charlie Brown, Paramount, 1977.
Bon Voyage, Charlie Brown (And Don't Come Back), Paramount, 1980.
It Was My Best Birthday Ever, Charlie Brown, 1997.

Film Director:
Wrinkles: In Need of Cuddles, 2006.

RECORDINGS

Albums:
(With Jymn Magon) *You're in Love, Charlie Brown*, Charlie Brown Records, 1979.
(With Magon, Ed Bogas, and Desiree Goyette) *Flashbeagle*, Charlie Brown Records, 1984.

WRITINGS

Television Specials:
(With others) *The Fabulous Funnies*, NBC, 1968.
(With Larry Markes and Charles Einstein) *The Wonderful World of Pizzazz*, NBC, 1969.
The Fantastic Funnies, CBS, 1980.
(With others) *Sunday Funnies*, NBC, 1983.
(With Bill Melendez) *You Don't Look 40, Charlie Brown* (also known as *Celebrating 40 Years in the Comics and 25 Years on Television*), CBS, 1990.
Here's to You, Charlie Brown: 50 Great Years, 2000.

Television Music; Specials:
(Special musical material) *The Fantastic Funnies*, CBS, 1980.

Television Miniseries:

(With others) *This is America, Charlie Brown!* (also known as *Charlie Brown and Snoopy's History of America* and *Charlie Brown's History of the U.S.*), CBS, 1988.

Screenplays:

Wrinkles: In Need of Cuddles, 1986.

Books:

Charlie Brown and Charles Schultz, World Publishing, 1970.

(With Bill Melendez) *A Charlie Brown Christmas,* HarperCollins, 2000.

MERCHANT, Paul
    See ELLISON, Harlan

MERLIN, Joanna 1931–

PERSONAL

Original name, Joann Ratner; born July 15, 1931, in Chicago, IL; daughter of Harry (a grocer) and Toni (maiden name, Merlin) Ratner; married Martin Lubner (an artist and teacher), December 17, 1950 (divorced, 1955); married David Dretzin (an attorney), March 1, 1964. *Education:* Attended University of California, Los Angeles, 1949–51, and American Shakespeare Festival Theatre and Academy, New York City, 1957–58; studied acting with Benjamin Zemach, 1947–50, Morris Carnovsky, 1948, Michael Chekhov, 1950–55, Fanny Bradshaw, 1957–58, Uta Hagen, 1961, and Tamara Daykarhanova, beginning 1962.

Career: Actress, casting director, and author.

Member: Actors' Equity Association, American Federation of Television and Radio Artists, Screen Actors Guild.

Awards, Honors: Artios Award, best casting for a dramatic feature film, Casting Society of America, 1988, for *The Last Emperor.*

CREDITS

Stage Appearances:
Too Many Marys, Chicago, IL, 1942.

Pilar, *Bullfight,* New Hampshire Playhouse, Hollywood, CA, 1956.

Athenian girl and understudy for Myrrhina, *Lysistrata,* Lenox Hill Playhouse, New York City, 1956.

Gina, *The Pigeon,* Temple Theatre, New York City, 1957.

Hamlet, American Shakespeare Festival, Stratford, CT, 1958.

A Midsummer Night's Dream, American Shakespeare Festival, 1958.

Emilia, *A Winter's Tale,* American Shakespeare Festival, 1958.

Isolde, *Tunnel of Love,* Rockland County Playhouse, NY, 1959.

Mrs. Frank, *The Diary of Anne Frank,* Rockland County Playhouse, 1959.

Helena, *Look Back in Anger,* Rockland County Playhouse, 1959.

Esther, *The Flowering Peach,* Rockland County Playhouse, 1959.

Rosetta, *No Trifling with Love,* St. Marks Playhouse, New York City, 1959.

Title role, *Major Barbara,* Murray Dodge Theatre, Princeton, NJ, 1960.

Catherine, *The Winslow Boy,* Tenthouse Theatre, Highland Park, IL, 1960.

Gina, *Right You Are,* McCarter Theatre, Princeton, NJ, 1960.

Anita di Speranza, *The Breaking Wall,* St. Marks Playhouse, 1960.

Silia Gala, *The Rules of the Game,* Gramercy Arts Theatre, New York City, 1960.

(Broadway debut) Gwendolyn, *Becket,* St. James Theatre, 1961, then Hudson Theatre, both New York City, 1961.

Martha Freud, *A Far Country,* Music Box Theatre, New York City, 1961.

Poppea Sabina, *The Emperor,* Maidman Playhouse, New York City, 1963 Stepdaughter, *Six Characters in Search of an Author,* Martinique Theatre, New York City, 1963.

Dawnthea, *Thistle in My Bed,* Gramercy Arts Theatre, 1963.

Geraldine, *Come to the Palace of Sin,* Theatre de Lys (now Lucille Lortel Theatre), New York City, 1963.

Rachel Apt, *The Wall,* Arena Stage, Washington, DC, 1964.

Tzeitl, *Fiddler on the Roof* (musical), Imperial Theatre, New York City, beginning 1964.

Gertrude Glass, *The Bird, the Bear and the Actress,* Eugene O'Neill Memorial Theatre, Waterford, CT, 1966.

Gloria, *Shelter* (musical), John Golden Theatre, New York City, 1973.

Standby for Sofya Alexandrovna, *Uncle Vanya,* Circle in the Square, Joseph E. Levine Theatre, New York City, 1973.

Title role, *Clytemnestra,* Cubiculo Theatre, New York City, 1976.

Mother, *Canadian Gothic* and Pat, *American Modern* (double–bill), Phoenix Theatre Company, Marymount Manhattan Theatre, New York City, 1976.

Anna Colonna, *The Grinding Machine,* American Place Theatre, New York City, 1978.

Leslie Nathan, *The Beach House,* Long Wharf Theatre, New Haven, CT, 1980 Zlatke, *The Survivor,* Morosco Theatre, New York City, 1981.

Liz, *Solomon's Child,* Little Theatre, New York City, 1982.

Deborah Brodsky, *The Yiddish Trojan Women,* American Jewish Theatre, New York City, 1996.

Also appeared as Madame Ranevskaya in *The Cherry Orchard* and as Mrs. Patrick Campbell in *Dear Liar,* both John Drew Theatre, Long Island, NY; appeared in *The Brooklyn Trojan Women.*

Major Tours:
Gwendolyn, *Becket,* U.S. Cities, 1960.
Martha Freud, *A Far Country,* 1961.

Film Appearances:
Jethro's daughter, *The Ten Commandments,* Paramount, 1956.

Myra, *The Key* (documentary), Campus, 1957.

The Pusher, United Artists, 1960.

Josie, *Weddings and Babies,* Twentieth Century–Fox, 1960.

Anatomy of a Disease (documentary), Vision Association, 1962.

Jake's landlady, *Hester Street,* 1975.

Nurse Pierce, *All That Jazz,* Twentieth Century–Fox, 1979.

Miss Berg, *Fame,* Metro–Goldwyn–Mayer, 1980.

Mrs. Sturgis, *Love Child,* Warner Bros., 1982.

Allan's mother, *Soup for One,* Warner Bros., 1982.

Mrs. Rosen, *Baby, It's You,* Paramount, 1983.

Schanberg's sister, *The Killing Fields,* Warner Bros., 1984.

Bag lady, *Prince of Darkness* (also known as *John Carpenter's "Prince of Darkness"*), Universal, 1987.

Margaret Arujo, *Mystic Pizza,* Samuel Goldwyn Films, 1988.

Estelle Ward, *Class Action,* Twentieth Century–Fox, 1991.

Loretta, *Mr. Wonderful,* Warner Bros., 1993.

Guendolina, *Two Bits* (also known as *A Day to Remember*), Miramax, 1995.

Doris, *MURDER and murder,* Zeitgeist Films, 1996.

Teresa Messinger, *City of Angels* (also known as *Stadt der engel*), Warner Bros., 1998.

Emily, *The Jimmy Show,* 2001.

Joan Kaufman, *The Invasion,* Warner Bros., 2007.

Television Appearances; Series:
Dr. Emily Cole, *Another World* (also known as *Another World: Bay City*), NBC, 1982.

Judge Brauer, *All My Children* (also known as *AMC*), ABC, 1997.

Judge Lena Petrovsky, a recurring role, *Law & Order: Special Victims Unit* (also known as *Law & Order: SVU* and *Special Victims Unit*), NBC, between 2000 and 2007.

Television Appearances; Movies:
Mrs. Farelli, *The Last Tenant,* ABC, 1978.

Nan Riley, *Nurse,* CBS, 1980.

Jacobo Timerman: Prisoner without a Name, Cell without a Number (also known as *Prisoner without a Name, Cell without a Number*), NBC, 1983.

Dr. Bromberg, *Murder in Black and White* (also known as *Janek: Cause of Death*), CBS, 1990.

Frances Silvano, *In a Child's Name,* CBS, 1991.

The Prosecutors, NBC, 1996.

Ann Benedetto, *Black and Blue,* CBS, 1999.

Cindy's mother, *Witness Protection,* HBO, 1999.

Sadie, *Just Another Story,* Showtime, 2003.

Television Appearances; Miniseries:
Rose Profaci, *Love, Honor & Obey: The Last Mafia Marriage,* NBC, 1993.

Television Appearances; Specials:
Inez Martin, "Starstruck," *ABC Afterschool Specials,* ABC, 1981.

Marian Rosenberg, "A Matter of Conscience" (also known as "Silent Witness"), *CBS Schoolbreak Specials,* CBS, 1989.

Dolly (some sources cite Emmy) Stieglitz, "A Marriage: Georgia O'Keeffe and Alfred Stieglitz" (also known as "An American Place, O'Keeffe and Stieglitz" and "The Eleventh Hour"), *American Playhouse,* PBS, 1991.

Flashback, HBO, 1997.

Television Appearances; Episodic:
Great Jewish Stories, WOR, 1957.

"The Oresteia," *Omnibus,* NBC, 1960.

Musya, "The Seven Who Were Hanged," *CBS Repertoire Workshop,* CBS, 1960.

Delgado's wife, *The Power and the Glory,* CBS, 1961.

Lucia Lopez, "It's War, Man" (premiere episode), *East Side/West Side,* CBS, 1962.

Gloria Werminski, "King Stanislaus and the Knights of the Round Table," *Naked City,* ABC, 1963.

Katy Martinez, "The Bagman," *The Defenders,* CBS, 1963.

Mariel/wealthy lady, "Gather Ye Acorns, *Amazing Stories* (also known as *Steven Spielberg's "Amazing Stories"*), 1986.

Ellen Kennedy, "Pump It Up," *L.A. Law,* NBC, 1991.

Carla Bowman, "Silence," *Law & Order,* NBC, 1992.

Carla Bowman, "Virus," *Law & Order,* NBC, 1992.

Gina Halbrook, *Baby Talk,* ABC, 1992.

Nadine Fleischman, "Birds of a Feather," *Northern Exposure,* CBS, 1993.

Deirdre Powell, "Virtue," *Law & Order,* NBC, 1994.

Deirdre Powell, "Atonement," *Law & Order,* NBC, 1996.

Carmella McNamara, "Going Platinum," *New York Undercover* (also known as *Uptown Undercover*), Fox, 1996.

Carmella McNamara, "Fade Out," *New York Undercover* (also known as *Uptown Undercover*), Fox, 1996.

Carmella McNamara, "Vendetta," *New York Undercover* (also known as *Uptown Undercover*), Fox, 1997.

Deirdre Powell, "Expert," *Law & Order,* NBC, 1998.

Jackie Ochs, "Too Jung to Die," *The Jury,* Fox, 2004.

Herself, "The Boy in the Bubble," *The American Experience,* PBS, 2006.

WRITINGS

Books:

Auditioning: An Actor–Friendly Guide, Vintage Books, 2001.

MESA, William
(Bill Mesa)

PERSONAL

Brother of John P. Mesa (a visual effects supervisor) and Tina Mesa (a visual effects producer); married, wife's name Penny A. (a visual effects production manager; separated); children: two, including Arthur.

Addresses: *Office*—Flash Film Works, 743 Seward Ave., Hollywood, CA 90038.

Career: Visual effects director, director, producer, and executive. Introvision International, Inc., worked as creative director, visual effects director, and visual effects supervisor; Flash Film Works, Hollywood, CA, founder, 1993, producer, director, and visual effects director, 1993—. Also worked as second unit photographer; worked on award–winning visual effects for commercials, including General Motors Onstar ads featuring Batman, 2001.

Awards, Honors: Emmy Award nomination (with graphic artist Tim Donahue), outstanding creative special achievement, 1982, for his contribution to *Inside the Third Reich;* Emmy Award (on behalf of Introvision International), outstanding special visual effects, 1985, for *The Hugga Bunch;* Academy Award (with others), technical achievement in film, 1988; Emmy Award (with special effects team), outstanding achievement in special visual effects, 1990, for *Miracle Landing;* Film Award nomination (with Roy Arbogast), best special effects, British Academy of Film and Television Arts, 1994, for train wreck sequence, *The Fugitive;* Visual Effects Society Award (with others), outstanding supporting visual effects in a motion picture, 2004, for *The Last Samurai.*

CREDITS

Film Visual Effects Director:

976–EVIL, New Line Cinema, 1988.

Fantasy sequence, *UHF* (also known as *The Vidiot from UHF*), Orion, 1989.

(As Bill Mesa) *The Karate Kid III,* Columbia, 1989.

Army of Darkness (also known as *Army of Darkness: The Ultimate Experience in Medieval Horror, Army of Darkness: Evil Dead 3, Bruce Campbell vs. Army of Darkness, Captain Supermarket, Evil Dead 3,* and *The Medieval Dead*), Universal, 1993.

(And producer and director) *Galaxis* (also known as *Galactic Force, Star Crystal,* and *Terminal Force*), Turner Home Video, 1995.

(And director and cinematographer) *The Darkening* (also known as *The Black Gate* and *Dark Encounters*), Inner Sky International, 1995.

Film Work; Other:

Visual effects producer, *The Waterboy,* Buena Vista, 1998.

Executive producer, *Colony 12,* Storm Entertainment, 2001.

Cinematographer, *Scene Stealer,* 2004.

Film Appearances:

Tropical Snow, PSM Entertainment, 1986.

Television Work; Movies:

Producer, creative director, and visual effects designer, *The Night They Saved Christmas,* ABC, 1984.

Director, coproducer, and visual effects producer, *DNA* (also known as *Genetic Code*), HBO, 1997.

RECORDINGS

Video Games:

Director, *Maximum Surge,* Cyber Cinema Interactive, 1996.

MESSNER, Johnny 1970–
(Johnny Mesner)

PERSONAL

Born April 11, 1970, in Syracuse, NY; father, in the U.S. Air Force. *Education:* Studied communications at San Diego State University.

Addresses: *Agent*—International Creative Management, 10250 Constellation Way, Ninth Floor, Los Angeles, CA 90067; (voice work) Special Artists Agency, 9465 Wilshire Blvd., Suite 890, Beverly Hills, CA 90212. *Manager*—McKeon Myones Management, 9100 Wilshire Blvd., Suite 350 West, Beverly Hills, CA 90212.

Career: Actor. Appeared in the short promotional film *DKNY Road Stories,* DKNY Jeans, 2004. Worked as a personal assistant to the film producer Andrew Stevens. Worked as a bartender.

CREDITS

Film Appearances:
Todd, *The Sweetest Thing* (also known as *Untitled Nancy Pimental Project, Allumeuses!, Bonjour l'amour, Edes kis semmiseg, La cosa mas dulce, La cosa piu dolce, Puicute bune, Radalla, Snygg, sexig & singel, Super suess und super sexy,* and *Tudo para ficar com ele*), Columbia/TriStar, 2002.
Vickers, *Operation Delta Force 4: Deep Fault* (also known as *Operation Zeus* and *Delta Force 4—Engano final*), Nu Image Films, 2002.
Kelly Lake, *Tears of the Sun* (also known as *Hostile Act, Hostile Rescue, Man of War, Rules of Engagement, L'ultima alba, Lagrimas del sol, Lagrimas do sol, Les larmes du soleil, Paeikese pisarad, Tears of the sun—auringon kyyneleet,* and *Traenen der Sonne*), Columbia/TriStar, 2003.
Nick, *Finding Home,* 2003, Castle Hill Productions, 2005.
Agent Grace, *Spartan* (also known as *Halastamatu*), Warner Bros., 2004.
Bill Johnson, *Anacondas: The Hunt for the Blood Orchid* (also known as *Anaconda 2, Anaconda 2: The Black Orchid, Anacondas 2: The Hunt for the Blood Orchid, Anaconda: Alla ricerca dell'orchidea maledetta, Anaconda 2—A cacada pela orquidea sangrenta, Anaconda 2: En busca de la orquidea sangrienta, Anacondas: A la poursuite de l'orchidee de sang, Anacondas: Die Jagd nach der Blut-Orchidee, Anacondas: La caceria por la orquidea sangrienta, Anakonda 2: To kynigi tis matomenis orhideas,* and *Anakondad: Jaht vereorhideedele*), Screen Gems, 2004.

Playboy, *Our Time Is Up* (short film), Station B, 2004.
Zevo, *The Whole Ten Yards* (also known as *The Whole Nine Yards 2, FBI: Protezione testimoni 2, Keine halben Sachen 2—Jetzt erst recht!, Koko potti 2, Le retour du nouveau voisin, Mas falsas apariencias, Meu vizinho mafioso 2, Mi vecino el asesino 2, Mon voisin le tueur 2,* and *Ti fod under*), Warner Bros., 2004.
Jason O'Malley, *One Last Thing ...,* Magnolia Pictures, 2005.
Mr. Jones, *Hostage* (also known as *Bajo amenaza, Gisslan, Hostage—Entfuehrt, Mdzevali, Otage, Otages de la peur, Panttivanki,* and *Refem*), Miramax, 2005.
Tommy "Tombs" Perello, *Running Scared* (also known as *Intre focuri, La peur au ventre, Traque,* and *Trexe grigora*), New Line Cinema, 2006.
Tony (the limousine driver), *Bottoms Up,* Sony Pictures Home Entertainment, 2006.
Bill, *The Poker Club,* Chesapeake Films/RAM Films, 2007.
Christopher Loren, *The Art of Travel,* Brenster Productions, 2007.
David Vaughn, *Believers,* Warner Bros., 2007.
Doug Wade, *Remarkable Power,* 2007.
Javon, *Loaded,* Arsenal Pictures, 2007.
Tito, *Caught on Tape,* Mindfire Entertainment, 2008.

Television Appearances; Series:
Rob Layne, *Guiding Light,* CBS, 1998.
Lance Baldwin, a recurring role, *The O.C.* (also known as *California Teens, Newport Beach, O.C., O.C., California, Orange County, A Narancsvidek, O.C.—Um estranho no paraiso,* and *Zycie na fali*), Fox, 2005.
Detective Jack Hale, *Killer Instinct* (also known as *Deviant Behavior, The Gate,* and *Pahuuden jaeljillae*), Fox, 2005–2006.

Television Appearances; Movies:
Officer Jenkins, *Dancing in September,* HBO, 2000.

Television Appearances; Episodic:
Cute podiatrist, "One Birthday at a Time," *Rude Awakening,* Showtime, 1999.
Kevin, "Lonely Hearts," *Angel* (also known as *Angel: The Series, Angel—Jaeger der Finsternis,* and *Skoteinos angelos*), The WB, 1999.
Ted Sallanger, "Cool Change," *CSI: Crime Scene Investigation* (also known as *C.S.I., CSI: Las Vegas, CSI: Weekends,* and *Les experts*), CBS, 2000.
Cash, "The One with Rachel's Date," *Friends* (also known as *Across the Hall, Friends Like Us, Insomnia Cafe,* and *Six of One*), NBC, 2001.
Handsome man, "Area 69," *Son of the Beach* (also known as *Babewatch, Hijo de la playa, Rantojen kunkku,* and *Strandloven*), fX Channel, 2001.

Jim, "Let Sleeping Dogs Lie," *Men, Women & Dogs* (also known as *Hombres, mujeres y perros*), The WB, 2001.

Detective Michael Foster, "Secrets and Lies," *Tarzan* (also known as *Tarzan and Jane*), The WB, 2003.

Himself, "The Family," *Miami Ink,* The Learning Channel, 2005.

While billed as Johnny Mesner, appeared in "Forget about Your Boss," an unaired episode of *Danny* (also known as *American Wreck* and *Community Center*), CBS.

Television Appearances; Pilots:

Detective Michael Foster, *Tarzan* (also known as *Tarzan and Jane*), The WB, 2003.

Connor McGreevy, *Ricochet,* Fox, c. 2004.

Detective Jack Hale, *Killer Instinct* (also known as *Deviant Behavior, The Gate,* and *Pahuuden jaeljillae*), Fox, 2005.

Gavin Lynch, *Judy's Got a Gun,* ABC, c. 2007.

Stage Appearances:

Appeared in regional theatre productions.

RECORDINGS

Videos:

Himself, *Journey to Safety: Making "Tears of the Sun"* (short), Columbia/TriStar Home Video, 2003.

Himself, *Running Scared: Through the Looking Glass* (short), Media 8 Entertainment, 2006.

Himself, *The Art of Travel: Production Webisodes* (short), Chop Shop Entertainment, 2007.

OTHER SOURCES

Periodicals:

Hollywood Reporter, October 6, 2004.
Movieline's Hollywood Life, March, 2004, p. 24.

MOON, Guy

PERSONAL

Full name, Guy Vernon Moon.

Addresses: *Agent*—Soundtrack Music Associates, 2229 Cloverfield Blvd., Santa Monica, CA 90405.

Career: Composer, orchestrator, song producer, and singer. Composed music for promotional purposes.

Awards, Honors: Daytime Emmy Award nomination (with others), outstanding music direction and composition, 1997, for *The Real Adventures of Johnny Quest;* Annie Award nomination (with Bill Burnett), outstanding individual achievement for music in an animated television production, International Animated Film Society, 1998, for "The Ugliest Weenie: Part 2," an episode of *Cow and Chicken;* Annie Award nomination, outstanding individual achievement for music score for an animated television production, 2001, BMI Cable awards, Broadcast Music Inc., 2002, 2003, and 2004, and Annie Award nomination (with others), outstanding individual achievement for music in an animated television production, 2003, all for *The Fairly OddParents;* Emmy Award nomination (with others), outstanding music and lyrics, 2002, for "I Wish Every Day Could Be Christmas," a song from "Christmas Every Day," an episode of *The Fairly OddParents;* BMI Cable Award, 2002, for *ChalkZone;* Emmy Award nominations, outstanding music and lyrics, both with others, both 2003, for "It's Great to Be A Guy" and "What Girls Love," both songs from "Love Struck," an episode of *The Fairly OddParents;* Emmy Award nomination (with others), outstanding music and lyrics, 2004, for "Wish Come True," a song from *The Fairly OddParents in: Abra Catastrophe!;* BMI Cable Award, 2004, for *Danny Phantom;* Golden Reel Award nomination (with others), best sound editing in animated television, Motion Picture Sound Editors, 2006, for "The Good Ol' Days/ Future Lost" an episode of *The Fairly OddParents.*

CREDITS

Television Work; Series:

Theme song performer, *Danny Phantom* (animated), Nickelodeon, 2004–2007.

Television Work; Movies:

Background vocalist, *The Fairly OddParents in: Abra Catastrophe!* (animated; also known as *Abra–Catastophe, The Fairly OddParents in Abra Catastrophe!,* and *The Fairly OddParents Movie*), Nickelodeon, 2003.

Backup singer, *The Fairly OddParents in School's Out! The Musical* (animated musical), Nickelodeon, 2004.

Television Work; Specials:

Theme song performer, *Danny Phantom: Reign Storm* (animated), Nickelodeon, 2005.

Theme song performer, *Danny Phantom: The Ultimate Enemy* (animated), Nickelodeon, 2005.

Television Work; Episodic:

Singer, "Boy Toy/Inspection Detection," *The Fairly Odd-Parents* (animated; also known as *The Fairly God-*

Parents, The Fairly Odd Parents, and *Oh My! God-Parents*), Nickelodeon, 2002.

Singer, "Shelf Life," *The Fairly OddParents* (animated; also known as *The Fairly GodParents, The Fairly Odd Parents,* and *Oh My! GodParents*), Nickelodeon, 2004.

Film Work:

Orchestrator, *Getting It Right* (also known as *Das Verflixte erste Mal, Jag har I allafall min vespa, Matkalla miehuuteen, Minha primeira transa,* and *Senza nessun timore*), Management Company Entertainment Group, 1989.

Orchestrator, *A Very Brady Sequel* (also known as *A volta de familia sol, la, si, do, Bradys faar tilloekning, Die Brady Family 2, El retorno de los Brady, Les nouvelles aventures de la famille Brady,* and *Les nouvelles aventures de la tribu Brady*), Paramount, 1996.

Song producer and performer of "Forbidden to Love," *Fight Club* (also known as *Borilacki klub, Clube de combate, Clube de luta, El club de la lucha, El club de la pelea, Harcosok klubja,* and *Klub boraca*), Twentieth Century–Fox, 1999.

Song producer of "Dance to the Music," and song producer and performer of "Jamal Dance Co. 1 & No. 2," *Black Knight* (also known as *Chevalier noir, El caballero negro, Enas ippotis mavra halia, Le chevalier Black, Locuras en la edad media, Loucuras na idade media,* and *Ritter Jamal—Eine schwarze Komoedie*), Twentieth Century–Fox, 2001.

Song producer, *Dr. Dolittle 2* (also known as *Doctor Dolittle 2, DR2, DR.2, Docteur Dolittle 2, Elaeintohtori 2,* and *Il Dottor Dolittle 2*), Twentieth Century–Fox, 2001.

Song producer of "The Ho Is Mine," *Brown Sugar* (also known as *I Used to Love Her, Seven Days, Codigo de amor,* and *No embalo do amor*), Twentieth Century–Fox, 2002.

Song producer of "Pine and Oats," *Minority Report* (also known as *Kueloenvelemeny, Minority Report—A nova lei, Minority report: Sentencia previa, Raport special, Rapport minoritaire, Sentencia previa,* and *Suvisni izvestaj*), Twentieth Century–Fox, 2002.

Some sources cite Moon as the editor of *The Runnin' Kind* (also known as *Una vita in fuga*), Metro–Goldwyn–Mayer/United Artists, 1989.

WRITINGS

Television Music; Series:

Baby Boom, NBC, 1988–89.

Theme music, *The Famous Teddy Z,* CBS, 1989–90.

(Including song "Curiosity") *Snoops,* CBS, 1989–90.

Elvis, ABC, 1990.

Man of the People, NBC, 1991.

Additional music, *The Heights,* Fox, 1992.

California Dreams (also known as *Dreams*), NBC, 1992–97.

Additional music, *2 Stupid Dogs* (animated; also known as *Dos perros tontos* and *Zwei dumme Hunde*), syndicated, 1993–95, also broadcast on the Cartoon Network.

The Real Adventures of Jonny Quest (animated), TBS, Cartoon Network, and syndicated, 1996–97.

Theme music, *The Bugs n' Daffy Show* (animated), The WB, 1996–97, Cartoon Network, 1996–2002.

(Including theme music) *Cow and Chicken* (animated; also known as *Cow and Chicken—Muh–Kuh und Chickie, Ku og kylling, La vaca y el pollito,* and *Vaca y pollo*), Cartoon Network, 1997–99.

Johnny Bravo (animated), Cartoon Network, 1997–2004.

Movie Stars, The WB, 1999–2000.

The Fairly OddParents (animated; also known as *The Fairly GodParents, The Fairly Odd Parents,* and *Oh My! GodParents*), Nickelodeon, 2001—.

(Including main title theme music) *Grim & Evil* (animated; also known as *The Grim Adventures of Billy & Mandy*), Cartoon Network, 2001—.

(Including theme song) *Danny Phantom* (animated), Nickelodeon, 2004–2007.

Tak & the Power of Juju (animated), Nickelodeon, beginning 2007.

Composer for other programs, including *Ghostbusters.*

Television Music; Miniseries:

Title song, *Glory! Glory!* (also known as *Gloria! Gloria!, Holy shit, de scorer kassen,* and *Taivaalliset huijarit*), CBS, 1989.

Television Music; Movies:

Additional music, *Pink Lightning* (also known as *Amor, traicao & cia, Cinque incredibili donne, El relampago rosa, Fem tjejer och en rosa cabriolet, 5 Tage noch, Traeume und kein Ende,* and *Vaaleanpunainen salama*), Fox, 1991.

Love and Curses … and All That Jazz (also known as *Verfluchte Liebe*), CBS, 1991.

Additional music, *Reason for Living: The Jill Ireland Story* (also known as *Life Lines, Uma razao para viver, Une vie brisee,* and *Usko elaemaeaen*), NBC, 1991.

Theme music, *Captive* (also known as *Capturada, Im Banne des Entfuehrers,* and *Porwanie*), ABC, 1991.

Out–of–Sync (also known as *Black Rebel*), Black Entertainment Television, 1995.

Come On, Get Happy: The Partridge Family Story (also known as *C'Mon, Get Happy: The Partridge Family Story, Come on, get happy—Die Partridge Familie, Den sanna historien om familjen Partridge,* and *Partridge familyn tarina*), ABC, 1999.

These Old Broads (also known as *Droles de retrou-vailles* and *Esa chicas fabulosas*), ABC, 2001.

The Way She Moves (also known as *When the Music Stops, Corazon latino, Kiihkeaet rytmit,* and *Ritmo da seducao*), VH1, 2001.

(Including song "Wish Come True") *The Fairly OddParents in: Abra Catastrophe!* (animated; also known as *Abra–Catastophe, The Fairly OddParents in Abra Catastrophe!,* and *The Fairly OddParents Movie*), Nickleodeon, 2003.

The Fairly OddParents in Channel Chasers (animated), Nickelodeon, 2004.

(Including theme song) *Danny Phantom: Reign Storm* (animated), Nickelodeon, 2005.

(Including theme song) *Danny Phantom: The Ultimate Enemy* (animated), Nickelodeon, 2005.

The Jimmy Timmy Power Hour 2: When Nerds Collide (animated), Nickelodeon, 2006.

Television Music; Specials:

Cartoon All–Stars to the Rescue (animated), multiple networks, 1990.

"Different Worlds: A Story of Interracial Love," *CBS Schoolbreak Special*, CBS, 1992.

The Steadfast Tin Soldier: An Animated Special from the "Happily Ever After: Fairy Tales for Every Child" Series (animated), HBO, 2000.

The Electric Piper (animated rock opera), Nickelodeon, 2003.

The Jimmy Timmy Power Hour (animated), Nickelodeon, 2004.

Television Music; Episodic:

Songs, "Jamal the Funny Frog/Thatta Boy/Hobart: The Weedkeeper," *Oh Yeah! Cartoons!* (animated), Nickelodeon, 1998.

Various songs, *The Fairly OddParents* (animated; also known as *The Fairly GodParents, The Fairly Odd Parents,* and *Oh My! GodParents*), Nickelodeon, beginning 2001.

Songs, "The Skrawl/Pie Day/Secret Passages," *Chalk-Zone* (animated), Nickelodeon, 2002.

Songs, "The Let's Twister Again/The Legend of the Golden Worms," *ChalkZone* (animated), Nickel-odeon, 2004.

"Sparkles & Gloom," *Random! Cartoons* (animated), Nickelodeon, 2007.

Also composer for other programs, including *Cousin Skeeter*, Nickelodeon; *Frank's Place*, CBS; *Jake and the Fatman*, CBS; and *Matlock*, NBC and ABC.

Television Composer; Pilots:

Theme song, *Brand New Life: The Honeymooners*, NBC, 1989.

Lost Cat (animated), Cartoon Network, 2000.

Uncle Gus in: For the Love of Monkeys (animated; also known as *Uncle Gus*), Cartoon Network, 2000.

Crash Nebula, Nickelodeon, 2004.

Film Composer:

Creepozoids (also known as *Creepzone* and *Creeps Zone*), Empire Pictures, 1987.

Sorority Babes in the Slimeball Bowl–o–Rama (also known as *The Imp*), Empire Pictures, 1988.

Deadly Weapon (also known as *A arma proibida*), Empire Pictures, 1989.

The Runnin' Kind (also known as *Una vita in fuga*), Metro–Goldwyn–Mayer/United Artists, 1989.

Additional music, *Second Sight* (also known as *A.A.A. Detective chiaroveggente offresi, Agencja "Trzecie Oko," Atlatnok, Detectives en folie, Henkimaail-man hommia, Mein Partner mit dem zweiten Blick, Olho vivo, Um detetive do outro mundo,* and *Un detective con mucha vista*), Warner Bros., 1989.

Diving In (also known as *Hoehenangst, Il campione di Beverly Hills, Suuri haaste,* and *Zanurzajac sie*), Skouras Pictures, 1990.

Additional music, *Family Prayers* (also known as *A Family Divided*), Arrow Releasing, 1993.

The Brady Bunch Movie (also known as *A familia sol, la, si, do, Bradyjeva klapa, Bradys klarar sivan!, Die Brady Family, La tribu de los Brady,* and *Rokkava Bradyn perhe*), Paramount, 1995.

Howling: New Moon Rising (also known as *Howling VII: Mystery Woman* and *Nuits de pleine lune*), New Line Home Video, 1995.

A Very Brady Sequel (also known as *A volta de familia sol, la, si, do, Bradys faar tilloekning, Die Brady Family 2, El retorno de los Brady, Les nouvelles aventures de la famille Brady,* and *Les nouvelles aventures de la tribu Brady*), Paramount, 1996.

The Rainbow Fish [and] *Dazzle the Dinosaur*, Sony Wonder, 1997.

Little Witch, Sony Wonder, 1999.

Additional music, *Soft Toilet Seats*, 1999, Phaedra Cinema, 2000.

Additional music (uncredited) and songwriter, *Black Knight* (also known as *Chevalier noir, El caballero negro, Enas ippotis mavra halia, Le chevalier Black, Locuras en la edad media, Loucuras na idade media,* and *Ritter Jamal—Eine schwarze Komo-edie*), Twentieth Century–Fox, 2001.

Mickey, Slugger Productions, 2004.

Some sources state that Moon composed music for *Mystic Pizza* (also known as *Pizza, pizza, Pizza, Pizza, 3 Girlfriends, 3 girlfriends, Amor e fantasia, Kaerester, Pizza Pizza—Ein Stuck vom Himmel, Pizzavarazs, Tre tjejer, Tres mulheres, tres amores,* and *Un pedazo de cielo*), Samuel Goldwyn, 1988.

Film Music; Songs:

"Cellar Dweller," "Creepozoids," and "Slave Girls from beyond Infinity," *The Occultist* (also known as

Maximum Threat and *Waldo Warren: Private Dick without a Brain*), Urban Classics, 1989.

"Rocky Road," *The Favor* (also known as *The Favour, The Indecent Favour, A letto con l'amico, Bana bir iyilik yap, El favor (The Favor), Ett farligt foerslag, The Favor—Hilfe, meine Frau ist verliebt!, Les fantasmes de Kathy, O favor,* and *Um favor indecente*), Orion, 1994.

"I Am Your Monster," *The Brady Bunch Movie* (also known as *A familia sol, la, si, do, Bradyjeva klapa, Bradys klarar sivan!, Die Brady Family, La tribu de los Brady,* and *Rokkava Bradyn perhe*), Paramount, 1995.

"Corn Festival," *Dudley Do–Right* (also known as *Allo la police, Allo, la police?, Dudley de la montana, Dudley es la policia montada, Peloton punatakki,* and *Policia desmontada*), Universal, 1999.

"Forbidden to Love," *Fight Club* (also known as *Borilacki klub, Clube de combate, Clube de luta, El club de la lucha, El club de la pelea, Harcosok klubja,* and *Klub boraca*), Twentieth Century–Fox, 1999.

"The Ho Is Mine," *Brown Sugar* (also known as *I Used to Love Her, Seven Days, Codigo de amor,* and *No embalo do amor*), Twentieth Century–Fox, 2002.

"Pine and Oats," *Minority Report* (also known as *Kueloenvelemeny, Minority Report—A nova lei, Minority report: Sentencia previa, Raport special, Rapport minoritaire, Sentencia previa,* and *Suvisni izvestaj*), Twentieth Century–Fox, 2002.

Videos:

Also composer for the series *The Beginner's Bible* and *See How They Grow,* both Sony Wonder; and for *Cave Kids* and *Timeless Tales from Hallmark,* both Hanna–Barbera.

MORGAN, Donald A.
(Don Morgan, Donald Morgan)

PERSONAL

Career: Cinematographer, lighting consultant, lighting designer, and lighting director.

Awards, Honors: Emmy Award nomination, outstanding lighting direction (electronic) for a comedy series, 1990, for *Bagdad Cafe;* Emmy Awards, outstanding individual achievement in lighting direction (electronic) for a comedy series, 1992, 1992, 1994, 1995, 1996, and outstanding lighting direction (electronic) for a comedy series, 1998, 1999, Emmy Award nomination, outstanding lighting direction (electronic) for a comedy series, 1997, all for *Home Improvement;* Emmy Award nomination, outstanding cinematography for a multi–camera series, 2003, for *Girlfriends.*

CREDITS

Film Work:

(As Donald Morgan) Aerial camera operator, *Bear Island* (also known as *Alistair MacLean's "Bear Island"*), Taft International Pictures, 1979.

Cinematographer, *Off the Wall,* Jensen Farley Pictures, 1983.

(As Don Morgan) Lighting technician for Tempe concert film crew, *U2: Rattle and Hum* (also known as *Rattle and Hum*), 1988.

Cinematographer, *Gas,* Twentieth Century–Fox Home Entertainment, 2004.

Cinematographer, *The Big Black Comedy Show, Vol. 2,* Twentieth Century–Fox Home Entertainment, 2005.

Co–executive producer and cinematographer, *Let Me Count the Ways* (short), 2006.

Television Cinematographer; Series:

227, NBC, 1985.
Pursuit of Happiness, ABC, 1987.
Marblehead Manson, NBC, 1987.
Sister Kate, NBC, 1989.
Home Improvement, ABC, 1991–92.
Rachel Gunn, R.N., Fox, 1992.
Where I Live, ABC, 1992–94.
Boy Meets World, ABC, 1993–94.
Thunder Alley, ABC, 1994.
Monty, Fox, 1994.
All–American Girl, ABC, 1994.
South Central, Fox, 1994.
The Parent 'Hood, The WB, 1994–95.
Martin, Fox, 1994–95.
The Preston Episodes, Fox, 1995.
Moesha, UPN, 1995–96.
Bedtime, Showtime, 1996.
Life ... and Stuff (also known as *Life & Stuff*), CBS, 1997.
Soul Man, ABC, 1997.
The Gregory Hines Show, CBS, 1997.
Built to Last, NBC, 1997.
Teen Angel, ABC, 1997.
Party Girl, Fox, 1997.
Linc's, Showtime, 1998.
Costello, Fox, 1998.
Oh Baby, Lifetime, 1998.
Damon, Fox, 1998.
Brother's Keeper, ABC, 1998.
Grown Ups, UPN, 1999–2000.
Daddio, NBC, 2000.
Girlfriends, UPN, then The CW, 2000–2007.
My Wife and Kids, ABC, 2001–2004.
Lost at Home, ABC, 2003.
The Tracy Morgan Show, NBC, 2003.
Nick Cannon Presents: Wild 'n Out, 2005.
Stacked, Fox, 2005.
(As Don Morgan) *The War at Home,* Fox, 2005–2007.
The Return of Jezebel James, 2007.

Television Lighting Director; Series:
The Facts of Life, NBC, 1979.
New Love American Style, ABC, 1985.
Mr. Belvedere, ABC, 1985.
The Last Chance Cafe, ABC, 1986.
The Robert Guillaume Show, ABC, 1989.
The Fresh Prince of Bel–Air, NBC, 1990–92.
Home Improvement, ABC, 1991–2000.
In the House, 1994–95.
Buddies, ABC, 1996.

Television Lighting Consultant; Series:
Homeroom, ABC, 1989.
Solo en America, Telemundo, 1998.
Viva Vegas!, Telemundo, 2000.
Reba, The WB then The CW, 2001.

Television Lighting Designer; Series:
The Golden Girls, NBC, 1985.

Television Lighting; Series:
The Golden Girls, NBC, 1985–86.

Television Work; Movies:
Cinematographer, *Saved by the Bell: Hawaiian Style,* NBC, 1992.

Television Cinematographer; Specials:
The Barbara Walters Special, ABC, 1993.
Martha Stewart's Christmas Dream, CBS, 2000.
The 38th NAACP Image Awards, Fox, 2007.

Television Lighting Director; Specials:
"Saved by the Bell" Graduation Special, NBC, 1993.

Television Lighting Designer; Specials:
(As Donald Morgan) *Count on Me,* PBS, 1993.
Merry Christmas, George Bailey, PBS, 1997.
The 32nd NAACP Image Awards, Fox, 2001.
NAACP Music Image Awards, The WB, 2001.
The 33rd Annual NAACP Image Awards, Fox, 2002.
The 34th Annual NAACP Image Awards, Fox, 2003.
The 2003 Essence Awards, Fox, 2003.
The 35th Annual NAACP Image Awards, Fox, 2004.
The 36th Annual NAACP Image Awards, Fox, 2005.
The 37th Annual NAACP Image Awards, Fox, 2006.
The 38th Annual NAACP Image Awards, Fox, 2007.

Television Cinematographer; Pilots:
Coming to America, CBS, 1989.
Home Improvement, ABC, 1991.
Clippers, CBS, 1991.
The Nanny, CBS, 1993.
Bouncers, UPN, 1997.
Brother's Keeper, 1998.

Reba, The WB, 2001.
The War at Home, Fox, 2005.

Television Photography; Pilots:
Hurricane Sam, CBS, 1990.

Television Lighting Designer; Pilots:
Changing Patterns, CBS, 1987.
Home Improvement, ABC, 1991.

Television Lighting Director; Pilots:
Cadets, ABC, 1988.
(As Don Morgan) *Somerset Gardens,* ABC, 1989.
(As Don Morgan) *In the House,* NBC, 1991.

Television Work; Episodic:
Lighting technician, "The Engagement," *The Golden Girls,* CBS, 1985.
Lighting director, "Dancing to the Max," *Saved by the Bell,* NBC, 1989.
Lighting director, "Screen's Woman," *Saved by the Bell,* NBC, 1989.
Lighting designer, "Nothing More Than Feelings," *Home Improvement,* ABC, 1991.
Lighting consultant, "The Honeymoon's Over or Now What?," *Reba,* The WB, 2001.
Cinematographer, "Where Everyone Knows My Name," *Girlfriends,* UPN, 2003.

RECORDINGS

Videos (as Cinematographer):
The Firm: Body Sculpting System—Cardio Sculpt, 2002.
Firm: Body Sculpting System—Body Sculpt, 2002.
(As Donald Morgan) *The Firm: Body Sculpting System—Abs Sculpt* (short), 2003.

MOYNIHAN, Christopher 1973–
(Chris Moynihan)

PERSONAL

Some sources cite original name as Christoph G. Moynihan; born April 1, 1973, in New York, NY.

Addresses: *Agent*—Lisa Harrison, Endeavor, 9601 Wilshire Blvd., Third Floor, Beverly Hills, CA 90210. *Manager*—Ron West, Thruline Entertainment, 9250 Wilshire Blvd., Suite 100, Beverly Hills, CA 90212.

Career: Actor and producer. Appeared in advertisements. Also worked as a pianist.

Awards, Honors: Seattle Film Critics Award, best music, 2003, and Florida Film Critics Circle Award, best ensemble cast, 2004, both with others, for *A Mighty Wind;* Gotham Award nomination (with others), best ensemble cast, IFP/New York, 2006, for *For Your Consideration.*

CREDITS

Film Appearances:
Rob, *Hiding in Walls* (short film), Out of Pocket Films, 2002.
Sean Halloran, *A Mighty Wind* (also known as *Untitled Christopher Guest Project*), Warner Bros., 2003.
Brian Chubb, *For Your Consideration,* Warner Independent Pictures, 2006.

Film Producer:
Last Night (short film), 2006.

Television Appearances; Series:
Jimmy, *The Hughleys,* UPN, between 1999 and 2001.
(As Chris Moynihan) Terry Fitzgerald, *The Fighting Fitzgeralds,* NBC, 2001.
Voice of Gary Newton, *Gary & Mike* (animated), UPN, 2001.
Chris, *According to Jim* (also known as *The Dad, Immer wieder Jim, Jim hat immer recht, Jims vaerld, La vita secondo Jim,* and *Perheen kalleudet*), ABC, between 2001 and 2003.
Jeff Clancy, *Coupling* (also known as *Coupling U.S.*), NBC, 2003.

Television Appearances; Episodic:
Guest, *The Test,* FX Channel, 2001.
Derek Roth, "Squid Pro Quo," *Boston Legal* (also known as *Fleet Street, The Practice: Fleet Street,* and *The Untitled Practice*), ABC, 2006.
Himself, *MTV News,* MTV, 2006.
Tom, "Game, Set ... Muuurder?," *Psych* (also known as *Psych—Dilis detektivek*), USA Network, 2007.

Also appeared as Deke in "A Girl's Gotta Come through in a Clutch," an unaired episode of *Jenny,* NBC.

Television Appearances; Pilots:
(As Chris Moynihan) Terry Fitzgerald, *The Fighting Fitzgeralds,* NBC, 2001.
Jack Stafford, *Foster Hall,* NBC, 2004.

Television Work; Pilots:
Executive producer, *Foster Hall,* NBC, 2004.

Producer for the pilot *The Institution,* Fox.

RECORDINGS

Albums; with Others; Soundtracks:
A Mighty Wind, Sony, 2003.
For Your Consideration, c. 2006.

WRITINGS

Teleplays; with Others; Pilots:
Foster Hall, NBC, 2004.

Wrote the pilot *The Institution,* Fox.

MULDOWNEY, Dominic 1952–

PERSONAL

Full name, Dominic John Muldowney; born July 19, 1952, in Southampton, Hampshire, England; son of William and Barbara Muldowney; married Diane Ellen Trevis, 1986; children: one daughter. *Education:* York University, B.A., B.Phil.

Addresses: *Agent*—Montana Artists Agency, 7715 Sunset Blvd., 3rd Floor, Los Angeles, CA 90046.

Career: Music director and composer. Southern Arts Association, composer in residence, 1974–76; National Theatre, London, England, beginning 1976.

Member: Performing Right Society.

CREDITS

Film Music Director:
The Ploughman's Lunch, Green Point/Samuel Goldwyn, 1983.
1984, Atlantic Releasing, 1984.

Film Music Conductor:
The Ploughman's Lunch, 1983.

WRITINGS

Film Scores:
The Ploughman's Lunch, Green Point/Samuel Goldwyn, 1983.
Loose Connections, Twentieth Century–Fox, 1983.
Betrayal, Twentieth Century–Fox, 1983.

Laughterhouse (also known as *Singleton's Pluck*), Green Point/Film Four International, 1984.
The Insurance Man, 1985.
Bloody Sunday (also known as *Sunday*), Paramount Classics, 2002.
Stella Street, Columbia TriStar, 2004.

Films Songs:
"Music of Oceania," "Oceania, 'Tis for Thee," "The Hiking Song," and "The Washerwoman's Song," *1984,* Atlantic Releasing, 1984.

Television Scores; Series:
Warrior Queens, Thames, 1978.

Television Scores; Miniseries:
Ginger Tree, BBC and PBS, 1989.
The Peacock Spring, BBC and PBS, 1996.
Sharpe's Challenge, ITV and BBC America, 2006.

Television Scores; Movies:
Baal, 1982.
The Burston Rebellion, BBC, 1985.
The Black Candle, 1991.
Growing Rich, 1992.
Sharpe's Rifles, PBS, 1993.
Sharpe's Eagle, PBS, 1993.
Sharpe's Company, PBS, 1994.
Sharpe's Enemy, PBS, 1994.
Sharpe's Honour, PBS, 1994.
Sharpe's Sword, 1995.
Sharpe's Mission, ITV, 1996.
Emma (also known as *Jane Austen's "Emma"*), Arts and Entertainment, 1996.
Eskimo Day (also known as *Interview Day*), BBC and PBS, 1996.
Sharpe's Revenge, 1997.
The Fix, BBC, 1997.
Copenhagen, PBS, 2002.
Holy Cross, BBC, 2003.

Television Scores; Specials:
The Merry Wives of Windsor (also known as *BBC Television Shakespeare: "The Merry Wives of Windsor"*), 1982.
"Tales from Hollywood," *American Playhouse,* PBS, 1992.
King Lear, BBC2 and PBS, 1998.
"Sharpe's Challenge": Behind the Scenes, ITV3, 2006.

Stage Scores:
Macbeth, National Theatre, London, 1994.
All My Sons, Cottesloe Theatre, Royal National Theatre, London, 2000.
Virginia in Brixton, Royal National Theatre, then John Golden Theatre, New York City, 2003.

The Talking Cure, Royal National Theatre, 2003.
The Night of the Iguana, Lyric Theatre, London, 2006.
A Moon for the Misbegotten, Brooks Atkinson Theatre, New York City, 2007.

Stage Incidental Music:
Wild Honey, Virginia Theatre, New York City, 1986–87.

Published Musical Compositions:
Piano Concerto, 1983.
The Duration of Exile, 1984.
Saxophone Concerto, 1985.
Sinfonietta, 1986.
Ars Subtilior, 1987.
Lonely Hearts, 1988.
Violin Concerto, 1989.
Three Pieces for Orchestra, 1990.
Percussion Concerto, 1991.
Oboe Concerto, 1992.

MUMY, Liliana 1994(?)–

PERSONAL

Full name, Liliana Berry Davis Mumy; born April 16, 1994 (some sources say 1995); daughter of Bill (an actor) and Eileen Mumy; sister of Seth Mumy (an actor). *Avocational Interests:* Softball, skateboarding, reading, swimming, dancing, and playing violin.

Addresses: *Agent*—Coast to Coast Talent, Inc., 3350 Barham Blvd., Los Angeles, CA 90068.

Career: Actress. Appeared in a television commercial for Six Flags theme parks.

Awards, Honors: Young Artist Award nomination, best performance in a television comedy or drama series—guest starring young actress age ten or under, 2003, for *My Wife and Kids;* Young Artist Award (with others), best young ensemble in a feature film, 2004, for *Cheaper by the Dozen;* Young Artist Award nomination (with others), best performance in a feature film—young ensemble cast, 2006, for *Cheaper by the Dozen 2.*

CREDITS

Film Appearances:
(English version) Voice of Nonoko, *Hohokekyo tonari no Yamada–kun* (animated; also known as *My Neighbors the Yamadas*), Walt Disney Company, 1999.

Lucy Miller, *The Santa Clause 2* (also known as *SC2, Santa Clause 2,* and *The Santa Clause 2: The Mrs. Clause*), Buena Vista, 2002.

Jessica Baker, *Cheaper by the Dozen,* Twentieth Century–Fox, 2003.

Voice of Myrtle Edmonds and others, *Stitch! The Movie* (animated; also known as *Disney's "Stitch! The Movie"*), Buena Vista Home Video, 2003.

Additional voices, *Mulan II* (animated), Buena Vista Home Video, 2004.

(English version) Voice of Madge, *Hauru no ugoku shiro* (animated; also known as *Howl's Moving Castle*), Buena Vista, 2004.

Voice of Amy, *Holly Hobbie and Friends: Surprise Party* (animated short), Paramount, 2005.

Voice of Myrtle, *Lilo & Stitch 2: Stitch Has a Glitch* (animated), Buena Vista Home Video, 2005.

Voice of Sister, *The Happy Elf* (animated), Anchor Bay Entertainment, 2005.

Jessica Baker, *Cheaper by the Dozen 2,* Twentieth Century–Fox, 2005.

Voice of Chick, *Barnyard* (animated; also known as *Barnyard: The Original Party Animals* and *Der tierisch verruckte Bauernhof*), Paramount, 2006.

Lucy Miller, *The Santa Clause 3: The Escape Clause,* Buena Vista, 2006.

Voice of Amy Morris, *Holly Hobbie and Friends: Christmas Wishes* (animated short), Paramount, 2006.

Voice of Amy Morris, *Holly Hobbie and Friends: Secret Adventures* (animated short), American Greetings Corp., 2007.

Television Appearances; Series:

Rachael, *My Wife and Kids,* ABC, 2002–2004.

Voice of Myrtle Edmonds, *Lilo & Stitch: The Series* (animated), Disney Channel, 2003–2004.

Voice of Twinkle, *Higglytown Heroes* (animated), Disney Channel, 2004–2005.

Voice of Human Kimberly, *Catscratch* (animated), Nickelodeon, 2005–2006.

Television Appearances; Movies:

Additional voices, *Leroy & Stitch* (animated), Disney Channel, 2006.

Television Appearances; Episodic:

Samantha Tanner, "My Old Lady," *Scrubs,* NBC, 2001.

Donna at age seven, "Class Picture," *That '70s Show,* Fox, 2002.

Annie, "Discharged," *Strong Medicine,* Lifetime, 2002.

Audrey Fremont, "It's Still a Good Life," *The Twilight Zone,* UPN, 2003.

Lena, "After Dark," *Crossing Jordan,* NBC, 2004.

Herself, "Child Stars II: Growing Up Hollywood," *Biography,* Arts and Entertainment, 2005.

Voice of Larry Simpson, "Bananas for Golf/Fruit Ball Heroes," *Coconut Fred's Fruit Salad Island!* (animated), 2005.

Voice of Olivia, "Fu and Tell," *American Dragon: Jake Long* (animated), Disney Channel, 2005.

Voice of Olivia Meers, "Switcheroo," *American Dragon: Jake Long* (animated), Disney Channel, 2007.

Help Me Help You, ABC, 2007.

RECORDINGS

Video Games:

Voice, *Stitch Experiment 626* (also known as *Disney's "Stitch: Experiment 626"*), 2002.

MYERS, Ruth 1940–

PERSONAL

Born 1940, in Manchester, Lancashire, England; married Richard Macdonald (a production designer; marriage ended). *Education:* Attended St. Martin's College of Art, London, and English Stage Company of the Royal Court Theatre, London.

Addresses: *Agent*—Marsh, Best, and Associates, 9150 Wilshire Blvd., Suite 220, Beverly Hills, CA 90212.

Career: Costume designer. Royal Court Theatre, London, wardrobe mistress, then designer, through 1963, then 1965–?; worked for a year with a repertory theatre in Oxford, c. 1964–65.

Awards, Honors: Film Award nomination, best costume design, British Academy of Film and Television Arts, 1970, for *Isadora;* Saturn Award nomination, best costumes, Academy of Science Fiction, Fantasy and Horror Films, 1984, for *Something Wicked This Way Comes;* CableACE Award, costume design, National Cable Television Association, 1988, for *Baja Oklahoma;* Academy Award nomination, best costume design, 1992, for *The Addams Family;* Academy Award nomination, best costume design, 1997, for *Emma;* Film Award nomination, best costume design, British Academy of Film and Televison Arts, 1998, for *L.A. Confidential;* Emmy Award (with others), outstanding costumes for a series, Costume Designers Guild Award (with Terry Dresbach), excellence in costume design for television—period/fantasy, 2004, both for *Carnivale.*

CREDITS

Film Costume Designer:

Work Is a 4–Letter Word (also known as *Work is a Four Letter Word*), 1967.

Smashing Time, 1967.

Isadora (also known as *The Loves of Isadora*), 1968.
Three into Two Won't Go, 1969.
The Virgin Soldiers, 1969.
A Nice Girl Like Me, 1969.
All the Right Noises, 1969.
The Twelve Chairs, 1970.
Romance of a Horsethief (also known as *Le roman d'un voleur de chevaux*), 1971.
The Ruling Class, 1972.
Cari genitori (also known as *Dear Parents*), 1972.
That'll Be the Day, 1973.
A Touch of Class, 1973.
Ghost in the Noonday Sun, 1973.
Stardust, 1974.
Little Malcolm (also known as *Little Malcolm and His Struggle Against the Eunuchs*), 1974.
The Romantic Englishwoman (also known as *Une anglaise romantique*), 1975.
Galileo (also known as *Galileo Galilei*), 1975.
The Adventures of Sherlock Holmes Smarter Brother (also known as *Sherlock Holmes "Smarter Brother"*), 1975.
The World's Greatest Lover, 1977.
Silver Bears (also known as *Fool's Gold*), 1977.
Magic, 1978.
... And Justice for All, 1979.
The Main Event, 1979.
It's My Turn (also known as *A Perfect Circle*), 1980.
In God We Tru$t (also known as *Gimme That Prime Time Religion*), 1980.
The Competition, 1980.
Altered States, 1980.
(American segment) *Sunday Lovers*, 1980.
First Monday in October, 1981.
Cannery Row (also known as *John Steinbeck's "Cannery Row"*), 1982.
Something Wicked This Way Comes, 1983.
The Woman in Red, 1984.
Teachers, 1984.
Electric Dreams, 1984.
Plenty, 1984.
Haunted Honeymoon, 1986.
The Accidental Tourist, 1988.
Vibes (also known as *Vibes: The Secret of the Golden Pyramids*), 1988.
Blood Red, 1988.
Blaze, 1989.
Bert Rigby, You're a Fool, 1989.
The Russia House, 1990.
The Marrying Man (also known as *Too Hot to Handle*), Buena Vista, 1991.
Another You, Columbia TriStar, 1991.
The Addams Family, Paramount, 1991.
Mr. Saturday Night, Columbia, 1992.
The Firm, Paramount, 1993.
Pontiac Moon, Paramount, 1994.
I.Q., Paramount, 1994.
Clean Slate, Metro–Goldwyn–Mayer, 1994.

How to Make an American Quilt, Universal, 1995.
Emma, Miramax, 1996.
Bogus, Warner Bros., 1996.
L.A. Confidential, Warner Bros., 1997.
A Thousand Acres, 1997.
Deep Impact, Paramount, 1998.
Cradle Will Rock, Buena Vista, 1999.
The Next Best Thing, Buena Vista, 2000.
Company Man, Paramount, 2000.
Center Stage (also known as *Centre Stage*), Sony Pictures Classics, 2000.
Proof of Life, Warner Bros., 2000.
The Four Feathers, Paramount, 2001.
Iris, 2001.
Nicholas Nickleby, United Artists, 2002.
Ella Enchanted, Miramax, 2004.
Connie and Carla, Universal, 2004.
Beyond the Sea, Lions Gate Films, 2004.
Half Light, First Look International, 2006.
Monster House (animated; also known as *Neighbourhood Crimes & Peepers*), Columbia, 2006.
Infamous, Warner Independent Pictures, 2006.
The Painted Veil, Warner Independent Pictures, 2006.
The Golden Compass (also known as *His Dark Materials: Northern Lights*), New Line Cinema, 2007.

Film Work; Other:
Wardrobe, *Isadora* (also known as *The Loves of Isadora*), 1968.
Costume consultant, *That'll Be the Day,* 1973.
Wardrobe designer, *First Monday in October,* 1981.

Film Appearances:
Herself, *Creating a Classic: The Making of "Nicholas Nickleby"* (documentary short), Metro–Goldwyn–Mayer Home Entertainment, 2003.
Herself, *Backstage with Connie and Carla* (documentary short), MCA/Universal Home Video, 2004.
Herself, *Dressing in Drag: "Connie and Carla"* (documentary short), Universal Studios Home Video, 2004.

Television Costume Designer; Movies:
Dracula (also known as *Bram Stoker's "Dracula"*), CBS, 1973.
Baja Oklahoma, HBO, 1988.

Television Costume Designer; Pilots:
"Milfay," *Carnivale,* HBO, 2003.
Big Love, HBO, 2006.

Television Appearances; Specials:
The Making of "The Addams Family," 1991.
The Magical World of "Ella Enchanted," 2004.
"Ella Enchanted": A Red Carpet Premiere Special, 2004.

N

NAIR, Mira 1957–

PERSONAL

Born October 15, 1957, in Bhubaneshwar, Orissa, India; daughter of a civil servant; married Mitch Epstein (a photographer; divorced); married Mahmood Mamdani (a political scientist); children: (second marriage) Zohran. *Education:* Attended Delhi University, 1975–76, and Harvard University, 1976–79.

Addresses: *Office*—Mirabai Films, 5 East 16th St., 12th Floor, New York, NY 10003. *Agent*—Creative Artists Agency, 2000 Avenue of the Stars, Los Angeles, CA 90067; Cinetic, 555 West 25th St., 4th Floor, New York, NY 10001.

Career: Director, producer, and screenwriter. Mirabai Films, principal. Columbia University, New York, NY, educator, 2002.

Awards, Honors: Best Documentary Prize, American Film Festival, Best Documentary Prize, Global Village Film Festival, 1985, both for *India Cabaret;* Golden Camera Award and Audience Award, Cannes Film Festival, Silver Lotus Award, best regional film—Hindi, National Film Awards, India, Prize of the Ecumenical Jury, Most Popular Film Award, and Jury Prize, Montreal World Film Festival, 1988, Academy Award nomination, best foreign film, Cesar Award nomination, best foreign film, Academie des Arts et Techniques du Cinema, 1989, Lillian Gish Award, excellence in feature film, Los Angeles Women in Film Festival, Filmfare Awards, best director and best film, and Film Award nomination, best film not in the English language, British Academy of Film and Television Arts, 1990, all for *Salaam Bombay!;* New Generation Award, Los Angeles Film Critics Association, 1988; Golden

Osella Award (with Sooni Taraporevala) and Golden Lion Award nomination, Venice Film Festival, Critics Special Award, Sao Paulo International Film Festival, 1991, Silver Ribbon Award, best director—foreign film, Italian National Syndicate of Film Journalists, 1992, Independent Spirit Award nomination (with Michael Nozik), best feature, Independent Spirit Awards, 1993, all for *Mississippi Masala;* Golden Seashell nomination, San Sebastian International Film Festival, 1996, for *Kama Sutra: A Tale of Love;* Muse Award, outstanding vision and achievement, New York Women in Film and Television, 1997; Vision Award, Boston Film Video Association, 1997; Rosebud Award nomination, best film, Verzaubert—International Gay and Lesbian Film Festival, 1999, for *My Own Country;* Special Mention Award (documentary and essay), Biarritz International Festival of Audiovisual Programming, 2000, for *The Laughing Club of India;* Audience Award, Canberra International Film Festival, Screen International Award nomination, European Film Awards, Golden Lion and Laterna Mgaica Prize, Venice Film Festival, 2001, Film Award nomination (with Caroline Bacon), best film not in the English language, British Academy of Film and Television Arts, Popular Award, special award for international cinema, Zee Cine Awards, 2002, all for *Monsoon Wedding;* UNESCO Award (with others), Venice Film Festival, 2002, Cesar Award nomination (with others), best European Union Film, for *11'09"01— September 11;* Golden Star Award nomination, Marrakech International Film Festival, 2003, for *Hysterical Blindness;* Faith Hubley Web of Life Award, High Falls Film Festival, 2004; Golden Lion Award nomination, Venice Film Festival, 2004, for *Vanity Fair.*

CREDITS

Film Work:

Director, *Jama Masjid Street Journal* (documentary), Mirabai, 1979.

Director, *So Far From India* (documentary), Mirabai, 1982.

Director, *Women and Development* (documentary), 1984.
Director, *India Cabaret* (documentary), Mirabai, 1985.
Director, *Children of a Desired Sex* (documentary), Mirabai, 1987.
Director, *Chull Bumbai Chull,* Mirabai, 1988.
Director and producer, *Salaam Bombay!,* Cinecom, 1988.
Director and (with Michael Nozik) producer, *Mississippi Masala,* Samuel Goldwyn, 1992.
Director and producer, *The Day the Mercedes Became a Hat,* 1993.
Director, *The Perez Family,* Samuel Goldwyn, 1995.
Director and producer, *Kama Sutra: A Tale of Love,* Trimark Pictures, 1996.
Director and producer, *The Laughing Club of India* (documentary), Mirabai, 1999.
Director, *Monsoon Wedding* (also known as *Le mariage des moussons* and *Monsoon wedding—matrimonio indiano*), Mirabai, 2001.
Director, "India," *11'09"01—September 11* (also known as *11 septembre 2001, 11'09"01: Onze minutes, neuf secondes, un cadre, Eleven Minutes, Nine Seconds, One Image: September 11,* and *September 11*), Empire Pictures, 2002.
Director, *Vanity Fair,* Focus Features, 2004.
Producer, *Still, the Children Are Here* (documentary), First Run/Icarus Films, 2004.
Director and producer, *The Namesake,* Fox Searchlight, 2006.
Director and executive producer, *Migration* (short), 2007.

Film Appearances:
Gossip number one, *Mississippi Masala,* Samuel Goldwyn, 1992.
Woman buying flowers, *The Perez Family,* Samuel Goldwyn, 1995.
Mira, *Bollywood Calling,* 2001.
(Uncredited) Voice of Mrs. Mehta, *Monsoon Wedding* (also known as *Le mariage des moussons* and *Monsoon wedding—matrimonio indiano*), 2001.
Herself, *Bollywood Remixed—Das indische kino erobert den westen* (documentary), 2004.
Herself, *Five Directors on "The Battle of Algiers"* (documentary short), Criterion Collection, 2004.

Television Work; Movies:
Director, *Children of a Desired Sex,* 1987.
Director and producer, *My Own Country,* Showtime, 1998.
Director, *Hysterical Blindness,* 2002.

Television Work; Specials:
Producer, *India Cabaret,* PBS, 1986.

Television Appearances; Movies:
Saryu Joshi, *My Own Country,* Showtime, 1998.

Television Appearances; Specials:
Women on Top: Hollywood and Power, AMC, 2003.
Presenter, *IFP Gotham Awards 2005,* 2005.
Wanderlust, Independent Film Channel, 2006.
Lights! Action! Music!, 2007.

Television Appearances; Episodic:
Drinks with LX, 2007.

WRITINGS

Screenplays:
(With Sooni Taraporevala) *Salaam Bombay!,* Cinecom, 1988.
Mississippi Masala, Samuel Goldwyn, 1992.
The Day the Mercedes Became a Hat, 1993.
Kama Sutra: A Tale of Love, Trimark Pictures, 1996.

Film Stories:
Salaam Bombay!, Cinecom, 1988.
Kama Sutra: A Tale of Love, Trimark Pictures, 1996.

OTHER SOURCES

Books:
Notable Asian Americans, Gale Research, 1995.
Women Filmmakers & Their Films, St. James Press, 1998.
Newsmakers, Issue 4, Gale Group, 2007.

Periodicals:
Cineaste, winter, 2004, p. 10.
Entertainment Weekly, March 21, 1997, p. 55; December 20, 2002, p. 38.
Interview, September, 1988, p. 114.
New Yorker, December 9, 2002, p. 100.
Time, September 6, 2004, p. 86.
UNESCO Courier, November, 1998, p. 46.

NAUGHTON, David 1951–

PERSONAL

Full name, David Walsh Naughton; born February 13, 1951, in Hartford, CT; son of Joseph (a teacher) and Rosemary (a teacher; maiden name, Walsh) Naughton; brother of James Naughton (an actor); uncle of Greg Naughton (an actor) and Keira Naughton (an actress); married Denise Stephen, 1977 (divorced); married Deborah Dutton, April 6, 1985 (divorced); married Seann Sara Sella, August 1, 2007; children: (second marriage) two. *Education:* University of Pennsylvania, B.A., English literature; studied acting at London Academy of Music and Dramatic Arts.

Addresses: *Agent*—House of Representatives, 400 South Beverly Dr., Suite 101, Beverly Hills, CA 90212. *Manager*—The Marshak/Zachary Company, 8840 Wilshire Blvd., 1st Floor, Beverly Hills, CA 90211.

Career: Actor and singer. Appeared as a singer and dancer in the "Be a Pepper" Dr. Pepper soft drink commercials, late 1970s and early 1980s; appeared in a television commercial for Mercedes Benz automobiles, 1997.

Awards, Honors: Gold record, Recording Industry Association of America, 1979, for "Makin' It."

CREDITS

Film Appearances:

Jerry Lansing, *Separate Ways,* Crown International, 1979.

Adam, *Midnight Madness,* Buena Vista, 1980.

David Kessler, *An American Werewolf in London* (also known as *American Werewolf*), Universal, 1981.

Dan O'Callahan, *Hot Dog … The Movie,* Metro–Goldwyn–Mayer/United Artists, 1984.

Barry Denver, *Not for Publication,* Thorn–EMI, 1984.

(In archival footage) *Terror in the Aisles* (also known as *Time for Terror*), 1984.

Richard Moore, *Separate Vacations,* RSL, 1986.

Bill, *The Boy in Blue* (also known as *La race des champions*), Twentieth Century–Fox, 1986.

Detective Vince McCarthy, *Kidnapped,* Fries Entertainment, 1987.

Mauro, *Ti presento un'amica* (also known as *Private Affairs* and *Quite by Chance*), Medusa, 1987.

She's Having a Baby, 1988.

Zach, *Desert Steel,* 1989.

Phillip, *Overexposed,* Concorde, 1990.

Jason McCree, *The Sleeping Car,* Triax, 1990.

Detective Clifford Dunn, *Steel and Lace,* Fries Home Video, 1990.

Dick Cutler, *Amityville: A New Generation* (also known as *Amityville 1993: The Image of Evil* and *Amityville 6*), Republic, 1993.

Phillip Marcus, *Wild Cactus,* Imperial Entertainment, 1993.

Mr. Ladd, *Beanstalk,* Paramount, 1994.

Caribbean Kill, 1994.

Detective Kobek, *Mirror Mirror III: The Voyeur,* Miranda Entertainment, 1995.

Martin Cassera, *Ice Cream Man,* A–Pix Entertainment, 1995.

Professor Byrd, *The Adventures of Black Feather,* 1995.

Joe Johnson, *Urban Safari,* Warwick Pictures, 1996.

Deadlock, 1998.

Voice of Buzz, *Little Insects* (animated), Crystal Sky Communications/MPA, 2000.

Empty man, *A Crack in the Floor,* Norris Johnson Productions, 2000.

Dr. Stephen North, *Flying Virus* (also known as *Killer Buzz* and *Abelhas–Ataque Mortal*), American Cinema International, 2001.

(English version) Voice, *Wonderful Days* (also known as *Sky Blue*), Engdame Entertainment, 2003.

Sheriff Joe Ruben, *Big Bad Wolf,* Screen Media Ventures, 2006.

Shopkeeper, *Hallows Point,* 2007.

Harry, *Brutal Massacre: A Comedy,* 2007.

Television Appearances; Series:

Billy Manucci, *Makin' It,* ABC, 1979.

Private Tony Baker, *At Ease,* ABC, 1983.

Jack Kincaid, *My Sister Sam* (also known as *Taking the Town*), CBS, 1986–87.

Television Appearances; Movies:

The Other Side of Victory, 1976.

David Balsiger, *I, Desire* (also known as *Desire, the Vampire*), ABC, 1982.

Micky Ritter, *Getting Physical,* CBS, 1984.

Ted Beckman, *Goddess of Love,* NBC, 1988.

Pete, "The Gas Station," *John Carpenter Presents "Body Bags"* (also known as *Body Bags*), Showtime, 1993.

Art Haber, *Chance of a Lifetime,* CBS, 1998.

Out of the Wilderness, Showtime, 1998.

Steven, *Mystery Woman: Sing Me a Murder,* 2005.

Television Appearances; Pilots:

Chris, *Belles of Bleecker Street,* ABC, 1991.

Television Appearances; Specials:

The Making of "An American Werewolf in London," 1981.

Brad, *Sex, Shock and Censorship in the 90s* (also known as *Basic Values: Sex, Shock & Censorship in the 90's*), Showtime, 1993.

I Love the 80's 3–D, VH1, 2005.

Television Appearances; Episodic:

Dr. Stole, "The Surgeon," *Planet of the Apes,* CBS, 1974.

Guest host, *Fridays,* 1981.

Just Men!, 1983.

"The Fountain of Youth/Bad Luck Cabin/Uncle Daddy," *The Love Boat,* ABC, 1983.

The $10,000 Pyramid, 1986.

Panelist, *The New Hollywood Squares,* 1987.

John Sellick, "Secret Service," *The Twilight Zone* (also known as *The New Twilight Zone*), 1988.

Ken Parrish, "Wearing of the Green," *Murder, She Wrote,* CBS, 1988.

LaManna, "Honest Abe," *MacGyver,* ABC, 1991.

Dick, "The Red Dot," *Seinfeld,* NBC, 1991.

Tom Larson, "My Four Husbands," *Diagnosis Murder,* CBS, 1994.

Lou Chandler, "Run, Billy, Run," *Melrose Place,* Fox, 1996.

Michael Russell, "Birthmarks," *Touched by an Angel,* CBS, 1996.

Norm Kipper, "Movin' Up," *Bailey Kipper's P.O.V.* (also known as *Bailey Kipper's Point of View*), 1996.

Norm Kipper, "Trust Me," *Bailey Kipper's P.O.V.* (also known as *Bailey Kipper's Point of View*), 1996.

Andy, "Bachelor Party," *Cybill,* CBS, 1997.

Andy, "Little Bo Peep," *Cybill,* CBS, 1997.

"K–Val," *V.I.P.* (also known as *V.I.P.—Die Bodyguards*), syndicated, 1999.

Paul Dinsman, "It's Never Too Late," *Chicken Soup for the Soul,* PAX, 1999.

"Signature Songs," *VH–1 Where Are They Now?,* VH1, 1999.

Detective Grady, "JAG TV," *JAG,* CBS, 2000.

Detective Grady, "Past Tense," *JAG,* CBS, 2001.

Ben Stevens, "Thy Will Be Done," *ER,* NBC, 2001.

Ames, "Tracy," *Kate Brasher,* CBS, 2001.

The Big Breakfast, Channel 4, 2002.

Voice of The Streak, "Legends: Parts 1 & 2," *Justice League* (animated; also known as *JL* and *Justice League Unlimited*), Cartoon Network, 2002.

District Attorney Jenetta, "Cruel & Unusual," *Crossing Jordan,* NBC, 2003.

Voice of orchestra conductor, "Say What?/Higgly Harmonies," *Higglytown Heroes* (animated), Disney Channel, 2005.

Stage Appearances:

(Professional debut) Player queen, Francisco, Osric, Fortinbras, and various soldiers in *Hamlet,* New York Shakespeare Festival, New York City, 1975.

Understudy Young Charlie, *Da,* Morosco Theatre, New York City, 1978–80.

Davey Weldman, *Poor Little Lambs,* Theatre at St. Peter's Church, New York City, 1982.

A Good Swift Kick (revue), Variety Arts Theatre, New York City, 1999.

also appeared in *All I Really Need to Know I Learned in Kindergarten,* Tiffany Theatre; *The Fantastics; Happy Holidays,* Pasadena Playhouse, Pasadena, CA; *John Brown's Body,* Lobero Theatre, Santa Barbara, CA.

Stage Work:

Assistant stage manager, *Da,* Morosco Theatre, New York City, 1978–80.

RECORDINGS

Singles:
"Makin' It," RSO, 1979.

Video Games:

Manfred, *Getting Up: Contents Under Pressure* (also known as *Marc Ecko's "Getting Up: Contents Under Pressure"*), 2005.

Voice of Mister Fantastic, *Marvel: Ultimate Alliance,* Activision, 2006.

NETTER, Jason

PERSONAL

Cousin of Christian Forte (a writer) and Julia Forte (an art director). *Education:* University of California, Los Angeles, B.A.; Pepperdine University, M.B.A.

Addresses: *Office*—Kickstart Entertainment, 11777 San Vicente Blvd., Suite 650, Los Angeles, CA 90049.

Career: Producer, digital effects expert, writer, and executive. Netter Digital Entertainment, visual effects designer and vice president for business development; Shanghai Digital Film Studio, Shanghai, China, creator; Kickstart Entertainment (some sources cite Kickstart Productions), Los Angeles, founder and president, beginning 2000. Created animated shorts for the Disney Channel. Also worked as animation supervisor.

CREDITS

Television Producer; Series:

Producer, *Voltron: The Third Dimension* (animated), syndicated, 1998–2000.

Executive producer, *Finley the Fire Engine* (animated), beginning 2006.

Executive producer, *Happy Monster Band* (animated), Disney Channel, beginning 2007.

Executive producer, *Painkiller Jane,* Sci–Fi Channel, beginning 2007.

Producer, *Wolverine & the X–Men* (animated), beginning 2007.

Television Work; Miniseries:

Visual effects producer, *Dune* (also known as *Frank Herbert's "Dune," Duna, Dyyni, Frank Herbert's "Dune"—Der Wuestenplanet,* and *Der Wuestenplanet*), Sci–Fi Channel, 2000.

Television Work; Movies:

Visual effects producer, *Alien Cargo* (also known as *Komiczy wirus* and *Medo real*), UPN, 1999.

Television Editor; Episodic:

Apprentice editor, "Acts of Sacrifice," *Babylon 5* (also known as *B5*), syndicated, 1995.

Apprentice editor, "Hunter, Prey," *Babylon 5* (also known as *B5*), syndicated, 1995.

Assistant editor, "Z'ha'dum," *Babylon 5* (also known as *B5*), syndicated, 1996.

Television Executive Producer; Pilots:

Co–executive producer, *Painkiller Jane,* Sci–Fi Channel, 2005.

The Amazing Screw–On Head (animated), Sci–Fi Channel, 2006.

Nobody, ABC Family Channel, 2007.

Film Producer:

Robotech 3000 (animated short film), FUNimation Entertainment, 2000.

Robotech: The Shadow Chronicles (animated; also known as *Robotech: Shadow Force*), FUNimation Entertainment, 2006.

Battle Chasers (also known as *Battlechasers*), Twentieth Century–Fox, 2008.

Wanted, Universal, 2008.

Some sources state that Netter produced other films.

Film Effects Producer:

Visual effects producer, *Children of the Corn V: Fields of Terror* (also known as *Children of the Corn 5, Children of the Corn V: Field of Screams, Colheita maldita 5—Campos do terror, Cosecha negra V: Siente el terror, Gli adoratori del male, Kinder des Zorns 5—Feld des Terrors, Los chicos del maiz 5: Campos de terror,* and *Maissilapset 5: Kuoleman pellot*), Dimension Films, 1998.

Visual effects executive producer, *Bats* (also known as *Blood Moon, Bats—Fliegende Teufel, La nuit des chauve–souris,* and *Murcielagos*), Columbia, 1999.

Visual effects executive producer, *From Dusk till Dawn 2: Texas Blood Money* (also known as *Aberto ate de madrugada 2, Abierto hasta el amanecer 2, Dal tramanto all'alba: Texas sangue e denaro, Del crepusculo al amanecer 2: Terror en Texas, Haemaer-*

aestae aamunkoittoon II, Haemaeraestae aamunkoittoon 2—Texas Blood Money, Um drink no inferno 2: Texas sangrento, and *Une nuit en enfer 2—Le prix du sang*), Amuse Pictures, 1999.

Visual effects executive producer, *From Dusk till Dawn 3: The Hangman's Daughter* (also known as *The Hangman's Daughter, Abierto hasta el amanecer 3: La hija del verdugo, Dal tramanto all'alba: la figlia del boia, Del crepusculo al amanecer 3: La hija del verdugo, Haemaeraestae aamunkoittoon 3, Haemaeraestae aamunkoittoon III—Pyoevelin tytaer, Um drink no inferno 3: A filha do carrasco,* and *Une nuit en enfer 3—La fille du bourreau*), Amuse Pictures, 2000.

Digital effects producer, *Driven* (also known as *Champs, Formula One, Into Thin Air, A toute vitesse, Alta velocidade, Felpoergetve, La viteza maxima, Mrboleli, Ruutulippu,* and *Voidusoit*), Warner Bros., 2001.

Visual effects executive producer, *Jay and Silent Bob Strike Back* (also known as *VA5* and *View Askew 5*), Miramax/Dimension Films, 2001.

RECORDINGS

Video Game Work:

Executive producer, *Spider–Man 2: Enter Electro,* Activision, 2001.

Video Appearances:

Himself, *Robotech: Birth of a Sequel* (also known as *The Making of Robotech: The Shadow Chronicles*), FUNimation Entertainment, 2007.

WRITINGS

Teleplays; with Others; Series:

Finley the Fire Engine (animated), beginning 2006.

OTHER SOURCES

Electronic:

Kickstart Entertainment, http://kickstartent.com, July 14, 2007.

NOSILLE, Nabrah
See ELLISON, Harlan

NUGIEL, Nellie
(Nellie Rachel Nugiel)

PERSONAL

Full name, Nellie Rachel Nugiel.

Addresses: *Agent*—Paradigm, 360 North Crescent Dr., North Building, Beverly Hills, CA 90210.

Career: Producer. HandMade Films, manager of U.S. production; Home Box Office (HBO), production executive; also worked as a line producer, unit production manager, and production accountant.

Awards, Honors: Annual CableACE Award, best dramatic or theatrical special, National Cable Television Association, and Emmy Award nomination, outstanding made–for–television movie, both with others, 1997, for *In the Gloaming;* Black Movie Award, outstanding television movie, and Emmy Award nomination, outstanding made–for–television movie, both 2005, Directors Guild of America Award, outstanding directorial achievement in movies for television, Christopher Award, television and cable category, Golden Laurel Award nomination, television producer of the year in longform, PGA Golden Laurel awards, Producers Guild of America, and Independent Spirit Award nomination, best first feature, Independent Features Project/West, all 2006, all with others, for *Lackawanna Blues.*

CREDITS

Film Producer:
Me and Veronica (also known as *Ich & Veronica, Io e Veronica, Minae ja Veronica,* and *Veronica e eu*), Arrow Releasing, 1993.
Line producer, *The Pallbearer* (also known as *Happy Blue, Amigo desconhecido, Der Zufallslover, El funebrero, Identitate furata, Le porteur, Mi desconocido amigo, Tre amici un matrimonio e un funerale,* and *Vaenner och flickvaenner*), Miramax, 1996.
(With others) *Commandments* (also known as *Alles unheil kommt von oben, Clamando al cielo, Jumalten hylkaeaemae,* and *Vastoin kaeskyjae*), Gramercy Pictures/Universal, 1997.
(With others) *People I Know* (also known as *Eyewitness, Influences, Der innere Kreis, Gente conhecida, Im inneren Kreis, La noche del crimen, O articulador,* and *Relaciones confidenciales*), New Films International, 2002, Miramax, 2003.
(With others) *Chasing Papi* (also known as *Bomba latina, Naistenmies pulassa, Papi chulo, 3 femmes pour un papillon,* and *Un amante para tres*), Twentieth Century–Fox, 2003.
(With others) *Bickford Shmeckler's Cool Ideas,* Screen Media Films, 2007.

Film Associate Producer:
Crossing Delancey (also known as *Ahava mimabat shlishi, Amor a segunda vista, Cruzando la calle,*

Dall'altro lato della strada, Izzy et Sam, Kaerlek paa Manhattan, Romanssi Manhattanilla, Sarah und Sam, and *Zmien kapelusz*), Warner Bros., 1988.
The House on Carroll Street (also known as *A casa suspeita, Das Haus an der Carroll Street, Dom przy Carroll Street, Huset paa Carroll Street, La casa de Carroll Street, Labirinto mortale, Pesadelo na rua Carroll, Talo Carroll Streetillae,* and *Une femme en peril*), Orion, 1988.
Come See the Paradise (also known as *Bem–vindos ao paraiso, Benvenuti in paradiso, Bienvenido al paraiso, Bienvenue au paradis, Ela na deis ton Paradeiso, Komm und sieh das Paradies, Przyjdz zobyczyc raj, Tervetuloa paratiisiin, Vaelkommen till paradiset,* and *Venha ver o Paraiso*), Twentieth Century–Fox, 1990.

Film Unit Production Manager:
Commandments (also known as *Alles unheil kommt von oben, Clamando al cielo, Jumalten hylkaeaemae,* and *Vastoin kaeskyjae*), Gramercy Pictures/Universal, 1997.
Evening (also known as *I teleftaia nyhta*), Focus Features, 2007.

Film Production Accountant:
Falling in Love (also known as *Amor a primeira vista, Der Liebe verfallen, Enamorarse, Encontro com o amor, Foeraelskade, Innamorarsi, Mia agapi gennietai, Rakastutaan,* and *Zakochac sie*), Paramount, 1984.
Reckless (also known as *Amare con rabbia, Jovens sem rumo, Jung und ruecksichtslos, Kovis, Mindenutt jo, de legjobb mashol, Na oslep, Rebeldes temerarios,* and *Reckless—Jung und Ruecksichtslos*), Metro–Goldwyn–Mayer, 1984.
The House on Carroll Street (also known as *A casa suspeita, Das Haus an der Carroll Street, Dom przy Carroll Street, Huset paa Carroll Street, La casa de Carroll Street, Labirinto mortale, Pesadelo na rua Carroll, Talo Carroll Streetillae,* and *Une femme en peril*), Orion, 1988.

Film Work; Other:
Production executive, *After Hours* (also known as *Lies, A Night in SoHo, After Hours—quelle nuit de galere, Depois de horas, Despues de hora, Die Zeit nach Mitternacht, En Natt i New York, Fuori orario, Illasta aamuun, Jo, que noche!, Liderces orak, Meta ta mesanyhta, Natt paa Manhattan, Nova Iorque fora de horas, Po godzinach,* and *Quina nit!*), Warner Bros., 1985.
Accounts department worker, *Track 29* (also known as *Armadilha sentimental, Mille pezzi di un delirio, Tor 29, Track 29—Ein gefaehrliches Spiel,* and *Vaeaerillae raiteilla*), Island Pictures, 1987.

Worked on other projects.

Television Work; Series:
Unit production manager, *Greek,* ABC Family Channel, beginning 2007.

Television Work; Miniseries:
Producer, *Crocodile Shoes* (also known as *Krokotiilikengaet*), BBC, 1994.

Television Producer; Movies:
Associate producer, *Death of a Salesman* (also known as *Der Tod eines Handlungsreisenden*), CBS, 1985.

(With others) *Women & Men 2: In Love There Are No Rules* (also known as *The Art of Seduction* and *Women & Men 2*), HBO, 1991.

Strapped (also known as *Armati di pistola, Atrapados por la violencia, Meurtres a Brooklyn,* and *Schule der Gewalt*), HBO, 1993.

In the Gloaming (also known as *Armadilha selvagem, I skymningen,* and *In der Abenddaemmerung*), HBO, 1997.

(With others) *61** (also known as *61*), HBO, 2001.

(As Nellie Rachel Nugiel) Producer, *Lackawanna Blues* (also known as *Notes storgis*), HBO, 2005.

Television Work; Other; Movies:
Production accountant, *Death of a Salesman* (also known as *Der Tod eines Handlungsreisenden*), CBS, 1985.

Unit production manager, *In the Gloaming* (also known as *Armadilha selvagem, I skymningen,* and *In der Abenddaemmerung*), HBO, 1997.

Unit production manager, *Lackawanna Blues* (also known as *Notes storgis*), HBO, 2005.

Executive for television projects.

Television Work; Specials:
Best boy, *Landscape with Waitress,* PBS, 1986.

Television Work; Pilots:
Producer, *Him and Us,* ABC, 2006.

O–P

OSMOND, Marie 1959–

PERSONAL

Full name, Olive Marie Osmond; born October, 13, 1959, in Ogden, UT; daughter of George Virl and Olive May Osmond; sister of Wayne Osmond (a singer), Alan R. Osmond (a singer), Merrill Osmond (a singer and theatre owner), Jay Osmond (a singer and producer), Jimmy Osmond (a singer), and Donny Osmond (a singer and actor); married Steve Craig (an actor and production designer), June 26, 1982 (divorced, 1985); married Brian Blosil, October 28, 1986 (separated, 2000); children: (first marriage) Stephen; (second marriage; five are adopted) Jessica, Rachael, Michael, Brandon, Brianna, Matthew R., Abigail. Religion: Church of Jesus Christ of Latter–day Saints (Mormon). *Religion:* Church of Jesus Christ of Latter–day Saints (Mormon). *Avocational Interests:* Sculpting dolls.

Addresses: *Agent*—Tim Curtis, William Morris Agency, 151 S. El Camino Dr., Beverly Hills, CA 90212–2775.

Career: Singer, actress, and producer. Member of the family singing group The Osmonds, 1966–73; appeared in commercials, including ads for Pepsi Twist soft drinks, 2003. Owner of a line of cosmetics sold at K–mart stores, 1977; created clothing patterns for Butterick, 1978; Marie Osmond Fine Porcelain Doll Collection, designer (with L. L. Knickerbocker), beginning 1990; Marian (porcelain doll company), co–owner, beginning 2000. Children's Miracle Network, co-founder and annual fundraising host, 1983.

Awards, Honors: American Music Award (with Dan Seals), best country band, duo, or group, 1975, for "Meet Me in Montana;" People's Choice Award, favorite television variety series, 1979; Country Music Associa-tion Award (with Seals), vocal duo of the year, 1986; Roy Acuff Award, Country Music Foundation, 1989, for work with *Children's Miracle Network;* Daytime Emmy Award nominations (with others), outstanding talk show, 2000, 2001, and Emmy Award nominations (with brother, Donny Osmond), outstanding talk show host, 2000, 2001, all for *Donny & Marie;* TV Land Award (with Donny Osmond), favorite singing siblings, TV Land network, 2006.

CREDITS

Television Appearances; Series:
Host, *Donny and Marie* (also known as *The Osmond Family Show*), ABC, 1975–78.
Marie Owens, *Marie,* 1979–80.
Host, *Marie,* NBC, 1980–81.
Host, *Ripley's Believe It or Not,* ABC, 1985–86.
Julia Wallace, *Maybe This Time,* ABC, 1995.
Host, *Donny & Marie* (also known as *Donny and Marie Hour*), syndicated, 1998–2000.
Making the Band, ABC, 2001.
Judge, *Celebrity Duets,* Fox, 2006.
Dancing with the Stars, ABC, 2007.

Television Appearances; Movies:
Beth Atherton, *The Gift of Love,* ABC, 1978.
Olive Osmond, *Side by Side: The True Story of the Osmond Family,* NBC, 1982.
Josephine "Josie" Marcus, *I Married Wyatt Earp,* NBC, 1983.
Inside the Osmonds (also known as *The Osmonds*), ABC, 2001.

Television Appearances; Specials:
The Bob Hope Show, NBC, 1973.
The Perry Como Sunshine Show, CBS, 1974.
The Osmonds Special, CBS, 1974.
Bob Hope's Christmas Party, NBC, 1975.
Host, *The Donny and Marie Osmond Show,* 1975.

Bob Hope's Bicentennial Star Spangled Spectacular, NBC, 1976.

The Paul Lynde Halloween Special, 1976.

Bob Hope Special: Happy Birthday, Bob!, NBC, 1978.

General Electric's All–Star Anniversary, ABC, 1978.

Tribute to "Mr. Television" Milton Berle, NBC, 1978.

The Barbara Walters Special (also known as *Barbara Walters: Interviews of a Lifetime* and *The Barbara Walters Summer Special*), 1978.

Paul Lynde Goes M–a–a–a–a–d, ABC, 1979.

The Donny and Marie Christmas Special, ABC, 1979.

Osmond Family Christmas Special, NBC, 1980.

The Bob Hope Christmas Show and All–Star Comedy Special (also known as *The Bob Hope Christmas Special*), NBC, 1980.

Doug Henning's World of Magic, NBC, 1981.

The Osmond Family Thanksgiving Special, NBC, 1981.

Bob Hope's 30th Anniversary Television Special (also known as *The Bob Hope Anniversary Show*), NBC, 1981.

Bob Hope's All–Star Comedy Birthday Party at West Point (also known as *All–Star Comedy Birthday Party from West Point*), NBC, 1981.

Walt Disney … One Man's Dream, CBS, 1981.

EPCOT Center: The Opening Ceremonies, 1982.

Bob Hope's Women I Love—Beautiful But Funny (also known as *Women I Love: Beautiful But Funny*), NBC, 1982.

The Suzanne Somers Special, 1982.

Bob Hope's Salute to NASA (also known as *Bob Hope Special: Bob Hope's Salute to NASA—25 Years of Reaching for the Stars*), NBC, 1983.

Hollywood's Private Home Movies, ABC, 1983.

Christmas in Washington, NBC, 1984.

Salute to Lady Liberty, CBS, 1984.

Fairy Princess and Velveteen Rabbit, *The Velveteen Rabbit,* 1984.

Disneyland's 30th Anniversary Celebration, NBC, 1985.

Here's Television Entertainment, syndicated, 1985.

ABC All–Star Spectacular, ABC, 1985.

American Bandstand's 33 1/3 Celebration, ABC, 1985.

Perry Como's Christmas in Hawaii, ABC, 1985.

Voice of Rose Petal, *Rose Petal Palace: Real Friends,* 1985.

Host, *Marie Osmond's Merry Christmas,* 1986.

53rd Annual King Orange Jamboree, NBC, 1986.

Lifetime Salutes Mom, Lifetime, 1987.

Sea World's All–Star Lone Star Celebration, CBS, 1988.

Country Music Crossroads, PBS, 1988.

Happy Birthday, Bob—Fifty Stars Salute Your Fifty Years with NBC, 1988.

Marie Osmond at Church Street Station, 1990.

Cohost, *Children's Miracle Network,* 1991.

Bob Hope's Christmas Cheer from Saudi Arabia, NBC, 1991.

Yellow Ribbon Party (also known as *Bob Hope's Yellow Ribbon Celebration*), NBC, 1991.

Host, *National Parenting Poll,* 1992.

Super Bowl Saturday Night, 1992.

Host, *International Motorsports Hall of Fame,* 1992.

Hats Off to Minnie Pearl: America Honors Minnie Pearl, 1992.

The Women of Country, 1993.

Star Spangled Branson, 1993.

(In archive footage) *A Bob Hope Christmas,* 1993.

Host, *Television's Christmas Classics,* 1994.

Backstage with Tanya Tucker, 1994.

Narrator, *The True Life of Barbie,* The Learning Channel, 1996.

67th Annual Hollywood Christmas Parade, UPN, 1998.

The Osmonds: Pure and Simple, Arts and Entertainment, 1999.

Cohost, *Miss America Pageant,* ABC, 1999, 2000.

The Four Freshmen: 50 Years Fresh!, PBS, 1999.

The Life and Times of the Osmonds, The Nashville Network, 2000.

Intimate Portrait: Marie Osmond, Lifetime, 2000.

"Andy Williams," *Biography,* Arts and Entertainment, 2003.

(In archive footage) *101 Biggest Celebrity Oops,* E! Entertainment Television, 2004.

Stadium of Fire: 25th Anniversary, American Forces Network, 2005.

The Osmonds 50th Anniversary, PBS, 2007.

Television Appearances; Pilots:

Sister Mae Davis, *Rooster,* ABC, 1982.

Voice of Rose Petal, *Rose Petal Place* (animated), syndicated, 1985.

Television Appearances; Episodic:

Musikladen, 1973.

Top of the Pops (also known as *All New Top of the Pops* and *TOTP*), 1974, 1979.

The Sonny and Cher Show, 1976.

The Brady Bunch Hour, ABC, 1977.

Solid Gold (also known as *Solid Gold in Concert*), 1982.

Maria Rosselli, "Venetian Love Song/The Arrangement/Arrividerci, Gopher/The Gigolo: Parts 1 & 2," *The Love Boat,* ABC, 1982.

Herself, "Pudding," *The Single Guy,* NBC, 1996.

Herself, "Heaven's Helper," *Almost Perfect,* 1996.

"Andy Gibb," *Behind the Music* (also known as *VH1's "Behind the Music"*), VH1, 1997.

Herself, "Bloody Valentine," *V.I.P.* (also known as *V.I.P.—Die Bodyguards*), syndicated, 1998.

Wheel of Fortune, syndicated, 1998.

Herself, "Return of the Owl," *V.I.P.* (also known as *V.I.P.—Die Bodyguards*), syndicated, 1999.

Herself, "The Mouth that Roared," *Diagnosis Murder,* CBS, 1999.

"Donny & Marie," *Behind the Music* (also known as *VH1's "Behind the Music"*), VH1, 1999.

Herself, "Video Gurl," *Movie Stars,* The WB, 2000.

"Marie Osmond," *Celebrity Profile,* 2000.

"70s Teen Idols," *VH–1 Where Are They Now?*, VH1, 2002.

Television Appearances; Awards Presentations:
Presenter, *The 28th Annual Primetime Emmy Awards*, ABC, 1976.
The 4th Annual American Music Awards, ABC, 1977.
The 39th Annual Golden Globe Awards, CBS, 1982.
19th Annual Country Music Association Awards, CBS, 1985.
20th Annual Country Music Association Awards, CBS, 1986.
20th Annual Music City News Country Awards, syndicated, 1986.
21st Annual Academy of Country Music Awards, NBC, 1986.
21st Annual Music City News Country Awards, syndicated, 1987.
The 22nd Annual Academy of Country Music Awards, NBC, 1987.
The 11th Annual ACE Awards, multiple networks, 1990.
The 26th Annual Academy of Country Music Awards, NBC, 1991.
Presenter, *25th Annual Music City News Country Awards*, The Nashville Network, 1991.
The 27th Annual Academy of Country Music Awards, NBC, 1992.
Host, *Music City News Country Songwriters Awards*, The Nashville Network, 1992.
The 28th Academy of Country Music Awards, NBC, 1993.
Presenter, *The 26th Annual Daytime Emmy Awards*, CBS, 1999.
Presenter, *The 26th Annual American Music Awards*, ABC, 1999.
Presenter, *The 27th Annual Daytime Emmy Awards*, ABC, 2000.
Presenter, *35th Annual Academy of Country Music Awards*, CBS, 2000.
Presenter, *Lifetime Presents: Disney's American Teacher Awards*, Lifetime, 2001.
The Fourth Annual TV Land Awards: A Celebration of Classic TV, TV Land, 2006.

Television Guest Appearances; Episodic:
The Mike Douglas Show, CBS, 1976.
Guest host, *The Big Show*, NBC, 1980.
The Tonight Show Starring Johnny Carson, NBC, 1981.
The Rosie O'Donnell Show, syndicated, 1996, 1998, 2001.
Hollywood Squares (also known as *H2* and *H2: Hollywood Squares*), 1999.
The Howard Stern Radio Show, syndicated, 2000.
The Oprah Winfrey Show (also known as *Oprah*), syndicated, 2000.
Late Night with Conan O'Brien, NBC, 2000.
Dale's All Stars, BBC1, 2000.
Jimmy Kimmel Live, ABC, 2004.

Larry King Live, Cable News Network, 2004, 2007.
The Tony Danza Show, syndicated, 2005.
The View, ABC, 2005, 2007.
Entertainment Tonight (also known as *Entertainment This Week, E.T., ET Weekend,* and *This Week in Entertainment*), syndicated, 2006.
The Late Late Show with Craig Ferguson, CBS, 2006.

Television Work; Series:
Costume designer, *The Osmond Brothers Special*, ABC, 1978.
Producer, *Donny & Marie* (series; also known as *Donny and Marie Hour*), syndicated, 1998–2000.

Film Appearances:
Vocalist, *Hugo the Hippo* (animated; also known as *Hugo, a vizilo*), Twentieth Century–Fox, 1976.
Marie, *Goin' Coconuts*, Osmond, 1978.
Voice of Queen, *Buster & Chauncey's Silent Night*, Columbia TriStar Home Video, 1998.
Herself, *Get Bruce*, 1999.
O' Christmas Tree, 1999.

Stage Appearances:
Anna Leonowens, *The King and I* (musical), Neil Simon Theatre, New York City, 1997.

Major Tours:
Maria, *The Sound of Music* (musical), U.S. cities, 1994–95, then Asian cities, 1997.

RECORDINGS

Albums:
Paper Roses, 1973.
In My Little Corner of the World, 1974.
I'm Leaving It All Up to You, 1974.
Who's Sorry Now, 1975.
(With Donny Osmond) *Make the World Go Away*, 1975.
This Is the Way I Feel, 1977.
Steppin' Stone, Curb, 1985.
There's No Stopping Your Heart, Curb, 1986.
I Only Wanted You, Curb, 1987.
All in Love, Curb, 1988.
Like a Hurricane, Curb, 1990.
The Best of Marie Osmond, Curb, 1990.
25 Hits Special Collection, Curb, 1995.

Also recorded *Donny and Marie Special, Goin' Coconuts, Greatest Hits, New Season, Rose Petal Place,* and *Winning Combination;* (with the Osmond Family) *All Time Greatest Hits of the Osmond Family, Around the World Live, Best of the Freedom Fest, The Best of the Osmonds, The Collector's Edition, Glory of America,*

Greatest Hits, Lo mejor de lo mejor de The Osmonds, Osmond Christmas, Osmond Family Christmas, The Osmonds Live, and *The Wonderful World of the Osmond Brothers.* Singles include (with Donny Osmond) "On Bad Apple," 1971; (solo) "Paper Roses," 1973; "Read My Lips," Curb, 1986; "You're Still New to Me," Curb, 1986; "I Only Wanted You," Curb, 1987; "What Kind of Man (Walks on a Woman)," Curb, 1995; (with Dan Seals) "Meet Me in Montana," Curb; and "There's No Stopping Your Heart," Curb.

Videos:
Marie Osmond's Merry Christmas, Winsor, 2001.
Celebrate the Season, Music Video Distributors, 2004.

Appeared in *The Best of Donny and Marie, Volumes 1 & 2.* Appeared in the Muppets music video "She Drives Me Crazy."

WRITINGS

Television Series:
Donny & Marie (also known as *Donny and Marie Hour*), syndicated, 1998–2000.

Books:
(With Rochelle Reed) *Fun, Fame, and Family,* New American Library, 1973.
(With Julie Davis) *Marie Osmond's Guide to Beauty, Health, and Style,* Simon & Schuster, 1980.
(With Elizabeth Noble) *Marie Osmond's Exercises for Mothers–to–Be,* New American Library, 1985.
(With Marcia Wilkie and Judith Moore) *Behind the Smile: My Journey Out of Postpartum Depression,* Warner Books, 2001.

OTHER SOURCES

Books:
Eldred, Patricia Mulrooney, *Donny and Marie,* 1978.
Encyclopedia of World Biography Supplement, Volume 27, Gale, 2007.
Osmond, Marie, Marcia Wilkie, Judith Moore, *Behind the Smile: My Journey Out of Postpartum Depression,* Warner Books, 2001.

Periodicals:
Entertainment Weekly, October 2, 1998, pp. 38–40.
TV Guide, September 26, 1998, pp. 34–38; October 30, 1999; November 13, 1999, pp. 40–44; May 20, 2000, pp. 18–27, 67.

Electronic:
Marie Osmond Official Site, http://www.marieosmond.com, August 26, 2007.

Television Specials:
The Osmonds: Pure and Simple, Arts and Entertainment, 1999.
The Life and Times of the Osmonds, The Nashville Network, 2000.
Intimate Portrait: Marie Osmond, Lifetime, 2000.

Television Movies:
Side by Side: The True Story of the Osmond Family, NBC, 1982.
Inside the Osmonds (also known as *The Osmonds*), ABC, 2001.

PARK, Sung Hee
See WHANG, Suzanne

PARKER, Bert
See ELLISON, Harlan

PARKER, David
(David M. Parker)

PERSONAL

Full name, David M. Parker.

Career: Actor.

CREDITS

Film Appearances:
(As David M. Parker) Bartender, *Sister Act* (also known as *Apaca show, Cambio de habito, Do cabare para o convento, En vaersting till syster, Halloj i klosteret, Mudanca de habito, Nune pojejo, Nunnia ja konnia, Rock 'n' nonne, Sister Act—Eine himmlische Karriere, Sister Act: una monja de cuidado, Sister Act—una svitata in abito da suora,* and *Una monja de cuidado*), Buena Vista, 1992.
Detective Troyer, *The Landlady,* Trimark Pictures, 1998.
Overweight man, *Speedway Junky,* 1999, Regent Releasing, 2001.
First dark suit man, *Ballistic: Ecks vs. Sever* (also known as *Ballistic, Ecks vs. Sever,* and *X vs. Sever*), Warner Bros., 2002.
Detective Boxer, *Willard,* New Line Cinema, 2003.

Ernie, *Fantastic Four* (also known as *Fantastic 4, Fantastik doertlue, Les quatre fantastiques, Los cuatro fantasticos,* and *Quarteto fantastico*), Twentieth Century–Fox, 2005.

Raymond, *Nursie,* Skouras Ventura Film Partners, 2005.

Mr. Eckerman, *Comeback Season,* Myriad Pictures/THINKFilm, 2006.

Police sergeant, *The Bracelet of Bordeaux,* Amusement Park Media/Eagle Productions/Eakin Films/Ontracc/Photographic Design Labs/Silver Rock Productions/TVman/Wagner Media/Zapata Deign, 2007.

Television Appearances; Series:

Detective Roosevelt, *John Doe,* Fox, 2003–2004.

Television Appearances; Movies:

James Whitmore, *James Dean* (also known as *James Dean: An Invented Life* and *Il etait une fois James Dean*), TNT, 2001.

(As David M. Parker) Officer, *She's No Angel* (also known as *D'une vie a l'autre* and *Truegerisches Glueck*), Lifetime, 2001.

Deputy Gunderson, *Video Voyeur: The Susan Wilson Story* (also known as *Acoso a la intimidad, L'enfer a domicile, Le voyeur, Video Voyeur—Verbotene Blicke,* and *Vigiados*), Lifetime, 2002.

Ted Leopold, *Damaged Care* (also known as *Negligencia medica, Rohkea valinta,* and *Testemunha da corrupcao*), Showtime, 2002.

Harry Zordich, *Stealing Christmas* (also known as *Ein Schlitzohr names Santa Claus, Otro cuento de navidad, Pere Noel de service,* and *Petit papa voleur*), USA Network, 2003.

Kalahane, *Word of Honor,* TNT, 2003.

Patrick, *I Want to Marry Ryan Banks* (also known as *The Reality of Love, Famoso y seductor, Juego de amor, La chiavi del cuore,* and *Qui veut m'epouser?*), ABC Family Channel, 2004.

Mark, *Shark Swarm,* The Hallmark Channel, 2008.

Television Appearances; Episodic:

Dwight McMillan, "Lights Out," *Pacific Blue,* USA Network, 1996.

Larry Sparks, "As Flies to Careless Boys …," *NYPD Blue,* ABC, 1997.

Lonnie, "St. Jude Took a Bullet," *EZ Streets,* CBS, 1997.

Phil Eggers, "Hard–Boiled Murder," *Diagnosis Murder,* CBS, 1997.

Garrett Stone, "Royal Heist," *Walker, Texas Ranger* (also known as *Walker*), CBS, 1998.

Officer Pearson, "Two," *Dark Angel* (also known as *James Cameron's "Dark Angel"*), Fox, 2001.

Police sergeant, "Home of the Brave," *The Chris Isaak Show,* Showtime, 2002.

"The Plague Year," *The Agency* (also known as *CIA: The Agency, The Agency—Im Fadenkreuz der C.I.A., Agentit, Espion d'etat,* and *La agencia*), CBS, 2002.

Police officer, "Memphis," *The Twilight Zone,* UPN, 2003.

Cal, "Day 1,385," *The Days,* ABC, 2004.

Lieutenant Dobbs, "Heros and Demons," *The Dead Zone* (also known as *Dead Zone, Stephen King's "Dead Zone," The Dark Half, La morta zona, La zona morta, La zona muerta,* and *Zona smrti*), USA Network, 2004.

Brennan Sommers, "Traffic," *Numb3rs* (also known as *Numbers* and *Num3ers*), CBS, 2006.

Mike Kroger, "The Perfect Storm," *Criminal Minds* (also known as *Quantico, Criminal Minds—FBI tutjijat, Esprits criminels, Gyilkos elmek, Kurjuse kannul,* and *Mentes criminales*), CBS, 2006.

Petey, "8 Years," *Cold Case* (also known as *Anexihniastes ypothesis, Caso abierto, Cold case—affaires classees, Cold Case—Kein Opfer ist je vergessen, Doegloett aktak, Kalla spaar, Todistettavasti syyllinen,* and *Victimes du passe*), CBS, 2006.

Gary Sutton, "A House Divided," *ER* (also known as *Emergency Room*), NBC, 2007.

Television Appearances; Pilots:

Twin brothers, *Cutty Whitman,* CBS, 1996.

PARKES, Walter F. 1951–
　(Walter Parkes)

PERSONAL

Born April 15, 1951, in Bakersfield, CA; married Laurie MacDonald (a producer); children: Jane MacDonald, Graham Joseph. *Education:* Yale University, B.A. (cum laude), 1973; Stanford University, M.A., communications.

Addresses: *Agent*—Creative Artists Agency, 2000 Avenue of the Stars, Los Angeles, CA 90067. *Office*—Parkes/MacDonald Productions, 100 Universal City Plaza, Universal City, CA 91608.

Career: Producer and writer. Amblin Entertainment, president, 1992—; DreamWorks SKG, head of Motion Picture Division (with wife, Laurie MacDonald), 1994—; Parkes/MacDonald Productions, Universal City, CA, principal. Also worked as a professional musician. Member of Global Business Network.

Member: Academy of Motion Picture Arts and Sciences, Writers Guild of America.

Awards, Honors: Academy Award nomination (with Keith Critchlow), best documentary feature, 1976, for *The California Reich;* Academy Award nomination (with Lawrence Lasker), best original screenplay, Saturn Award nomination (with Lasker), best writing, Academy of Science Fiction, Fantasy, and Horror Films, Writers Guild of America Screen Award nomination (with Lasker), best drama written directly for the screen, 1984, both for *WarGames;* Academy Award nomination (with Lasker), best picture, 1991, for *Awakenings;* Edgar Allan Poe Award nomination (with Lasker and Phil Alden Robinson), best motion picture, Mystery Writers of America, 1993, for *Sneakers;* Golden Satellite Award (with Laurie MacDonald), best animated or mixed–media motion picture, International Press Academy, 1998, for *Men in Black;* ShoWest Award (with MacDonald), producer of the year, National Association of Theatre Owners, 1998.

CREDITS

Film Work:

Producer (with Keith Critchlow), director, cinematographer, and editor, *The California Reich* (documentary), Intercontinental, 1975.

Producer (with Richard Shepherd), *Volunteers,* TriStar, 1985.

Producer (with Lawrence Lasker), *Project X,* Twentieth Century–Fox, 1987.

Producer (with Lasker), *True Believer* (also known as *Fighting Justice*), Columbia, 1990.

Producer (with Lasker), *Awakenings,* Columbia, 1990.

Producer (with Lasker), *Sneakers,* Universal, 1992.

Executive producer, *Little Giants,* Warner Bros., 1994.

Executive producer, *How to Make an American Quilt,* Universal, 1995.

Executive producer, *To Wang Foo, Thanks for Everything, Julie Newmar,* Universal, 1995.

(As Walter Parkes) Executive producer, *Twister,* Warner Bros., 1996.

(As Walter Parkes) Executive producer, *The Trigger Effect,* Gramercy, 1996.

Producer, *Men in Black* (also known as *MIB*), Columbia, 1997.

(As Walter Parkes) Producer, *The Peacemaker,* DreamWorks Distribution, 1997.

(As Walter Parkes) Executive producer, *Amistad,* DreamWorks Distribution, 1997.

(As Walter Parkes) Executive producer, *Deep Impact,* Paramount/DreamWorks Distribution, 1998.

(As Walter Parkes) Executive producer, *Small Soldiers,* DreamWorks, 1998.

Executive producer, *The Mask of Zorro,* TriStar, 1998.

Executive producer, *Gladiator,* DreamWorks, 2000.

Executive producer, *A.I. Artificial Intelligence* (also known as *Artificial Intelligence: A.I.*), Warner Bros., 2001.

Studio executive, *The Last Castle,* DreamWorks, 2001.

Producer and studio executive, *The Time Machine,* Warner Bros., 2002.

Producer and studio executive, *Minority Report,* Twentieth Century–Fox, 2002.

Producer, *Men in Black II* (also known as *MIB2* and *MIIB*), Columbia TriStar, 2002.

Executive producer, *Road to Perdition,* DreamWorks, 2002.

Executive producer, *The Tuxedo,* DreamWorks, 2002.

Producer, *The Ring,* DreamWorks, 2002.

Producer, *Catch Me If You Can,* DreamWorks, 2002.

Studio executive, *Collateral,* DreamWorks, 2004.

Producer, *Terminal,* DreamWorks, 2004.

Producer, *Lemony Snicket's A Series of Unfortunate Events* (also known as *Lemony Snicket—Ratselhafte Ereignisse*), Paramount, 2004.

Producer, *The Ring Two* (also known as *Samara, The Ring 2,* and *Samara: Ring 2*), DreamWorks, 2005.

Producer, *The Island,* DreamWorks, 2005.

Producer, *Just Like Heaven,* DreamWorks, 2005.

Producer, *The Legend of Zorro* (also known as *Z*), Columbia, 2005.

(As Walter Parkes) Producer, *The Lookout,* Miramax, 2007.

Executive producer, *The Kite Runner,* DreamWorks, 2007.

Producer, *Sweeney Todd: The Demon Barber of Fleet Street* (also known as *Sweeney Todd*), DreamWorks, 2007.

Producer, *A Tale of Two Sisters,* DreamWorks, 2008.

Also producer (with Lasker) of *The Dark Horse.*

Film Appearances:

Himself, *Barry Sonnenfeld's "Intergalactic Guide to Comedy"* (documentary shorts), Columbia TriStar Home Video, 2002.

Himself, *"Catch Me If You Can": Behind the Camera* (documentary short), DreamWorks Home Entertainment, 2003.

Himself, *"Catch Me If You Can": The Casting of the Film* (documentary short; also known as *Cast Me If You Can*), DreamWorks Home Entertainment, 2003.

Himself, *The Making of "Sneakers"* (documentary short), Universal Studios Home Video, 2003.

(As Walter Parkes) Himself, *A Terrible Tragedy: Alarming Evidence from the Making of the Film—A Woeful World* (documentary), Paramount, 2004.

(As Walter Parkes) Himself, *Taking Off: Making "The Terminal"* (documentary short), DreamWorks, 2004.

Himself, *Booking the Flight: The Script, the Story* (documentary short), DreamWorks Home Entertainment, 2004.

Himself, *Strength and Honor: Creating the World of "Gladiator"* (documentary), DreamWorks Home Entertainment, 2005.

Television Work; Series:

Creator, *Eddie Dodd* (also known as *True Believer*), ABC, 1991.

Creator (with Scott Frank) and executive producer, *Bird-land,* ABC, 1994.

Executive producer, *Men in Black: The Series* (also known as *Men in Black: The Animated Series*), The WB, 1997.

Television Work; Pilots:

Executive producer (with Lawrence Lasker), *Eddie Dodd,* ABC, 1991.

Television Appearances; Specials:

Inside "The Terminal," HBO, 2004.

Television Appearances; Episodic:

"Catch Me If You Can," *HBO First Look,* HBO, 2002.
"Inside 'The Terminal'," *HBO First Look,* HBO, 2004.
"The Making of 'The Ring Two'," *HBO First Look,* HBO, 2005.
"Just Like Heaven," *HBO First Look,* HBO, 2005.

WRITINGS

Screenplays:

(With Lawrence Lasker) *WarGames,* Metro–Goldwyn–Mayer/United Artists, 1983.
(With Lasker) *Sneakers,* Universal, 1992.

Television Pilots:

The Compass, NBC, 2000.

Television Episodes:

Eddie Dodd, 1991.
Birdland, ABC, 1994.

Other Writings:

Contributor to the magazine *Omni.*

OTHER SOURCES

Books:

Newsmakers, Issue 1, Gale Group, 2004.

Periodicals:

Forbes, March 3, 2003, p. 86.

PAUP, Theresa
  See **RUSSELL, Theresa**

PENA, Elizabeth 1959–
  (Elizabeth Anne Dicknson)

PERSONAL

Born September 23, 1959, in Elizabeth, NJ; daughter of Mario (an actor, writer, and director) and Estella Margarita (a producer and arts administrator; maiden name, Toirac) Pena; married William Stephan Kibler (a teacher and former talent agency), 1988 (marriage ended); married Hans Rolla (a carpenter and contractor), 1994; children: (second marriage) one daughter, one son. *Education:* Graduated from the New York High School of the Performing Arts, 1977; studied acting with Curt Dempster at the Ensemble Studio Theatre and with Endre Hules at La Mama Experimental Theatre Club, both New York, NY.

Addresses: *Office*—Film Independent, 9911 West Pico Blvd., 11th Floor, Los Angeles, CA 90035. *Agent*—Innovative Artists, 1505 10th St., Santa Monica, CA 90401. *Manager*—Rugolo Entertainment, 195 South Beverly Dr., Suite 400, Beverly Hills, CA 90212.

Career: Actress. Film Independent, Los Angeles, CA, member of board of directors.

Member: Actors' Equity Association, Screen Actors Guild, American Federation of Television and Radio Artists.

Awards, Honors: Woman of the Year Award, Hispanic Women's Council, 1988; New York Image Award, 1988; U.S. Congressional Award, U.S. Congress, 1988; Nosotros Golden Eagle Award, best actress, 1991; Bravo Award, outstanding actress in a feature film, National Council of La Raza, 1996, Independent Spirit Award, best supporting female, Independent Project Features West, 1997, both for *Lone Star;* ALMA Award nomination, outstanding actress in a feature film, American Latin Media Arts Awards, 1998, for *Gridlock'd;* ALMA Award, outstanding actress in a made–for–television movie or mini–series, 1998, for *Contagious;* ALMA Award nomination, outstanding actress in a made–for–television movie or miniseries, 1999, for *Aldrich Ames: Traitor Within;* ALMA Award, outstanding actress in a feature film, Blockbuster Entertainment Award nomination, favorite supporting actress in an action/adventure film, 1999, both for *Rush Hour;* ALMA Award, outstanding actress in a new television series, 2001, for *Resurrection Blvd;* ALMA Award, outstanding supporting actress in a motion picture, 2002, for *Tortilla Soup.*

CREDITS

Film Appearances:

Aurelita, *El Super,* New Yorker Films, 1979.

Disco hostess, *Times Square,* Associated Film Distributors, 1980.

Rita, *They All Laughed,* 1981.

Liz Garcia, *Crossover Dreams,* Crossover Films, Ltd., 1984.

Carmen, *Down and Out in Beverly Hills,* Buena Vista, 1985.

Rosie Morales, *La Bamba,* Columbia, 1986.

Marisa Esquivel, **batteries Not Included,* 1987.

Consuela, *Vibes* (also known as *Vibes: The Secret of the Golden Pyramids*), Columbia, 1988.

Tracy Perez, *Blue Steel,* Metro–Goldwyn–Mayer/United Artists, 1990.

Jezebel, *Jacob's Ladder* (also known as *Dante's Inferno*), TriStar, 1990.

Herself, *Building "Jacob's Ladder,"* 1990.

Rosa, *The Waterdance,* Samuel Goldwyn, 1992.

Vivian "Viv" Saunders, *Dead Funny,* 1994, A–Pix Entertainment, 1995.

Carmen, *Across the Moon,* Hemdale, 1994.

Kate Haley, *Free Willy 2: The Adventure Home* (also known as *Sauvez Willy 2*), Warner Bros., 1995.

Recon, 1996.

Pilar Cruz, *Lone Star,* Sony Pictures Classics, 1996.

(As Elizabeth Anne Dickenson) Admissions person, *Gridlock'd,* 1997.

Zeena, *The Pass* (also known as *Highway Hitcher*), York Entertainment, 1998.

Demolition specialist Tania Johnson, *Rush Hour,* New Line Cinema, 1998.

Toni Gage, *Strangeland* (also known as *Dee Snider's "StrangeLand"*), Artisan Entertainment, 1998.

Martha, *Seven Girlfriends,* Castle Hill Productions, 1999.

Herself, *A Piece of the Action: Behind the Scenes of "Rush Hour,"* 1999.

Connie, *On the Borderline,* Avalanche Home Entertainment, 2000.

Carmen, *Things Behind the Sun,* Behind the Sun Productions, 2001.

Leticia Naranjo, *Tortilla Soup,* Samuel Goldwyn Company, 2001.

Ten Tiny Love Stories (also known as *Women Remember Men*), Lions Gate Films Home Entertainment, 2001.

Midwife, *Imposter,* Dimension Films, 2002.

Ms. Tate, *ZigZag,* Silver Nitrate Films, 2002.

Narrator, *Adio Kerida* (documentary), 2002.

Voice of Mirage, *The Incredibles* (animated), Buena Vista, 2004.

How the Garcia Girls Spent Their Summer, 2005.

Margaret, *Transamerica,* IFC Films, 2005.

Gale, *Down in the Valley,* ThinkFilm, 2005.

Holly, *Keep Your Distance,* Lunacy Pictures, 2005.

Miliciana Munoz, *The Lost City,* Lions Gate Films, 2005.

Mirabela, *Sueno,* Destination Films, 2005.

Isabel Parades, *Adrift in Manhattan,* 2007.

Agent Linda Perez, *D–War* (also known as *Dragon Wars*), Freestyle Releasing, 2007.

Rosa Maria, *Goal II: Living the Dream,* Walt Disney Pictures, 2007.

Esperanza, *Love Comes Lately,* 2007.

Storyteller, *A Single Woman,* 2007.

Mrs. Castro, *Por vida,* 2008.

Also appeared in *Fat Chance.*

Television Appearances; Series:

Officer Connie Rivera, *Tough Cookies,* CBS, 1986.

Dora Calderon, *I Married Dora,* ABC, 1987–88.

Lucy Acosta, *Shannon's Deal,* NBC, 1990–91.

Beatriz "Bibi" Corrales, *Resurrection Blvd.,* Showtime, 2001–2003.

Voice of Rosa Santos, *Maya & Miguel,* PBS, 2004.

Also appeared in *As the World Turns.*

Television Appearances; Miniseries:

Mika Camarena, *Drug Wars: The Camarena Story* (also known as *Desperados: The Miki Camarena Story* and *Desperados: The Camarena Story*), NBC, 1990.

Ellen Garza, *The Invaders,* The WB, 1995.

Television Appearances; Movies:

Flo Martin, *Fugitive Among Us,* CBS, 1992.

Lisa, *Roommates,* NBC, 1994.

Elizabeth Gaitan, *Two,* 1995.

Ellen Fields, *It Came from Outer Space II,* Sci–Fi Channel, 1996.

Detective Lou Rojas, *Contagious* (also known as *Virus*), USA Network, 1997.

Christina, *The Second Civil War,* HBO, 1997.

Rosario Ames, *Aldrich Ames: Traitor Within,* Showtime, 1998.

Maria, *Border Line,* NBC, 1999.

Theresa Shoe, *The Hollywood Mom's Mystery,* Hallmark Channel, 2004.

Clara Harris, *Suburban Madness,* CBS, 2004.

Flores, *Racing for Time,* Lifetime, 2008.

Television Appearances; Specials:

Funny, You Don't Look 200: A Constitutional Vaudeville (also known as *Funny, You Don't Look 200*), ABC, 1987.

The 4th Annual Desi Awards, syndicated, 1992.

The 1995 NCLR Bravo Awards, Fox, 1995.

The 1996 NCLR Bravo Awards, Fox, 1996.

Canned Ham: "Rush Hour," Comedy Central, 1998.

The 2001 IFP/West Independent Spirit Awards, IFC, 2001.

Presenter, *The 17th Annual IFP/West Independent Spirit Awards,* IFC, 2002.

The 100 Scariest Movie Moments, Bravo, 2004.

Margaret, *La noche desperada,* 2007.

Television Appearances; Pilots:
Lucy Acosta, *Shannon's Deal,* NBC, 1989.

Television Appearances; Episodic:
Adelita Carrena, "Ordinary Hero," *Cagney & Lacey,* CBS, 1985.
Maria, "Ripoff," *T. J. Hooker,* CBS, 1985.
Alice, "Come and Get It," *Hill Street Blues,* 1986.
Debra, "Super Freak," *Dream On,* 1993.
Jinx Baldasseri, "Leap of Faith," *L.A. Law,* NBC, 1993.
Jinx Baldasseri, "Pacific Rimshot," *L.A. Law,* NBC, 1993.
Jinx Baldasseri, "Eli's Gumming," *L.A. Law,* NBC, 1993.
Jinx Baldasseri, "Whistle Stop," *L.A. Law,* NBC, 1994.
Dr. Jennifer Martinez, "Living Hell," *The Outer Limits* (also known as *The New Outer Limits*), Showtime and syndicated, 1995.
Gisella, "Fortune Teller," *Dead Man's Gun,* Showtime, 1997.
Aunt Ida, "Charts & Graphs: The Dessert Derby," *The Eddie Files,* 1998.
Superintendent Elizabeth Vasquez, "Chapter Forty–Seven," *Boston Public,* Fox, 2002.
Superintendent Elizabeth Vasquez, "Chapter Fifty–Four," *Boston Public,* Fox, 2003.
Mercedes Escalante, "Simple Man," *CSI: Miami,* CBS, 2003.
FBI Agent Lina Reyes, "Terminal Leave," *Navy NCIS: Naval Criminal Investigative Service* (also known as *NCIS* and *NCIS: Naval Criminal Investigative Service*), CBS, 2004.
Dennis Miller, CNBC, 2004.
Voice of Paran Dul, "Starcrossed: Parts 1, 2 & 3," *Justice League* (animated; also known as *JL* and *Justice League Unlimited*), Cartoon Network, 2004.
Voice of Paran Dul, "Hunter's Moon," *Justice League* (animated; also known as *JL* and *Justice League Unlimited*), Cartoon Network, 2005.
Rosie Diez, "Neither Rain Nor Sleet," *Without A Trace* (also known as *W.A.T.*), CBS, 2005.
Sonya Benavides, "Assassin," *Numb3rs* (also known as *Num3ers*), CBS, 2005.
Voice of Maria/Gold Digger, "Landon in Love," *Minoriteam* (animated), Cartoon Network, 2006.
Voice of store owner, "American Dream Factory," *American Dad!* (animated), Fox, 2007.

Also appeared in *Dellaventura; Feeling Good,* PBS; *Saturday Night Live,* NBC.

Television Director; Episodic:
"Justica," *Resurrection Blvd.,* Showtime, 2002.

Stage Appearances:
Jesse, *Dog Lady,* International Arts Relations Theatre, New York City, 1984.
Jane, *Becoming Garcia,* Louis Abron Arts for Living Center, New York City, 1984.

Appeared as barmaid, *Act One and Only,* Public Theatre, New York City; Maria, *Bring on the Night,* Sutton Theatre; Teresa, *Italian–American Reconciliation,* GNU Theatre; Teresa, *La Morena,* Henry Street Playhouse, New York City; Beba, *Night of the Assassins,* La Mama Experimental Theatre Club, New York City; Juliet, *Romeo and Juliet,* Gramercy Arts Theatre, New York City; and Cynthia, *Shattered Image,* American Theatre of Actors, New York City; also appeared in *Antigone, Blood Wedding,* and *Cinderella,* off–Broadway productions.

Major Tours:
Toured as Juliet, *Romeo and Juliet.*

RECORDINGS

Video Games:
Voice of Mirage, *The Incredibles,* 2004.

Music Videos:
Appeared in Alabama's "She and I."

OTHER SOURCES

Books:
Dictionary of Hispanic Biography, Gale Research, 1996.
Notable Hispanic American Women, Book 1, Gale Research, 1993.

Periodicals:
Parade, February 14, 1999.
People Weekly, May 13, 1991, pp. 107–08.

PENNER, Jonathan 1962–

PERSONAL

Full name, Jonathan Lindsay Penner; born March 5, 1962, in New York, NY; married Stacy Title (a director, producer, and writer); children: two, including Ava. *Education:* Sarah Lawrence College, graduated; attended London Academy of Music and Dramatic Arts; studied acting with Larry Moss and Julie Bovasso, voice with Therman Bailey, Andrew Jack, and Robert Palmer, dance and movement with Trish Arnold and Ben Bennison, and stage combat with Steve Vaughn and Henry Marshal.

Addresses: *Agent*—Elise Henderson, William Morris Agency, 1 William Morris Pl., Beverly Hills, CA 90212; (theatre) Joe Vance, Domain, 9229 Sunset Blvd., Suite

415, Los Angeles, CA 90069. *Manager*—Lisa Suzanne Blum, Modus Entertainment, 110 South Fairfax Ave., Suite 250, Los Angeles, CA 90036.

Career: Actor, producer, and writer. Title/Penner Productions, partner and executive vice president. Also worked as assistant director and second unit director.

Awards, Honors: Academy Award nomination (with Stacy Title), best short live–action film, 1994, for *Down at the Waterfront;* Prix SACD (with Title), Avignon Film Festival, 2000, for *Let the Devil Wear Black;* Drama-Logue Award, best actor, for *Zastrozzi.*

CREDITS

Film Appearances:
Morris Codman, *Religion, Inc.* (also known as *A Fool and His Money*), Chronicle Films, 1989.
Marv Miller, *White Palace,* Universal, 1990.
Dr. Leonard Stafford, *Amityville 1992: It's about Time,* Republic, 1992.
Studio executive, *Dragon: The Bruce Lee Story,* Universal, 1993.
Air traffic captain, *Coneheads,* Paramount, 1993.
Al Cohn, *Down at the Waterfront* (short film), Strand Releasing, 1993, later broadcast as a television special by PBS, 1994.
Marc, *The Last Supper,* Columbia, 1995.
Dominick, *Raging Angels,* Borde Releasing, 1995.
Desk sergeant, *Excessive Force II: Force on Force,* Cinetel Films, 1995.
Johnny Marvosa, *Bloodfist VII* (also known as *Manhunt*), Concorde–New Horizons, 1995.
Radio voice, *Judgement,* 1995.
Seaman Stanley "Spots" Sylversterson, *Down Periscope,* Twentieth Century–Fox, 1996.
Matt Smith, *Wedding Bell Blues,* Legacy Releasing, 1996.
First cop, *For Better or Worse,* Columbia, 1996.
Jerry, *Anarchy TV,* Asylum, 1997.
Jon, *Cleopatra's Second Husband,* 1998, Indican Pictures, 2000.
Adam, *Inconceivable,* Asylum, 1998.
Man, *Flying with the Angels,* Green Building Films, 1998.
Jack Lyne, *Let the Devil Wear Black,* Trimark Pictures, 1999.
Guy, *Would I Lie to You?,* 2002.
Fowler, *Hood of Horror* (also known as *Snoop Dogg's "Hood of Horror"*), Xenon Pictures/Freestyle Releasing, 2006.

Also appeared in *Baby It's You, Fighting Fish* (short film), and *Spirit.*

Film Work:
Producer (with wife, Stacy Title), *Down at the Waterfront* (short film), Strand Releasing, 1993, later broadcast as a television special by PBS, 1994.
Co–executive producer, *The Last Supper,* Columbia, 1995.
Co–executive producer, *Let the Devil Wear Black,* Trimark Pictures, 1999.
Co–executive producer, *Hood of Horror* (also known as *Snoop Dogg's "Hood of Horror"*), Xenon Pictures/Freestyle Releasing, 2006.

Television Appearances; Series:
Nick Columbus, *The Naked Truth* (also known as *Wilde Again*), NBC, 1995–97.
Dave Parelli, *Rude Awakening,* Showtime, 1998–2001.
Contestant and juror, *Survivor,* CBS, 2006.

Television Appearances; Pilots:
Danny Imperiali, *The Nanny,* CBS, 1993.
Brad, *Grapevine,* CBS, 2000.

Television Appearances; Episodic:
David Klein, "The Allison and Ken Story," *Grapevine,* CBS, 1992.
David Klein, "The Jessica and Tony Story," *Grapevine,* CBS, 1992.
Joel, "Married to It," *Melrose Place,* Fox, 1993.
Danny Imperiali, "Franny's Choice," *The Nanny,* CBS, 1994.
Michael, *Madman of the People,* 1994.
Paul, "Gale Gets a Life," *LateLine,* ABC, 1998.
Zach, "The Bookstore," *Seinfeld,* NBC, 1998.
Steve Filberg/the champion, "The Big Leagues," *The Tick,* Fox, 2001.
Detective Fellows, "Not without My Daughter," *Arrested Development,* Fox, 2004.
Detective Travis, "Viva Las Vegas," *CSI: Crime Scene Investigation* (also known as *C.S.I., CSI: Las Vegas,* and *Les experts*), CBS, 2004.
FBI Agent Jaffe, "Five Pillars," *E–Ring,* NBC, 2006.
Newt Glick, "Run Silent, Run Deep," *CSI: NY,* CBS, 2006.

Television Appearances; Other:
Jim, *Under the Car* (special), Showtime, 1993.
Larry Reese, *The Courtyard* (movie), Showtime, 1995.

Television Work; Movies:
Executive producer, *The Lone Ranger,* The WB, 2003.

Stage Appearances:
Appeared in *Blue Is the Boys,* Corner Loft Theatre, New York City; *A Midsummer Night's Dream,* Texas Shakespeare Festival; *This Wooden O,* Wings Theatre Company, New York City; *Triplets,* Skylight Theatre;

Twelfth Night, Texas Shakespeare Festival; *What the Butler Saw,* Forum Theatre Group, New York City; and in title role, *Zastrozzi* (also known as *Zastrozzi: The Master of Discipline*), Beverly Hills Playhouse, Beverly Hills, CA.

Major Tours:

Toured U.S. cities in *Mornings of April and May;* toured U.S. cities as actor and stage manager in *I Giularri di piazza.*

Stage Work:

Coproducer, *Zastrozzi* (also known as *Zastrozzi: The Master of Discipline*), Beverly Hills Playhouse, Beverly Hills, CA.

WRITINGS

Screenplays:

(With Stacy Title) *Down at the Waterfront* (short film), Strand Releasing, 1993, later broadcast as a television special by PBS, 1994.
Let the Devil Wear Black, Trimark Pictures, 1999.

Television Movies:

The Lone Ranger, The WB, 2003.

Stage Plays:

Author of *Zastrozzi* (also known as *Zastrozzi: The Master of Discipline*), Beverly Hills Playhouse, Beverly Hills, CA.

PERRY, Luke 1965–

PERSONAL

Full name, Coy Luther Perry III; born October 11, 1965, in Mansfield, OH; son of Coy (a steelworker) and Ann (a homemaker) Perry; stepson of Steve Bennett (a construction worker); married Rachel "Minnie" Sharp (a former model), November 20, 1993 (divorced, 2003); children: Jack, Sophie. *Education:* Graduated from Fredricktown High School, Fredricktown, OH.

Addresses: *Agent*—Paradigm, 360 North Crescent Dr., North Bldg., Beverly Hills, CA 90210. *Manager*—Himber Entertainment, 211 South Beverly Dr., Suite 208, Beverly Hills, CA 90212. *Publicist*—Rogers and Cowan Public Relations, 8687 Melrose Ave., Pacific Design Center, 7th Floor, Los Angeles, CA 90069.

Career: Actor. Midwest Productions, founder. Appeared in television commercials for Pizza Hut, 1997; appeared in print ads for Faded Glory Jeans, 1994. Worked in a doorknob factory, a hotel, as an asphalt layer, a cook, chauffeur, shoe salesperson, painter, construction worker, and store clerk.

Awards, Honors: Video Premiere Award nomination, best supporting actor, DVD Exclusive Awards, 2001, for *Attention Shoppers;* TV Land Award nomination, favorite teen dream—male, 2004, TV Land Award nomination (with Shannen Doherty), break up that was so bad it was good, 2007, both for *Beverly Hills, 90210.*

CREDITS

Film Appearances:
Sweet Trash, 1989.
Ray Ray, *Scorchers* (also known as *Jumper: Hot Lover*), 1991.
John Hunter, *Terminal Bliss,* Cannon Pictures, 1992.
Pike, *Buffy the Vampire Slayer,* Twentieth Century–Fox, 1992.
Garbage guy, *The Webbers* (also known as *At Home with the Webbers* and *Webber's World*), Den Films, 1993.
Lane Frost, *8 Seconds* (also known as *The Lane Frost Story*), New Line Cinema, 1994.
Himself, *Vacanze di Natale 95,* Filmauro Distribuzione, 1995.
Chris Anderson, *Normal Life,* Fine Line Features, 1996.
Johnny, *American Strays,* A–Pix Entertainment/Unapix Entertainment, 1996.
Billy, *The Fifth Element* (also known as *Le cinquieme element*), Columbia/TriStar, 1997.
Martin Devoe, *Lifebreath* (also known as *Last Breath*), 1997.
Frankie, *The Florentine,* Bcb Productions, 1999.
Jack, *The Heist,* 1999.
Dr. Ron Young, *Storm* (also known as *Storm Trackers*), 1999.
Mark, *Attention Shoppers,* Metro–Goldwyn–Mayer Home Entertainment, 2000.
Attorney, *Dirt,* Canned Pictures, 2001.
Dr. Michael Ashton, *The Enemy* (also known as *Todliche Formel*), 2001.
Bob, *Fogbound,* 2002.
Narrator, *Cowboy Up: Inside the Extreme World of Bull Riding* (documentary), 2002.
David, *Down the Barrel* (also known as *Luxury of Love*), 2003.
Tony, *Dishdogz,* Lionsgate, 2005.
Ben McKinley, *Alice,* Lionsgate, 2007.
Tommy, *The Sandlot 3* (also known as *The Sandlot: Heading Home*), Twentieth Century–Fox, 2007.

Television Appearances; Series:
Ned Bates, *Loving,* ABC, 1987–88.

Kenny, *Another World* (also known as *Another World: Bay City*), NBC, 1988.

Dylan McKay, *Beverly Hills, 90210,* Fox, 1990–95, 1998–2000.

Voice of Napoleon Brie, *Biker Mice from Mars* (animated), 1994–95.

Voice of Sub–Zero, *Mortal Kombat: The Animated Series* (animated; also known as *Mortal Kombat: Defenders of the Realm*), USA Network, 1995.

Voice of Rick Jones, *The Incredible Hulk,* UPN, 1996.

Voice of Stewart Walldinger, *Pepper Ann* (animated; also known as *Disney's "Pepper Ann"*), ABC, 1997–99.

Reverend Jeremiah Cloutier, *Oz,* HBO, 2001–2002.

Title role, *Jeremiah,* Showtime, 2002–2004.

Peter Schaefer, *Windfall,* NBC, 2006.

Linc Stark, *John from Cincinnati,* HBO, 2007.

Television Appearances; Miniseries:

Beau Stark, *Invasion* (also known as *Robin Cook's "Invasion"*), NBC, 1997.

Harry Hammett, *Johnson County War,* Hallmark Channel, 2002.

Television Appearances; Movies:

Martin Devoe, *The Last Breath* (also known as *Lifebreath*), 1991.

Boomer, "Empty," *Riot* (also known as *Riot in the Streets*), Showtime, 1997.

Michael Nash, *Indiscreet,* HBO, 1998.

Dr. Ron Young, *Storm,* Fox Family Channel, 1999.

The Last Buckaroo, TBS, 2000.

Stu Sheridan, *The Triangle,* 2001.

Dr. Jake Rollins, *Descent,* Sci–Fi Channel, 2005.

Dr. Chris Richardson, *Supernova,* Hallmark Channel, 2005.

Television Appearances; Specials:

Entertainers '91: The Top Twenty of the Year, ABC, 1991.

Idols, Fox, 1991.

The 43rd Annual Primetime Emmy Awards Presentation, Fox, 1991.

The 18th Annual People's Choice Awards, CBS, 1992.

The 49th Annual Golden Globe Awards, TBS, 1992.

Presenter, *The 1992 MTV Movie Awards,* MTV, 1992.

MTV Video Music Awards 1992, MTV, 1992.

First Person with Maria Shriver, NBC, 1992.

Fox/MTV Guide to Summer 92, Fox, 1992.

Star–athon 92: A Weekend with the Stars, syndicated, 1992.

Oliver Pike, *Buffy the Vampire Slayer: Featurette,* 1992.

Presenter, *The Walt Disney Company Presents the American Teacher Awards,* 1992.

Presenter, *The 18th Annual People's Choice Awards,* CBS, 1992.

Back to School '92, 1992.

In a New Light '93, 1993.

Edna Time, Fox, 1993.

90210: Behind the Scenes, 1993.

The 29th Annual Academy of Country Music Awards, NBC, 1994.

In a New Light '94, 1994.

Host, *The 1995 World Music Awards,* ABC, 1994.

A 90210 Christmas Special, 1994.

Presenter, *The Blockbuster Entertainment Awards,* CBS, 1995, UPN, 1996.

"Beverly Hills 90210": Our Favorite Moments, Fox, 1998.

The 1999 Teen Choice Awards, Fox, 1999.

Presenter, *TNN Music City News Country Awards,* TNN, 1999.

Voice of Brom Bones, *The Night of the Headless Horseman* (animated), Fox, 1999.

Just for Laughs: Montreal Comedy Festival, 1999.

The Mod Squad: The E! True Hollywood Story, E! Entertainment Television, 2000.

Beverly Hills 90210: The Final Goodbye, Fox, 2000.

"Beverly Hills, 90210": The E! True Hollywood Story, E! Entertainment Television, 2001.

John Wayne Made Me Cry: Our Western Heros (also known as *John Wayne Made Me Cry: Our Western Heroes*), TMC, 2002.

"Beverly Hills, 90210": 10–Year High School Reunion, Fox, 2003.

Shannen Doherty: The E! True Hollywood Story, E! Entertainment Television, 2003.

The 3rd Annual TV Land Awards, TV Land, 2005.

Television Appearances; Episodic:

The Tonight Show Starring Johnny Carson, NBC, 1991.

Himself, "Geek Tragedy," *Parker Lewis Can't Lose* (also known as *Parker Lewis*), 1992.

"Tonarsserien Beverly Hills en succe for TV4," *Nyhetsmorgon,* 1992.

Voice, "Krusty Gets Kancelled," *The Simpsons* (animated), Fox, 1993.

Guest host, *Saturday Night Live* (also known as *SNL*), NBC, 1993.

Peter Brinkley, "The Time Has Come Today," *Beverly Hills, 90210,* Fox, 1994.

Billy McCoy/Marshall Jedediah Southwit, "The Real McKay," *Beverly Hills, 90210,* Fox, 1995.

Spence, "Kiss Me, Stupid," *Spin City,* ABC, 1997.

The Rosie O'Donnell Show, syndicated, 1997, 1999, 2002.

Hollywood Squares (also known as *H2* and *H2: Hollywood Squares*), syndicated, 1998.

The Howard Stern Radio Show, 1999.

Howard Stern, 1999.

Voice of himself, "The Story on Page 1," *Family Guy* (animated; also known as *Padre de familia*), Fox, 2000.

Voice of himself, "Luke Perry's Guide to Love," *Johnny Bravo* (animated), Cartoon Network, 2000.

Dr. Michael Sears, "Now He's Coming Up the Stairs," *Night Visions,* Fox, 2001.

Himself and Oliver Pike, "Buffy the Vampire Slayer," *Backstory* (also known as *Hollywood Backstories*), AMC, 2002.

The Late Late Show with Craig Kilborn (also known as *The Late Late Show*), CBS, 2002.

Late Night with Conan O'Brien, NBC, 2002, 2006.

Late Show with David Letterman (also known as *The Late Show*), CBS, 2002.

Voice of Ponce de Leon, "Litter Kills: Litterally," *Clone High* (animated; also known as *Clone High, U.S.A.*), MTV, 2003.

Jimmy Kimmel Live!, ABC, 2003, 2006.

Judge, *Pet Star,* Animal Planet, 2003.

GMTV, ITV, 2004.

Richard & Judy, Channel 4, 2004.

T4, Channel 4, 2004.

Today with Des and Mel, ITV, 2004.

Aaron, "The Birds and the Bees," *Will & Grace,* NBC, 2005.

Todd, "Dangerous Liaison," *What I Like About You,* The WB, 2005.

Todd, "My Boyfriend's Back," *What I Like About You,* The WB, 2005.

Todd, "Enough Is Enough," *What I Like About You,* The WB, 2005.

Ellen: The Ellen DeGeneres Show, syndicated, 2005.

Todd, "I Want My Baby Back," *What I Like About You,* The WB, 2005.

Live with Regis and Kelly, syndicated, 2005.

(Uncredited) Dylan McKay, *Headline News,* CNN, 2006.

Last Call with Carson Daly, NBC, 2006.

Friday Night Smackdown!, 2006.

Also appeared as voice, *Fanatic* (also known as *MTV's "Fanatic"*), MTV.

Television Work; Series:

Executive producer, *Jeremiah,* Showtime, 2002.

Television Work; Movies:

Executive producer, *Indiscreet,* HBO, 1998.

Television Director; Episodic:

"Fortune Cookie," *Beverly Hills, 90210,* Fox, 1999.

"Laying Pipe," *Beverly Hills, 90210,* Fox, 1999.

Stage Appearances:

Guest, *The J. Keith van Straaten Show,* ACME Comedy Theatre, Los Angeles, 2001.

(Broadway debut) Brad Majors, *The Rocky Horror Show,* Circle in the Square Theatre, New York City, 2001.

Harry, *When Harry Met Sally,* West End production, 2004.

RECORDINGS

Videos:

Time Out: The Truth about HIV, AIDS, and You, Paramount, 1992.

For Our Children, 1993.

Music Videos:

Twisted Sister: Come Out and Play, 1986.

OTHER SOURCES

Books:

Newsmakers 1992, Gale, 1992.

Reisfeld, Randi, *Loving Luke: The Unauthorized Luke Perry Story in Facts and Photos,* Bantam Books, 1991.

Periodicals:

People, August 26, 1991, pp. 38–39; September 9, 1991; November 4, 1991, pp. 95–102; May 5, 1997, p. 19; November 23, 1998, p. 27.

Rolling Stone, February 20, 1992.

Vanity Fair, July, 1992, pp. 92–96, 146–51.

Electronic:

Luke Perry Website, http://www.lukeperry.com, October 10, 2007.

PETRARCA, David 1962–

PERSONAL

Born November 10, 1962, in Warwick, RI. *Education:* New York University, B.F.A., 1983. *Avocational Interests:* Collecting folk art.

Addresses: *Agent*—Creative Artists Agency, 2000 Avenue of the Stars, Los Angeles, CA 90067. *Manager*—Rosalie Swedlin, Industry Entertainment, 955 South Carrillo Dr., 3rd Floor, Los Angeles, CA 90048.

Career: Director and producer. Limbo Theatre, New York City, artistic director, 1982–85; Cincinnati Playhouse, Cincinnati, OH, artistic associate, 1984–85; Chelsea Theatre Center, New York City, associate artistic director, 1985–86; Goodman Theatre, Chicago, IL, resident director, 1987—. Faculty member at North Carolina School of the Arts and Northwestern University. National Endowment for the Arts, onsite evaluator, 1990—.

Member: Society of Stage Directors and Choreographers, Dramatists Guild.

Awards, Honors: Helen Hayes Award nomination, Washington Theatre Awards Society, 1986, for *As Is*; directing fellowship, Theatre Communication Group and National Endowment for the Arts, 1987; Joseph Jefferson Award nomination, 1990, Outer Critics Circle Award nomination, and London Fringe Award nomination, all for *Marvin's Room*; Joseph Jefferson award, c. 1995, for *The House of Martin Guerre*; named Chicagoan of the year, *Chicago Tribune*, 1996.

CREDITS

Stage Director:

The Tooth of Crime, Hartford Stage Company, Hartford, CT, 1986.

As Is, 1986.

Lloyd's Prayer, Remains Theatre, Chicago, IL, 1988.

Three Postcards, Northlight Theatre, Evanston, IL, 1988.

Mill Fire, Goodman Theatre, Chicago, IL, then Apple Corps Theatre, New York City, 1989.

Nothing Sacred, Northlight Theatre, 1989.

Peacekeeper, 1990.

Marvin's Room, Goodman Theatre, 1990, then Hartford Stage Company, 1991, Playwrights Horizons Theatre, New York City, 1991–92, Minetta Lane Theatre, New York City, 1992, and Comedy Theatre, New York City, 1993, later John F. Kennedy Center for the Performing Arts, Washington, DC, and Hampstead Theatre Club, London.

The Visit, Goodman Theatre, 1991.

Deep in a Dream of You, Goodman Theatre, then Public Theatre, New York City, both 1991.

A Midsummer Night's Dream, Dallas Theatre Center, Dallas, TX, 1991.

Richard II, Goodman Theatre, 1993.

Sin, Goodman Theatre, 1994, then Second Stage, McGinn–Cazale Theatre, New York City, 1995.

The House of Martin Guerre, Goodman Theatre, 1995, then Canadian Stage Company, Bluma Appel Theatre, Toronto, Ontario, Canada, 1997.

The Water Children, Playwrights Horizons Theatre, 1997.

Dinah Was, Workshop of the Players Art, Gramercy Theatre, New York City, 1998, then Kreeger Theatre, Arena Stage, Washington, DC, 2000.

Red, Long Wharf Theatre, New Haven, CT, and Manhattan Theatre Club Stage II, New York City, 1999.

Fuddy Meers, Manhattan Theatre Club Stage II, 1999–2000, then Minetta Lane Theatre, 2000.

Current Events, Manhattan Theatre Club Stage II, 2000.

The Man Who Would Be King, Goodman Theatre, 2000.

Schoolgirl Figure, Goodman Theatre, 2000.

A Year with Frog and Toad (musical), Children's Theatre, Minneapolis, MN, 2002, then Cort Theatre, New York City, 2003.

Kimberly Akimbo, Manhattan Theatre Club Stage I, 2003.

Juvenilia, Playwrights Horizons Theatre, 2003.

Also directed productions of *Away,* Northlight Theatre, Chicago, IL; *Dark Rapture,* American Conservatory Theatre, San Francisco, CA; *Design for Living,* Goodman Theatre, Chicago; *Down the Shore; Light Up the Sky,* Goodman Theatre; *Northeast Local,* Trinity Repertory Theatre and Seattle Repertory Theatre, Seattle, WA; *Peacekeeper,* American Blues Theatre, Chicago; *The Skin of Our Teeth,* Goodman Theatre; and *Somebody Else's House.*

Major Tours:

Director of *Dinah Was,* U.S. cities.

Television Director; Series:

Dawson's Creek, The WB, multiple episodes, 2000–2002.

Everwood (also known as *Our New Life in Everwood*), The WB, multiple episodes, between 2002 and 2006.

Television Director; Episodic:

"The Coldest Night of the Year," *Nothing Sacred,* ABC, 1998.

"Hung Jury," *Cupid,* ABC, 1998.

"Pseudos, Sex, and Sidebars," *Jack & Jill,* The WB, 1999.

"Lovers and Other Strangers," *Jack & Jill,* The WB, 2000.

"Hope in a Jar," *Popular,* The WB, 2000.

"Paris Is Burning," *Gilmore Girls* (also known as *Gilmore Girls: Beginnings*), The WB, 2001.

"Seriously, All Coma Proposals Aside," *Jack & Jill,* The WB, 2001.

"Caution: Parents Crossing," *Jack & Jill,* The WB, 2001.

"Hostile Environment," *Pasadena,* 2001.

"The Last Thanksgiving," *Felicity,* The WB, 2001.

"Bringeth It On," *Joan of Arcadia,* CBS, 2003.

"Big Waves," *Summerland,* The WB, 2004.

"And Justice for All," *Jack & Bobby,* The WB, 2004.

"The First Lady," *Jack & Bobby,* The WB, 2004.

"Chess Lessons," *Jack & Bobby,* The WB, 2005.

"A New Frontier," *Jack & Bobby,* The WB, 2005.

"The Long Lead Story," *Studio 60 on the Sunset Strip* (also known as *Studio 60*), NBC, 2006.

"Helpy Helperpants," *State of Mind,* Lifetime, 2007.

"Family Day," *Brothers & Sisters,* ABC, 2007.

"Surstromming or a Slice," *Six Degrees,* ABC, 2007.

"Objects in the Mirror," *Six Degrees,* ABC, 2007.

Also directed episodes of *Early Edition,* CBS, and *Glory Days* (also known as *Demontown*), The WB.

Television Work; Other:
Producer, *Everwood* (series; also known as *Our New Life in Everwood*), The WB, 2004, 2005.

Film Director:
Save the Last Dance 2 (also known as *Steppin' Up*), Paramount Home Video, 2006.

PHILLIPS, Michelle 1944–

PERSONAL

Original name, Holly Michelle Gilliam; born June 4, 1944, in Long Beach, CA; daughter of Gardner Burnett (a merchant marine) and Joyce Leon (an accountant; maiden name, Poole) Gilliam; married John Phillips (a musician, composer, actor, and producer), December 31, 1962 (divorced, 1968 or 1970); married Dennis Hopper (an actor and director), October 31, 1970 (divorced November 8, 1970); married Robert Burch (a radio executive), May 21, 1978 (divorced, 1980); married Grainger Hines (an actor, producer, and director; divorced); married Steven Zax (a plastic surgeon), March, 2000; children: (first marriage) Gilliam Chynna (a singer and songwriter); (fourth marriage) Austin Devereux, Aron Scott Wilson; stepchildren: Bijou Phillips (an actress), Mackenzie Phillips (an actress), Jeffrey Phillips.

Addresses: *Agent*—Origin Talent Agency, 4705 Laurel Canyon, Suite 306, Studio City, CA 91607. *Manager*—Josh Scherr, Candy Entertainment, 8833 West Sunset Blvd., Suite 402, Los Angeles, CA 90069.

Career: Actress, singer, and writer. Francis Gill Agency, New York City, model, 1962–64; performed with the Journeymen, early 1960s, then cofounder of the New Journeymen; member of the Mamas and the Papas (folk rock band), 1965–68.

Member: American Federation of Television and Radio Artists, Screen Actors Guild.

Awards, Honors: Grammy Award (with the Mamas and the Papas), best contemporary (rock and roll) group performance, National Academy of Recording Arts and Sciences, 1966, for "Monday, Monday"; Golden Globe Award nomination, most promising female newcomer, 1974, for *Dillinger;* Medal of Honor, Stop War Toys Campaign, Alliance for Survival, 1987; *Soap Opera Digest* Award, outstanding prime–time villainess, 1991, and *Soap Opera Digest* Award nomination, outstanding prime–time actress, 1992, both for *Knots Landing;* inducted (with the Mamas and the Papas) into Rock and Roll Hall of Fame, 1997; four gold albums (with the Mamas and the Papas), Recording Industry Association of America.

CREDITS

Television Appearances; Series:
Ruby Ashford, *Search for Tomorrow,* 1983.
Elizabeth Bradshaw Cabot, a recurring role, *Hotel* (also known as *Arthur Hailey's "Hotel"*), 1983–86.
Anne W. Matheson Sumner, *Knots Landing,* CBS, 1989–93.
Joanna, *Second Chances,* CBS, 1993–94.
Suki Walker, *Malibu Shores,* CBS, 1996.
Voice of Raven, *Spicy City,* 1997.
Abby Malone, a recurring role, *Beverly Hills, 90210,* Fox, 1997–98.

Television Appearances; Movies:
Maggie, *The California Kid,* ABC, 1974.
Joyce Kreski, *The Death Squad,* ABC, 1974.
Marina Brent, *The Users,* ABC, 1978.
Meredith Tyne, *Moonlight,* CBS, 1982.
Chris Jameson, *Murder Me, Murder You* (also known as *Mickey Spillane's "Mike Hammer: Murder Me, Murder You"*), CBS, 1983.
Katie Jordan, *Secrets of a Married Man,* NBC, 1984.
Claire Noble, *Covenant,* NBC, 1985.
Paint Me a Murder (also known as *Hammer House of Mystery and Suspense: Paint Me a Murder*), USA Network, 1985.
Jennifer Clayton, *Stark: Mirror Image* (also known as *Stark II*), CBS, 1986.
Madge Evers, *Assault and Matrimony,* NBC, 1987.
Suzanna Hollander, *Trenchcoat in Paradise,* CBS, 1989.
Leora Van Treas, "Murder Takes All" (also known as "Mike Hammer in Las Vegas"), *Mickey Spillane's "Mike Hammer,"* CBS, 1989.
Jordana Orwitz, *Rubdown,* USA Network, 1993.
Laura Collins, *No One Would Tell,* NBC, 1996.
Mrs. Stepanek, *Pretty Poison,* 1996.
Nancy Nevins, *Sweetwater* (also known as *Sweetwater: A True Rock Story*), VH1, 1999.

Television Appearances; Miniseries:
Gloria Osborne, *Aspen* (also known as *The Innocent and the Damned*), NBC, 1977.
Jennie Barber, *The French Atlantic Affair,* ABC, 1979.
Anne W. Matheson Sumner, *Knots Landing: Back to the Cul–de–Sac,* CBS, 1997.

Television Appearances; Episodic:
(With the Mamas and the Papas) *Shindig!,* 1965.
(With the Mamas and the Papas) *Hullabaloo,* 1966.
(With the Mamas and the Papas) *Where the Action Is,* 1966.
(With the Mamas and the Papas) *The Hollywood Palace,* 1966.
(With the Mamas and the Papas) *Bandstand* (also known as *AB* and *American Bandstand*), 1966, 1967.
(With the Mamas and the Papas) *Toast of the Town* (also known as *The Ed Sullivan Show*), 1966, 1967.
(With the Mamas and the Papas) "Rodgers & Hart Today," *ABC Stage 67,* ABC, 1967.
"The Prowler," *Owen Marshall, Counselor at Law,* ABC, 1973.
Anne Winston Matheson, *Knots Landing,* CBS, 1979.
Princess Nyah the Mermaid, "The Mermaid," *Fantasy Island,* ABC, 1979.
The Tonight Show Starring Johnny Carson, NBC, 1979.
"Ladies in Blue," *Vegas* (also known as *Vega$*), ABC, 1980.
Officer Cassandra Hunt, "Golden Gate Cop Killer: Parts 1 & 2," *Vegas* (also known as *Vega$*), ABC, 1980.
Princess Nyah the Mermaid, "The Mermaid Returns," *Fantasy Island,* ABC, 1980.
Sheila Godfrey, "Lady Godiva," *Fantasy Island,* ABC, 1981.
Barbara Carroll, "The Three R's," *The Love Boat,* ABC, 1981.
Sheila Godfrey, "Man–Beast/Ole Island Oprey," *Fantasy Island,* ABC, 1981.
Valerie, "The Magic Camera/Mata Hari/Valerie," *Fantasy Island,* ABC, 1982.
"Legends," *Fantasy Island,* ABC, 1982.
Linda, "Doc's Nephew," *The Love Boat,* ABC, 1982.
Glenda Collins, "Shark Bait," *Matt Houston,* ABC, 1982.
Fay Charles, "The Chameleon," *The Fall Guy,* ABC, 1983.
Helen Sinclair, "Three's a Crowd," *Fantasy Island,* ABC, 1983.
"No More Alimony," *The Love Boat,* ABC, 1983.
Veronica Everly, "Murder Take One," *Automan,* ABC, 1984.
Princess Nyah the Mermaid, "The Mermaid and the Matchmaker," *Fantasy Island,* ABC, 1984.
Alicia Marsh, "Yesterday's Child," *Finder of Lost Loves,* ABC, 1984.
Regina Kellijian, "Death Casts a Spell," *Murder, She Wrote,* CBS, 1984.
Teri Sherman, "Love Story," *T. J. Hooker,* ABC, 1985.
"Murder on the Half Shell," *Scene of the Crime,* NBC, 1985.
"The Matriarch," *Glitter,* ABC, 1985.
Rich robbery victim, *Santa Barbara,* NBC, 1985.
Katherine Clark, "If Looks Could Kill," *Alfred Hitchcock Presents,* USA Network, 1988.
Jenice Manheim, "We'll Always Have Paris," *Star Trek: The Next Generation* (also known as *Star Trek: TNG*), syndicated, 1988.

Denise Zima, "Who Killed the Starlet?" *Burke's Law,* CBS, 1994.
Sandra Clayton, "A Head in the Polls," *Herman's Head,* Fox, 1994.
Christine Radford–Shaw, "A Very Fatal Funeral," *Diagnosis Murder,* CBS, 1994.
"Stepping Out," *Heaven Help Us,* 1994.
Joanna Russell, "Save the Last Dance for Me," *Second Chances,* 1994.
Joanna Russell, "Swimming through Mud," *Second Chances,* 1994.
Joanna Russell, "Living In Between," *Second Chances,* 1994.
Claudette Wilder, "Target: Jimmy Olsen," *Lois & Clark: The New Adventures of Superman* (also known as *Lois & Clark* and *The New Adventures of Superman*), ABC, 1995.
Karen Reeves, "Donny's Mother," *Too Something* (also known as *New York Daze*), Fox, 1996.
Cassandra, "Foreplay," *Pauly,* Fox, 1997.
"The Mamas and the Papas," *Behind the Music* (also known as *BH1's Behind the Music*), VH1, 1998.
Maude Standish, "Witness," *The Magnificent Seven,* CBS, 1998.
Quinn Ford, "True Course," *The Love Boat: The Next Wave,* UPN, 1998.
Maude Standish, "Sins of the Past," *The Magnificent Seven,* CBS, 1999.
Blair Mason, "If Memory Serves," *Providence,* NBC, 1999.
Vivian, "Dude Awakening," *Rude Awakening,* Showtime, 1999.
Vivian, "Trude Awakening," *Rude Awakening,* Showtime, 1999.
Livia Parkinson, "The Flame," *Diagnosis Murder,* CBS, 1999.
Edwina Lewis, "Old Flames," *Twice in a Lifetime,* PAX, 2000.
Maude Standish, "The Trial," *The Magnificent Seven,* CBS, 2000.
Hellacious Akers, "Style and Substance Abuse," *Popular,* The WB, 2000.
Hellacious Akers, "Ur–ine Trouble," *Popular,* The WB, 2000.
Juliana Merrick, "The Scare," *All About Us,* 2001.
Joan Moore, "The Wedding Scammer," *Spin City,* ABC, 2001.
"Sex in the Suburbs," *That's Life,* 2001.
Lily, "Regrets," *7th Heaven* (also known as *Seventh Heaven* and *7th Heaven: Beginnings*), The WB, 2001.
"Michelle Phillips," *Autograph,* 2002.
Christine Newton, "The Mama and the Papa," *Abby,* UPN, 2003.
Lily, "Don't Speak Ill of the Living or the Dead," *7th Heaven* (also known as *Seventh Heaven* and *7th Heaven: Beginnings*), The WB, 2004.
Lily, "Two Weddings, an Engagement, and a Funeral," *7th Heaven* (also known as *Seventh Heaven* and *7th Heaven: Beginnings*), The WB, 2004.

(With the Mamas and the Papas; in archive footage) "Lo veraniego," *La tierra de la 1000 musicas,* 2005.

Television Appearances; Specials:

Youth 68: Everything's Changing ... or Maybe It Isn't, 1968.
NBC team member, *Battle of the Network Stars III,* ABC, 1977.
Circus of the Stars #3, CBS, 1979.
Lifetime Salutes Mom, Lifetime, 1987.
2 Years ... Later, NBC, 1990.
Host from Hawaii, *CBS All–American Thanksgiving Day Parade,* CBS, 1990.
The Very Best of the Ed Sullivan Show, CBS, 1991.
Knots Landing Block Party, CBS, 1993.
Host, *Rock 'n' Roll Revolution: The British Invade America* (also known as *Ed Sullivan Presents: Rock 'n' Roll Revolution; The British Invade America*), CBS, 1995.
The History of Rock 'n' Roll, Vol. 4 (also known as *Plugging In*), The WB, 1995.
Mackenzie Phillips: The E! True Hollywood Story, E! Entertainment Television, 1998.
Narrator, *Rock n' Roll Forever: Ed Sullivan's Greatest Hits,* 1999.
Straight Shooter: The Story of the Mamas and the Papas, 1999.
Intimate Portrait: Mackenzie Phillips, Lifetime, 2000.
Intimate Portrait: Janis Joplin, Lifetime, 2000.
Mama Cass Elliot: The E! True Hollywood Story, E! Entertainment Television, 2001.
Narrator, *Carnie Wilson,* Arts and Entertainment, 2001.
Intimate Portrait: Michelle Phillips, Lifetime, 2002.
Intimate Portrait: Carnie Wilson, Lifetime, 2003.
Host, *Rock Gardens,* Home and Garden Television, 2003.
California Dreamin': The Songs of "The Mamas & and Papas," PBS, 2005.
Anne W. Matheson Sumner, *Knots Landing Reunion: Together Again,* CBS, 2005.

Television Appearances; Pilots:

Don't Call Me Mama Anymore, CBS, 1973.
Joanna Russell, *Second Chances,* 1994.
Suki Walker, *Malibu Shores,* CBS, 1996.

Television Appearances; Awards Presentations:

The 25th Annual Grammy Awards, 1983.
American Video Awards, syndicated, 1987.
The 8th Annual Soap Opera Digest Awards, NBC, 1992.

Television Appearances; Other:

Appearances, 1990.
919 Fifth Avenue (also known as *Dominick Dunne's "919 Fifth Avenue"*), 1995.

Film Appearances:

(With the Mamas and the Papas) *Monterey Pop,* 1968.
The banker's daughter, *The Last Movie* (also known as *Chinchero*), 1971.
Billie Frechette, *Dillinger,* American International Pictures, 1973.
Trixie, *Miracle,* 1975.
Natasha Rambova, *Valentino,* United Artists, 1977.
Vivian Nichols, *Bloodline* (also known as *Sidney Sheldon's "Bloodline"* and *Blutspur*), Paramount, 1979.
Gena, *The Man with Bogart's Face* (also known as *Sam Marlowe, Private Eye*), Twentieth Century–Fox, 1980.
Maggie, *Savage Harvest,* Twentieth Century–Fox, 1981.
Linda Tevere, *American Anthem,* Sony Pictures Releasing, 1986.
Mrs. Davis, *Let It Ride,* Paramount, 1989.
Ann Carter, *Scissors,* Paramount, 1991.
Keep on Running, 1991.
Esther Severence, *Army of One* (also known as *Joshua Tree*), 1993.
DeeDee Westbrook (Miss M), *Lost in the Pershing Point Hotel,* Northern Arts Entertainment, 2000.
Mrs. Rye, *The Price of Air,* Artistic License, 2000.
Joan, *March,* Kanan/Hammerschlag, 2001.
June, *Jane White Is Sick & Twisted,* Asylum, 2001.
(In archive footage) *Mayor of the Sunset Strip,* 2003.
Mother, *Harry + Max,* TLA Releasing, 2004.
Singer, *Kids in America,* Slowhand Cinema Releasing, 2005.
Erma, *Unbeatable Harold,* Visual Factory, 2006.
3055 Jean Leon (documentary), 2006.

Film Work:

Song performer, "No Love Today," *Mother, Jugs & Speed,* 1976.

RECORDINGS

Albums; With the Mamas and the Papas:

If You Can Believe Your Eyes and Ears, MCA, 1966.
The Mamas and The Papas, 1966.
Farewell to First Golden Era, MCA, 1967.
Deliver, MCA, 1967.
Golden Era, Vol. 2, 1968.
The Papas and the Mamas, MCA, 1968.
The Mamas and the Papas Book of Songs, 1968.
16 Greatest Hits, MCA, 1970.
Monterey International Pop Festival, One Way Records, 1971.
A Gathering of Flowers, 1971.
Biggest Hits, 1971.
People Like Us, Laserlight, 1971.
20 Golden Hits, 1973.
Monday, Monday, 1973.
California, 1974.
The ABC Collection: Greatest Hits, 1976.
The Best of the Mamas and the Papas, Arcade, 1977.

California Dreamin', M&S, 1978.
20 Greatest Hits, 1980.
Presented By, 1980.
Hits of Gold, MCA, 1981.
The Best of the Mamas and the Papas, MCA, 1987.
The Papas and The Mamas, MCA, 1987.
Deliver, MCA, 1987.
Collection, 1988.
The Very Best of the Mamas and the Papas, Arcade, 1988.
Elliott, Phillips, Gilliam, Doherty, 1988.
The Very Best of the Mamas and the Papas, Platinum Music, 1988.
Mamas and the Papas, MCA, 1990.
Best of the Mamas and the Papas, Alex, 1991.
Daydream, Ariola, 1992.
Creeque Alley/The History of The Mamas and the Papas, MCA, 1991.
Words of Love, Pair, 1993.
California Dreamin', Universal Special Products, 1994.
Very Best of the Mamas and the Papas, Universal/Polygram, 1996.
California Dreamin': Live in Concert, Prism, 1998.
Greatest Hits, MCA, 1998.
Great: Live, Goldies, 1998.
Deliver/Papas and Mamas, 1999.
Before They Were the Mamas and the Papas ... The Magic Circle, Varese Vintage, 1999.
Best of the Mamas and the Papas: 20th Century Masters, MCA, 1999.
California Dreamin', Columbia River, 1999.
Universal Masters Collection: Classic, Universal/Polygram, 1999.
The Mamas and the Papas: Magic Collection, Magic Collection, 2000.
All the Leaves Are Brown: The Golden Era Collection, MCA, 2001.
California Dreamin', Laserlight, 2002.
Live at the Savoy 1982, Sold Out, Ryodisc USA, 2003.
The Mamas and the Papas, Delta, 2004.
Gold: Greatest Hits, Universal International, 2004.
Complete Anthology, Universal/MCA, 2005.
Gold, Geffen, 2005.
Dreamin' Live, Legacy, 2005.
The Ultimate Collection, Geffen, 2005.
California Dreamin', Falcon, 2005.
Best Selection, Universal, 2006.
California Dreamin': The Best of the Mamas and the Papas, Universal, 2006.
Best One, Universal/MCA, 2006.
Colour Collection, Universal, 2007.

Singles with the Mamas and the Papas include "California Dreamin/Monday Monday," Universal/Polygram, 2002.

Albums; Other:
Victim of Romance, A&M, 1977.

Videos:
Flashing on the Sixties: A Tribal Document, 1990.
(With the Mamas and the Papas) *Straight Shooter*, Rhino, 1991.
The Very Best of the Mamas and the Papas, Music Video Distributors, 2001.
California Dreamin': The Songs of the Mamas and the Papas, Hip–O, 2005.

WRITINGS

Books:
California Dreamin': The Story of The Mamas and the Papas, Warner Books, 1986.

Songs Featured in Films:
Writer (with John Phillips) of the hit song "California Dreamin'," recorded by the Mamas and the Papas; this song has been featured in numerous films, from *Free and Easy* in 1967 to *Forrest Gump*, 1994, *The Big Tease*, 1999, and *After the Sunset*, 2004.

OTHER SOURCES

Books:
Greenwald, Matthew, editor, *Go Where You Wanna Go: The Oral History of the Mamas & the Papas*, Cooper Square Press, 2002.
Phillips, Michelle, *California Dreamin': The Story of The Mamas and the Papas*, Warner Books, 1986.

Periodicals:
People Weekly, January 26, 1998, p. 85.

Other:
Straight Shooter: The Story of the Mamas and the Papas (television special), 1999.
Intimate Portrait: Michelle Phillips (television special), Lifetime, 2002.

PINKSTON, Rob 1988–
(Robby Pinkston)

PERSONAL

Full name, William Robert Pinkston IV; born January 30, 1988, in Atlanta, GA. *Education:* Studied acting.

Addresses: *Agent*—TalentWorks, 3500 West Olive Ave., Suite 1400, Burbank, CA 91505. *Manager*—Mark Robert Management, P.O. Box 1549, Studio City, CA

91614. *Publicist*—Scott Appel, Scott Appel Public Relations, 13547 Ventura Blvd., Suite 203, Sherman Oaks, CA 91423.

Career: Actor and voice performer. Appeared in advertisements. Affiliated with the theme park attractions *Bugs Bunny World* and *Looney Tunes Spooky Town,* both Six Flags Magic Mountain.

Member: Screen Actors Guild, American Federation of Television and Radio Artists.

CREDITS

Film Appearances:
Damien, *Plays Well with Others,* c. 1999.
Taylor, *Open Spaces,* Blue Horizon International, c. 1999.
Smartmouth kid, *The Honor System* (short film), Tight-lipped Films, 2003.
Rapper kid, *Undercover Kids,* Artist View Entertainment, 2004.
Chuck Overton, *The Derby Stallion,* Scorpio Pictures, 2005.
Maynard Keyes, *The Sasquatch Dumpling Gang,* Sony BMG Feature Films, 2006.
Young drinker, *If I Had Known I Was a Genius* (also known as *Genius: If Only I Had Known*), Gibraltar Entertainment, 2006.
Griffin, *Parental Guidance Suggested,* Dimension Films, 2007.

Appeared in other films, including an appearance as Johnny, *My Dollar's Gone,* Little Mexican Productions; and an appearance as a video boy, *20 Minutes.*

Film Additional Voices:
Meet the Robinsons (animated; also known as *Beetle, A Day with Wilbur Robinson, A familia do futuro, Bienvenue chez les Robinsons, Conociendo a los Robinsons, Familjen Robinson, Gnoriste tous Robinson, I Robinson—Una famiglia spaziale, La familia del futuro, La famille Robinson, Riemukas Robinsonin perhe, Robinson ailesi, Robinsonid, Robinsonovi,* and *Triff die Robinsons*), Buena Vista, 2007.
The Legend of Secret Pass (animated), JC2 Animated Entertainment/Lords Productions/Strategic Dreamers, 2008.

Television Appearances; Series:
Coconut Head, *Ned's Declassified School Survival Guide* (also known as *Neds ultimativer Schulwahnsinn*), Nickelodeon, beginning 2004.

Voice of Guy, *Danger Rangers* (animated), beginning 2005.

Television Appearances; Movies:
(As Robby Pinkston) Student, *The Metro Chase,* 2003.

Television Appearances; Episodic:
Field agent, *Punk'd* (also known as *Harassment*), MTV, multiple episodes in 2005.
Voice of Todd Maplewood, "Under Wraps," *Ben 10* (animated), Cartoon Network, 2007.
Voice of Todd Maplewood, "The Visitor," *Ben 10* (animated), Cartoon Network, 2007.
Voice, "I'm Trying to Be a Leader Here," *Kid Nation,* CBS, 2007.
Son, *Nick Cannon Presents: Short Circuitz,* MTV, 2007.

Television Appearances; Pilots:
Appeared in *Enter Mode 5,* Cartoon Network.

RECORDINGS

Videos:
Appeared as Sam Smith in the instructional video *Ride Operations Safety Training,* Six Flags; and as Ryan in the video *School of Duel,* Your Turn Products.

OTHER SOURCES

Electronic:
Rob Pinkston, http://www.robpinkston.com, June 25, 2007.

POLK, Stephen
(Steven Polk)

PERSONAL

Son of Louis F. "Bo" (a film executive) and Sally Boyd Polk. *Education:* Graduated from Kenyon College and Westminster College; studied at the New York University Film School; studied acting at the Neighborhood Playhouse, New York, NY, and with Tony Greco, Stella Adler, and Harry Mastrogeorge. *Avocational Interests:* Dancing, singing, and sports.

Addresses: *Office*—Providence Productions, PO Box 785, Malibu, CA 90265.

Career: Actor, producer, and screenwriter. Children's Theater Company, Minneapolis, MN, member; Providence Productions (a production company), Malibu,

CA, founder and president, 1999—. The Foundation of Conscious Humanity, president; worked with child advocacy groups, Boys and Girls Clubs, and Youth at Risk groups.

CREDITS

Film Appearances:
Williams, *By the Sword,* Hansen Entertainment, 1991.
Surveillance man, *Thelma & Louise,* Metro–Goldwyn–Mayer, 1991.
(Uncredited) Donald, *Where Sleeping Dogs Lie,* 1992.
American soldier number one, *Heaven & Earth* (also known as *Entre ciel et terre*), Warner Bros., 1993.
Farm boy, *The Pickle* (also known as *The Adventures of the Flying Pickle*), Columbia, 1993.
Director, *Playmaker* (also known as *Private Teacher*), Orion, 1994.
Desk Sergeant Yardley, *Indecent Behavior II,* 1994.
Graham, *Destination Vegas,* New Concorde, 1995.
Detective Croft, *Bolt* (short), 1997.
Charles Blakely, *God, Sex & Apple Pie,* Warner Bros., 1998.
Drowning on Dry Land, Cargo Films, 1999.
Patron number one, *Clubland,* Legacy Releasing Corp., 1999.
Fred, *Resolution,* Alpine Pictures, 2001.
Bill, *Amy's Orgasm* (also known as *Amy's O* and *Why Love Doesn't Work*), Magic Lamp Releasing, 2001.
Joyce, *Cherish,* 2002.
Sergeant, *Go for Broke,* Artisan Entertainment, 2002.
Sheriff, *The Wooden Gun,* Golden Show Pictures, 2002.
Michael Dare, *Dr. Rage* (also known as *The Straun House*), 2005.
Fred, *In a Dark Place,* 2005.
Kidman, *Pirate Camp,* 2007.
Detective Earl Holiday, *Black Dahlia Movie,* 2007.

Film Producer:
Resolution, 2001.
The Gospel of Lou, Foundation for Conscious Humanity, 2003.
Dr. Rage (also known as *The Straun House*), 2005.
In a Dark Place, 2005.
Revolution, Louniversal Releasing, 2006.
Pirate Camp, 2007.

Film Executive Producer:
The Wooden Gun, Golden Show Pictures, 2002.

Film Coproducer:
Dead Air, 2008.

Television Appearances; Movies:
Gambler, *Puss in Boots,* 1982.

Frog footman, *Alice in Wonderland* (also known as *Lewis Carroll's "Alice in Wonderland"*), 1982.

Television Appearances; Pilots:
District attorney, *Homeland Security* (movies), NBC, 2004.

Stage Appearances:
Appeared in *Truss't,* Children's Theatre Company, Minneapolis, MN.

Stage Work:
Worked in *Truss't,* Children's Theatre Company, Minneapolis, MN.

WRITINGS

Screenplays:
Dr. Rage (also known as *The Straun House*), 2005.
Pirate Camp, 2007.

PORIZKOVA, Paulina 1965–

PERSONAL

Original name, Pavlina Porizkova; born April 9, 1965, in Prostejov, Czechoslovakia (now Czech Republic); immigrated to Sweden, c. 1975, then the United States, 1982; naturalized U.S. citizen; daughter of Anna Porizkova; married Ric Ocasek (a musician and actor), August 23, 1989; children: Jonathan Raven, Oliver Orion; four stepsons: Adam Otcasek, Eron Otcasek, Christopher Otcasek, Derek Otcasek. *Avocational Interests:* Playing classical piano.

Addresses: *Agent*—Paradigm, 360 North Crescent Dr., North Bldg., Beverly Hills, CA 90210.

Career: Actress. Also worked as a model, beginning at age three; spokesperson for Estee Lauder cosmetics, 1988–95; appeared in print ads for Sprite, 1985, Joanie Char fashions, 1986, Diet Sprite, 1987, Christian Dior, 1987, and various Estee Lauder products; appeared in television commercial for FreshDirect online grocer, 2006.

Awards, Honors: Selected as "one of the fifty most beautiful people in the world," *People Weekly,* c. 1990 (some sources cite 1992).

CREDITS

Film Appearances:
Elite model, *Portfolio,* 1983.

Covergirl (also known as *Dreamworld*), New World Pictures, 1984.

Krystyna, *Anna,* Vestron Pictures, 1987.

Nina, *Her Alibi,* Warner Bros., 1989.

Millie, *Arizona Dream* (also known as *The Arrowtooth Waltz*), 1993, Warner Bros., 1995.

Langley Flynn, *Female Perversions* (also known as *Phantasien einer frau*), 1996, October Films, 1997.

Tanya, *Wedding Bell Blues,* Legacy Releasing, 1996.

Diane Thwaite, *Long Time Since,* Lucius Films, 1997.

Dallas, *Thursday,* PolyGram, 1998.

Chi Chi Chemise, *The Intern* (also known as *Intern*), Moonstone Entertainment, 2000.

Wallis P. Longsworth, *Partners in Crime,* Artisan Entertainment, 2000.

Ellen Maxfield, *After the Rain,* 2000.

Eliza, *Roommates,* 2001.

Maggie, *Asylum* (also known as *Dark Asylum* and *Return to Death Row*), Lions Gate Films, 2001.

Mary Rafelson, *Au plus pres du paradis* (also known as *Lo mas cercano al cielo* and *Nearest to Heaven*), Pyramide Distribution, 2002.

Dr. Anna Fahri, *People I Know* (also known as *Im innerern kreis* and *Der innere kreis*), Miramax, 2002.

Allison, *Second Best,* THINKFilm, 2004.

Lily Kildear, *Knots* (also known as *Sex, Love, and Lies*), Lions Gate Films Home Entertainment, 2004.

Nearest to Heaven, 2005.

Film Work:

Dialogue coach for subtitle translation, *Anna,* Vestron Pictures, 1987.

Director, *Roommates,* 2001.

Television Appearances; Series:

Dancing with the Stars, ABC, 2007.

Television Appearances; Specials:

The Making of a Model, 1988.

"People Magazine" on TV, 1990.

Why Bother Voting?, 1992.

"Sports Illustrated" Behind the Scenes: Official Swimsuit Video, HBO, 1992.

Herself, "I Hate the Way I Look," *ABC Afterschool Specials,* ABC, 1994.

Retrosexual: The 80's, VH1, 2004.

"Sports Illustrated" 40th Anniversary Swimsuit Special: *American Beauty,* Spike TV, 2004.

Television Appearances; Episodic:

Late Night with David Letterman, NBC, 1986.

Saturday Night Live (also known as *SNL*), NBC, 1987, 1989.

Sally Jessy Raphael, 1992.

"Beauty," *Understanding,* 1994.

(Uncredited) Alexa Miroslav, "Model Husband," *Ned and Stacey,* Fox, 1995.

Teresa, "About Being Gay," *Talk to Me,* ABC, 2000.

The Howard Stern Radio Show, syndicated, 2000.

Howard Stern, E! Entertainment Television, 2000.

Jimmy Kimmel Live, ABC, 2007.

Entertainment Tonight (also known as *E.T.*), syndicated, 2007.

The Colbert Report, Comedy Central, 2007.

Also appeared as herself, "Anna," *15 Minutes* (also known as *Andy Warhol's "15 Minutes"*).

RECORDINGS

Videos:

A Private Lesson, Estee Lauder, 1991.

Music Videos:

The Cars' "Drive," 1984.

Also appeared in The Cars' "You Might Think."

WRITINGS

Screenplays:

Roommates, 2001.

Books:

(With Joanne Russell) *The Adventures of Ralphie the Roach* (juvenile), illustrated by Adam Ocasek, Doubleday (New York City), c. 1992.

OTHER SOURCES

Books:

Contemporary Newsmakers 1986, Issue Cumulation, Gale, 1987.

Periodicals:

Entertainment Weekly, August 18, 1995, p. 68.

New Woman, April, 1997, pp. 62, 64.

PORTER, Linda

PERSONAL

Career: Actress. Appeared in television commercials, including Nature Valley Cereal.

CREDITS

Film Appearances:
Painter, *Twins,* Universal, 1988.
Newscast auditioner, *The Truth About Cats & Dogs,* Twentieth Century–Fox, 1996.
Mrs. Boman, *Tumbleweeds,* Fine Line Features, 1999.
The wise old woman, *The Mating Habits of the Earthbound Human,* Columbia TriStar Home Video, 1999.
Alice, *Stanley's Gig,* Cut Entertainment Group, 2000.
Mrs. Crabbleman, *Dude, Where's My Car?,* Twentieth Century–Fox, 2000.
Old biddy number two, *Duplex* (also known as *Der Appartement–Schreck* and *Our House*), Miramax, 2003.
Mrs. Wadsworth, *Queen of Cactus Cove* (short), 2005.

Television Appearances; Miniseries:
Dr. Einwohner, *Baby M,* ABC, 1988.
Old woman, *The Phantom Eye* (also known as *Roger Corman's "The Phantom Eye"*), AMC, 1999.

Television Appearances; Movies:
Mayna, *Who Gets the Friends?,* CBS, 1988.
Older woman, *Partners,* 2000.
Old woman, *When Billie Beat Bobby* (also known as *Billie contre Bobby: La bataille des sexes*), ABC, 2001.

Television Appearances; Pilots:
Woman in elevator, *Committed,* NBC, 2005.

Television Appearances; Episodic:
Elizabeth, "Ozymandias," *Beauty and the Beast,* CBS, 1988.
Clerk, "The Witch's Curse," *Murder, She Wrote,* CBS, 1992.
Mary, "Flour Child," *Frasier,* NBC, 1994.
Bev's friend, "Shower the People You Love with Stuff," *Roseanne,* ABC, 1995.
Mark's grateful patient, "New Year's Eve," *Mad About You,* 1995.
Elderly patient, *Mad About You,* NBC, 1995.
Little Old Lady, "Wingless: Part 2," *Wings,* NBC, 1996.
Martha, "Style Before Substance," *Hang Time,* NBC, 1996.
Edwina, "The Unsinkable Nora Wilde," *The Naked Truth* (also known as *Wilde Again*), NBC, 1997.
Inga Paulson, "Exodus," *ER,* NBC, 1998.
Elderly woman, "Drive," *The X–Files,* Fox, 1998.
Nun, "The Daughterboy," *Melrose Place,* Fox, 1999.
Mother character, "To Be or Not to Be Evil," *G vs E* (also known as *Good vs Evil*), USA Network, 1999.
Office assistant, "Passages," *Get Real,* Fox, 1999.
Irma, *Clueless,* 1999.
Woman, *Ladies Man,* CBS, 1999.

Miss Winkle, "A Resting Place," *Diagnosis Murder,* CBS, 2000.
French teacher, "Secrets and Spies," *Even Stevens,* Disney Channel, 2000.
Becky, "Sleepless in San Francisco," *Dharma & Greg,* ABC, 2000.
Ms. Duncan, "The Burden of Perspective," *Judging Amy,* CBS, 2000.
Old woman number two, *Spin City,* ABC, 2000.
Audrey, "Evacuation," *Malcolm in the Middle,* Fox, 2001.
Fran, "Red Light on the Wedding Night," *Gilmore Girls,* The WB, 2001.
Fran, "The Ins and Outs of Inns," *Gilmore Girls,* The WB, 2001.
Fran, "Happy Birthday, Baby," *Gilmore Girls,* The WB, 2003.
Mrs. Nussbaum, "The Pact," *Girlfriends,* UPN, 2003.
"Temperatures Rising," *Strong Medicine,* Lifetime, 2003.
Grandma Berwick, *Phil of the Future,* Disney Channel, 2003.
Old woman, "We'll Miss Gittle a Little," *What I Like About You,* The WB, 2004.
Old woman, *Scrubs,* NBC, 2004.
Eloise, "Buy Curious," *The King of Queens,* CBS, 2005.
Doris, "Guilt Trip," *Out of Practice,* CBS, 2005.
Mind of Mencia, Comedy Central, 2005.
Edith, *Joey,* NBC, 2005.
Gertie Grossman, "The Four Aces," *That's So Raven* (also known as *That's So Raven!*), Disney Channel, 2006.

RECORDINGS

Music Videos:
Appeared in Tenacious D's "Tribute."

PORTER, Steven M.
> (Stephen M. Porter, Steve Porter, Steven Porter, Steven M. Potter)

PERSONAL

Addresses: *Agent*—Schiowitz, Connor, Ankrum, Wolf, Inc., 1680 Vine St., Suite 1016, Los Angeles, CA 90028; KSA (Kazarian/Spencer & Associates, Inc.), 11969 Ventura Blvd., Third Floor, Box 7409, Studio City, CA 91604.

Career: Actor. Appeared in advertisements.

Member: Screen Actors Guild, American Federation of Television and Radio Artists, Actors' Equity Association.

CREDITS

Film Appearances:

Yo–Yo Charlie, *Angel* (also known as *Angel killer, Angel—sista natten, Angel—Strasse ohne Ende, Aniol zemsty,* and *Mathitria to proi, porni to vrady*), New World Pictures, 1984.

Yo–Yo Charlie, *Avenging Angel* (also known as *Angel 2, Angel kehrt zurueck, Angel 2, haemnden, Ekdikisi apo enan angelo, Kadun enkelin kosto,* and *La vengeance de l'ange*), New World Pictures, 1985.

Reporter, *The Scout* (also known as *Der Scout, El cazatalentos, La revelation,* and *O pancada*), Twentieth Century–Fox, 1994.

Bart, *Nothing to Lose* (also known as *Ce–am avut si ce–am pierdut, Ei mitaeaen menetettaevaeae, Inget att foerlora, Kaybedecek bir sey yok, Nada a perder, Nada que perder, Nekem 8, Nic ni izgubljeno, Niente da perdere, Nix zu verlieren,* and *Rien a perdre*), Buena Vista, 1997.

Higgins, *Almost Heroes* (also known as *Almost History, Edwards and Hunt, Edwards and Hunt: The First American Road Trip, From Here to There, Westward Ho, Bohaterowie z przypadku, Casi heroes, Fast Helden, Heroes por casualidad, Les premiers colons, Melkein sankareita,* and *Os quase herois*), Warner Bros., 1998.

(As Steve Porter) Second detective, *I Woke Up Early the Day I Died* (also known as *Ed Wood's "I Woke Up Early the Day I Died," I Awoke Early the Day I Died, Ed Wood's "Der Tag, an dem ich starb," Me levante temprano el dia de mi muerte,* and *O ultimo dia de minha vida*), Cinequanon Pictures International, 1998.

Berry Grady, *Leprechaun in the Hood* (also known as *Leprechaun 5, Leprechaun 5: Leprechaun in the Hood,* and *El duende 5*), Trimark Pictures, 2000.

(As Steve Porter) Bulge, *Best in Show* (also known as *Dog Show* and *Dogumentary*), Warner Bros., 2000.

(As Steven Porter) Person in chicken suit, *The Big Tease* (also known as *Scissors Cup, Con mucho estilo, Der Grosse Mackenzie, Je m'appelle Crawford,* and *Sukkelat sakset*), Warner Bros., 2000.

Marshall Geller, *Boat Trip* (also known as *Croisiere en folie, Cruzeiro das loucas,* and *El crucero de las locas*), Artisan Entertainment, 2002.

Sixth referee, *Million Dollar Baby* (also known as *Rope Burns, Golpes del destino, La fille a un million de dollars, Menina de ouro, Miljoni dollari tuedruk,* and *Za wszelka cene*), Warner Bros., 2004.

Jen's father, Dick, and Buford T., *Embedded,* Cinema Libre Studio, 2005.

(As Steven Porter) Floor manager, *For Your Consideration,* Warner Independent Pictures, 2006.

Tourist, *Flags of Our Fathers* (also known as *A conquista da honra, Atalarimizin bayraklari, Banderas de nuestros padres, Isiemme liput, La conquista del honor, Meie isade lipud, Memoires de nos peres, Oi simaies ton progonon mas, Sztandar chwaly, Vaara faeders fanor,* and *Zastave nasih oceva*), DreamWorks, 2006.

Albert Cromley, *The Poughkeepsie Tapes* (documentary), Brothers Dowdle Productions, 2007.

Rails & Ties, Warner Independent Pictures, 2007.

Television Appearances; Movies:

Rusty Valentine, *Ernie Kovacs: Between the Laughter* (also known as *Ernie Kovacs: Detras de las risas*), ABC, 1984.

(As Steve Porter) Hayes, *Voices Within: The Lives of Truddi Chase* (also known as *Shattered, Menneisyyden riivaama,* and *Schreie aus dem Innern*), ABC, 1990.

Gary Anderson, *Crash Landing: The Rescue of Flight 232* (also known as *A Thousand Heroes*), ABC, 1992.

Second reporter, "Greed," *Favorite Deadly Sins* (also known as *National Lampoon's "Favorite Deadly Sins"*), Showtime, 1995.

Hal, *Jake's Women* (also known as *Neil Simon's "Jake's Women"*), CBS, 1996.

Modern Vampires (also known as *Revenant, The Revenant, Vamps, Revenant—Sie kommen in der Nacht, Revenant—Vampiros modernos, Sie kommen in der Nacht,* and *Vampiros modernos*), 1998.

Television Appearances; Specials:

Fuller, "Dangerous Company," *CBS Afternoon Playhouse,* CBS, 1982.

Television Appearances; Episodic:

(As Steve Porter) Waiter, "And Ma Makes Three," *The Golden Girls* (also known as *Golden Girls, Miami Nice, Bnot Zahav, Cuori senza eta, Las chicas de oro, Les craquantes, Los anos dorados, Oereglanyok, Pantertanter,* and *Tyttoekullat*), NBC, 1988.

(As Steve Porter) Waiter, "Scared Straight," *The Golden Girls* (also known as *Golden Girls, Miami Nice, Bnot Zahav, Cuori senza eta, Las chicas de oro, Les craquantes, Los anos dorados, Oereglanyok, Pantertanter,* and *Tyttoekullat*), NBC, 1988.

Attendant, "In Vino Veritas," *Growing Pains,* ABC, 1991.

Out–of–towner, "Token Friend," *Mad about You* (also known as *Loved by You*), NBC, 1992.

(As Steve Porter) Injured man, "An Old Friend for Dinner," *Danger Theatre,* Fox, 1993.

(As Steve Porter) Bellhop, "Reporters Make Strange Bedfellows," *Murphy Brown,* CBS, 1994.

(As Steve Porter) Dog owner, "Hey, Nineteen," *Wings,* NBC, 1994.

Max Davis, "Last One into the Water," *Bakersfield P.D.,* Fox, 1994.

(As Stephen M. Porter) Sal Rourke (some sources cite Dale Rourke), "Mi Casa, Su Casa," *Nurses,* NBC, 1994.

(As Stephen M. Porter) Bill, "A River Runs through His Head," *The George Wendt Show*, CBS, 1995.

Bobby, "New York on $2,000 a Day," *Platypus Man*, UPN, 1995.

Roger, "Selfish Dick," *3rd Rock from the Sun* (also known as *Life as We Know It* and *3rd Rock*), NBC, 1996.

Security guard, "The One after the Superbowl: Part 2," *Friends* (also known as *Across the Hall, Friends Like Us, Insomnia Cafe*, and *Six of One*), NBC, 1996.

(As Steve Porter) Tom, "Broads for Broader Horizons," *Grace under Fire* (also known as *Grace under Pressure*), ABC, 1996.

Coco the clown, "Point of No Return," *Party of Five*, Fox, 1997.

Harold, "Elegy," *The X–Files*, Fox, 1997.

Vendor, "Top o' the World, Ma," *Working*, NBC, 1997.

Frankie Zimmer, "Hooked on Heroine," *The Naked Truth* (also known as *Wilde Again*), NBC, 1998.

Vendor, "Equality," *Working*, NBC, 1998.

Bryce, "Sabrina's Real World," *Sabrina, the Teenage Witch* (also known as *Sabrina* and *Sabrina Goes to College*), ABC, 1999.

(As Stephen M. Porter) Jack, "Beer Bad," *Buffy the Vampire Slayer* (also known as *BtVS, Buffy, Buffy the Vampire Slayer: The Series, Nightfall, Bafi, ubica vampira, Buffy, a vampirok reme, Buffy, cacadora de vampiros, Buffy contre les vampires, Buffy i vampirofonissa, Buffy—Im Bann der Daemonen, Buffy, l'ammazzavampiri, Buffy, la cazavampiros, Buffy och vampyrerna, Buffy—Vampyrdaeberen, Buffy vampyrdoedaren, Buffy—Vampyrenes skrekk, Buffy—Vampyrernes skraek*, and *Buffy, vampyyrintappaja*), The WB, 1999.

Jim, "Laurie Loses It," *The Norm Show* (also known as *Norm*), ABC, 2000.

(As Steven Porter) Mr. Mann, "The Rumor," *Becker*, CBS, 2000.

Mr. Pularski, "Rock, Paper, Scissors," *ER* (also known as *Emergency Room*), NBC, 2001.

(As Steven M. Potter) Ralphie, "Lost and Found," *Citizen Baines* (also known as *The Second Act*), CBS, 2001.

(As Steven M. Potter) Ralphie, "The Whole Thump–Thump–Thump," *Citizen Baines* (also known as *The Second Act*), CBS, 2001.

Clive Ryder, "Sabrina Unplugged," *Sabrina, the Teenage Witch* (also known as *Sabrina* and *Sabrina Goes to College*), The WB, 2002.

"House Call," *Strong Medicine*, Lifetime, 2002.

Health inspector, "The Importance of Being Phoebe," *Charmed*, The WB, 2003.

Bob, "The War of the Rose," *Freddie*, ABC, 2005.

Kevin Willhite, "Smile," *Boston Legal* (also known as *Fleet Street, The Practice: Fleet Street*, and *The Untitled Practice*), ABC, 2006.

Appeared as Cyrus in *Likely Suspects*, Fox. Appeared in other programs, including *The Big Easy* (also known as *Big Easy—Strassen zur Suende, The big easy—Corrupcio a New Orleans*, and *Flic de mon coeur*), USA Network.

Television Appearances; Pilots:
Bar patron, *Earth Scum*, ABC, c. 1998.

Stage Appearances:
Milton Callabus Cork, *Alagazam*, Actors' Gang, Los Angeles, 2002.

PRESSMAN, Michael 1950–

PERSONAL

Born July 1, 1950, in New York, NY; son of David (a stage and television director) and Sasha (a dancer; maiden name, Katz) Pressman. *Education:* Attended Carnegie–Mellon University; California Institute of the Arts, B.F.A., 1972; also studied with Alexander Mackendrick.

Addresses: *Agent*—Glick Agency, 1250 Sixth St., Suite 100, Santa Monica, CA 90401. *Manager*—Judy Hofflund, Hofflund/Polone, 9465 Wilshire Blvd., Suite 420, Beverly Hills, CA 90212.

Career: Director, producer, and actor. California Institute of the Arts, Valencia, CA, member of board of trustees.

Member: Directors Guild of America.

Awards, Honors: Emmy Awards (with others), outstanding drama series, 1993 and 1994, both for *Picket Fences*; Emmy Award nomination (with others), outstanding drama series, and Directors Guild of America Award nomination (with others), outstanding direction in a nighttime dramatic series, both 1995, for *Chicago Hope*.

CREDITS

Film Director:
The Great Texas Dynamite Chase (also known as *Dynamite Woman* and *Dynamite Women*), New World, 1976.

The Bad News Bears in Breaking Training (also known as *Breaking Training*), Paramount, 1977.

Boulevard Nights, Warner Bros., 1977.

(And producer) *Those Lips, Those Eyes,* United Artists, 1980.
Some Kind of Hero, Paramount, 1982.
Dr. Detroit, Universal, 1983.
Teenage Mutant Ninja Turtles II: The Secret of the Ooze, New Line Cinema, 1991.
To Gillian on Her 37th Birthday, Triumph Releasing, 1996.
Frankie and Johnny Are Married, IFC Films, 2004.

Film Producer:
Lake Placid (also known as *Lac Placid*), Twentieth Century–Fox, 1999.

Film Appearances:
News manager, *Teenage Mutant Ninja Turtles II: The Secret of the Ooze,* New Line Cinema, 1991.
Himself, *Frankie and Johnny Are Married,* IFC Films, 2004.
Himself, *Mackendrick on Film* (documentary), Sticking Place Films, 2004.

Television Work; Series:
Co–executive producer, *Picket Fences,* CBS, 1992–93.
Producer, *Chicago Hope,* CBS, 1994.
Executive producer, *Picket Fences,* CBS, 1995–96.
Executive producer, *Michael Hayes,* 1997.
Executive producer, *The Guardian,* CBS, 2001.
Executive producer and director, *The Brotherhood of Poland, New Hampshire,* CBS, 2003.
Director, *Law & Order,* NBC, multiple episodes, between 2005 and 2007.

Television Work; Specials:
Director, *On Our Way,* CBS, 1985.
Director, "And the Children Shall Lead," *WonderWorks,* PBS, 1985.
Producer, *The Eighties,* NBC, 1989.
Senior producer, *Childhood in America,* PBS, 1991.
Producer, "Children of Divorce," *Families in Crisis* (also known as *Brokaw Report*), NBC, 1992.
Producer, "Norwood Ohio USA," *The Lost Generation* (also known as *Brokaw Report*), NBC, 1992.
Producer, "The Violent Media," *America the Violent,* NBC, 1992.
Producer, *A Day at the White House,* NBC, 1993.
Field producer, *Spinal Tap Goes to 20,* Independent Film Channel, 2004.
Producer and director, *IFC News Special: The Comic–Con Chronicles,* Independent Film Channel, 2005.
Executive producer and director, *IFC News Special: The Comic–Con Chronicles,* Independent Film Channel, 2005.

Television Director; Movies:
Like Mom, Like Me, CBS, 1978.
The Imposter, ABC, 1984.

Final Jeopardy, NBC, 1985.
The Christmas Gift, CBS, 1986.
"Sirens," *CBS Summer Playhouse,* CBS, 1987.
Haunted by Her Past (also known as *Secret Passions*), NBC, 1987.
To Heal a Nation, NBC, 1988.
Shootdown, NBC, 1988.
The Revenge of Al Capone (also known as *Capone*), NBC, 1989.
Incident at Dark River (also known as *Dark River—A Father's Revenge* and *The Smell of Money*), TNT, 1989.
(And producer) *Man Against the Mob: The Chinatown Murders,* NBC, 1989.
Joshua's Heart, NBC, 1990.
Quicksand: No Escape, USA Network, 1992.
Miracle Child (also known as *Miracle at Clements Pond*), NBC, 1993.
Saint Maybe (also known as *Anne Tyler's "Saint Maybe"*), CBS, 1998.
"A Season for Miracles," *Hallmark Hall of Fame,* CBS, 1999.

Television Director; Pilots:
Private Sessions, NBC, 1985.
Chicago Hope, CBS, 1994.
(And executive producer) *Cashmere Mafia,* ABC, 2007.

Television Director; Episodic:
"The Green Bay Chopper," *Picket Fences,* CBS, 1992.
"Thanksgiving," *Picket Fences,* CBS, 1992.
"The Lullaby League," *Picket Fences,* CBS, 1993.
"The Bus Stops Here," *Picket Fences,* CBS, 1995.
Apartment supervisor, *Michael Hayes,* 1997.
"Part I," *The Practice,* ABC, 1997.
"Reasonable Doubts," *The Practice,* ABC, 1997.
"Chapter Ten," *Boston Public,* Fox, 2001.
"Baby Boom," *Law & Order: Trial by Jury,* NBC, 2005.
"Number One with a Bullet," *Kidnapped,* NBC, 2006.
"The Good Lawyer," *Boston Legal,* ABC, 2007.
"Saving Face," *The Closer,* TNT, 2007.

Also directed episodes of *The Guardian,* CBS, and *The $treet,* Fox.

Television Appearances; Movies:
Bernie, *Man Against the Mob: The Chinatown Murders,* NBC, 1989.
Agent, *The Revenge of Al Capone* (also known as *Capone*), NBC, 1989.

Television Appearances; Episodic:
Dr. Marvin Rosenzweig, "With the Greatest of Ease," *Chicago Hope,* CBS, 1994.

Television Appearances; Other:
Ophthalmologist, *Baby M* (miniseries), ABC, 1988.
Alex Steele, *The Guardian* (pilot), CBS, 2001.

Stage Director:
Come Back, Little Sheba, Center Theatre Group, Kirk Douglas Theatre, Culver City, CA, 2007, then Manhattan Theatre Club, Biltmore Theatre, New York City, 2008.

RECORDINGS

Videos:
The Making of "Teenage Mutant Ninja Turtles:" Behind the Shells, Northshore Investments, 1991.

WRITINGS

Film Scripts:
Frankie and Johnny Are Married, IFC Films, 2004.

PURL, Linda 1955–

PERSONAL

Born September 2, 1955, in Greenwich, CT; daughter of Raymond (a business executive) and Marcie Purl; married William Broyles, Jr. (a screenwriter and journalist; divorced); married Desi Arnaz, Jr. (an actor and singer), January 13, 1980 (divorced 1981); married Alexander Cary (a writer); children: (third marriage) Lucius Cary. *Education:* Attended Finch College; trained for the stage with Marguerite Beale, 1970–71, at the Lee Strasberg Theatre and Film Institute, 1972–74, with Milton Katselas, beginning in 1978, at the Toho Geino Academy, Japan, and with Robert Lewis. *Avocational Interests:* Painting, swimming, horseback riding, mountain climbing.

Addresses: *Agent*—Don Buchwald & Associates, 6500 Wilshire Blvd., Suite 2200, Los Angeles, CA 90048.

Career: Actress and singer. Tokyo International Players, Tokyo, Japan, member; cabaret appearances include performances at the Gardenia, Roosevelt's Cinegrill, the Rose Tattoo, and the Jazz Bakery, all Los Angeles, and at Town Hall and 88's, both New York City; also a concert performer at various venues. Colorado Festival of World Theatre, Colorado Springs, CO, founder and founding executive director; and affiliated with the Rubicon International Theatre Festival. Affiliated with various charities, including the AIDS Project Los Angeles, the Christopher Reeve Paralysis Foundation, the Cystic Fibrosis Foundation, and the Haven House Domestic Abuse Shelter, Los Angeles.

Member: Actors' Equity Association, Screen Actors Guild, American Federation of Television and Radio Artists.

Awards, Honors: Tokyo Music Festival awards, best song and best performance, 1974; Robby Award and *DramaLogue* Award, both best actress, 1981, for *The Merchant of Venice; DramaLogue* awards, best actress, 1982 (two awards), for *A Doll's House* and *The Man Who Could See through Time,* 1984, for *Beyond Therapy,* 1985, for *Romeo and Juliet,* and 1986, for *The Real Thing;* Connecticut Drama Critics Circle Award, outstanding performance in a play, c. 1990, for *The Baby Dance.*

CREDITS

Television Appearances; Series:
Doreen Post, *The Secret Storm,* CBS, 1973–74.
Betsy Bullock, *Beacon Hill,* CBS, 1974–75.
Gloria, *Happy Days* (also known as *Happy Days Again*), ABC, 1974–75.
Deborah Randal, *The Oregon Trail* (also known as *Pioneer Trail* and *Westwaerts nach Oregon*), NBC, 1977, also broadcast on BBC–2.
Molly Beaton, *The Young Pioneers* (also known as *Young Pioneers* and *Los jovenes pioneros*), ABC, 1978.
Ashley Pfister, *Happy Days* (also known as *Happy Days Again*), ABC, 1982–83.
Weekends, ABC, beginning 1983.
Charlene Matlock, *Matlock,* NBC, 1986–87.
Kate Del'Amico, *Under Cover* (also known as *The Company*), Fox, 1991.
Brett Robin, *Robin's Hoods* (also known as *Robins Club, A toca de Robin, Les anges gardiens,* and *Mis cinco delincuentes*), syndicated, 1994–95.
Claire Wright, *Port Charles* (also known as *Port Charles: Desire, Port Charles: Fate, Port Charles: The Gift, Port Charles: Miracles Happen, Port Charles: Naked Eyes, Port Charles: Secrets, Port Charles: Superstitions, Port Charles: Surrender, Port Charles: Tainted Love, Port Charles: Tempted, Port Charles: Time in a Bottle,* and *Port Charles: Torn*), ABC, 2000.
Sarah Novelli, *First Monday,* CBS, 2002.

Host of a program on NHK–TV (National Educational Network), Tokyo, Japan, beginning c. 1962.

Television Appearances; Miniseries:
Alice Roosevelt, "Eleanor and Franklin," *ABC Theatre,* ABC, 1976.
Mavis Eaton, *Testimony of Two Men,* syndicated, 1977.

Nydia, *The Last Days of Pompeii*, ABC, 1978.

Deirdre O'Manion, *The Manions of America*, ABC, 1981.

Television Appearances; Movies:

Laurie Mathews, *Bad Ronald*, ABC, 1974.

Laura Gorman, *Having Babies* (also known as *Giving Birth*), ABC, 1976.

Anne Macarino, *Black Market Baby* (also known as *A Dangerous Love* and *Don't Steal My Baby*), ABC, 1977.

Hailey Atkins, *Little Ladies of the Night* (also known as *Diamond Alley*), ABC, 1977.

Emmaline Nevada "Vada" Holtz, *The Flame Is Love* (also known as *Rakkauden liekki*), NBC, 1979.

Jennifer Scott, *Women at West Point*, CBS, 1979.

Sharon Muir, *A Last Cry for Help*, ABC, 1979.

Virginia Rae Hensler, *Like Normal People*, ABC, 1979.

Brenda Farrell, *The Night the City Screamed*, ABC, 1980.

Nellie Bly, *The Adventures of Nellie Bly* (also known as *The Amazing Nellie Bly*), NBC, 1981.

Annie Gilson, *Money on the Side*, ABC, 1982.

Arlene Robbins, *Outrage!*, CBS, 1986.

Eve Harper, *Pleasures*, ABC, 1986.

Susan Andrews, *In Self Defense* (also known as *Hollow Point*), ABC, 1987.

Beverly Rossmore, *Spies, Lies & Naked Thighs* (also known as *Spie, pasticci & bugie* and *Spione, ueberall Spione*), CBS, 1988.

Cassie Robbins, *Addicted to His Love* (also known as *Sisterhood*), ABC, 1988.

Lauren Hall, *Web of Deceit*, USA Network, 1990.

Kate Del'Amico, *Before the Storm* (also known as *Undercover 2—Operation C–Waffe*; consists of re–edited episodes of *Under Cover*), ABC, 1991.

Kate Del'Amico, *Spy Games* (consists of re–edited episodes of *Under Cover*), ABC, 1991.

Jane Adams, *Secrets* (also known as *Danielle Steel's "Secrets"*), NBC, 1992.

Norma, *Body Language*, USA Network, 1992.

Helen Davis, *Incident at Deception Ridge* (also known as *Terror at Deception Ridge*), USA Network, 1994.

Maryanne Bellman, *Accidental Meeting*, USA Network, 1994.

Ellie Porter, *Born Free: A New Adventure* (also known as *Born Free 2, A historia de Elza—Parte 2,* and *Foedd fri 2—Lejonet Elsa blir stor*), ABC, 1996.

Jean Dalton, *The Absolute Truth*, CBS, 1997.

Joan Wolrod, *Holy Joe* (also known as *Man of Miracles, O homem dos milagres,* and *Par miracle*), CBS, 1999.

Narrator, *The Griffin and the Minor Canon* (animated), West Virginia Public Broadcasting, 2002.

Dr. Christy Blanchard, *Frozen Impact* (also known as *Cataclysme*), PAX TV, 2003.

Katherine Norris, *Stranger at the Door* (also known as *Un etranger parmi nous*), Lifetime, 2004.

Kirsten Sorenen, *Criminal Intent* (also known as *Amour et premeditation*), Lifetime, 2005.

Laci Collins, *Maid of Honor* (also known as *Dama de honor* and *Damigella d'onore*), Lifetime, 2006.

Television Appearances; Specials:

Shelley Hewitt, *I Do, I Don't,* 1983.

Life's Most Embarrassing Moments, 1984.

Herself, *Circus of the Stars and Sideshow* (also known as *The All New Circus of the Stars and Sideshow XVII* and *Circus of the Stars #17*), CBS, 1992.

Detective, *Story First: Behind the Unabomber*, Lifetime, 1996.

True Stories from Touched by an Angel, CBS, 1998.

Herself, *Happy Days 30th Anniversary Reunion*, ABC, 2005.

Television Appearances; Awards Presentations:

Presenter, *The 48th Annual Golden Globe Awards*, TBS, 1991.

Television Appearances; Episodic:

Alicia, "The Spoilers," *The Waltons*, CBS, 1974.

Diane, "Thirteen Going on Twenty," *Lucas Tanner*, NBC, 1974.

Julie, "The Pregnancy," *Sons and Daughters*, CBS, 1974.

Kim, "Us against the World," *Medical Story*, NBC, 1975.

Leslie, "Street Girl," *Medical Center*, CBS, 1975.

Ruth Martin, "The Hostage," *Hawaii Five–O* (also known as *McGarrett*), CBS, 1975.

Magda, "Sanctuary," *Serpico*, ABC, 1977.

Vanessa, "The Heartbreaker," *The Waltons*, CBS, 1977.

Student, "The Girl Who Always Said No," *What Really Happened to the Class of '65?*, NBC, 1978.

Lisa Tate, "Revenge," *Alfred Hitchcock Presents* (also known as *Alfred Hitchcock esittaeae, Alfred Hitchcock presenta, Alfred Hitchcock presente,* and *Alfred Hitchcock zeigt*), NBC, 1985.

Terry Shannon, "Murder at the Oasis," *Murder, She Wrote*, CBS, 1985.

"Call Me Grandma/A Gentleman of Discretion/The Perfect Divorce/Letting Go: Part 1," *The Love Boat*, ABC, 1985.

Crystal Wendle, "Mourning among the Wisterias," *Murder, She Wrote*, CBS, 1988.

Laura, "The Sad Professor," *Trying Times*, PBS, 1989.

(In archive footage) Charlene Matlock, "The Kidnapper," *Matlock*, NBC, 1990.

Nicky DeSilva, "The Last Time I Saw Paris," *Jack's Place*, ABC, 1992.

Kate Richards, "Her Life as a Dog," *The Hidden Room* (also known as *La chambre secrete*), Lifetime, 1993.

Laura Ann Callan, "Dead Eye," *Murder, She Wrote*, CBS, 1993.

Kelly Harris, "Who Killed the Legal Eagle?," *Burke's Law*, CBS, 1994.

Lynn Maxfield, "It's a Family Affair," *Crisis Center,* NBC, 1997.

Barbara Conway (some sources cite role as Barbara Cortino), "Crusader," *Walker, Texas Ranger* (also known as *Walker*), CBS, 1998.

Sally Buckall, "Flights of Angels," *Touched by an Angel,* CBS, 1998.

Joan, "Conspiracy," *Crossing Jordan* (also known as *Untitled Tim Kring Project*), NBC, 2003.

Diane Moore (2005), "Schadenfreude," *Cold Case* (also known as *Anexihniastes ypothesis, Caso abierto, Cold case—affaires classees, Cold Case—Kein Opfer ist je vergessen, Doegloett aktak, Kalla spaar, Todistettavasti syyllinen,* and *Victimes du passe*), CBS, 2005.

Herself, "Being Bad behind the Scenes," *TV Land Confidential* (also known as *TV Land Confidential: The Untold Stories*), TV Land, 2005.

Also appeared in other programs, including *Merv Griffin Show,* NBC, syndicated, and CBS.

Television Appearances; Pilots:

Bobbie Jean Shaw, *State Fair,* 1976.

Deborah Randal, *The Oregon Trail* (also known as *Pioneer Trail* and *Westwaerts nach Oregon*), NBC, 1976.

Molly Beaton, *The Young Pioneers* (also known as *Young Pioneers, Los jovenes pioneros,* and *Wildes neues Land*), ABC, 1976.

Molly Beaton, *The Young Pioneers' Christmas* (also known as *Young Pioneers' Christmas* and *La Navidad de los jovenes pioneros*), ABC, 1976.

Sarah, *Midas Valley* (also known as *ABC Thursday Night Movie*), ABC, 1985.

Shellane Victor, *Dark Mansions,* ABC, 1986.

Judith Lumley, "Day to Day," *CBS Summer Playhouse,* CBS, 1987.

Kate Del'Amico, *Under Cover* (also known as *The Company*), Fox, 1991.

Sarah Novelli, *First Monday,* CBS, 2002.

Film Appearances:

Time Travelers, c. 1964 (some sources cite 1966).

Rose Allen, *Aru heishi no kake* (also known as *One Soldier's Gamble* and *The Walking Major*), 1970.

Amy, *Jory,* Avco–Embassy, 1972.

Cheryl, *Crazy Mama,* New World Pictures, 1975.

Ingenue, *W. C. Fields and Me,* Universal, 1976.

Loree, *Leo and Loree* (also known as *Starmakers*), United Artists, 1980.

Sheila Munroe, *Visiting Hours* (also known as *The Fright, Get Well Soon,* and *Terreur a l'hopital central*), Twentieth Century–Fox, 1980.

Kathy, *High Country* (also known as *The First Hello*), 1981.

Voice of Delilah, *Samson & Delilah* (short animated film), 1985.

Laura McCalla, *Viper* (also known as *Codename Viper, Codigo Vibora, Dossier Viper,* and *Tuhon tuojat*), Fries Entertainment, 1988.

Jessie MacCarthy, *Natural Causes,* 1994.

Dr. Ruth Young, *Mighty Joe Young* (also known as *Mighty Joe*), Buena Vista, 1998.

Emily, *Sunday,* 1999.

Jessica Michaels, *The Perfect Tenant,* Trimark Pictures, 2000.

Sandy Bilings, *Fear of the Dark,* Screen Media, 2002.

Film Work:

Associate producer, *The Perfect Tenant,* Trimark Pictures, 2000.

Stage Appearances:

Joe Egg, *A Day in the Death of Joe Egg,* Tokyo International Players, Tokyo, Japan, 1966.

Helen Keller, *The Miracle Worker,* Tokyo International Players, Imperial Theatre, Tokyo, Japan, 1967.

The Relapse, Tokyo International Players, Tokyo, Japan, 1967.

Bet, *Oliver!* (musical), Imperial Theatre, 1968.

Louis, *The King and I* (musical), Imperial Theatre, 1968.

Isobel, *Hallelujah,* CBS Workshop, Los Angeles, 1973.

Fourth Floor Walk Up, CAST Theatre, Los Angeles, 1977.

Sandy, *Grease* (musical), San Bernardino Civic Light Opera, San Bernardino, CA, 1980.

Spoon River Anthology, Theatre 40, Los Angeles, 1980.

Portia, *The Merchant of Venice,* Globe Theatre, Los Angeles, 1981.

Ellen, *The Man Who Could See through Time,* South Coast Repertory Theatre, Costa Mesa, CA, 1982.

Nora, *A Doll's House,* Allied International Productions, Matrix Theatre, 1982.

Betty, *Snacks,* Los Angeles, 1984.

Daisy, *On a Clear Day You Can See Forever* (musical), San Bernardino Civic Light Opera, 1984.

Prudence, *Beyond Therapy,* Los Angeles Public Theatre, Los Angeles, 1984.

Juliet, *Romeo and Juliet,* Los Angeles Public Theatre, then Starlight Theatre, Los Angeles, 1985.

Annie, *The Real Thing,* Mark Taper Forum, Los Angeles, 1986.

Thea, *Hedda Gabler,* Mark Taper Forum, 1986.

Bell, *Tusitala,* Berkshire Theatre Festival, Stockbridge, MA, 1988.

Jane, *Fallen Angels,* Olney Theatre, Olney, MD, 1989.

Wanda, *The Baby Dance,* Williamstown Theatre Festival, The Other Stage, Williamstown, MA, Long Wharf Theatre, New Haven, CT, and Pasadena Playhouse, Pasadena, CA, all 1990, and Lucille Lortel Theatre, New York City, 1991.

Lucy Brown, *The Threepenny Opera* (musical theatre), Williamstown Theatre Festival, Main Stage, Williamstown, MA, 1992.

Title role, *Nora,* Williamstown Theatre Festival, Main Stage, 1993.

Mary Follet, *All the Way Home,* Williamstown Theatre Festival, Main Stage, 1995.

Barbara Webster, *Johnny on a Spot,* Williamstown Theatre Festival, Main Stage, 1997.

Elsa, *The Road to Mecca,* Long Wharf Theatre, 1997.

John Brown's Body, Lobero Stage Company, c. 1997.

Karen, *Dinner with Friends,* Actors Theatre of Louisville, Louisville, KY, 1998.

Victoria Phillips, *Getting and Spending,* Old Globe, San Diego, CA, and Helen Hayes Theatre, New York City, both 1998.

Regina Giddens, *The Little Foxes,* Rubicon Theatre Company, Ventura, CA, c. 1999–2000.

No. 9 rue d'Antin, Pacific Resident Theatre, Venice, CA, 2000.

Aunt Polly, *The Adventures of Tom Sawyer* (musical), Minskoff Theatre, New York City, 2001.

Blanche DuBois, *A Streetcar Named Desire,* Rubicon Theatre Company, 2003.

Phaidra, *Hippolytos,* Getty Villa, Barbara & Lawrence Fleischman Theater, Pacific Palisades, CA, 2006.

Mrs. Van Daan, *The Diary of Anne Frank,* Rubicon Theatre Company, 2007.

Appeared in other productions, including an appearance as the title role, *Camille* (musical); and an appearance in *Hallelujah Hallelujah,* off–off–Broadway production.

Stage Work:

Producer, *The Baby Dance,* Williamstown Theatre Festival, The Other Stage, Williamstown, MA, Long Wharf Theatre, New Haven, CT, and Pasadena Playhouse, Pasadena, CA, all 1990, and Lucille Lortel Theatre, New York City, 1991.

Radio Appearances:

Voice of Sally O'Mally, *Milford–Haven, U.S.A.,* BBC Radio 5 and syndicated, beginning c. 1992.

Performed in *Broken Glass,* National Public Radio; and in *Nora,* L.A. Theatre Works, National Public Radio.

RECORDINGS

Albums:

Alone Together, Varese Sarabande, 1998.

Out of This World (Live), LML Records, 2005.

Albums; with Others:

Teaching English (spoken word recording), Columbia, 1967.

Song "If We Could Turn Back Time," *Leo and Loree* (soundtrack), c. 1980.

George and Ira Gershwin: A Musical Celebration, MCA, 1994.

A Hollywood Christmas, MCA Special Products, 1996.

Cole Porter: A Musical Toast, Varese Sarabande, 1997.

The Burt Bacharach Album: Broadway Sings the Best of Burt Bacharach, Varese Sarabande, 1998.

OTHER SOURCES

Electronic:

www.lindapurl.net, http://www.lindapurl.net, June 19, 2007.

R

REDICAN, Dan
(Dan Redicam)

PERSONAL

Married Carol Commisso, April 7, 1990; children: two.

Addresses: *Manager*—Protocol Entertainment, 8899 Beverly Blvd., Suite 606, Los Angeles, CA 90048.

Career: Actor, writer, producer, and creative consultant. The Frantics (a comedy troupe), founding member, 1979–89, 2004—; also worked as a puppeteer.

Awards, Honors: Gemini Award nomination (with others), best performance in a variety/entertainment/performing arts program or series, Academy of Canadian Cinema and Television, 1986, for *Four on the Floor;* Gemini Award nomination, best performance in a comedy program or series—individual or ensemble, 1995, for *The Dan Redican Comedy Hour;* Canadian Comedy Award nomination, television—pretty funny male performance, 2003, 2004, Gemini Award nomination (with others), best ensemble performance in a comedy program or series, 2005, all for *Puppets Who Kill;* Gemini Award nomination, best writing in a comedy or variety program or series, 2006, for *Burnt Toast.*

CREDITS

Film Appearances:
Ken Daly, *The Wrong Guy,* Hollywood Pictures Home Video, 1997.
Freaky Freddy, *Superstar,* Paramount, 1999.
Karl, *If I See Randy Again, Do You Want Me to Hit Him with the Axe?* (short), Flow Distribution, 2006.

Television Appearances; Series:
Various, *Four on the Floor* (also known as *The Frantics: Four on the Floor*), Showtime, 1985.
Anthony, Zsa Zsa Pork Mustard, *The Jim Henson Hour,* NBC, 1989.
George, *Mosquito Lake,* CBC, 1989.
Voice of Maurice, *Freaky Stories,* YTV and Fox Family, 1997.
Voice of Joel, *The Chimp Channel,* 1999.
Dan Barlow, *Puppets Who Kill,* Comedy Central, 2002–2006.

Television Appearances; Miniseries:
Marty Blaine, *Woman on the Run: The Lawrencia Bembenek Story* (also known as *Woman on Trial: The Lawrencia Bembenek Story*), 1993.
Terry Franks, *The Judge* (also known as *Steve Martini's "The Judge"*), NBC, 2001.

Television Appearances; Movies:
Tom Fitzgerald, *Elvis Meets Nixon,* Showtime, 1997.
(As Dan Redicam) Director, *The Pooch and the Pauper,* ABC, 1999.

Television Appearances; Specials:
Various, *Dan Redican Comedy Hour,* 1994.
Host, *Cream of Comedy* (also known as *The 8th Annual Tim Sims Encouragement Fund Award* and *Tim Sims Award*), 2003.
The 2004 Gemini Award, CBC, 2004.
The Frantics TV Special, 2005.
Lab technician, *Burnt Toast,* 2005.

Television Appearances; Pilots:
Head of CBC, *Getting Along Famously,* CBC, 2005.

Television Appearances; Episodic:
Sergeant James, "Defective Vision," *Seeing Things,* CBC, 1985.

The museum guard, "Museum," *Sharon, Lois & Bram's Elephant Show* (also known as *The Elephant Show*), 1988.

Coworker, "The Call," *The Twilight Zone,* CBS, 1988.

Lanny Reese, "Late Night Harry," *Maniac Mansion,* Family Channel, 1991.

Howard Rossiter, "Crossroads," *Street Legal,* CBC, 1994.

Howard Rossiter, "The Morning After," *Street Legal,* CBC, 1994.

Ed, "The Debt Collectors," *The Hardy Boys,* 1995.

"A Bad Day," *The Newsroom,* CBC, 1996.

Judd Wainwright, "Four Walls and a Roof: Part 2," *Wind at My Back,* CBC, 1996.

Judd Wainwright, "A Family of Independent Means," *Wind at My Back,* CBC, 1996.

Judd Wainwright, "Aunt Grace's Wedding," *Wind at My Back,* CBC, 1997.

Carl Pillar, "Frozen in Time," *PSI Factor: Chronicles of the Paranormal,* syndicated, 1997.

Nikita's neighbor, "Fuzzy Logic," *La Femme Nikita* (also known as *Nikita*), USA Network, 1998.

Carl Spiffy, "The Magic Key," *Noddy,* PBS, 1998.

Booth announcer, "Dr. Longball," *Due South* (also known as *Un tandem du choc*), CTV, 1998.

Open Mike with Mike Bullard (also known as *Open Mike* and *The Mike Bullard Show*), Global, 2002.

Jack, "Watch Your Back," *Train 48,* Global, 2004.

The Regina Official, "Meery Gasmas," *Corner Gas,* CTV, 2005.

Television Work; Series:

Supervising producer and story editor, *The Kids in the Hall,* CBC and HBO, 1988.

Story editor, *Boogie's Diner,* syndicated, 1994.

Consulting producer, *The Chimp Channel,* TBS, 1999.

Creative consultant, *The War Next Door,* USA Network, 2000.

Executive producer, *The Lyricist Lounge Show,* MTV, 2000.

Editor, *Blackfly,* Global, 2001.

Producer, *Not This But This,* 2007.

Creative consultant, *Little Mosque on the Prairie,* CBC, 2007.

Also worked as producer, *Jenny McCarthy Show,* MTV.

Television Work; Specials:

Director and producer, *The Frantics TV Special,* 2005.

Television Work; Episodic:

Story editor, "Swimming Up Stream," *Little Mosque on the Prairie,* CBC, 2007.

Stage Appearances:

Toured in numerous one–man shows, including *Stop Being Stupid.*

WRITINGS

Television Specials:

Burnt Toast, 2005.
The Frantics TV Special, 2005.

Television Episodes:

Stickin' Around, Fox, 1996.
Freaky Stories, YTV and Fox Family, 1997.
The Chimp Channel, TBS, 1999.
Puppets Who Kill, Comedy Central, 2004–2006.
Not This But This, 2007.

Also wrote "Lucky Day," *Little Mosque on the Prairie,* CBC; *Blackfly,* Global.

REED, Daphne Maxwell
   See MAXWELL REID, Daphne

REED, Rex 1938–

PERSONAL

Full name, Rex Taylor Reed; born October 2, 1938, in Fort Worth, TX; son of James M. (an oil company executive) and Jewell (maiden, name Smith) Reed. *Education:* Louisiana State University, B.A., journalism, 1960.

Career: Critic, writer, and actor. Publicity writer, including work as a copy boy for Twentieth Century–Fox; *Women's Wear Daily,* film critic, 1965–69; *Stereo Review,* music critic, 1968–75; *Daily News,* New York City, film critic, 1971–75; *Observer,* columnist, 1990s; *Talk,* contributing editor; worked as a film critic for various periodicals, including *Cosmopolitan, Gentleman's Quarterly* (also known as *GQ*), *Holiday, Status, Vogue,* and the *New York Post;* worked as a syndicated columnist, Chicago Tribune–New York Daily News syndicate; jury member at various film festivals, including the Berlin International Film Festival, Montreal Film Festival, Venice International Film Festival, and the U.S.A. Film Festival; also a lecturer and wrote album liner notes for various performers. Worked as a jazz singer, record salesperson, and a cook, c. 1960–65.

Member: National Society of Film Critics, New York Film Critics Circle.

Awards, Honors: Louisiana Hall of Fame, inductee, 1993; multiple Grammy awards, National Academy of Recording Arts and Sciences; Brandeis University, honorary degree.

CREDITS

Television Appearances; Series:
Panelist, *The Gong Show,* syndicated, 1976–80.
Host, *Rex Reed's "Movie Guide,"* syndicated, beginning 1980.
Correspondent, *Inside America,* ABC, 1982.
Cohost, *At the Movies,* syndicated, 1986–90.

Also appeared as a regular, *Tomorrow* (also known as *Tomorrow Coast to Coast*), NBC.

Television Appearances; Specials:
That Was the Year That Was, NBC, 1976.
Himself, *The Making of "Superman: The Movie,"* c. 1978.
Judy Garland: The Concert Years, PBS, 1985.
Night of 100 Stars III (also known as *Night of One Hundred Stars*), NBC, 1990.
(In archive footage) Himself, *Playboy: The Party Continues,* 2000.
Himself, *The Big O! True West Hollywood Story* (also known as *The Daily Show with Jon Stewart Presents "Frank DeCaro: The Big O! True West Hollywood Machine"*), Comedy Central, 2002.

Television Appearances; Episodic:
Guest, *The Dick Cavett Show,* ABC, 1968, 1969, 1970.
Himself, *The Mike Douglas Show,* syndicated, 1969, 1970, 1974, 1977.
Himself, *Playboy after Dark,* syndicated, c. 1970.
Himself, *The Tonight Show Starring Johnny Carson* (also known as *The Best of Carson*), NBC, various episodes, 1970–73.
Himself, *Dinah's Place,* NBC, 1974.
Himself, *You Don't Say,* ABC, multiple episodes in 1975.
Himself, *The New Hollywood Squares,* syndicated, 1987.
Voice of himself, "Uneasy Rider," *The Critic* (animated), ABC, 1994.
Voice of himself, "Siskel & Ebert & Jay & Alice," *The Critic* (animated), Fox, 1995.
Himself, *Howard Stern* (also known as *The Howard Stern Show*), E! Entertainment Television, 1996.
"Raquel Welch," *Biography* (also known as *A&E Biography: Raquel Welch*), Arts and Entertainment, 1999.
Himself, *The Howard Stern Radio Show,* syndicated, 1999.
Himself, *Intimate Portrait: Jacqueline Susann,* Lifetime, 1999.
Himself, "Jacqueline Susann," *Life and Times,* CBC, 2000.
"Jacqueline Susann: The Writing Machine," *Biography* (also known as *A&E Biography: Jacqueline Susann*), Arts and Entertainment, 2000.

Television Appearances; Pilots:
Hellzapoppin', ABC, 1972.

Film Appearances:
(Uncredited) Farmer, *Hurry Sundown* (also known as *E venne la notte, Foerbjudet omraade, Huomenna on uusi paeivae, La noche deseada, Lad natten komme, Morgen ist ein neuer Tag, O incerto amanha,* and *Que vienne la nuit*), Paramount, 1967.
Myron, *Myra Breckinridge* (also known as *Gore Vidal's "Myra Breckinridge," Il caso Myra Breckinridge,* and *Myra—herkkua helmoissa*), Twentieth Century–Fox, 1970.
Himself, *Superman* (also known as *Superman—The Movie, Superman: The Movie, Super–Homem, Superman: el film, Superman—Le film, Superman—O filme, Superman—teraesmies,* and *Supermann*), Warner Bros., 1978.
(Scenes deleted) Longfellow, *Inchon* (also known as *Inchon!, Oh, Inchon!,* and *Ladowanie w Inchon*), Metro–Goldwyn–Mayer/United Artists, 1981.
Entertainment editor, *Irreconcilable Differences* (also known as *Triple Trouble, Deosebiri ireconciliabile, Diferencias irreconciliaveis, Divorce a Hollywood,* and *Inhimilliset erot*), Warner Bros., 1984.
Voice of himself on radio, *Lost in America* (also known as *Relax, Eksyksissae Amerikassa, Eksynyt Amerikassa, Jaeljet katoavat Amerikkaan, Kopfueber in Amerika,* and *Pubblicitario offresi*), Warner Bros., 1985.
Himself, *Ballad of the Nightingale* (also known as *Los Angeles—Cannes solo andata*), August Entertainment, 1998.
Himself, *People I Know* (also known as *Eyewitness, Influences, Der innere Kreis, Gente conhecida, Im inneren Kreis, La noche del crimen, O articulador,* and *Relaciones confidenciales*), New Films International, 2002, Miramax, 2003.
Himself, *Broadway: The Golden Age, by the Legends Who Were There* (documentary; also known as *Broadway, Broadway: The Golden Age,* and *Broadway: The Movie*), Dada Films, 2003.
The Needs of Kim Stanley (documentary), Frozen Motion Films, 2005.

Stage Appearances:
Night of 100 Stars III (also known as *Night of One Hundred Stars*), Radio City Music Hall, New York City, 1990.

Host and narrator of the *Lyrics and Lyrics* series, 92nd Street Y, New York City.

Radio Appearances:
Himself, *Howard Stern* (also known as *The Howard Stern Show*), 1996.
Himself, *The Howard Stern Radio Show,* 1999.

RECORDINGS

Videos:

(In archive footage) Himself, *Playboy: Farrah Fawcett, All of Me,* Playboy Video Enterprises, 2000.

Himself, *Sex at 24 Frames per Second* (documentary; also known as *Playboy Presents "Sex at 24 Frames per Second: The Ultimate Journey through Sex in Cinema"*), Playboy Entertainment Group/Image Entertainment, 2003.

WRITINGS

Teleplays; Series:

Rex Reed's "Movie Guide," syndicated, beginning 1980.

At the Movies, syndicated, 1986–90.

Teleplays; with Others; Episodic:

Inside America, ABC, 1982.

Nonfiction:

Do You Sleep in the Nude?, New American Library, 1968.

Conversations in the Raw, World Publishing, 1970.

Big Screen, Little Screen, Macmillan, 1971.

Contributor of the piece "Ava: Life in the Afternoon," *The New Journalism,* by Tom Wolfe and others, edited by Wolfe and E. W. Johnson, Harper & Row, 1973.

People Are Crazy Here, Delacorte, 1974.

Valentines and Vitriol, Delacorte, 1977.

Travolta to Keaton, Morrow, 1979.

Rex Reed's "Guide to Movies on TV and Video," Warner, 1992.

Contributor to periodicals, including *Esquire, Harper's Bazaar, Ladies Home' Journal, New York, Playboy,* and the *New York Times.*

Fiction:

Personal Effects (novel), Arbor House, 1986.

OTHER SOURCES

Books:

Dictionary of Literary Biography, Volume 185: *American Literary Journalists, 1945–1995,* First Series, Gale, 1997.

RICHTER, Andy 1966–

PERSONAL

Full name, Paul Andrew Richter; born October 28, 1966, in Grand Rapids, MI; father, a university teacher of Russian; mother, a designer of kitchen cabinets; married Sarah Thyre (a writer and actress), March 18, 1994; children: Mercy, William. *Education:* Attended University of Illinois at Urbana–Champaign, 1984–86; studied film at Columbia College, Chicago, IL; studied improvisation with Del Close and Mick Napier.

Addresses: *Agent*—Creative Artists Agency, 2000 Avenue of the Stars, Los Angeles, CA 90067. *Manager*—Brillstein Entertainment Partners, 9150 Wilshire Blvd., Suite 350, Beverly Hills, CA 90212. *Publicist*—Baker/Winokur/Ryder, 9100 Wilshire Blvd., 6th Floor, West Tower, Beverly Hills, CA 90212.

Career: Actor and writer. Performed with improvisational groups in Chicago, IL, including Annoyance Theatre, Gambrinus King of Beer, Comedy Underground, and Improv Olympia. Appeared in television commercial for Reach toothbrushes, 1997.

Awards, Honors: Emmy Award nominations (with others), outstanding writing for a variety, music, or comedy program, 1996, 1997, 1998, 1999, 2000, Writers Guild of America Television Awards (with others), best comedy/variety series, 1997, 2000, Writers Guild of America Television Award nominations (with others), best comedy/variety series, 1999, 2001, all for *Late Night with Conan O'Brien*; Gemini Award nomination (with others), best performance or host in a variety program or series, Academy of Canadian Cinema and Television, 2003, for *The True Meaning of Christmas Specials.*

CREDITS

Film Appearances:

Kenny, *Cabin Boy,* Buena Vista, 1994.

Happy, *Good Money,* 1996.

Ken Irpine, *The Thin Pink Line,* 1998.

Himself, *Barenaked in America* (documentary), 1999.

Himself, *Royal Rumble,* 2000.

Eli, *Dr. T and the Women,* Artisan Entertainment, 2000.

Father Kerris, *Scary Movie II* (also known as *Scary Movie 2* and *Scarier Movie*), Dimension Films, 2001.

Eugen Wilson, *Dr. Doolittle 2* (also known as *DR.2* and *DR2*), Twentieth Century–Fox, 2001.

Record executive, *Pootie Tang,* Paramount, 2001.

Big Trouble, Buena Vista, 2001.

Kevin, *The Guest,* Dimension Films, 2001.

Himself, *"Kids in the Hall": Same Guys, New Dresses* (documentary), Eclectic DVD Distribution, 2001.

Himself, cohost, and panelist, *Wild Desk Ride* (also known as *Conan O'Brien's "Wild Desk Ride"*), 2001.

Network executive number two, *Run Ronnie Run,* New Line Cinema, 2002.

Maitre 'D, *Martin & Orloff,* Spit & Glue Distribution, 2002.

Jack Pendick/Ralph Pendick, *Big Trouble,* 2002.

(English version) Voice of Natoru, *Neko no ongaeshi* (animated; also known as *The Cat Returns*), Buena Vista Home Video, 2002.

Himself, *Gigantic (A Tale of Two Johns)* (documentary), Cowboy Pictures, 2002.

Herb, *Frank McKlusky, C.I,* Buena Vista, 2002.

Drinky Crow, *God Hates Cartoons* (animated), 2002.

Red Taylor, *My Boss's Daughter,* Dimension, 2003.

Morris, *Elf,* New Line Cinema, 2003.

(Uncredited) Himself, *End of the Century* (documentary; also known as *End of the Century: The Story of the Ramones*), Magnolia Pictures, 2003.

Voice of Lenny, *Lenny the Wonder Dog,* North by Northwest Entertainment, 2004.

Congressman Jack Levanyt, *Death and Taxes,* 2004.

Bennie Bang, *New York Minute,* Warner Bros., 2004.

Carl, *Seeing Other People,* Lantern Lane Entertainment, 2004.

Himself, *Sesame Street: Happy Healthy Monsters,* Genius Products, 2004.

"*Late Night with Conan O'Brien*": The Best of Triumph the Insult Comic Dog, Lions Gate Films Home Entertainment, 2004.

Voice of Mort, *Madagascar* (animated), DreamWorks, 2005.

Himself, *The Aristocrats* (documentary; also known as *The @r!St* (r@t$)*), THINKFilm, 2005.

Jerry Lillard, *Clark and Michael* (short), Innertube, 2006.

Gregory, *Talladega Nights: The Ballad of Ricky Bobby,* Columbia, 2006.

If I Had Known I Was a Genius (also known as *Genius: If Only I Had Known*), Gibraltar Entertainment, 2007.

Mountie number one, *Blades of Glory,* DreamWorks, 2007.

Bobby Dee, *Semi–Pro,* New Line Cinema, 2008.

Voice of Mort, *Madagascar: The Crate Escape* (animated), Paramount, 2008.

Film Work:

Production assistant, *All the Love in the World,* 1992.

Television Appearances; Series:

Sidekick, *Late Night with Conan O'Brien* (also known as *Conan O'Brien*), NBC, 1993–2000.

Andy Richter, *Andy Richter Controls the Universe,* Fox, 2002–2003.

Bob Chase, *Quintuplets,* Fox, 2004–2005.

Andy Barker, *Andy Barker, P.I.,* NBC, 2007.

Television Appearances; Movies:

Police officer, *The Positively True Adventures of the Alleged Texas Cheerleader–Murdering Mom,* HBO, 1993.

Harry, *Harry's Girl,* 2003.

Television Appearances; Pilots:

(Uncredited) Himself, *DAG,* NBC, 2000.

Andy Barker, *Andy Barker, P.I.,* 2007.

Voice, *Mighty B,* Nickelodeon, 2008.

Television Appearances; Specials:

NBC's New Year's Eve with "Friday Night," NBC, 1995.

Late Night with Conan O'Brien 5, NBC, 1998.

The 52nd Annual Primetime Emmy Awards, ABC, 2000.

Host, *The 2001 Creative Arts Emmy Awards,* E! Entertainment Television, 2001.

Narrator, *Brilliant But Cancelled* (also known as *The Perfect Pitch* and *Brilliant But Cancelled: The Perfect Pitch*), Trio, 2002.

The 54th Annual Primetime Emmy Awards, NBC, 2002.

Priest, *The True Meaning of Christmas Specials,* CBC, 2002.

(Uncredited) Scooter the PA, *The 2003 MTV Movie Awards,* MTV, 2003.

Late Night with Conan O'Brien: 10th Anniversary Special, NBC, 2003.

Host, *Comedy Central Presents: The Commies,* Comedy Central, 2003.

Conan O'Brien 10th Anniversary Special, NBC, 2003.

VH1 Goes Inside Live with Regis and Kelly, VH1, 2004.

Donald Lohan, *The 2004 MTV Movie Awards,* MTV, 2004.

Performer, *A.S.S.S.S.C.A.T. Improv,* Bravo, 2005.

Television Appearances; Episodic:

Himself, "The Cry of a Hungry Baby," *Mr. Show,* HBO, 1995.

Hansel, "Story of the Toad," *Upright Citizens Brigade,* Comedy Central, 1998.

Himself, *SexTV,* 1998.

Himself, Pearce on Conan," *LateLine,* ABC, 1999.

Himself, *The Awful Truth,* Bravo, 1999.

The career wizard, "Yes You Can't," *Strangers with Candy,* Comedy Central, 2000.

Tweetzie railroad Indian, "Trail of Tears," *Strangers with Candy,* Comedy Central, 2000.

Pharmacist, "Blank Relay," *Strangers with Candy,* Comedy Central, 2000.

Alan, "Choosing to Be Super," *Just Shoot Me,* NBC, 2000.

Barney Sticuzo, "Youth Bandits," *Ed,* NBC, 2002.

Dr. Kennedy, "Clip Show," *Malcolm in the Middle,* Fox, 2002.

Himself, *Primetime Glick,* Comedy Central, 2002.

Himself, "Bullies," *Dennis Miller Live,* HBO, 2002.

The Daily Show (also known as *The Daily Show with Jon Stewart, The Daily Show with Jon Stewart Global Edition,* and *Jon Stewart*), Comedy Central, 2002, 2004.

Last Call with Carson Daly, NBC, 2002, 2005, 2007.

The Tonight Show with Jay Leno, NBC, 2002, 2007.

Kelly Robbins, "Ex," *The Lyon's Den,* NBC, 2003.

On the Shot, The WB, 2003.

Clerk, *Happy Family,* NBC, 2003.

Dr. Bob, "Philip in a China Shop," *It's All Relative,* ABC, 2004.

Voice of Nelson "Bong–Bong," "What's Black and White and Depressed All Over?," *Father of the Pride* (animated), NBC, 2004.

Audience member, *American Idol: The Search for a Superstar* (also known as *American Idol*), Fox, 2004.

Voice of Lloyd, *Crank Yankers,* Comedy Central, 2004, 2005.

Celebrity Poker Showdown, Bravo, 2004, 2005.

Dale, "The Old Man and the Sea," *Will & Grace,* NBC, 2005.

Himself, "Switch Hitter," *Arrested Development,* Fox, 2005.

"Madagascar: Welcome to the Jungle," *HBO First Look,* HBO, 2005.

Today (also known as *The Today Show*), NBC, 2005.

The Big Idea with Donny Deutsch, CNBC, 2005.

Weekends at the DL, Comedy Central, 2005.

Cohost, *Live with Regis and Kelly,* syndicated, 2005, 2007.

Donnie Richter, Chareth Richter, Rocky Richter–Wang, Emmett Richter, and himself, "S.O.B.s," *Arrested Development,* Fox, 2006.

Voice of Philip, "Rough Trade," *American Dad* (animated), Fox, 2006.

Stan, "Supertramp," *The New Adventures of Old Christine,* CBS, 2006.

Stan, "A Long Day's Journey into Stan," *The New Adventures of Old Christine,* CBS, 2006.

Stan, "The Champ," *The New Adventures of Old Christine,* CBS, 2006.

Voice of J. F. Amarth, "Dethstars," *Metalocalpyse,* Comedy Central, 2006.

"Andy Richter," *Talkshow with Spike Feresten,* Fox, 2006.

"Top Ten Musical Moments," *TV Land's Top Ten,* TV Land, 2006.

Howard Stern on Demand, 2007.

Hal, "Mr. Monk Makes a Friend," *Monk,* USA Network, 2007.

Mayor William Q. Lefawn, "Key to the City," *The Naked Trucker and T–Bones Show,* 2007.

Also appeared in "One–Star Hotel," *On the Spot.*

Television Work; Series:
Producer and supervising producer, *Andy Richter Controls the Universe,* Fox, 2002–2003.

Television Work; Pilots:
Andy Barker, P.I., NBC, 2007.

Television Work; Episodic:
Producer, "Fairway, My Lovely," *Andy Barker, P.I.,* NBC, 2007.

Stage Appearances:
Mike, *Real Live TV Night,* Top of the Gate, New York City, 1991–92.

Incident at Cobblers Knob, Lincoln Center Festival, New York City, 1997.

Also appeared as Mike Brady, *The Real Live Brady Bunch,* New York City and Los Angeles productions.

WRITINGS

Television Episodes:
Late Night with Conan O'Brien (also known as *Conan O'Brien*), NBC, 1993–2000.

OTHER SOURCES

Periodicals:
Entertainment Weekly, August 14, 1998; May 26, 2000.
TV Guide, March 27, 1999; May 20, 2000.

RIEGEL, Eden 1981–

PERSONAL

Full name, Eden Sonja Jane Riegel; born January 1, 1981, in Washington, D.C.; daughter of Kurt and Lenore Riegel; engaged to Andrew Miller, March 2007. *Education:* Studied political and social theory at Harvard University, Cambridge, MA, 1998–2000; studied voice with Abbe Harkavy, Maestro Franco Iglesius, and Brad Ross. *Avocational Interests:* Figure skating.

Addresses: *Office*—c/o *All My Children* Studios, 320 W. 66th St., New York, NY 10023. *Agent*—International Creative Management, 10250 Constellation Way, 9th fl., Los Angeles, CA 90067.

Career: Actress and singer. Began career as a child performing dinner theater in suburban Washington; member of Broadway Kids. White House intern, 2000.

Member: Screen Actors Guild, American Federation of Television and Radio Artists, Actors Equity Association.

Awards, Honors: Daytime Emmy Award nominations, outstanding younger actress in a drama series, 2001, 2002, 2004, *Soap Opera Digest* Award, outstanding female newcomer, 2001, and outstanding younger lead actress, Favorite OUT Image of the Year Award, GLAAD Media Awards, 2004, Daytime Emmy Award, outstanding young actress in a drama series, 2005, all for *All My Children.*

CREDITS

Film Appearances:

(Uncredited) Choir member, *Home Alone 2: Lost in New York,* Twentieth Century–Fox, 1992.

Voice, *Richard Scarry's Best Learning Songs Video Ever!* (animated), 1993.

Voice, *Richard Scarry's Best Busy People Video Ever!* (animated), 1993.

Princess, *The Frog King,* 1994.

Joan, *Duo: The True Story of a Gifted Child with Down Syndrome* (short), 1996.

Voice of Young Miriam, *The Prince of Egypt* (animated), DreamWorks, 1998.

Sarah, *American Pie,* Universal, 1999.

Nicole Hill, *Henry Hill* (also known as *Play for Me*), The Asylum, 1999.

Elisabeth, *Semmelweis* (short), 2001.

Television Appearances; Series:

Heather, *As the World Turns,* CBS, 1998.

Bianca Christine Montgomery, *All My Children,* ABC, 2001—.

Television Appearances; Specials:

Voice, *Smoke Alarm: The Unfiltered Truth About Cigarettes,* HBO, 1996.

The 27th Annual Daytime Emmy Awards, ABC, 2000.

The 28th Annual Daytime Emmy Awards, NBC, 2001.

The 29th Annual Daytime Emmy Awards, CBS, 2002.

The 18th Annual "Soap Opera Digest" Awards, SoapNet, 2003.

Intimate Portrait: Susan Lucci, Lifetime, 2003.

The 30th Annual Daytime Emmy Awards, ABC, 2003.

Tribeca Film Festival Presents, 2003.

Totally Gay! (also known as *VH–1's "Totally Gay!"*), VH1, 2003.

Bianca Montgomery, *SOAPnet Revels ABC Soap Secrets,* SoapNet, 2004.

The 56th Annual Writers Guild Awards, 2004.

The 31st Annual Daytime Emmy Awards, NBC, 2004.

The 32nd Annual Daytime Emmy Awards, CBS, 2005.

Television Appearances; Episodic:

Meghan Cooper, "Digital Underground," *New York Undercover* (also known as *Uptown Undercover*), Fox, 1995.

Meghan Cooper, "The Solomon Papers," *New York Undercover* (also known as *Undercover*), Fox, 1997.

Natalie, "Mad Dog," *Law & Order,* NBC, 1997.

Soap Center, 2001.

American Dreams, NBC, 2002.

"All My Children," *Biography,* Arts and Entertainment, 2003.

The View, ABC, 2003.

SoapTalk, SoapNet, 2003, 2004, 2005.

Protestor, "Shoot the Moon," *American Dreams* (also known as *Our Generation*), NBC, 2004.

Bianca Montgomery, *One Life to Live,* ABC, 2004, 2005.

"Alicia Minshew," *Soapography,* SoapNet, 2004.

"Susan Lucci's Stars," *Party Planner with David Tutera,* Discovery Channel, 2005.

Also appeared as herself, "Young, Sexy and ... Soapy," *Young, Sexy & ....*

Stage Appearances:

Young Cosette and alternate Young Eponine, *Les Miserables,* New York City, c. 1990–92.

Freddy Rogers, James Rogers, and Mary Rogers, *The Will Rogers Follies,* Palace Theatre, New York City, 1991–93.

Also appeared as Roper, *The Will Rogers Follies;* Becca, *Spittin' Image,* Form Theater; Kaila, *Little Match Girl;* Polly, *Vanity and Vexation;* Becca, *My Good Name,* Bay Street Theatre; Ginya, *Nine Armenians,* Manhattan Theatre Club, New York City; Mary, *In No Man's Land,* The Women's Project; Tamara, *Lost and Found,* Circle Repertory Theatre Lab, New York City; in *Broadway Kids Sing Broadway,* John Houseman Theater, New York City.

Major Tours:

Young Cosette, *Les Miserables,* U.S. cities, c. 1988–90.

Stage Work:

Worked as assistant stage manager, *Broadway Kid Sing Broadway.*

RECORDINGS

Videos:

Bianca Montgomery, *Daytime's Greatest Weddings,* Buena Vista Home Video, 2004.

Taped Readings:

Ella Enchanted by Gail Carson Levine, Random House Audio Books, 1988.

Albums:

Appeared on *Broadway Kids Sing,* Light–year Entertainment; Michael Jackson's *HIStory,* Epic; Jewel's *Joy: A Holiday Collection,* Atlantic Records; *Home Alone Two,* Twentieth Century–Fox; *The Crossing Guard,* Metro–Goldwyn–Mayer; *Songs of Virtue,* Peter Pan Records.

OTHER SOURCES

Periodicals:
The Harvard Crimson, July 14, 2000.

RIMMER, Shane 1932(?)–

PERSONAL

Born 1932 (some sources cite 1936), in Toronto, Ontario, Canada.

Career: Actor, voice artist, and writer.

CREDITS

Film Appearances:
Running Bear, *Flaming Frontier,* Twentieth Century–Fox, 1958.

Nancy's father, *A Dangerous Age,* Ajay Film Company, 1959.

Captain G. A. "Ace" Owens, *Dr. Strangelove or: How I Learned to Stop Worrying and Love the Bomb* (also known as *Dr. Strangelove, A Delicate Balance of Terror, Edge of Doom, Docteur Folamour, Docteur Folamour, ou: Comment j'ai appris a ne plus m'en faire et a aimer la bombe, Dr. Estranho Amor, Dr. Fantastico, Dr. Folamour, Dr. Insolito, Dr. Insolito o: Como aprendi a dejar de preocuparme y amar la bomba, Dr. Seltsam oder Gebrauchsanweisung fuer Anfaenger in der sorgenfreien Liebe zu Atomwaffen, Dr. Seltsam, oder wie ich lemte, die Bombe zu lieben, Dr. Strangelove, avagy rajoettem, hogy nem kell felni a bombatol, meg is lehet szeretni, Dr. Strangelove eller: Hur jag laerde mig sluta aengslas och aelska bomben, Dr. Strangelove eller: Hur jag slutade aengslas och laerde mig aelska bomben, Dr. Strangelove lub: jak przestalem sie martwic i pokochalem bombe, Il dottor Stranamore, ovvero come imparai a non preoccuparmi e ad amare la bomba, Telefono rojo?, volamos hacia Moscu, Tri Outolempi,* and *Tri Outolempi, eli: Kuinka lakkasin olemasta huolissani ja opin rakastamaan pommia*), Columbia, 1964.

Seaman first class C.I.C., *The Bedford Incident* (also known as *Alarm ved Gronland, Aux postes de combat, Estado de alarma, Fremmed u–baad jages, Hyoekkaeys Jaeaemerellae, Jakt paa frammande ubaat, Stato d'allarme, Vythisate to ypovryhio U–128,* and *Zwischenfall im Atlantik*), Columbia, 1965.

Voice of Scott Tracy, *Thunderbirds Are Go* (also known as *Thunderbirds Are GO, Feuervoegel startbereit, Guardianes del espacio, Thunderbirds et l'odyssee du cosmos,* and *Thunderbirds: i cavalieri dello spazio*), United Artists, 1966.

(Uncredited) Hawaii radar operator, *You Only Live Twice* (also known as *Ian Fleming's "You Only Live Twice," James Bond 5, Agent 007—du lever kun 2 gange, Agente 007, si vive solo due volte, Ata Rak Hai Pa'ama'im, Com 007 so se vive duas vezes, Elaet vain kahdesti, Insan iki kere yasar, James Bond i Japan, James Bond 007—Man lebt nur zweimal, Man lever bara tvaa gaanger, Nomes es viu dues vegades, On ne vit que deux fois, Solo de vive dos veces,* and *007—So se vive duas vezes*), United Artists, 1967.

Voice of Scott Tracy, *Thunderbird 6* (also known as *Thunderbird Six, L'odyssee du cosmos,* and *Thunderbirds et Lady Penelope*), United Artists, 1968.

(Uncredited) Tom, *Diamonds Are Forever* (also known as *Ian Fleming's "Diamonds Are Forever," Agente 007, una cascata di diamnati, Brylanty sa na zawsze, Diamanter varer evig, Diamanter varer evigt, Diamantes para la eternidad, Diamants per a l'eternitat, James Bond 007—Diamantenfieber, Les diamants sont eternels, Los diamantes son eternos, Oeluemsuez elmaslar, Timantit ovat ikuisia,* and *007—Os diamantes sao eternos*), United Artists, 1971.

(Uncredited) Police officer in hotel, *Scorpio* (also known as *Scorpio, der Killer* and *Skorpioni*), United Artists, 1973.

Take Me High (also known as *Hot Property*), Anglo–EMI Film Distributors, 1973.

Hessler, *S*P*Y*S* (also known as *S.P.Y.S, Wet Stuff, Das Chaos–Duo, Les "S" pions,* and *S.P.Y.S.—vauhkot vakoojat*), Twentieth Century–Fox, 1974.

Carter (CIA), *The "Human" Factor* (also known as *The Human Factor* and *Il giustiziere*), Bryanston Distributing, 1975.

Rusty (team executive), *Rollerball* (also known as *Rollerball—Os gladiadores do futuro*), United Artists, 1975.

Colonel Alexander B. Franklin, *Twilight's Last Gleaming* (also known as *Nuclear Countdown* and *Das Ultimatum*), Allied Artists, 1977.

Commander Carter, *The Spy Who Loved Me* (also known as *Aelskade spion, Agente 007, la spia che mi amava, Beni seven casus, Ha–Meragel She Ahav Oti, James Bond 007—Der Spion, der mich liebte, L'espia que em va estimar, L'espion qui m'aimait, La espia que me amo, Spionen der elskede mig, Spionen som elsket meg, 007—Agente irresistivel, 007—O espiao que me amava,* and *007 rakastettuni*), United Artists, 1977.

(Uncredited) Customs officer, *Julia* (also known as *Giula* and *Muistojeni Julia*), Twentieth Century–Fox, 1977.

Hogan, *The People That Time Forgot,* American International Pictures, 1977.

(Uncredited) InCom engineer, *Star Wars* (also known as *Star Wars: Episode IV—A New Hope, Star Wars IV: A New Hope, The Star Wars, The Star Wars: From the Adventures of Luke Starkiller, Adventures of the Starkiller: Episode 1—The Star Wars, The Adven-*

tures of Luke Starkiller as Taken from the "Journal of the Whills": Saga I—Star Wars, A guerra das estrelas, Csillagok haboruja, Guerra nas estrelas, Guerre stellari: Episodio IV—Una nuova speranza, Gwiezdne wojny, Hvezdne valky, Kreig der Sterne, Kreig der Sterne—Episode IV: Eine neue Hoffnung, La guerra de las estrellas, La guerra de las galaxias, La guerra de las galaxies, La guerra de las galaxies: Una nova esperanca, La guerre des etoiles, La guerre des etoiles—Un nouvel espoir, Ratovi zvezda—Nova nada, Ratovi zvijezda, Star wars: Episode IV, la guerre des etoiles, Star Wars: Episode IV—Neue Hoffnung, Star wars: Episodio IV—Una nueva esperanza, Star wars IV—Taehtien sota: Uusi toivo, Stjaemornas krig, Stjemekrigen, Stjoemustrio, Suta wozu: Aratanaru kibou, Taehtien sota, and Yildiz savalari), Twentieth Century–Fox, 1977.

Officer, *Nasty Habits* (also known as *The Abbess*), Brut Productions, 1977.

American banker, *Silver Bears* (also known as *Fool's Gold*), Columbia, 1978.

Captain Daniels, *Warlords of Atlantis* (also known as *Warlords of the Deep*), Columbia, 1978.

Abu, *Arabian Adventure* (also known as *Alfombras magicas, Awentura araba, Im Banne des Kalifen, Le tresor de la montagne sacree, O ekdikitis me to iptameno hali, O tapete voador, 1001 peripeteies stin aravia, Prinssi Hassanin seikkailut,* and *Przygoda arabska*), Warner Bros., 1979.

Colonel Ronald Bart, *Hanover Street* (also known as *Ao encontro da guerra e do amor, Das Toedliche Dreieck, Guerre et passion, I skuggan av ett krig, La calle del adios, Muistojen katu,* and *Una strada, un amore*), Columbia, 1979.

Second controller, *Superman II* (also known as *Staalmannen II, Superman II—Allein gegen alle,* and *Superman 2—Aventyret fortsaetter*), Warner Bros., 1980, alternate version released as *Superman II: The Richard Donner Cut*, Warner Home Video, 2006.

Chief immigration officer, *Priest of Love* (also known as *Modlitwa o milosc, Rakkauden apostoli,* and *Sacerdote del amor*), Filmways Pictures, 1981.

Dr. Oaks, *The Dogs of War* (also known as *Caes de guerra, Die Hunde des Krieges, I mastini della guerra, Krigshundarna, Les chiens de guerre, Los perros de la guerra, Psy wojny,* and *Sodan koirat*), United Artists, 1981.

MacAlpine, *Reds* (also known as *Adoomim, Czerwoni, Les rouges, Punaiset, Rojos,* and *Voeroesoek*), Paramount, 1981.

Radio commentator at funeral, *Gandhi* (also known as *Richard Attenborough's Film: "Gandhi"*), Columbia, 1982.

Adolph Fannon, *The Lonely Lady* (also known as *Chica solitaria, Karriere durch alle Betten, Kultanainen,* and *Tie huipulle*), Universal, 1983.

Jelinek, *The Hunger* (also known as *Aclik, Az ehseg, Begierde, Blodsghunger, El ansia, Fome de viver, Les predateurs, Miriam si sveglia a mezzanotte,* and *Verenjano*), Metro–Goldwyn–Mayer, 1983.

State police officer, *Superman III* (also known as *Superman vs. Superman, Staalmannen gaar paa en kryptonit,* and *Superman III—Der staehlerne Blitz*), Warner Bros., 1983.

Ambassador Larry Smith, *White Nights* (also known as *Biale noce, Die Nacht der Entscheidung, Hvide naetter, Il sole a mezzanote, Noches del sol, O sol da meia–noite, O sol da meia noite, Sol de medianoche, Valkeat yoet, Vita naetter,* and *White Nights—Nacht der Entscheidung*), Columbia, 1985.

Belknap (farm manager), *Out of Africa* (also known as *Africa mia, Africa minha, Benim Afrikam, Jenseits von Afrika, La mia Africa, Memorias de Africa, Memories d'Africa, Minun Afrikkani, Mit Afrika, Mitt Afrika, Out of Africa—Souvenirs d'Afrique, Pera apo tin Afriki, Pozegnanie z Afryka, Souvenirs d'Afrique,* and *Tavol Afrikatol*), Universal, 1985.

Lieutenant Miles, *The Holcroft Covenant* (also known as *A Holcroft egyezmeny, Der 4 1/2 Billionen Dollar Vertrag, El pacto de Berlin, El pacto Holcroft, Holkroftova pogodba, Il ritorno delle aquile,* and *Verirahat*), Universal, 1985.

Melvin, *Morons from Outer Space* (also known as *Space Cracks, Aeaelioet ulkoavaruudesta, Glupcy z kosmosu, Ineptos interplanetarios, Les debiles de l'espace, Naerkontakt av vaersta greden, Os tarados do espaco,* and *Star Cracks—Die irre Bruchlandung der Ausserirdischen*), Universal, 1985.

Mr. Marl, *Dreamchild* (also known as *Das Wahre Leben der Alice im Wunderland, Dziecko z marzen, Ihmelapsi, Ihmemaan lapsi,* and *No mundo dos sonhos*), Universal, 1985.

Marvin Gelber (U.S. Secretary of State), *Whoops Apocalypse* (also known as *As golpadas da politica, Die Bombe fliegt, La loca guerra de la Gran Bretana, Se on menoa nyt, Se on ydinsota nyt, Una signora chiamata presidente, Whoops—Apocalipse Ja!,* and *Zu splaet—Die Bombe fliegt*), ITC Entertainment Group, 1986, Metro–Goldwyn–Mayer, 1988.

Mr. Mather, *Crusoe* (also known as *Crusoe—Etelameren seikkailija, Robinson Crusoe—Reise ins Abenteuer,* and *Robinson Kruse*), Island Pictures, 1989.

Chairman of Maxine Gray Cosmetics, *Company Business* (also known as *Companhia de assassinos, De sista dubbelagenterna, Espias sin fronteras, Oi teleftaioi diploi praktores, Patriotes, Spie contro, Venaelaeinen ruletti,* and *Wewnetrzna sprawa CIA*), Metro–Goldwyn–Mayer, 1991.

Commissioner Malley (some sources cite role as Commissioner Mallet), *A Kiss before Dying* (also known as *Besame antes de morir, Der Kuss vor dem Tode, Een kus voor je sterft, En Kyss foere doeden, Pocalunek przed smiercia, Suudelma ennen kuolemaa, Um beijo antes de morrer, Um beijo ao morrer, Um beijo para a morte, Un bacio prima di morire, Un baiser avant de mourir,* and *Un beso antes de morir*), Universal, 1991.

T. T. Kelleher, *Year of the Comet* (also known as *Das Jahr des Kometen, Den vilda jakten paa vinet, El ano del cometa, Komeettakanuunat, L'anno della cometa,* and *O ano do cometa*), Columbia, 1992.

Mr. Hughes, *Piccolo grande amore* (also known as *Pretty Princess, Pretty Princess: Pequeno gran amor,* and *Um pequeno grande amor*), [Italy], 1993.

Coach, *A Kid in King Arthur's Court* (also known as *Aventuras en la corte del rey Arturo, Chlopak na dworze kroka Artura, Egy koelyoek Artur kiraly udvaraban, Firlama soevalye, Knightskater—Ritter auf Rollerblades, Le kid et le roi, Uma viagem a corte do rei Artur, Un joven en la corte del rey Arturo,* and *Un ragazzo alla corte di re Artu*), Buena Vista, 1996.

E. J. Saggs, *Space Truckers* (also known as *Star Truckers, Camioneros del espacio, Guerra espacial, Piratas do espaco, Space Truckers: transporte espacial,* and *Urkamionosok*), Pachyderm Productions, 1996.

Parnell Thomas, *One of the Hollywood Ten* (documentary; also known as *Punto de mira* and *Punto di vista*), Alibi Films International, 2000.

Estate agent, *Spy Game* (also known as *Jeux d'espionnage, Jogo de espioes, Juego de espias, Kemjatszma, Spioni di elita, Spy Game—Der finale Countdown, Spy game—Jeu d'espions, Spy game: Juego de espias,* and *Zawod: Szpieg*), Universal, 2001.

Voice of Tantive Base operative, *The War of the Starfighters* (animated), 2003.

Anderson, *Mee–Shee: The Water Giant* (also known as *The Water Giant, Mee–Shee—Le secret des profondeurs, Mee–Shee, to thalassio elefantaki,* and *Ogopogo*), ContentFilm, 2005.

Older Gotham Water Board technician, *Batman Begins* (also known as *Batman 5, Batman: Intimidation, The Intimidation Game, Batman alustab, Batman comienza, Batman: El comienza, Batman inicia,* and *Batman: Le commencement*), Warner Bros., 2005, IMAX version released as *Batman Begins: The IMAX Experience.*

Colonel, *Alien Autopsy* (also known as *Alien—I aftopsia, Autopsia de un alien,* and *Avaruusolennon ruumiinavus*), Warner Bros., 2006.

Television Appearances; Series:

Host, *Come Fly with Me*, CBC, 1958.

Russell Corrigan, *Compact*, BBC, 1963–64.

Voices of Scott Tracy and other characters, *Thunderbirds* (also known as *Tairnearan Tar As*), Associated Television and Incorporated Television Company, 1965–66.

Khan, *Orlando*, Rediffusion, 1966.

Voices of various characters, *Captain Scarlet and the Mysterons* (also known as *Captain Scarlet*), Incorporated Television Company and syndicated, 1967–68.

Joe Donnelli, *Coronation Street* (also known as *Corrie, Florizel Street,* and *Where No Bird Sings*), Independent Television and CBC, c. 1967–70.

Various voices, *Joe 90,* Incorporated Television Company, 1968–69.

Various characters, *Space: 1999* (also known as *Spazio: 1999*), Incorporated Television Company and syndicated, 1975–76.

Ed Condon, *Oppenheimer*, BBC–2, 1980, broadcast on *American Playhouse*, PBS, 1982.

Voice of Dick Spanner, *Dick Spanner, P.I.* (also known as *Dick Spanner*), Channel 4 (England), beginning 1986.

Malcolm Reid, *Coronation Street* (also known as *Corrie, Florizel Street,* and *Where No Bird Sings*), Independent Television and CBC, c. 1988.

Lieutenant colonel Trekker, *Lipstick on Your Collar* (musical), Channel 4, 1993.

Television Appearances; Miniseries:

(Uncredited) Reporter outside court, *QB VII*, ABC, 1974.

Willoughby, *A Man Called Intrepid*, NBC, 1979.

Sergeant Ed Kusborski, *The Rose Medallion*, BBC, 1981.

Carroll, *Master of the Game* (also known as *El amo del juego, La padrona del gioco, Maitre du jeu, Timanttidynastia,* and *Timantti Dynastia*), CBS, 1984.

Duffy, *Ellis Island*, CBS, 1984.

Harry Klein, *Mistral's Daughter*, CBS, 1984.

Press agent, *Lace*, ABC, 1984.

General Quigley, *Space* (also known as *James A. Michener's "Space"*), CBS, 1985.

Harvey Coward, *Anastasia: The Mystery of Anna* (also known as *Anastasia, Anastacia—O misterio de Ana,* and *Anasztazia*), NBC, 1986.

Doorman, *The Two Mrs. Grenvilles*, NBC, 1987.

General Conklin, *The Bourne Identity* (also known as *Agent ohne Namen, Conspiracion terrorista: el caso Bourne, El caso Bourne, Identitet okaend, La memoire dans la peau, Medusan verkko,* and *Tozsamosc Bourne'a*), ABC, 1988.

Reilly, *The Fortunate Pilgrim* (also known as *Mario Puzo's "The Fortunate Pilgrim"* and *Mamma Lucia*), NBC, 1988.

Secretary of state, *A Very British Coup*, Channel 4 (England), 1988, broadcast on *Masterpiece Theatre* (also known as *ExxonMobil Masterpiece Theatre* and *Mobil Masterpiece Theatre*), PBS, c. 1988.

Ambassador Dodd, *The Nightmare Years*, TNT, 1989.

Skip Harrier, *Fiendens fiende* (also known as *Enemy's Enemy*), TV4 Sweden, 1990.

Morton Fendig, *Stanley and the Women*, Independent Television (England), 1991.

Warren Oliver, *Only Love* (also known as *Erich Segal's "Only Love"*), CBS, 1998.

Television Appearances; Movies:

Track announcer, *Baffled!*, NBC, 1973.

(Uncredited) Voice of Eagle pilot, *Alien Attack* (also known as *Alien Attack—Die Ausserirdischen schlagen zu* and *Angriff auf Alpha 1;* re–edited episodes of *Space: 1999*), Incorporated Television Company, 1976.

Bob Grodin, *Alternative 3* (also known as *Science Report* and *Science Report: "Alternative 3"*), 1977.

American colonel, *The One and Only Phyllis Dixey* (also known as *Peek–A–Boo*), Thames Television and PBS, 1978.

Braley, *Charlie Muffin* (also known as *A Deadly Game* and *L'abbraccio dell'orso*), Euston Films, 1979.

Mr. Gardner, *Nairobi Affair*, CBS, 1984.

Jay, *Gulag*, HBO, 1985.

Joe Szyluk, *Reunion at Fairborough*, HBO, 1985.

Brod Sarnton, *Mr. and Mrs. Edgehill* (also known as *Noel Coward Stories: Mr. and Mrs. Edgehill* and *Star Quality: Mr. and Mrs. Edgehill*), BBC, 1985, broadcast as part of *Star Quality: Noel Coward Stories* on *Masterpiece Theatre* (also known as *ExxonMobil Masterpiece Theatre* and *Mobil Masterpiece Theatre*), PBS, 1987.

Colonel, *Of Pure Blood* (also known as *The Nazis: Of Pure Blood*), CBS, 1986.

Dr. Lawrence Ball (a colonel), *The Last Days of Patton* (also known as *Kenraali Patton—viimeinentaistelu*, *Les derniers jours de Patton*, and *Los ultimos dias de Patton*), CBS, 1986.

Doc, *Riviera*, ABC, 1987.

Hogan, *Roman Holiday* (also known as *A princesa e o plebeu*, *Loma Roomassa*, and *Vacanze romane 2*), NBC, 1987.

Stark, *The Return of Sherlock Holmes*, CBS, 1987.

Admiral Reilly, *Tailspin: Behind the Korean Airliner Tragedy* (also known as *Coded Hostile*), HBO, 1989.

Bob Harrison, *The Software Murders*, syndicated, 1989.

General, *Red King, White Knight*, HBO, 1989.

Double Vision (also known as *Double vision—l'une pour l'autre*), 1992.

President Hoover, *Ivar Kreuger*, 1998.

American longshoreman, *Dockers*, 1999.

Father, *Caught in the Act* (also known as *Mind of the Crime*), Lifetime, 2004.

Byrnes, *Hiroshima*, BBC, 2005.

Television Appearances; Specials:

Marine sergeant, "Lee Oswald: Assassin," *Play of the Month*, BBC, 1966.

Stone, "Professional Foul," *BBC2 Play of the Week*, BBC–2, 1977.

Ambassador Bingham, "Speed King," *BBC2 Playhouse*, BBC–2, 1979.

George Schultz, *The Summit: A Nuclear Age Drama*, PBS, 1987.

Narrator, *The "Space: 1999" Documentary*, 1996.

Himself, *Mr. Thunderbird: The Gerry Anderson Story*, 2000.

Himself, *I Love Christmas*, BBC, 2001.

Television Appearances; Episodic:

Campbell, "Roast Goose and Walnut Stuffing," *Armchair Theatre*, Associated British Picture Corporation, 1959.

Major Smith, "The Hi–Jackers," *The Saint*, Independent Television (England), 1964.

Buchanan, "The Mercenaries," *Danger Man* (also known as *Secret Agent* and *Secret Agent aka Danger Man*), Independent Television, 1965.

Bud Burdine, "The Flipside," *Thirty–Minute Theatre*, BBC, 1966.

Ramsey, "All Roads Lead to Callaghan," *Court Martial*, ABC, 1966.

Seth Harper, "Don't Shoot the Pianist," *Doctor Who*, BBC, 1966.

Seth Harper, "A Holiday for the Doctor," *Doctor Who*, BBC, 1966.

Lieutenant Bill Johnson, "Identified," *UFO*, syndicated, 1970.

CIA agent, "Confetti Check A–OK," *UFO*, syndicated, 1971.

(Uncredited) Lieutenant Bill Johnson and an alien, "Computer Affair," *UFO*, syndicated, 1971.

Lomax, "Element of Risk," *The Persuaders!*, ABC, 1972.

Police sergeant Warren, "In the Confessional," *Great Mysteries* (also known as *Orson Welles' "Great Mysteries"*), Independent Television, 1973.

Vickers, "Vocal," *The Protectors*, Independent Television, 1973.

Zeke, "Zeke's Blues," *The Protectors*, Independent Television, 1973.

Harry Brent, "Thundersky," *Quiller*, BBC, 1975.

Peter Kovacs, "Value for Money," *You're on Your Own*, 1975.

Harold Giles Hoffman, "The Lindbergh Kidnapping," *Second Verdict*, BBC, 1976.

Pollack, "Divorce," *Hadleigh*, Yorkshire Television, 1976.

Mr. Henning, "Five on Finniston Farm," *The Famous Five* (also known as *Enid Blyton's "Famous Five"*), Independent Television, 1978.

"Two Birds, One Stone," *The Standard*, BBC, 1978.

Canadian commandant, "The Execution," *Secret Army*, BBC, 1979.

Falco, "Dragonseed," *Return of the Saint* (also known as *The Son of the Saint*), Independent Television, 1979.

Arthur Beauchamp, "My Lady Love, My Dove," *Tales of the Unexpected* (also known as *Roald Dahl's "Tales of the Unexpected"*), Anglia Television and syndicated, 1980.

Dick Leonard, "Fathers," *Nanny*, BBC, 1982.

John Smith, "A Man with a Fortune," *Tales of the Unexpected* (also known as *Roald Dahl's "Tales of the Unexpected"*), Anglia Television and syndicated, 1982.

Detective, "Smart Aleck Kill," *Philip Marlowe, Private Eye*, HBO, 1983.

Hersh, "Last Video and Testament," *Hammer House of Mystery and Suspense*, 1984.

Alas Smith & Jones (also known as *Smith and Jones*), BBC, multiple episodes in 1984.

Hank Ryder, "The Crackler," *Agatha Christie's "Partners in Crime"* (also known as *Partners in Crime, Partners in Crime, Series II, Companeros en el crimen, Detektei Blunt,* and *Pareja en el crimen*), London Weekend Television, 1984, broadcast on *Mystery!,* PBS, 1986.

Agent Biddle, "Don Danko," *Dirty Dozen: The Series* (also known as *Doce del patibulo* and *Les douze salopards*), Fox, 1988.

Detective Barnes, "Basketball Story," *Street Legal,* CBC, 1989.

Lovell J. Wallace, "A Sudden Silence," *Van der Valk,* Independent Television, 1991.

Bob, "The Authentic Taste of England," *Land of Hope and Gloria,* Thames Television, 1992.

William Kingsley, "Brooklyn Bridge," *Seven Wonders of the Industrial World,* BBC, 2003.

Television Appearances; Pilots:

Appeared as Lieutenant Chuck Brogan in *Space Police* (also known as *Star Laws*), the unaired pilot for *Space Precinct* (also known as *Brigada espacial* and *Space Cops—Tatort Demeter City*), syndicated and Sky One.

RECORDINGS

Videos:

Himself, *Inside "Diamonds Are Forever"* (short), Sony Pictures Home Entertainment, 2000.

Himself, *Inside the Making of "Dr. Strangelove"* (also known as *Inside "Dr. Strangelove"*), Columbia, 2000.

WRITINGS

Teleplays; Episodic:

"Avalanche," *Captain Scarlet and the Mysterons* (also known as *Captain Scarlet*), Incorporated Television Company and syndicated, 1967.

"Expo 2068," *Captain Scarlet and the Mysterons* (also known as *Captain Scarlet*), Incorporated Television Company and syndicated, 1968.

"Inferno," *Captain Scarlet and the Mysterons* (also known as *Captain Scarlet*), Incorporated Television Company and syndicated, 1968.

Joe 90, Incorporated Television Company, multiple episodes in 1968–69.

"Hole in One," *The Secret Service,* 1969.

"Zeke's Blues," *The Protectors,* Independent Television (England), 1973.

"Blockbuster," *The Protectors,* Independent Television, 1974.

Wrote unproduced teleplays for *Space: 1999* (also known as *Spazio: 1999*), Incorporated Television Company and syndicated.

ROBINSON, Andrew 1942–
(Andrew J. Robinson, Andy Robinson)

PERSONAL

Full name, Andrew Jordt Robinson; born February 14, 1942, in New York, NY; son of William Hurlin and Agnes Corcoran (maiden name, Jordt) Robinson; married Irene Dobjanskis, March 9, 1970; children: Rachel (an actress). *Education:* Attended University of New Hampshire; New School for Social Research, New York, NY, B.A., 1964; studied acting at London Academy of Music and Dramatic Arts, 1964–65.

Addresses: Manager—The Firm, 9465 Wilshire Blvd., 6th Floor, Beverly Hills, CA 90212.

Career: Actor, director, and writer. Milwaukee Repertory Theatre, Milwaukee, WI, actor, 1965–66; Playhouse in the Park, Cincinnati, OH, actor, 1966–67; Trinity Playhouse, Providence, RI, member of Trinity Square Repertory Company, 1966–67; Matrix Theatre Company, Los Angeles, founding member, c. 1993—; worked as an actor with LaMama Plexus (experimental theatre group), New York City. Queens College of the City University of New York, teacher, 1968–69; University of Southern California, teacher at Idyllwild School of Music and the Arts, 1982–83, faculty member and director of M.F.A. program in acting, 2006; University of California, Los Angeles, teacher, 1990. Also worked as a carpenter and construction worker.

Member: Academy of Motion Picture Arts and Sciences (fellow), Screen Actors Guild (member of board of directors, 1991).

Awards, Honors: Fulbright scholar in England, 1964–65; Daytime Emmy Award nomination, outstanding actor in a daytime drama series, 1978, for *Ryan's Hope;* Los Angeles Drama Critics Circle Award, best actor, 1984, for *In the Belly of the Beast;* Los Angeles Drama Critics Circle awards, best director, 1995, for *Endgame,* and 1996, for *The Homecoming;* L.A. Ovation Award, Los Angeles Stage Alliance, and *Back Stage West* Award, both 1998, for *Yield of the Long Bond;* Feature Film Award, best supporting actor, New York International Independent Film and Video Festival, 2003, for *The Making of Daniel Boone.*

CREDITS

Stage Appearances:

(Off–Broadway debut) *MacBird!,* Village Gate Theatre, 1967.

Woyzeck, La Mama Experimental Theatre Club, New York City, between 1967 and 1970.

Inside Out, LaMama Experimental Theatre Club, between 1967 and 1970.

Sheriff Tom Sluck, *Futz!,* Theatre De Lys, then Actors Playhouse, both New York City, 1968.

Klaus, *The Cannibals,* American Place Theatre, New York City, 1968.

Dante, "The Young Master Dante," in *Trainer, Dean, Liepolt, and Company,* American Place Theatre, 1968.

Young man, *Operation Sidewinder,* Vivian Beaumont Theatre, Lincoln Center, New York City, 1970.

Prince Myshkin, *Subject to Fits,* New York Shakespeare Festival, Public Theatre, New York City, 1971.

Sir William Davison, *Mary Stuart,* Vivian Beaumont Theatre, Lincoln Center 1971.

The Idiot, New York Shakespeare Festival, Public Theatre, 1971.

Kiro, *Narrow Road to the Deep North,* Vivian Beaumont Theatre, Lincoln Center, 1972.

The Death and Life of Jesse James, New Theatre for Now, Ahmanson Theatre, Los Angeles, 1974.

Gogol, a Mystery Play, New York Shakespeare Festival, Public Theatre, 1976.

The Bacchae, Los Angeles Actors Theatre, Los Angeles, 1979.

Macbeth, Los Angeles Actors Theatre, 1980.

The Man Who Came to Dinner, Long Beach Theatre Festival, Long Beach, CA, 1980.

Professor Leo Lehrer, *The Genius,* Center Theatre Group, Mark Taper Forum, Los Angeles, 1984.

Jack Henry Abbot, *In the Belly of the Beast,* Center Theatre Group, Mark Taper Forum, 1984, then Joyce Theatre, New York City, 1985.

The Aristocrats, Mark Taper Forum, 1989.

Richard II, Mark Taper Forum, 1991.

M. Butterfly, Seattle Repertory Theatre, Seattle, WA, 1991.

Wanderings of Odysseus, J. Paul Getty Museum Theatre, Los Angeles, 1992.

(Broadway debut) Gus Brower, *Any Given Day,* Longacre Theatre, New York City, 1993.

The Tavern, Matrix Theatre Company, Los Angeles, 1993.

Memoirs of Jesus (solo show), Matrix Theatre Company, 1993.

Habeas Corpus, Matrix Theatre Company, 1994.

Adelaide MacKenzie, *The Fading Day* (workshop performance), New Work Festival, Falcon Theatre, Burbank, CA, 1997.

Yield of the Long Bond, Matrix Theatre Company, 1998.

Death of a Salesman, Falcon Theatre, Burbank, CA, 1998.

Vienna Lusthaus (Revisited), New York Theatre Workshop, New York City, 2002.

Also appeared in *The Changing Room,* Odyssey Theatre, Los Angeles; and *Curse of the Starving Class,* Tiffany Theatre, Los Angeles.

Stage Director:

Endgame, Matrix Theatre Company, Los Angeles, 1995.

The Homecoming, Matrix Theatre Company, 1996.

Dangerous Corner, Matrix Theatre Company, 1997–98.

A Moon for the Misbegotten, Matrix Theatre Company, 1997–98.

Yield of the Long Bond, Matrix Theatre Company, 1998.

Death of a Salesman, Falcon Theatre, Burbank, CA, 1998.

Visiting Mr. Green, Pasadena Playhouse, Pasadena, CA, 1999.

Waiting for Godot, Matrix Theatre Company, 2000.

Television Appearances; Series:

Frank Ryan, a recurring role, *Ryan's Hope,* ABC, 1975–77.

(Sometimes credited as Andrew J. Robinson) Elim Garak, *Star Trek: Deep Space Nine* (also known as *Deep Space Nine, DS9,* and *Star Trek: DS9*), UPN, 1993–99.

Cousin Yuri, *Days of Our Lives* (also known as *Days* and *DOOL*), 1996.

Television Appearances; Miniseries:

Reb Rayburne, *Once an Eagle,* NBC, 1976.

Sergeant Maylon Stark, *From Here to Eternity,* NBC, 1979.

Jack Mallard, *The Atlanta Child Murders,* CBS, 1985.

Dr. Phillip Eckhart, *Telling Secrets* (also known as *Contract for Murder*), ABC, 1993.

Television Appearances; Movies:

Sheriff Moore, "House of Evil," *ABC Mystery Movie,* ABC, 1974.

Paul Kendra, "Right to an Attorney," *Chase,* 1974.

Frank Berlin, *Someone I Touched,* ABC, 1975.

Dr. Royce, *Not My Kid,* CBS, 1985.

Title role, *Liberace,* ABC, 1988.

Andrew Simms, *The Lady Forgets,* CBS, 1989.

Henry Willson, *Rock Hudson,* ABC, 1990.

Mort, *Appearances,* NBC, 1990.

Commissioner Garth, *Prime Target,* 1991.

Sheriff Aaron (some sources cite Anson) Starett, *Into the Badlands,* USA Network, 1991.

Sheriff Childs, *Fatal Charm,* Showtime, 1992.

Frank Spears, *Criminal Behavior,* ABC, 1992.

Senator, *Homeland Security,* NBC, 2004.

Television Appearances; Pilots:

Andy, *The Catcher,* CBS, 1972.

Butch Kovack, *The Family Kovack,* CBS, 1974.

Willie Norman, *Lanigan's Rabbi* (also known as *Friday the Rabbi Slept Late*), NBC, 1976.

Frank Morrella, *Reward,* ABC, 1980.

(As Andy Robinson) Beau, *Big Bend Country,* 1981.

Seamus, *Desperate,* ABC, 1987.

Television Appearances; Episodic:

"Three–Fifty–Two," *N.Y.P.D.*, 1969.

(As Andy Robinson) John Harper, "Forever: Parts 1 & 2," *Bonanza* (also known as *Ponderosa*), 1972.

(As Andy Robinson) Lee Borden, "To Taste of Terror," *The Rookies*, 1972.

(As Andy Robinson) German major, "Incident at Vichy," *Hollywood Theatre*, PBS, 1973.

(As Andy Robinson) Johnny, "Crossties," *Kung Fu*, 1974.

(As Andy Robinson) Billy Kempson, "Prelude to Vengeance," *The Rookies*, 1974.

(As Andy Robinson) "Come Eleven, Come Twelve," *Ironside* (also known as *The Raymond Burr Show*), 1974.

(As Andy Robinson) "The Case of the Violent Valley," *The New Perry Mason*, 1974.

Drew, "Each Day a Miracle," *Marcus Welby, M.D.* (also known as *Robert Young, Family Doctor*), 1975.

Archie Kimbro, "Spooks for Sale," *The Streets of San Francisco*, 1975.

(As Andy Robinson) Leon, "I Want to Report a Dream," *Kojak*, 1975.

Jim Bracken, "Reflections," *Harry O*, 1975.

Shipping clerk, "The Sentry," *Kolchak: The Night Stalker* (also known as *The Night Stalker*), 1975.

"And Sorrow for Angels," *Doctors' Hospital*, 1975.

"The Book of Fear," *Bert D'Angelo/Superstar*, 1976.

Sonny Holland, "Band of Evil," *Barnaby Jones*, 1976.

"Any Second Now," *S.W.A.T.*, 1976.

Ron "Ronnie" McGuire, "The Cannibals," *The Streets of San Francisco*, 1977.

Roger Layton, "Photo Must Credit Joe Paxton," *Kojak*, 1978.

Dr. Dan Rhodes, "Life and Death," *The Incredible Hulk*, 1978.

McTieg, "The Con Caper," *The Amazing Spiderman*, 1978.

"Murder on the Flip Side," *The Eddie Capra Mysteries*, 1978.

Bill Clayton, "Hot Wheels," *CHiPs* (also known as *CHiPs Patrol*), 1979.

Robert Curtis, "Echo of a Distant Battle: Parts 1 & 2," *Barnaby Jones*, 1979.

Mick Steele, "This Lady Is Murder," *Hart to Hart*, 1979.

Mitchell, "The Valley Strangler," *Mrs. Columbo* (also known as *Kate Columbo, Kate Loves a Mystery*, and *Kate the Detective*), 1979.

"A Family of Winners," *Insight*, 1979.

Sangree, "Makin' Tracks," *Young Maverick*, 1980.

Phil Devine, "Murder in the Key of C," *Barnaby Jones*, 1980.

Derek Razzio, "Golden Gate Cop Killer: Parts 1 & 2," *Vega$*, 1980.

Billy Joe Pruitt, "The Hazzardville Horror," *The Dukes of Hazzard*, 1980.

Wilson, "Hostages," *240–Robert*, 1981.

Phil Eberhardt, "The Candidate," *Falcon Crest*, 1982.

Chris Stofford, "Resurrection of Carlini," *The Greatest American Hero*, 1982.

Billy Joe Pruitt, "The Treasure of Soggy Marsh," *The Dukes of Hazzard*, 1982.

The New F.B.I., 1982.

Mike Huntington, "Emily, by Hart," *Hart to Hart*, 1983.

"Eye Witness Blues," *The Rousters*, 1983.

Jackson, "The Beast from the Belly of a Boeing," *The A–Team*, 1983.

Deputy Rance, "The White Ballot," *The A–Team*, 1983.

Jonathan Redfield, "Here's Another Fine Mess," *Matt Houston*, 1983.

Frank Kelly, "Filial Duty," *Cagney & Lacey*, CBS, 1985.

Oliver Bancroft, "Death Trap," *Matt Houston*, 1985.

"The Face of Gabriel Ortiz," *This Is the Life*, 1985.

President John F. Kennedy, "Profile in Silver," *The Twilight Zone*, CBS, 1986.

Mr. Nelson, "Family Connections," *Cagney & Lacey*, CBS, 1986.

Mr. Williams, "Private Channel," *The Twilight Zone*, CBS, 1987.

Leslie Hunziger, "Plastic Fantastic Lovers," *Moonlighting*, 1989.

Stanley Hayden, "The Broker," *Matlock*, NBC, 1990.

Gregory Edmonson, "He's a Crowd," *L.A. Law*, NBC, 1991.

Frank Hayes, "The Defense," *Matlock*, NBC, 1991.

Phillip Marietta, "Consultation," *Law & Order*, NBC, 1992.

Leo Cabe, "A Shadow in the Night," *Walker, Texas Ranger* (also known as *Walker*), CBS, 1993.

Ambrose Griffith, "A Killing in Cork," *Murder, She Wrote*, 1993.

Solomon Box, "To Prey in Darkness," *M.A.N.T.I.S.*, Fox, 1994.

Solomon Box, "Thou Shalt Not Kill," *M.A.N.T.I.S.*, Fox, 1994.

Solomon Box, "Revelation," *M.A.N.T.I.S.*, Fox, 1994.

James Harris, "An Egg to Die For," *Murder, She Wrote*, CBS, 1994.

Michael Foster, "The Person Formerly Known as Lowell," *Wings*, NBC, 1995.

(As Andrew J. Robinson) "Sleeping Dogs," *Nothing Sacred*, 1998.

Dr. Ian Detweiler, "Alpha," *The X–Files*, Fox, 1999.

(As Andrew J. Robinson) Admiral Thomas Kly, "Rogue," *JAG*, CBS, 1999.

(As Andrew J. Robinson) Robert Dunlop, "The Waiting Room," *The Sentinel*, 1999.

(As Andrew J. Robinson) Lieutenant Jenkins, "Flesh & Blood," *The Pretender*, NBC, 1999.

(As Andrew J. Robinson) Richard Tynan, "No Quarter," *Martial Law*, The Nashville Network, 2000.

(As Andrew J. Robinson) Daniel Wade, "Pianissimo," *Profiler*, NBC, 2000.

Daniel McGill, "Gray vs. Gray," *Judging Amy*, CBS, 2000.

Jesse, "Secrets," *Presidio Med*, CBS, 2002.

Jesse, "Once Upon a Family," *Presidio Med*, CBS, 2002.

(As Andrew J. Robinson) Edmond Solomon, "The Firm," *The Practice*, ABC, 2004.

Carl Monroe, "Upstairs Downstairs," *Without a Trace* (also known as *W.A.T.*), CBS, 2004.

(As Andrew J. Robinson) Admiral Thomas Kly, "Whole New Ball Game," *JAG*, CBS, 2004.

Television Appearances; Other:

Gregory Waples, "The Trial of Bernhard Goetz" (special), *American Playhouse*, PBS, 1988.

Kenneth, *Matt's Million*, 1996.

Television Director; Series:

Judging Amy, CBS, multiple episodes, between 2001 and 2005.

Television Director as Andrew J. Robinson; Episodic:

"Looking for par'Mach in All the Wrong Places," *Star Trek: Deep Space Nine* (also known as *Deep Space Nine*, *DS9*, and *Star Trek: DS9*), UPN, 1996.

"Blood Fever," *Star Trek: Voyager*, UPN, 1996.

"Unforgettable," *Star Trek: Voyager*, UPN, 1998.

Film Appearances:

(As Andy Robinson) Scorpio killer, *Dirty Harry*, Warner Bros., 1971.

Harman Sullivan, *Charley Varrick* (also known as *Kill Charley Varrick*), Universal, 1973.

(As Andy Robinson) Pat Reaves (some sources cite Pat Reavis), *The Drowning Pool*, Warner Bros., 1975.

Coley Phipps, *Mackintosh and T. J.*, Penland, 1975.

Steve McCoy, *A Woman for All Men* (also known as *Deadly Intrigue* and *Part Time Wife*), 1975.

Dr. Vinton, *Mask* (also known as *Peter Bogdanovich's "Mask"*), Universal, 1985.

Detective Monte, *Cobra*, Warner Bros., 1986.

Larry Cotton and Frank Cotton, *Hellraiser* (also known as *Clive Barker's "Hellraiser"*), New World, 1987.

Pretty Boy Floyd, *The Verne Miller Story* (also known as *Gangland* and *Verne Miller*), 1987.

Harvey, *Shoot to Kill* (also known as *Deadly Pursuit*), Buena Vista, 1988.

Larry Cotton (in archive footage), *Hellbound: Hellraiser II*, 1988.

Sergeant Botnick, *Child's Play 3* (also known as *Child's Play 3: Look Who's Stalking*), Universal, 1991.

Commissioner, *Prime Target*, 1991.

Colonel Daddy Muthuh, *Trancers III* (also known as *Death Lives*, *Future Cop III*, and *Trancers 3: Deth Lives*), 1992.

Frank, *There Goes My Baby* (also known as *The Last Days of Paradise*), Orion, 1993.

Hawthorne, *The Puppet Masters* (also known as *Robert Heinlein's "The Puppet Masters"*), Buena Vista, 1994.

Sheriff Sean Braddock, *Pumpkinhead II: Blood Wings* (also known as *Pumpkinhead II*, *Pumpkinhead 2: The Demon Returns*, and *The Revenge of Pumpkin-*

head: Blood Wings), Motion Picture Corporation of America, 1994.

Newspaperman, *The Moravian Massacre*, 1996.

(As Andrew J. Robinson) Captain Don Gibbs, *Running Woman*, Concorde, 1998.

The super, *Archibald the Rainbow Painter* (also known as *The Homefront*), 1998.

Larry Cotton and Frank Cotton (in archive footage), *Boogeymen: The Killer Compilation*, Flixmix, 2001.

Timothy Flint, *The Making of Daniel Boone*, 2003.

Dr. Albert Krentz, *A Question of Loyalty* (short film), 2005.

RECORDINGS

Videos:

(As Andy Robinson) Voice of Sheriff Sean Braddock, *Bloodwings: Pumpkinhead's Revenge* (video game), 1995.

Voice of Elim Garak, *Star Trek: Deep Space Nine—The Fallen* (video game), 1999.

(As Andy Robinson) *Dirty Harry: The Original*, Warner Home Video, 2001.

(As Andy Robinson) Voice of Theodoric Cassel, *Earth and Beyond* (video game), Electronic Arts, 2002.

WRITINGS

Plays:

Memoirs of Jesus (solo show), Matrix Theatre Company, Los Angeles, 1993.

Author of *Last Chance Saloon* and *Springvoices*, both LaMama Experimental Theatre Club, New York City.

Other Writings:

Author of a science fiction novel, *A Stitch in Time*.

OTHER SOURCES

Periodicals:

Cinefantastique, November, 1997, pp. 56–58.

Cult Times, March, 1998, pp. 20–23.

Starlog, April, 1997.

Star Trek Monthly, June, 1998; January, 2000; July, 2000, pp. 72–75.

TV Zone Special, July, 1999, pp. 34–38.

ROEG, Theresa
    See RUSSELL, Theresa

ROONEY, Andy 1920–
  (Andrew A. Rooney)

PERSONAL

Full name, Andrew Aitken Rooney; born January 14, 1920, in Albany, NY; son of Walter Scott and Elinor (maiden name, Reynolds), Rooney; married Marguerite Howard (a teacher), April 21, 1942 (died April 27, 2004); children: Ellen, Martha, Emily (a broadcast journalist and news producer), Brian. *Education:* Attended Colgate University, Hamilton, NY, c. 1941.

Addresses: *Office*—c/o *60 Minutes,* CBS News, 51 West 52nd Street, New York, NY 10019. *Agent*—N. S. Bienstock, 1740 Broadway, 24th Floor, New York, NY 10019.

Career: Broadcast journalist, commentator, producer, writer, columnist, and essayist. Metro–Goldwyn–Mayer, Hollywood, CA, worked briefly as a writer; freelance magazine writer, 1947–49; CBS News, New York City, writer and producer, 1959–70; WNET–TV, New York City, broadcaster and writer, 1970–71; ABC–TV, writer, 1971–72; CBS News, writer and producer, 1972—. *Military service:* U.S. Army, journalist with *Stars & Stripes,* 1941–45; served in European theatre; became sergeant; received Bronze Star.

Member: Writers Guild of America, American Federation of Television and Radio Actors.

Awards, Honors: Writers Guild of America Awards, best written television documentary, 1966, for "The Great Love Affair," 1968, for "Black History: Lost, Stolen, or Strayed," 1971, for "An Essay on War," 1975, for "Mr. Rooney Goes to Washington," 1976, for "Mr. Rooney Goes to Dinner," and 1979, for "Happiness: The Elusive Pursuit"; Emmy Awards, outstanding individual achievement in news documentary programs, 1969, for the report "Black History: Lost, Stolen, or Strayed," *CBS News Hour,* outstanding writing for news or documentary programs, 1979, for "Who Owns What in America: A Few Minutes with Andy Rooney," *60 Minutes,* outstanding producer/reporter for news program segments, 1981, for "Grain: A Few Minutes with Andy Rooney," *60 Minutes,* and outstanding correspondent, 1981, for "Tanks: A Few Minutes with Andy Rooney," *60 Minutes;* George Foster Peabody Broadcasting Award, Henry W. Grady School of Journalism and Mass Communications, University of Georgia, 1975, for the report "Mr. Rooney Goes to Washington"; Walter Cronkite Award, Walter Cronkite School of Journalism and Mass Communications, Arizona State University, 2003; Ernie Pyle Lifetime Achievement Award, National Society of Newspaper Columnists, 2003.

CREDITS

Television Appearances; Series:
Commentator, *CBS News Hour,* CBS, 1968.
Commentator, *The Great American Dream Machine,* WNET (New York City), 1970–72.
Commentator, *60 Minutes,* CBS, 1979—.

Television Appearances; Specials:
A Year with Andy Rooney: 1989, CBS, 1989.
Share a Moment with the World, CBS, 1992.
60 Minutes … 25 Years, CBS, 1993.
Presenter, *51st Alfred I. Dupont/Columbia University Awards,* PBS, 1993.
10th Annual TV Academy Hall of Fame, Disney Channel, 1994.
The NFL at 75: An All–Star Celebration, ABC, 1995.
Cronkite Remembers, CBS, 1996.
"Arthur Godfrey: Broadcasting's Forgotten Giant," *Biography,* Arts and Entertainment, 1996.
Correspondent, *1996 Republican National Convention,* CBS, 1996.
Correspondent, *1996 Democratic National Convention,* CBS, 1996.
Correspondent for "Eye on People" segments, *60 Minutes More,* CBS, 1997.
Walter Cronkite: Eyewitness to History, Arts and Entertainment, 1998.
G.I. Joe: The Ernie Pyle Story, PBS, 1998.
CBS: The First 50 Years, CBS, 1998.
Don Hewitt: 90 Minutes on 60 Minutes, CBS, 1998.
60 Minutes at 30, CBS, 1998.
Heroes and Icons: People of the Century; CBS News/Time 100, CBS, 1999.
The 20th Century: Yesterday's Tomorrows (also known as *Barry Levinson on the Future in the 20th Century: Yesterday's Tomorrows*), Showtime, 1999.
Holocaust: The Untold Story, History Channel, 2001.
"Walter Cronkite: Witness to History," *American Masters,* PBS, 2006.
Mr. Conservative: Goldwater on Goldwater, HBO, 2006.
That's the Way It Is: Celebrating Cronkite at 90, CBS, 2007.

Television Appearances; Episodic:
Late Night with David Letterman, NBC, 1982.
Late Show with David Letterman (also known as *The Late Show* and *Late Show Backstage*), CBS, 1993.
ESPN SportsCentury, ESPN, 2001, 2004.
Himself as reporter for *Stars & Stripes,* "Ball Turret Gunners," *Modern Marvels,* History Channel, 2003.
Larry King Live, Cable News Network, 2003, 2006.
"Realness," *Da Ali G Show* (also known as *Ali G in da USAiii*), HBO, 2004.

Television Appearances; Miniseries:
(Uncredited; in archive footage) *Cronkite Remembers,* CBS, 1997.

Television Work; Series:
Director, *CBS News Hour*, CBS, 1968.
News coeditor, *60 Minutes*, CBS, 1968.

Television Work; Specials:
Producer, *A Year with Andy Rooney: 1989*, CBS, 1989.

Documentary Film Appearances:
I, Curmudgeon, 2004.
Silent Wings: The American Glider Pilots of World War II, Inecom Entertainment, 2007.

WRITINGS

Television Series:
Arthur Godfrey's Talent Scouts, CBS, 1949–55.
The Great American Dream Machine, WNET (New York City), 1970–72.
60 Minutes, CBS, 1979—.

Contributor to other news programs, including *Adventure, Calendar, The Morning Show with Will Rogers, Jr., News of America,* and *The Twentieth Century;* also worked as writer for television personalities such as Sam Levenson and Victor Borge.

Radio Series:
The Garry Moore Show, CBS, 1959–65.

Other:
(With Oram C. Hutton) *Air Gunner*, Farrar & Rinehart, 1944.
(With Hutton) *The Story of the "Stars and Stripes,"* Farrar & Rinehart, 1946.
(With Hutton) *Conquerors' Peace: A Report to the American Stockholders*, Doubleday, 1947.
(Editor, with Dickson Hartwell, and author of commentary and notes) *Off the Record: The Best Stories of Foreign Correspondents*, Doubleday, 1952.
The Fortunes of War: Four Great Battles of World War II, Little, Brown, 1962.
A Few Minutes with Andy Rooney, Atheneum, 1981.
My War (memoir), Public Affairs Press, 1981.
And More by Andy Rooney, Atheneum, 1982.
The Complete Andy Rooney, Warner Books, 1983.
Pieces of My Mind, Scribner, 1984.
And More by Andy Rooney, Scribner, 1985.
The Most of Andy Rooney, Macmillan, 1986.
Word for Word, Putnam, 1986.
Not that You Asked ..., Easton Press, 1989.
Sweet and Sour, Putnam, 1992.
Sincerely, Andy Rooney, Public Affairs Press, 1999.
Common Nonsense, Public Affairs Press, 2002.

Years of Minutes: The Best of Rooney from 60 Minutes, Public Affairs Press, 2003.
Out of My Mind, Public Affairs Press, 2006.

Tribune Media Services, syndicated columnist, 1979—. Contributor to magazines, including *Esquire, Harper's, Life, Look,* and *Reader's Digest*. Some writings appear under name Andrew A. Rooney.

OTHER SOURCES

Books:
Rooney, Andy, *My War*, Public Affairs Press, 1997.

Periodicals:
People Weekly, May 8, 1995, pp. 207–216.
Rolling Stone, August 8, 1996, p. 65.
Time Out New York, May 22, 2003, p. 180.

RUBINSTEIN, Michael
   See WESTON, Michael

RUSSELL, Theresa 1957–
   (Theresa Paup, Theresa Roeg)

PERSONAL

Original name, Theresa Lynn Paup; born March 20, 1957, in San Diego, CA; daughter of Jerry Russell Paup and Carole (maiden name, Mall) Platt; married Nicolas Jack Roeg (a director), February 12, 1986 (divorced); children: Stratten Jack, Maximillian. *Education:* Attended high school in Burbank, CA; studied acting at Lee Strasberg Theatre Institute.

Addresses: *Agent*—Innovative Artists, 1505 Tenth St., Santa Monica, CA 90401. *Manager*—Evolution Entertainment, 901 North Highland Ave., Los Angeles, CA 90038

Career: Actress. Began modeling at age twelve.

Member: Screen Actors Guild.

Awards, Honors: Star of Tomorrow Award, National Association of Theatre Owners, 1986; Mystfest Award, best actress, 1988, Newcomer of the Year Award, both for *Track 29*.

CREDITS

Film Appearances:

Cecilia Brady, *The Last Tycoon,* Paramount, 1976.

Jenny Mercer, *Straight Time,* Warner Brothers, 1978.

Milena Flaherty, *Bad Timing: A Sensual Obsession* (also known as *Bad Timing*), 1980.

Tracy, *Eureka,* United Artists, 1983.

Sophie, *The Razor's Edge,* Columbia, 1984.

The actress, *Insignificance,* Island Alive, 1985.

King Zog, "Un ballo in maschera," *Aria,* Virgin Vision, 1987.

Catharine, *Black Widow* (also known as *Bulleseye*), Twentieth Century–Fox, 1987.

Linda Henry, *Track 29,* Island, 1988.

Jenny Hudson, *Physical Evidence,* Columbia, 1989.

Lottie Mason, *Impulse,* Warner Brothers, 1990.

Liz, *Whore* (also known as *If You're Afraid to Say It ... Just See It*), Trimark Pictures, 1991.

Gabriela, *Kafka,* Miramax, 1992.

Marie Davenport, *Cold Heaven,* Hemdale, 1992.

The storyteller, *Being Human,* Warner Bros., 1993.

Mary Ann Curran/Alex Canis, *The Flight of the Dove* (also known as *The Spy Within*), New Horizon, 1994.

Lady Harriet Coal, *The Grotesque* (also known as *Gentlemen Don't Eat Poets* and *Grave Indiscretion*), Live Entertainment, 1995.

Morgan Le Fay, *A Young Connecticut Yankee in King Arthur's Court* (also known as *Arbalete et rock'n roll*), Filmline International, 1995.

Hotel Paradise (also known as *Erotic Tales II*), Regina Ziegler Filmproduktion, 1995.

Kate, *Public Enemies* (also known as *Public Enemy #1* and *Public Enemy No. 1*), Trimark Pictures, 1996.

Margo Anthony, *Once You Meet a Stranger,* Warner Bros., 1996.

Catherine Morgan, *The Proposition,* A–Pix Entertainment, 1997.

Sandra Van Ryan, *Wild Things* (also known as *wildthings*), Columbia, 1998.

Emily Russo, *Running Woman,* Concorde, 1998.

The Velocity of Gary (Not His Real Name), 1999.

Stella, *Luckytown Blues* (also known as *Lucky Town* and *Luckytown*), A Plus Entertainment, 2000.

Dori Wilson, *Now and Forever* (also known as *Now & Forever*), Illumaire Entertainment, 2000.

Lina Moebius, *The Believer,* Fireworks Pictures, 2001.

Helen Schmidt, *The House Next Door,* Trinity Home Entertainment, 2002.

Lois Vargas, *Passionada,* Samuel Goldwyn Films, 2002.

Herself, *Searching for Debra Winger* (documentary), 2002.

Jackie O'Connor, *Save It For Later* (also known as *Water Under the Bridge*), Lightyear Entertainment, 2003.

Dora Baker, *The Box,* MTI Home Video, 2003.

Herself, *Morality and the Code: A How–To Manual for Hollywood* (documentary short), Warner Home Video, 2006.

Herself, *Prohibition Opens the Floodgates* (documentary short), Warner Home Video, 2006.

Herself, *Molls and Dolls: The Women of Gangster Films* (documentary short), Warner Home Video, 2006.

Stool Pigeons and Pine Overcoats: The Language of Gangster Films (documentary short), 2006.

Welcome to the Big House (documentary short), Warner Home Video, 2006.

Gangsters: The Immigrant's Hero (documentary short), Warner Home Video, 2006.

Emma Marko, *Spider–Man 3,* Columbia, 2007.

Mrs. Williams, *Chinaman's Chance,* Plus Entertainment, 2007.

Nicole, *Dark World,* 2007.

Aunt Kay, *Jolene,* 2007.

Television Appearances; Series:

Hazel Walker, *Glory Days* (also known as *Demontown*), The WB, 2002.

Television Appearances; Miniseries:

Maureen Dean, *Blind Ambition* (also known as *The John Dean Story*), CBS, 1979.

Rose, *A Woman's Guide to Adultery,* ITV, 1993.

Charlene, *Empire Falls,* HBO, 2005.

Television Appearances; Movies:

Debbie/Jo, *Thicker Than Water,* Arts and Entertainment, 1993.

Jackie Daniels, *Trade Off,* 1995.

Trixie Grillo, *Earth vs. the Spider,* Cinemax, 2001.

Dr. Nancy Burnham, *Project Viper,* Sci–Fi Channel, 2002.

Sarah Graham, *Love Comes Softly,* Hallmark Channel, 2003.

Joanna Bartlett, *Blind Injustice,* Lifetime, 2005.

Television Appearances; Specials:

Sandra After Dark, With Your Hostess, Sandra Bernhard, HBO, 1992.

Hollywood Women, 1994.

Complicated Women, TCM, 2003.

Z Channel: A Magnificent Obsession, Independent Film Channel, 2004.

Television Appearances; Episodic:

Late Night with David Letterman, NBC, 1989.

Reesa Tussel, "To Be or Not to Be Evil," *G vs E* (also known as *Good vs Evil*), USA Network, 1999.

Sarah Williams/Ellen Holiday, "Jackpot: Parts 1 & 2," *Nash Bridges,* CBS, 2000.

Regina Reid, "On Fire," *Law & Order: Criminal Intent* (also known as *Law & Order: CI*), NBC, 2006.

Jordan Wakefield, "Lions and Tigers and Bears," *American Heiress,* 2007.

Television Work; Specials:
Complicated Women, TCM, 2003.

Radio Appearances:
Phyllis Nirdlinger, *Double Indemnity,* BBC Radio, 1993.

OTHER SOURCES

Periodicals:
American Film, April, 1989, p. 34.
Interview, November 5, 1985, p. 70.

RYAN, Amy

PERSONAL

Addresses: *Manager*—Framework Entertainment, 9057 Nemo St., Suite C, West Hollywood, CA 90069.

Career: Actress.

Awards, Honors: Antoinette Perry Award nomination, best actress in a featured role—play, 2000, for *Uncle Vanya;* Antoinette Perry Award nomination, best actress in a featured role—play, Outer Critics Circle Award, outstanding featured actor in a play, 2005, both for *A Streetcar Named Desire.*

CREDITS

Film Appearances:
Judy, *Roberta,* 1999.
Beth, *A Pork Chop for Larry,* 2000.
Rachel Louise Prescott, *You Can Count on Me,* Paramount Classics, 2000.
Lynn Bedik, *Keane,* Magnolia Pictures, 2004.
Neighbor with toddler, *War of the Worlds,* Paramount, 2005.
Marie Dewey, *Capote,* Sony Pictures Classics, 2005.
Emily Brooks, *Looking for Comedy in the Muslim World,* Warner Independent, 2005.
Queenie, *Marvelous,* 2006.
Mom, *Shiner* (short), 2006.
Forward (short), 2007.
Carolyn Cassady, *Neal Cassady,* 2007.
Martha, *Before the Devil Knows You're Dead,* Think-Film, 2007.
Eileen, *Dan in Real Life,* Buena Vista, 2007.
Helene McCready, *Gone Baby Gone,* Miramax, 2007.

Television Appearances; Series:
Renee, *As the World Turns,* CBS, 1990.
Chloe Banks, *The Naked Truth* (also known as *Wilde Again*), ABC, 1995–96.
Rebecca Rifkind, *100 Centre Street,* Arts and Entertainment, 2001–2002.
Officer Beatrice "Beadie" Russell, *The Wire,* HBO, 2003–2006.
Marcie Futteman, *M.O.N.Y.,* NBC, 2007.

Television Appearances; Miniseries:
Carrie Baker, *A Will of Their Own,* NBC, 1998.

Television Appearances; Movies:
Beth, *In the Deep Woods,* NBC, 1992.
Elaine Devlin, *Remembering Sex* (also known as *Getting Off*), 1998.

Television Appearances; Pilots:
Marcie Futteman, *M.O.N.Y.,* NBC, 2007.

Television Appearances; Specials:
Peggy, *The Women,* PBS, 2002.
The 59th Annual Tony Awards, CBS, 2005.

Television Appearances; Episodic:
Libby McBain, "Raped—June 20, 1980," *Quantum Leap,* NBC, 1991.
Young Sophie, "Old Fools," *Brooklyn Bridge,* CBS, 1991.
Robin, "Luck Be a Taylor Tonight," *Home Improvement,* ABC, 1992.
Parkie Sasser, "All in the Life," *I'll Fly Away,* NBC, 1992.
Parkie Sasser, "Desperate Measures," *I'll Fly Away,* NBC, 1992.
Parkie Sasser, "Eighteen," *I'll Fly Away,* NBC, 1992.
Parkie Sasser, "Since Walter," *I'll Fly Away,* NBC, 1992.
Amy, "Jurisdiction," *Law & Order,* NBC, 1993.
April Ward, "The Abduction," *Sirens,* syndicated, 1995.
Sister, "Love Among the Ruins," *ER,* NBC, 1995.
Helen Sherwood, "Liver, Hold the Mushrooms," *Chicago Hope,* CBS, 1998.
Erika Cullen, "A Case of Do or Die," *Homicide: Life on the Street* (also known as *Homicide*), NBC, 1999.
Lorraine Hensen, "Bad Blood," *Law & Order: Special Victims Unit* (also known as *Law & Order: SVU* and *Special Victims Unit*), NBC, 2000.
"Out of the Ashes," *Hack,* CBS, 2003.
Julie Turner, "Suite Sorrow," *Law & Order: Criminal Intent* (also known as *Law & Order: CI*), NBC, 2003.
Dr. Jenny Hanson, "Last Will and Testament," *Third Watch,* NBC, 2004.
Luzena Wilson, "Gold Rush," *The American Experience,* PBS, 2006.
Valerie Messick, "Family Friend," *Law & Order,* NBC, 2006.

Maureen, "Number One with a Bullet," *Kidnapped,* NBC, 2006.

Edie Nelson, "Rocket Man," *Law & Order: Criminal Intent* (also known as *Law & Order: CI*), NBC, 2007.

Stage Appearances:

Lena Truitt, *The Rimers of Eldritch,* McGinn–Cazale Theatre, New York City, 1988.

Tess Goode, *The Sisters Rosensweig,* Ethel Barrymore Theatre, New York City, 1993–94.

Natalya Ivanova, *The Three Sisters,* Criterion Center Stage Right, New York City, 1997.

Amber, back–up singer, secretary, Bethany, and Ginny, *As the Bees in Honey Drown,* Lucille Lortel Theatre, New York City, 1997–98.

The Author's Voice & Imagining Brad, Greenhouse Theatre, New York City, 1999.

Sofya Alexandrovna, *Uncle Vanya,* Brooks Atkinson Theatre, New York City, 2001.

Saved, American Place Theatre, New York City, 2001.

Meg, *Crimes of the Heart,* Second Stage Theatre, New York City, 2001.

Peggy, *The Women,* American Airlines Theatre, New York City, 2001–2002.

Cammie, *The Distance from Here,* Almeida Theatre, London, 2002.

Stella Kowalski, *A Streetcar Named Desire,* Studio 54, New York City, 2005.

Sarah, *On the Mountain,* Playwrights Horizons Theatre, New York City, 2005.

Susan, *The 24 Hour Plays 2006,* American Airlines Theatre, 2006.

S

SCHNEIDER, Paul

PERSONAL

Career: Director and producer.

CREDITS

Film Work:
Director, *Sweetwater*, 1983.
Director, *Willy/Milly* (also known as *I Was a Teenage Boy* and *Something Special*), Cinema Group, 1986.
Associate producer, *Options*, 1989.
Director, *The Wall*, Marvista Entertainment, 2007.

Television Work; Series:
Associate producer, *First Person*, Bravo and Independent Film Channel, 2000.

Television Director; Movies:
The Leftovers, ABC, 1986.
14 Going on 30, ABC, 1988.
Dance 'Till Dawn, NBC, 1988.
Babycakes, CBS, 1989.
My Boyfriend's Back, NBC, 1989.
How to Murder a Millionaire, CBS, 1990.
Guess Who's Coming for Christmas? (also known as *UFO Cafe*), NBC, 1990.
The Entertainers, ABC, 1991.
Maid for Each Other, NBC, 1992.
Highway Heartbreaker, CBS, 1992.
A House of Secrets and Lies, CBS, 1992.
Empty Cradle, ABC, 1993.
Honor Thy Father and Mother: The True Story of the Menendez Murders (also known as *Honor Thy Father and Mother: The Menendez Killings*), Fox, 1994.

For the Love of Nancy, ABC, 1994.
Roseanne: An Unauthorized Biography, Fox, 1994.
With Hostile Intent (also known as *With Hostile Intent: Sisters in Black and Blue*), CBS, 1995.
Have You Seen My Son?, ABC, 1996.
Murder on the Iditarod Trail (also known as *The Cold Heart of a Killer*), CBS, 1996.
Sudden Terror: The Hijacking of School Bus #17, ABC, 1996.
The Bachelor's Baby (also known as *Here Comes the Son*), CBS, 1996.
When the Cradle Falls, CBS, 1997.
You Lucky Dog, Disney Channel, 1998.
When He Didn't Come Home, CBS, 1998.
Can of Worms, Disney Channel, 1999.
Lethal Vows, CBS, 1999.
The Retrievers, Animal Planet, 2001.
Big Spender, Animal Planet, 2003.
Seventeen & Missing, Lifetime, 2006.
Love Thy Neighbor, 2006.
Roller Palace, 2006.
Cries in the Dark, Lifetime, 2006.
Vivid Dreams, Lifetime, 2007.

Television Work; Movies:
Coproducer, *Maid for Each Other*, NBC, 1992.
Co–associate producer, *Malaika*, HBO, 1999.

Television Director; Specials:
Daniel and the Towers, PBS, 1987.

Television Director; Episodic:
"Sparky Brackman R.I.P.????–1987," *L.A. Law*, NBC, 1987.
Once a Hero, ABC, 1987.
"Home Cort," *Baywatch*, NBC, 1990.
"Muddy Waters," *Baywatch*, NBC, 1990.
"Eclipse," *Baywatch*, NBC, 1990.
"Fame Is Where You Find It," *Beverly Hills, 90210*, Fox, 1991.

"Moving Targets," *Beverly Hills, 90210,* Fox, 1993.
"Radar Love," *Beverly Hills, 90210,* Fox, 1993.
"Heartbreaker," *Beverly Hills, 90210,* Fox, 1994.
"Impact," *JAG,* CBS, 1997.
MythQuest, PBS and CBC, 2001.

Television Appearances; Specials:
Intimate Portrait: Tracey Gold, Lifetime, 2003.

Stage Work:
Assistant director, *Ti–Jean and His Brothers,* Delacorte Theatre, New York City, 1972.
Director, *The Children,* Joseph Papp Public Theatre, New York City, 1972–73.

SCHOFIELD, Andrew
(Drew Schofield)

PERSONAL

Career: Actor.

CREDITS

Television Appearances; Series:
Mersey Pirate, ITV, 1979.
Norman Mannion, *Coronation Street* (also known as *Corrie*), ITV, 1979.
Franny Scully, *Scully,* Channel 4, 1984.
Chief vigilante, *Needle,* 1990.

Television Appearances; Miniseries:
Ransome, *Kidnapped* (also known as *Die Abenteuer des David Balfour* and *Les Aventures de David Balfour*), Scottish Television, 1978.
Nosebleed policeman, *Boys from the Blackstuff,* BBC, 1982.
Leadbitter, *The Marksman,* BBC, 1987.
Peter Grenville, *GBH,* Channel 4, 1991.
Jake's Progress, 1995.
Charlton Ffoulkes, *Melissa,* Channel 4, 1997.
Toby Crackitt, *Oliver Twist,* PBS, 1999.

Television Appearances; Movies:
Franny Scully, "Scully's New Year's Eve," *Play for Today,* BBC, 1978.
(As Drew Schofield) Baz, "Bobby Wants to Meet Me," *BBC2 Playhouse,* BBC2, 1981.
Skinhead leader, "The Garland," *Play for Today,* BBC1, 1981.
Eddie, *The Long Roads* (also known as *The Screen Two: Long Roads*), BBC, 1993.

Clint, *Self Catering* (also known as *Alan Bleasdale Presents "Self Catering"*), Channel 4, 1994.
Rocky, *Requiem Apache* (also known as *Alan Bleasdale Presents "Requiem Apache"*), Channel 4, 1994.
(As Drew Schofield) Paul, *Doomsday Gun,* HBO, 1994.
Post Office supervisor, *Blood on the Dole* (also known as *Alan Bleasdale Presents "Blood on the Dole"*), Channel 4, 1994.
Pope, *Sharpe's Mission,* ITV, 1996.
Television pundit, television interviewer, and deputy head, *I'm a Juvenile Delinquent, Jail Me!,* BBC, 2004.

Television Appearances; Pilots:
Eric, *Rules of Engagement,* 1997.

Television Appearances; Episodic:
Terry Cosgrave, "Exposure," *Z Cars,* BBC, 1978.
Ade, "Spanish Eyes," *El C.I.D.,* ITV, 1990.
Hotel porter, "Some Lie and Some Die," *Ruth Rendell Mysteries,* PBS, 1990.
Caplan, "Shingle Beach," *Stay Lucky,* Yorkshire, 1991.
Gavin, "The Sharp End," *Boon,* ITV, 1992.
Michael Chater, "No One Likes to See That," *Thief Takers,* ITV, 1996.
Pete North, "Trust," *Casualty,* BBC1, 1998.
Mulholland, "Respect," *City Central,* BBC, 2000.
Ron Turner, "Every Cloud," *Holby City* (also known as *Holby*), BBC, 2002.
Deputy Inspector Paul McArdle, premiere episode, *Donovan,* ITV, 2004.
Thorpe, "Strongbox," *Murphy's Law,* BBC, 2005.
Barry Lake, *New Street Law,* BBC, 2006.

Film Appearances:
Nocker, *No Surrender,* Circle Films, 1985.
Johnny Rotten, *Sid and Nancy* (also known as *Sid and Nancy: Love Kills*), New Line Cinema, 1986.
Les, *Distant Voices, Still Lives,* Avenue, 1988.
Young lord, *Hamlet* (also known as *William Shakespeare's "Hamlet"*), Columbia, 1996.
Desk clerk, *Three Businessmen,* 1998.
Shark Hunt, 1998.
Wreckingham referee, *There's Only One Jimmy Grimble* (also known as *Jimmy Grimble*), Pathe, 2000.
Uncle Tom, *Liam,* Lions Gate Films, 2000.
A Heap of Trouble (short film), Tumble Hill Productions, 2001.
Second man, *Dead Drunk* (short film), Hurricane Films, 2002.
Carlo, *Revengers Tragedy,* Cable Hogue, 2002.
Joe Potts, *Under the Mud,* Hurricane Films, 2006.
Hawk, *Dead Man's Cards,* Peacock Films, 2007.

Stage Appearances:
Terry, *Feels Like the First Time,* Oldham Coliseum, Manchester, England, 2006.

WRITINGS

Songs Featured in Films:
"We're Gonna Die," *No Surrender,* Circle Films, 1985.

SCOTT, Campbell 1961(?)–

PERSONAL

Born July 19, 1961 (some sources cite 1962), in New York, NY; son of George C. Scott (an actor, director, and producer) and Colleen Dewhurst (an actress); brother of Alexander Scott (a writer and stage manager); married, wife's name Anne (a painter), July, 1991 (divorced, c. 2002); children: Malcolm. *Education:* Lawrence University, Appleton, WI, B.A., 1983; studied acting with Geraldine Page and Stella Adler.

Addresses: *Agent*—Clifford Stevens, Paradigm, 360 North Crescent Dr. N., Beverly Hills, CA 90210.

Career: Actor, producer, and director.

Awards, Honors: MTV Movie Award nomination, best breakthrough performance, 1992, for *Dying Young;* Independent Spirit Award nomination, best male lead, Independent Features Project West, 1995, for *Mrs. Parker and the Vicious Circle;* Boston Society of Film Critics Award, best new filmmaker, New York Film Critics Circle Award, best new director, nomination for Grand Jury Prize, dramatic category, Sundance Film Festival, and nomination for Grand Special Prize, Deauville Film Festival, all (with Stanley Tucci) 1996, Independent Spirit Award nomination (with others), best first feature, and nomination for Golden Precolumbian Circle (with Tucci), best film, Bogota Film Festival, both 1997, all for *Big Night;* Video Premiere Award nomination, best actor, DVD Exclusive Awards, 2001, for *Top of the Food Chain;* career achievement award, Westchester County Film Festival, 2002; National Board of Review Award, best actor, 2002, and Independent Spirit Award nomination, best actor, 2003, both for *Roger Dodger;* DVD Premiere Award nomination, DVD Exclusive Awards, 2003, for *Lush;* Maverick Award and Taos Land Grant Award, both Taos Talking Picture Festival, 2003, and Audience Award, best drama, Sarasota Film Festival, 2004, both for *Off the Map;* Chlotrudis Award nomination, best actor, 2004, for *The Secret Lives of Dentists;* Genie Award nomination, best supporting actor, Academy of Canadian Cinema and Television, 2006, for *Saint Ralph.*

CREDITS

Film Appearances:
Cop, *Five Corners,* Cineplex Odeon, 1987.

Bobby, *From Hollywood to Deadwood,* Island Pictures, 1988.
Willy, *Longtime Companion,* Samuel Goldwyn Company, 1989.
Fletcher Kane, *Ain't No Way Back* (also known as *The Ghost of Fletcher Ridge* and *No Way Back*), DSL Entertainment, 1990.
George Tunner, *The Sheltering Sky* (also known as *Il te nel deserto*), Warner Bros., 1990.
Victor "Vic" Geddes, *Dying Young* (also known as *The Choice of Love*), Twentieth Century–Fox, 1991.
Doug, *Dead Again,* Paramount, 1991.
Steve Dunne, *Singles,* Warner Bros., 1992.
Leonard Markham, *The Innocent* (also known as *Und der Himmel steht still*), Miramax, 1993.
Robert Benchley, *Mrs. Parker and the Vicious Circle* (also known as *Mrs. Parker and the Round Table*), Fine Line, 1994.
Bob, *Big Night,* Samuel Goldwyn Films, 1996.
Eddie Masler, *The Daytrippers* (also known as *En route vers Manhattan*), Columbia TriStar, 1996.
Joseph A. "Joe" Ross, *The Spanish Prisoner,* Sony Pictures Classics, 1997.
Meistrich, *The Imposters,* Twentieth Century–Fox, 1998.
Ray, *Hi–Life,* Lions Gate Films, 1998.
Dr. Karel Lamonte, *Top of the Food Chain* (also known as *Invasion!* and *Welcome to Exceptional Vista*), Equinox Entertainment/Red Sky Entertainment, 1999.
Frederickson, *Spring Forward,* IFC Productions, 1999.
Lionel "Ex" Exley, *Lush,* 1999.
John, *Other Voices,* A–Pix Entertainment, 2000.
Kevin, *Delivering Milo,* IMMI Pictures, 2001.
Roger Swanson, *Rodger Dodger,* Artisan Entertainment, 2002.
David Hurst, *The Secret Lives of Dentists,* Manhattan Pictures International, 2003.
Marie and Bruce, New Films International, 2004.
Father George Hibbert, *Saint Ralph,* Samuel Goldwyn Films, 2005.
Jeffrey Tishop, *The Dying Gaul,* Strand Releasing, 2005.
Peter, *Duma,* Warner Bros., 2005.
Ethan Thomas, *The Exorcism of Emily Rose,* Screen Gems, 2005.
Paul's father, *Loverboy,* Screen Media Films/ThinkFilm, 2006.
Voice of Bernard Berenson, *Stolen* (documentary), International Film Circuit, 2006.
Richard, *Crashing,* Existential Films/Pendragon Film, 2007.
Sloan Cates, *Music and Lyrics,* Warner Bros., 2007.
Narrator, *No End in Sight* (documentary), Magnolia Pictures, 2007.

Film Producer:
Coproducer (and director; with Stanley Tucci) *Big Night,* Samuel Goldwyn Films, 1996.
Executive producer, *The Daytrippers* (also known as *En route vers Manhattan*), Columbia TriStar, 1996.

(And director) *Final,* Lions Gate Films, 2001.
Rodger Dodger, Artisan Entertainment, 2002.
The Secret Lives of Dentists, Manhattan Pictures International, 2003.
(And director) *Off the Map,* Manhattan Pictures International, 2003.
The Dying Gaul, Strand Releasing, 2005.

Television Appearances; Series:
Steven Caseman, *Six Degrees,* ABC, 2006–2007.

Television Appearances; Miniseries:
Joseph P. Kennedy, Jr., *The Kennedys of Massachusetts* (also known as *The Fitzgeralds and the Kennedys*), ABC, 1990.
Thomas Jefferson, *Liberty! The American Revolution,* PBS, 1997.
Title role, *Hamlet,* Odyssey Network, 2000.
Robert Hart, *The Pilot's Wife* (also known as *La femme du pilote*), CBS, 2002.
William Prescott, "Independence," and Harold Ickes, "Depression and War," *Freedom: A History of Us,* PBS, 2003.
Narrator, *Ten Days that Unexpectedly Changed America,* History Channel, 2005.
William Phillips, *Final Days of Planet Earth,* Hallmark Channel, 2006.

Television Appearances; Movies:
Carter Blair, *The Perfect Tribute,* ABC, 1991.
Gabriel, *Let It Be Me* (also known as *Love Dance*), Starz!, 1995.
Scott Corrigan, *The Love Letter,* ABC, 1998.
Ben Carlyle, *The Tale of Sweeney Todd,* Showtime, 1998.
David McClune, *Follow the Stars Home* (also known as *A Second Chance*), CBS, 2001.

Television Appearances; Specials:
Commentator, *Would You Kindly Direct Me to Hell? The Infamous Dorothy Parker,* Arts and Entertainment, 1994.
Title role, "F. Scott Fitzgerald: Winter Dreams," *American Masters,* PBS, 2001.
Voice, *Echoes from the White House,* PBS, 2001.
Intimate Portrait: Lisa Gay Hamilton, Lifetime, 2002.
Narrator, *Kinsey,* PBS, 2005.
Title role, *Ambrose Bierce: Civil War Stories,* 2006.
Narrator, "Hijacked," *The American Experience,* PBS, 2006.
Narrator, "The Boy in the Bubble," *The American Experience,* PBS, 2006.

Television Appearances; Episodic:
Officer Clayton, "Sidney, the Dead–Nosed Reindeer," *L.A. Law,* 1986.

Eric Matthews, "Invasion of the Psychologist Snatchers," *Family Ties,* 1987.
"Off the Map," *Anatomy of a Scene,* Sundance Channel, 2004.
Bernard Berenson, "Stolen," *Independent Lens,* PBS, 2005.
Talking Movies, BBC, 2005.

Television Appearances; Pilots:
Steven Caseman, *Six Degrees,* ABC, 2007.

Television Work; Miniseries:
Producer and director, *Hamlet,* Odyssey Network, 2000.

Stage Appearances:
Soldier, *The Queen and the Rebels,* Plymouth Theatre, New York City, 1982.
Brodie, *The Real Thing,* Plymouth Theatre, 1984.
George, *Our Town,* Seattle Repertory Theatre, Seattle, WA, 1984.
Sandy Tyrell, *Hay Fever,* Music Box Theatre, New York City, 1985–86.
Master Richard Rich, *A Man for All Seasons,* Roundabout Theatre Company, Union Square Theatre, New York City, 1986.
Fritz, *Dalliance,* Long Wharf Theatre, New Haven, CT, 1986.
Parker Smith, *Copperhead,* Workshop of the Players Art Theatre, New York City, 1987.
Arthur Miller, *Ah, Wilderness!* Yale Repertory Theatre, New Haven, CT, 1987–88, then Neil Simon Theatre, New York City, 1988.
Edmund Tyrone, *Long Day's Journey into Night,* Yale Repertory Theatre, 1987–88, then Neil Simon Theatre, 1988.
Dr. Fellowes, *Paradise for the Worried,* Theatre at St. Clement's Church, New York City, 1990.
Title role, *Hamlet,* Old Globe Theatre, San Diego, CA, 1990.
Title role, *Pericles,* New York Shakespeare Festival, Estelle R. Newman Theatre, Public Theatre, New York City, 1991.
Farker/Frank, *On the Bum,* Playwrights Horizons Theatre, New York City, 1992.
Title role, *Hamlet,* Huntington Theatre Company, Boston, MA, 1996.

Also appeared as Angelo, *Measure for Measure,* Mitzi E. Newhouse Theatre, New York City; and as Iago, *Othello,* Philadelphia Drama Guild, Philadelphia, PA.

Stage Director:
The Recruiting Officer, Lawrence University Theatre, Appleton, WI, 1993.

RECORDINGS

Videos:

Are We Alone?, Echo Bridge Home Entertainment, 2006.

Complexities of War: The Making of "Civil War Stories," Hannover House, 2006.

Audio Books; Narrator:

From Time to Time, Simon & Schuster, 1995.

Touched, Bantam, 1996.

Sacrament by Clive Barker, HarperAudio, 1996.

The Notebook by Nicholas Sparks, Time Warner, 1996.

The Burning Man by Phillip M. Margolin, Random House Audio, 1996.

Into the Wild by Jon Krakauer, Random House Audio, 1996.

The Forgetting Room by Nick Bantock, HarperAudio, 1997.

Omega, by Patrick Lynch, Random House Audio, 1997.

The Rum Diary: The Long Lost Novel by Hunter S. Thompson, Simon & Schuster Audio, 1998.

Where Serpents Lie by T. Jefferson Parker, Random House Audio, 1998.

Bringing Out the Dead by Joe Connelly, Random House Audio, 1999.

Fountain Society by Wes Craven, Simon & Schuster Audio, 1999.

Gravity by Tess Gerritsen, Audioworks, 1999.

The Marching Season by Daniel Silva, Random House Audio, 1999.

The Paperboy by Pete Dexter, Random House Audio, 1999.

The Reader by Bernhard Schlink, Random House Audio, 1999.

Time Stops for No Mouse: A Hermux Tantamoq Adventure by Michael Hoeye and K. L. Going, Listening Library, 2000.

Seabiscuit by Laura Hillenbrands, Random House, 2001.

War Letters: Extraordinary Correspondence from American Wars by Andrew Carroll, Simon & Schuster Audio, 2001.

The Sands of Time by Michael Hoeye, Listening Library, 2001.

The Stories of F. Scott Fitzgerald, Caedmon, 2001.

The English Assassin by Daniel Silva, Random House Audio, 2002.

One More for the Road: A New Story Collection by Ray Bradbury, HarperAudio, 2002.

The Devil's Banker by Christopher Reich, Random House Audio, 2003.

Oryx and Crake by Margaret Atwood, Random House Audio, 2003.

The Big Bounce by Elmore Leonard, HarperAudio, 2004.

Hear No Evil by James Grippando, HarperAudio, 2004.

Murder on the Leviathan by Boris Akunin, Random House Audio, 2004.

No Time Like Show Time by Michael Hoeye, Listening Library, 2004.

Public Enemies by Bryan Burrough, Simon & Schuster Audio, 2004.

Shadow Divers: The True Adventures of Two Americans Who Risked Everything to Solve One of the Last Mysteries of World War II by Robert Kurson, Random House Audio, 2004.

Be Cool by Elmore Leonard, HarperAudio, 2005.

The Lost Painting by Jonathan Harr, Random House Audio, 2005.

The Shining by Stephen King, Simon & Schuster Audio, 2005.

The Sunflower: A Novel by Richard Paul Evans, Simon & Schuster Audio, 2005.

Cell by Stephen King, Simon & Schuster Audio, 2006.

Close Range: Wyoming Stories by Annie Proulx, Simon & Schuster Audio, 2006.

For Whom the Bell Tolls by Ernest Hemingway, Simon & Schuster Audio, 2006.

The Abstinence Teacher by Tom Perrotta, Audio Renaissance, 2007.

WRITINGS

Television Miniseries:

Hamlet (based on the play by Shakespeare), Odyssey Network, 2000.

OTHER SOURCES

Periodicals:

American Theatre, April, 1996, p. 24.

Empire, September, 2003, pp. 94–96.

Entertainment Weekly, April 25, 2003, p. 88.

Rolling Stone, June 14, 1990.

Time, September 23, 1996, p. 72.

SCOTT, Donna W.
(Donna Scott, Donna Wilson)

PERSONAL

Married Tony Scott, November 27, 1994; children: Max, Frank.

Addresses: *Manager*—TRC Entertainment, 8424A Santa Monica Blvd., Suite 770, West Hollywood, CA 90069.

Career: Actress.

CREDITS

Film Appearances:

(As Donna Wilson) Darlene, *Days of Thunder,* Paramount, 1990.

(As Donna Wilson) Sleeping party girl, *The Last Boy Scout,* Warner Bros., 1991.

Screaming woman, *Get Shorty,* United International, 1995.

Deborah, *Dark Breed,* Bellevue, 1996.

Fembot, *Austin Powers: International Man of Mystery* (also known as *Austin Powers–Das Scharfste, was ihre majestat zu bieten hat*), New Line Cinema, 1997.

(As Donna Scott) Quikie Mart patron, *Plump Fiction,* Manga, 1997.

(As Donna Scott) Jen, Carla's friend, *Enemy of the State,* 1998.

(As Donna Scott) Nurse, *Idle Hands,* Columbia 1999.

Fiona, *Beat Boys Beat Girls,* 2003.

(As Donna Scott) Agent Dina Wilson, *Domino,* New Line Cinema, 2005.

(As Donna Scott) Beth, *Deja Vu* (also known as *Feline*), Buena Vista, 2006.

Dr. Schulman, *The Uninvited,* Canal, 2007.

Television Appearances; Episodic:

Donna, "High Impact," *Nash Bridges* (also known as *Bridges*), 1996.

Tamara Van Zant, "Bombshell," *Nash Bridges* (also known as *Bridges*), 1997.

(As Donna Scott) Pamela Sue Amsterdam, "Movies," *Tracey Takes On ...,* 1997.

Beautiful dame, *Buddy Fargo,* CBS, 1998.

Tamara Van Zant, "High Fall," *Nash Bridges* (also known as *Bridges*), 1998.

(As Donna Scott) Lieutenant Grace, "Deja Vu," *Soldier of Fortune, Inc.* (also known as *S.O.F. Special Ops Force, S.O.F., Inc.,* and *SOF, Inc.*), syndicated, 1998.

(As Donna Scott) Lieutenant Grace, "Apres Vu," *Soldier of Fortune, Inc.* (also known as *S.O.F. Special Ops Force, S.O.F., Inc.,* and *SOF, Inc.*), syndicated, 1998.

(As Donna Scott) "Lap Dance," *Nash Bridges* (also known as *Bridges*), 2000.

(As Donna Scott) "Something Borrowed," *Nash Bridges* (also known as *Bridges*), 2001.

Christina Braverton, "Convictions," *The District,* 2002.

(As Donna Scott) Waitress Nancy, "Revenge is Best Served Cold," *CSI: Crime Scene Investigation* (also known as *C.S.I., CSI: Las Vegas,* and *Les Experts*), 2002.

Cat, "Friends, Lovers, Others, and Brothers," *South of Nowhere,* 2005.

Cat, "Put Out or Get Out," *South of Nowhere,* 2005.

Cat, "Say It Ain't So, Spencer," *South of Nowhere,* 2006.

SEIDELMAN, Susan 1952–

PERSONAL

Born December 11, 1952, in Abington, PA; daughter of Michael (a hardware manufacturer) and Florence (a teacher) Seidelman; companion of Jonathan Brett (a producer); children: (with Brett) Oscar. *Education:* Drexel University, B.A.; New York University, M.F.A.

Addresses: *Manager*—Gary Pearl, Pearl Pictures and Management, 10956 Weyburn Ave., Suite 200, Los Angeles, CA 90024–2834.

Career: Director, producer, and writer. Worked as an assistant television producer at a local station in Philadelphia, PA, 1982; also worked as a freelance editor and a production assistant for television commercials. Berlin International Film Festival, member of jury, 1994.

Member: Directors Guild of America.

Awards, Honors: Student Academy award, Academy of Motion Picture Arts and Sciences, 1977, for *And You Act like One, Too;* American Film Institute grant, c. 1976; awards from Chicago Film Festival, American Film Festival, and Athens International Film Festival, all c. 1979, for *Yours Truly, Andrea G. Stern;* nomination for Golden Palm, Cannes Film Festival, 1982, for *Smithereens;* Cesar Award nomination, best foreign film, Academie des Arts et Techniques du Cinema, 1986, for *Desperately Seeking Susan;* Academy Award nomination (with Jonathan Brett), best achievement in live–action short films, 1994, for *The Dutch Master.*

CREDITS

Film Director:

And You Act like One, Too (short film), 1976.

Deficit (short film), 1977.

Yours Truly, Andrea G. Stern (short film), 1978.

(And producer and film editor) *Smithereens,* New Line Cinema, 1982.

Desperately Seeking Susan, Orion, 1985.

(And executive producer) *Making Mr. Right,* Orion, 1987.

(And executive producer) *Cookie,* Warner Bros., 1989.

(And producer) *She–Devil,* Orion, 1989.

The Dutch Master (short film; also known as *Der Flaemische meister*), 1995, released as a segment of *Tales of Erotica* (also known as *Erotic Tales*), Trimark Pictures, 1996.

(And executive producer) *Gaudi Afternoon* (also known as *Tardes de Gaudi*), Lola Films, 2000.

(And producer) *The Boynton Beach Bereavement Club* (also known as *Boynton Beach Club*), Samuel Goldwyn Films, 2006.

Film Work; Other:

Associate producer, *The Night We Never Met*, Miramax, 1993.

Film Appearances:

50 Years of Action!, 1986.

Herself, *Calling the Shots*, 1988.

Television Director; Movies:

The Barefoot Executive, ABC, 1995.

A Cooler Climate, Showtime, 1999.

Power and Beauty, Showtime, 2001.

The Ranch, Showtime, 2004.

Television Director; Specials:

Confessions of a Suburban Girl (also known as *Paradise Paved*), BBC Scotland, 1992.

Television Director; Episodic:

Premiere episode, *Sex and the City*, HBO, 1998.

"The Power of Female Sex," *Sex and the City*, HBO, 1998.

"The Baby Shower," *Sex and the City*, HBO, 1998.

"Office Party," *Stella*, Comedy Central, 2005.

"Paper Route," *Stella*, Comedy Central, 2005.

Also directed episodes of *Early Edition*, CBS; and *Now and Again*, CBS.

Television Appearances; Specials:

Chambre 666 (also known as *Room 666*), 1982.

Premiere Presents: Christmas Movie '89, Fox, 1989.

Confessions of a Suburban Girl (also known as *Paradise Paved*), BBC Scotland, 1992.

Television Appearances; Episodic:

Guest for an episode of *Independent View*, PBS.

RECORDINGS

Videos:

Director of the music video "Into the Groove" by Madonna.

WRITINGS

Screenplays:

The Dutch Master (short film; also known as *Der Flaemische meister*), 1995, released as a segment of

Tales of Erotica (also known as *Erotic Tales*), Trimark Pictures, 1996.

The Boynton Beach Bereavement Club (also known as *Boynton Beach Club*), Samuel Goldwyn Films, 2006.

Television Specials:

Confessions of a Suburban Girl (also known as *Paradise Paved*), BBC Scotland, 1992.

ADAPTATIONS

The 1982 film *Smithereens* was based on a story by Seidelman.

OTHER SOURCES

Books:

Authors and Artists for Young Adults, Volume 68, Gale, 2006.

International Dictionary of Films and Filmmakers, Volume 2: *Directors*, 4th edition, St. James Press, 2000.

Women Filmmakers & Their Films, St. James Press, 1998.

Periodicals:

New York Times, July 2, 2006, p. 14.

Rolling Stone, Sept. 21, 1989, p. 47–48.

SERKIS, Andy 1964–

PERSONAL

Born April 20, 1964, in London, England; father, a doctor; mother, a special education teacher; married Lorraine Ashbourne (an actress and singer), July 22, 2002; children: Ruby, Sonny, Louis George. *Education:* Studied visual arts at Lancaster University. *Avocational Interests:* Painting, mountaineering, and charity work for groups such as The Hope Foundation.

Addresses: *Agent*—Lou Coulson Associates, 37 Berwick St., London W1V 3RF United Kingdom; The Gersh Agency, 232 North Canon Dr., Beverly Hills, CA 90210. *Manager*—Principal Entertainment, 1964 Westwood Blvd., Suite 400, Los Angeles, CA 90025. *Publicist*—True Public Relations, 6725 Sunset Blvd., Suite 570, Los Angeles, CA 90028.

Career: Actor. Served as an apprentice to Jonathan Petherbridge at the Dukes Playhouse, Lancaster, England; appeared in television commercial for Greenpeace.

Awards, Honors: Phoenix Film Critics Society Award (with others), best acting ensemble, Screen Actors Guild Award nomination (with others), outstanding performance by the cast of a theatrical motion picture, 2002, all for *The Lord of the Rings: The Fellowship of the Ring;* Saturn Award, best supporting actor, Academy of Science Fiction, Fantasy and Horror, DVD Exclusive Award nomination (with others), best audio commentary (new for DVD), Empire Award nomination, best British actor, Online Film Critics Society Award (with others), best ensemble, Online Film Critics Society Award nomination, best supporting actor, Phoenix Film Critics Society Award (with others), best acting ensemble, Screen Actors Guild Award nomination (with others), outstanding performance by the cast of a theatrical motion picture, Visual Effects Society Award (with others), best performance by an actor in an effects film, 2003, all for *The Lord of the Rings: The Two Towers;* Empire Award, best British actor, National Board of Review Award (with others), best acting by an ensemble, 2003, Saturn Award, best supporting actor, Academy of Science Fiction, Fantasy and Horror, Broadcast Film Critics Association Award (with others), best acting ensemble, Chicago Film Critics Association Award nomination, best supporting actor, Online Film Critics Society Award nomination, best supporting actor, Phoenix Film Critics Society Award nomination (with others), best acting ensemble, Screen Actors Guild Award (with others), outstanding performance by a cast in a motion picture, Visual Effects Society Award (with others), outstanding character animation in a live action motion picture, 2004, all for *The Lord of the Rings: The Return of the King;* Special Citation, Toronto Film Critics Association, 2005, Empire Award nomination, best actor, Visual Effects Society Award (with others), outstanding animated character in a live action motion picture, 2006, all for *King Kong; Manchester Evening News* Award, best actor, for *Decadence.*

CREDITS

Film Appearances:

Torstem, *Prince of Jutland* (also known as *Royal Deceit, Amled, prinsen af Jylland,* and *Prinsen af Jylland*), Miramax, 1994.

Bunny, *The Near Room,* 1995.

Fitz, *Stella Does Tricks,* Strand Releasing, 1996.

Mr. Evans, *Career Girls,* October Films, 1997.

Sid Potts, *Mojo,* Channel 4 Films, 1997.

Bill, *Loop,* 1997.

Bob, *Among Giants,* Twentieth Century–Fox, 1998.

Leo King, *The Tale of Sweety Barrett* (also known as *Sweety Barrett* and *Aulabarour*), Handmade Films, 1998.

The Righteous Babes, 1998.

David, *Clueless,* 1998.

Harry, *Insomnia,* 1998.

John Duban, *Topsy–Turvy,* October Films, 1999.

Chester, *Five Seconds to Spare,* Winchester Films, 1999.

Spider, *The Jolly Boys Last Stand,* 2000.

John Thelwall, *Pandemonium,* Moonstone Entertainment, 2000.

Mel, *Shiner,* Miramax, 2000.

Shaun, *Jump,* 2000.

Ricky Barnes, *The Escapist,* Trinity Home Entertainment, 2001.

Gollum, *The Lord of the Rings: The Fellowship of the Ring* (also known as *The Fellowship of the Ring* and *The Lord of the Rings: The Fellowship of the Ring: The Motion Picture*), New Line Cinema, 2001.

Martin Hannet, *24 Hour Party People* (also known as *Twenty Four Hour Party People*), United Artists, 2001.

Private Thomas Quinn, *Deathwatch* (also known as *La tranchee*), Lions Gate Films, 2002.

Gollum, *The Lord of the Rings: The Two Towers* (also known as *Der Herr der ringe: die zwei turme* and *The Two Towers*), New Line Cinema, 2002.

Himself, *The Making of "Lord of the Rings"* (short), 2002.

Gollum, Smeagol, and character voices, *The Lord of the Rings: The Return of the King* (also known as *Der Herr der ringee: die ruckkehr des konigs* and *The Return of the King*), New Line Cinema, 2003.

Himself and Richard Kneeland, *Making of a Teen Dream* (short), 2004.

Granny, Rastafarian, and Hunter Jackson, *Standing Room Only* (short), Buena Vista, 2004, released as segment of *Stories of Lost Souls,* America Video, 2005.

Richard Kneeland, *13 Going on 30* (also known as *Suddenly 30*), Columbia, 2004.

Father Carlo, *Blessed,* DEJ Productions, 2004.

Ringens disipler (documentary short), SF Norge A/S, 2004.

Kong and Lumpy, *King Kong* (also known as *Kong: The Eighth Wonder of the Year* and *Peter Jackson's "King Kong"*), Universal, 2005.

Himself, *Ringers: Lord of the Fans* (documentary), Sony Pictures Home Entertainment, 2005.

Himself, *Du kommst nicht vorbei–fans im bann des ringes* (short), Traumflieger, 2005.

Himself, *"King Kong": Peter Jackson's Production Diaries* (documentary), 2005.

Voice of Stingray, *Stingray* (short), 2006.

Mr. Grin, *Stormbreaker* (also known as *Alex Rider: Operation Stormbreaker*), Weinstein Company, 2006.

Alley, *The Prestige,* Buena Vista, 2006.

Voice of Spike, *Flushed Away* (animated), Paramount, 2006.

Himself, *Bryan's Journals* (documentary), 2006.

Himself, *"King Kong": The Post–Production Diaries* (documentary), Universal Studios Home Video, 2006.

Himself, *Recreating the Eighth Wonder: The Making of "King Kong"* (documentary), Universal Studios Home Video, 2006.

Hoodwink, *Sugarhouse Lane* (also known as *Sugarhouse*), Slingshot Studios, 2007.

The interrogator, *Rendition,* 2007.

Erickson, *Freezing Time,* 2007.

Capricorn, *Inkheart,* New Line Cinema, 2008.

The Cottage, Screen Gems, 2008.

Film Work:

Assistant location manager, *The Long and Short of It,* 2003.

Producer and director, *Freezing Time,* 2007.

Director, *Addict,* 2008.

Also directed *Snake* (short).

Television Appearances; Series:

Owen, *Streetwise,* 1989.

Tom, *Finney,* ITV, 1995.

Television Appearances; Miniseries:

Pyotr, *Grushko,* BBC, 1993.

Michael Lawler, *Touching Evil III,* PBS, 1999.

Styeman, *Shooting the Past,* PBS, 1999.

Bill Sikes, *Oliver Twist,* ITV and PBS, 1999.

Kasim, *Arabian Nights,* NBC, 2000.

Television Appearances; Movies:

Sergeant Corrigan, *The Pale Horse* (also known as *Agatha Christie's "The Pale Horse"*), Arts and Entertainment, 1996.

Steven Brunos, *The Jump,* 1998.

Ian Brady, *Longford,* HBO, 2006.

Albert Einstein, *Einstein and Eddington,* HBO, 2007.

Television Appearances; Specials:

Potts, *Venice Report,* 1997.

Bill Sikes, *Oliver Twist,* PBS, 1999.

"*The Lord of the Rings: The Two Towers,*" *Return to Middle Earth,* The WB, 2002.

The 2003 MTV Movie Awards, MTV, 2003.

1st Annual Spaceys, Space Channel, 2003.

DNZ: The Real Middle Earth, TVNZ, 2004.

The Orange British Academy Film Awards, BBC, 2004.

The Ultimate Film, Channel 4, 2004.

Sci Fi Inside: "King Kong," Sci–Fi Channel, 2005.

06 Spaceys, Space Channel, 2006.

The Prestige: Now That's Magic, ITV, 2006.

Also appeared in *Made in Spain; The Chief; Kavanagh QC.*

Television Appearances; Episodic:

Peter Moran, "A Wapping Conspiracy," *The New Statesman,* ITV1, 1989.

Peter Moran, "The Haltemprice Bunker," *The New Statesman,* ITV1, 1989.

Dudin, "Into Africa," *Saracen,* Central, 1989.

Greville, "Le Grand Weekend," *The Darling Buds of May,* ITV, 1992.

Alex Rackin, "Return to Sender," *The Bill,* ITV1, 1993.

"Passion Fruit Fool," *Pie in the Sky,* BBC, 1994.

The Screensavers, Tech TV, 2003.

Himself, "Filmland Special—Ringenes Herre: kongen vender tilbage," *Filmland,* 2003.

Tinseltown TV, International Channel, 2003.

Frids film, 2003.

"Kuninkaan paluu—tarun paatos," *4Pop,* 2003.

Voice of Cleanie, "Dude, Where's My Ranch?," *The Simpsons* (animated), Fox, 2003.

Riff, "Celebrity," *Spooks* (also known as *MI–5*), BBC, 2004.

Richard & Judy, Channel 4, 2004.

The Sharon Osbourne Show, syndicated, 2004.

Late Night with Conan O'Brien, NBC, 2004, 2006.

Corazon de ..., 2005.

The Film Programme (also known as *Film 2005*), BBC, 2005.

HypaSpace (also known as *HypaSpace Daily* and *HypaSpace Weekly*), Space Channel, 2006.

"Down the Loo: The Making of 'Flushed Away,'" *HBO First Look,* HBO, 2006.

Vincent Van Gogh, "Van Gogh," *Simon Schama's Power of Art,* 2006.

Voice of the driver, "Underground," *Arena,* BBC, 2007.

Stage Appearances:

Macbeth, Royal Exchange Theatre, Manchester, England, 1989.

Dogboy, *Hush,* Royal Court Theatre, London, 1993.

Potts, *Mojo,* Royal Court Theatre, 1995.

Hurlyburly, Old Vic Theatre, London, then Queen's Theatre, London, 1997.

Jake, *A Lie of the Mind,* Donmar Warehouse, London, 2001.

Made stage debut in *Privates on Parade,* Lancaster, England; also appeared in *Volpone, The Good Person of Szechwan,* and *A Midsummer Night's Dream,* all Dukes Playhouse, Lancaster, England; *Faust,* Lyric Theatre–Hammersmith, London; *Decadence,* Bolon Octagon; *Cabaret,* Crucible Theatre, Sheffield, England; *She Stoops to Conquer, Your Home in the West, True Nature of Love,* and *Unidentified Human Remains,* all Royal Exchange Theatre, Manchester, England; *Decadence;* as the fool, *King Lear,* Royal Court Theatre, London; Macheath, *The Threepenny Opera,* Bubble Theatre; Jerry, *Some Like It Hot,* West Yorkshire Playhouse, Leeds, England.

Stage Work:
Director, *The Double Bass*, Southwark Playhouse, London, 2003.

RECORDINGS

Video Games:
Voice of Gollum, *The Lord of the Rings: The Return of the King*, EA Games, 2003.
Gollum, *The Lord of the Rings: The Third Age*, Electronic Arts, 2004.
Voice of Lumpy, *King Kong: The Official Game of the Movie* (also known as *Kong: The 8th Wonder of the World*), Ubi Soft Entertainment, 2005.
King, *Heavenly Sword*, Sony Computer Entertainment America, 2007.

Music Videos:
Neneh Cherry's "Woman," 1996.

WRITINGS

Screenplays:
Wrote *Snake* (short).

Books:
Wrote *Gollum*, Houghton Mifflin.

OTHER SOURCES

Periodicals:
Empire, August, 1998, p. 28.

Electronic:
Andy Serkis Website, http://www.serkis.com, September 15, 2007.

SESSIONS, John 1953–

PERSONAL

Original name, John Gibb Marshall; born January 11, 1953, in Largs, Scotland. *Education:* University of Wales, M.A., English literature; did Ph.D. research at McMaster University; studied at the Royal Academy of Dramatic Art.

Addresses: *Agent*—Markham and Froggatt, Ltd., 4 Windmill St., London W1P 1HF, England.

Career: Actor. Appeared in the short trailer "The Comedy Trail: A Shaggy Dog Story," BBC, 1999.

Member: Royal Academy of Dramatic Art (associate member).

Awards, Honors: Film Discovery Jury Award, best actor, U.S. Comedy Arts Festival, 2004, for *Stella Street.*

CREDITS

Film Appearances:
The Sender (also known as *Il messaggero della morte*, *Nadawca*, *Nattens saang*, and *Teuflische Signale*), Paramount, 1982.
John Smith, *The Bounty* (also known as *Bounty—kapina laivalla*, *Die Bounty*, *I antarsia tou Bounty*, *Il Bounty*, *Lazadas a Bountyn*, *Le Bounty*, *Motin a bordo*, and *Revolta de pe Bounty*), Orion, 1984.
Flight, *Sky Bandits* (also known as *Gunbus*), Galaxy International Releasing, 1986.
Man in pub, *Castaway*, Cannon, 1986.
Mr. Sweetzer, *Whoops Apocalypse* (also known as *As golpadas da politica*, *Die Bombe fliegt*, *La loca guerra de la Gran Bretana*, *Se on menoa nyt*, *Se on ydinsota nyt*, *Una signora chiamata presidente*, *Whoops—Apocalipse Ja!*, and *Zu splaet—Die Bombe fliegt*), ITC Entertainment Group, 1986, Metro–Goldwyn–Mayer, 1988.
MacMorris, *Henry V* (also known as *Enrico V*, *Enrique V*, *Henric al V–lea*, *Henrich V.*, *Henrik V*, *Henrique V*, *Kuningas Henrik V*, and *V. Henrik*), Samuel Goldwyn, 1989.
Dino, *The Pope Must Die* (also known as *The Pope Must Diet*), Miramax, 1991.
Voices of Scotty and other characters, *Freddie the Frog* (animated; also known as *Freddie as F.R.O.7*, *Agent Freddie—I hans majeststaets hemliga tjaenst*, *Freddie agent O.7.*, *Freddie, der Superfrosch*, *Fredi sammakko*, and *Froen Freddy*), Miramax, 1992.
Prince regent, *Princess Caraboo* (also known as *La princesa Caraboo*, *La principessa degli intrighi*, *Princesse Caraboo*, *Prinsessa Caraboo*, and *Prinzessin Caraboo*), TriStar, 1994.
Voices of William S. Burroughs and Ken Kesey, *Drug–Taking and the Arts* (documentary), 1994.
Terry Du Bois and Queen Gertrude, *In the Bleak Midwinter* (also known as *A Midwinter's Tale*), Sony Pictures Classics, 1995.
Schoolmaster, *The Adventures of Pinocchio* (also known as *Carlo Collodi's "Pinocchio,"* *Pinocchio*, *As aventuras de Pinocchio*, *Die Legende von Pinocchio*, *Las aventuras de Pinocho*, *Les aventures de Pinocchio*, *Oi peripeteies tou Pinocchio*, *Ostrzek*, *Pinocchion seikkailut*, *Pinocchios aeventyr*, *Pinocho, la leyenda*, *Pinokyo*, and *Przygody Pinokia*), New Line Cinema, 1996.

Humphrey Gould, *The Scarlet Tunic,* Scarlet Films, 1998.

Musical director, *Cousin Bette,* Fox Searchlight Pictures, 1998.

Philostrate, *A Midsummer Night's Dream* (also known as *William Shakespeare's "A Midsummer Night's Dream"* and *Sogno di una notte di mezza estate*), Fox Searchlight Pictures, 1999.

Voice of Chudley, *Faeries* (animated; also known as *Entfuhrung ins Elfenreich*), 1999.

Voice of Passepartout, *Around the World in 80 Days* (animated; also known as *La vuelta al mundo en 80 dias*), 1999.

Paul Jarrico, *One of the Hollywood Ten* (documentary; also known as *Punto de mira* and *Punto di vista*), Alibi Films International, 2000.

Director, *High Heels and Low Lives* (also known as *Blackmail, Kiristaejaet piikkikoroissa, Ladrones de lujo, Mulheres e chantagens, Perigo de saltos altos, Rouge a levres (& arme a feu), Rouge a levres et arme a feu, Toc inalt si minte brici,* and *Verbrechen verfuhrt*), Buena Vista, 2001.

Harry Watkins and Lincoln, *Gangs of New York* (also known as *Gang of New York, Gangs de Nova Iorque, Gangues de Nova York, Knufiot New York, Les gangs de New York, New Yorgi jougud,* and *Pandillas de Nueva York*), Miramax, 2002.

Mr. Reynard, *Lighthouse Hill,* Flamingo Films, 2004.

Peasemarsh, *Five Children and It* (also known as *5 Children & It* and *Cinq enfants et moi*), Capitol Films, 2004.

Salerio, *The Merchant of Venice* (also known as *William Shakespeare's "The Merchant of Venice"* and *Il mercante di Venezia*), Metro–Goldwyn–Mayer/Sony Pictures Classics, 2004.

Various characters, *Stella Street,* Columbia/TriStar, 2004.

Voice of Kelpie, *The Loch Ness Kelpie* (animated short film), Scottish Screen, 2004.

Felix Miles Sty, *Rag Tale,* Becker Films International, 2005.

Valentin Mironov and Yuri Modin, *The Good Shepherd* (also known as *Den innersta kretsen, Der Gute Hirte, Dobar pastir, El buen pastor, Hea karjane, Kirli sirlar, O kathodigitis,* and *Raisons d'etat*), Universal, 2006.

Finbar "Finn" Darrow, *Art in Las Vegas,* Scion Films/Pembridge Pictures/Prospero Pictures, 2007.

Joe, *Intervention* (also known as *Funny Farm*), Scion Films/Pembridge Pictures/Prospero Pictures, 2007.

Dylan, Rafford Films, 2008.

Television Appearances; Series:

Various characters, *Laugh??? I Nearly Paid My Licence Fee,* BBC, beginning 1984.

Various voices, *Spitting Image* (also known as *Spitting Back*), Central Television, 1984–94 and 1996.

Himself, *Whose Line Is It Anyway?* (also known as *Whose Line* and *WLiiA*), Channel 4 (England),

1988–91, and appeared in archive footage in various compilations.

Various characters, *John Sessions,* beginning 1989.

Various characters, *John Sessions' "Tall Tales,"* BBC, 1991.

James Boswell, *Screenplay: Boswell & Johnson's Tour of the Western Isles* (also known as *Boswell & Johnson's Tour of the Western Isles*), [Great Britain], beginning 1993.

Tippit, *Nice Day at the Office,* BBC, 1994.

Various characters, *John Sessions' "Likely Stories,"* BBC, 1994.

Various characters, *Stella Street,* BBC–2, beginning 1997.

Television Appearances; Miniseries:

Young Scot, *Tender Is the Night,* Showtime, 1985.

Lionel Zipser, *Porterhouse Blue,* Channel 4 (England), 1987.

Larry Knight, *Menace Unseen* (also known as *Naekymaetoen uhka*), Independent Television (England), 1988.

McMurdo, *Jute City,* BBC, 1991.

Henry Fielding, *The History of Tom Jones, a Foundling* (also known as *Henry Fielding's "The History of Tom Jones," Henry Fielding's "Tom Jones,"* and *Historia de Tom Jones enjeitado*), BBC, 1997, Arts and Entertainment, 1998.

Hercules Fortescue, *In the Red* (also known as *Dans le rouge* and *Murhatunnari*), BBC, 1998.

Dr. Prunesquallor, *Gormenghast,* BBC–2 and BBC America, 2000.

Mr. Hansell, *The Lost Prince* (also known as *El principe* and *Kadonnut prinssi*), BBC, 2003, broadcast on *Masterpiece Theatre* (also known as *ExxonMobil Masterpiece Theatre* and *Mobil Masterpiece Theatre*), PBS, 2005.

Professor Barry Lennox, *Low Winter Sun,* Channel 4 and BBC America, 2006.

Mr. Sowerberry, *Oliver Twist,* BBC, 2007.

Television Appearances; Movies:

Croser, *A Day in the Summer,* Yorkshire Television, 1989.

John, *Sweet Revenge* (also known as *Une femme parfaite*), TNT, 1990.

John Locke, *Citizen Locke,* 1994.

Daniel, *My Night with Reg,* BBC, 1996.

Redman, *The Treasure Seekers,* 1996.

Jerry Barnes, *The Man,* 1999.

Dennis Sciama, *Hawking,* BBC, 2004.

Ridley, *The English Harem,* Independent Television (England), 2005.

Professor Bell, *Reichenbach Falls* (also known as *The Acid Test*), BBC, 2007.

Television Appearances; Specials:

Voice, *Spitting Image: Down and Out in the White House,* NBC, 1986.

The Madness Museum, 1986.

Voice, *Spitting Image: The Ronnie and Nancy Show,* NBC, 1987.

Himself, *A Night of Comic Relief 2,* BBC, 1989.

Frosch, *Die Fledermaus* (opera), BBC, 1990.

Voices of Laurens and Acco Bouvaix, *David Macaulay: Roman City* (live action and animated; also known as *City*), PBS, 1994.

Himself, *Live from Lighthouse,* 1998.

The owl, *Queen's Park Story* (short), BBC, 1998.

George Henry Lewes, *George Eliot: A Scandalous Life,* BBC, 2002.

Voice of Shadrack Moore, *Mill Times* (live action and animated), PBS, 2002.

Spencer, *The Key,* BBC, 2003.

Rival editor, *The Legend of the Tamworth Two,* BBC, 2004.

Presenter, *The Proms,* BBC, 2006.

Himself, *Stephen Fry: 50 Not Out,* BBC Four, 2007.

Various characters, *Comic Relief 2007: The Big One,* 2007.

Television Appearances; Awards Presentations:

Voice, *Spitting Image: The 1987 Movie Awards,* NBC, 1987.

Television Appearances; Episodic:

Dean, "Cassie," *Happy Families,* BBC, 1985.

The Lenny Henry Show, BBC, 1985.

Barney Spitz, "Box 13," *Boon,* Independent Television (England), 1986.

Rodney, "Who's Ya Uncle Shelley?," *Girls on Top,* Independent Television, 1986.

Radio voices, "Four and Twenty Blackbirds," *Poirot* (also known as *Agatha Christie's "Poirot"* and *Hercule Poirot*), Independent Television, 1989, broadcast on *Mystery!,* PBS, c. 1990.

Voice of snooker competition entrant, "Dramatic Fever," *One Foot in the Grave,* BBC, 1990.

Himself, *Saturday Night Clive* (also known as *Clive James*), Channel 4 (England), 1990, 1994.

Lord Penistone, "Let Them Sniff Cake," *The New Statesman,* Independent Television, 1991.

Himself, *Wogan* (also known as *The Wogan Years*), BBC, 1991.

Himself, *Have I Got News for You* (also known as *HIGNFY, Have I Got 1992 for You, Have I Got Old News for You,* and *Have I Got the 90s for You,* longer version known as *Have I Got a Little Bit More News for You*), BBC, 1992 (multiple episodes).

Himself, *Aspel & Company,* Independent Television, 1992, 1993.

Himself, *The Full Wax,* BBC, 1993.

Himself, *Bore of the Year Awards,* c. 1993.

Himself, "Kings of Comedy," *Light Lunch,* Channel 4, 1997.

Himself, "Richard Briers: A Good Life," *Funny Turns,* BBC, 2000.

Combe Fishacre, "O Happy Isle," *Randall & Hopkirk (Deceased)* (also known as *Randall & Hopkirk*), BBC, 2001.

Professor Rutherford, "The Kingdom of Bones," *Murder Rooms* (also known as *Murder Rooms: The Kingdom of Bones*), BBC, 2001.

Himself, *Later with Jools Holland* (also known as *A Little Later*), BBC, 2001.

Brian Cantwell, QC (queen's counsel), "Political Expediency," *Judge John Deed,* BBC, 2002.

Charlie Penn, "Dialogues of the Dead," *Dalziel and Pascoe,* BBC, 2002.

John Corntel, "Well Schooled in Murder," *The Inspector Lynley Mysteries,* BBC, 2002, also broadcast on *Mystery!,* PBS.

Barrett Filby, "Painted in Blood," *Midsomer Murders,* Independent Television, BBC, and Arts and Entertainment, 2003.

Brian Cantwell, QC (queen's counsel), "Conspiracy," *Judge John Deed,* BBC, 2003.

Himself, "A Life in the Day," *Grumpy Old Men,* BBC, 2003.

Himself, *QI* (also known as *Quite Interesting*), BBC, episodes from 2003–2006.

Brian Cantwell, QC (queen's counsel), "Defence of the Realm," *Judge John Deed,* BBC, 2005.

John Kennedy, "Spinning America," *Absolute Power,* BBC, 2005.

Himself, *The Culture Show,* BBC, 2005.

Cardew Pye, "The Moving Finger," *Marple* (also known as *Agatha Christie—"Marple: The Moving Finger," Agatha Christie's "Marple," Agatha Christie's "Miss Marple," Marple: The Moving Finger, Miss Marple, Miss Marple, Series II: The Moving Finger,* and *Miss Marple—La plume empoisonnee*), Independent Television, 2006, also broadcast on Arts and Entertainment and CBC.

Storyteller, "Muddle Earth," *Jackanory,* BBC, 2006.

Himself, *Sunday AM,* 2006.

Voice of himself, *Who Wants to Be a Millionaire,* syndicated, 2006.

Dr. Finlay McKenzie, "Casualty," *New Tricks,* BBC, 2007.

Himself, "Bullets, Bombs and Bridges: The Story of the War Film," *British Film Forever* (documentary), BBC, 2007.

Himself, "Longing, Loving and Leg–Overs: The Story of British Romance," *British Film Forever* (documentary), BBC, 2007.

Donovan Credo, *Hotel Babylon,* BBC, 2007.

Radio Appearances:

Panelist, *Whose Line Is It Anyway?* (also known as *Whose Line* and *WLiiA*), BBC Radio 4, beginning c. 1987.

Voice of Manfred Strumer, *Private Passions,* BBC Radio 3, multiple episodes, including 1997.

Voices of various characters, *Dead Man Talking,* BBC Radio 4, beginning c. 2001.

Stage Appearances:
Appeared in *Paint Said Fred,* Royal Academy of Art. Also appeared in other productions, including *Life of Napoleon* and *Traveling Tails.*

Internet Appearances:
General Tannis, "Death Comes to Time" (miniseries), *Doctor Who,* BBCi Cult, c. 2001.

RECORDINGS

Videos:
Himself, *A Profile of "Brief Encounter"* (short), Carlton International Media, 2000.
(In archive footage) Himself, *The Very Best of "Have I Got News for You,"* Video Collection International, 2002.
Himself, *"Merchant of Venice": Shakespeare Through the Lens* (short), Sony Pictures Home Entertainment, 2005.

Audiobooks:
Paul Stewart and Chris Riddell, *Muddle Earth,* Macmillan Audio Books, 2004.
Rene Goscinny and Albert Uderzo, *Asterix and the Golden Sickle,* Orion Books, 2005.
Goscinny and Uderzo, *Asterix and the Goths,* Orion Books, 2005.
Goscinny and Uderzo, *Asterix the Gaul,* Orion Books, 2005.
Goscinny and Uderzo, *Asterix the Gladiator,* Orion Books, 2005.
Goscinny and Uderzo, *Asterix and the Big Fight,* Orion Books, 2006.
Paul Torday, *Salmon Fishing in the Yemen,* Orion Books, 2007.

WRITINGS

Screenplays:
Stella Street, Columbia/TriStar, 2004.
Additional dialogue, *Churchill: The Hollywood Years,* Pathe, 2004.

Teleplays; Series:
(With others) *Laugh??? I Nearly Paid My Licence Fee,* BBC, beginning 1984.
(With others) *Whose Line Is It Anyway?* (also known as *Whose Line* and *WliiA*), Channel 4 (England), 1988–91, and material appeared as archive footage in various compilations.
John Sessions, beginning 1989.

John Sessions' "Tall Tales," BBC, 1991.
John Sessions' "Likely Stories," BBC, 1994.
(With others) *Stella Street,* BBC–2, beginning 1997.

OTHER SOURCES

Periodicals:
The Face, August, 1987, pp. 19–21.
Radio Times, May 14, 1994, pp. 24–26; February 17, 1996, p. 10.

SHANDLING, Garry 1949–

PERSONAL

Born November 29, 1949, in Chicago, IL; son of Irving (a print shop owner) and Muriel (a pet store proprietor) Shandling. *Education:* Earned a degree in marketing from University of Arizona.

Addresses: *Agent*—Endeavor, 9601 Wilshire Blvd., 3rd Floor, Beverly Hills, CA 90210; International Creative Management, 10250 Constellation Way, 9th Floor, Los Angeles, CA 90067. *Publicist*—I/D Public Relations, 8409 Santa Monica Blvd., West Hollywood, CA 90069.

Career: Comedian and actor. Wrote scripts for situation comedies; performed standup comedy at the Comedy Store, Los Angeles.

Awards, Honors: CableACE Award nomination, performance in a comedy special, National Cable Television Association, Television Critics Association Award, best comedy series, 1987, both for *It's Garry Shandling's Show—25th Anniversary Special;* American Comedy Award, funniest male performer in a leading role in a television series, 1988, Emmy Award nomination (with Alan Zweibel), outstanding writing in a comedy series, 1988, CableACE Award nomination, actor in a comedy series, 1990, all for *It's Garry Shandling's Show;* CableACE Award (with others), comedy series, 1993, 1994, 1995, 1996, Emmy Award nominations, outstanding lead actor in a comedy series, 1993, 1995, 1996, 1997, 1998, outstanding individual achievement in writing for a comedy series (with others), 1993, 1994, 1995, 1996, 1997, and outstanding comedy series (with others), 1993, 1994, 1995, 1996, 1997, 1998, Golden Globe Award nominations, best actor in a comedy or musical television series, 1995, 1996, American Comedy Award nomination, funniest male performer in a leading role in a television series, 1996, American Comedy Award, funniest male performer in a leading role in a television series, 1998, 1999, Writers

Guild of America Television Award nomination (with others), best episodic comedy, 1996, 1998, Golden Satellite Award nominations, best actor in a comedy or musical television series, International Press Academy, 1997, 1998, Emmy Award (with Peter Tolan), outstanding writing for a comedy series, 1998, Television Award, best international television program, British Academy of Film and Television Arts, 1999, all for *The Larry Sanders Show*; American Comedy Award nomination, funniest male performer in a leading role in a television series, 2001, for *The 52nd Annual Primetime Emmy Awards*.

CREDITS

Film Appearances:
Himself, *Doctor Duck's Super Secret All–Purpose Sauce*, 1985.
(Uncredited) Mr. Vertisey, dental patient, *The Night We Never Met*, 1993.
Kip DeMay, *Love Affair*, 1994.
Stanley Tannenbaum, *Mixed Nuts* (also known as *Lifesavers*), 1994.
Voice of male pigeon, *Doctor Doolittle*, Twentieth Century–Fox, 1998.
Artie, *Hurlyburly*, Fine Line Features, 1998.
Harold Anderson, *What Planet Are You From?*, Columbia, 2000.
Griffin, *Town and Country* (also known as *Town & Country*), New Line Cinema, 2001.
Himself, *Run Ronnie Run*, 2002.
Comedian, *Comedian* (documentary), 2002.
Himself, *Shandling Talks ... No Flipping!* (short; also known as *Garry Shandling Talks ... No Flipping!*), Columbia TriStar Home Entertainment, 2002.
Himself, *Catalina View* (short), 2004.
Dr. Beekman, *Trust the Man*, Fox Searchlight, 2005.
Himself, *Special Thanks to Roy London*, Special Thanks to Roy London, 2005.
Voice of Verne, *Over the Hedge* (animated), Paramount, 2006.
Himself, *Meet the Cast of "Over the Hedge"* (documentary short), 2006.
Voice of Verne, *Hammy's Boomerang Adventures* (animated short), Paramount Home Entertainment, 2006.
Himself, *The Making of "The Larry Sanders Show"* (documentary), Sony Pictures Home Entertainment, 2007.

Film Work:
Producer, *What Planet Are You From?*, Columbia, 2000.
Executive producer, *The Making of "The Larry Sanders Show"* (documentary), Sony Pictures Home Entertainment, 2007.

Television Appearances; Series:
It's Garry Shandling's Show, Showtime, then Fox, 1986–90.
Title role, *The Larry Sanders Show*, HBO, 1992–98.

Television Appearances; Movies:
Jack, *Mother Goose Rock 'n' Rhyme*, Disney Channel, 1990.
Himself, *The Rutles 2: Can't Buy Me Lunch*, 2002.

Television Appearances; Pilots:
Michael Nesmith in Television Parts, NBC, 1985.
The Ben Stiller Show, 1992.

Television Appearances; Specials:
The Tonight Show Starring Johnny Carson: 19th Anniversary Special, NBC, 1981.
Garry Shandling ... Alone in Las Vegas, Showtime, 1984.
The Tonight Show Starring Johnny Carson: 23rd Anniversary Special, NBC, 1985.
Joan Rivers and Friends Salute Heidi Abromowitz, 1985.
Michael Nesmith in Television Parts, 1985.
Host, "It's Garry Shandling's Show 5th Anniversary Special," *Showtime Comedy Spotlight*, Showtime, 1986.
Disneyland's Summer Vacation Party, NBC, 1986.
Comic Relief, HBO, 1986.
Caesar's 20th Birthday Celebration, Showtime, 1987.
The Comedy Store 15th Year Class Reunion (also known as *Class Reunion* and *Comedy Store Reunion*), NBC, 1988.
The "I'm Exhausted" Concert (also known as *Richard Lewis: I'm Exhausted* and *Richard Lewis: The "I'm Exhausted" Concert*), 1988.
Merrill Markoe's Guide to Glamorous Living, *Cinemax Comedy Experiment,*.
Cinemax, 1988.
The Tonight Show Starring Johnny Carson: 26th Anniversary Special, NBC, 1988.
A Comedy Celebration: The Comedy and Magic Club's 10th Anniversary, Showtime, 1989.
Comic Relief III, HBO, 1989.
(Uncredited) Audience member, "*Saturday Night Live*": *15th Anniversary*, NBC, 1989.
Sunday Night with Larry King, NBC, 1990.
"Garry Shandling: Stand Up," *HBO Comedy Hour*, HBO, 1991.
Alan King: Inside the Comedy Mind, 1991.
Johnny Caron's 29th Anniversary, 1991.
American Bandstand 40th Anniversary Special, 1992.
Comic Relief V, HBO, 1992.
HBO's 20th Anniversary—We Hardly Believe It Ourselves, HBO, 1992.
The Comedy Store's 20th Birthday, 1992.
Bob Hope: The First Ninety Years (also known as *Bob Hope: A 90th Birthday Celebration*), NBC, 1993.
Comic Relief VI, HBO, 1994.
Host, *The 1995 Young Comedians Show Hosted by Garry Shandling*, HBO, 1995.
20 Years of Comedy on HBO, HBO, 1995.
A Comedy Salute to Andy Kaufman, NBC, 1995.
Who Makes You Laugh?, 1995.

Classic Stand–Up Comedy of Television, 1996.

The Late Show with David Letterman Video Special 2, CBS, 1996.

Host, *Hollywood Salutes Arnold Schwarzenegger: An American Cinematheque Tribute,* TNT, 1998.

Intimate Portrait: Brett Butler, Lifetime, 1998.

Jerry Seinfeld: I'm Telling You for the Last Time, HBO, 1998.

Influences: From Yesterday to Today, CBS, 1999.

The Award Show Awards Show, Trio, 2003.

Intimate Portrait: Dana Delaney, Lifetime, 2003.

Comedy Central Presents: 100 Greatest Stand–Ups of All Time, Comedy Central, 2004.

"T4" Goes "Over the Hedge," 2006.

Ricky Gervais Meets ... Garry Shandling, 2006.

Jerry Seinfeld: The Comedian Award, HBO, 2007.

Television Appearances; Awards Presentations:

The 39th Annual Emmy Awards, Fox, 1987.

The 40th Annual Emmy Awards, Fox, 1988.

The 2nd Annual American Comedy Awards, ABC, 1988.

Host, *The 32nd Annual Grammy Awards,* CBS, 1990.

Host, *The 33rd Annual Grammy Awards,* CBS, 1991.

Presenter, *The 44th Annual Primetime Emmy Awards,* Fox, 1992.

Presenter, *The 14th Annual CableACE Awards,* Lifetime, 1993.

Host, *The 35th Annual Grammy Awards,* 1993.

Presenter, *The 45th Annual Primetime Emmy Awards,* ABC, 1993.

Presenter, *The American Television Awards,* ABC, 1993.

Presenter, *The 15th Annual CableACE Awards,* TNT, 1994.

Host, *The 36th Annual Grammy Awards,* CBS, 1994.

Presenter, *The 46th Annual Primetime Emmy Awards,* ABC, 1994.

Presenter, *The 47th Annual Primetime Emmy Awards,* Fox, 1995.

Presenter, *The 1996 Emmy Awards,* ABC, 1996.

Presenter, *The 49th Annual Primetime Emmy Awards,* CBS, 1997.

The 12th Annual American Comedy Awards, Fox, 1998.

Presenter, *The 50th Emmy Awards,* NBC, 1998.

Screen Actors Guild 4th Annual Awards, TNT, 1998.

Presenter, *The 51st Annual Primetime Emmy Awards,* Fox, 1999.

The 13th Annual American Comedy Awards, Fox, 1999.

Host, *The 52nd Annual Primetime Emmy Awards,* ABC, 2000.

The 72nd Annual Academy Awards, ABC, 2000.

The 15th Annual American Comedy Awards, Comedy Central, 2001.

Cohost, *The 55th Annual Primetime Emmy Awards,* Fox, 2003.

Host, *The 56th Annual Primetime Emmy Awards,* ABC, 2004.

The 3rd Annual TV Land Awards, TV Land, 2005.

Television Appearances; Episodic:

Rock Concert (also known as *Don Kirshner's "Rock Concert"*), 1979.

The Tonight Show with Johnny Carson, NBC, 1981.

Guest host, *The Tonight Show with Johnny Carson,* NBC, 1981, 1986, 1987.

Host, *Saturday Night Live* (also known as *SNL*), 1987.

Late Night with David Letterman, NBC, 1989.

"Episode with Garry Shandling," *The Ben Stiller Show,* 1992.

The Howard Stern Interview (also known as *The Howard Stern "Interview"*), 1992.

"Other People's Failures," *Dennis Miller Live,* HBO, 1994.

The Tonight Show with Jay Leno, NBC, 1995, 1996, 2004, 2006.

"Happiness," *Dennis Miller Live,* HBO, 1996.

Voice of Garry, "Sticky Notes," *Dr. Katz, Professional Therapist* (animated), Comedy Central, 1996.

The Rosie O'Donnell Show, syndicated, 1996, 1997, 1998.

The Late Show with David Letterman (also known as *The Late Show*), CBS, 1997, 2007.

Former patient, "Caroline and the Marriage Counselor: Part 1," *Caroline in the City,* NBC, 1998.

Himself, "Hollywood A.D.," *The X–Files,* Fox, 2000.

Dinner for Five, Independent Film Channel, 2001.

"Commitment Phobias," *Dennis Miller Live,* HBO, 2002.

"Death Be Not Pre–Empted," *Wednesday 9:30 (8:30 Central)* (also known as *My Adventures in Television*), ABC, 2002.

The Late, Late Show with Craig Kilborn (also known as *The Late Late Show*), CBS, 2004.

Ellen: The Ellen DeGeneres Show, syndicated, 2005.

"Over the Hedge: Off the Strip & Onto the Screen," *HBO First Look,* HBO, 2006.

Voice of Captain Pat Lewellen, "Couple's Therapy," *Tom Goes to the Mayor* (animated), Cartoon Network, 2006.

Live with Regis & Kelly, syndicated, 2007.

The Daily Show (also known as *Jon Stewart, The Daily Show with Jon Stewart,* and *The Daily Show with Jon Stewart Global Edition*), Comedy Central, 2007.

Late Night with Conan O'Brien (also known as *Conan O'Brien*), NBC, 2007.

The Late, Late Show with Craig Ferguson, CBS, 2007.

Television Work; Series:

Executive producer (with others) and creator, *It's Garry Shandling's Show,* Showtime, then Fox, 1986–90.

Creator and executive producer, *The Larry Sanders Show,* HBO, 1992–98.

Television Work; Specials:

Producer, *Garry Shandling—Alone in Las Vegas,* Showtime, 1984.

Executive producer, "It's Garry Shandling's Show—25th Anniversary Special," *Showtime Comedy Spotlight,* Showtime, 1986.

Executive producer, "Garry Shandling: Stand Up," *HBO Comedy Hour,* HBO, 1991.

Writing supervisor and comedy sketch producer, *The 56th Annual Primetime Emmy Awards,* ABC, 2004.

Television Director; Episodic:

"As My Career Lay Dying," *The Larry Sanders Show,* HBO, 1998.

"Adolf Hankler," *The Larry Sanders Show,* HBO, 1998.

"I Buried Sid," *The Larry Sanders Show,* HBO, 1998.

WRITINGS

Screenplays:

What Planet Are You From?, Columbia, 2000.

Television Theme Song Lyrics:

It's Garry Shandling's Show, Showtime, then Fox, 1986–90.

Television Specials:

Garry Shandling ... Alone in Las Vegas, Showtime, 1984.

"It's Garry Shandling's Show 5th Anniversary Special," *Showtime Comedy Spotlight,* Showtime, 1986.

Comic Relief, 1986.

"Garry Shandling: Stand Up," *HBO Comedy Hour,* HBO, 1991.

The 35th Annual Grammy Awards, CBS, 1993.

The 52nd Annual Primetime Emmy Awards, ABC, 2000.

The 56th Annual Primetime Emmy Awards, ABC, 2004.

Television Awards Presentations:

The 35th Annual Grammy Awards, 1993.

The 52nd Annual Primetime Emmy Awards, 2000.

Television Episodes:

"Sanford and Rising Son," *Sanford and Son,* 1975.

"The Camping Trip," *Sanford and Son,* 1975.

"Committee Men," *Sanford and Son,* 1975.

"Horshack vs. Carvelli," *Welcome Back, Kotter,* 1976.

"The One Where Harvey Won't Change," *The Harvey Korman Show,* 1978.

It's Garry Shandling's Show, Showtime, then Fox, 1986–90.

The Larry Sanders Show, HBO, 1992–98.

Also wrote episodes of *Three's Company.*

Other Writings:

Confessions of a Late–Night Talk Show Host: The Autobiography of Larry Sanders, Simon & Schuster (New York City), 1998.

OTHER SOURCES

Books:

Newsmakers 1995, Issue 4, Gale, 1995.

Contemporary Authors Online, Gale, 2003.

Periodicals:

Entertainment Weekly, May 22, 1998, p. 34.

Esquire, July, 1998, pp. 64–69.

Newsweek, April 6, 1998, p. 59.

Playboy, December, 1994, p. 61.

Rolling Stone, February 26, 1990; September 8, 1994.

TV Guide, March 14, 1998, pp. 56–60.

SHANNON, Michael 1946–
(Michael J. Shannon, Michael J Shannon)

PERSONAL

Born in 1946, in Chicago, IL; married Vickery Turner (an actress; died, April 4, 2006).

Career: Actor.

CREDITS

Film Appearances:

Purcell, *Shoot It Black, Shoot It Blue,* Levitt–Pickman, 1974.

(As Michael J. Shannon) Lieutenant Davis, *That Lucky Touch* (also known as *Bleib mir ja vom leib*), Allied Artists Pictures, 1975.

Peter, *Never Never Land,* Sharp Features, 1980.

(As Michael J. Shannon) President's aide, *Superman II,* Warner Bros., 1980.

Philip Ames, *Sheena* (also known as *Sheena: Queen of the Jungle*), Columbia, 1984.

Bishop Holmes, *Death of an Angel,* Twentieth Century–Fox, 1986.

(As Michael J. Shannon) Television reporter, *Little Shop of Horrors,* Warner Bros., 1986.

Neil Turkle, *Nervous Energy,* 1995.

(Uncredited) Voice, *Balto,* Universal, 1995.

Old luvvie, *Beginner's Luck,* Guerilla Films, Ltd., 2001.

(As Michael J. Shannon) Jerry, *American Gun,* IFC Films, 2005.

(As Michael J. Shannon) President's aide, *Superman II* (also known as *"Superman II": The Richard Donner Cut*), Warner Bros., 2006.

Television Appearances; Series:
Jim McCarren, *Search for Tomorrow*, CBS, 1971–72.
Dr. Bill Hoffman, *All My Children*, ABC, 1972.
Carl "Tubes" Benson, *Rock Follies*, ITV, 1976.
Officer Haven, *Future Cop*, ABC, 1977–78.
Major Jim Kiley, *We'll Meet Again*, ITV, 1982.
Jack Daniels, *A Very Peculiar Place*, BBC, 1986.
Milton Macrae, *The Peter Principle* (also known as *The Boss*), BBC, 1997.
Robert, *A Legend to Ride* (also known as *13, ratsastaja, 13th Rider,* and *Pony Track*), 1997.

Television Appearances; Miniseries:
Freddie Gebhard, *Lillie*, BBC, 1978.
Patrick Callahan, *The Best Place to Be*, NBC, 1979.
Jack Fisher, *The Two Mrs. Grenvilles*, NBC, 1987.
(As Michael J. Shannon) *Poor Little Rich Girl: The Barbara Hutton Story*, NBC, 1987.
Toby Dehring, *Anything More Would Be Greedy*, 1989.
David, *The Big Battalions*, 1992.
(As Michael J. Shannon) Jake Hunter, *Prime Suspect 3* (also known as *Prime Suspect 3: The Keeper of Souls*), ITV and PBS, 1993.
Maxwell, *Scarlett*, CBS, 1994.
(As Michael J. Shannon) Dr. Duncan, *Only Love* (also known as *Erich Segal's "Only Love"*), CBS, 1998.

Television Appearances; Movies:
Second to the Right on Till Morning, ITV, 1979.
(As Michael J. Shannon) Edward Boyne, *Afterward*, 1985.
Senator John Tunney, *The Ted Kennedy Jr. Story*, NBC, 1986.
Bruce Nelson, *The Ladies*, NBC, 1987.
Frank Osbourne, *Out of the Shadows*, Showtime, 1988.
Ivanov, *Murder on the Moon* (also known as *Murder by Moonlighting* and *Murder in Space*), CBS, 1989.
Grover, *Tailspin: Behind the Korean Airliner Tragedy* (also known as *Coded Hostile*), HBO, 1989.
Chapinski, *Pride and Extreme Prejudice*, USA Network, 1990.
Blackbeard, *Merlin of the Crystal Cave*, BBC, 1991.
(As Michael J. Shannon) Senator Scanlon, *Royce*, Showtime, 1994.
(As Michael J. Shannon) U.S. ambassador, *Fatherland*, HBO, 1994.
Denis Prince, *Paparazzo*, ITV, 1995.
(As Michael J. Shannon) Martin Schraeder, *Night Watch* (also known as *Alistair MacLean's "Night Watch"* and *Detonator 2: Night Watch*), USA Network, 1995.
Captain Ford, *The Affair*, 1995.
Admiral, *Hostile Waters* (also known as *Im fahrwasser des todes* and *Peril en mer*), HBO, 1997.

Graham, *30 Years to Life*, UPN, 1998.
Brayton Jennings, *You've Got a Friend*, 2007.

Television Appearances; Pilots:
Haven, *Future Cop* (movie), ABC, 1976.
John Haven, *Cops and Robin* (movie), NBC, 1978.
Robert Harwell, *Behind Enemy Lines* (movie; also known as *92 Grosvenor Street*), NBC, 1985.
Milton Macrae, *The Peter Principle* (also known as *The Boss*), BBC, 1995.

Television Appearances; Episodic:
Milton Webber, "Grail and Platter," *The Hanged Man*, 1975.
"Here a Spy, There a Spy," *The Feather and Father Gang*, ABC, 1977.
Bradley, "Rogue's Gallery," *Target*, BBC, 1978.
Cameron, "The Boy Who Knew Her Secret: Parts 1 & 2," *Wonder Woman* (also known as *The New Adventures of Wonder Woman* and *The New Original Wonder Woman*), CBS, 1979.
Tim Stone, "Rosemary for Remembrance," *Charlie's Angels*, ABC, 1979.
Mac McIvor, "Gambling," *Lou Grant*, CBS, 1979.
Ben Catron, "If the Glass Slipper Fits," *Eight is Enough*, ABC, 1981.
Brice Landis, "Honkytonk," *Riker*, CBS, 1981.
(As Michael J. Shannon) "Perfect Shadows," *BBC2 Playhouse*, BBC2, 1983.
(As Michael J. Shannon) Dr. Sutro, "Smart Aleck Kill," *Philip Marlowe, Private Eye*, HBO, 1983.
Morrison, *The Paper Chase: The Second Year*, Showtime, 1983.
"Afterward," *Shades of Darkness*, PBS, 1984.
"The Setup," *Partners in Crime* (also known as *50/50*), ITV and PBS, 1984.
Frank Bigelow, "Now You Steele It, Now You Don't," *Remington Steele*, NBC, 1985.
Dr. Claude Dreyer, "Out-of-Town Blues," *Simon & Simon*, CBS, 1985.
Dr. Scardelli, "The Eyes Have It," *Scarecrow and Mrs. King*, CBS, 1986.
Balloon vender, "Heaven on Earth," *Highway to Heaven*, NBC, 1986.
(As Michael J. Shannon) Carl Conrad, "The Burning: Parts 1 & 2," *Dempsey & Makepeace*, ITV, 1986.
Randy Anderson, "The Grey Team," *The A-Team*, NBC, 1986.
(As Michael J. Shannon) Peter Shelley, "Sickness and Health," *Boon*, ITV, 1989.
(As Michael J. Shannon) J. Baker Wood, "Double Sin," *Poirot* (also known as *Agatha Christie's "Poirot"*), ITV and PBS, 1990.
Josie, 1991.
Patrick Mulligan, *Angel Street*, CBS, 1992.
(As Michael J. Shannon) Oswald Clark, "Maigret and the Hotel Majestic," *Maigret*, Granada, 1993.

(As Michael J. Shannon) Dr. Henry Jansen, "Flash," *Space Precinct,* syndicated, 1995.

(As Michael J. Shannon) Ed Murrow, "Between the Devil and the Deep Blue Sea," *Goodnight Sweetheart,* BBC, 1995.

(As Michael J. Shannon) John F. Kennedy, "Tikka to Ride," *Red Dwarf,* BBC, 1997.

Merle, *Early Edition,* CBS, 1997.

Stryker, "Phoenix," *CI5: The New Professionals,* syndicated, 1999.

General Plesac, "War Stories," *JAG,* CBS, 1999.

General Plesac, "Baby, It's Cold Outside," *JAG,* CBS, 2001.

(As Michael J. Shannon) "Dead in the Water," *Crossing Jordan,* NBC, 2004.

Ashley Tutt, *The Riches,* FX Channel, 2006.

Stage Appearances:

Cass, *Shoppers Carried by Escalators into the Flames,* Dimson Theatre, New York City, 2002.

SHANNON, Michael 1974–
(Mike Shannon)

PERSONAL

Born in 1974, in Lexington, KY.

Addresses: *Agent*—SDB Partners, 1801 Avenue of the Stars, suite 902, Los Angeles, CA 90067. *Manager*—Wetzel Management, 200 Park Ave. South, 8th Floor, New York, NY 10001. *Contact*—A Red Orchid Theatre, 151 N. Wells St., Chicago, IL 60610.

Career: Actor.

Awards, Honors: Lucille Lortel Award nomination, outstanding lead actor, League of off–Broadway Theatres and Producers, 2004, for *Bug.*

CREDITS

Film Appearances:

Fred Kleiser, *Groundhog Day,* Columbia, 1993.

Flower delivery man, *Chain Reaction,* Twentieth Century–Fox, 1996.

Crack head, *Chicago Cab* (also known as *Hellcab*), Castle Hill Productions, 1998.

Jimmy, *The Ride,* 1999.

(As Mike Shannon) Dundun, *Jesus' Son,* Lions Gate Films, 1999.

Mulitt (short), 2000.

(As Mike Shannon) Petie, *Cecil B. DeMented,* Artisan Entertainment, 2000.

Sergeant Filmore, *Tigerland,* Twentieth Century–Fox, 2000.

Lieutenant Gooz Wood, *Pearl Harbor* (also known as *Pearl Harbour*), Buena Vista, 2001.

Stanton, *New Port South,* Buena Vista, 2001.

Aaron, *Vanilla Sky,* Paramount, 2001.

Troy Abbott, *High Crimes,* Twentieth Century–Fox, 2002.

Greg Buehl, *8 Mile,* Universal, 2002.

Frankie Lombardo, *Kangaroo Jack,* Warner Bros., 2003.

Floyd Poteet, *Bad Boys II* (also known as *Good Cops: Bad Boys II*), Columbia, 2003.

Larry Oster–Berg, *Grand Theft Parsons,* Swipe Films, 2003.

Rosen, *The Woodsman,* Newmarket Films, 2004.

Walt, Zamboni man, *Zamboni Man* (short), 2004.

Gene, *Criminal,* Warner Independent Pictures, 2004.

Clyde, *Dead Birds,* 2004.

Bobby Matherson, *Water,* 2004.

Himself, *Showboat & Boonie* (documentary short), Sony Pictures Entertainment, 2005.

Himself, *Making "Dead Birds"* (documentary short), Columbia TriStar Home Video, 2005.

Himself, *The Making of "World Trade Center"* (documentary), Paramount Home Entertainment, 2006.

John, *Marvelous,* 2006.

Peter Evans, *Bug,* Lions Gate Films, 2006.

Dave Karnes, *World Trade Center,* Paramount, 2006.

Lynard, *Let's Go to Prison,* Universal, 2006.

Son Hayes, *Shotgun Stories,* Vertigo Films, 2007.

Murl, *Blackbird,* 2007.

Ray Zumbro, *Lucky You,* Warner Bros., 2007.

Dex, *Before the Devil Knows You're Dead,* ThinkFilm, 2007.

Television Appearances; Movies:

Brayton Jennings, *You've Got a Friend,* Hallmark Channel, 2007.

Television Appearances; Pilots:

Patrick Mulligan, *Angel Street* (movie), CBS, 1992.

Young man, *Overexposed* (movie), ABC, 1992.

Man number one, *Turks,* CBS, 1999.

Television Appearances; Episodic:

(As Mike Shannon) Mr. Andrews, "Take Me Out to the Ballgame," *Early Edition,* CBS, 1999.

Avery Shaw, "Quarry," *Law & Order: Special Victims Unit* (also known as *Law & Order: SVU* and *Special Victims Unit*), NBC, 2005.

Student, "Galileo and the Sinful Spyglass," *Man, Moment, Machine,* 2007.

Stage Appearances:

Bug, Gate Theatre, London, 1996.

Chris Smith, *Killer Joe,* Soho Playhouse, New York City, 1998.

Peter Evans, *Bug,* Barrow Street Theatre, New York City, 2004.

The Pillowman, Steppenwolf Theatre Company, Chicago, IL, 2006.

Grace, Northlight Theatre, Chicago, IL, 2006.

Also appeared in *Winterset,* Illinois Theatre Center, Park Forest, IL; *Woyzeck,* West End production, London; *Killer Joe,* West End production, London; as Harry Brown, *Man from Nebraska,* Steppenwolf Theatre, Chicago, IL; Eddie, *Gargarin Way,* Red Orchid Theatre, Chicago, IL.

Stage Director:

Directed *Hunger and Thirst,* Red Orchid Theatre, Chicago, IL.

SHAW, Fiona 1958(?)–

PERSONAL

Full name, Fiona Mary Wilson; born July 10, 1958 (some sources say 1955), in Cork, Ireland; father, an eye surgeon; mother, physicist; married Hugh; children: two daughters. *Education:* Graduated from the Royal Academy of Dramatic Art; studied philosophy at the University College, Cork, Ireland.

Addresses: *Agent*—International Creative Management, 10250 Constellation Way, 9th Floor, Los Angeles, CA 90067.

Career: Actress. Royal Academy of Dramatic Art, London, associate member. University of Missouri at Kansas City, teacher at acting workshop, 1996.

Awards, Honors: Bancroft Gold Medal, Royal Academy of Dramatic Art, 1982; London Critics Circle Theatre Award, best actress, 1989, for *Electra* and *The Good Person of Sichuan;* Laurence Olivier awards, best actress, Society of West End Theatre, 1990, for *Electra, As You Like It,* and *The Good Person of Sichuan;* London Critics Circle Theatre Award, best actress, 1991, for *Hedda Gabler;* Plays and Players London Theatre Critics Awards, best actress, 1991, for *Hedda Gabler* and *Electra; Evening Standard* Theatre Award, best actress, 1993, Laurence Olivier Theatre Award, best actress, Society of West End Theatre, 1994, both for *Machinal;* Chlotrudis Award nomination, best supporting actress, Chlotrudis Society for Independent Film, 1996, for *Persuasion;* Drama Desk Awards,

outstanding one–person show and best solo/one–woman show, *Theatre World* Award, 1997, both for *The Waste Land;* Commander of the Order of the British Empire, 2001; *Evening Standard* Theatre Award, best actress, 2002, Antoinette Perry Award nomination, best actress in a play, Drama Desk Award nomination, outstanding actress in a play, Obie Award, best performance, *Village Voice,* 2003, all for *Medea;* Phoenix Film Critics Society Award nomination (with others), best acting ensemble, 2003, for *Harry Potter and the Chamber of Secrets.*

CREDITS

Stage Appearances:

(Stage debut) Rosaline, *Love's Labour's Lost,* Royal Shakespeare Company, London, 1983.

Julia Melville, *The Rivals,* National Theatre Company, Olivier Theatre, London, 1983.

Mary Shelley, *Bloody Poetry,* Hampstead Theatre Club, London, 1984.

Celia, *As You Like It,* Royal Shakespeare Company, Stratford–on–Avon, England, then Barbican Theatre, London, both 1985.

Madame de Volanges, *Les liaisons dangereuses,* Royal Shakespeare Company, Stratford–on–Avon, 1985, then Pit Theatre, London, 1986.

Tatyana Vasilyevna, *The Philistines,* Royal Shakespeare Company, Stratford–on–Avon, 1985, then Pit Theatre, 1986.

Erika Bruckner, *Mephisto,* Royal Shakespeare Company, Barbican Theatre, London, 1986.

Prudence, *The New Inn,* Royal Shakespeare Company, Swan Theatre, Stratford–on–Avon, England, 1987.

Mistress Carol, *Hyde Park,* Royal Shakespeare Company, Swan Theatre, 1987, then Pit Theatre, 1988.

Katherine, *The Taming of the Shrew,* Royal Shakespeare Company, Stratford–on–Avon, 1987, then Barbican Theatre, 1988.

Title role, *Mary Stuart,* Greenwich Theatre, London, 1988.

Title role, *Electra,* Royal Shakespeare Company, Pit Theatre, 1988–89.

Rosalind, *As You Like It,* Old Vic Theatre, London, 1989.

Shen The/Shui Ta, *The Good Person of Sichuan,* National Theatre Company, Olivier Theatre, 1989–90.

Shakespeare—As He Liked It, Haymarket Theatre, London, 1990.

The Waste Land (solo dramatic reading), Kunsten Festival des Arts, Brussels, Belgium, 1995, then Liberty Theatre, New York City, 1996–97.

Title role, *Richard II,* Royal National Theatre, London, 1996.

The Prime of Miss Jane Brodie, London, 1998.

Medea, *Medea,* Abbey Theatre, Dublin, Ireland, 2000, Queen's Theatre, London, 2001, Brooks Atkinson Theatre, New York City, 2002–2003.

Happy Days, National Theatre, London, 2002.

The Powerbook, Royal National Theatre, London, 2002.

Calpurnia, *Julius Caesar,* Barbican Theatre, London, 2005.

Also appeared in the title role, *Hedda Gabler,* Abbey Theatre, Dublin, Ireland, then West End production, London; in *Footfalls,* Garrick Theatre, London; *Machinal,* Royal National Theatre, London; *Titus Andronicus,* Royal Shakespeare Company.

Major Tours:

Portia, *The Merchant of Venice,* Royal Shakespeare Company, British cities, 1986–87.

Beatrice, *Much Ado About Nothing,* Royal Shakespeare Company, British cities, 1986–87.

Calpurnia, *Julius Caesar,* French and Spanish cities, 2005.

Major Tours; as Director:

Widowers' Houses, Royal National Theatre, London, 1999.

Film Appearances:

Laura, *The Man Who Shot Christmas,* 1984.

Sister Felicity, *Sacred Hearts,* Reality/Film Four, 1984.

Dr. Eileen Cole, *My Left Foot* (also known as *My Left Foot: The Story of Christy Brown*), Miramax, 1989.

Isabel Arundell, Mrs. Burton in 1861, *Mountains of the Moon,* TriStar, 1990.

Miss Lomax, *Three Men and a Little Lady* (also known as *3 Men and a Little Lady*), 1990.

Headley, *London Kills Me,* 1991.

Lena, *Super Mario Bros.,* 1993.

Novacek, *Undercover Blues,* 1993.

Pauline, *Maria's Child,* 1993.

Mrs. Croft, *Persuasion,* 1995.

The Waste Land, 1995.

Mrs. Reed, *Jane Eyre* (also known as *Charlotte Bronte's "Jane Eyre"*), Miramax, 1996.

Lydia, *Anna Karenina* (also known as *Anna Karenine*), Warner Bros., 1997.

Mrs. Nugent, *The Butcher Boy,* Warner Bros., 1997.

Father, *The Avengers,* Warner Bros., 1998.

Marda Norton, *The Last September,* Trimark Pictures, 1999.

Frances O'Neil, *Mind Games,* 2000.

Aunt Petunia Dursley, *Harry Potter and the Sorcerer's Stone* (also known as *Harry Potter and the Philosopher's Stone*), Warner Bros., 2001.

Leontine, *The Triumph of Love* (also known as *Il trionfo dell'amore*), Paramount Classics, 2001.

Professor Catherine Lebourg, *Doctor Sleep* (also known as *Close Your Eyes* and *Hypnotic*), First Look International, 2002.

Aunt Petunia Dursley, *Harry Potter and the Chamber of Secrets* (also known as *Harry Potter und die kammer des schreckens*), Warner Bros., 2002.

Herself, *Interviews with Professors & More* (documentary short), 2003.

Herself, *Head to Shrunken Head* (documentary short), 2004.

Aunt Petunia Dursley, *Harry Potter and the Prisoner of Azkaban,* Warner Bros., 2004.

(English versions) Voice of the witches, *El sueno de una noche de San Juan* (animated; also known as *Midsummer Dream*), 2005.

Ramona Linscott, *The Black Dahlia* (also known as *Black Dahlia*), Universal, 2006.

Ellen Douglas, *Catch and Release,* Columbia, 2006.

Judge Robinson, *Fracture,* New Line Cinema, 2007.

Aunt Petunia Dursley, *Harry Potter and the Order of the Phoenix,* Warner Bros., 2007.

Television Appearances; Series:

Various characters, *The Last Machine,* 1995.

Television Appearances; Miniseries:

Gillian Savage, *For the Greater Good,* BBC, 1991.

Herself, "Girls Who Are Boys," "It's a Family Affair," and "Like a Virgin," *Conjuring Shakespeare,* 1997.

Irma Prunesquallor, *Gormenghast,* BBC and BBC America, 2000.

Presenter, "William Shakespeare," *Great Britons,* 2002.

Fulvia, *Empire,* ABC, 2005.

Television Appearances; Movies:

Young Deirdre, *Love Song,* Anglia Television, then *Masterpiece Theatre,* PBS, 1987.

Clytemnestra, *Iphigenia at Aulis,* 1990.

Pauline, "Maria's Child," *Screen Two,* BBC, 1992.

Seascape, 1994.

Cosima Wagner, *Wagner's Women,* 1995.

Richard II, 1997.

Hedda Hopper, *RKO 281* (also known as *RKO 281: The Battle Over Citizen Kane*), HBO, 1999.

Frances O'Neil, *Mind Games,* 2001.

Mrs. Gourdon, *The Seventh Stream,* CBS, 2001.

Trial and Retribution XIV: Mirror Image, 2007.

Also appeared in *Fireworks for Elspeth.*

Television Appearances; Specials:

Title role and program host, "Hedda Gabler," *Masterpiece Theatre,* PBS, 1993.

The Waste Land, BBC, 1995.

The 57th Annual Tony Awards, CBS, 2003.

The Evening Standard Awards, ITV3, 2005.

Television Appearances; Episodic:

Miss Morrison, "The Crooked Man," *The Adventures of Sherlock Holmes* (also kwon as *Sherlock Holmes*), PBS, 1985.

Voice of Viola, "Twelfth Night," *Shakespeare: The Animated Tales* (animated), HBO, 1992.
Ruby, BBC, 1997.
This Week, BBC, 2005.

RECORDINGS

Audio Books:
The Banyan Tree, Time Warner, 2000.

WRITINGS

Stage Plays:
(With Jeannette Winterson and Deborah Warner) *The Powerbook,* Royal National Theatre, London, 2002.

Nonfiction:
Composing Myself: A Journey through Postpartum Depression, Steerforth, 1998.

OTHER SOURCES

Periodicals:
American Theatre, March, 1997, p. 12.
Newsweek, January 15, 1996, p. 67.

SHAW, Vinessa 1976–

PERSONAL

Full name, Vinessa Elizabeth Shaw; born July 19, 1976, in Los Angeles, CA; daughter of Larry (a psychologist) and Susan (an actress; maiden name, Damante) Shaw. *Education:* Attended Barnard College, New York, NY.

Addresses: *Agent*—William Morris Agency, 1 William Morris Pl., Beverly Hills, CA 90212. *Manager*—The Collective, 9100 Wilshire Blvd., Suite 700 W, Beverly Hills, CA 90212. *Publicist*—Megan Moss, I/D Public Relations, 8409 Santa Monica Blvd., West Hollywood, CA 90069.

Career: Actress. Elite Models, became a model, c. 1989; appeared in commercials, including an advertisement for Calvin Klein eyeglasses, 2000. Performed with folk singer Peter Alsop as a child.

Awards, Honors: Young Artist Award nominations (with others), best young actress costarring in a motion picture and outstanding young ensemble in a motion picture, both 1993, for *Ladybugs;* Young Artist Award nomination, best young actress recurring in a television series, 1993, for *Great Scott;* Young Artist Award nomination, best leading youth actress in a motion picture comedy, 1994, for *Hocus Pocus;* Young Artist Award nomination, best youth actress in a drama series, 1995, for *McKenna;* Young Artist Award nomination, best guest–starring television performance by a youth actress, 1995, for *Murder, She Wrote.*

CREDITS

Film Appearances:
Angel, *Home Sweet Home* (also known as *Slasher in the House*), 1981.
Kimberly Mullen, *Ladybugs,* Paramount, 1992.
Allison, *Hocus Pocus,* Buena Vista, 1993.
Callie Carpenter, *Coyote Summer,* Leucadia Film Corp., 1996.
Barbara, *L.A. Without a Map* (also known as *I Love L.A.* and *Los Angeles Without a Map*), United Media, 1998.
Domino, *Eyes Wide Shut* (also known as *EWS*), Warner Bros., 1999.
Cordelia, *Wayward Son,* Arthur Kananack and Associates, 1999.
Anethe Christenson, *The Weight of Water* (also known as *Le poids de l'eau*), Lions Gate Films, 2000.
Agent Kate Russo, *Corky Romano* (also known as *Corky Romano: "Special" Agent*), Buena Vista, 2001.
Nicole, *40 Days and 40 Nights* (also known as *40 jours et 40 nuits*), Miramax, 2002.
Stacey Fox, *Melinda and Melinda,* Fox Searchlight, 2005.
Lynn Carter Bukowski, *The Hills Have Eyes,* Fox Searchlight, 2006.
Sally, *Garden Party,* Lookout Films, 2007.
Emmy Roberts, *3:10 to Yuma,* Lions Gate Films, 2007.
Nora, *Badlands,* Badland Corp., 2007.

Television Appearances; Movies:
Clara Tarpin, *Long Road Home,* NBC, 1991.
Molly, *Bereft,* 2004.
Nell, *Fathers and Sons,* Showtime, 2005.

Television Appearances; Pilots:
Heather Calhoun, *Country Estates,* ABC, 1993.
Cassidy McKenna, *McKenna,* ABC, 1994.
World of Trouble, NBC, 2005.

Television Appearances; Episodic:
Meredith Reed, "Swear Not by the Moon," *The Torkelsons,* 1992.
Jeannie Streeter, "The Quiet Room," *Fallen Angels,* Showtime, 1993.
Gloria Bryce, "Murder by Twos," *Murder, She Wrote,* CBS, 1994.

Krista McCauley, "Young, Beautiful, and Dead," *New York Undercover* (also known as *Uptown Undercover*), Fox, 1995.

Television Appearances; Other:
Carolyn Cole, a recurring role, *Great Scott* (series), Fox, 1992.
Narrator, *Jackie: Behind the Myth* (special), PBS, 1999.
Eileen Wells, *The 70s* (miniseries), NBC, 2000.

Stage Appearances:
Gallows Humor, Laurelgrove Theatre, Los Angeles, 2001.

RECORDINGS

Videos:
Surviving the Hills: Making of "The Hills Have Eyes," Twentieth Century–Fox, 2006.

OTHER SOURCES

Periodicals:
In Style, July, 1999.
Premiere, September, 2001, p. 19.
Us Weekly, May 8, 2000, p. 16.
Vogue, July, 1998, p. 51.

SHERIDAN, Nicollette 1963–
(Nicolette Sheridan)

PERSONAL

Original name, Colette Sheridan; born November 21, 1963, in Worthing, Sussex, England; immigrated to the United States, c. 1973; daughter of Sally (an actress; maiden name, Adams; later surname, Savalas) Sheridan; stepdaughter of Telly Savalas (an actor); married Harry Hamlin (an actor), September 7, 1991 (divorced, 1993). *Avocational Interests:* Horseback riding, animal welfare activities.

Addresses: *Agent*—Marcia Hurwitz, Innovative Artists Talent and Literary Agency, 1505 10th St., Santa Monica, CA 90401. *Publicist*—Nicole T. Perna, Baker/Winokur/Ryder, 9100 Wilshire Blvd., 6th Floor W., Beverly Hills, CA 90212.

Career: Actress and model. Worked for Elite Modeling Agency, New York City; appeared in print ads and in television commercials for 7Up soft drinks, 2005, and other products.

Awards, Honors: *Soap Opera Digest* Awards, outstanding lead actress in a prime–time show, 1990, and outstanding heroine in a prime–time show, 1991, both for *Knots Landing;* Golden Globe Award nomination, best supporting actress in a television series, miniseries, or movie, 2005, Screen Actors Guild Awards, 2005, 2006, and Screen Actors Guild Award nomination, 2007, all outstanding ensemble in a comedy series (with others), all for *Desperate Housewives.*

CREDITS

Television Appearances; Series:
Taryn Blake, *Paper Dolls,* ABC, 1984.
Paige Matheson, *Knots Landing,* CBS, 1986–93.
Edie Britt, *Desperate Housewives,* ABC, 2004—.

Television Appearances; Movies:
Banda Drake, *Dark Mansions,* ABC, 1985.
(As Nicolette Sheridan) Hattie Stubbs, *Dead Man's Folly* (also known as *Agatha Christie's "Dead Man's Folly"*), CBS, 1986.
Lucky Santangelo Richmond Stanislopolous Golden, *Lucky/Chances* (also known as *Jackie Collins's "Lucky/Chances"*), NBC, 1990.
Adrienne Erickson, *Deceptions,* Showtime, 1990.
Sara, *Somebody's Daughter,* 1992.
Jenny Barton, *A Time to Heal* (also known as *Jenny's Story*), NBC, 1994.
Rowena Ecklund, *Shadows of Desire* (also known as *The Devil's Bed*), CBS, 1994.
Marissa Blumenthal, *Virus* (also known as *Formula for Death, Robin Cook's "Formula for Death," Robin Cook's "Outbreak,"* and *Robin Cook's "Virus"*), 1995.
Michelle Hughes, *The Silver Strand,* 1995.
Grace, *Indictment: The McMartin Trial,* 1995.
Anna Morse, *The People Next Door,* CBS, 1996.
Callain Pearson, *Murder in My Mind,* CBS, 1997.
Alexandra Elston, *Dead Husbands* (also known as *Last Man on the List*), USA Network, 1998.
Helen Chapel, *The Spiral Staircase* (also known as *Le secret du manoir*), Fox, 2000.
Donna Randal, *Deadly Betrayal* (also known as *Trahison mortelle*), Lifetime, 2002.
Eliza/Kate/Emily Winton, *Haven't We Met Before?* (also known as *Mary Higgins Clark's "Haven't We Met Before"* and *Mary Higgins Clark: Vous souvenez–vous?*), Ion, 2002.
Ann Culver, *Deadly Visions* (also known as *Possessed*), Lifetime, 2004.

Television Appearances; Specials:
Host from Hawaii, *CBS All–American Thanksgiving Day Parade,* CBS, 1987.
Battle of the Network Stars XIX, ABC, 1988.
Member of choir, *Voices that Care,* 1991.

The Knots Landing Block Party, 1993.

The Rich and Famous 1993 World's Best, 1993.

Tsunami Aid: A Concert of Hope, multiple networks, 2005.

Knots Landing Reunion: Together Again, CBS, 2005.

The Women of Desperate Housewives: The E! True Hollywood Story, E! Entertainment Television, 2005.

Keith Barry: Extraordinary, CBS, 2006.

Edie Britt (in archive footage), *Celebrity Debut,* ABC, 2006.

Television Appearances; Episodic:

"Murder on the Rocks," *Scene of the Crime,* NBC, 1985.

Lily, "Twenty–four Hours," *Paradise* (also known as *Guns of Paradise*), 1988.

Herself, "The Matchmaker," *The Larry Sanders Show,* HBO, 1997.

Eleanor, "New Wave," *The Legend of Tarzan* (also known as *Disney's "The Legend of Tarzan"*), 2001.

Voices of Darcy and Miss Moore, "Toys in the Hood," *Static Shock,* The WB, 2003.

Dr. Danielle Morty, "24," *Will & Grace,* NBC, 2003.

Anna, "A First Class Flight," *Becker,* CBS, 2003.

Edie Britt, "Philadelphia at Dallas," *NFL Monday Night Football* (also known as *ABC Monday Night Football* and *Monday Night Football*), ABC, 2004.

(In archive footage) *'80s,* 2005.

Edie Britt (in archive footage), *Las cinco caras de David LaChapelle,* 2006.

Punk'd, MTV, 2006.

(In archive footage) "Coses d'ahir I avui," *La rentadora,* 2006.

Television Appearances; Awards Presentations:

The 43rd Annual Primetime Emmy Awards Presentation, Fox, 1991.

Presenter, *The 48th Annual Golden Globe Awards,* TBS, 1991.

Presenter, *The 17th Annual CableACE Awards,* TNT, 1995.

Presenter, *The 62nd Annual Golden Globe Awards,* NBC, 2005.

11th Annual Screen Actors Guild Awards, TNT, 2005.

77th Annual Academy Awards—UK, Sky (England), 2005.

ESPY Awards, ESPN, 2005.

The 57th Annual Primetime Emmy Awards, CBS, 2005.

The 32nd Annual People's Choice Awards, CBS, 2006.

Presenter, *The 62nd Annual Golden Globe Awards,* NBC, 2006.

Presenter, *The 63rd Annual Golden Globe Awards,* NBC, 2006.

12th Annual Screen Actors Guild Awards, TBS, 2006.

Television Guest Appearances; Episodic:

The Tonight Show Starring Johnny Carson, NBC, 1990.

The Rosie O'Donnell Show, syndicated, 1996.

The Late Late Show with Craig Kilborn (also known as *The Late Late Show*), CBS, 2004.

The Oprah Winfrey Show (also known as *Oprah*), syndicated, 2004, 2005.

Live with Regis and Kelly, syndicated, multiple appearances, between 2004 and 2007.

The Tonight Show with Jay Leno, NBC, 2005.

Late Show with David Letterman, CBS, 2005.

The Tony Danza Show, syndicated, 2005.

Richard & Judy, Channel 4, 2005.

Rove Live, Ten Network, 2005.

The View, ABC, 2005, 2007.

Jimmy Kimmel Live, ABC, 2005, 2007.

Ellen: The Ellen DeGeneres Show, syndicated, 2005, 2007.

Late Night with Conan O'Brien, NBC, 2006.

Corazon de ..., 2006.

Entertainment Tonight (also known as *Entertainment This Week, E.T., ET Weekend,* and *This Week in Entertainment*), syndicated, 2007.

Television Appearances; Other:

(Uncredited) Paige Matheson, *Knots Landing: Back to the Cul–de–Sac* (miniseries), CBS, 1997.

Edie Britt, *Desperate Housewives* (pilot), ABC, 2004.

(In archive footage) *Retrosexual: The 80's* (miniseries), VH1, 2004.

Film Appearances:

Title role, *The Sure Thing,* Embassy, 1985.

Herself, *Dirty Tennis,* 1989.

Brooke Ashton/Vicki, *Noises Off,* Buena Vista, 1992.

Veronique Ukrinsky, Agent 3.14, *Spy Hard,* Buena Vista, 1996.

Allison Page/Sally Jones, *Beverly Hills Ninja,* TriStar, 1997.

Ballroom woman, *I Woke Up Early the Day I Died* (also known as *Ed Wood's "I Woke Up Early the Day I Died"* and *I Awoke Early the Day I Died*), Cinequanon Pictures, 1998.

Izabel Sauvestre, *Raw Nerve,* York Entertainment, 1999.

Misty Brummel, *.com for Murder,* Omega Entertainment, 2001.

Voice of Eleanor, *Tarzan & Jane* (animated), Buena Vista Home Video, 2002.

Carrie, *Lost Treasure,* Blockbuster Video, 2003.

Voice of white cat, *The Karate Dog,* Paradise Group, 2004.

Diane, *Code Name: The Cleaner,* New Line Cinema, 2007.

Nadia, *Fly Me to the Moon,* nWave Pictures/Illuminata Pictures, 2007.

RECORDINGS

Videos:

Appeared in the music video "Voices that Care."

OTHER SOURCES

Periodicals:
Parade, December 24, 2006, p. 16.
Sly, January, 2006, pp. 54–63.

SHORTHOUSE, Dame Edith
    See CRAWFORD, Michael

SIMMONS, Richard 1948–

PERSONAL

Full name, Richard Milton Teagle Simmons; born July 12, 1948, in New Orleans, LA; son of Leonard (a dancer) and Shirley (a dancer) Simmons. *Education:* Studied art in Florence, Italy. *Avocational Interests:* Collecting art dolls and art glass.

Addresses: *Office*—Slimmons, 9306 Santa Monica Blvd., Beverly Hills, CA 90210. *Agent*—(voice work and commercials) Tim Curtis, William Morris Agency, 1 William Morris Pl., Beverly Hills, CA 90212. *Manager*—Celebrities Plus, 8899 Beverly Blvd., Suite 500, Los Angeles, CA 90048.

Career: Physical fitness specialist, television personality, producer, and writer. Anatomy Asylum, Beverly Hills, CA, founder, 1975; Slimmons (workout studio), founder and aerobics teacher; Ruffage (health food restaurant), founder, 1975; Reach Foundation (fitness centers for the disabled), founder; owner of a national chain of exercise salons; creator of Deal–a–Meal Food Plan; inventor of Deal–a–Meal and FoodMover devices; Carnival Cruise Lines, leader of weight–loss cruises; appeared in commercials for Fruit of the Loom apparel, 1996, Sprint telecommunications, 2000, and other products. Worked for Coty Cosmetics, beginning 1971; also worked as a maitre d' at Derrick's restaurant, Los Angeles.

Awards, Honors: Emmy Award nomination, 1981, for *The Richard Simmons Show.*

CREDITS

Television Appearances:
Himself, *General Hospital,* ABC, 1979.
Host, *The Richard Simmons Show,* syndicated, 1980–84.
Host, *Here's Richard,* 1982.
Host, *Richard Simmons Slim Cooking,* 1987.
Voice of Physedipus, *Hercules* (animated; also known as *Disney's "Hercules"*), ABC and syndicated, 1998.
Host, *DreamMaker* (also known as *Richard Simmons' "DreamMaker"*), syndicated, 1999.

Television Appearances; Specials:
All Star Salute to Mother's Day, 1981.
Anne Murray's Caribbean Cruise, 1983.
Birthing coach, *From Here to Maternity,* Cinemax, 1985.
What're My True Colors?, 1987.
Host, *Value Television,* 1987.
Circus of the Stars #12, CBS, 1987.
Circus of the Stars #15, CBS, 1990.
Circus of the Stars and Sideshow (also known as *Circus of the Stars #17*), CBS, 1992.
Regis Philbin: Made for TV, 1998.
Richard Simmons: The E! True Hollywood Story, E! Entertainment Television, 2000.
"Richard Simmons: Fit for Life," *Biography,* Arts and Entertainment, 2001.
Big Fat Documentary (also known as *Victoria Wood's "Big Fat Documentary"*), BBC, 2004.
Half Ton Man, Channel 4, 2005.

Television Appearances; Episodic:
Assistant, *All American Ultra Quiz,* NBC, 1981.
Himself, "Meet the New Guy," *CHiPs* (also known as *CHiPs Patrol*), 1982.
Himself, "Teachers," *Fame,* syndicated, c. 1983.
Himself, "Remote Control Man," *Amazing Stories* (also known as *Steven Spielberg's "Amazing Stories"*), 1985.
Super Password, 1986.
Fame, Fortune & Romance, 1986.
The Match Game (also known as *Match Game '90*), 1990.
Himself, "Harlan Deals–a–Meal," *Evening Shade,* 1992.
Himself, "The Warmth Episode," *The Larry Sanders Show,* HBO, 1992.
Voice of Richard Simmons dinosaur, "Nature Calls," *Dinosaurs* (animated), ABC, 1992.
Aerobics instructor, "No Pain, No Gain/Who Gives a Buck?," *Rocko's Modern Life,* 1993.
Hi–Octane, Comedy Central, 1995.
Panelist, *Figure It Out* (also known as *Figure It Out: Family Style* and *Figure It Out: Wild Style*), 1999.
Whose Line Is It Anyway? (also known as *Whose Line?* and *W.L.I.A.*), ABC, 2003.
Himself, "Bringing Up Buster," *Arrested Development,* Fox, 2003.
Voice, "Get Shovelized/T Is for Trouble," *Johnny Bravo* (animated), Cartoon Network, 2004.
(In archive footage) *CMT Insider,* Country Music Television, 2006.
(In archive footage) *20 to 1,* Nine Network, 2006.

Panelist on the series *Body Language,* CBS; also appeared in episode of *Real People.*

Television Guest Appearances; Episodic:
The Tonight Show Starring Johnny Carson, NBC, 1981.
The New Hollywood Squares, 1986, 1987, 1988.
The Howard Stern Show, syndicated, 1990, 1991, 1992.
Saturday Night Live (also known as *NBC's Saturday Night* and *SNL*), NBC, 1994.
The Late Show with David Letterman (also known as *The Late Show*), CBS, multiple appearances, between 1994 and 2006.
The Tonight Show with Jay Leno, NBC, 1995, 2000.
Howard Stern, 1996, 1999.
The Rosie O'Donnell Show, syndicated, multiple appearances, between 1996 and 2001.
The Howard Stern Radio Show, 1999.
Hollywood Squares (also known as *H2* and *H2: Hollywood Squares*), syndicated, 1999, 2001, 2003.
SoapTalk, Soap Network, 2004.
On–Air with Ryan Seacrest, syndicated, 2004.
Martha, syndicated, 2005.
The Tony Danza Show, syndicated, 2005, 2006.
Your World w/ Neil Cavuto, Fox News Channel, 2006.
Ellen: The Ellen DeGeneres Show, syndicated, 2006.
The Megan Mullally Show, syndicated, 2006.
"Richard Simmons," *Howard Stern on Demand* (also known as *Howard TV on Demand*), 2006.
"Richard Simmons Cries," *Howard Stern on Demand* (also known as *Howard TV on Demand*), 2007.

Also appeared as guest on talk shows hosted by Phil Donahue, Mike Douglas, Merv Griffin, and Charlie Rose.

Television Appearances; Pilots:
Host, *Here's Richard,* syndicated, 1982.

Television Work; Series:
Coproducer, *Richard Simmons Slim Cooking,* 1987.
Co–executive producer, *DreamMaker* (also known as *Richard Simmons' "DreamMaker"*), syndicated, 1999.

Film Appearances:
Cameo appearances, *Satyricon,* 1969.
Cameo appearance, *The Crowns,* 1970.
Himself on television, *In & Out,* Paramount, 1997.
Voice of Boone, *Rudolph the Red–Nosed Reindeer: The Movie* (animated), Legacy Releasing, 1998.
(Uncredited) Himself, *What Women Want,* 2000.

RECORDINGS

Videos:
Richard Simmons: Get Started, 1985.

Richard Simmons and the Silver Foxes (also known as *Richard Simmons and the Silver Foxes: Fitness for Senior Citizens*), 1986.
(And producer) *Sweatin' to the Oldies,* 1988.
(And executive producer) *Sweatin' to the Classics,* 1991.
(And producer) *Sweat & Shout: An Aerobic Workout,* 1992.
(And producer) *Sweatin' to the Oldies 2,* 1992.
Richard Simmons—Sweat & Shout: An Aerobic Workout, 1994.
(And producer) *Sweatin' to the Oldies 3,* 1995.
(And producer) *Disco Sweat,* 1995.
Tone and Sweat, 1998.
Love to Stretch, 1998.
Farewell to Fat, 1998.
Tonin' Uptown/Tonin' Downtown, 1998.
Voice of Physedipus, *Hercules: Zero to Hero* (animated), 1999.
The Silver Foxes 2: Shape Up America, 2001.

More than fifty other exercise videos include *Blast Off the Pounds, Dance Your Pants Off, Platinum Sweat, Sit Tight,* and *Sweatin' to the Oldies 4.*

Audio Books:
Narrator, *Never Give Up: Inspirations, Reflections, Stories of Hope,* Audio Renaissance, 1993.

Albums:
Reach, Elektra, 1982.
Vocalist for the song "It's the Most Flattering Time of the Year," Bob Rivers, *Twisted Christmas,* 1997.

WRITINGS

(With Suzy Kalter) *Richard Simmons' Never–Say–Diet Book,* Warner Books, 1980.
Richard Simmons' Better Body Book, Warner Books, 1983.
Reach for Fitness: A Special Book of Exercises for the Physically Challenged, Warner Books, 1986.
(With Winifred Morice) *Deal–a–Meal Cook Book,* Deal–a–Meal (Beverly Hills, CA), 1987.
Richard Simmons' Never Give Up: Inspirations, Reflections, Stories of Hope, Warner Books, 1993.
(With Morice) *Richard Simmons' Farewell to Fat Cookbook: Homemade in the USA,* photographs by Ed Ouellette, GT Publishing, 1996.
Sweetie Pie: The Richard Simmons Private Collection of Dazzling Desserts, GT Publishing, 1997.
FoodMover Cookbook, GT Merchandising and Licensing, 1999.
Still Hungry After All These Years: My Story (autobiography), GT Publishing, 1999.
Richard Simmons Cookin' on Broadway, edited by Lynn Hamlin, GT Merchandising and Licensing, 2000.

Author of "Simmons Says," a column in *Soap Opera Digest,* beginning in 1981. Contributor to periodicals.

OTHER SOURCES

Books:

Simmons, Richard, *Still Hungry After All These Years: My Story,* General Publishing, 1999.

Periodicals:

Los Angeles Times, May 11, 2000.

Electronic:

Richard Simmons Official Site, http://www. richardsimmons.com, August 11, 2007.

SINGER, Marc 1948–

PERSONAL

Born January 29, 1948, in Vancouver, British Columbia, Canada; son of Jacques (a symphony conductor) and Leslie (a concert pianist) Singer; brother of Lori Singer (an actress and cellist); cousin of Bryan Singer (a film director, producer, and screenwriter); married Haunani Minn (an actress). *Education:* Attended Indiana University and other schools; studied acting and martial arts. *Avocational Interests:* Boxing, martial arts, motorcycling, playing the piano, running, sailing, skiing.

Addresses: *Agent*—David Shapira & Associates, 193 North Robertson Blvd., Beverly Hills, CA 90211.

Career: Actor. Participant at entertainment industry conventions.

CREDITS

Film Appearances:

Captain Al Olivetti, *Go Tell the Spartans,* Avco–Embassy, 1978.

Dar (title role), *The Beastmaster* (also known as *Beastmaster—Der Befreier, Dar l'invincible, El senor de las bestias, Kaan principe guerriero, Kungasonen, O guerreiro sagrado, Varvos mahitis, Voittamaton kostaja,* and *Wladca zwierzat*), Metro–Goldwyn–Mayer, 1982.

Tom Sullivan, *If You Could See What I Hear* (also known as *Au–dela du regard*), Jensen Farley Pictures, 1982.

Kenny Landruff, *Born to Race,* Metro–Goldwyn–Mayer/United Artists, 1987.

Paul Ferguson, *Watchers II* (also known as *Alterazione genetica II, Ihmisjahti,* and *Watchers II—Augen des Terrors*), Concorde Pictures, 1990.

Tom Redding, *Body Chemistry,* Columbia/TriStar, 1990.

Von Kraut, *A Man Called Sarge,* Cannon, 1990.

Dar (the beastmaster), *Beastmaster 2: Through the Portal of Time* (also known as *Beastmaster 2—Der Zeitspringer, Beastmaster 2—genom tidsbarriaeren, Beastmaster 2—petojen herra, Dar l'invincible 2—La puerta del tiempo, En senor de las bestias 2: La puerta del tiempo, O portal do tempo,* and *Wladca zwierzat 2*), New Line Cinema, 1991.

Ken Strom, *In the Cold of the Night,* Omega Entertainment, 1991.

Krieger, *Dead Space* (also known as *DeadSpace*), Concorde Pictures, 1991.

Harry Spangler, *The Berlin Conspiracy* (also known as *Complotto a Berlino, Conspiracion en Berlin, Die Berlin–Verschwoerung,* and *Iskuryhmae Berliini*), Concorde–New Horizons, 1992.

Jonathan Sullivan, *Ultimate Desires* (also known as *Beyond the Silhouette*), 1992.

Steve Cotton, *Sweet Justice* (also known as *Killer Instincts*), 1992.

Baker, *Silk Degrees* (also known as *Target Witness*), New City Releasing, 1994.

Voice of Adam, *Animated Stories from the Bible: Music Video—Volume 1* (animated), 1994.

Jack Ford, *Droid Gunner* (also known as *Cyberzone, Cyber Zone,* and *Phoenix 2*), New Horizon Picture Corporation, 1995.

Peter Starky, *Victim of Desire* (also known as *Implicated*), Concorde–New Horizons, 1995.

Dar (the beastmaster), *Beastmaster: The Eye of Braxus* (also known as *Beastmaster III, Beastmaster III: The Eye of Braxus, Beastmaster—Das Auge des Braxus, Beastmaster—L'occhio di Braxus, Dar l'invincible III—l'oeil de Braxus, En senor de las bestias 3. El ojo de Braxus, O varvaros mahitis epistrefei,* and *Wladca zwierzat 3*), MCA Home Entertainment, 1996.

Mike Justus, *Street Corner Justice,* New City Releasing, 1996.

Lancelot du Lac (title role), *Lancelot: Guardian of Time* (also known as *Lancelot, guardian del tiempo*), Alpine Pictures, 1997.

Sam Steele, *L.A.P.D.: To Protect and to Serve* (also known as *LAPD, LAPD Conspiracy, Die Todesengel von L.A., LAPD: Policia de Los Angeles,* and *Policia de Los Angeles—Corrupcion total*), Fries Film Group, 2001.

Dr. Martin Gites, *Angel Blade* (also known as *Forbidden Angel*), Vegas Knights Film Productions, 2002.

Himself, *UnConventional* (documentary), Revolution Earth Productions, 2004.

Television Appearances; Series:

Johnny Captor, *The Contender,* CBS, 1980.

Mike Donovan, *V* (also known as *V: The Series*) NBC, 1984–85.

The Quest for Power, beginning 1988.

Chet, *The Young and the Restless* (also known as *Y&R, The Innocent Years, Atithasa niata, Les feux de l'amour, Schatten der Leidenschaft,* and *Tunteita ja tuoksuja*), CBS, c. 1998–99.

Dartunus, *BeastMaster* (also known as *BeastMaster—Herr der Wildnis, BeastMaster, le dernier des survivants,* and *O arhontas ton zoon*), syndicated, 2001–2002.

Television Appearances; Miniseries:

Ross Savitch, *Harold Robbins' "79 Park Avenue"* (also known as *79 Park Avenue*), NBC, 1977.

Andy Warner, *Roots: The Next Generations* (also known as *Racines 2, Raices: Las siguientes generaciones,* and *Roots—Die naechsten Generationen*), ABC, 1979.

Mike Donovan, *V* (also known as *V: The Original Miniseries*), NBC, 1983.

Mike Donovan, *V: The Final Battle,* NBC, 1984.

Mike Donavan, *V: The Second Generation,* NBC, 2008.

Television Appearances; Movies:

(Uncredited) Young television doctor, *Columbo: Double Shock,* CBS, 1973.

Andy Gerlach, *Things in Their Season,* CBS, 1974.

David Hartman, *Journey from Darkness,* NBC, 1975.

John Cappelletti, *Something for Joey,* CBS, 1977.

Jason Cole, *Sergeant Matlovich vs. the U.S. Air Force,* NBC, 1978.

David Reynolds, *The Two Worlds of Jennie Logan,* CBS, 1979.

Dalton, *Forgotten City of the Planet of the Apes* (also known as *The Forgotten City of the Planet of the Apes;* consists of *Planet of the Apes* episodes combined and re–edited as a television movie), c. 1981.

Stan Novak, *For Ladies Only* (also known as *Club Max*), NBC, 1981.

Mark Rogers, *Her Life as a Man,* NBC, 1984.

Bruce, *Shades of Love: Indigo Autumn,* [Canada], 1987.

Brad Mueller, *High Desert Kill,* USA Network, 1989.

Dan Turner, *Dan Turner, Hollywood Detective* (also known as *The Raven Red Kiss–Off*), syndicated, 1990.

Jake Kellogg, *Deadly Game,* USA Network, 1991.

Johnson, *The Sea Wolf* (also known as *Der Seewolf, El lobo de mar, La nave fantasma, Le loup de mers, Merisusi,* and *O lobo do mar*), TNT, 1993.

Ziegfield von Trotta, *Savate* (also known as *The Fighter*), HBO, 1995.

Reese Williams, *Determination of Death* (also known as *Disparition programmee, Halalos elszantsag, La desaparicion de risk, Morte suspeita, Resolu a mourir, Seguro de morte,* and *Tod auf Abruf*), Lifetime, 2001.

Curt Seavers, *Snowman's Pass* (also known as *What Lies Above, Ascenso mortal, Desfiladeiro da morte,* and *Traque en haute montagne*), Lifetime, 2004.

Captain Varney, *Lesser Evil,* Lifetime, 2006.

Television Appearances; Specials:

Christian de Neuvillette, "Cyrano de Bergerac," *Great Performances,* PBS, 1974.

Petruchio, "The Taming of the Shrew" (also known as "La fierecilla domada"), *Great Performances,* PBS, 1976.

NBC team member, *Battle of the Network Stars XVII* (also known as *Battle of the Network Stars*), ABC, 1984.

Himself, *Re–Decision 2003: The California Recall,* Comedy Central, 2003.

Television Appearances; Episodic:

Dalton, "The Gladiators," *Planet of the Apes* (also known as *A majmok bolygoja, Apinoiden planeetta, Apornas planet, El planeta de los simios, La planete des singes,* and *Planet der Affen*), CBS, 1974.

"No Place to Hide," *Nakia,* ABC, 1974.

Feather Tanner, "Trap Play," *Barnaby Jones,* CBS, 1975.

Jeff Heywood, "Target? The Lady," *Hawaii Five–O* (also known as *McGarrett*), CBS, 1975.

Randy, "Bomb, Bomb, Who's Got the Bomb?," *Hawaii Five–O* (also known as *McGarrett*), CBS, 1975.

Tally Morgan, "The Price of Terror," *Barnaby Jones,* CBS, 1975.

Blair Winfield, "Journey to Oblivion," *The Rookies,* ABC, 1976.

Wade Bedell, "Death at the Party," *Jigsaw John,* NBC, 1976.

Wade Bedell, "Eclipse," *Jigsaw John,* NBC, 1976.

Wade Bedell, "Homicide 96403: John Smith," *Jigsaw John,* NBC, 1976.

Wade Bedell, "The Mourning Line," *Jigsaw John,* NBC, 1976.

"Escape," *Visions,* PBS, 1978.

Himself, *Just Men!,* NBC, 1983.

John Neary, "My Mother, My Chaperone/The Present/The Death and Life of Sir Alfred Demerest/Welcome Aboard: Parts 1 & 2," *The Love Boat,* ABC, 1984.

Matt Cantrell, "The Deadly Game," *Dallas* (also known as *Oil*), CBS, 1986.

Matt Cantrell, "Missing," *Dallas* (also known as *Oil*), CBS, 1986.

Lieutenant commander Tom Hardison, "Past Tense," *Hotel* (also known as *Arthur Hailey's "Hotel"*), ABC, 1987.

Monty Hanks and Ed Harrier, "Extra Innings," *The Twilight Zone,* CBS, 1988.

Ray McGuinness, "Love Song of Abigail Marsh," *Simon & Simon,* CBS, 1988.

Rick Barton (some sources cite role as Rick Banner), "The Search for Peter Kerry," *Murder, She Wrote,* CBS, 1989.

Robert Lewis, "Code Liz," *The Hitchhiker* (also known as *Deadly Nightmares* and *Le voyageur*), USA Network, 1989.

Caleb Cole, "Mountain Man," *Highlander* (also known as *Highlander: The Series*), syndicated, 1992.

Commander Trask, "The Long Rain," *The Ray Bradbury Theater* (also known as *The Bradbury Trilogy, Mystery Theatre, Ray Bradbury Theater, Le monde fantastique de Ray Bradbury,* and *Ray Bradbury presente*), HBO, 1992.

Voices of Dr. Kirk Langstrom and Man–Bat, "On Leather Wings," *Batman* (animated; also known as *The Adventures of Batman & Robin* and *Batman: The Animated Series*), Fox, 1992.

Voices of Dr. Kirk Langstrom and Man–Bat, "Terror in the Sky," *Batman* (animated; also known as *The Adventures of Batman & Robin* and *Batman: The Animated Series*), Fox, 1992.

Voices of Dr. Kirk Langstrom and Man–Bat, "Tyger Tyger," *Batman* (animated; also known as *The Adventures of Batman & Robin* and *Batman: The Animated Series*), Fox, 1992.

Caleb Cole, "The Watchers," *Highlander* (also known as *Highlander: The Series*), syndicated, 1993.

Bruce Waller, "Gun Play: Parts 1 & 2," *Sirens,* syndicated, 1994.

Voice of Mitchell Stramm, "AMOK," *The Real Adventures of Jonny Quest* (animated; also known as *Jonny Quest: The Real Adventures*), TBS, Cartoon Network, and syndicated, 1996.

Voice of Montague, "The Alchemist," *The Real Adventures of Jonny Quest* (animated; also known as *Jonny Quest: The Real Adventures*), TBS, Cartoon Network, and syndicated, 1996.

Bob, "Honey, It's Doomsday," *Honey, I Shrunk the Kids: The TV Show* (also known as *Disney's "Honey, I Shrunk the Kids: The TV Show"* and *Honey, I Shrunk the Kids*), syndicated, 1998.

Himself, *The Daily Show* (also known as *The Daily Show with Jon Stewart, The Daily Show with Jon Stewart Global Edition, Ha–Daily Show,* and *I satira tou Jon Stewart*), Comedy Central, 2003.

Voice of Kirk Manlord, "Bonafide Hero: Captain Duck Dodgers," *Duck Dodgers* (animated; also known as *Duck Dodgers in the 24 1/2th Century*), Cartoon Network, 2005.

(In archive footage) Mike Donovan, *La imagen de tu vida,* Television Espanola (TVE, Spain), 2006.

Television Appearances; Pilots:

Tim Donahue, *Never Con a Killer* (also known as *The Feather & Father Gang*), ABC, 1977.

Wesley Miles, *Paper Dolls,* ABC, 1982.

Stage Appearances:

Christian de Neuvillette, *Cyrano de Bergerac,* American Conservatory Theater (ACT), San Francisco, CA, beginning c. 1974.

Petruchio, *The Taming of the Shrew,* American Conservatory Theater (ACT), 1975.

Appeared in regional theatre and summer stock productions.

RECORDINGS

Videos:

Himself and Dar (the beastmaster), *The Making of "Beastmaster 2: Through the Portal of Time"* (short), Republic Pictures Home Video, 1991.

Himself, *The Saga of "The Beastmaster,"* Anchor Bay Entertainment, 2005.

Working with a Master: Don Coscarelli (short), Anchor Bay Entertainment, 2006.

Video Work:

Footage work, *The Saga of "The Beastmaster,"* Anchor Bay Entertainment, 2005.

OTHER SOURCES

Periodicals:
Starlog, July, 1984, pp. 24–25, 95.

Electronic:
Marc Singer.com, http://www.marc-singer.com, June 18, 2007.

SODERBERGH, Steven 1963–
(Peter Andrews, Mary Ann Bernard, Sam Lowry)

PERSONAL

Full name, Steven Andrew Soderbergh; born January 14, 1963, in Atlanta, GA; son of Peter Andrew (a university professor and administrator) and Mary Ann (maiden name, Bernard) Soderbergh; married Elizabeth Jeanne "Betsy" Brantley (an actress), December 1, 1989 (divorced, October, 1994); married Jules Asner (a model and television reporter), May 10, 2003; children: (first marriage) Sarah. *Politics:* Democrat.

Addresses: *Agent*—International Creative Management, 10250 Constellation Way, 9th Floor, Los Angeles, CA 90067.

Career: Producer, director, writer, cinematographer, film and sound editor, and composer. Section Eight (production company), founder (with George Clooney),

1999, co–owner, 1999–2006. Member of jury, Sundance Film Festival, 1990, and Cannes International Film Festival, 2003. Provided director's commentaries for DVD releases of several of his films. Once worked at a video production house and as a video director for local bands, both in Louisiana, early 1980s.

Member: Academy of Motion Picture Arts and Sciences, Directors Guild of America (national vice president, beginning 2002).

Awards, Honors: Grammy Award nomination (with others), best long–form music video, National Academy of Recording Arts and Sciences, 1987, for *9012 Live;* Audience Award and nomination for grand jury prize, both dramatic category, Sundance Film Festival, 1989, Golden Palm and FIPRESCI Prize, best feature–length film, Cannes International Film Festival, Independent Spirit Award, best director, Independent Features Project West, Academy Award nomination, best original screenplay, Golden Globe Award nomination, best screenplay for a motion picture, Writers Guild Award nomination, best original screenplay, Film Award nomination, best original screenplay, British Academy of Film and Television Arts, and Cesar Award nomination, best foreign film, Academie des Arts et Techniques du Cinema, 1990, all for *Sex, Lies, and Videotape;* nomination for Golden Palm, Cannes International Film Festival, 1993, for *King of the Hill;* Golden Satellite Award nomination (with others), best comedy or musical motion picture, International Press Academy, 1999, for *Pleasantville;* National Society of Film Critics Award, best director, 1999, for *Out of Sight;* Independent Spirit Award nomination, best director, 2000, for *The Limey;* directing awards include Toronto Film Critics Association Award, 2000, Phoenix Film Critics Society Award, 2000, Academy Award, Golden Globe Award nomination, Directors Guild of America Award nomination, Golden Satellite Award, Southeastern Film Critics Association Award, Chicago Film Critics Association Award, Dallas–Fort Worth Film Critics Association Award, Kansas City Film Critics Circle Award, Vancouver Film Critics Circle Award, nomination for silver ribbon, best director of a foreign film, Italian National Syndicate of Film Journalists, and Online Film Critics Society Award nomination, all 2001, and Kinema Junpo Award, best foreign language film director, and Empire Award nomination, both 2002, cinematography awards include Golden Satellite Award nomination, Best Cinematography Award nomination, British Society of Cinematographers, Chicago Film Critics Association Award nomination, and Online Film Critics Society Award nominations, all 2001, nomination for Golden Berlin Bear, Berlin International Film Festival, 2001, Amanda Award nomination, best foreign feature film, 2001, Cesar Award nomination, best foreign film, 2002, Bodil Award nomination, best American film, 2002, and Kinema Junpo Award, best foreign language film, 2002, all for *Traffic;* Screen

International Award nomination, U.S. category, European Film Awards, 2000, Amanda Award nomination, best foreign feature film, 2000, and Academy Award nomination, London Film Critics Circle Award nomination, Golden Globe Award nomination, Directors Guild of America Award nomination, and Golden Satellite Award nomination, all best director, all 2001, for *Erin Brockovich;* Sierra Award, Las Vegas Film Critics Society, National Board of Review Award, New York Film Critics Circle Award, and Los Angeles Film Critics Association Award, 2000, and National Society of Film Critics Award, Broadcast Film Critics Association Award, and Florida Film Critics Circle Award, all best director, and nomination for David Lean Award for Direction, British Academy of Film and Television Arts, all 2001, for both *Traffic* and *Erin Brockovich;* nomination for Golden Berlin Bear, 2003, for *Solaris;* Cesar Award nomination, best foreign film, and Empire Award nomination, best director, both 2003, for *Ocean's Eleven;* National Board of Review Award and Golden Globe Award nomination, both best picture, 2005, for *Good Night, and Good Luck;* nomination for Golden Berlin Bear, 2007, for *The Good German;* Independent Spirit Award nomination, best director, 2007, for *Bubble.*

CREDITS

Film Director:
Winston (short film), 1987.
(And film editor and uncredited sound editor) *Sex, Lies, and Videotape* (also known as *Sex, Lies …*), Miramax, 1989.
(And film editor) *Kafka,* Miramax, 1991.
(And film editor) *King of the Hill,* Gramercy, 1993.
Underneath, Gramercy, 1995.
Gray's Anatomy, 1996, Northern Arts Entertainment, 1997.
(And film editor and uncredited cinematographer) *Schizopolis* (also known as *Steven Soderbergh's "Schizopolis"*), Universal, 1996.
Out of Sight, Universal, 1998.
The Limey, Artisan Entertainment, 1999.
Erin Brockovich, Universal, 2000.
(And cinematographer, as Peter Andrews) *Traffic* (also known as *Traffic—Die Macht des kartells*), USA Films, 2000.
(And cinematographer, as Andrews) *Ocean's Eleven* (also known as *11* and *O11*), Warner Bros., 2001.
(And cinematographer, as Andrews) *Full Frontal,* Miramax, 2002.
(And cinematographer, as Andrews; and film editor, as Mary Ann Bernard) *Solaris,* Twentieth Century–Fox, 2002.
(And cinematographer, as Andrews) *Ocean's Twelve,* Warner Bros., 2004.
(And cinematographer, as Andrews; and film editor, as Bernard) "Equilibrium," *Eros,* Warner Independent Pictures, 2005.

(And cinematographer, as Andrews; and film editor, as Bernard) *Bubble,* Magnolia Pictures, 2006.

(And producer; and cinematographer, as Andrews; and film editor, as Bernard) *The Good German,* Warner Bros., 2006.

(And executive producer; and cinematographer, as Andrews) *Ocean's Thirteen* (also known as *13*), Warner Bros., 2007.

Film Executive Producer:

Suture, Samuel Goldwyn, 1993.

Insomnia, Warner Bros., 2002.

Far from Heaven (also known as *Loin du paradis*), Focus Features, 2002.

Naqoyqatsi (documentary; also known as *Naqoyqatsi: Life as War*), Miramax, 2002.

Confessions of a Dangerous Mind (also known as *Confessions d'un homme dangereux*), Miramax, 2002.

Able Edwards, 2004, Heretic Films, 2007.

Keane, Magnolia Pictures, 2005.

Symbiopsychotaxiplasm: Take 2 ½, 2005.

Good Night, and Good Luck, Warner Independent Pictures, 2005.

Syriana, Warner Bros., 2005.

Rumor Has It …, Warner Bros., 2005.

A Scanner Darkly (animated), Warner Independent Pictures, 2006.

The Half Life of Timofey Berezin, Picturehouse Entertainment, 2006.

Wind Chill, TriStar, 2007.

Michael Clayton, Warner Bros., 2007.

Leatherheads, Universal, 2007.

Film Producer:

The Daytrippers (also known as *En route vers Manhattan*), 1996, Cinepix Film Properties, 1997.

Pleasantville, New Line Cinema, 1998.

Welcome to Collinwood (also known as *Safecrackers oder diebe haben's schwer*), Warner Bros., 2002.

Criminal, Warner Independent Pictures, 2004.

The Jacket, Warner Independent Pictures, 2005.

Film Appearances:

(Uncredited) Smoking guy at concert, *The Underneath,* Gramercy, 1995.

(Uncredited) Fletcher Munson/Dr. Jeffrey Korchek, *Schizopolis* (also known as *Steven Soderbergh's "Schizopolis"*), Universal, 1996.

Interviewee on television, *Waking Life,* Fox Searchlight, 2001.

(Uncredited) Vault–bombing thief, *Ocean's Eleven* (also known as *11* and *O11*), Warner Bros., 2001.

Man reflected in digital screens, *Naqoyqatsi* (documentary; also known as *Naqoyqatsi: Life as War*), Miramax, 2002.

(Uncredited) *Full Frontal,* Miramax, 2002.

Television Executive Producer; Series:

(And film editor) *K Street,* HBO, 2003.

Unscripted, HBO, 2005.

Television Executive Producer; Specials:

Who Is Bernard Tapie?, 2001.

Tribute (also known as *Tribute: A Rockumentary*), Showtime, 2001.

Television Director; Episodic:

"The Quiet Room," *Fallen Angels,* Showtime, 1993.

Television Work; Other:

Film editor, *Games People Play* (series), 1981.

Television Appearances; Specials:

Independent's Day, Sundance Channel, 1998.

Lesley Ann Warren: A Cinderella Story (also known as *Celebrity: Lesley Ann Warren*), 2000.

Spotlight on Location: Erin Brockovich (also known as *The Making of "Erin Brockovich"*), 2000.

Inside Traffic: The Making of "Traffic," 2000.

"The Making of 'Ocean's Eleven,'" *HBO First Look,* HBO, 2001.

"Inside 'Solaris,'" *HBO First Look,* HBO, 2002.

Intimate Portrait: Erin Brockovich, Lifetime, 2003.

"The Making of 'Ocean's Twelve,'" *HBO First Look,* HBO, 2004.

Bleep! Censoring Hollywood, AMC, 2005.

"Ocean's Thirteen" *HBO First Look,* HBO, 2007.

Television Appearances; Awards Presentations:

The 73rd Annual Academy Awards, ABC, 2001.

Presenter, *The 2006 Gotham Awards,* 2006.

Television Appearances; Episodic:

American Cinema, 1995.

+ de cinema, 2002.

Sen kvaell med Luuk, 2003.

MovieReal, Arts and Entertainment, 2004.

(In archive footage) *Cinema mil,* 2005.

20 heures le journal, 2007.

Stage Director:

Geniuses, Swine Palace Productions, Baton Rouge, LA, 1996.

RECORDINGS

Videos:

Director, *9012 Live* (concert performance; also known as *Yes: 9012 Live*), 1986.

Inside "Out of Sight," Universal Studios Home Video, 1998.

Day for Night: The Making of "Insomnia," Warner Home Video, 2002.

"Ocean's Eleven:" The Look of the Con, Warner Home Video, 2002.

"Solaris:" Behind the Planet, Twentieth Century–Fox Home Entertainment, 2003.

Five Directors on "The Battle of Algiers," Criterion Collection, 2004.

WRITINGS

Screenplays:
Winston (short film), 1987.

Sex, Lies, and Videotape (also known as *Sex, Lies ...),* Miramax, 1989, published with journal, Harper (New York City), 1990.

King of the Hill, Gramercy, 1993.

(As Sam Lowry) *The Underneath,* Gramercy, 1995.

(And uncredited composer) *Schizopolis* (also known as *Steven Soderbergh's "Schizopolis"),* Universal, 1996.

Nightwatch, Miramax/Dimension Films, 1998.

Solaris, Twentieth Century–Fox, 2002.

(As Sam Lowry) *Criminal,* Warner Independent Pictures, 2004.

"Equilibrium," Eros, Warner Independent Pictures, 2005.

Leatherheads, Universal, 2007.

Television Episodes:
K Street, HBO, 2003.

Books:
(With Richard Lester) *Getting Away with It: or, The Further Adventures of the Luckiest Bastard You Ever Saw,* Faber, 1999.

OTHER SOURCES

Books:
Authors and Artists for Young Adults, Volume 43, Gale, 2002.

Encyclopedia of World Biography Supplement, Volume 25, Gale, 2005.

International Dictionary of Films and Filmmakers, Volume 2: *Directors,* St. James Press, 4th edition, 2000.

Newsmakers, Issue 4, Gale, 2001.

Periodicals:
Entertainment Weekly, February 23, 2001, p. 105; March 2, 2001, p. 20; November 15, 2002, pp. 43–50.

Film Comment, July–August, 1989, pp. 22–28; January, 2001, pp. 26–31.

Interview, July, 1998, p. 60.

Los Angeles, January, 2001, p. 82.

Madison, September, 1999, pp. 126–129.

Movieline, December, 2000, pp. 62–66, 118; December, 2001, pp. 50–62.

Newsweek, January 8, 2001, p. 62.

New York Times, July 23, 1989.

New York Times Magazine, November 3, 1991, pp. 34–40, 83.

Rolling Stone, April 12, 2001, pp. 120–122, 152.

Time, January 8, 2001, p. 62.

SOLO, Jay
  See ELLISON, Harlan

SOMERS, Suzanne 1946–
  (Susane Somers, Suzy Somers)

PERSONAL

Full name, Suzanne Marie Somers; born October 16, 1946, in San Bruno, CA; daughter of Francis (a gardener and laborer) and Marion Elizabeth (a medical secretary; maiden name, Turner) Mahoney; married Bruce Somers, April 14, 1965 (divorced, c. 1967); married Alan Hamel (an actor, producer, and business manager), November 11, 1977; children: (first marriage) Bruce (a television commercial director); (second marriage; stepchildren) Stephen (a film producer), Leslie. *Education:* Attended San Francisco College for Women; trained for the stage with Charles Conrad. *Religion:* Roman Catholic. *Avocational Interests:* Gourmet cooking.

Addresses: *Agent*—Michael Pick, MPI Talent Agency, 9255 West Sunset Blvd., Suite 407, Los Angeles, CA 90069.

Career: Actress, producer, and singer. Worked as fashion model and television commercial actress; spokesperson for jewelry and other products on Home Shopping Network; Body Solutions, spokesperson for exercise equipment, including ThighMaster, and for FaceMaster, Torso Track, and Somersize products. Performer at nightclubs in Las Vegas, NV, and elsewhere, including touring performer of Pacific military theatre with United Service Organizations; Suzanne Somers Institute for the Effects of Addictions on Families, founder, 1990, and director; Suzanne Somers Foundation (research organization), founder.

Member: National Association for Children of Alcoholics (honorary national chair).

Awards, Honors: People's Choice Award, favorite actress in a new television series, 1977, and Golden Globe Award nomination, best television actress in a musical or comedy, 1979, both for *Three's Company;* named Las Vegas female entertainer of the year, 1986; People's Choice Award, favorite actress in a new television series, 1991, for *Step by Step;* Humanitarian Award, National Council on Alcoholism, 1991; shared Mother of the Year Award, National Mother's Day Committee, 1992; award for distinguished achievement in public service, U.S. Department of Health and Human Services, 1992; received star on Hollywood Walk of Fame, 2003; President's Award, Association of American Drug Counselors.

CREDITS

Television Appearances; Series:
Prize model, *Anniversary Game,* c. 1968.
Assistant, *High Rollers* (also known as *The New High Rollers*), 1974–80.
Christmas "Chrissy" Snow, *Three's Company,* ABC, 1977–81.
Sheriff Hildy Granger, *She's the Sheriff* (also known as *Suddenly Sheriff*), syndicated, 1987–89.
Carol Foster Lambert, *Step By Step,* ABC, 1991–97, CBS, 1997–98.
Host, *The Suzanne Somers Show,* syndicated, 1994.
Host, *VH1's 8–Track Flashback,* VH1, 1995.
Cohost, *Candid Camera,* CBS, 1998–2000.

Television Appearances; Movies:
Female reporter, *Sky Hei$t,* NBC, 1975.
(As Susane Somers) Gloria Henderson, *It Happened at Lake Wood Manor* (also known as *Ants!* and *Panic at Lakewood Manor*), ABC, 1977.
Mattie, *Happily Ever After* (also known as *Tonight's the Night*), CBS, 1978.
Bonnie Katt, *Zuma Beach,* NBC, 1978.
Paige, *Rich Men, Single Women,* ABC, 1990.
Herself, *Keeping Secrets,* ABC, 1991.
Marcy Singer, *Exclusive,* ABC, 1992.
Leigh Lindsay, *Seduced by Evil,* USA Network, 1994.
Sally McCormick, *Devil's Food,* Lifetime, 1996.
Emma Poleski, *No Laughing Matter,* USA Network, 1998.
Clara Hagen/Emily Shepherd, *The Darklings,* Fox Family Channel, 1999.

Television Appearances; Specials:
ABC team member, *Battle of the Network Stars III,* ABC, 1977.
Celebrity Challenge of the Sexes, CBS, 1977, 1979.
Host, *Battle of the Network Stars IV,* ABC, 1978.
The Carpenters ... Space Encounters, ABC, 1978.
Paul Anka in Monte Carlo, CBS, 1978.
General Electrics All–Star Anniversary, ABC, 1978.

Rich Little's Washington Follies, 1978.
NBC Salutes the 25th Anniversary of the Wonderful World of Disney, NBC, 1978.
Host, *Echoes of the Sixties,* NBC, 1979.
The Barbara Walters Special, ABC, 1979.
John Ritter: Being of Sound Mind and Body, 1980.
Host, *The Suzanne Somers Special,* CBS, 1982, 1983.
Joan Rivers and Friends Salute Heidi Abromowitz, 1985.
Charlie Sorrell and Charlene Sorrell, *Goodbye, Charlie,* ABC, 1985.
A Star–Spangled Celebration, ABC, 1987.
Host, *Suzanne,* syndicated, 1987.
Super Bloopers & New Practical Jokes, NBC, 1988.
Director, *Disney's Totally Minnie* (also known as *Totally Minnie*), NBC, 1988.
Suzanne Somers Presents: Showtime's Triple Crown of Comedy, Showtime, 1988.
The Disney/MGM Studios Theme Park Grand Opening, NBC, 1989.
TGIF Comedy Preview, ABC, 1991.
Host, *The Saturday Morning Preview Special,* ABC, 1992.
The Best of the Hollywood Palace, ABC, 1992.
Carol, *ABC's Saturday Morning Preview,* ABC, 1992.
Robin Leach's Private Files: The Price of Fame, 1993.
More of "The Best of the Hollywood Palace," 1993.
Carol Foster Lambert, *ABC Sneak Peek with Step by Step,* 1994.
People's 20th Birthday, 1994.
All–New Return of TV Censored Bloopers, 1994.
Host, *Will You Marry Me?,* ABC, 1994, 1995.
The NFL at 75: An All–Star Celebration, 1995.
Celebrity First Loves, 1995.
Host, *Walt Disney World Very Merry Christmas Parade,* 1996.
Caesar's Palace 30th Anniversary Celebration, 1996.
The Making of "American Graffiti," 1998.
Intimate Portrait: Suzanne Somers, Lifetime, 1998.
Three's Company: The E! True Hollywood Story, E! Entertainment Television, 1998.
TV Guide's Truth Behind the Sitcom Scandals: Three's Company, Brady Bunch, and Partridge Family, 1999.
Headliners & Legends: Suzanne Somers, 2000.
The '70s: The Decade that Changed Television, ABC, 2000.
(In archive footage) *Entertainment Tonight Presents: TV's Greatest Scandals,* syndicated, 2000.
"John Ritter: In Good Company," *Biography,* Arts and Entertainment, 2002.
Suzanne Somers: The E! True Hollywood Story, E! Entertainment Television, 2002.
"American Graffiti," *VH–1 Where Are They Now?,* VH1, 2002.
TVography: Suzanne Somers—Mastering Success, Arts and Entertainment, 2002.
Host, *Latin Dancesport Championship 2001,* Arts and Entertainment, 2002.

Inside TV Land: 40 Greatest Theme Songs, TV Land, 2002.

Inside TV Land: Taboo TV, TV Land, 2002.

John Ritter: The E! True Hollywood Story, E! Entertainment Television, 2002.

Inside TV Land: Style and Fashion, TV Land, 2003.

A Life of Laughter: Remembering John Ritter, ABC, 2003.

Commentator, *TV Revolution,* Bravo, 2003.

(In archive footage) *101 Biggest Celebrity Oops,* E! Entertainment Television, 2004.

Playboy: Celebrity Centerfolds, 2006.

Television Appearances; Miniseries:

Gina Germaine, *Hollywood Wives,* ABC, 1985.

Heroes of Comedy: Women on Top, Comedy Central, 2003.

(In archive footage) *The Ultimate Hollywood Blonde,* E! Entertainment Television, 2004.

(In archive footage) *I Love the '90s: Part Deux,* VH1, 2005.

Television Appearances; Episodic:

(As Suzy Somers) Collie Smith, "If There Were Dreams to Sell," *Ben Casey,* ABC, 1963.

Linda Banning, "High Water," *Lassie* (also known as *Jeff's Collie* and *Timmy and Lassie*), CBS, 1965.

Panelist, *Mantrap* (talk show), syndicated, 1971.

Contestant, *The Dating Game,* 1973.

Virginia Nelson, "The Big Ripoff," *The Rockford Files* (also known as *Jim Rockford, Private Investigator*), NBC, 1974.

Gloria, "Bummy's Girl," *Lotsa Luck,* 1974.

Sally Ann Sloan, "Savage Saturday," *Starsky and Hutch,* ABC, 1975.

"Julie the Waitress," *One Day at a Time,* CBS, 1976.

Linda Offenbecker, "The Vampire," *Starsky and Hutch,* ABC, 1976.

Lorraine Hoffman, "One if by Land," *The Love Boat,* ABC, 1977.

Jane Hutton, "Murder Ward," *Starsky and Hutch,* ABC, 1977.

Jenny Fraser, "The Cheshire Project," *Six Million Dollar Man,* ABC, 1977.

Match Game 73 (also known as *Match Game 77*), 1977.

Billy, CBS, 1979.

Chrissy Snow, "The Surprise Party" (also known as "The Party"), *The Ropers* (also known as *Three's Company's Friends, the Ropers*), ABC, 1979.

On Stage America, syndicated, 1984.

Host, *The Late Show,* Fox, 1986.

Public People, Private Lives, syndicated, 1988.

Guest host, *Studio 59* (also known as *Into the Night*), ABC, 1991.

Herself, "Moving Pictures," *Sisters,* NBC, 1993.

Herself, "Larry Loses Interest," *The Larry Sanders Show,* HBO, 1993.

Herself, "Love on the Rocks," *Full House,* ABC, 1994.

Herself, "Star and Comet Collide! Giant Bugs Invade!" *The Naked Truth* (also known as *Wilde Again*), 1995.

Voice, "The Day the Violence Died," *The Simpsons* (animated), Fox, 1996.

Chrissy, *The Jenny McCarthy Show,* MTV, 1997.

Host, "Millennium Episode," *I Can't Believe I Wore That,* WE Network, 2005.

"Wacky Neighbors," *TV Land's Top Ten,* TV Land, 2005.

"Perfect 10's the Women," *TV Land's Top Ten,* TV Land, 2005.

"Sexiest Men," *TV Land's Top Ten,* TV Land, 2005.

Also appeared in *Us Against the World.*

Television Guest Appearances; Episodic:

The Tonight Show Starring Johnny Carson, NBC, multiple appearances, between 1974 and 1984.

Sabado noche, 1988.

Late Night with Conan O'Brien (also known as *Conan O'Brien*), NBC, 1994, 2000.

Howard Stern, E! Entertainment Television, multiple appearances, between 1994 and 2001.

The Rosie O'Donnell Show, syndicated, multiple appearances, between 1997 and 2001.

The Howard Stern Radio Show, syndicated, 2000.

Entertainment Tonight (also known as *Entertainment This Week, Entertainment Tonight Weekend, E.T., ET Weekend,* and *This Week in Entertainment*), syndicated, 2003, 2006, 2007.

Jimmy Kimmel Live!, ABC, 2004.

The Wayne Brady Show, syndicated, 2004.

The Sharon Osbourne Show (also known as *Sharon*), syndicated, 2004.

The O'Reilly Factor, Fox News Channel, 2004.

Good Day Live, syndicated, 2004, 2005.

The Tony Danza Show, syndicated, 2004, 2005.

Larry King Live, Cable News Network, 2004, 2006, 2007.

The Late Late Show with Craig Ferguson, CBS, 2005.

Live with Regis and Kelly, syndicated, 2005.

Scarborough Country, MSNBC, 2005.

Corazon de ..., 2005.

The View, ABC, 2005, 2006.

Appeared as a guest for other talk shows, including *The Danny Thomas Hour, Good Morning America, Inside Edition, Phil Donahue,* and *Sally Jesse Raphael.*

Television Appearances; Awards Presentations:

Presenter, *The American Movie Awards,* 1980.

The 47th Annual Golden Globe Awards, TBS, 1990.

Presenter, *The 2nd Annual Quill Awards,* NBC, 2006.

Television Appearances; Other:

One for the Road, 1989.

Venus, *Love–Struck,* The Family Channel, 1997.

Television Work:

Executive producer, *Keeping Secrets* (movie), ABC, 1991.

Co–executive producer, *Exclusive* (movie), ABC, 1992.

Executive producer, *The Suzanne Somers Show* (special), syndicated, 1994.

Film Appearances:

(Uncredited) Bit part, *Bullitt,* Warner Bros., 1968.

(Uncredited) Extra, *Daddy's Gone a–Hunting,* National General, 1969.

Fools, Cinerama, 1970.

Girl in white Thunderbird, *American Graffiti,* Universal, 1973.

(Uncredited) Pool girl, *Magnum Force,* Warner Bros., 1973.

Party girl, *Billy Jack Goes to Washington,* 1977.

Cloudy Martin, *Yesterday's Hero,* 1979.

Abigail Adams, *Nothing Personal,* 1980.

Herself, *Serial Mom,* Savoy Pictures, 1994.

Voice of Malley the dog, *Rusty: A Dog's Tale* (also known as *Rusty: The Great Rescue*), Saban Entertainment, 1997.

(Uncredited) Herself, *Say It Isn't So,* Twentieth Century–Fox, 2001.

Stage Appearances:

The Blonde in the Thunderbird (solo show), Brooks Atkinson Theatre, New York City, 2005.

Appeared in stock productions of *Annie Get Your Gun, The Boyfriend, Guys and Dolls,* and *The Sound of Music.* Cabaret singer in "Moulin Rouge," performed at Las Vegas Hilton Hotel, Las Vegas, NV.

RECORDINGS

Videos:

Somersize Part 1, Suzanne Somers: Eat Great, Lose Weight, 1996.

Somersize Part 2, Suzanne Somers: Think Great, Look Great, 1996.

"Liberian Girl" segment, *Michael Jackson: HIStory on Film—Volume II,* 1997.

Candid Camera: 5 Decades of Smiles, Rhino, 2005.

Appeared in various workout videos.

Albums:

Suzanne Somers' How to Change Your Life, Audio Renaissance, 1999.

WRITINGS

Television Music; Series:

Theme song, *The Jenny McCarthy Show,* MTV, 1997.

Books:

Touch Me Again (poetry), Workman Publishing, 1973.

Keeping Secrets (autobiography), Warner Books, 1988.

Wednesday's Children: Adult Survivors of Abuse Speak Out (interviews), Putnam, 1992.

Suzanne Somers' Eat Great, Lose Weight, illustrated by Leslie Hamel, Crown, 1997.

After the Fall: How I Picked Myself Up, Dusted Myself Off, and Started All Over Again (autobiography), Crown, 1998.

Suzanne Somers' Get Skinny on Fabulous Food, illustrated by Hamel, Crown, 1999.

Suzanne Somers' 365 Ways to Change Your Life, Crown, 1999.

Eat, Cheat, and Melt the Fat Away, illustrated by Hamel, Crown, 2001.

Somersize Desserts, Crown, 2001.

Suzanne Somers' Fast and Easy: Lost Weight the Somersize Way with Quick, Delicious Meals for the Entire Family!, illustrated by Hamel, Crown, 2002.

Sexy Years: Discover the Natural Hormone Connection—The Secret to Fabulous Sex, Great Health, and Vitality for Women and Men, Crown, 2004.

Somersize Chocolate: 30 Delicious, Guilt–Free Desserts for the Carb–Conscious Chocolate–Lover, Crown, 2004.

Somersize Cocktails: 30 Sexy Libations from Cool Classics to Unique Concoctions, Crown, 2005.

Somersize Appetizers: 30 Scintillating Starters to Tantalize Your Tastebuds at Every Occasion, Crown, 2005.

Suzanne Somers' Slim and Sexy Forever: The Hormone Solution for Permanent Weight Loss and Optimal Living, illustrated by Hamel, Crown, 2005.

Ageless: The Naked Truth about Bioidentical Hormones and Beyond, Crown, 2006.

ADAPTATIONS

Keeping Secrets was adapted for television and broadcast on ABC, 1991, with Somers as executive producer.

OTHER SOURCES

Books:

Business Leader Profiles for Students, Volume 2, Gale, 2002.

Newsmakers 2000, Issue 1, Gale, 2000.

Somers, Suzanne, *Keeping Secrets,* Warner Books, 1988.

Somers, Suzanne, *After the Fall: How I Picked Myself Up, Dusted Myself Off, and Started All Over Again,* Crown, 1998.

Periodicals:

Alternative Medicine Digest, November, 1997.

Better Nutrition, July, 2004, pp. 36–39.

Biography, February, 2001.

Fortune, June 14, 2004, p. 44.
Ladies Home Journal, May, 1998, p. 92.
Parade, May 13, 2001, p. 14.
People Weekly, January 21, 1980, pp. 24–25; March 1, 1982, pp. 76–80; August 9, 1982, pp. 76–80; April 18, 1988, pp. 100–111; November 11, 1991, pp. 99–103; March 3, 1997, p. 42; May 25, 1998, p. 41; April 30, 2001, pp. 72–78, 81; April 30, 2001, p. 72; May 19, 2003, p. 131.
Publishers Weekly, September 13, 2004, p. 74.
Saturday Evening Post, May–June, 2007, p. 46.
Time, August 9, 1999, p. 73.
TV Guide, December 28, 2002, p. 10.
USA Today, June 22, 1999, p. 8D.
Washington Post, July 1, 2005, pp. N1, N7.
Woman's Day, May 4, 2004, p. 91.

Television Specials:

Intimate Portrait: Suzanne Somers, Lifetime, 1998.
TV Guide's Truth behind the Sitcom Scandals: Three's Company, Brady Bunch, and Partridge Family, 1999.
Headliners & Legends: Suzanne Somers, 2000.
Suzanne Somers: The E! True Hollywood Story, E! Entertainment Television, 2002.
TVography: Suzanne Comers—Mastering Success, Arts and Entertainment, 2002.

SPICE, Scary
See BROWN, Melanie

SPIVAK, Alice 1935–

PERSONAL

Born August 11, 1935, in Brooklyn, NY.

Career: Actress.

CREDITS

Film Appearances:

(Uncredited) Lonely girl, *Lilith,* Columbia, 1964.
Harriet Mitchell, *Fun and Games,* Audubon Productions, 1973.
Nurse at hospital, *Stardust Memories,* United Artists, 1980.
Magda, *Times Square,* Anchor Bay Entertainment, 1980.
Customer in Pete's, *The Muppets Take Manhattan,* TriStar, 1984.

Claire Rolfe, *Garbo Talks* (also known as *Garbo Talks!*), Metro–Goldwyn–Mayer, 1984.
Woman applicant, *Deadly Illusion* (also known as *I Love You do Death* and *Love You to Death*), Cinetel, 1987.
Engagement party guest, *Another Woman,* Orion, 1988.
Dispatcher, *See No Evil, Hear No Evil,* TriStar, 1989.
The "Producer," *How to Be Louise,* 1990.
Jenny, *Privilege,* Zeitgeist, 1990.
Louise Robinson, *Electric Moon,* 1992.
Josie, *Home of Angels,* Bridgestone Media, 1994.
Bunny, *Trouble* (short), 1995.
Elegant middle–aged woman, *If Lucy Fell,* TriStar, 1996.
Customer from Hell, *The Waiting Game,* Seventh Art Releasing, 1999.
Female judge, *Find Me Guilty* (also known as *Find Me Guilty: The Jacke Dee Story*), Yari Film Group Releasing, 2006.
Receptionist, *Before the Devil Knows You're Dead,* ThinkFilm, 2007.

Film Work:

Dialogue coach, *Buck and the Preacher,* Columbia, 1972.
Creative consultant, *The Fan,* Paramount, 1981.

Television Appearances; Series:

Bailiff Naomi, *100 Centre Street,* Arts and Entertainment, 2001–2002.

Television Appearances; Movies:

Deputy number three, *A Summer to Remember,* CBS, 1985.
Mrs. Reeseman, *Gryphon,* 1990.

Television Appearances; Specials:

We the Women, CBS, 1974.
Mrs. Reeseman, *Gryphon,* PBS, 1988.
Bus stop woman, *Pulp Comics: Caroline Rhea,* Comedy Central, 1999.

Television Appearances; Episodic:

"Last Port of Call," *N.Y.P.D.,* ABC, 1968.
Acting teacher, "Unnatural Causes," *The Equalizer,* CBS, 1986.
Esther Fein, "Prince of Darkness," *Law & Order,* NBC, 1992.
Rita, "Change of a Dress," *Sex and the City,* HBO, 2002.
Mrs. Wing, "Cherry Red," *Law & Order: Criminal Intent* (also known as *Law & Order: CI*), NBC, 2003.
Herself/acting coach, "The Girl Who Drives Everyone Crazy," *America's Next Top Model* (also known as *ANTM, Top Model,* and *America's Next Top Model with Tyra Banks*), UPN, 2003.

Television Work; Series:

Acting coach, *Encyclopedia,* HBO, 1988.

Television Work; Miniseries:
Acting coach, *Harem,* ABC, 1986.

Television Work; Movies:
Dialogue coach, *Tarzan in Manhattan,* CBS, 1989.

Stage Appearances:
Sylvia and Mildred, "Take Me To Bed," *Time for Bed/ Take Me to Bed,* Provincetown Playhouse, New York City, 1969.
Nelie, *A Backer's Audition,* American Jewish Theatre, New York City, 1992.
Tzawrah Shotsky, *Chaim's Love Song,* Raymond J. Greenwald Theatre, New York City, 1998–99.
A Last Dance for Sybil, New Federal Theatre, New York City, 2002.
Landlady, *Funnyhouse of a Negro,* Harlem School of the Arts Theatre, New York City, 2006.

Also appeared as Renee, *After–Play,* Theatre 4; Shirley, *South Side,* George Street Playhouse, New Brunswick, NJ; Mrs. Levine, *Sheldon & Mrs. Levine,* Penguin Repertory Theatre, Stony Point, NY.

STAIT, Brent 1959–

PERSONAL

Born September 9, 1959, in The Pas, Manitoba, Canada. *Education:* Attended the Banff School of Fine Arts and the Ryerson Theatre School. *Avocational Interests:* Hockey, physical fitness, reading, snowboarding.

Career: Actor. Hudson Bay Mining and Smelting Company, miner, c. 1977–78.

Awards, Honors: Gemini Award nomination, best performance by an actor in a featured supporting role in a dramatic program or miniseries, Academy of Canadian Cinema and Television, 1998, for *For Those Who Hunt the Wounded Down.*

CREDITS

Film Appearances:
Burt, *Termini Station* (also known as *Paeaeteasema*), 1989, Northern Arts Entertainment, 1991.
Jim Blessing, *Showdown at Williams Creek* (also known as *Kootenai Brown, The Legend of Kootenai Brown,* and *Wer erschoss Jim Blessing?*), National Film Board of Canada/Festival Films, 1991.

Second military police officer in psychiatric ward, *Cadence* (also known as *Count a Lonely Cadence, Stockade, A marcha da revolta, A Megtoerhetetlen, Cadence—Ein fremder Klang, Ein fremder Klang, Kadencja, Karcer, Kompania karna, Straffkompaniet,* and *Uomini al passo*), New Line Cinema, 1991.
Mechanic, *North of Pittsburgh* (also known as *Ao norte de Pittsburgh* and *La nord de Pittsburgh*), Acme Motion Pictures/Telefilm Canada, 1992.
Vince, *Tokyo Cowboy* (also known as *Yin Yang*), 1994.
Sartech, *Far from Home: The Adventures of Yellow Dog* (also known as *Yellow Dog*), Twentieth Century–Fox, 1995.
Walt Shannon, *Gunfighter's Moon,* Rysher Entertainment, 1995.
Kevin Holt, *Mystery, Alaska* (also known as *Disney's "Hockey Project," The Game, Pond Rules, Alaska ardiente, Alaska escaldante, Esquentando o Alasca, Mistery, Alaska,* and *Mystery—New York: Ein Spiel um die Ehre*), Buena Vista, 1999.
Father, *Speak* (short film), 2001.
Wade, *On the Corner,* TVA Films, 2003.
Father and rich man, *My Old Man* (short film), 2004.
Photographer, *Capture* (short film), 2004.
Dr. Dean, *Dysfunction* (short film), 2006.
The man, *Fracture* (short film), 2006.

Television Appearances; Series:
Rev Bem, *Andromeda* (also known as *Gene Roddenberry's "Andromeda"*), Sci–Fi Channel, 2000–2004.

Television Appearances; Miniseries:
Ballenger, *A Good Day to Die* (also known as *Children of the Dust, Cacada brutal, Die Rache der Gejagten,* and *La croisee des destins*), CBS, 1995.
Irish bunkmate, *Titanic* (also known as *Titanic 2* and *Le Titanic*), CBS, 1996.
Jim Woltz, *Intensity* (also known as *Dean Koontz's "Intensity"*), Fox, 1997.
Sheriff Kerby, "Acid Test," *Taken* (also known as *Steven Spielberg Presents "Taken"*), Sci–Fi Channel, 2002.
Royce, *Into the West,* TNT, 2005.

Television Appearances; Movies:
Corporal Bloggs, *Le peloton d'execution* (also known as *Firing Squad* and *Teloitusryhmae*), 1991.
Eddie, *I Still Dream of Jeannie,* NBC, 1991.
Mica, *Omen IV: The Awakening* (also known as *A profecia maldita, La malediction IV—L'eveil, La profecia IV: el renacer, Omen IV—Das Erwachen, Omen IV: Ondskans haemnd, Omen IV: presagio infernale,* and *Omen IV: riivaajan paluu*), Fox, 1991.
Billy, *Blind Man's Bluff,* USA Network, 1992.
Mort, *The Man Upstairs* (also known as *CBS Sunday Movie, Kein Engel auf Erden, Mannen i oevervaaningen,* and *Un homme au grenier*), CBS, 1992.

Francois, *Call of the Wild* (also known as *Apelo selvagem, Der Ruf der Wildnis, Eraemaan kutsu, L'appel de la foret, Skriet fraan vildmarken,* and *Zew krwi*), CBS, 1993.

Peter Terriglio, *Sidney Sheldon's "A Stranger in the Mirror"* (also known as *A Stranger in the Mirror*), ABC, 1993.

Raymond, *Born to Run,* Fox, 1993.

Scott, *Whose Child Is This? The War for Baby Jessica* (also known as *Ma fille Jessica, Pour l'amour de Jessica,* and *Tout pour ma fille*), ABC, 1993.

O. T. Betsill, *A Christmas Romance* (also known as *Eingeschneit—Weihnachten im Schneesturm, Jouluromanssi, La romance de Noel, Romance de Natal, Romance de Navidad,* and *Un romance en Navidad*), CBS, 1994.

Evan Soika, *Broken Trust* (also known as *Court of Honor*), TNT, 1995.

Larry Devore, *Deceived by Trust: A Moment of Truth Movie* (also known as *Abus d'autorite, Obcecada por justica,* and *Vom Lehrer bedraengt—Missbrauch an der Schule*), NBC, 1995.

Gary Percy Rils, *For Those Who Hunt the Wounded Down,* CBC, 1996.

Richard Thinbill, *In the Lake of the Woods* (also known as *Le lac du doute* and *Truque do medo*), Fox, 1996.

Sheriff, *The Limbic Region,* Showtime, 1996.

Wendel Pone, *Hostile Force* (also known as *The Heist* and *Alarm fuer Security 13*), 1996.

SWAT team leader, *Five Desperate Hours* (also known as *Amenazada, Epaetoivon tunnit, 5 horas de desespero,* and *Fuenf Stunden Todesangst*), NBC, 1997.

Vye, *Nights below Station Street,* CBC, 1997.

Captain Phillips, *Roswell: The Aliens Attack* (also known as *Roswell—Alien Attack, Roswell, invasion extraterrestre,* and *Roswell, les aliens attaquent*), UPN, 1999.

Mel, *The Sheldon Kennedy Story* (also known as *Un reve abime*), CTV (Canada), 1999.

Ozone, "H–E Double Hockey Sticks" (also known as "Demons et merveilles," "Entrando numa fria," and "Griffelkin—Ein Teufel auf Abwegen"), *The Wonderful World of Disney,* ABC, 1999.

Griffin, *The Virginian* (also known as *Land der Gesetzlosen, Mannen fraan Virginia,* and *Omul din Virginia*), TNT, 2000.

Roger Walker, *Touched by a Killer* (also known as *Interview mit einem Killer*), Lifetime, 2001.

Alfred Baker, *A Crime of Passion* (also known as *Mary Higgins Clark's "A Crime of Passion"* and *Mary Higgins Clark: "Un crime passionnel"*), PAX TV, 2003.

FBI commander Hall, *Meltdown* (also known as *American Meltdown* and *Angst ueber Amerika*), fX Channel, 2004.

Roger Shapiro, *A Job to Kill For* (also known as *The Protege* and *Fascination criminelle*), Lifetime, 2006.

Crawford, *Smokejumpers* (also known as *Smoke Jumpers*), 2008.

Television Appearances; Specials:

Reverend Fuller, *Secrets of the Unknown,* CBS, 1991.

"Ellen Foster" (also known as "Ellen Foster—Ein Kind kampft um sein Glueck" and "La maison bleue"), *Hallmark Hall of Fame,* CBS, 1997.

Television Appearances; Episodic:

Donald Young, "The Pimp," *Night Heat,* CBS, 1987.

Carl, "No Regrets," *Night Heat,* CBS, 1988.

Jim Sweeney, "Prism," *Alfred Hitchcock Presents* (also known as *Alfred Hitchcock esittaeae, Alfred Hitchcock presenta, Alfred Hitchcock presente,* and *Alfred Hitchcock zeigt*), USA Network, 1988.

John, "The Eden Road," *Captain Power and the Soldiers of the Future* (live action and animated), syndicated, 1988.

Bob Drake, "Vigilante," *Bordertown* (also known as *Les deux font la loi*), Family Channel and CanWest Global Television, 1989.

Jim Sweeney, "Mirror Mirror," *Alfred Hitchcock Presents* (also known as *Alfred Hitchcock esittaeae, Alfred Hitchcock presenta, Alfred Hitchcock presente,* and *Alfred Hitchcock zeigt*), USA Network, 1989.

Tall man, "Next Victim," *21 Jump Street,* Fox, 1989.

Tim, "Lost Weekend," *Knightwatch,* ABC, 1989.

"Fatal Obsession," *Katts and Dog* (also known as *Rin Tin Tin: K–9 Cop*), CTV (Canada) and Family Channel, 1989.

Axel Whitman, "Dead Right," *Wiseguy,* CBC, 1990.

"The Mighty Quinn," *Neon Rider,* syndicated, 1990.

"Time Wounds All Heels," *Mom P.I.,* CBC, 1991.

Eddie Doyle, "Mountain Men," *Highlander* (also known as *Highlander: The Series*), syndicated, 1992.

B. B. Davenport, "Scali, P.I.," *The Commish,* ABC, 1993.

Corporal Taylor, "Fallen Angel," *The X–Files,* Fox, 1993.

Scott, "Hello ... Again," *Street Justice,* syndicated, 1993.

"Law and Order," *Lonesome Dove: The Series,* syndicated, 1994.

Colonel Ramsey, "The Wrath of Kali," *Highlander* (also known as *Highlander: The Series*), syndicated, 1995.

Officer Fitch (some sources cite role as Officer Finch), "The Ballad of Lucas Burke," *The Marshal,* ABC, 1995.

"Hester," *Hawkeye,* syndicated, 1995.

McBride, "The Siege," *The Sentinel,* UPN, 1996.

Terry Edward Mayhew (some sources cite role as Timothy Mayhew), "Terma," *The X–Files,* Fox, 1996.

Terry Edward Mayhew (some sources cite role as Timothy Mayhew), "Tunguska," *The X–Files,* Fox, 1996.

Jimmy, "Chain Gang," *Two* (also known as *Gejagt—Das zweite Gesicht*), CTV (Canada) and syndicated, 1997.

John Wesley Richter, "Finding Richter," *Poltergeist: The Legacy* (also known as *Poltergeist, El legado, Poltergeist—Die unheimliche Macht, Poltergeist: El legado,* and *Poltergeist, les aventuriers du surnaturel*), Showtime and syndicated, 1997.

"Cupid," *Profit* (also known as *Jim Profit—Ein Mann geht ueber Leichen*), Fox, 1997.

Major Louis Ferretti, "Within the Serpent's Grasp," *Stargate SG–1* (also known as *La porte des etoiles* and *Stargaate SG–1*), Showtime and syndicated, 1998.

Miller, "Prisoner X," *The Sentinel,* UPN, 1998.

Simon LeShane, "Hot Potato," *Viper,* syndicated, 1998.

Vic Hester, "Mountie on the Bounty: Parts 1 & 2," *Due South* (also known as *Un tandem de choc*), CTV (Canada), syndicated, and TNT, 1998.

Edwin Brucks, "The Collector," *Seven Days* (also known as *7 Days* and *Seven Days: The Series*), UPN, 1999.

Maguire, "Prayer for the White Man," *First Wave,* USA Network, 1999.

McBride, "Four Point Shot," *The Sentinel,* UPN, 1999.

Vince Baxter, "What Will the Neighbors Think?," *The Outer Limits* (also known as *The New Outer Limits*), Showtime, Sci–Fi Channel, and syndicated, 1999.

"The Grid," *The Outer Limits* (also known as *The New Outer Limits*), Showtime, Sci–Fi Channel, and syndicated, 2000.

Stan Amado, "Something Fishy," *Mysterious Ways* (also known as *One Clear Moment, Anexegeta phainomena, Les chemins de l'etrange, Mysterious ways—les chemins de l'etrange, Rajatapaus,* and *Senderos misteriosos*), NBC and PAX TV, 2002.

John Watts, "Killing Time," *Cold Squad,* CTV (Canada), 2003.

Mason, "Bastille Day," *Battlestar Galactica* (also known as *Galactica, Galactica—Estrella de combate,* and *Taisteluplaneetta Galactica*), Sci–Fi Channel, 2004.

Frank Vanner, "Suffer the Children," *The 4400,* USA Network and Sky, 2005.

Ziereis, "The Historian," *The Collector,* Space Television and City TV, 2005.

Damek, "Angels & Demons," *Blade: The Series* (also known as *Blade* and *Blade—Die Jagd geht weiter*), Spike, 2006.

Damek, "Delivery," *Blade: The Series* (also known as *Blade* and *Blade—Die Jagd geht weiter*), Spike, 2006.

John Reddle, "The Damned Thing," *Masters of Horror,* Showtime, 2006.

Michael Kenmore, "Allies," *Stargate: Atlantis* (also known as *Atlantis, Csillagkapu—Atlantisz, La porte d'Atlantis,* and *Stargaate: Atlaantis*), Sci–Fi Channel, 2006.

Scotty, "Scarecrow," *Supernatural* (also known as *Sobrenatural*), The WB, 2006.

Television Appearances; Pilots:

Jackson, *Green Dolphin Beat* (also known as *Green Dolphin Street*), Fox, 1994.

Major Louis Ferretti, "Children of the Gods," *Stargate SG–1* (also known as *Stargate SG–1: Children of the Gods, La porte des etoiles,* and *Stargaate SG–1*), Showtime and syndicated, 1997.

Stage Appearances:

Appeared as Danny, *Danny and the Deep Blue Sea,* Vancouver, British Columbia, Canada. Appeared in *King Lear, The Merchant of Venice, Romeo and Juliet,* and *Twelfth Night* (also known as *Twelfth Night, or What You Will*); appeared in theatre productions at the Stratford Festival of Canada, Stratford, Ontario, Canada.

OTHER SOURCES

Periodicals:

TV Zone, February, 2001, pp. 36–39.

STAR, Darren 1961–

PERSONAL

Born 1961; father, an orthodontist; mother, a freelance writer; companion of Dennis Erdman (a director). *Education:* Attended University of Southern California and University of California, Los Angeles.

Addresses: *Office*—Darren Star Productions, 10202 West Washington Blvd., 2210 Fred Astaire Bldg., Culver City, CA 90232. *Agent*—William Morris Agency, 1 William Morris Pl., Beverly Hills, CA 90212.

Career: Producer, director, and writer. Darren Star Productions, Culver City, CA, president.

Awards, Honors: Golden Globe Awards, best musical or comedy television series, 1999, 2000, 2001, Emmy Award nominations, 1999, 2000, and Emmy Award, 2001, all outstanding comedy series, Golden Satellite Award, best musical or comedy television series, International Press Academy, 2000, 2001, and Danny Thomas Producer of the Year Award in Episodic Television, Golden Laurel Awards, Producers Guild of America, 2001, 2002, all (with others) for *Sex and the City.*

CREDITS

Television Work; Series:

Creator and coproducer, *Beverly Hills, 90210,* Fox, 1990.

Supervising producer, *Beverly Hills, 90210,* Fox, 1991–92.

Executive producer, *Beverly Hills, 90210,* Fox, 1992–95.

Creator and executive producer, *Melrose Place,* Fox, 1992–95.

Creator and executive producer, *Central Park West* (also known as *C.P.W.*), CBS, 1995.

Creator and executive producer, *Sex and the City*, HBO, 1999–2000.

Creator and executive producer, *The $treet*, Fox, 2000.

Creator and executive producer, *Grosse Pointe*, The WB, 2000.

Creator and executive producer, *Miss Match*, NBC, 2003–2005.

Executive producer, *Kitchen Confidential*, Fox, 2005–2006.

Television Executive Producer; Pilots:

Producer, *Central Park West*, CBS, 1995.

Runaway, CW Network, 2006.

Cashmere Mafia, ABC, 2007.

Manchild, Showtime, 2007.

Literary Superstar, ABC, 2007.

Television Director; Episodic:

"Spring Dance," *Beverly Hills, 90210*, Fox, 1991.

"A Walsh Family Christmas," *Beverly Hills, 90210*, Fox, 1991.

"The Monogamists," *Sex and the City*, HBO, 1998.

"Twenty–Something Girls vs. Thirty–Something Women," *Sex and the City*, HBO, 1999.

"Passion Fish," *Grosse Pointe*, The WB, 2001.

"Exile on Main Street," *Kitchen Confidential*. Fox, 2005.

"Aftermath," *Kitchen Confidential*. Fox, 2005.

Television Director; Pilots:

Miss Match, NBC, 2003.

Television Appearances; Specials:

A Day in the Lives of Melrose Place, Fox, 1994.

Love Thy Neighbor: The Baddest and the Best of Melrose Place, Fox, 1995.

Intimate Portrait: Kim Cattrall, Lifetime, 2000.

What Is a Producer?, E! Entertainment Television, 2001.

The Women of "Sex and the City," E! Entertainment Television, 2001.

Intimate Portrait: Cynthia Nixon, Lifetime, 2002.

Inside TV Land: Taboo TV, TV Land, 2002.

The Perfect Pitch (also known as *Brilliant but Cancelled: The Perfect Pitch*), Trio, 2002.

Melrose Place: The E! True Hollywood Story, E! Entertainment Television, 2003.

Brilliant but Cancelled: Pilot Season, Trio, 2003.

Commentator, *TV Revolution*, Bravo, 2003.

When Melrose Place Ruled the World, VH1, 2004.

Heather Locklear: The E! True Hollywood Story, E! Entertainment Television, 2004.

Sex and the City: A Farewell, HBO, 2004.

"Heather Locklear," *Biography*, Arts and Entertainment, 2005.

Television Appearances; Episodic:

"Darren Star," *Lauren Hutton and ...*, 1995.

(Uncredited) Executive in limousine, "You Gotta Have Heart," *Beverly Hills, 90210*, Fox, 1995.

Television Appearances; Miniseries:

Heroes of Comedy: Women on Top, Comedy Central, 2003.

TV Land Moguls, TV Land, 2004.

RECORDINGS

Videos:

Himself, *A Recipe for Comedy*, Trailer Park, 2007.

WRITINGS

Television Pilots:

Bill and Ted's Excellent Adventures (animated), Fox, 1992.

Television Series:

Beverly Hills, 90210, Fox, 1990–2000.

Melrose Place, Fox, 1992–99.

Bill & Ted's Excellent Adventures (animated), Fox, 1992.

Central Park West (also known as *C.P.W.*), CBS, 1995–96.

Sex and the City, HBO, 1998–2004.

The $treet, Fox, 2000–2001.

Grosse Pointe, The WB, 2000–2001.

Miss Match, NBC, 2003–2005.

Screenplays:

Doin' Time on Planet Earth (also based on story by Star), Warner Bros. Home Video, 1988.

If Looks Could Kill (also known as *Teen Agent*), Warner Bros., 1991.

OTHER SOURCES

Periodicals:

Los Angeles, November, 2000, p. 68.

Newsweek, October 2, 2000, p. 68.

STEEN, Jessica 1965–

PERSONAL

Born December 19, 1965, in Toronto, Ontario, Canada; daughter of Jan Steen (a director and actor) and Joanna Noyes (an actress).

Addresses: *Agent*—Innovative Artists Talent and Literary Agency, 1505 10th St., Santa Monica, CA 90401; Colleen Schlegel, Bauman–Redanty and Shaul, 5757 Wilshire Blvd., Suite 473, Los Angeles, CA 90036; Lesa Kirk, Kirk Talent Agencies, Inc., 134 Abbott St., Suite 402, Vancouver, British Columbia, Canada V6B 2K4.

Career: Actress. Appeared in numerous television commercials, including advertisements for McDonald's restaurants, Mr. Clean cleaning products, Sears department stores, Doritos chips, Coca–Cola, and Firestone tires.

Member: Screen Actors Guild, Alliance of Canadian Cinema, Television, and Radio Artists.

Awards, Honors: Gemini Award nomination, best actress in a continuing dramatic role, Academy of Canadian Cinema and Television, 1988, for *Captain Power and the Soldiers of the Future;* Gemini Award, best actress in a dramatic program or miniseries, 1996, for *Small Gifts;* DVD Premiere Award nomination, best actress, DVD Exclusive Awards, 2003, for *Slap Shot 2: Breaking the Ice.*

CREDITS

Television Appearances; Series:
Corporal Jennifer "Pilot" Chase, *Captain Power and the Soldiers of the Future,* syndicated, 1987.
Patricia "Trisha" Alden Sowolsky Hartman McKenzie, *Loving,* ABC and Lifetime, 1991.
Linda Metcalf, *Homefront,* ABC, 1991–93.
Dr. Julia Heller, *Earth 2,* NBC, 1994–95.
Special Agent Paula Cassidy, a recurring role, *Navy NCIS: Naval Criminal Investigative Service* (also known as *NCIS* and *NCIS: Naval Criminal Investigative Service*), CBS, between 2003 and 2007.
Dr. Francine Klepp, a recurring role, *Killer Instinct,* Fox, 2005.

Television Appearances; Movies:
Gail Pennoyer, *When We First Met,* HBO, 1984.
Donna, *Gentle Sinners,* CBC, 1985.
Lowni Striker, *Striker's Mountain* (also known as *Im Reich der weissen berge*), 1985.
Mellisa Stotts, *Workin' for Peanuts,* HBO, 1985.
Tracy Gordon, *Young Again,* ABC, 1986.
Wendy Robinson, *Easy Prey,* ABC, 1986.
Girlfriend, *The Rocket Boy,* 1989.
Jennifer McPhail, "High Country," *C.B.C.'s Magic Hour,* CBC, 1991.
Kathi Davidson, *To Save the Children,* CBS, 1994.
Nora Delany, *Small Gifts,* CBC, 1994.
Janet, *Dogwatch,* Dog Watch Productions, 1996.

Celia Shine, *Principal Takes a Holiday,* Disney Channel, 1998.
Andrea Roberts, *Question of Privilege* (also known as *Piege mortel*), Lifetime, 1999.
Sara Barnes, *Smart House,* Disney Channel, 1999.
Allison Beauchamp, *On Hostile Ground,* TBS, 2000.
Terry Best, *Society's Child* (also known as *Le combat d'une mere*), CBC, 2001.
Detective Anne–Marie Marrone, *The Pact,* Lifetime, 2002.
Susan Holme, *The Paradise Virus,* PAX, 2003.
Linda, *Rapid Fire,* USA Network, 2005.

Television Appearances; Pilots:
Melonie, *Home Free,* CBC, 1985.
Tracy Steelgrave, *Wiseguy,* CBS, 1987.
Kate Hightower, *The Great Pretender* (also known as *Dead End Brattigan*), NBC, 1991.
Linda Metcalf, *Homefront,* ABC, 1991.
Dr. Julia Heller, *Earth 2,* NBC, 1994.
Kate, *Kojak,* USA Network, 2005.
Dr. Francine Klepp, *Killer Instinct,* Fox, 2005.
Katherine "Kat" Baines, *Canooks,* 2007.

Television Appearances; Specials:
Kate, "The Day They Came to Arrest the Book," *CBS Schoolbreak Special,* CBS, 1986.
Kay, *The Truth About Alex,* HBO, 1986.
Eileen Morgan, *Christmas in America* (also known as *Christmas in America: A Love Story*), NBC, 1990.

Television Appearances; Episodic:
Uncle Bobby, c. 1968.
The Sunrunners, c. 1973.
Girl wearing green towel, "It's a Wonderful Film," *SCTV Channel,* Cinemax, 1983.
"Slim Obsession," *For the Record,* CBC, 1984.
"Enemy of Weston," *The Edison Twins,* CBC, 1984.
Michelle Parker, "The Source," *Night Heat,* CBS, 1985.
Leslie "Torque" Davidson, "Torque," *The Littlest Hobo,* syndicated, 1985.
Elaine, "What Goes Up," *The Edison Twins,* CBC, 1986.
Lindsay, "Little White Lies," *Kay O'Brien,* CBS, 1986.
Officer Kelly Miller, "Stand Off," *True Confessions,* c. 1986.
Angela Rivera, "Fighting Back," *Night Heat,* CBS, 1986.
Amanda, "Blinded by Love," *The Campbells,* syndicated, 1986.
Sally Carlyle, "Man on the Edge," *Alfred Hitchcock Presents,* NBC, 1987.
Karen MacNeil, "Softshell," *Street Legal,* CBC, 1990.
Patricia Poston, "Dead Men Tell," *Sweating Bullets* (also known as *Tropical Heat*), CBS, 1991.
Heather, "When Hairy Met Hermy," *Herman's Head,* Fox, 1993.
Karen Hardy, "True Lies," *ER,* NBC, 1996.

Nurse Gina Beaumont, "The Refuge," *The Outer Limits* (also known as *The New Outer Limits*), Showtime and syndicated, 1996.

The 1996 Gemini Awards, CBC, 1996.

Paige Weikopf, "Chapter 9, Year Two," *Murder One,* ABC, 1997.

Paige Weikopf, "Chapter 10, Year Two," *Murder One,* ABC, 1997.

Paige Weikopf, "Chapter 11, Year Two," *Murder One,* ABC, 1997.

Paige Weikopf, "Chapter 12, Year Two," *Murder One,* ABC, 1997.

Sarah Bingham, "Full Moon," *Touched by an Angel,* CBS, 1997.

Rachel, "The Assassin," *The Pretender,* NBC, 1999.

Maggie MacKenzie, "Hunting Season," *Due South* (also known as *Un tandem de choc*), CTV, 1999.

Stephanie Sawyer, "Essence of Life," *The Outer Limits,* Showtime and syndicated, 1999.

Brianna Hatfield, "Marooned," *The Practice,* ABC, 1999.

Kathrine, "The Grid," *The Outer Limits,* Showtime and syndicated, 2000.

Dr. Sarah Ford, "Inter Arma Silent Leges," *The Practice,* ABC, 2001.

Myra Teal, "Mr. Monk and the Billionaire Mugger," *Monk,* USA Network, 2002.

Amy Wenzel, "The Cutting of the Swath," *Dragnet* (also known as *L.A. Dragnet*), ABC, 2003.

Dr. Sara Stanton, "The Taking of Crows," *Mutant X,* syndicated, 2003.

Dr. Elizabeth Weir, "Lost City: Parts 1 & 2," *Stargate SG–1* (also known as *La porte des etoiles*), Sci–Fi Channel, 2004.

Amy Connors, "Kimber Henry," *Nip/Tuck,* FX Network, 2004.

Ruth Brody, "Ordinary Witches," *Charmed,* The WB, 2005.

Holly Gibson, "Shots," *Eyes,* ABC, 2005.

Officer Kathleen, "The Benders," *Supernatural,* The WB, 2006.

Donna Basset, "Toe Tags," *CSI: Crime Scene Investigation* (also known as *C.S.I., CSI: Las Vegas,* and *Les experts*), CBS, 2006.

Katherine "Kat" Baines, "The City LA," *Canooks,* 2007.

Appeared as D'arcy in an episode of *Hangin' In,* CBC.

Film Appearances:

Tracy Vrain, *Threshold,* Twentieth Century–Fox International Classics, 1981.

Melinda Coverdale, *A Judgment in Stone* (also known as *The Housekeeper*), Castle Hill, 1986.

Carly Simmons, *Flying* (also known as *Dream to Believe* and *Teenage Dream*), Sony Pictures Releasing, 1986.

Faith, *John and the Missus,* Cinema Group, 1987.

Nellie Ambrose, *Still Life* (also known as *Art Killer Framed* and *Still Life: The Fine Art of Murder*), Bucko Pictures, 1988.

Hannah Gottschalk, *Sing,* TriStar, 1989.

Sharon, *Showtime Gospel* (short film), Canadian Centre for Advanced Film Studies, 1989.

Elizabeth Gardner, *Trial and Error,* New Line Cinema, 1997.

Copilot Jennifer Watts, *Armageddon,* Buena Vista, 1998.

Clara Kaufman, *The Ride Home* (short film), Spitting Cobra Films, 2000.

Victoria "Vicky" Thorn, *Apocalypse IV: Judgment* (also known as *Judgment* and *O.N.E.: One Nation Earth*), Cloud Ten Pictures, 2001.

Jessie Dage, *Slap Shot 2: Breaking the Ice,* Universal Home Entertainment, 2002.

Sue, *Flip Phone* (short film), 2003.

Carolyn Miller, *Left Behind: World at War,* Columbia, 2005.

Karen Cross, *Chaos* (also known as *Hit & Blast*), Lions Gate Films, 2007.

Stage Appearances:
Cathryn Aldridge, *Ms. Trial,* Court Theatre, West Hollywood, CA, 2002.

OTHER SOURCES

Periodicals:
Movieline, July, 1998, p. 16.
Smoke, summer, 1998.
Starlog, April, 1995; September, 1998, pp. 14–17.
Winnipeg Sun, October 5, 2000.

Electronic:
Jessica Steen Official Site, http://www.jessicasteen.com, August 11, 2007.

STOCKWELL, John 1961–

PERSONAL

Original name, John Stockwell Samuels IV; born March 25, 1961, in Galveston, TX; son of John Samuels III (an attorney); married Helene Henderson (owner and operator of a catering company); children: Cecelia, Casper, additional child. *Education:* Harvard University, B.A., visual and environmental studies; studied acting at the Royal Academy of Dramatic Art, London, and with Hal Asprey at the Actors Workshop, New York University School of the Arts; studied voice technique with Marv Duff at the National Theatre, London.

Addresses: *Agent*—International Creative Management, 10250 Constellation Way, 9th Floor, Los Angeles, CA 90067.

Career: Actor, screenwriter, and director. The Brood (a New York City–based rock group), rhythm guitarist and lead singer.

Awards, Honors: Emmy Award nomination, outstanding writing for a miniseries or a movie, 2000, for *Cheaters*.

CREDITS

Stage Appearances:
Appeared as Lobo, *Camino Real,* Williamstown Theatre Festival, Williamstown, MA; Hal, *Loot;* in *The Merry Wives of Windsor,* Houston Shakespeare Festival, Houston, TX; *Macbeth,* Houston Shakespeare Festival, Houston, TX; *Spring's Awakening,* Brighton Festival, Brighton, England; *Three Boys,* Playwrights Horizons, Theatre, New York City; in *Ah, Wilderness!.*

Film Appearances:
(Film debut) Jim Sterling, *So Fine,* Warner Bros., 1981.
Dennis Guilder, *Christine* (also known as *John Carpenter's "Christine"*), Columbia, 1983.
Keith Livingston, *Eddie and the Cruisers,* Embassy, 1983.
Spider, *Losin' It,* Embassy, 1983.
Leland ("Lee"), *City Limits,* Atlantic, 1985.
Michael Harlan, *My Science Project,* Buena Vista, 1985.
Randy McDevitt, *Dangerously Close* (also known as *Campus '86* and *Choice Kill*), Cannon, 1986.
Phillip Marlowe, *Radioactive Dreams,* De Laurentiis Entertainment Group, 1986.
Cougar, *Top Gun,* Paramount, 1986.
David Phipps, *Miliardi* (also known as *Billions, Miliardi/ Millions,* and *Millions*), Prism Pictures, 1991.
Captain Jack Hassler, *Born to Ride,* Warner Bros., 1991.
Andy Aldrich, *Aurora: Operation Intercept,* Trimark Pictures, 1995.
Grant, *I Shot a Man in Vegas* (also known as *I Shot a Man in Reno*), Arrow Entertainment, 1995.
Staffer number one, *Nixon,* Buena Vista, 1995.
Jack Martin, *The Nurse,* Live Entertainment, 1997.
Victor Mallick, *Stag,* New City Releasing, 1997.
Adam, *Legal Deceit* (also known as *The Promised Land*), Spectrum Films, 1997.
Robert Renaud, *Breast Men,* Home Box Office Home Video, 1997.
Himself, *"Christine": Ignition* (documentary short), Columbia TriStar Home Entertainment, 2004.
Himself, *"Christine": Finish Line* (documentary short), Columbia TriStar Home Entertainment, 2004.

Himself, *"Christine": Fast & Furious* (documentary short), Columbia TriStar Home Entertainment, 2004.
Himself, *Into the Blue: Diving Deeper into the Blue* (documentary short), Sony Pictures Home Entertainment, 2004.
Male backpacker, *Turistas* (also known as *Paradise Lost*), Fox Atomic, 2006.

Film Work:
(With Scott Fields) Director, *Under Cover,* Cannon, 1987.
Director, *Crazy/Beautiful,* Buena Vista, 2001.
Director, *Blue Crush,* 2002.
Director, *Into the Blue,* 2005.
Producer and director, *Turistas* (also known as *Paradise Lost*), Fox Atomic, 2006.

Television Appearances; Series:
Made professional debut in *The Guiding Light,* CBS.

Television Appearances; Miniseries:
Billy Hazard, *North and South,* ABC, 1985.
Brad Sedgwick, *Billionaire Boys Club,* NBC, 1987.

Television Appearances; Movies:
Scott Massey, *Quarterback Princess,* CBS, 1983.
Peter Rubin, *"Hart to Hart": Crimes of the Hart,* 1994.
News producer, *Cheaters,* HBO, 2000.

Television Appearances; Specials:
Maxwell Fletcher, *"A Family Tree," Trying Times,* PBS, 1987.
Women of the Beach, E! Entertainment Television, 2002.

Television Appearances; Pilots:
Mick, *Too Good to Be True,* ABC, 1983.

Television Appearances; Episodic:
Gilmore, *Miami Vice,* NBC, 1986.
Maxwell Fletcher, *"A Family Tree," Trying Times,* PBS, 1987.
Tim Ayres, *"Badge of Honor," Friday the 13th* (also known as *Friday the 13th: The Series* and *Friday's Curse*), syndicated, 1988.
Malcolm Barrington, *"The Eyes of the Panther," Nightmare Classics,* 1990.
Bill Barlow, *"Dark Brother," The Young Riders,* ABC, 1992.
Professor Sinclair, *Relativity,* ABC, 1996.
"Top Gun," VH–1 Behind the Movie, VH1, 2002.
Sunday Morning Shootout, AMC, 2005.
"Lacy Lilting Lyrics," The L Word, Showtime, 2007.

Television Work; Movies:
Director, *Cheaters,* 2000.

Television Director; Episodic:
"Lez Girls," *The L Word,* Showtime, 2007.
"Literary License to Kill," *The L Word,* Showtime, 2007.

WRITINGS

Screenplays:
(With Scott Fields and Marty Ross) *Dangerously Close* (also known as *Campus '86* and *Choice Kill*), Cannon, 1986.
(With Scott Fields) *Under Cover,* Cannon, 1987.
Breast Men, Home Box Office Video, 1997.
Rock Star, Warner Bros., 2001.
(Rewrite) *Blue Crush,* Universal, 2002.

Television Movies:
Cheaters, 2000.

STOLTZ, Eric 1961–

PERSONAL

Full name, Eric Cameron Stoltz; born September 30, 1961, in Whittier, CA; son of Jack (an elementary schoolteacher) and Evelyn B. (a violinist and schoolteacher) Stoltz; brother of Catherine Stoltz (an opera singer). *Education:* Attended University of Southern California, 1979–81; trained for the stage at the Loft Studio with Stella Adler, Peggy Fury, and William Traylor.

Addresses: *Agent*—Creative Artists Agency, 2000 Avenue of the Stars, Los Angeles, CA 90067. *Manager*—Landmark Artists Management, 4116 West Magnolia Blvd., Suite 101, Burbank, CA 91505.

Career: Actor and producer. Actors Studio, member. As a teenager, piano player for local musical theatre productions.

Awards, Honors: ShoWest Award, male star of tomorrow, National Association of Theatre Owners, 1985; Golden Globe Award nomination, best supporting actor in a motion picture, 1986, for *Mask;* Antoinette Perry Award nomination, best featured actor in a play, Drama Desk Award nomination, outstanding featured actor in a play, *Theatre World* Award, 1989, all for *Our Town;* Independent Spirit Award nomination, best supporting

actor, Independent Features Project West, 1995, for *Pulp Fiction;* Indie Supporter Award, Los Angeles Independent Film Festival, 1998; Daytime Emmy Award nomination, outstanding directing in a children's special, 2002, for *My Horrible Year!.*

CREDITS

Film Appearances:
(Film debut) One of the "stoner buds," *Fast Times at Ridgemont High,* Universal, 1981.
Bill Conrad, *The Wild Life,* Universal, 1983.
Roy "Rocky" Dennis, *Mask,* Universal, 1984.
Chuck, *Surf II* (also known as *Surf II: The End of the Trilogy*), International Film Marketing, 1984.
Danny Hicks, *Running Hot* (also known as *Highway to Hell* and *Lucky 13*), New Line Cinema, 1984.
Mark, *The New Kids* (also known as *Striking Back*), Columbia, 1985.
Andy Wheeler, *Code Name: Emerald* (also known as *Deep Cover* and *Emerald*), Metro–Goldwyn–Mayer/United Artists, 1985.
Robert Nerra, *Lionheart* (also known as *Lionheart: The Children's Crusade*), Orion, 1987.
Keith Nelson, *Some Kind of Wonderful,* Paramount, 1987.
Christopher, *Manifesto* (also known as *A Night of Love*), Cannon, 1988.
Matt Rutledge, *Sister, Sister,* New World, 1988.
Percy Shelley, *Haunted Summer,* 1988.
The narrator, *Greasy Lake,* 1988.
Martin Brundle, *The Fly II,* Twentieth Century–Fox, 1989.
Vahlere, *Say Anything …* (also known as *… Say Anything …* , Twentieth Century–Fox, 1989.
Sergeant Danny Daly, *Memphis Belle,* Warner Bros., 1990.
Franck Cimballi, *Money,* 1991.
Joel Garcia, *The Waterdance,* Samuel Goldwyn Company, 1992.
Mime, *Singles,* Warner Bros., 1992.
Sid, *Bodies, Rest & Motion,* Fine Line Features, 1993.
Jake Briggs, *Naked in New York,* Fine Line Features, 1994.
Zed, *Killing Zoe,* October Films, 1994.
John Brooke, *Little Women,* Columbia, 1994.
Lance, *Pulp Fiction,* Miramax, 1994.
Joseph, *Sleep with Me,* United Artists, 1994.
MacDonald, *Rob Roy,* United Artists, 1995.
Jeff Newman, *Fluke,* Metro–Goldwyn–Mayer, 1995.
Simon, *The Prophecy* (also known as *God's Army* and *God's Secret Army*), Miramax/Dimension Films, 1995.
Chet, *Kicking and Screaming,* Trimark Pictures, 1995.
Stop N Start manager, *Killing Time,* 1995.
Howard Cazsatt, *Grace of My Heart,* Gramercy, 1996.

Wes Taylor, *Two Days in the Valley,* Metro–Goldwyn–Mayer, 1996.

Ethan Valhere, *Jerry Maguire,* TriStar, 1996.

Lance (in archival footage), *You're Still Not Fooling Anybody* (documentary short), Impossible Funky Productions, 1997.

Richter Boudreau, *Keys to Tulsa,* Gramercy, 1997.

Dr. Steven Cale, *Anaconda,* Columbia, 1997.

Lester Grimm, *Mr. Jealousy,* 1997.

The man, *The Rocking Horse Winner,* 1997.

Himself, *Pitch* (documentary), 1997.

(Uncredited) *The Definite Maybe,* DJM Films/Kaufman Astoria Studios/Definite Maybe, 1997.

Darlen, *Highball,* 1997.

Jimmy, *Hi–Life,* Sterling Home Entertainment, 1998.

Himself, *Reliving Our Fast Times at Ridgemont High* (documentary short), Universal Studios Home Video, 1999.

Voice of Theseus, the Grim Avenger, *Hercules: Zero to Hero* (animated), 1999.

Thurman Parks III, *A Murder of Crows,* 1999.

Sam Donovan, *The Simian Line,* DaWa Movies/S.L. Productions, 2000.

Lawrence Selden, *The House of Mirth* (also known as *Chez les heureux du monde* and *Haus Bellomont*), Capitol Films, 2000.

(Uncredited) Topeka partier, *Almost Famous,* DreamWorks Distribution, 2000.

Jesus, *Jesus and Hutch,* Boulder Films/Flying Pescado Pictures, 2000.

Mr. Stoltz, *It's a Shame About Ray,* 2000.

Dan, *Things Behind the Sun,* Behind the Sun Productions, 2001.

Teddy, *Harvard Man,* Lions Gate Films, 2001.

(Uncredited) Eric Stoltz, *Hollywood Palms,* Moonstone Entertainment, 2001.

Levine, *Happy Hour,* 2001.

Mr. Lance Lawson, *The Rules of Attraction* (also known as *Die regein des spiels*), Lions Gate Films, 2002.

Himself, *Pulp Fiction: The Facts* (documentary short), Buena Vista Home Entertainment, 2002.

Levine, *Happy Hour,* Davis Entertainment Filmworks, 2003.

Otto, *When Zachary Beaver Came to Town,* Echo Bridge Entertainment, 2003.

George Miller, *The Butterfly Effect,* New Line Cinema, 2004.

Fresno Burnbaum, *Childstar,* Hart Sharp Video, 2004.

Max, *Hello* (short), 2005.

William Davis, *The Honeymooners,* Paramount, 2005.

Narrator, *Odyssey in Rome* (documentary), 2005.

Mickey, *The Lather Effect,* 2006.

Josh, *The Grand Design* (short), 2007.

Film Work:

Production assistant, *Illegally Yours,* 1988.

Production assistant, *Say Anything,* Twentieth Century–Fox, 1989.

Producer, *Bodies, Rest & Motion,* Fine Line Features, 1993.

Producer, *Sleep with Me,* United Artists, 1994.

Executive producer, *Mr. Jealousy,* 1997.

Executive producer and director, *The Bulls* (short), 2005.

Executive producer and director, *The Grand Design* (short), 2007.

Television Appearances; Series:

Alan Tofsky, *Mad About You,* NBC, 1994–98.

Director Weller, *The Lot,* American Movie Classics, 1999.

August Dimitri, *Once and Again,* ABC, 2001–2002.

Mark Colm, *Out of Order,* Showtime, 2003–2004.

Host, *Character Studies,* 2005.

Television Appearances; Miniseries:

Boy, *The Seekers,* syndicated, 1979.

Mark Colm, *Out of Order,* 2003.

Howard Thomas, *The Triangle,* Sci–Fi Channel, 2005.

Television Appearances; Movies:

Joey and Redhawk, 1978.

First boy, *The Seekers,* 1979.

Steve Benson, *The Grass Is Always Greener over the Septic Tank,* CBS, 1980.

Pete Brady, *The Violation of Sarah McDavid,* CBS, 1982.

Steve, *Paper Dolls,* 1982.

Thursday's Child, CBS, 1983.

Ricky Tison, *A Killer in the Family,* ABC, 1983.

Younger Edward, *Sensibility and Sense,* PBS, 1990.

Frank Cimballi, *Money,* 1991.

Franz Bueller, *A Woman at War* (also known as *Ma guerre dans la Gestapo*), 1991.

Fred Turner, *Foreign Affairs,* TNT, 1993.

David Leader, *The Heart of Justice,* TNT, 1993.

Bill Thomas, *Roommates,* NBC, 1993.

Marty Strydom, *Inside,* Showtime, 1996.

Jesse Parish, *Don't Look Back,* HBO, 1996.

John Dantley, *Blackout Effect* (also known as *747*), NBC, 1998.

Robert Laurino, *Our Guys: Outrage at Glen Ridge* (also known as *Outrage in Glen Ridge*), ABC, 1999.

Nathaniel Brandon, *The Passion of Ayn Rand,* Showtime, 1999.

Thurman Parks III, *A Murder of Crows,* Cinemax, 1999.

Johnny Burroughs, *Common Ground,* Showtime, 2000.

Captain Walker Randall, *One Kill,* Showtime, 2000.

Thirty, 2000.

Todd Cope, *The Last Dance,* CBS, 2000.

Television Appearances; Specials:

George Gibbs, "Our Town," *Great Performances,* PBS, 1989.

Memphis Belle and the Glory Boys, Arts and Entertainment, 1990.

The 1995 MTV Movie Awards, MTV, 1995.

Voice, *U.S.–Mexican War (1846–1848),* 1998.

Presenter, *The 15th Annual IFP/West Independent Spirit Awards,* Independent Film Channel and Bravo, 2000.

Presenter, *The 2001 IFP/West Independent Spirit Awards,* Independent Film Channel, 2001.

Uncle Charlie, *My Horrible Year!,* Showtime, 2001.

The 2002 IFP/West Independent Spirit Awards, IFC and Bravo, 2002.

Still Cher, BBC, 2002.

Roy L. "Rocky" Dennis, *Cher: The Farewell Tour,* NBC, 2003.

Retrosexual: The 80's, VH1, 2004.

Happy Birthday Oscar Wilde, BBC, 2004.

Narrator, *Mornings with Shirley Povich: A Century of Writing Sports,* ESPN, 2005.

Television Appearances; Pilots:
Neil Troutman, *Things Are Looking Up,* CBS, 1984.

Television Appearances; Episodic:
(Television debut) *Class of '65,* NBC, 1980.

Kurt Harper, "Finally Grad Night," *Eight Is Enough,* 1980.

First senior boy, "The Valediction," *The Waltons,* 1980.

"The Killing of McNeal County's Children," *Walking Tall,* 1981.

Luke, "Man of the Hour," *Knots Landing,* CBS, 1981.

Steve, *Paper Dolls,* ABC, 1982.

Eddie Carson, "Under Pressure," *St. Elsewhere,* NBC, 1983.

Eddie Carson, "Entrapment," *St. Elsewhere,* NBC, 1983.

Eddie Carson, "All About Eve," *St. Elsewhere,* NBC, 1983.

Juice, *The Fall Guy,* 1983.

Younger Edward, "Sensibility and Sense," *American Playhouse,* PBS, 1990.

Voice of Don, "Miracle on Third or Fourth Street," *Frasier,* NBC, 1993.

Cameron, "How Long Does It Take to Cook a 22–Pound Turkey?," *Partners,* Fox, 1995.

Nick Ballestier, "A Dime a Dance," *Fallen Angels,* 1995.

The Rosie O'Donnell Show, syndicated, 1996.

Drew Kellerman, "Wu's on First?," *Homicide: Life on the Street,* NBC, 1997.

Voice of Theseus, "Hercules and the Minotaur," *Hercules* (animated; also known as *Disney's "Hercules"*), ABC and syndicated, 1998.

Dr. Robert Yeats, "Wag the Doc," *Chicago Hope,* CBS, 1998.

Dr. Robert Yeats, "McNeil and Pray," *Chicago Hope,* CBS, 1998.

Dr. Robert Yeats, "Curing Cancer," *Chicago Hope,* CBS, 1998.

Voice of Theseus, the Grim Avenger, "The Grim Avenger," *Hercules* (animated; also known as *Disney's "Hercules"*), ABC and syndicated, 1999.

"Music Movie Stars," *VH–1 Where Are They Now?,* VH1, 2000.

Voice of reader, "War Letters," *The American Experience,* PBS, 2001.

Ray Stanard Baker, "Woodrow Wilson: Episode One—A Passionate Man," *The American Experience,* PBS, 2002.

Ray Stanard Baker, "Woodrow Wilson: Episode Two—The Redemption of the World," *The American Experience,* PBS, 2002.

Father Michael Sweeney, "Silence," *Law & Order: Special Victims Unit* (also known as *Law & Order: SVU* and *Special Victims Unit*), NBC, 2002.

V Graham Norton, Channel 4, 2003.

Rocked with Gina Gershon, 2004.

Tom Cassidy, "Kiss and Tell," *Will & Grace,* NBC, 2005.

Tom, "Friends with Benefits," *Will & Grace,* NBC, 2005.

Sonny Troyer, "We Had a Dream," *Medium,* NBC, 2007.

Detective Chris Veeder, "Drink the Cup," *Close to Home,* CBS, 2007.

Detective Chris Veeder, "Fall from Grace," *Close to Home,* CBS, 2007.

Detective Chris Veeder, "Eminent Domain," *Close to Home,* CBS, 2007.

Also appeared as himself, "Ally Sheedy," *Celebrity Profile,* E! Entertainment Television.

Television Director; Specials:
My Horrible Year!, Showtime, 2001.

Television Director; Episodic:
"Falling in Place," *Once and Again,* ABC, 2002.

"Tombstone," *Law & Order,* NBC, 2005.

"Dumping Bella," *Boston Legal,* ABC, 2007.

Stage Appearances:
(Stage debut) Winthrop, *The Music Man,* 1973.

Billy Bibbitt, *One Flew Over the Cuckoo's Nest,* Santa Barbara, CA, 1978.

Barnaby, *Hello, Dolly!,* 1979.

Konstantin, *The Seagull,* Theatre at University of Southern California, Los Angeles, 1980.

Billy, *Album,* Edinburgh Festival, Edinburgh, Scotland, 1981.

Eddie, *Runaways,* Edinburgh Festival, 1981.

Snoopy, *You're a Good Man Charlie Brown,* Edinburgh Festival, 1981.

(Off–Broadway debut) Horace Robadeaux, *The Widow Claire,* Circle in the Square, New York City, 1987.

(Broadway debut) George Gibbs, *Our Town,* Lyceum Theatre, 1988–89.

Gil Harbison, *The American Plan,* Manhattan Theatre Club, New York City, 1990.

Dion Boucicault, *Two Shakespearean Actors,* Cort Theatre, New York City, 1991–92.

William Reach, *Down the Road,* Atlantic Theatre, New York City, 1993.

The Importance of Being Earnest, Irish Repertory Theatre, New York City, 1996.

Baron Tuzenbach, *Three Sisters,* Roundabout Theatre, then Criterion Theatre, both New York City, 1997.

Arms and the Man, 1997.

The Glass Menagerie, off–Broadway production, 1998.

Prelude to a Kiss, Theatre at Skirball Cultural Center, Los Angeles, 2000.

Light Up the Sky, Williamstown Theatre Festival, Williamstown, MA, 2000.

Betrayal, Los Angeles, 2001.

Simon Able, *Sly Fox,* Ethel Barrymore Theatre, New York City, 2004.

McReele, 2005.

Major Tours:

Joe Crowell, *Our Town,* 1974.

Oliver!, 1976.

RECORDINGS

Audio Books:
Raveling, Time Warner, 2000.

Videos:
Himself, *Film–Fest DVD: Issue 1—Sundance,* 1999.

WRITINGS

Screenplays:
The Grand Design (short), 2007.

Film Scores:
The Bulls, 2005.

OTHER SOURCES

Periodicals:
Entertainment Weekly, April 14, 1995, p. 43.
Movieline, June, 1992, p. 44.
Premiere, August, 1998, p. 36.

T

TAYLOR–YOUNG, Leigh 1945(?)–
(Leigh Taylor Young)

PERSONAL

Born January 25, 1945 (some sources say 1944), in Washington, DC; daughter of Carol Taylor (a diplomat) and Pauline Young; step–daughter of Donald Young (an executive); married Ryan O'Neal (an actor), February, 1967 (divorced, 1973); married Guy McElwaine (an agent and director), 1978 (divorced, c. 1985); married Mark Holmes (a doctor of oriental medicine), c. 1987 (divorced, February, 1992); children: (first marriage) Patrick (an actor and sportscaster). *Education:* Studied economics and theater at Northwestern University, Evanston, IL, 1963–64; entered the master's program at the Peace Theological Seminary and College of Philosophy, Los Angeles, 1993; studied acting with Sanford Meisner, Alvina Krause, and Stella Adler at the Neighborhood Playhouse.

Addresses: *Agent*—House of Representatives, 400 South Beverly Dr., Suite 101, Beverly Hills, CA 90212. *Manager*—Daniel Sladek Entertainment Corp., 8306 Wilshire Blvd., Suite 510, Beverly Hills, CA 90211.

Career: Actress. Eagles Mere Summer Repertory Theatre, Eagles Mere, PA, apprentice actress; hosted the Muscular Dystrophy Telethon; provided voice for the "Search for Serenity" series of audio meditations from "The Course in Miracles" training. Movement of Spiritual Inner Awareness, ordained minister; United Nations Environment Program, special advisor in arts and media; Goodwill Ambassador for United Nations for ICEBRIDGE: First Arctic Environmental Forum, 1995; spoke on behalf of the Institute for Individual and World Peace; worked with Better World Society, Hands Across America, Heartfelt Foundation, American Cancer Society.

Awards, Honors: Golden Globe Award nomination, most promising newcomer–female, 1969, for *I Love You, Alice B. Toklas!;* Emmy Award, outstanding supporting actress in a drama series, 1994, and Golden Globe Award nomination, best performance by an actress in a supporting role in a series, 1995, both for *Picket Fences.*

CREDITS

Stage Appearances:
(Stage debut) Assistant, *Catastrophe,* Harold Clurman Theatre, New York City, 1983.
Dead End Kids: A History of Nuclear Power, New Theatre for Now, Center Theatre Group, Mark Taper Forum, Los Angeles, 1984.
Made in America, New Theatre for Now, Center Theatre Group, Mark Taper Forum, 1984.
Pass/Fail, New Theatre for Now, Center Theatre Group, Mark Taper Forum, 1984.
Cakewalk, New Theatre for Now, Center Theatre Group, Mark Taper Forum, 1984.
Beckett! Beckett! Beckett!, New Theatre for Now, Center Theatre Group, Mark Taper Forum, 1984.
Sally, *Sleeping Dogs,* Center Theatre Group, Mark Taper Forum, 1985.

Also appeared as the lawyer, *Knives;* Jeanette, *Three Bags Full.*

Film Appearances:
Nancy, *I Love You, Alice B. Toklas!* (also known as *Kiss My Butterfly*), Warner Bros., 1968.
Nancy Barker, *The Big Bounce,* Warner Bros./Seven Arts, 1969.
Amparo, *The Adventurers,* Paramount, 1970.
(Uncredited) College co–ed, *The Games,* 1970.
Manny, *Buttercup Chain,* Columbia, 1971.
Angela Palumbo, *The Gang That Couldn't Shoot Straight,* Metro–Goldwyn–Mayer, 1971.

Zereh, *The Horsemen,* Columbia, 1971.

Shirl, *Soylent Green,* Metro–Goldwyn–Mayer, 1973.

Herself, *A Look at the World of "Soylent Green"* (documentary), 1973.

Herself, *Aliens from Spaceship Earth,* 1977.

Claudie Walters, *Can't Stop the Music,* Associated, 1980.

Jennifer Long, *Looker,* Warner Bros., 1981.

Elizabeth Frimple, *Secret Admirer* (also known as *The Letter*), Orion, 1985.

Virginia Howell, *The Jagged Edge,* Columbia, 1985.

Beryl Chambers, *Accidents,* 1988.

Doris, *Honeymoon Academy* (also known as *For Better or for Worse*), 1990.

Dr. Sharon Kawai, *Dreamrider,* 1993.

Redhead, *Bliss,* Sony Pictures Entertainment, 1997.

Patrice, *Addams Family Reunion,* Warner Bros. Home Video, 1998.

Valerie Patton, *Slackers* (also known as *Les complices*), Screen Gems, 2002.

Teresa, *Klepto,* Showcase Entertainment, 2003.

(As Leigh Taylor Young) Mom, *A–List,* 2006.

The psychiatrist, *Spiritual Warriors,* 2006.

Mrs. James, *Dirty Laundry,* Codeblack Entertainment, 2006.

Klepto, 2006.

Diana, *Coffee Date,* TLA Releasing, 2006.

Television Appearances; Series:

Rachael Welles, *Peyton Place,* ABC, 1966–67.

Lauren Dane, *The Devlin Connection,* NBC, 1982.

Lee Chadway, *The Hamptons,* ABC, 1983.

Kimberly Cryder, *Dallas,* CBS, 1987–89.

Mayor Rachel Harris, *Picket Fences,* CBS, 1993–95.

Elaine Stevens, *Sunset Beach,* NBC, 1997.

Katherine Barrett Crane, a recurring role, *Passions* (also known as *Harmony's Passions*), NBC, 2004–2007.

Television Appearances; Miniseries:

Madame de Stael, *Napoleon and Josephine: A Love Story,* ABC, 1987.

Television Appearances; Movies:

Jennifer, *Under the Yum Yum Tree,* 1969.

Barrie Johnson, *Marathon,* CBS, 1980.

Maura McGuire, *Perry Mason: The Case of the Sinister Spirit,* NBC, 1987.

Aggie Harden, *Who Gets the Friends?,* CBS, 1988.

Eve's mother, *Clowning Around 2,* PBS, 1993.

Dr. Sharon Kawai, *Dreamrider,* Showtime, 1993.

Barbara Hansen, *Murder or Memory? A Moment of Truth Movie* (also known as *Murder or Memory?* and *Moment of Truth: Murder or Memory?*), NBC, 1994.

Cynthia Connor, *An Unfinished Affair,* ABC, 1996.

Margot, *Stranger in My Home,* CBS, 1997.

Television Appearances; Specials:

NBC team member, *Battle of the Network Stars XIII,* CBS, 1982.

Hollywood Women, syndicated, 1988.

An All Star Party for Aaron Spelling, ABC, 1998.

The O'Neals: The E! True Hollywood Story, E! Entertainment Television, 2001.

Television Appearances; Pilots:

Police Sergeant, *Houston Knights,* CBS, 1987.

Elizabeth Strack, *Ghost Writer,* Fox, 1990.

Nita Davenport, *Silverfox,* ABC, 1991.

Meredith, *JAG,* NBC, 1995.

Television Appearances; Episodic:

Dateline: Hollywood, 1967.

(As Leigh Taylor Young) Bonnie Foster, "Bonnie and McCloud," *McCloud,* 1976.

Leslie Tarleton, "I Want to Get Married/The Jewel Thief," *Fantasy Island,* ABC, 1978.

Ann, "Folks from Home/The Captain's Cup/Legal Eagle," *The Love Boat,* ABC, 1978.

Victoria Wilder, "Deep in the Hart of Dixieland," *Hart to Hart,* 1982.

Carole, "Secrets," *Hotel* (also known as *Arthur Hailey's "Hotel"*), 1983.

Stephanie McMullen, "Identities," *Hotel* (also known as *Arthur Hailey's "Hotel"*), 1985.

Sharon Lockwood, "Pressure Points," *Hotel* (also known as *Arthur Hailey's "Hotel"*), 1986.

Alicia Carlisle, "Angel of Desolation," *Spenser: For Hire,* 1986.

"Tintype," *Outlaws,* 1987.

Lieutenant Sherina McLaren, "Mirrors," *Houston Knights,* CBS, 1987.

Adalaide Walker, "Murder Party," *Alfred Hitchcock Presents,* 1988.

Beck Kincaid, "Wood's Thirtieth Reunion," *Evening Shade,* CBS, 1991.

Polly, "Lessons Learned," *The Young Riders,* 1992.

"Denise and De Nuptials," *Civil Wars,* ABC, 1992.

"A Liver Runs Through It," *Civil Wars,* ABC, 1993.

Gwen Langley, "Grandma, What Big Eyes You Have," *Empty Nest,* NBC, 1995.

Laney Sherman Boswell, "A Quaking in Aspen," *Murder, She Wrote,* CBS, 1995.

Mrs. Green, "The Competitive Edge," *Malibu Shores,* NBC, 1996.

Naomi Sandburg, "Spare Parts," *The Sentinel,* UPN, 1996.

Naomi Sandburg, "Private Eyes," *The Sentinel,* UPN, 1997.

Nora Chambers, "Don't Take My Love Away," *7th Heaven* (also known as *Seventh Heaven*), The WB, 1997.

Michelle Lucca Stamatis, "Bulletproof," *The Pretender,* NBC, 1998.

Blythe Hunter, "The Morning After," *Beverly Hills, 90210,* Fox, 1998.

Blythe Hunter, "Dealer's Choice," *Beverly Hills, 90210,* Fox, 1998.

Blythe Hunter, "Don't Ask Don't Tell," *Beverly Hills, 90210,* Fox, 1998.

Michelle Lucca Stamatis, "Parole," *The Pretender,* NBC, 1998.

Michelle Lucca Stamatis, "Flesh & Blood," *The Pretender,* NBC, 1999.

Yanas Tigan, "Prodigal Daughter," *Star Trek: Deep Space Nine* (also known as *DS9, Deep Space Nine,* and *Star Trek: DS9),* 1999.

Naomi Sandburg, "The Sentinel by Blair Sandburg," *The Sentinel,* UPN, 1999.

(As Leigh Taylor Young) Catherine Beecher–Douglas, "Maternal Mirrors," *Strong Medicine,* Lifetime, 2003.

OTHER SOURCES

Electronic:

Leigh Taylor–Young Website, http://www.lty.com, August 20, 2007.

THOMPSON, John

PERSONAL

Career: Producer. Began career in Italian film industry, 1980s–90s; Millennium Films, head of production, 1997—.

Awards, Honors: Video Premiere Award nomination (with others), best live–action video premiere, DVD Exclusive Awards, 2001, for *Replicant.*

CREDITS

Film Associate Producer:
Hospital Massacre, 1980.
The Assisi Underground, Cannon, 1985.
The Berlin Affair (also known as *Interno berlinese* and *Leidenschaften),* Cannon, 1985.
Salome, 1986.
Un complicato intrigo di donne, vicoli et delitti (also known as *A Complex Plot About Women, Alleys and Crimes, Camorra, Camorra (A Story of Streets, Women and Crime),* and *Camorra: The Naples Connection),* Cannon, 1986.
Dumb Dicks, 1986.
Dancers (also known as *Giselle),* Cannon, 1987.
Haunted Summer, 1988.

Sinbad of the Seven Seas, 1989.
The Comfort of Strangers (also known as *Cortesie per gli ospiti),* Skouras Pictures, 1990.

Film Producer:
Shadows and Lights (also known as *Joni Mitchell: Shadows and Lights),* Warner Home Video, 1980.
The Barbarians, 1987.
Looking for Lola, Nu Image Films, 1998.
Shadrach, Columbia, 1998.
The 4th Floor, A–Pix Entertainment, 1999.
Takedown (also known as *Hackers 2: Takedown* and *Track Down),* Dimension Films, 2000.
Forever Lulu (also known as *Along for the Ride),* Artisan Entertainment, 2000.
Nobody's Baby, Artisan Entertainment, 2001.
Replicant, Artisan Entertainment, 2001.
The Order (also known as *Jihad Warrior),* TriStar, 2001.
Run for the Money (also known as *Hard Cash),* Artisan Entertainment, 2002.
In Hell (also known as *The Savage* and *The Shu),* Starmedia Home Entertainment, 2003.
Shadow of Fear, Mainline Productions, 2004.
Edison (also known as *Edison Force),* Sony Pictures Home Entertainment, 2005.
16 Blocks, Warner Bros., 2006.
The Wicker Man, Warner Bros., 2006.
King of California, First Look International, 2007.
Until Death, Sony, 2007.
Hero Wanted, Nu Image Films, 2007.
John Rambo, Lions Gate Films, 2008.

Film Coproducer:
No Code of Conduct, Dimension Films, 1998.
Mary/Mary, 2002.

Film Executive Producer:
Hercules (also known as *Ercole),* Cannon, 1983.
Le avventure dell'incredible Ercole (also known as *Le avventure di Ercole 2, Hercules II,* and *The Adventures of Hercules),* Cannon, 1985.
Otello, Cannon, 1986.
The Barbarians (also known as *I barbari, The Barbarian Brothers,* and *The Barbarians and Co.),* Cannon, 1987.
Twin Sitters (also known as *The Babysitters),* Global Pictures, 1994.
Some Girl (also known as *Girl Talk* and *Men),* Millennium Films, 1998.
Outside Ozona, TriStar, 1998.
Guinevere, Miramax, 1999.
The Brass Ring, Big Brass Ring, Inc., 1999.
For the Cause (also known as *Final Encounter),* Dimension Films, 2000.
Prozac Nation, Miramax, 2001.
Undisputed (also known as *Undisputed—Seig ohne ruhm),* Miramax, 2002.

Try Seventeen (also known as *All I Want*), Try Seventeen Productions, Inc., 2002.
Blind Horizon, Lions Gate Films, 2003.
Belly of the Beast, Columbia TriStar Home Entertainment, 2003.
Control, Lions Gate Films, 2004.
Loverboy, Screen Media Films, 2005.
Mansquito (also known as *Mosquitoman*), First Look International, 2005.
Mozart and the Whale, 2005.
Undisputed II: Last Man Standing (also known as *Undisputed 2*), New Line Home Video, 2006.
Lonely Hearts (also known as *Lonely Hearts Killer*), Millennium, 2006.
The Black Dahlia (also known as *Black Dahlia*), Universal, 2006.
Wicked Little Things, AfterDark Films, 2006.
Home of the Brave, Metro–Goldwyn–Mayer, 2006.
88 Minutes, TriStar, 2007.
When Nietzsche Wept, First Look International, 2007.
More Than You Know, Columbia, 2007.
Blonde Ambition, Sony, 2007.

Film Co–Executive Producer:
October 22, Millennium Films, 1998.
How to Kill Your Neighbor's Dog (also known as *Mad Dogs and Englishmen*), Artistic License, 2000.

Film Work:
Production manager, *Rust Never Sleeps,* International Harmony, 1979.
First assistant producer, *Neil Young: Human Highway,* Warner Home Video, 1982.
Line producer, *Deathline* (also known as *Armageddon* and *Redline*), Ascot Video, 1997.
Executive in charge of production, *American Perfekt,* 1997.

Film Appearances:
(Uncredited) Udo, *Deathline* (also known as *Armageddon* and *Redline*), Ascot Video, 1997.
Himself, *Absolute Power: The Making of "Edison Force"* (short), Sony, 2006.

Television Executive Producer; Movies:
Hammerhead: Shark Frenzy (also known as *Hammerhead* and *SharkMan*), Sci–Fi Channel, 2005.
The Snake King, Sci–Fi Channel, 2005.
Larva, Sci–Fi Channel, 2005.
L'Inchiesta (also known as *En busca de la tumba de Cristo, The Final Inquiry,* and *The Inquiry*), 2006.
Gryphon, Sci–Fi Channel, 2007.

Television Co–Executive Producer; Movies:
The Mary Kay Letourneau Story: All–American Girl, USA Network, 2000.

Television Appearances; Episodic:
The Tonight Show Starring Johnny Carson, NBC, 1970.

WRITINGS

Film Stories:
Looking for Lola, 1998.

Television Movie Stories:
Alien Lockdown (also known as *PredatorMan*), Sci–Fi Channel, 2004.

THOMPSON, Randy 1954–

PERSONAL

Born September 25, 1954, in Fort Wayne, IN.

Career: Actor, director, producer, writer.

CREDITS

Film Appearances:
Zukini, *Brenda Starr,* Triumph, 1989.
Andy Miller, *Stages,* 1990.
Tony Conway, *Edge of Honor,* 1991.
Andy Miller, *The Montana Run,* New City, 1992.
Stu, *Singles,* Warner Bros., 1992.
Businessman, *The Year of My Japanese Cousin,* Michi, 1995.
Library guard, *Desperate Measures,* TriStar, 1998.

Film Work:
Director and producer, *Stages,* 1990.
Director, producer and editor, *The Montana Run,* 1992.

Television Appearances; Episodic:
Peter, "Heroes," *Northern Exposure,* CBS, 1992.
Sean McCarthy, "A Haunting Case," *Under Suspicion,* 1995.
Lawyer, "The Quest," *Northern Exposure,* CBS, 1995.
Blind author, "Blind Man's Bluff," *Medicine Ball,* 1995.
Mr. Hardy, "The Enemy Within," *Nowhere Man,* 1995.
Network executive, "Fame," *Tracey Takes On ...,* HBO, 1996.
Swat team leader, "A Mad Tea Party," *L.A. Firefighters,* FOX, 1996.
Medical examiner, "Second Chances," *Chicago Hope,* 1997.
Gun shop owner, "Heroes," *Michael Hayes,* 1997.
Cop, "One Hundred Tears Away," *Ally McBeal,* 1997.

Guard, "Starry Night," *Boy Meets World,* 1998.

Fred, "Tool–Thousand–One: A Space Oddyssey," *Home Improvement,* 1998.

Phone caller, "When Ellen Talks, People Listen," *Ellen* (also known as *These Friends of Mine*), ABC, 1998.

Parent, "Slam Dunkin' Donuts," *DiResta,* UPN, 1999.

Cafe owner, *Passions,* NBC, 1999.

Supervisor, *Sunset Beach,* NBC, 1999.

Deputy, "Primrose Empath," *Charmed,* 2000.

Bailiff, "The Unsinkable Sydney Hansen," *Providence,* 2000.

Dr. Kriegel, "Shadow," *Buffy the Vampire Slayer* (also known as *BtVS, Buffy,* and *Buffy the Vampire Slayer: The Series*), The WB, 2000.

Dr. Kriegel, "Listening to Fear," *Buffy the Vampire Slayer* (also known as *BtVS, Buffy,* and *Buffy the Vampire Slayer: The Series*), The WB, 2000.

Dr. Kriegel, "Into the Woods," *Buffy the Vampire Slayer* (also known as *BtVS, Buffy,* and *Buffy the Vampire Slayer: The Series*), The WB, 2000.

Dr. Kriegel, "The Body," *Buffy the Vampire Slayer* (also known as *BtVS, Buffy,* and *Buffy the Vampire Slayer: The Series*), The WB, 2001.

Goodwill driver, "The Not–So–Hostile Takeover," *For Your Love,* 2001.

Tytell, "Busted," *Roswell* (also known as *Roswell High*), UPN, 2001.

Executive donor number one, "Bartlet for America," *The West Wing,* 2001.

Policeman, "One Hundred Tears," *Ally McBeal,* 2001.

Gaffer, "Daddy Dearest," *The Lot,* 2001.

JKX: The Jamie Kennedy Experiment, The WB, 2001.

Cop, "Charity," *Malcolm in the Middle,* 2001.

Colonel Isaac Phillips, "Felonious Monk," *CSI: Crime Scene Investigation* (also known as *C.S.I., CSI: Las Vegas,* and *Les Experts*), 2002.

Cop Frank, "Going Down," *Judging Amy,* 2003.

William Fennerty, "The Firm," *The Practice,* 2004.

Officer, "Reese Joins the Army: Part 2," *Malcolm in the Middle,* 2004.

Roger Sommers, *24,* 2004.

CIA agent, "What Dreams May Come," *American Dreams* (also known as *Our Generation*), 2004.

Detective, *The Young and the Restless* (also known as *Y&R*), CBS, 2004.

Dock worker, *Secret Lives,* Lifetime, 2005.

Detective, *The Young and the Restless* (also known as *Y&R*), CBS, 2006.

Bailiff, "Don't Mess with Sloppy," *The Jake Effect,* Bravo, 2006.

Officer Carl Ralston, "Race Ipsa," *Boston Legal,* 2006.

Officer Carl Ralston, "Can't We All Get a Lung," *Boston Legal,* 2006.

J. R. 'Smitty' Smith, "Jones," *Criminal Minds,* 2007.

Officer Carl Ralston, "Son of the Defender," *Boston Legal,* 2007.

Frank Waring, "Time After Time," *Grey's Anatomy,* ABC, 2007.

Television Appearances; Movies:

First marshall, *Witness Protection,* 1999.

Dock worker, *Secret Lives,* Lifetime, 2005.

Television Appearances; Pilots:

Politician, *Seven Days,* UPN, 1998.

WRITINGS

Screenplays:

Stages, 1990.

The Montana Run, 1992.

Film Scores:

Stages, 1990.

The Montana Run, 1992.

TIGER, Derry
   See ELLISON, Harlan

TIMME, Reinhold
   See EBERT, Roger

TRAVIS, Nancy 1961–

PERSONAL

Full name, Nancy Ann Travis; born September 21, 1961, in (or near) New York, NY; married Robert N. Fried (a studio executive and producer), 1994; children: Benjamin, Jeremy. *Education:* New York University, B.A.

Addresses: *Agent*—Leanne Coronel, Endeavor, 9601 Wilshire Blvd., 3rd Floor, Beverly Hills, CA 90210.

Career: Actress, voice performer, and producer. Circle in the Square, New York City, apprentice at Professional Theatre School; Naked Angels (theatre company), founding member, 1987. Appeared in television commercials, including advertisements for Excedrin pain reliever, Eggo Nutri–Grain waffles, and Canada Dry ginger ale.

CREDITS

Film Appearances:

(Film debut) Sylvia Bennington, *3 Men and a Baby,* Buena Vista, 1987.

Lyria (some sources cite Lyra) Williams, *Eight Men Out,* Orion, 1988.

Karen Lutnick, *Married to the Mob,* Orion, 1988.

Corinne Landreaux, *Air America,* TriStar, 1990.

Kathleen Avila, *Internal Affairs,* Paramount, 1990.

Riva, *Loose Cannons,* TriStar, 1990.

Sylvia Bennington, *Three Men and a Little Lady,* Buena Vista, 1990.

Cassie Slocombe, *Passed Away,* Buena Vista, 1992.

Joan Barry, *Chaplin* (also known as *Charlot*), TriStar, 1992.

Harriet Michaels, *So I Married an Axe Murderer,* TriStar, 1993.

Rita Baker, *The Vanishing,* Twentieth Century–Fox, 1993.

Robin Hunter, *Greedy,* Universal, 1994.

Lucille, *Destiny Turns On the Radio,* Savoy Pictures, 1995.

Kate, *Lieberman in Love,* Chanticleer Films, 1995.

Carol Johnson, *Fluke,* Metro–Goldwyn–Mayer, 1995.

Lorraine Franklin, *Bogus,* Warner Bros., 1996.

Carol, *Auggie Rose* (also known as *Beyond Suspicion*), New City Releasing, 2000.

Lydia Rodman, *The Sisterhood of the Traveling Pants* (also known as *The Sisterhood of the Travelling Pants*), Warner Bros., 2005.

Cat, *The Jane Austen Book Club,* Sony Pictures Classics, 2007.

Television Appearances; Series:

Kim Cooper, *Almost Perfect,* CBS, 1995–97.

Julie Better, *Work with Me,* CBS, 1999.

Chris Connor, *Becker,* CBS, 2002–2004.

Susan Pearson, *The Bill Engvall Show,* TBS, 2007.

Television Appearances; Miniseries:

Jessica Gray, *Harem,* ABC, 1986.

Professor Joyce Reardon, *Rose Red* (also known as *Stephen King's "Rose Red"*), ABC, 2001.

Television Appearances; Movies:

Ann, *Malice in Wonderland* (also known as *The Rumor Mill*), CBS, 1985.

Leah Bundy, *I'll Be Home for Christmas,* NBC, 1988.

T. J. Harlow, *Body Language,* HBO, 1995.

Jenny Pryce, *Running Mates,* TNT, 2000.

April Brenner, *The Party Never Stops: Diary of a Binge Drinker,* Lifetime, 2007.

Television Appearances; Specials:

Judy, "High School Narc," *ABC Afterschool Special,* ABC, 1985.

Night of About 14 CBS Stars, CBS, 1996.

Television Appearances; Awards Presentations:

The Movie Awards, CBS, 1991.

Presenter, *The 29th Annual People's Choice Awards,* CBS, 2003.

Television Appearances; Episodic:

"Serenade for Dead Lovers," *Worlds Beyond,* 1986.

Laura, "My Own Place," *Tales from the Darkside,* 1987.

Bette Allison, "The Frightening Frammis," *Fallen Angels,* Showtime, 1993.

Voices of Beatrice, Bernice, and Beverly, "About Face," *Duckman: Private Dick/Family Man* (animated), USA Network, 1994.

Voices of Beatrice, Bernice, and Beverly, "Papa Oom M.O.W. M.O.W.," *Duckman: Private Dick/Family Man* (animated), USA Network, 1995.

Late Show with David Letterman (also known as *The Late Show*), CBS, 1995.

The Rosie O'Donnell Show, syndicated, 1996, 1999.

Voice of Bernice, "Grandma–ma's Flatulent Adventure," *Duckman: Private Dick/Family Man* (animated), USA Network, 1996.

Herself, "Lowenstein's Lament," *Cybill,* CBS, 1996.

Voice of Spencer, "Rage's Burning Wheel," *The Real Adventures of Jonny Quest* (animated; also known as *Jonny Quest: The Real Adventures*), TNT, 1996.

Diane Esheo, "Ricochet," *Gun* (also known as *Robert Altman's "Gun"*), ABC, 1997.

Voice of Grandma–ma Sophia, "Crime, Punishment, War, Peace, and the Idiot," *Duckman: Private Dick/Family Man* (animated), USA Network, 1997.

Voice of Darci Mason, "Obsession," *Superman* (animated; also known as *Superman: The Animated Series*), The WB, 1998.

Voice of cat, "Queen of Denial," *The Wild Thornberrys* (animated), Nickelodeon, 2000.

Television Appearances; Other:

Susan Morton (some sources cite Susan Allen), *My Last Love* (also known as *To Live For*), ABC, 1999.

Windsor, *Talk Show Diaries* (pilot), UPN, 2005.

Television Work:

Producer, *My Last Love* (also known as *To Live For*), ABC, 1999.

Co–executive producer, *Work with Me* (series), CBS, 1999.

Stage Appearances:

(Off–Broadway debut) Betty Shapiro, *Its Hard to Be a Jew,* American Jewish Theatre, 1984.

(Broadway debut) Laurie, *I'm Not Rappaport,* Booth Theatre, between 1985 and 1988.

A. C., *The Signal Season of Dummy Hoy,* Hudson Guild Theatre, New York City, 1987–88.

Appeared in *Aven–U Boys* and *King of Connecticut,* both Naked Angels productions, and *My Children, My*

Africa, La Jolla Playhouse, La Jolla, CA; also appeared at New Jersey Shakespeare Festival, Madison, NJ, 1981.

Major Tours:
Understudy for Nora, *Brighton Beach Memoirs,* 1980.

OTHER SOURCES

Periodicals:
Interview, January, 1990, p. 34.
People Weekly, April 8, 1996, p. 15; September 2, 1996, p. 44.
Premiere, August, 1990, pp. 46–47.

TURMAN, Glynn 1946–

PERSONAL

Full name, Glynn Russell Turman; born January 31, 1946, in New York, NY; married Aretha Franklin (a singer) April 11, 1978 (divorced, 1984); married Jo–Ann Allen (a real estate broker); children: (second marriage) Glynn, Jr. (deceased), Delena Joy, Darryl, Stephanie. *Education:* Attended High School of the Performing Arts.

Addresses: *Manager*—Elkins Entertainment, 134 S. Rossmore Ave., Los Angeles, CA 90004.

Career: Actor, director, and composer. Inner City Repertory Theatre, Los Angeles, member of company and teacher, 1972–73; also worked at Tyrone Guthrie Theatre, Minneapolis, MN. Camp Gid D Up (a non profit children's cam), cofounder with Jo–Ann Allen.

Member: Screen Actors Guild.

Awards, Honors: TOR Award, best actor in the black theatre, 1974; Image Award, National Association for the Advancement of Colored People, 1978; AUDELCO Award, 1979, for *A Raisin in the Sun;* Image Award nomination, outstanding supporting actor in a drama series, 2007, for *The Wire;* Image Award and Drama–Logue Award, both for *Eyes of the American;* Los Angeles Critics Award nomination and Dramalogue Award, both for *The Wine Sellers;* Image Award, direction, for *Deadwood Dick.*

CREDITS

Film Appearances:
Muhammed G, *A.W.O.L.* (also known as *A.W.O.L.—Avhopparen*), 1972.

Gideon, *Five on the Black Hand Side,* United Artists, 1973.
Jomo, *Thomasine and Bushrod,* Columbia, 1974.
Dr. Johnson, *The Together Brothers,* Twentieth Century–Fox, 1974.
Voice, *The Nine Lives of Fritz the Cat* (animated), American International Pictures, 1974.
Jeff Williams, *The River Niger,* Cine Artists, 1975.
Robert "Preach" Morris, *Cooley High,* American International Pictures, 1975.
Isaac "Ike," *J. D.'s Revenge,* American International Pictures, 1976.
Nigeria, *A Hero Ain't Nothin' But a Sandwich,* New World, 1977.
Monroe, *The Serpent's Egg* (also known as *Das Schlangenei*), Paramount, 1977.
Charles, *Penitentiary II* (also known as *Championship Fight*), Metro–Goldwyn–Mayer/United Artists, 1982.
Roy Hanson, *Gremlins,* Warner Bros., 1984.
Lieutenant Delgado, *Out of Bounds,* Columbia, 1986.
Russell Stevens, Sr., *Deep Cover,* New Line Cinema, 1992.
Spencer Phillips, *The Inkwell* (also known as *No Ordinary Summer*), Buena Vista, 1994.
Psalms from the Underground, Humble Journey Films, 1996.
Stallworth Hubbs, *Subterfuge,* 1996.
Dr. Shakespeare, *How Stella Got Her Groove Back,* Twentieth Century–Fox, 1998.
Principal Armstrong, *Light It Up,* Twentieth Century–Fox, 1999.
Al Rheingold, *The Visit,* Urbanworld Films, 2000.
Chief Floyd, *Men of Honor* (also known as *Men of Honour*), Twentieth Century–Fox, 2000.
Air Rage, New City Releasing, 2001.
Derrick's dad, *The Seat Filler,* DEJ Productions, 2004.
Himself, *TV in Black: The First Fifty Years* (documentary), Koch Vision, 2004.
Himself, *Macked, Hammered, Slaughtered and Shafted* (documentary), 2004.
Dr. Frank Hopper, *Sahara* (also known as *Sahara—Abenteuer in der wuste*), Paramount, 2005.
Himself, *Black Theater Today: 2005,* 2005.
Kevin Sawyer, *City Teacher,* 2007.
Clarence Brown, *Kings of the Evening,* 2007.
Himself, *Broadway: Beyond the Golden Age* (documentary; also known as *B.G.A. 2* and *Broadway: The Golden Age Two*), 2008.

Television Appearances; Series:
Lew Miles, *Peyton Place,* ABC, 1968–69.
Secretary of State LaRue Hawkes, *Hail to the Chief,* ABC, 1985.
Colonel Bradford "Brad" Taylor, *A Different World,* NBC, 1988–93.
Bobby Davis, *Resurrection Blvd.,* 2000–2002.
Ted Olsen, *Big Apple,* CBS, 2001.
Mayor Clarence V. Royce, *The Wire,* HBO, 2004–2006.

Television Appearances; Miniseries:
Nate Person, *Centennial*, NBC, 1978.

Television Appearances; Movies:
George Brightman, *Carter's Army* (also known as *Black Brigade*), ABC, 1970.
Bodhi, *In Search of America*, ABC, 1971.
Theo, *Ceremonies in Dark Old Men*, 1975.
Edwin Beall, *The Blue Knight*, 1975.
This Far by Faith, 1977.
Harry Brown, Jr., *Minstrel Man*, CBS, 1977.
Preston de Cordiva, *Katie: Portrait of a Centerfold*, NBC, 1978.
Raymond Franklin, *Attica*, ABC, 1980.
James Thornwell, *Thornwell*, CBS, 1981.
Righteous Apples, 1981.
Jesse, *Secrets of a Married Man* (also known as *Portrait of a John* and *Trick Eyes*), NBC, 1984.
Joshua, *Charlotte Forten's Mission: Experiment in Freedom* (also known as *Half–Slave, Half–Free 2*), PBS, 1985.
Joe Franklin, 1985.
Essence, 1986.
Solomon, *Race to Freedom: The Underground Railroad*, Family Channel Black Entertainment, 1994.
Judge Roullard, *Someone Else's Child* (also known as *Lost and Found*), 1994.
Circle of Pain, 1996.
Coach Powell, *Rebound: The Legend of Earl "the Goat" Manigault* (also known as *Rebound*), HBO, 1996.
Sergeant Joshua "Joyu" Judges Ruth, *Buffalo Soldiers*, TNT, 1997.
"T–Bone" Lanier, *Freedom Song*, TNT, 2000.
Robert Aimes, Sr., *Fire and Ice*, Black Entertainment Television, 2001.

Made television debut in *Sing a Song*.

Television Appearances; Specials:
The Richard Pryor Special, 1977.
Lenny Johnson, "The Rag Tag Champs," *ABC Afterschool Special*, ABC, 1978.
Two of Hearts, HBO, 1982.
Lloyd Lyman, *Ask Max*, ABC, 1986.
Eric, "Gwendolyn," *AFI Comedy Special* (also known as *NBC Presents the AFI Comedy Special*), NBC, 1987.
Ebony/Jet Showcase, 1987.
The 7th Annual Stellar Gospel Music Awards, syndicated, 1992.
Rough Riders & Black Cowboy Legends, 2004.
Black in the 80s, VH1, 2005.

Television Appearances; Pilots:
Edwin Beall, *The Blue Knight*, CBS, 1975.
Officer Woodrow Freeman, *Cass Malloy*, CBS, 1982.
Tyrone C. Earl, *Manimal*, CBS, 1983.

Jonathan Kingsley, *Poor Richard*, CBS, 1984.
Roger Donnely, "The Doctors Wilde" (also known as "Zoo Vets"), *CBS Summer Playhouse*, CBS, 1987.
Lieutenant Caspersons, *J. J. Starbuck*, NBC, 1987.

Television Appearances; Episodic:
Jimmy James, "The Undergraduate," *Julia*, NBC, 1969.
Jackson, "Sadbird," *CBS Playhouse*, CBS, 1969.
"Dreams of Glory," *Room 222*, ABC, 1970.
"Marathon," *Storefront Lawyers* (also known as *Men at Law*), CBS, 1971.
"Kill Gently, Sweet Jessie," *Mod Squad*, ABC, 1972.
Jamal, "Deadly Hostage," *Cannon*, CBS, 1973.
Harley Dartson, "Tricks Are No Treats," *Hawaii Five–0*, CBS, 1973.
Jimmy, "Blood Brother," *The Rookies*, ABC, 1973.
Axis, "The Tapestry/Circles," *Visions*, 1976.
"New Found Franklin," *The Tony Randall Show*, CBS, 1977.
"Charlie Smith and the Fritter Tree," *Visions*, PBS, 1978.
Mr. Livingston, "Moot Court," *The Paper Chase*, CBS, 1978.
Ron Taylor, "A Few Good Men," *The White Shadow*, CBS, 1980.
"The Old Sister," *Palmerstown, U.S.A.*, CBS, 1980.
Captain, "The Devil and the Deep Blue Sea," *The Greatest American Hero*, ABC, 1982.
Ben Pettit, "Class Act," *Fame*, NBC, 1982.
Magnum, P.I., CBS, 1983.
"Detroit: The Price of Freedom" (also known as "The Prisoner"), *Lottery*, ABC, 1983.
"Bojangles and the Dancer," *Fantasy Island*, ABC, 1984.
"Hit or Miss America," *The Love Boat*, ABC, 1984.
"Anatomy of a Killing," *T. J. Hooker*, ABC, 1984.
"Goodbye, I Love You," *Hot Pursuit*, NBC, 1984.
"Reprise for the Lord," *This Is the Life*, 1984.
Tyrone Diamond, "Prisoner of War," *Riptide*, NBC, 1985.
Ben Coleman, "Murder to a Jazz Beat," *Murder, She Wrote*, CBS, 1985.
Joshua, "Charlotte Forten's Mission: Experiment in Freedom" (also known as "Half–Slave, Half–Free 2"), *American Playhouse*, PBS, 1985.
"Whatever Happened to …?," *Detective in the House*, CBS, 1985.
"Games People Play," *Detective in the House*, CBS, 1985.
Riptide, NBC, 1985.
Billy Kinetta, "Paladin of the Lost Hour," *The Twilight Zone*, CBS, 1985.
"High School Blues," *The Redd Foxx Show*, ABC, 1986.
Lloyd Lyman, "Ask Max," *The Disney Sunday Movie*, ABC, 1986.
Stan Lassiter, "Deadline for Murder," *Murder, She Wrote*, CBS, 1986.
Major Dennis Orlando, "The Court–Martial: Parts 1 & 2," *Matlock*, NBC, 1987.
Earl Browder, "Jack and Bill," *Murder, She Wrote*, CBS, 1989.

Dr. Redman, "Life Sentence," *Freddy's Nightmares* (also known as *Freddy's Nightmares: A Nightmare on Elm Street*), 1990.

Storytime, 1994.

James Glen, "Wide Open," *Millennium,* Fox, 1997.

Wade Beecher, "Skin," *Strange World,* ABC, 1999.

Achilles Thompson, "Achilles," *The Magnificent Seven,* CBS, 1999.

Negro y Moreno, *Resurrection Blvd.,* 2000.

Himself, "Ben Vereen: The Hard Way," *Biography,* Arts and Entertainment, 2000.

Sheriff Guthrie, "Finger of God," *Touched by an Angel,* CBS, 2000.

Sub captain, "Mixed Messages," *JAG,* CBS, 2001.

Roy Hines, "Pravda," *Law & Order: Criminal Intent* (also known as *Law & Order: CI*), NBC, 2003.

Calvin, Bernie's brother, "Family Reunion," *The Bernie Mac Show,* Fox, 2004.

Carl, "Who Gives This Bride," *The Bernie Mac Show,* Fox, 2005.

Dr. Young, "Infected," *Law & Order: Special Victims Unit* (also known as *Law & Order: SVU* and *Special Victims Unit*), NBC, 2006.

Earl, "The Courtship of Robert's Father," *All of Us,* 2006.

Earl, "Like Father, Like Son, Like Hell!," *All of Us,* 2006.

Earl, "My Two Dads," *All of Us,* 2006.

Also appeared as Phil Cherot, "Duty to Serve," *The Lyon's Den,* NBC.

Television Director; Movies:
Buffalo Soldiers, TNT, 1997.

Television Director; Episodic:
"Sister to Sister, Sister," *A Different World,* NBC, 1991.

"Prisoner of Love," *A Different World,* NBC, 1992.

"Baby, It's Cold Outside," *A Different World,* NBC, 1992.

"Great X–Pectations," *A Different World,* NBC, 1993.

"Security," *Hangin' with Mr. Cooper,* 1997.

Also directed episodes of *The Parent 'Hood,* The WB; *The Wayans Bros.,* The WB.

Stage Appearances:
(Stage debut) Travis Younger, *A Raisin in the Sun,* Ethel Barrymore Theatre, New York City, 1959.

Tim, Jr., *Who's Got His Own,* Theatre at St. Clements Church, New York City, 1966.

Junebug, *Junebug Graduates Tonight!,* Chelsea Theatre Center, New York City, 1967.

The Adventures of the Black Girl in Her Search for God, Center Theatre Group, Mark Taper Forum, Los Angeles, 1968–69.

Revolution, Center Theatre Group, New Theatre for Now, Music Center, Los Angeles, 1972–73.

Steve Carlton, *What the Wine–Sellers Buy,* New Federal Theatre, New York City, 1973, later Vivian Beaumont Theatre, New York City, 1974.

Steve Carlton, *The Wine Sellers,* Center Theatre Group, New Theatre for Now, Mark Taper Forum, 1973.

A Raisin in the Sun, Pilgrim Theatre, New York City, 1979.

Do Lord Remember Me, American Place Theatre, then Town Hall Theatre, New York City, 1982–83.

Proud, 1984.

James Horsford Ottley III, *Eyes of the American,* Negro Ensemble Company, Theatre Four, New York City, 1985, then Los Angeles Theatre Center, 1986.

Nat Turner and other roles, *Do Lord Remember Me,* New Federal Theatre, Sylvia and Danny Kaye Playhouse, New York City, 1997.

The Sons of Lincoln, Lillian Theatre, Hollywood, CA, 2000.

Thomas Thurman, *Good Boys,* Guthrie Theatre, Minneapolis, MN, 2002.

Also appeared as member of chorus, *Puccini's Tosca,* Amato Opera; in *Good Boys,* Repertory Theatre; *Harper's Ferry,* Repertory Theatre; *The Visit,* Repertory Theatre; *The House of Atreus,* Repertory Theatre; *Ceremonies in Dark Old Men; Don't Get God Started; One in a Crowd; Slow Dance on the Killing Ground,* Los Angeles; *The Toilet.*

Major Tours:
I'm Not Rappaport, 1987.

Stage Director:
Directed *Deadwood Dick,* Inner City Cultural Center, Los Angeles.

WRITINGS

Film Music:
Stickin' Together, 1992.

Television Episodes:
Writer for *Peyton Place,* ABC.

Songs:
Coauthor of the song "I'm Your Speed," recorded by Aretha Franklin on the album *Almighty Fire.*

V–W

VAN WORMER, Steve 1969–

PERSONAL

Born December 8, 1969, in Grand Blanc, MI; *Education:* Attended Michigan State University, 1987–1991.

Addresses: *Agent*—Innovative Artists, 1505 10th St., Santa Monica, CA 90401.

Career: Actor and comedian.

CREDITS

Film Appearances:
Turbo Man float parade worker, *Jingle All the Way,* Twentieth Century–Fox, 1996.
Tony, *Hijacking Hollywood,* Curb, 1997.
Stew Deedle, *Meet the Deedles,* Buena Vista, 1998.
Curtis, *Idle Hands,* Columbia, 1999.
Chris, *Rubbernecking,* Media Vision, 2000.
Extreme Adventures of Super Dave, MGM, 2000.
Deejay, *The Extreme Adventures of Super Dave* (video), Warner Home Video, 2000.
Mark's friend, *Bubble Boy,* Buena Vista, 2001.
Double D, *The Anarchist Cookbook,* American World, 2002.
Jason Anderson, *Timecop: The Berlin Decision* (video), Universal, 2003.

Television Appearances; Episodic:
The Tonight Show with Jay Leno (also known as *Jay Leno*), NBC, 1998.
Chris, "After the Pilot," *Turks,* 1999.
Voice of Jason, "Every Little Bit Alps," *The Wild Thornberrys* (animated), Nickelodeon, 2000.

Kevin, "End Game," *Without a Trace* (also known as *W.A.T.*), 2005.

Television Appearances; Movies:
Randy, *Johnny Tsunami,* 1999.

RECORDINGS

Voice of Maxi, *Soul Calibur III* (also known as *Soul Calibur III: Arcade Edition*), Namco, 2005.
American Wasteland (also known as *Tony Hawk's "American Wasteland"*), Activision, 2005.
Voice of John Allerdyce, *X–Men: The Official Game,* Activision, 2006.
Tales of the World: Radiant Mythology, Namco, 2007.
Ace combat 6: Kaiho e no senka (also known as *Ace Combat 6: Fires of Liberation*), Namco Bandai, 2007.

VENABLES, Bruce

PERSONAL

Married Judy Nunn (an actress).

Career: Actor.

CREDITS

Film Appearances:
Metcalfe, *A Cry in the Dark* (also known as *Evil Angels*), Warner Bros., 1988.
Limousine driver, *Emerald City,* 1988.
Bug man, *Weekend with Kate,* Video Search of Miami, 1990.

First police detective, *Heaven Tonight,* New City Releasing, 1990.

Stu, *The Girl Who Came Late* (also known as *Daydream Believer*), 1991.

Archie, *Deadly,* 1992.

McPherson, *Seeing Red,* 1992.

Mr. Hartley, *Big Ideas,* 1992.

John Tyke, *Shotgun Wedding,* 1993.

Crimetime, 1993.

Semi–trailer driver, *Spider & Rose,* 1994.

Security guard, *The Roly Poly Man,* 1994.

Petersen, *Dad and Dave: On Our Selection,* Roadshow Entertainment, 1995.

Gutser, *Mr. Reliable* (also known as *Mr. Reliable: A True Story* and *My Entire Life*), Gramercy, 1996.

Barman, *Flynn,* Beyond Distribution Sydney, 1996.

Chris's father, *River Street,* 1996.

Artie, *Paperback Hero,* PolyGram Filmed Entertainment, 1998.

Williams, *Bootmen,* Twentieth Century–Fox, 2000.

Uncle, *Breathe,* 2000.

Henry the butcher, *You Can't Stop the Murders,* Buena Vista International, 2003.

Second Meatworks owner, *The Honourable Wally Norman,* Becker Entertainment, 2003.

Wally, *The Crop,* Elliot Bros. Film Distribution, 2004.

Television Appearances; Movies:

Gospel singer, *Future Past,* 1987.

Oily master of ceremonies, *Outback Bound,* CBS, 1988.

Frank, *Touch the Sun: Peter & Pompey,* ABC (Australia), 1988.

George Shooks, *Mortgage,* Nine Network, 1989.

Mr. Hartley, *Big Ideas,* 1992.

Slampacker, *Stark,* ABC (Australia), 1993.

Merton, *Singapore Sling,* Nine Network, 1993.

Willie Monk, *Good Guys Bad Guys* (also known as *Good Guys Bad Guys: Only the Young Die Good*), 1997.

John Webb, *My Husband My Killer,* Ten Network, 2001.

Television Appearances; Episodic:

Sergio, *Heartbreak High,* ABC (Australia), 1997.

Tom "Chubb" Clancy, "All at Sea," *Water Rats,* Nine Network, 1997.

Gerard Gault, "Many Unhappy Returns," *Murder Call,* Nine Network, 1998.

Tony Kelso, *Wildside,* ABC (Australia), 1998, 1999.

Lance Petersen, "Late September," *Grass Roots,* ABC (Australia), 2000.

Stan Morrow, "We Could Be Heroes," *Water Rats,* Nine Network, 2000.

Bosco, "Valley of the Shadow: Parts 1 & 2," *All Saints,* Seven Network, 2000.

Haro, "Sisters Are Doing It for Themselves," *Always Greener,* Seven Network, 2001.

Haro, "The Mating Urge," *Always Greener,* Seven Network, 2001.

Haro, "What's in a Name?," *Always Greener,* Seven Network, 2002.

Haro, "A Man Walks into a Bar," *Always Greener,* Seven Network, 2002.

Michael Nitti, *White Collar Blue,* Ten Network, 2002, 2003.

Garbo, *Snobs,* Nine Network, 2003.

Ned Quade, "Begging for It," *All Saints,* Seven Network, 2005.

Television Appearances; Other:

Dadah Is Death (miniseries; also known as *Barlow and Chambers: A Long Way from Home, Deadly Decision,* and *A Long Way from Home*), CBS, 1988.

Policeman, *Home and Away* (pilot), Seven Network, 1988.

Bates, *Chances* (series), Nine Network, 1991.

WRITINGS

Screenplays:
Crimetime, 1993.

VERVEEN, Arie 1966–

PERSONAL

Born in 1966, in Ireland.

Addresses: *Agent*—Global Artist Agency, 1648 N. Wilcox Ave., Los Angeles, CA 90028. *Manager*—Insomnia Media Group, 100 Universal City Plaza, Bungalow 7151, Universal City, CA 91608.

Career: Actor.

Awards, Honors: Special Achievement award, outstanding new talent, International Press Academy Golden Satellite Awards, and Independent Spirit Award nomination, best debut performance, Independent Spirit Features Project West, both 1997, for *Caught.*

CREDITS

Film Appearances:

Nick, *Caught* (also known as *Atrapados*), Columbia TriStar, 1996.

Private Charlie Dale, *The Thin Red Line* (also known as *La Mince ligne rouge*), 1998.

Buddy, *Killers,* Dancebuy, 1999.

Adult Richard, *Running Free,* Columbia, 1999.

Horace Marywell, *The Journeyman,* Dream, 2001.

Henry the hermit, *Cabin Fever,* Lions Gate Films, 2002.

Flowers, *Briar Patch* (also known as *Plain Dirty*), Aipi 2003.

Edgar Allan Poe, *Descendant* (also known as *Descendent, Descendent*), Mainline, 2003.

Doctor, *Red Roses and Petrol,* World Wide, 2003.

Marty, *Sins,* Columbia TriStar, 2003.

Cabin Fever: Beneath the Skin, 2004.

Murphy, *Sin City* (also known as *Frank Miller's "Sin City"*), Dimension, 2005.

Television Appearances; Movies:

Calvin McCall, *Suspect,* 2007.

Television Appearances; Episodic:

Marlon Chambers, "The Siege," *UC: Undercover,* 2001.

Paul, "Homewrecker's Ball," *The Handler,* 2003.

Aaron Hensleigh, "The New World," *Vanished,* 2006.

Aaron Hensleigh, "The Cell," *Vanished,* 2006.

VIRTUE, Tom 1957–

(Thomas Virtue)

PERSONAL

Full name, Thomas Virtue; born November 19 (some sources cite November 18), 1957, in Sherman, TX. *Education:* Graduated from Northwestern University, 1979.

Addresses: *Agent*—The Gage Group, 14724 Ventura Blvd., Suite 505, Sherman Oaks, CA 91403.

Career: Actor.

CREDITS

Television Appearances; Series:

Stanley Michaels, *The Building,* CBS, 1993.

Camera operator Tom Vandoozer, *The Bonnie Hunt Show* (also known as *Bonnie* and *Human Interest*), CBS, 1995–96.

Steve Stevens, *Even Stevens* (also known as *Spivey's Kid Brother* and *La guerre des Stevens*), Disney Channel, 1999–2003.

Eddie, *The Comeback* (also known as *Mon comeback*), HBO, 2005.

Television Appearances; Movies:

Police officer, *Seeds of Tragedy,* Fox, 1991.

Reporter, *Majority Rule* (also known as *Majority City*), Lifetime, 1992.

Chuck Arnett, *For My Daughter's Honor* (also known as *Innocent Seduction*), CBS, 1996.

Movie dad, *Under Wraps,* Disney Channel, 1997.

Science teacher, *Brink!,* Disney Channel, 1998.

Dr. Jim Meyer, *The Darwin Conspiracy,* UPN, 1999.

Investment banker, *Horse Sense,* Disney Channel, 1999.

Miami comedian, *Introducing Dorothy Dandridge* (also known as *Face of an Angel*), HBO, 1999.

Announcer, *Miracle in Lane 2,* Disney Channel, 2000.

Steve Stevens, *The Even Stevens Movie* (also known as *The Stevens Get Even, Die Stevens schlagen zurueck,* and *Droles de vacances*), Disney Channel, 2003.

Trevor Martin, *Jane Doe: Vanishing Act,* The Hallmark Channel, 2005.

Ralph Bartlett, *Read It and Weep,* Disney Channel, 2006.

George, *A Grandpa for Christmas,* The Hallmark Channel, 2007.

Television Appearances; Specials:

Prison guard, *Public Enemy Number 2,* Showtime, 1991.

Herb Miller, *Sex, Shock and Censorship in the 90s,* MTV, 1993.

Television Appearances; Episodic:

Tom, "Lobocop," *Roseanne,* ABC, 1989.

Voice of caller, "Next Victim," *21 Jump Street,* Fox, 1989.

Father John, "Georgie and Grace," *Newhart,* CBS, 1990.

Jimmy, "The Healing," *Grand,* NBC, 1990.

Forest ranger, "Christmas Show," *The Fresh Prince of Bel–Air,* NBC, 1991.

John Doe, "Reversal of Grandpa," *Nurses,* NBC, 1991.

(As Thomas Virtue) "Spleen It to Me, Lucy," *L.A. Law,* NBC, 1991.

Police officer, "Robbing the Banks," *The Fresh Prince of Bel–Air,* NBC, 1992.

Doctor, "Top Copy," *Lois & Clark: The New Adventures of Superman* (also known as *Lois & Clark* and *The New Adventures of Superman*), ABC, 1994.

Professor Peter Needham, "Something in the Shadows: Parts 1 & 2," *Walker, Texas Ranger* (also known as *Walker*), CBS, 1994.

Lieutenant Walter Baxter, "Eye of the Needle," *Star Trek: Voyager* (also known as *Voyager*), syndicated, 1995.

Lieutenant Walter Baxter, "The 37s," *Star Trek: Voyager* (also known as *Voyager*), syndicated, 1995.

Lieutenant Walter Baxter, "Twisted," *Star Trek: Voyager* (also known as *Voyager*), syndicated, 1995.

Doctor, "Sleepless in Orlando," *Coach,* ABC, 1996.

"All Jammed Up," *Pacific Blue,* USA Network, 1996.

Andrew Steel, "Oil & Water," *Team Knight Rider* (also known as *El equipo fantastico, Nom de code: TKR, Oi ippotes tis asfaltou,* and *Ritariaessaet*), ABC, 1997.

Big Lou, "Driving," *The Secret World of Alex Mack* (also known as *Alex Mack*), Nickelodeon, 1997.

Dan Buelow, "Knockout," *Nash Bridges* (also known as *Bridges*), CBS, 1997.

Mr. Cummings, "Aloha Beverly Hills: Part 1," *Beverly Hills 90210,* Fox, 1997.

Nurse Bruce, "Who Do You Truss?," *Murphy Brown,* CBS, 1997.

Brad, *The Secret Lives of Men* (also known as *Ellos se lo cuentan todo, Salaiset ansiot,* and *Trois hommes sur le green*), ABC, 1998.

Mr. Atkinson, "Equality," *Working,* NBC, 1998.

Mitch Burgess, "Risky Business," *Chicago Hope,* CBS, 1998.

Victor Mott, "Overdrive," *Nash Bridges* (also known as *Bridges*), CBS, 1998.

"One Christmas, to Go," *Party of Five,* Fox, 1998.

Cyril Morton, "Nitro Man," *Martial Law* (also known as *Le flic de Shanghai, Ley marcial,* and *Piu forte ragazzi*), CBS, 1999.

Dave Klein, "Arcadia," *The X-Files,* Fox, 1999.

Marcus Behr, "Nine Yolks Whipped Lightly," *Beverly Hills 90210,* Fox, 1999.

Mr. Miller, "Dharma and Greg on a Hot Tin Roof," *Dharma and Greg,* ABC, 1999.

Dr. Jamison, "Mr. Freeze," *Malibu, CA* (also known as *Malibu*), syndicated, 2000.

Juror, "Twelve Angry People," *7th Heaven* (also known as *Seventh Heaven* and *7th Heaven: Beginnings*), The WB, 2000.

Marcus Behr, "Tainted Love," *Beverly Hills 90210,* Fox, 2000.

Mr. Cavanaugh, "Sabrina's Perfect Christmas," *Sabrina, the Teenage Witch* (also known as *Sabrina* and *Sabrina Goes to College*), The WB, 2000.

Mr. Sampson, "Girlfriends and Boyfriends," *Freaks and Geeks* (also known as *Freaks & Geeks, Freaks og Geeks, Nollor och noerdar,* and *Voll daneben, voll im Leben*), NBC, 2000.

Mr. Sampson, "Kim Kelly Is My Friend," *Freaks and Geeks* (also known as *Freaks & Geeks, Freaks og Geeks, Nollor och noerdar,* and *Voll daneben, voll im Leben*), NBC, 2000.

Priest, "Home Alone 4," *Malcolm in the Middle* (also known as *Fighting in Underpants*), Fox, 2000.

Supervisor, "Workforce: Parts 1 & 2," *Star Trek: Voyager* (also known as *Voyager*), syndicated, 2001.

Voice of Jonas Foutley, "Piece of My Heart," *As Told by Ginger* (animated; also known as *Gingers Welt* and *To imerologio tis Ginger*), Nickelodeon, 2001.

Dr. "Mr." Casey, "Is It Just Us?," *Life with Bonnie* (also known as *Alles dreht sich um Bonnie* and *Viata cu Bonnie*), ABC, 2002.

Father Matthew, "Swearin' to God," *Grounded for Life* (also known as *Freaky Finnertys, Familietrobbel, Keine Gnade fuer Dad,* and *Parents a tout prix*), Fox, 2002.

Pompous doctor, "Ariel," *Firefly* (also known as *Firefly: The Series* and *Firefly—Der Aufbruch der Serenity*), Fox, 2002.

Voice of Jonas Foutley, "Losing Nana Bishop," *As Told by Ginger* (animated; also known as *Gingers Welt* and *To imerologio tis Ginger*), Nickelodeon, 2002.

Warrant officer Scoggins, "All Ye Faithful," *JAG,* CBS, 2002.

"The Enemy Within," *The Agency* (also known as *CIA: The Agency, The Agency—Im Fadenkreuz der C.I.A., Agentit, Espion d'etat,* and *La agencia*), CBS, 2002.

Doctor, "Random Acts of Violence," *CSI: Crime Scene Investigation* (also known as *C.S.I., CSI: Las Vegas, CSI: Weekends,* and *Les experts*), CBS, 2003.

Dr. "Mr." Casey, "No Matter Where You Go, There You Are," *Life with Bonnie* (also known as *Alles dreht sich um Bonnie* and *Viata cu Bonnie*), ABC, 2003.

FBI agent, "Escobar Gallardo," *Nip/Tuck,* fX Channel, 2003.

Other coach, "Mr. Monk Goes to the Ballgame," *Monk,* USA Network, 2003.

Senator Bowles, "Human Error," *Mister Sterling,* NBC, 2003.

Coach Class, "All Growed Up," *Reba* (also known as *Deep in the Heart, Family Planning,* and *Sally*), The WB, 2004.

Dr. Horn, "Numb and Numb–er," *That's So Raven* (also known as *Absolutely Psychic, That's So Raven!, Es tan Raven, Phenomene Raven,* and *Raven blickt durch*), Disney Channel, 2004.

Edward Gorodetsky, "Bomb Shelter," *Six Feet Under,* HBO, 2004.

The man, "Come Back to Me," *Desperate Housewives* (also known as *Beautes desespereees, Desperate housewives—I segreti di Wisteria Lane, Desupareto na tsuma tachi, Esposas desesperadas, Frustrerte fruer, Gotowe na wszystko, Kucanice, Meeleheitel koduperenaised, Mujeres desesperadas, Noikokyres se apognosi, Szueletett felesegek,* and *Taeydelliset naiset*), ABC, 2004.

Mr. Dietrich, "Victor's Other Family," *Malcolm in the Middle* (also known as *Fighting in Underpants*), Fox, 2004.

Referee, "Wand Does the Sky," *Wanda Does It,* Comedy Central, 2004.

Saunders, "Out of Sight," *Crossing Jordan* (also known as *Untitled Tim Kring Project*), NBC, 2004.

Voice of Jonas Foutley, "Ten Chairs," *As Told by Ginger* (animated; also known as *Gingers Welt* and *To imerologio tis Ginger*), Nickelodeon, 2004.

Angry man, "Charmageddon," *Charmed,* The WB, 2005.

Gil Clurman, "Won't Get Fooled Again," *Criminal Minds* (also known as *Quantico, Criminal Minds—*

FBI tutjijat, Esprits criminels, Gyilkos elmek, Kurjuse kannul, and *Mentes criminales*), CBS, 2005.

Juilliard administrator, "Fallout," *Everwood* (also known as *Our New Life in Everwood*), The WB, 2005.

Kell (car salesperson), "Queen for a Day," *Arrested Development* (also known as *AD, Arrested development—Les nouveaux pauvres, Firma Ruffel & Baag, Firma Ruffel & Bygg, Sukuvika,* and *Ti presento i miei*), Fox, 2005.

Man with stutter, "The Bowtie," *Curb Your Enthusiasm* (also known as *Curb*), HBO, 2005.

Mr. Landry, "Slippery Slope," *The King of Queens* (also known as *King of Queens, El rey de Queens, Kellarin kunkku, Kongen af Queens, Kongen av Queens, Kung av Queens, O rei do bairro,* and *Un gars du Queens*), CBS, 2005.

Moderator, "Debates and Dead People," *Barbershop,* Showtime, 2005.

Lieutenant Bilbo, *Days of Our Lives* (also known as *Cruise of Deception: Days of Our Lives, Days, DOOL, Des jours et des vies, Horton–sagaen, I gode og onde dager, Los dias de nuestras vidas, Meres agapis, Paeivien viemaeae, Vaara baesta aar, Zeit der Sehnsucht,* and *Zile din viata noastra*), NBC, 2005.

Support group testimonial person, *Unscripted,* HBO, 2005.

Doctor with kidney, "Everybody Hates Kris," *Everybody Hates Chris* (also known as *Alle hassen Chris* and *Todo el mundo odia a Chris*), The CW, 2006.

Donald Payne, "Crucified," *Justice* (also known as *American Crime*), Fox, 2006.

Law firm partner, "Moving Day," *What about Brian,* ABC, 2006.

Major Doten, "Orphans," *Over There* (also known as *Kaukana kotoa*), fX Channel, 2006.

Matthew (1968), "Debut," *Cold Case* (also known as *Anexihniastes ypothesis, Caso abierto, Cold case—affaires classees, Cold Case—Kein Opfer ist je vergessen, Doegloett aktak, Kalla spaar, Todistettavasti syyllinen,* and *Victimes du passe*), CBS, 2006.

Mr. Nelson, "No Good Deed," *The Closer* (also known as *L.A.: Enquetes prioritaires* and *Se apostasi anapnois*), TNT, 2006.

Student advisor, "True Love Is Dead—Film at Eleven," *Pepper Dennis,* The WB, 2006.

Team owner (some sources cite role as general manager), "Superstar Treatment," *My Boys,* TBS, 2006.

Larry Reiner, "Scarlet Fever," *Shark,* CBS, 2007.

Mr. Roland, "Eric Punches Drake," *Drake & Josh,* Nickelodeon, 2007.

Mr. Roland, "Josh Is Done," *Drake & Josh,* Nickelodeon, 2007.

Pilot, "No Cannes Do," *Entourage* (also known as *El sequito, I koustodia,* and *Toertetoek*), HBO, 2007.

"K & R," *Studio 60 on the Sunset Strip* (also known as *Studio 7 on the Sunset Strip* and *Studio 60*), NBC, 2007.

Professor Walter Brauer, *Days of Our Lives* (also known as *Cruise of Deception: Days of Our Lives, Days,*

DOOL, Des jours et des vies, Horton–sagaen, I gode og onde dager, Los dias de nuestras vidas, Meres agapis, Paeivien viemaeae, Vaara baesta aar, Zeit der Sehnsucht, and *Zile din viata noastra*), NBC, 2007.

Provided the voice of Jonas Foutley in "The Wedding Frame," an episode of *As Told by Ginger* (animated; also known as *Gingers Welt* and *To imerologio tis Ginger*), Nickelodeon; appeared as Tyler's other father in "Upper West Side Story," an unaired episode of *Four Kings,* NBC.

Television Appearances; Pilots:
Clown, *Pride & Joy,* NBC, 1995.
Ally's father, *Ally McBeal,* Fox, 1997.
Steve Stevens, *Even Stevens* (also known as *Spivey's Kid Brother* and *La guerre des Stevens*), Disney Channel, 1999.
Dr. "Mr." Casey, *Life with Bonnie* (also known as *Alles dreht sich um Bonnie* and *Viata cu Bonnie*), ABC, 2002.
Eddie, *The Comeback* (also known as *Mon comeback*), HBO, 2005.
Eddie, *Side Order of Life,* Lifetime, 2007.

Film Appearances:
Bob Collins, *Tex* (also known as *Un ragazzo chiamato Tex*), Buena Vista, 1982.
Tom Kendrick, *We Met on the Vineyard* (also known as *The Big Day*), Monarch Films/Menemsha Entertainment, 1999.
Doctor Senderak, *Return to Me* (also known as *Distance Calls, Dos vidas contigo, Droit au coeur, Feitico do coracao, Hechizo del corazon, Palaa luokseni, Regressa para mim, Reviens–moi,* and *Zurueck zu dir*), Metro–Goldwyn–Mayer, 2000.
Voice of Reuben, *Joseph: King of Dreams* (animated musical; also known as *Giuseppe il re dei sogni, Joosef—unten kuningas, Jose: El rey de los suenos, Josef—droemmarnas konung,* and *Joseph—Koning der Traeume*), DreamWorks Home Entertainment/ Universal Home Video, 2000.
Fred Bizzert, *Detonator,* Cinetel Films, 2003.
Agent Scott, *Hair Show,* Innovation Film Group/ UrbanWorks Entertainment, 2004.
Basil Fogarty, *Trust Me,* Shoreline Entertainment, 2005.
Track and field coach, *Kicking & Screaming* (also known as *Kicking and Screaming, Soccer Dads, Untitled Will Ferrell Soccer Comedy, Cris et coups de pieds, Derby in famiglia, Fussballfieber—Elfmeter fuer Daddy, Gritando y pateando, Papai bate um bolao, Pelkoa ja inhoa nappulaliigassa,* and *Un entrenador genial*), Universal, 2005.
Floor manager, *Blades of Glory* (also known as *Die Eisprinzen, Escorregando para e gloria, Hokkarihemmot, Les rois du patin, Lezviya slavy—zvezduny na Idu,* and *Patinando a la gloria*), Paramount, 2007.
Attorney Apley, *Fracture,* New Line Cinema, c. 2007.

Stage Appearances:
Appeared in *MegaFun,* Practical Theatre Company, Chicago, IL; appeared with The Second City.

WARONOV, Mary
    See WORONOV, Mary

WARREN, Dan
    See WOREN, Dan

WEEZER, Lillian
    See JOHNSON, Kenneth

WELLS, David

PERSONAL

Addresses: *Agent*—Cunningham, Escott, Slevin and Doherty Talent Agency, 10635 Santa Monica Blvd., Suite 140, Los Angeles, CA 90025.

Career: Actor and voice performer.

CREDITS

Television Appearances; Movies:
James Watt, *To Heal a Nation,* NBC, 1988.
Minister, *A Cry for Help: The Tracey Thurman Story,* NBC, 1989.
Doctor Alex Wells, *Do You Know the Muffin Man?,* CBS, 1989.
Jury Duty: The Comedy (also known as *The Great American Sex Scandal*), ABC, 1990.
Tom Kelley, *Marilyn and Me,* ABC, 1991.
Quish, *Grand Tour: Disaster in Time* (also known as *Disaster in Time, The Grand Tour,* and *Timescape*), Showtime, 1992.
Campbell, *Prey of the Chameleon,* 1992.
Mailman, *Doorways,* 1993.
Medical examiner, *Black Widow Murders: The Blanche Taylor Moore Story,* NBC, 1993.
Third reporter at dock, *Amelia Earhart: The Final Flight,* TNT, 1994.
Young doctor, *Lightning in a Bottle,* Lifetime, 1994.
Father Martin, *Not Like Us,* Showtime, 1995.

Croupier, *Yesterday's Target,* 1996.
Lewis, *Breast Men,* 1997.
Harold, *Buried Alive II,* USA Network, 1997.
Mayor Carter, *Inherit the Wind,* Showtime, 1999.
Dr. Richard "Dick" Secor, *Judgment Day,* HBO, 1999.
Hardy, *Ali: An American Hero,* Fox, 2000.
Russ, *Terminal Error* (also known as *Peace Virus*), PAX, 2002.
Proprietor, *Avenging Angel,* Hallmark Channel, 2007.

Television Appearances; Miniseries:
Cruel Doubt, NBC, 1992.
Mr. Seaman, *Love, Honor and Obey: The Last Mafia Marriage,* NBC, 1993.

Television Appearances; Episodic:
Carl, "A Little Help," *Knots Landing,* 1984.
Communications officer, "The Adjuster," *Street Hawk,* 1985.
Third man, "Village of the Motorpigs," *Otherworld,* 1985.
Miller, "Many Happy Returns," *Knight Rider,* 1985.
"Dead Run" segment, "The Leprechaun–Artist/Dead Run," *The Twilight Zone,* 1986.
"Sleep Talkin' Guy," *Moonlighting,* 1986.
Davis, "They Shoot Fat Women, Don't They?," *Designing Women,* CBS, 1989.
Sandy, "Al Bundy, Shoe Dick," *Married ... with Children,* Fox, 1991.
Mueller, "In My New Country," *Nurses,* NBC, 1992.
Mueller, "Solitary Man," *Nurses,* NBC, 1992.
Mueller, "Love and Death," *Nurses,* NBC, 1993.
Marianne's father, *Route 66,* NBC, 1993.
Deputy District Attorney Peter Haskins, "The Accused," *Matlock,* ABC, 1994.
Protester, "Thanksgiving 1994," *Roseanne,* ABC, 1994.
Phil, "Lucky Suit," *Weird Science,* 1995.
Waiter, "9 ½ Days," *Dream On,* 1995.
Mousy man, "These Successful Friends of Mine," *Ellen* (also known as *These Friends of Mine*), ABC, 1995.
Mitchell Conklin, "Stress Related," *The Fresh Prince of Bel–Air,* NBC, 1995.
Avery, "It Takes a Thief," *The Wayans Bros.,* The WB, 1995.
Zalman Bain, "Mind over Murder," *Diagnosis Murder,* CBS, 1996.
Arli$$, HBO, 1996.
Archbishop, *Homeboys in Outer Space,* UPN, 1996.
Norm Skogland, "Road Work," *Nash Bridges* (also known as *Bridges*), CBS, 1997.
Mr. Chambers, "Baby Oprah," *The Parent 'Hood,* The WB, 1997.
Jason Mallory, *Michael Hayes,* CBS, 1997.
Jonathan Cramer, "Trial and Error," *The Practice,* ABC, 1997.
Lloyd, "Then and Now," *Murphy Brown,* CBS, 1998.

Tim, "Yes, We Have No Bananas (or Anything Else for That Matter)," *Dharma & Greg,* ABC, 1998.

Commander William Nils, "Sleeping in Light," *Babylon 5* (also known as *B5*), 1998.

Mr. Franco, "Sabrina, the Teenage Writer," *Sabrina, the Teenage Witch* (also known as *Sabrina* and *Sabrina Goes to College*), ABC, 1999.

Pharmacist, "Slipping Away," *Beverly Hills, 90210,* Fox, 1999.

Mr. Babbitt, "Rush," *The X–Files,* Fox, 1999.

Detention monitor, "Passages," *Get Real,* Fox, 1999.

Detention monitor, "Anatomy of a Rumor," *Get Real,* Fox, 1999.

Eddie, *Rescue 77,* The WB, 1999.

Bradley Perkins, "Frontier Dad," *Diagnosis Murder,* CBS, 2000.

"Broke," *7th Heaven* (also known as *7th Heaven: Beginnings*), The WB, 2000.

Mr. Whitaker, *Resurrection Blvd.,* Showtime, 2000.

Carrington, "Dog Day Afternoon," *Martial Law,* CBS, 2000.

Cheese man, "Restless," *Buffy the Vampire Slayer* (also known as *BtVS, Buffy,* and *Buffy the Vampire Slayer: The Series*), The WB, 2000.

Bland funeral director, "Life's Too Short," *Six Feet Under,* HBO, 2001.

Reverend Conrad Coates, "Answered Prayers," *JAG,* CBS, 2001.

Loan officer, "Childs in Charge," *Girlfriends,* UPN, 2002.

Jeff Murphy, "Sticks and Stones," *Dragnet* (also known as *L.A. Dragnet*), ABC, 2003.

Elliot Beckman, "Crow's Feet," *CSI: Crime Scene Investigation* (also known as *C.S.I., CSI: Las Vegas,* and *Les experts*), CBS, 2004.

Clyde, "The Seven Year Itch," *Charmed,* The WB, 2005.

Pharmacist, "Kamikaze Bingo," *Curb Your Enthusiasm,* HBO, 2005.

Chief Usher Waverly, "First Choice," *Commander in Chief,* ABC, 2005.

Chief Usher Waverly, "First ... Do No Harm," *Commander in Chief,* ABC, 2005.

Chief Usher Waverly, "The Mom Who Came to Dinner," *Commander in Chief,* ABC, 2005.

Father Sorenseon, "The Two that Got Away," *Freddie,* ABC, 2006.

Harley Frankel, "The Man with the Bone," *Bones,* Fox, 2006.

Appeared as interpreter, *Just Legal,* The WB; delivery man, *My Wife and Kids,* ABC; and priest, *The Naked Truth,* ABC.

Film Appearances:

Dispatcher, *Beverly Hills Cop,* Paramount, 1984.

Fox's assistant, *Starman* (also known as *John Carpenter's "Starman"*), Columbia, 1984.

Jury foreman, *The Ladies Club* (also known as *The Sisterhood* and *The Violated*), New Line Cinema, 1986.

Assistant District Attorney Durkee, *The Jigsaw Murders,* Metro–Goldwyn–Mayer, 1988.

Sergeant Burt, *Society,* Republic, 1989.

Detective Burt, *Silent Night, Deadly Night 4: Initiation* (also known as *Bugs* and *Initiation: Silent Night, Deadly Night 4*), 1990.

Granger, *Other People's Money* (also known as *Riqueza ajena*), Warner Bros., 1991.

Doctor Gordon, *The Guyver* (also known as *Mutronics*), New Line Cinema, 1991.

Polygraph examiner, *Basic Instinct* (censored version titled *Ice Cold Desire*), TriStar, 1992.

Salesman, *Wild Cactus,* 1993.

Mr. Banks, *The Skateboard Kid,* 1993.

Laboratory technician, *Return of the Living Dead 3* (also known as *Return of the Living Dead Part III*), Trimark Pictures, 1993.

Pinstripes, *Philadelphia Experiment II,* Trimark Pictures, 1993.

Dr. Evans, *Future Shock,* Hemdale Home Video, 1993.

Bennett, *Twin Sitters* (also known as *The Babysitters*), Global Pictures, 1994.

Alan, *Cracking Up,* Phaedra Cinema, 1994.

Priest, *Best Men,* Metro–Goldwyn–Mayer, 1997.

Dr. Duke Kelly, *The Progeny,* Sterling Home Entertainment, 1999.

Halifax man, *One Heart Broken into Song,* 1999.

Principal, *The Extreme Adventures of Super Dave,* Metro–Goldwyn–Mayer, 2000.

Dell Maxwell, *Contagion* (also known as *Epidemic* and *The Last Breath*), PorchLight Entertainment, 2001.

Recruiting sergeant, *Starship Troopers 2: Hero of the Federation,* Columbia TriStar Home Video, 2004.

Jesus the Driver, Rexomatic Productions, 2004.

Father Patrick, *Demon Hunter,* Anchor Bay Entertainment, 2005.

Ralf Coleman, *He Was a Quiet Man,* Neo Art & Logic, 2007.

Stage Appearances:

Glengarry Glen Ross, Third Stage Theatre, Los Angeles, 2000.

Additional Particulars, Third Stage Theatre, 2000.

RECORDINGS

Video Games:

Voice of Mr. Morris, *Goosebumps: Escape from Horrorland,* 1996.

WESTON, Michael 1973–
(Michael Rubinstein, Mike Weston)

PERSONAL

Original name, Michael Rubinstein; born October 25, 1973, in New York, NY; son of John Rubinstein (an actor, singer, composer, and director); grandson of Arthur Rubinstein (a pianist). *Education:* Northwestern University, B.S.

Addresses: *Agent*—Stephanie Ritz, Endeavor, 9601 Wilshire Blvd., 3rd Floor, Beverly Hills, CA 90210. *Manager*—Lainie Stolhanske, Management 360, 9111 Wilshire Blvd., Beverly Hills, CA 90210.

Career: Actor.

Member: Screen Actors Guild.

Awards, Honors: Grand Jury Prize, best supporting actor, New York International Independent Film and Video Festival, 2000, for *Sally.*

CREDITS

Film Appearances:
Jimmy, *Getting to Know You* (also known as *Getting to Know All About You;* later broadcast as television movie), 1999.
(As Michael Rubinstein) Bugs, *Sally,* 2000.
Danny, *Coyote Ugly,* Buena Vista, 2000.
Ben, *Cherry Falls,* USA Films/October Films, 2000.
Larry, *Lucky Numbers* (also known as *Le bon numero*), Paramount, 2000.
S1mone, New Line Cinema, 2001.
W. Roy Potts, *Hart's War,* Metro–Goldwyn–Mayer, 2001.
Kenny, *Evil Alien Conquerors,* Nada Pictures, 2002.
Brett Bumpers, *Wishcraft,* Media Cooperation One, 2002.
Harry, *Final Draft,* Shoreline Entertainment, 2003.
Kenny, *Garden State,* Fox Searchlight, 2004.
Deputy Enos Strate, *The Dukes of Hazzard,* Warner Bros., 2005.
Peter, *Looking for Sunday,* I–On Films/Suntaur Entertainment, 2006.
Izzy, *The Last Kiss,* DreamWorks/Paramount, 2006.
Ted, *The Pleasure of Your Company* (also known as *The Next Girl* and *Wedding Daze*), Metro–Goldwyn–Mayer, 2006.
Jake, *Pathology,* Metro–Goldwyn–Mayer, 2007.

Television Appearances; Movies:
Bobby Beausoleil, *Helter Skelter,* CBS, 2004.

Television Appearances; Episodic:
(As Mike Weston) "Chrome II," *Night Man,* syndicated, 1998.
Ice sculptor, "Daphne Does Dinner," *Frasier,* NBC, 2003.
Morris, "Mr. Monk and the Employee of the Monty," *Monk,* USA Network, 2004.
Jake, "That's My Dog," *Six Feet Under,* HBO, 2004.
Jake, "Coming and Going," *Six Feet Under,* HBO, 2004.
Jake, "Untitled," *Six Feet Under,* HBO, 2004.
Jake, "All Alone," *Six Feet Under,* HBO, 2005.
Tim Reston, "The Lady & the Tiger," *Saved,* TNT, 2006.
Rafe Hendricks, "21 Guns," *ER,* NBC, 2006.
Rafe Hendricks, "Bloodline," *ER,* NBC, 2006.
Adam Hornstock, "Cloudy ... with a Chance of Murder," *Psych,* USA Network, 2007.
Private Brian Dancer, "His Story IV," *Scrubs,* NBC, 2007.
Private Brian Dancer, "My Perspective," *Scrubs,* NBC, 2007.
Private Brian Dancer, "My Therapeutic Month," *Scrubs,* NBC, 2007.
Private Brian Dancer, "Fishbowl," *Scrubs,* NBC, 2007.
Simon Marsden, "Philadelphia," *Law & Order: Special Victims Unit* (also known as *Law & Order: SVU* and *Special Victims Unit*), NBC, 2007.
Simon Marsden, "Florida," *Law & Order: Special Victims Unit* (also known as *Law & Order: SVU* and *Special Victims Unit*), NBC, 2007.
Simon Marsden, "Screwed," *Law & Order: Special Victims Unit* (also known as *Law & Order: SVU* and *Special Victims Unit*), NBC, 2007.

Stage Appearances:
Dead End, 1997.
Misha's Party, 1997.
Johnny on a Spot, 1997.
The Matchmaker, Williamstown Theatre Festival, Williamstown, MA, 1998.
Young man, *Snakebit,* Century Center for the Performing Arts, New York City, 1999, then Coast Playhouse, West Hollywood, CA, 2000.
Daniel Reed, *The Waverly Gallery,* Pasadena Playhouse, Pasadena, CA, 2002.

OTHER SOURCES

Periodicals:
Parade, October 29, 2000, p. 14.

WHANG, Suzanne 1962–
(Sung Hee Park)

PERSONAL

Born September 28, 1962, in Arlington, VA. *Education:* Yale University, B.A., psychology; Brown University, M.S., cognitive psychology; studied acting at the Beverly Hills Playhouse with Milton Katselas, Richard Lawson, and Gary Imhoff, the William Esper Studio with Maggie Flanigan, and with Jeannie Lindheim and Jan Egleson. *Avocational Interests:* Rock climbing, watching the Washington Redskins.

Addresses: *Agent*—The Culbertson Group, 8430 Santa Monica Blvd., Suite 210, West Hollywood, CA 90069. *Manager*—Kragen and Company, 14039 Aubrey Rd., Beverly Hills, CA 90210. *Publicist*—Sharp and Associates, 8721 Sunset Blvd., Suite 208, Los Angeles, CA 90069.

Career: Actress and television show host. Also hosts and emcees pageants, charity events, and awards ceremonies; works as a stand–up comedian. Previously worked as a foot model in Boston.

Awards, Honors: Best Up & Coming Comedian, Las Vegas Comedy Festival, 2002; First Annual Andy Kaufman Award, New York Comedy Festival, 2004.

CREDITS

Film Appearances:
Moseby's secretary, *HouseSitter,* 1992.
Fed Ex person, *Twice as Dead,* 2001.
Sung He Park, *Seoul Mates* (short), Factory 515, 2002.
Sock puppet actor, *Date or Disaster,* 2003.
Commentator, *Homeless in America* (documentary short), Wiseau–Films, 2004.
Rosa, *Traci Townsend,* 2005.
Mother, *Constantine,* Warner Bros., 2005.
Medical examiner, *Edison* (also known as *Edison Force*), Sony Pictures Home Entertainment, 2005.
Television news anchor, *Materials Girls,* Metro–Goldwyn–Mayer, 2006.
Your Mommy Kills Animals (documentary), Halo8 Releasing, 2007.

Film Work:
Graphic writer, *Date or Disaster,* 2003.

Television Appearances; Series:
Road warrior, *Breakfast Time,* 1994.

Road warrior, *Fox After Breakfast* (also known as *The Vicki Lawrence Show*), Fox, 1996.
Cohost, *The Pet Department,* 1996.
Cohost, *TV Censored Bloopers 98,* NBC, 1998.
Cohost, *New Attitudes,* 1998.
Host, *House Hunters,* HGTV, 1999.
Polly, *Las Vegas,* NBC, 2005–2007.

Television Appearances; Movies:
Television reporter, *Ring of Darkness,* 2004.
Second reporter, *The Perfect Husband: The Laci Peterson Story,* USA Network, 2004.

Television Appearances; Specials:
Host, *Weddings of a Lifetime,* Lifetime, 1997.
Host, *Blitz Build 2000,* HGTV, 2000.
Host and narrator, *Homes of Our Heritage: Great American Women,* HGTV, 2000.
Host, *The Making of the Rose Parade 2005,* 2004.
Host, *The Making of the Rose Parade 2006,* 2005.
The 2006 Asian Excellence Awards, 2006.

Also appeared as host, *Holiday Windows,* HGTV; host, *Homes of Pasadena,* HGTV.

Television Appearances; Pilots:
Appeared in *Student Affairs,* UPN.

Television Appearances; Episodic:
Field host, *Personal FX: The Collectible Show,* FX Channel, 1994.
Diana Lu, "Mao Better Blues," *V.I.P.* (also known as *V.I.P.—Die Bodyguards*), syndicated, 1999.
"Legacy of Blood," *18 Wheels of Justice,* The Nashville Network, 2000.
Woman number three, "Norm vs. Homelessness," *The Norm Show* (also known as *Norm*), ABC, 2001.
Christy Kwan, "Bring Me the Head of Tucker Burns," *The Chronicle* (also known as *News from the Edge*), Sci–Fi Channel, 2001.
Dr. Kim, "Lies Like a Rug," *NYPD Blue,* ABC, 2001.
Dr. Sporich, "Stages," *Strong Medicine,* Lifetime, 2002.
Reporter, "In/Famous," *Robbery Homicide Division* (also known as *R.H.D./LA: Robbery Homicide Division/Los Angeles*), CBS, 2002.
Foreperson, "The Good Fight," *The Practice,* ABC, 2002.
Patron, "Still Looking for Love," *Still Standing,* CBS, 2004.
Anesthesiologist, "Smell the Umbrella Stand," *Two and a Half Men,* CBS, 2005.
Nurse Lee, "Momma Boone," *Nip/Tuck,* FX Channel, 2005.
Reporter, "Poison," *Criminal Minds,* CBS, 2006.
Juror number one, "Shock and Oww!," *Boston Legal,* ABC, 2006.

Linda Porter, "Shattered," *Without a Trace* (also known as *W.A.T.*), CBS, 2006.

Host, "Dream Home in the Bahamas," *House Hunters International*, 2006.

Mrs. Lee in 1984, "The River," *Cold Case*, CBS, 2006.

Carly, "Mistakes Were Made: Part 1," *Brothers & Sisters*, ABC, 2006.

Oprah, syndicated, 2007.

Stage Appearances:

Appeared in *24 Hour Play*, Los Angeles Theater Company, Los Angeles; *To Live, Love and Get Loaded*, McCadden Place Theatre, Los Angeles; *Nikki & Bobby*, The Coast Playhouse, Los Angeles; *Angry Tuxedos*, Improv Comedy Troupe, Boston, MA; *The Escort*, Seraphim Theatre Company, New York City; *My Sister Eileen*, West End Theatre, New York City; *And Nobody Says Stop*, New Dramatists, New York City; *A Balancing Act*, Performers Ensemble, Boston, MA; *Toying Around*, Theater of Newburyport, Newburyport, MA; *Guys and Dolls*, Yale University, New Haven, CT.

WRITINGS

Books:

(With Bruce W. Cook) *Suzanne Whang's Guide to Happy Home Buying*, HGTV, 2006.

Also contributed to *Audrey*.

OTHER SOURCES

Electronic:

Suzanne Whang Website, http://www.suzannewhang.com, September 15, 2007.

WHITFIELD, Lynn 1953(?)–
(Lynn C. Whitfield)

PERSONAL

Born May 6, 1953 (some sources cite February 15, 1954), in Baton Rouge, LA; daughter of Valerian (a dentist, composer, conductor, and playwright) and Jean (a finance officer and fashion coordinator; maiden name, Butler) Smith; married Vantile Whitfield (an artistic director), c. 1974 (divorced, c. 1978); married Brian Gibson (a producer, director, and writer), July 4, 1990 (divorced, 1992); children: (second marriage) Grace. *Education:* Attended Southern University; Howard University, B.F.A., 1974.

Addresses: *Agent*—Innovative Artists Talent and Literary Agency, 1505 10th St., Santa Monica, CA 90401. *Manager*—Danielle Allman–Del, Allman/Rea Management, 141 Barrington, Suite E, Los Angeles, CA 90049.

Career: Actress. Black Repertory Theatre, Washington, DC, actress; Links, Inc., member.

Awards, Honors: Emmy Award, best actress in a miniseries or special, 1991, Golden Globe Award nomination, best actress in a television miniseries or movie, 1992, Image Award, outstanding actress in a drama series, miniseries, or television movie, National Association for the Advancement of Colored People, 1993, and Annual CableACE Award, National Cable Television Association, all for *The Josephine Baker Story*; Image Award, outstanding actress in a television movie, miniseries, or drama special, 1992, for *Stompin' at the Savoy*; Alumni Achievement Award, Howard University, 1992; Image Award, outstanding actress in a drama series, miniseries, or television movie, 1994, for *I'll Fly Away*; Image Award, outstanding supporting actress in a drama series, 1998, for *Touched by an Angel*; Image Award nomination, outstanding lead actress in a motion picture, 1998, for *Eve's Bayou*; Image Award nomination, outstanding lead actress in a television movie, miniseries, or drama special, 1999, for *The Wedding*; Image Award, outstanding performance in a youth or children's series or special, 2000, for *The Planet of Junior Brown*; Black Reel Award nomination, best network or cable television actress, 2000, for *Love Songs*; Image Award nomination, outstanding actress in a television movie, miniseries, or dramatic special, 2000, for *Dangerous Evidence: The Lori Jackson Story*; Image Award nomination, outstanding performance in a youth or children's program, and Black Reel Award nomination, best supporting actress on television, both 2004, for *The Cheetah Girls*; BET Comedy Award nomination, outstanding supporting actress in a box–office movie, Black Entertainment Television, 2004, for *Head of State*; Image Award, outstanding actress in a television movie, miniseries, or dramatic special, and Black Reel Award, best network or cable television actress, both 2005, for *Redemption: The Stan Tookie Williams Story*; Black Movie Award nomination, outstanding supporting actress, 2006, for *Madea's Family Reunion*.

CREDITS

Television Appearances; Movies:

Bobbie Maxwell, *The George McKenna Story* (also known as *Hard Lessons*), CBS, 1986.

Title role, *Johnnie Mae Gibson: F.B.I.* (also known as *Agent Gibson: Undercover FBI, Johnnie Gibson F.B.I.*, and *The Johnnie Gibson Story*), CBS, 1986.

Natala Bell, *A Triumph of the Heart: The Ricky Bell Story*, CBS, 1991.

Title role, *The Josephine Baker Story,* HBO, 1991.
Esther Tolbert, *Stompin' at the Savoy,* CBS, 1992.
Carolyn Hunter, *Taking the Heat,* Showtime, 1993.
Dehlia Johnson, *State of Emergency,* HBO, 1994.
Bobbie Mallory, *Thicker than Blood: The Larry McLinden Story* (also known as *The Larry McLinden Story*), CBS, 1994.
Sophie Cooper (title role), *Sophie & the Moonhanger,* Lifetime, 1995.
Mrs. Brown, *The Planet of Junior Brown* (also known as *Junior's Groove*), 1997.
Minnie McGhee, *The Color of Courage,* USA Network, 1999.
Corrine Burrell, *Deep in My Heart,* CBS, 1999.
Lori Jackson, *Dangerous Evidence: The Lori Jackson Story,* Lifetime, 1999.
Jean, "A Love Song for Jean and Ellis," *Love Songs,* Showtime, 1999.
Dorothea Garibaldi, *The Cheetah Girls,* Disney Channel, 2003.
Barbara Becnel, *Redemption: The Stan Tookie Williams Story,* FX Network, 2004.
Dorothea Garibaldi, *The Cheetah Girls 2,* Disney Channel, 2006.

Television Appearances; Specials:
(As Lynn C. Whitfield) "For Colored Girls Who Have Considered Suicide/When the Rainbow Is Enuf," *American Playhouse,* PBS, 1982.
Behind the Scenes with "Jaws: The Revenge," 1987.
"Zora Is My Name!" *American Playhouse,* PBS, 1990.
19th Annual Black Filmmakers Hall of Fame, 1992.
Intimate Portrait: Josephine Baker, Lifetime, 1998.
Intimate Portrait: Patti LaBelle, Lifetime, 1998.
Host, *An Evening of Stars: A Celebration of Educational Excellence,* NBC, 2000.
"Martin Lawrence: Comic Trip," *Biography,* Arts and Entertainment, 2002.

Television Appearances; Miniseries:
Ciel, *The Women of Brewster Place,* ABC, 1989.
Corinne Coles, *The Wedding* (also known as *Oprah Winfrey Presents: "The Wedding"*), ABC, 1998.
Nia Morgan, *A Girl Thing,* Showtime, 2001.

Television Appearances; Series:
Dr. Cory Banks, *Heartbeat* (also known as *Private Practice* and *Women's Medical*), ABC, 1988–89.
Maggie Mayfield, a recurring role, *Equal Justice,* ABC, 1990–91.
Paula Van Doren, a recurring role, *Without a Trace* (also known as *W.A.T.*), CBS, between 2002 and 2006.

Television Appearances; Pilots:
Dr. Cory Banks, *Heartbeat,* ABC, 1988.

Barbara Lorenz, *The Cosby Mysteries* (also known as *Guy Hanks I*), NBC, 1994.
Bellaridere, *Lost in Oz,* The WB, 2002.
Dorothea, *The Cheetah Girls,* Disney Channel, 2004.
Anita Astin, *Shark,* CBS, 2006.

Television Appearances; Episodic:
Jill Thomas, "Can World War III Be an Attitude?," *Hill Street Blues,* 1981.
Jill Thomas, "Fecund Hand Rose," *Hill Street Blues,* 1981.
Jill Thomas, "Chipped Beef," *Hill Street Blues,* 1981.
"The Centerfold Murders," *Matt Houston,* 1983.
Norma, "Certain Arrangements," *This Is the Life,* 1983.
"How Shall We Then Live?," *This Is the Life,* 1985.
Eleanor Taggart, "Who Says It's Fair: Parts 1 & 2," *Cagney & Lacey,* 1985.
Odette Ribaud, "Bought and Paid For," *Miami Vice,* NBC, 1985.
Jeanne, "Escape Claus," *The Fall Guy,* 1985.
Della Marvel, "Harlem Nocturne," *Mike Hammer* (also known as *Mickey Spillane's "Mike Hammer"* and *The New Mike Hammer,* CBS, 1986.
Bustin' Loose, syndicated, 1987.
Pollie Ann, "John Henry," *Shelley Duvall's Tall Tales and Legends* (also known as *Shelley Duvall Presents: American Tall Tales and Legends* and *Tall Tales and Legends*), Showtime, 1987.
Annie Callan, "Curtains," *St. Elsewhere,* 1988.
Angela Page, "The Informer: Parts 1 & 2," *Matlock,* NBC, 1990.
"Domestic Silence," *The Trials of Rosie O'Neill,* 1991.
ABC in Concert, ABC, 1991.
Barbara Lorenz, "One Day at a Time," *The Cosby Mysteries,* NBC, 1994.
Barbara Lorenz, "Home, Street Home," *The Cosby Mysteries,* NBC, 1994.
Ellen, "Goin' Overboard: Parts 1 & 2," *Martin,* Fox, 1997.
Dr. Serena Hall, "Amazing Grace: Part 1," *Touched by an Angel,* CBS, 1997.
Louanna Harper, "Chapter Twenty–Six," *Boston Public,* Fox, 2001.
Louanna Harper, "Chapter Twenty–Eight," *Boston Public,* Fox, 2001.
Louanna Harper, "Chapter Twenty–Nine," *Boston Public,* Fox, 2001.
"Head of State," *HBO First Look,* HBO, 2003.
Dr. Marshall, "Race for a Cure," *Strong Medicine,* Lifetime, 2004.
"Tyler Perry: Madea's Family Reunion," *The Tyra Banks Show,* UPN, 2006.
Tavis Smiley, PBS, 2006.

Television Appearances; Awards Presentations:
The 43rd Annual Primetime Emmy Awards, Fox, 1991.
The 13th Annual ACE Awards, TNT, 1992.
Presenter, *The 1995 ESPY Awards,* ESPN, 1995.

Presenter, *The 16th Annual CableACE Awards,* TNT, 1995.

The 27th Annual NAACP Image Awards, Fox, 1996.

Presenter, *The 28th NAACP Image Awards,* 1997.

Presenter, *The 29th NAACP Image Awards,* Fox, 1998.

Cohost, *Essence Awards,* Fox, 1998.

Presenter, *The 30th NAACP Image Awards,* Fox, 1999.

5th Annual Screen Actors Guild Awards, TNT, 1999.

Host, *The 2000 Trumpet Awards,* TBS, 2000.

The 2006 Black Movie Awards, 2006.

The 37th Annual NAACP Image Awards, Fox, 2006.

Film Appearances:

Thelma Cleland, *Doctor Detroit,* Universal, 1983.

Rae Johnson, *Silverado,* Columbia, 1985.

Tina Alvarado, *The Slugger's Wife* (also known as *Neil Simon's "The Slugger's Wife"*), Columbia, 1985.

Louisa, *Jaws: The Revenge* (also known as *Jaws 4*), Universal, 1987.

Sheila Freeman, *Dead Aim* (also known as *Mace*), 1987, Double Helix, 1990.

Sergeant Ladd, *In the Army Now* (also known as *You're in the Army Now*), Buena Vista, 1994.

Brandi Web, *A Thin Line Between Love and Hate,* New Line Cinema, 1996.

Angie, *Gone Fishin',* Buena Vista, 1997.

Roz Batiste, *Eve's Bayou,* Trimark Pictures, 1997.

Dr. P. Sweikert, *Stepmom,* TriStar, 1998.

Linda Derricks, *A Time for Dancing,* East of Doheny, 2000.

Debra Lassiter, *Head of State,* DreamWorks, 2003.

Victoria, *Madea's Family Reunion,* Lions Gate Films, 2006.

Dr. Page, *Confessions* (also known as *Confessions of a Call Girl*), Codeblack Entertainment, 2007.

Gracie, *Kings of the Evening,* Picture Palace Films, 2007.

Lillian Winter, *Mama, I Want to Sing!,* Bigger Picture, 2007.

Stage Appearances:

Owen's Song, Black Repertory Theatre, John F. Kennedy Center for the Performing Arts, Washington, DC, 1974–75.

Showdown, New Federal Theatre, New York City, 1976.

Leionah, *The Great MacDaddy* (musical), Negro Ensemble Company, Theatre de Lys (now Lucille Lortel Theatre), New York City, 1977.

Georgiane, *Tamer of Horses,* Tom Bradley Theatre, Los Angeles Theatre Center, Los Angeles, 1986–87.

White Chocolate, Century Center for the Performing Arts, New York City, 2004–2005.

Appeared in *Changes,* Black Repertory Theatre; also appears in benefit performances.

Major Tours:

Toured in *For Colored Girls Who Have Considered Suicide (When the Rainbow Is Enuf),* U.S., British, and Australian cities, and *The Great MacDaddy,* U.S. cities.

RECORDINGS

Videos:

Appeared in the music video "Cheater (to all the Girls)" by Wyclef Jean.

OTHER SOURCES

Books:

Contemporary Black Biography, Volume 18, Gale, 1998.

Notable Black American Women, Book 3, Gale, 2002.

Periodicals:

BET Weekend, November, 1997, pp. 8–10.

Ebony, May, 1999, p. 72.

Essence, February, 1991, p. 72.

People Weekly, March 25, 1991, p. 87; February 13, 1995, p. 161.

WILLIAMS, Bernard
(Bernie Williams)

PERSONAL

Career: Producer and production manager.

CREDITS

Film Work:

Unit manager, *The Quiller Memorandum,* Twentieth Century–Fox, 1966.

Production manager, aerial unit, *Battle of Britain* (also known as *The Battle of Britain*), United Artists, 1969.

Production manager, *Country Dance* (also known as *Brotherly Love* and *The Sam Skin*), Metro–Goldwyn–Mayer, 1970.

Associate producer, *A Clockwork Orange* (also known as *Stanley Kubrick's "A Clockwork Orange"*), Warner Bros., 1971.

Associate producer, *Lady Caroline Lamb* (also known as *Peccato d'amore*), United Artists, 1972.

Associate producer, *Barry Lyndon,* Warner Bros., 1975.

(As Bernie Williams) Line producer and production supervisor, *Sky Riders,* Twentieth Century–Fox, 1976.

(As Bernie Williams) Line producer, *The Last Remake of Beau Geste,* Universal, 1977.

(As Bernie Williams) Associate producer and line producer, *The Big Sleep,* United Artists, 1978.

(As Bernie Williams) Executive producer, *Flash Gordon,* Universal, 1980.

Executive producer, *Ragtime* (also known as *Love and Glory*), Paramount, 1981.

(As Bernie Williams) Executive producer, *Amityville II: The Possession,* Orion, 1982.

Producer, *The Bounty,* Orion, 1984.

(As Bernie Williams) Producer, *The Miracles,* Orion, 1986.

Executive producer and unit production manager, *Manhunter* (also known as *Red Dragon: The Curse of Hannibal Lecter* and *Red Dragon: The Pursuit of Hannibal Lecter*), De Laurentiis Entertainment Group, 1986.

Producer and first assistant director, *Wisdom,* Twentieth Century–Fox, 1986.

(As Bernie Williams) Producer, *Who's That Girl?,* Warner Bros., 1987.

Producer and first assistant director, *Dirty Rotten Scoundrels,* Orion, 1988.

(As Bernie Williams) Producer and unit production manager, *War Party* (also known as *War Game*), Hemdale Film Corp., 1988.

(As Bernie Williams) Producer, *Navy Seals,* Orion, 1990.

Coproducer, *What About Bob?,* Buena Vista, 1991.

(As Bernie Williams) Executive producer and unit production manager, *HouseSitter,* Universal, 1992.

(As Bernie Williams) Executive producer and unit production manager, *So I Married an Axe Murderer,* TriStar, 1993.

(As Bernie Williams) Executive producer and unit production manager, *Star Trek: Generations* (also known as *Star Trek 7*), Paramount, 1994.

(As Bernie Williams) Executive producer and unit production manager, *The Indian in the Cupboard,* Paramount, 1995.

(As Bernie Williams) Executive producer and unit production manager, *Blood and Wine* (also known as *Blood & Wine*), Fox Searchlight, 1996.

(As Bernie Williams) Executive producer and unit production manager, *Bowfinger,* Universal, 1999.

(As Bernie Williams) Executive producer and unit production manager, *The Score,* Paramount, 2001.

(As Bernie Williams) Executive producer and unit production manager, *Daredevil* (also known as *Daredevil: A Daring New Vision*), Twentieth Century–Fox, 2003.

(As Bernie Williams) *Charlotte's Web,* Paramount, 2006.

Film Appearances:

(As Bernie Williams) London airport guard number one, *Daredevil* (also known as *Daredevil: A Daring New Vision*), Twentieth Century–Fox, 2003.

Himself, *"Charlotte's Web": Where Are They Now?* (documentary short), 2007.

Himself, *"Charlotte's Web": Making Some Movie* (documentary short), 2007.

Himself, *"Charlotte's Web": How Do They Do That?* (documentary short), 2007.

Television Work; Series:

Line producer, *The Prisoner,* 1967.
Production manager, *The Prisoner,* ITV, 1967–68.

Television Appearances; Specials:

(As Bernie Williams) Himself, *The 100 Greatest War Films,* Channel 4, 2005.

WILSON, Donna
   See SCOTT, Donna W.

WINTER, Ralph 1952–

PERSONAL

Full name, Ralph Frederick Winter; born April 24, 1952, in Glendale, CA; son of Charles Frederick and Effie Audrey (maiden name, Crawford) Winter; married Judy Beth Brown, April 19, 1974; children: Benjamin Charles, Beth Elaine. *Education:* University of California, Berkeley, B.A., 1974.

Addresses: *Agent*—International Creative Management, 10250 Constellation Way, 9th Floor, Los Angeles, CA 90067. *Office*—Ralph Winter Productions, 10201 West Pico Blvd., Bldg. 6, Suite 101, Los Angeles, CA 90035.

Career: Producer and studio executive. Walt Disney Co., Burbank, CA, producer, 1978; Paramount Pictures, television producer, 1979–81, director of post–production for television, 1981; Harve Bennett Productions, worked as executive in charge of production, c. 1982; Ralph Winter Productions, Los Angeles, CA, principal and producer. University of Iowa, Iowa City, Geneva Lecturer, 1999; Dove Foundation, member of advisory board.

Member: Directors Guild of America, Academy of Motion Picture Arts and Sciences.

Awards, Honors: Saturn Award nomination, best special effects, Academy of Science Fiction, Fantasy, and Horror Films, 1985, for *Star Trek III: The Search for*

Spock; Saturn Award nomination (with Bruce Nicholson), best special effects, Academy of Science Fiction, Fantasy, and Horror Films, 1986, for *Explorers;* Video Premiere Award nomination (with others), best live-action video premiere, 2001, for *Left Behind.*

CREDITS

Film Executive Producer:

Star Trek IV: The Voyage Home (also known as *The Voyage Home: Star Trek IV*), Paramount, 1986.
Star Trek V: The Final Frontier, Paramount, 1989.
The Perfect Weapon, Paramount, 1991.
Captain Ron, Buena Vista, 1992.
Hocus Pocus, Buena Vista, 1993.
Inspector Gadget, Buena Vista/Walt Disney Pictures, 1999.
Left Behind: The Movie, Cloud Ten Pictures, 2000.
Planet of the Apes, Twentieth Century–Fox, 2001.
Blizzard, Premiere Group, 2003.
Lost, Warner Home Video, 2004.
In My Sleep, 2007.

Film Producer:

Star Trek VI: The Undiscovered Country, Paramount, 1991.
The Puppet Masters (also known as *Robert A. Heinlein's "The Puppet Masters"*), Buena Vista, 1994.
Hackers, Metro–Goldwyn–Mayer/United Artists, 1995.
The Spittin' Image (short film), Make Believe Films, 1997.
Opie Gone Mad (short film), 1999.
X–Men (also known as *X–Men 1.5*), Twentieth Century–Fox, 2000.
Left Behind: The Movie (also known as *Left Behind*), Cloud Ten Pictures, 2000.
Shoot or Be Shot (also known as *Shooting Stars*), Iron Entertainment, 2000.
X2 (also known as *X–Men 2, X–2, X–Men 3: X–Men United,* and *X2: X–Men United*), Twentieth Century–Fox, 2003.
Hangman's Curse (also known as *The Vertias Project*), Twentieth Century–Fox, 2003.
Frank Peretti: From Page to Screen (documentary short), Twentieth Century Fox Home Entertainment, 2004.
The Spider Wrangler: The Spiders of "Hangman's Curse" (documentary short), Twentieth Century Fox Home Entertainment, 2004.
Fantastic Four, Twentieth Century–Fox, 2005.
The Visitation, Twentieth Century–Fox, 2006.
X–Men: The Last Stand (also known as *X–Men 3* and *X3*), Twentieth Century–Fox, 2006.
Thou Shalt Laugh, 2006.
Thr3e (also known as *Three*), Twentieth Century–Fox, 2006.
4: Rise of the Silver Surfer (also known as *Fantastic Four: Rise of the Silver Surfer*), 2007.

House, Twentieth Century–Fox, 2007.
The Screwtape Letters, 2008.

Film Work; Other:

(Uncredited) Post–production supervisor, *Star Trek: The Wrath of Khan* (also known as *Star Trek II: The Wrath of Kahn* and *Star Trek II: The Wrath of Khan—The Director's Cut*), 1982.
Associate producer, *Star Trek III: The Search for Spock,* Paramount, 1984.
Visual effects coordinator, *Explorers,* Paramount, 1985.
Co–executive producer, *Flight of the Intruder,* Paramount, 1991.
Supervising producer, *Mighty Joe Young* (also known as *Mighty Joe*), Buena Vista, 1998.
Co–producer, *The Bridge* (short), 2004.

Film Appearances:

Fourth vice president, *Hackers,* Metro–Goldwyn–Mayer/United Artists, 1995.
Himself, *X–Men Production Scrapbook* (documentary), Twentieth Century–Fox, 2003.
Himself, *The Uncanny Suspects* (documentary short), Twentieth Century Fox Home Entertainment, 2003.
Himself, *X–Factor: The Look of "X–Men"* (documentary short), Twentieth Century–Fox Home Entertainment, 2003.
Himself, *Cosmic Thoughts* (documentary short), Paramount Home Video, 2003.
Himself, *The Second Uncanny Issues of X–Men! Making "X2"* (also known as *The Second Uncannny Issue of X–Men;* documentary), Twentieth Century–Fox, 2003.
Himself, *Frank Peretti: From Page to Screen* (documentary short), Twentieth Century Fox Home Entertainment, 2004.
(Uncredited) Ship worker, *Fantastic Four,* 2005.

Television Work; Series:
Producer, *High Incident,* ABC, 1996.

Television Work; Miniseries:
Executive in charge of production (Harve Bennett Productions), *The Jesse Owens Story,* 1984.

Television Work; Movies:
Postproduction supervisor, *A Woman Called Golda,* 1982.
Postproduction supervisor, *The Jesse Owens Story,* 1984.

Television Work; Pilots:
Co–executive producer, *Plymouth,* 1991.

Television Work; Episodic:
High Incident, ABC, 1996.

Television Appearances; Specials:
The Making of "Planet of the Apes," 2001.
X–Pose: X2 Mutants Uncovered, Fox, 2003.

Television Appearances; Episodic:
"The Making of 'Planet of the Apes'," *HBO First Look,* HBO, 2001.
"Ralph Winter," *Life After Film School,* Fox Movie Channel, 2006.

OTHER SOURCES

Periodicals:
Starlog, April, 1992; September, 1993.

WOOF, Emily 1967–

PERSONAL

Born 1967, in Newcastle upon Tyne, England. *Education:* Attended Oxford University.

Addresses: *Agent*—Lorraine Hamilton, Hamilton Hodell Ltd., 66–68 Margaret St., 5th Floor, London W1W 8SR, England.

Career: Actress, director, and writer.

Awards, Honors: Screen Actors Guild Award (with others), outstanding cast performance, 1998, for *The Full Monty;* Australian Film Institute Award nomination, best supporting actress, 1999, for *Passion;* London Critics Circle Film Award nomination, British supporting actress of the year, 2005, for *Wondrous Oblivion.*

CREDITS

Film Appearances:
Mandy, *The Full Monty,* Fox Searchlight, 1997.
Linda, *Photographing Fairies* (also known as *Apparition*), PolyGram Video, 1997.
Grace Melbury, *The Woodlanders,* Miramax, 1997.
Shannon, *Velvet Goldmine,* Miramax, 1998.
Letitia/Claudia, *Fast Food,* Finnkino, 1998.
Alice, *This Year's Love,* Entertainment Film Distributors, 1999.
Karen Holten, *Passion* (also known as *Passion: The Story of Percy Grainger*) Motion International, 1999.
Dorothy Wordsworth, *Pandaemonium,* USA Films, 2000.

Anna, *Going Going,* 2000.
Rachel Stewart, *Silent Cry,* INmotion Pictures, 2002.
Ruth, *Wondrous Oblivion,* Momentum Pictures, 2003.
Kelly, *School for Seduction,* Redbus Film Distribution, 2004.
Lindsay, *The League of Gentlemen's Apocalypse,* United International Pictures, 2005.
Helen, *Meeting Helen,* APT Films, 2007.

Film Director:
Between the Wars (short film), Whatever Pictures, 2002.
Meeting Helen, APT Films, 2007.

Television Appearances; Miniseries:
Lydgate's maid, *Middlemarch,* PBS, 1994.
Susie, *Killer Net* (also known as *Lynda La Plante's "Killer Net"*), Channel 4, 1998.
Paula Sullivan, *Daylight Robbery,* 1999.
Nancy, *Oliver Twist,* PBS, 1999.
Paula Sullivan, *Daylight Robbery 2,* 2001.
Rowena Waddy, *Marple: Nemesis* (also known as *Miss Marple: Nemesis*), PBS, 2007.

Television Appearances; Specials:
Lise Meitner, *E=mc2,* Channel 4, 2005, broadcast in the United States as "Einstein's Big Idea," an episode of *Nova,* PBS, 2005.
Ann Fleming, *Ian Fleming: Bondmaker,* BBC, 2005.
The Evening Standard British Film Awards, ITV3, 2005.
The True Voice of Rape, More4, 2006.

Television Appearances; Movies:
Rita, *Born Equal,* BBC, 2006.
Janet Bailey, "The Animal Within," *Midsomer Murders,* Arts and Entertainment, 2007.

Television Appearances; Episodic:
Policewoman, *Casualty,* 1995.
Guest, *Breakfast,* BBC, 2004.

Appeared in "Perfect Day," *Crime Monologues,* More4, and *The Ronni Ancona Show,* BBC.

Stage Appearances:
Bullet, 1998.
Title role, *Salome,* 1998.

Radio Appearances:
Appeared as Miss Fife, *The Laughter of Stafford Girls' High,* and as Gretel, *Slicing the Gingerbread,* both BBC–Radio.

WRITINGS

Screenplays:
Going Going, 2000.
Meeting Helen, APT Films, 2007.

WOREN, Dan
(Jackson Daniels, Warren Daniels, Dan Warren)

PERSONAL

Career: Actor.

CREDITS

Film Appearances:
(As Jackson Daniels; English version) Voice, *Kido senshi gandamu I* (animated; also known as *Mobile Suit Gundam I*), Bandai, 1981.
Roger, *Goin' All the Way,* Saturn, 1982.
Voice of Cobra, *Space Adventure Cobra* (animated), Tara, 1982.
(English version) Voice, *Hadashi no Gen* (animated; also known as *Barefoot Gen*), Tara, 1983.
Jagi, *Hokuto no ken* (animated; also known as *Fist of the North Star*), Streamline, 1986.
(As Jackson Daniels; English version) Voice, *Juichi–nin iru!* (animated; also known as *11 People!*, *There Are 11,* and *They Were 11*), JONU, 1986.
(As Jackson Daniels; English version) Voice, *Amagae-dun uzu* (animated; also known as *Armageddon*), Manga, 1986.
(As Warren Daniels; English version) Voice, Nekkerout, *Oritsu uchugun oneamisu no tsubasa* (animated; also known as *Starquest, Wings of Honneamise,* and *Wings of Honneamise: Royal Space Force*), Tara, 1987.
(English version) Supervisor, *Dati pea Gekijo–ban* (animated; also known as *Dirty Pair, Dirty Pair: The Movie,* and *Original Dirty Pair: Project Eden*), Shochiku, 1987.
Clerk, *Casual Sex?,* 1988.
(As Jackson Daniels) *Akira* (also known as *Akira: The Special Edition*), Manga, 1988.
Problem Child, Universal, 1990.
Policeman number one, *Beastmaster 2: Through the Portal of Time,* New Line Cinema, 1991.
Terry, *Shelter from the Storm,* 1994.
Royce, *For All It's Worth,* USC, 1994.
Lenny, *The Granny* (also known as *The Granny: A Blood Relative*), A*Vision, 1995.
Borg, *Star Trek: First Contact,* Paramount, 1996.

(As Jackson Daniels; English version) Voice of Nicholas Doris, *Burakku jakku* (animated; also known as *Black Jack*), Manga, 1996.
Jim Goodman, *Attitudes,* Jackson, 1997.
(As Jackson Daniels) Auctioneer, *Sol Bianca: The Legacy,* 1999.
UN representative, *Devadasy,* 1999.
(As Jackson Daniels) Enra, *Hunt for the Sword Samurai,* 2000.
Skunk, *Metoroporisu* (also known as *Osamu Tezuka's "Metropolis," Metropolis, Osamu Tezuka's "Metoroporisu,"* and *Robotic Angel*), Columbia TriStar, 2001.
Lester Reams, *IceMaker,* Xenon, 2003.
Voice of General Reinhardt, *Robotech: The Shadow Chronicles,* Madman, 2006.
Ray C., *Taken by Force,* Fantastic, 2007.

Television Appearances; Episodic:
Officer, "The Least Dangerous Game," *Simon & Simon,* CBS, 1981.
Intern, "And Never Brought to Mind," *Knots Landing,* CBS, 1983.
Army Lieutenant, Red Star, "Shadow of the Hawke: Part 1," *Airwolf* (also known as *Lobo del aire*), CBS, 1984.
Voice of Roy Fokker, "Boobytrap," *Robotech,* syndicated, 1985.
Sergeant, "Firing Line," *The A–Team,* NBC, 1986.
Public defender, "The Best Defense," *Hill Street Blues,* NBC, 1986.
Police Officer number two, "How Am I Driving?," *L.A. Law,* NBC, 1994.
Bartender, "Confessions and Lamentations," *Babylon 5* (also known as *B5*), syndicated, 1995.
Man, "Jimmy Goes Away," *Grace Under Fire,* ABC, 1995.
Dr. Sturges, "The Rock," *Silk Stalkings,* USA Network, 1997.
Major Dunn, "Hitchhiker," *Night Man,* syndicated, 1998.
Voice of Kendall Tachikawa, a recurring role, *Digimon: Digital Monsters* (animated; also known as *Digimon 02, Digimon 03,* and *Digimon: Season 3*), Fox, 1999–2002.
Voice of Medicon, "Short–Circuited," *Power Rangers Time Force,* Fox, 2001.
Voice of Zen–Aku, "Curse of the Wolf," *Power Rangers Wild Force,* Fox, 2002.
Voice of Zen–Aku, "Battle of the Zords," *Power Rangers Wild Force,* Fox, 2002.
Voice of Zen–Aku, "Predazord, Awaken," *Power Rangers Wild Force,* Fox, 2002.
Voice of Onikage, "The Master's Herald: Part 1 & 2," *Power Rangers Wild Force,* 2002.
Voice of driver, a recurring role, *Gungrave* (animated), 2003–2004.
Voice of Uno, "Blue Monday," *Kokyo shihen Eureka Seven* (animated; also known as *Eureka 7* and *Psalms of Planets Eureka Seven*), Cartoon Network, 2005.

Television Appearances; Movies:

Voice of Roy Fokker, *Codename: Robotech* (animated), 1985.

Policeman, *The Richest Cat in the World,* ABC, 1986.

Neighbor number one, *Don't Touch My Daughter* (also known as *Nightmare*), NBC, 1991.

Broker, *An Element of Truth,* CBS, 1995.

Coroner, *The Beneficiary,* HBO, 1997.

Firetrap, HBO, 2001.

Television Appearances; Series:

Voice of Cobra, *Space Adventure Cobra* (animated), 1982.

Sheldon, *Days of Our Lives* (*DOOL* and *Days*), NBC, 1987–1990.

Voice of Bandit leader, *Street Fighter II: V* (animated; also known as *Street Fighter II: Victory*), 1995.

(As Jackson Daniels) Voice of Rob, *Kido senshi Gunam: Dai 08 MS shotai* (animated; also known as *Mobile Suite Gundam: The 08th MS Team*), Cartoon Network, 1996.

Voice of Hydro Contaminator, "Graduation Blues," *Power Rangers Zeo* (also known as *ZeoRangers*), Fox, 1996.

Voice of Drill Master, "It Came from Angel Grove," *Power Rangers Zeo* (also known as *ZeoRangers*), Fox, 1996.

Voice of Drill Master, "A Golden Homecoming," *Power Rangers Zeo* (also known as *ZeoRangers*), Fox, 1996.

Voice of Chapel The Evergreen, *Trigun* (animated; also known as *Toraigan* and *Trigun #1: The $$60,000,000,000 Man*), Cartoon Network, 1998.

Voice of Saiyo Wong, *Outlaw Star* (animated), Cartoon Network, 1998.

Preview narrator, *Kauboi bibappu* (animated; also known as *Cowboy Bebop*), Cartoon Network, 1998.

Chesire Cat poser, *Serial Experiments: Lain,* TechTV, 1998.

Voice of Pa, *Monster Farm* (animated), Fox Family, 1998.

Cougar, *Arc the Lad,* 1999.

Dennis, *Wild ARMs: Twilight Venom,* 1999.

(As Jackson Daniels) Voice of Gengo Kisaki, *Rorouni Kenshin* (animated), Cartoon Network, 2000.

Jinzo ningen Kikaida: The Animation (animated; also known as *Androide Kikaider: The Animation, Humanoid Kikaider: The Animation,* and *Kikaider*), Cartoon Network, 2000.

(As Jackson Daniels) Voice of Mr. Nishiya, *Gate Keepers* (animated; also known as *Gate Keepers 21*), 2001.

Crosswise, *Transformers: Robots in Disguise,* Fox, 2001.

Voice of Ken, *Kaze no yojinbo* (animated; also known as *Bodyguard of the Wind, Kaze no yojimbo,* and *Yojimbo of the Wind*), 2001.

Voice of Mr. Yasu, *Saibogu 009* (also known as *Cyborg 009: The Cyborg Soldier* and *Cyborg 009*), Cartoon Network, 2001.

(As Jackson Daniels) Voice of Lionel "Pops" Racer, *Speed Racer X* (animated), Nickelodeon, 2002.

Naruto (animated), Cartoon Network, 2002.

Gene Glen, *Heat Guy J,* 2002.

Voice of Fon, *Mouse,* 2002.

(As Jackson Daniels) Voice of Gwendal Von Voltaire, *Kyo kara mao!* (animated; also known as *God, Save Our King!*), 2004.

(As Jackson Daniels) Voice of man in black, *Shin getter robo* (animated; also known as *New Getter Robo*), 2004.

Voice of Matsunosuke Shibui, *Samurai champloo* (animated), Fuji and Cartoon Network, 2004.

(As Jackson Daniels) Voice of Hashimoto, teacher, *Grenadier: Hohoemi no senshi* (animated), 2004.

Voice of Takamine, *Paranoia Agent* (animated), Cartoon Network, 2004–2005.

Television Appearances; Specials:

Mr. McDunn, *Lost in Dinosaur World,* NBC, 1993.

Chasing the Sun, PBS, 2001.

Television Appearances; Miniseries:

(As Jackson Daniels) Voice of Colonel Killing, *Kido senshi Gunam 0080 pocket no naka no sensou* (animated; also known as *Gundam 0800: A War in the Pocket* and *Mobile Suit Gundham 0080: A War in the Pocket*), Cartoon Network, 1989.

Television Appearances; Pilots:

Gallery guard, *The Invisible Woman,* 1983.

Army Lieutenant, Red Star, *Airwolf,* 1984.

RECORDINGS

Video Games:

Voice of Kandoc, Grak the Traitor, *Stonekeep,* 1994.

(As Dan Warren) *Might and Magic VII: For Blood and Honor,* 1999.

Vampire: The Masquerade–Redemption, 2000.

Legends of Might and Magic, Interplay, 2001.

Might and Magic IX, New World, 2002.

Heroes of Might and Magic IV, New World, 2002.

(As Dan Warren) *.hack//Osen kakudai vol. 1* (also known as *.hack//Infection* and *.hack//Infections Part 1*), Atari, 2002.

(As Jackson Daniels) *WarCraft III: Reign of Chaos,* Blizzard, 2002.

(As Dan Warren) *.hack//Akusei heni vol. 2* (also known as *.hack//Mutation* and *.hack//Mutation Part 2*), Atari, 2002.

Voice of Roy Fokker/Zeraal, *Robotech: Battlecry,* TDK Mediactive, 2002.

(As Dan Warren) *.hack//Shinsoku vol. 3* (also known as *.hack//Outbreak* and *.hack//Outbreak Part 3*), Atari, 2002.

Voice of Liu Bei/Lu Bu, *Shin sangoku muso 3* (also known as *Dynasty Warriors 4, Dynasty Warriors 4: Hyper* and *Shin sangoku musou–Hyper*), KOEI, 2003.

(As Jackson Daniels) *Delta Force: Black Hawk Down,* Novalogic, 2003.

(As Dan Warren) *.hack//Zettai houi vol. 4* (also known as *.hack//Quarantine* and *.hack//Quarantine Part 4*), Atari, 2003.

Voice of Liu Bei, *Sangokushi senki* (also known as *Dynasty Tactics 2*), KOEI, 2003.

(As Jackson Daniels) *Warcraft III: The Frozen Throne,* Sierra, 2003.

Voice of Liu Bei/Lu Bu, *Shin sangoku muso 3 mushoden* (also known as *Dynasty Warriors 4: Xtreme Legends*), KOEI, 2003.

Lords of Everquest, Sony, 2003.

Voice of Liu Bei/Lu Bu, *Shin sangoku muso 3: Empires* (also known as *Dynasty Warriors 4: Empires*), 2004.

Voice of Date Vasal/Lu Bu, *Sengoku muso* (also known as *Samurai Warriors*), KOEI, 2004.

Voice of Lu Bu, *Sengoku muso mushoden* (also known as *Samurai Warriors: Xtreme Legends*), KOEI, 2004.

The Bard's Tale, Acclaim, 2004.

Minna no gorufu portable, Sony, 2004.

Voice of Thanos, *Radiata Stories,* Square Enix, 2005.

Voice of Liu Bei, *Shin sangoku muso 4,* KOEI, 2005.

Voice of Archibald, *Wild ARMS: The 4th Detonator* (also known as *Wild Arms 4*), Sony, 2005.

Voice of Liu Bei, *Shin sangoku muso 4 mushoden,u,* KOEI, 2005.

Soul Calibur III (also known as *Soul Calibur III: Arcade Edition*), Namco, 2005.

Dirge of Cerberus: Final Fantasy VII, Square Enix, 2006.

Liu Bei, *Shin sangoku muso 4: Empires,* KOEI, 2006.

WORONOV, Mary 1943–

(Penny Arcade, Mary Waronov)

PERSONAL

Born December 8, 1943, in Brooklyn, NY (some sources cite Palm Beach, FL); daughter of Victor D. (stepfather; a doctor) and Carol (maiden name, Eschholz) Woronov; married Theodore Gershuny (a bond broker, director, and producer), c. 1969 (marriage ended, 1973); married Ted Whitehead (a race car driver and agent), 1979. *Education:* Attended Cornell University, Ithaca, NY.

Addresses: *Manager*—Studio Talent Group, 1328 12th St., Santa Monica, CA 90401.

Career: Actress, director, and writer. Andy Warhol's Silver Factory, member of entourage, beginning c. 1964; Velvet Underground, go–go dancer for Exploding Plastic Inevitable shows. Otis College of Art and Design, Los Angeles, CA, writing instructor. Painter, with work exhibited in New York City and London, and occasionally used as set decorations for her films.

Awards, Honors: *Theatre World* Award, 1974, for *The Boom Boom Room;* Saturn Award nomination, best actress, Academy of Science Fiction, Fantasy, and Horror Films, 1983, for *Eating Raoul;* Saturn Award nomination, best supporting actress, 1985, for *Night of the Comet;* Independent Spirit Award nomination, best supporting female, 1990, for *Scenes from the Class Struggle in Beverly Hills;* Spirit of Silver Lake Award, Los Angeles Silver Lake Film Festival, 2000; Santa Fe Film Festival Award, 2001.

CREDITS

Film Appearances:
Screen Test #1, 1965.

(Uncredited) *Screen Test #3* (also known as *Suicide*), 1966.

(Uncredited) *Screen Test #4,* 1966.

Dancer, *Salvador Dali,* Andy Warhol Films, 1966.

Dancer, *The Velvet Underground and Nico,* Andy Warhol Films, 1966.

Superboy, 1966.

Shower, 1966.

Milk, 1966.

Kiss the Boot, 1966.

Policewoman, *Hedy* (also known as *The 14–Year–Old Girl* and *Hedy, the Shoplifter*), 1966.

Jean Harlow, *The Beard,* 1966.

**** (also known as *The 24 Hour Movie*), 1967.

Four Stars, 1967.

The Beard, 1967.

Hanoi Hannah, *Chelsea Girls,* Filmmakers' Distribution Center, 1967.

Mary Wonderly, *Kemek* (also known as *For Love or Murder*), GHM, 1970.

Camila Stone, *Sugar Cookies* (also known as *Love Me My Way*), General Film, 1973.

Mikki Hughes, *Seizure* (also known as *Queen of Evil* and *Tango macabre*), American International Pictures, 1974.

Diane Adams, *Silent Night, Bloody Night* (also known as *Death House* and *Night of the Dark Full Moon*), Cannon, 1974.

Calamity Jane, *Death Race 2000,* New World, 1975.

Diane, *Cover Girl Models,* New World, 1975.

Sandy Harris, *Cannonball* (also known as *Car Quake*), New World, 1976.

Mary McQueen, *Hollywood Boulevard,* New World, 1976.

Pearl, *Jackson County Jail* (also known as *The Innocent Victim*), New World, 1976.

(As Mary Waronov) Julie, *Hollywood Man* (also known as *Stoker*), 1976.

(Uncredited) *Mr. Billion* (also known as *The Windfall*), Twentieth Century–Fox, 1977.

Hackett, *Bad Georgia Road,* Dimension Films, 1977.

Arlene, *The One and Only,* Paramount, 1978.

Woman bankrobber, *The Lady in Red* (also known as *Guns, Sin, and Bathtub Gin* and *Touch Me and Die*), New World, 1979.

Evelyn Togar, *Rock 'n' Roll High School* (also known as *Girls' Gym*), New World, 1979.

Samantha Vitesse, *The Protectors, Book I* (also known as *Angel from H.E.A.T.* and *Angel of H.E.A.T.*), Studios Pan Imago, 1981.

Party house owner, *Heartbeeps,* Universal, 1981.

Secretary, "Success Wanters," *National Lampoon Goes to the Movies* (also known as *National Lampoon's "Movie Madness"*), Metro–Goldwyn–Mayer, 1981.

Mary Bland, *Eating Raoul,* Twentieth Century–Fox, 1982.

Violetta, *Get Crazy* (also known as *Flip Out*), Embassy, 1983.

Audrey, *Night of the Comet,* Atlantic Releasing, 1984.

Dr. Fletcher, *Hellhole,* Arkoff, 1985.

Dancing Mary, *Nomads,* Atlantic Releasing, 1985.

My Man Adam, TriStar, 1985.

Miss Blackwell, *The Movie House Massacre* (also known as *Blood Theatre*), Movie House, 1986.

Mary Bland, *Chopping Mall* (also known as *Killbots* and *R.O.B.O.T.*), Concorde, 1986.

Raquel Putterman, *TerrorVision,* Empire Releasing, 1986.

Shelley, *Black Widow* (also known as *Bullseye*), Twentieth Century–Fox, 1987.

Kappa, 1987.

Mary Purcell, *Mortuary Academy,* Skouras, 1988.

Channeller, *Warlock* (also known as *Warlock: The Magic Wizard*), Trimark Pictures, 1989.

Quinella, *Let It Ride,* Paramount, 1989.

Lisabeth Hepburn–Saravian, *Scenes from the Class Struggle in Beverly Hills,* Cinecom International, 1989.

Welfare person, *Dick Tracy,* Buena Vista, 1990.

Dr. Glatman, *Watchers II,* Concorde, 1990.

Dr. Vadar, *Rock 'n' Roll High School Forever,* 1990.

Jezebel, *Club Fed,* 1990.

Jane, *Buster's Bedroom,* 1991.

Kidnapping wife, *Motorama,* Two Moon Releasing, 1991.

Woman tourist, *Where Sleeping Dogs Lie,* 1992.

Daisy, *The Living End,* October Films, 1992.

Herself, *Invasion of the Scream Queens,* See More Video, 1992.

(As Penny Arcade) Eugene's aunt, *Hellroller,* 1992.

Attorney, *Grief,* Strand Releasing, 1993.

Wilamena LaRue, *Good Girls Don't,* 1993.

Stranger than Love, 1993.

Wedding coordinator, *Number One Fan,* 1995.

Mrs. Crump, *Glory Daze,* Columbia TriStar, 1996.

Lou Reed: Rock and Roll Heart, Films Transit International, 1997.

Sales woman, *Sweet Jane,* Phaedra Cinema, 1998.

Dr. Klein, *Mom, Can I Keep Her?,* New Horizons Home Video, 1998.

Aunt Felicity, *Secrets of a Chambermaid,* Mystique Films, 1998.

Olivia, *Invisible Mom II,* New Horizons Home Video, 1999.

Prunella, *Zoo,* 1999.

Mom, *Perfect Fit,* 1999.

Dr. Wright, *Straight Right,* 2000.

Lisa LaStrada, *The New Women,* Ariztical Entertainment/Vagrant Films, 2000.

Mary Richman, *Citizens of Perpetual Indulgence,* 2000.

Receptionist, *The Vampire Hunters Club* (short film), Doodle Barnett Productions/Irena Belle Films, 2001.

Dyanne She–Bitch Slutface, *Prison-a-Go-Go!,* EI Independent Cinema, 2003.

Voices of Acme vice president and Bad Ideas, *Looney Tunes: Back in Action* (animated; also known as *Looney Tunes Back in Action: The Movie*), Warner Bros., 2003.

Sister Cecelia, *The Halfway House,* Shoreline Entertainment, 2004.

Doctor, *Frog-g-g!,* End of All Cinema, 2004.

Dr. Larraz, *I Pass for Human,* Arcanum Entertainment, 2004.

Abbie, *The Devil's Rejects* (also known as *TDR—The Devil's Rejects*), Lions Gate Films, 2005.

Get Froggged! Behind the Scenes of Frog-g-g!, Go Kart Films, 2005.

Notes on Marie Menken (documentary), First Run/Icarus Films, 2006.

Television Appearances; Movies:

Bartender, *In the Glitter Palace* (also known as *A Woman Accused*), NBC, 1977.

Mary Garritee, *Challenge of a Lifetime,* ABC, 1985.

Miss Renfro, *A Bunny's Tale,* ABC, 1985.

Receptionist, *Acting on Impulse* (also known as *Eyes of a Stranger, Roses Are Dead, Secret Lies,* and *Secret Lives*), Showtime, 1993.

E. Joyce Togar, *Shake, Rattle and Rock,* Showtime, 1994.

Mrs. Dimwitty, *Here Come the Munsters,* Fox, 1995.

Mrs. Dimwitty, *The Munsters' Scary Little Christmas,* Fox, 1996.

Television Appearances; Specials:

Cheech and Chong: Get Out of My Room (also known as *Get Out of My Room*), Showtime, 1985.

Andy Warhol: The E! True Hollywood Story, E! Entertainment Television, 1998.

Nurse Goines, *Seed: A Love Story,* Lifetime, 1998.

Andy Warhol: The Complete Picture, Arts and Entertainment, 2002.

Psychedelic Revolution '67, 2007.

Jack Smith and the Destruction of Atlantis, Sundance Channel, 2007.

Television Appearances; Series:

Stephanie Dillard, *Somerset* (also known as *Another World: Somerset* and *Somerset: Bay City*), NBC, 1974–75.

Television Appearances; Episodic:

Maxine, "Angels in Chains," *Charlie's Angels,* 1976.

Irene, "Capture," *Logan's Run,* CBS, 1977.

Fran Strickland, "Nardo Loses Her Marbles," *Taxi,* ABC, 1979.

Kate's fellow inmate, "Off the Record," *Mrs. Columbo* (also known as *Kate Columbo, Kate Loves a Mystery,* and *Kate the Detective*), 1979.

Phyl & Mikhy, 1980.

Nola, "A Dream of Jennifer," *Buck Rogers in the 25th Century,* NBC, 1980.

Clavell, "The Dog Who Knew Too Much," *Hart to Hart,* 1984.

Brady, "Jessica behind Bars," *Murder, She Wrote,* CBS, 1985.

Dr. Von Furst, "Knight of the Juggernaut: Parts 1 & 2," *Knight Rider,* NBC, 1985.

Cheryl, "The Letter," *Mr. Belvedere,* 1985.

Nurse, "Secret Cinema," *Amazing Stories* (also known as *Steven Spielberg's "Amazing Stories"*), NBC, 1986.

Governess, "The Princess Who Had Never Laughed," *Faerie Tale Theatre* (also known as *Shelley Duvall's "Faerie Tale Theatre"*), Showtime, 1986.

"Nothing up My Sleeve," *St. Elsewhere,* 1986.

Dr. Flynn (some sources cite Dr. Quinn), "Where the Sun Don't Shine," *You Again?,* NBC, 1986.

Bean Sweeney, "The Upstairs Gardener," *Shell Game,* CBS, 1987.

Jill Taylor, "The Spa Who Loved Me," *Sledge Hammer!* (also known as *Sledge Hammer: The Early Years*), ABC, 1987.

Officer Burdette, *Trial and Error,* CBS, 1988.

Viki, "Pillow Talk," *Monsters,* 1988.

Officer Gwen, "Money Talks," *Parker Lewis Can't Lose* (also known as *Parker Lewis*), Fox, 1992.

Mona Savage, "The Player," *Flying Blind,* Fox, 1993.

Lydia Detmeir, "The Gift: Part 2," *Wings,* NBC, 1993.

Mona Savage, "My Dinner with Brad Schimmel," *Flying Blind,* Fox, 1993.

Mona Savage, "Unforgiving," *Flying Blind,* Fox, 1993.

Mona Savage, "The Bride of Marsh Man 2: The Spawning," *Flying Blind,* Fox, 1993.

Ko'Dath, "Born to the Purple," *Babylon 5* (also known as *B5*), 1994.

Dr. Linda Shields, "Pressure," *My So–Called Life,* ABC, 1994.

Rita Luce, "They Also Serve," *Highlander* (also known as *Highlander: The Series*), 1995.

Mrs. Ramsay, "Swine Lake," *Family Matters,* ABC, 1996.

Television Director; Episodic:

Women, 1996.

"Blind Love," *Women: Stories of Passion,* Showtime, 1996.

"The Little Vampire," *Women: Stories of Passion,* Showtime, 1997.

"The Gigolo," *Women: Stories of Passion,* Showtime, 1997.

"Astral Eros," *Women: Stories of Passion,* Showtime, 1997.

Stage Appearances:

Hanoi Hanna, *Vinyl,* Theatre of the Lost Continent, Cafe Cino, New York City, 1967.

Tamberlaine, *Conquest of the Universe,* Playhouse of the Ridiculous, Bouwerie Lane Theatre, New York City, 1967.

Lutetia, *Arenas of Lutetia,* Judson Poets' Theatre, New York City, 1968.

Big Mama, La Mama Experimental Theatre Club, New York City, 1969.

Jackie Onassis and the Queen of Greece, La Mama Experimental Theatre Club, 1969.

Bubi, *Night Club,* Cafe La Mama, New York City, 1970.

Jo, *Kitchenette,* Theatre of the Lost Continent, New York City, 1971.

Hypolyta, *Two Noble Kinsmen,* Mercer Brecht Theatre, New York City, 1973.

Susan, *The Boom Boom Room,* New York Shakespeare Festival, Vivian Beaumont Theatre, Lincoln Center, New York City, 1973.

Cleaning House, Workshop of the Players Art Theatre, New York City, 1973.

Gloria Jean Kojax, *Women Behind Bars,* Theatre of the Eye Repertory Company, New York Theatre Ensemble, New York City, 1974.

Godzilla, Beyond Baroque Theatre, Los Angeles, 1984.

Appeared as magician, *The Illusion,* Los Angeles Theatre Center, Los Angeles; and *Kennedy's Children,* Lobero Theatre, Santa Barbara, CA.

RECORDINGS

Videos:

Kicks and Crashes, Blue Underground, 2004.

30 Days in Hell (also known as *30 Days in Hell: The Making of "The Devil's Rejects"*), Lions Gate Films Home Entertainment, 2005.

Playing the Game: Looking Back at "Death Race 2000"—Death Race 2000 Special Edition DVD, Buena Vista Home Entertainment, 2005.

Back to School: A Retrospective—"Rock 'n' Roll High School" Rock On Edition DVD, Buena Vista Home Entertainment, 2005.

Appeared in the music videos "Institutionalized" and "Possessed to Skate" by Suicidal Tendencies, "One Time for Old Times" by .38 Special; and "Something to Believe In" by the Ramones.

WRITINGS

Television Episodes:

"Blind Love," *Women: Stories of Passion,* Showtime, 1996.

"The Little Vampire," *Women: Stories of Passion,* Showtime, 1997.

"The Gigolo," *Women: Stories of Passion,* Showtime, 1997.

Books:

Wake for the Angels: Paintings and Stories, Journey Editions, 1994.

Swimming Underground: My Years on the Warhol Factory, Journey Editions, 1995.

Snake (novel), Serpent's Tail, 2000.

Niagara (novel), Serpent's Tail, 2002.

Eye Witness to Warhol (essays), Victoria Dailey, 2002.

Blind Love (short stories), High Risk Books, 2004.

OTHER SOURCES

Books:

Woronov, Mary, *Swimming Underground: My Years on the Warhol Factory,* Journey Editions, 1995.

Periodicals:

Femme Fatales, October, 2000, pp. 52–55; May, 2002, pp. 20–22.

Film Comment, January, 2004, pp. 66, 68–70.

Psychotronic Video, Volume 1, issue 27, 1998, pp. 34–41.

Electronic:

Mary Woronov Official Site, http://www.maryworonov.com, August 15, 2007.

Y–Z

YANG, Jack

PERSONAL

Education: Attended the Art Center College of Design, Pasadena, CA, and the American Academy of Dramatic Arts; trained with the South Coast Repertory Theatre, Costa Mesa, CA.

Career: Actor and cinematographer. Worked as model and appeared in advertisements.

CREDITS

Film Appearances:
Jack, *The Yellow Truth* (short film), Commando Films, 2003.
Shadow Chaser (short film), Superba Films, 2003.
The designer, *Skin Trade* (short film), Commando Films, 2004.
Page, *The Seat Filler,* The Momentum Experience, 2004.

Film Cinematographer:
The Yellow Truth (short film), Commando Films, 2003.

Television Appearances; Episodic:
Ricky Yao, "Debt," *Law & Order: Special Victims Unit* (also known as *Law & Order's Sex Crimes, Law & Order: SVU,* and *Special Victims Unit*), NBC, 2004.
Harry, "He–Male Trouble," *All of Us,* UPN, 2005.
Shawn Kimsey, "Three–Way," *CSI: Miami,* CBS, 2005.
Walter, "Thanks for the Memories," *Grey's Anatomy* (also known as *Complications, Procedure, Surgeons, Under the Knife,* and *Grey's Anatomy—Die jungen Aerzte*), ABC, 2005.
Chiyo, "Gala Gallardo," *Nip/Tuck,* FX Network, 2006.

Chiyo, "Liz Cruz," *Nip/Tuck,* FX Network, 2006.
Chiyo, "Reefer," *Nip/Tuck,* FX Network, 2006.
Ha Huang, "Yi vs. Li," *The Evidence,* ABC, 2006.
Patient, "My Buddy's Booty," *Scrubs* (also known as *Foersta hjalpen, Helt sykt, Klinika, Meditsinskaya akademiya, Scrubs—Die Anfaenger, Toubib or not toubib,* and *Tuho–osasto*), NBC, 2006.
Walter, "Where the Boys Are," *Grey's Anatomy* (also known as *Complications, Procedure, Surgeons, Under the Knife,* and *Grey's Anatomy—Die jungen Aerzte*), ABC, 2006.
Walter, "Testing 1–2–3," *Grey's Anatomy* (also known as *Complications, Procedure, Surgeons, Under the Knife,* and *Grey's Anatomy—Die jungen Aerzte*), ABC, 2007.

YOUNG, Leigh Taylor
See TAYLOR–YOUNG, Leigh

YU, Jessica 1966–

PERSONAL

Full name, Jessica Lingman Yu; born 1966; married Mark Salzman (a writer and actor); children: Ava. *Education:* Yale University, B.A., English (summa cum laude).

Addresses: *Manager*—Adam Shulman, The Firm, 9465 Wilshire Blvd., Sixth Floor, Beverly Hills, CA 90212.

Career: Documentary filmmaker, director, writer, producer, and editor. Diorama Films, principal; participant in the John Wells Director Diversity Program; director of commercials; Isabella Stewart Gardner

Museum, Boston, MA, artist in residence, 2000; lecturer at educational institutions and other venues, including the Sun Valley Writers Conference. Competed as a fencer at various events, including the World Championships and U.S. Olympic Festivals.

Member: International Documentary Association (member of the board of directors), Directors Guild of America, Writers Guild of America, West, Phi Beta Kappa.

Awards, Honors: Named a member of the all–decade women's fencing team, National Collegiate Athletic Association (NCAA), 1991; Santa Barbara Film Festival Award, best live–action short film, c. 1993, for *Sour Death Balls;* Edward R. Murrow Award for journalism, Skeptics Society, 1995; International Documentary Association Award (with others), short documentaries category, 1995, for *89 mm od Europy;* Academy Award, best documentary, short subject, 1996, International Documentary Association Award, short documentaries category, 1996, Annual CableACE Award, best directing of a documentary special, National Cable Television Association, 1997, and Best Short Film Award, documentary category, Shorts International Film Festival, 1997, all for *Breathing Lessons: The Life and Work of Mark O'Brien;* Asian Media Award, Asian American International Film Festival, 1997; nomination for Grand Jury Prize, documentary category, Sundance Film Festival, 1999, and First Prize for Short Drama, New York Festival, all for *The Living Museum;* Gotham Award nomination, best documentary, Independent Feature Project, Ojai Film Festival Award, best documentary feature, and nomination for Grand Jury Prize, documentary category, Sundance Film Festival, all 2004, nomination for Documentary Screenplay Award, Writers Guild of America, 2005, and Emmy Award nomination (with others), exceptional merit in nonfiction filmmaking, 2006, all for *In the Realms of the Unreal;* nomination for Grand Jury Prize, documentary category, Sundance Film Festival, 2007, for *Protagonist;* Emmy Award for directing commercials; Dream Media Award, Western Law Center for Disability Rights; received other awards and recognition from film festivals; MacDowell Colony fellow and Yaddo fellow.

CREDITS

Film Director:
Home Base: A Chinatown Called Heinlenville (short documentary), American Film Foundation/Carousel Films, c. 1991.
The Conductor (short musical), Inscrutable Films, 1994.
Breathing Lessons: The Life and Work of Mark O'Brien (short documentary), Inscrutable Films/Pacific News Service, 1996.
Better Late (short film), 1998.

In the Realms of the Unreal (documentary; also known as *In the Realms of the Unreal: The Mystery of Henry Darger*), Wellspring Media, 2004.
Ping Pong Playa, Cherry Sky Films, 2007.
Protagonist (documentary), IFC Films, 2007.

Film Producer:
Associate producer, *Rose Kennedy: A Life to Remember* (short documentary), 1990.
The Conductor (short musical), Inscrutable Films, 1994.
Associate producer, *Maya Lin: A Strong Clear Vision* (documentary; also known as *Maya Lin's Monument*), Ocean Releasing, 1995.
Breathing Lessons: The Life and Work of Mark O'Brien (short documentary), Inscrutable Films/Pacific News Service, 1996.
In the Realms of the Unreal (documentary; also known as *In the Realms of the Unreal: The Mystery of Henry Darger*), Wellspring Media, 2004.
Protagonist (documentary), IFC Films, 2007.

Film Editor:
Breathing Lessons: The Life and Work of Mark O'Brien (short documentary), Inscrutable Films/Pacific News Service, 1996.
In the Realms of the Unreal (documentary; also known as *In the Realms of the Unreal: The Mystery of Henry Darger*), Wellspring Media, 2004.
Protagonist (documentary), IFC Films, 2007.

Film Work; Other:
Production assistant, *Iron & Silk* (also known as *Ferro & seta, Im Reich des Drachen, Iron & Silk—O regresso da aguia,* and *Svaerd och siden*), Prestige Films, 1990.
Script advisor, *Picture Bride* (also known as *A mulher prometida, Alesul din fotografie, Bijo photo, Brud per fotografi, Das Geheimnis der Braut, La foto del compromiso, Ocean hozott, Postorderbruden,* and *Synoikesio*), Miramax, 1994.

Worked on other films, including *89 mm od Europy* (short documentary; also known as *89mm from Europe*), c. 1993.

Television Director; Specials:
Sour Death Balls, PBS, 1993.
Men of Reenaction, Independent Television Service, c. 1994.
The Living Museum, HBO, 1998.

Television Editor; Specials:
Sour Death Balls, PBS, 1993.
The Living Museum, HBO, 1998.

Television Director; Episodic:

"Somebody's Going to Emergency, Somebody's Going to Jail," *The West Wing* (also known as *West Wing* and *El ala oeste de la Casablanca*), NBC, 2001.

"Bygones," *ER* (also known as *Emergency Room*), NBC, 2002.

"Angel Maintenance," *The West Wing* (also known as *West Wing* and *El ala oeste de la Casablanca*), NBC, 2003.

"Real–to–Reel," *American Dreams* (also known as *Bandstand, Miss American Pie,* and *Our Generation*), NBC, 2004.

"The Supremes," *The West Wing* (also known as *West Wing* and *El ala oeste de la Casablanca*), NBC, 2004.

"Begin the Begin," *Grey's Anatomy* (also known as *Complications, Procedure, Surgeons, Under the Knife,* and *Grey's Anatomy—Die jungen Aerzte*), ABC, 2006.

"Let the Angels Commit," *Grey's Anatomy* (also known as *Complications, Procedure, Surgeons, Under the Knife,* and *Grey's Anatomy—Die jungen Aerzte*), ABC, 2006.

"Getting an Addict into Treatment: The CRAFT Approach" segment, *Addiction* (also known as *Addiction: The Supplementary Series*), HBO, c. 2007.

Also directed other programs, including *The Guardian* (also known as *El guardia, The Guardian—Retter mit Herz, Le protecteur, O allos mou eaftos, Ochita bengoshi Nick Fallin, Ochita bengoshi Nick Fallin 2,* and *Oikeuden puolesta*), CBS. Directed "Sins of the Father," an unaired episode of *Mister Sterling,* NBC.

Television Producer; Episodic:

"Getting an Addict into Treatment: The CRAFT Approach" segment, *Addiction* (also known as *Addiction: The Supplementary Series*), HBO, c. 2007.

Television Director; Pilots:

The Lyon's Den (also known as *I lovens hule* and *Lain luola*), NBC, 2003.

Television Appearances; Awards Presentations:

The 69th Annual Academy Awards, ABC, 1997.

WRITINGS

Screenplays:

The Conductor (short musical), Inscrutable Films, 1994.

Breathing Lessons: The Life and Work of Mark O'Brien (short documentary), Inscrutable Films/Pacific News Service, 1996.

In the Realms of the Unreal (documentary; also known as *In the Realms of the Unreal: The Mystery of Henry Darger*), Wellspring Media, 2004.

Ping Pong Playa, Cherry Sky Films, 2007.
Protagonist (documentary), IFC Films, 2007.

Teleplays; Specials:

Sour Death Balls, PBS, 1993.
The Living Museum, HBO, 1998.

Nonfiction:

Contributor of articles to periodicals, including *Buzz,* the *Los Angeles Times,* and *Worth.*

OTHER SOURCES

Periodicals:

Entertainment Weekly, fall, 2000, pp. 99, 102–104.

ZALAZNICK, Lauren 1963–

PERSONAL

Born January 18, 1963; married; children: three. *Education:* Brown University, B.A., English and premedical studies, 1984. *Avocational Interests:* Cooking, reading, watching films with her children.

Addresses: *Office*—Bravo Networks, 30 Rockefeller Plaza, 14th Floor East, New York, NY 10112.

Career: Producer and executive. Film and television producer, 1986–94; VH1 (cable television network), vice president for on–air productions, 1994–c. 1996, then senior vice president for original programming, c. 1996–2002; Bravo Networks, New York City, involved with various projects and affiliated with Trio Network, beginning 2002, executive vice president of Trio Network, president, beginning 2005. Worked as a line producer, production executive, production manager, and location assistant; producer of public service announcements, music videos, commercials, and promotional pieces.

Awards, Honors: Houston Film Festival Silver Medal (with others), best public service announcement, 1991, for "Too Much"; Independent Spirit Award nomination (with Christine Vachon), best feature, Independent Features Project/West, 1996, for *Safe;* Daytime Emmy Award nominations (with others), outstanding special class program, 1999, and outstanding special class series, 2000, 2001, and 2002, all for *Pop Up Video;* Emmy Award nomination (with others), outstanding nonfiction program (special class), 2001, for *Bands on the Run.*

CREDITS

Television Executive Producer; Series:
The RuPaul Show, VH1, beginning 1996.
Storytellers (also known as *VH1 Storytellers* and *VH1's "Storytellers"*), VH1, beginning 1996.
Mixology, VH1, beginning 1998.
My Generation, VH1, beginning 1998.
Pop Up Video '80s, VH1, beginning 1998.
Vinyl Justice, VH1, beginning 1998.
The List, VH1, beginning 1999.
Pop Up Video, VH1, beginning 1999.
Random Play, VH1, beginning 1999.
Rock Candy, VH1, beginning 1999.
Video Timeline, VH1, beginning 1999.
Pop Up Quiz, VH1, beginning 2000.
Rock of Ages, VH1, beginning 2000.
RockStory, VH1, beginning 2000.
Sound Affects, VH1, beginning 2000.
20 to 1, VH1, beginning 2000.
VH1 Confidential, VH1, beginning 2000.
VH1 FanClub, VH1, beginning 2000.
Bands on the Run, VH1, beginning 2001.
Name That Video, VH1, beginning 2001.
Road to Fame, VH1, beginning 2001.
What's My 20?, VH1, beginning 2001.

Executive producer of other programs, including *The Game behind the Music* and *Love & Harmony,* both VH1.

Television Executive in Charge of Production; Series:
Legends (also known as *VH1's "Legends"*), VH1, beginning 1996.
Storytellers (also known as *VH1 Storytellers* and *VH1's "Storytellers"*), VH1, beginning 1996.
Strange Frequency, VH1, 2001.

Network executive for various programs.

Television Work; Other; Series:
Development executive, *Rock & Roll Jeopardy!,* VH1, beginning 1998.
Supervising producer, *Pop Up Video,* VH1, beginning 1999.
Creator, *VH1 FanClub,* VH1, beginning 2000.

Television Executive Producer; Miniseries:
The 100 Greatest Artists of Rock and Roll, VH1, 1998.
100 Greatest Women of Rock & Roll, VH1, 1999.
100 Greatest Artists of Hard Rock, VH1, 2000.
The 100 Greatest Dance Songs of Rock & Roll (also known as *The 100 Greatest Dance Songs*), VH1, 2000.
The 100 Greatest Rock & Roll Moments on TV, VH1, 2000.

100 Greatest Songs of Rock & Roll, VH1, 2000.
From the Waist Down: Men, Women & Music, VH1, 2001.
100 Greatest Albums of Rock & Roll, VH1, 2001.
100 Most Shocking Moments in Rock & Roll, VH1, 2001.
VH1 Presents the '80s, VH1, 2001.
100 Greatest Teen Stars, VH1, 2006.

Television Executive Producer; Specials:
Celine, Aretha, Gloria, Shania and Mariah: Divas Live, VH1, 1998.
Madonna Rising, VH1, 1998.
Billboard 40 Top Forty Singles (1959–1998), VH1, 1999.
VH1 Divas Live '99, VH1, 1999.
VH1's "Celebrity Karaoke Cabaret," VH1, 1999.
It's Only Rock 'n' Roll, ABC, 2000.
Men Strike Back (also known as *VH1: Men Strike Back*), VH1, 2000.
My VH1 Music Awards Pre–Show, VH1, 2000.
VH1 Divas 2000: A Tribute to Diana Ross, VH1, 2000.
Video Killed the Radio Star, VH1, 2000.
KISS: Beyond the Makeup, VH1, 2001.
Rock to Erase MS, VH1, 2001.
VH1 Divas Live: The One and Only Aretha Franklin—A Benefit Concert for VH1 Save the Music Foundation, VH1, 2001.

Television Line Producer; Specials:
"Summer Stories: The Mall," *ABC Afterschool Specials,* ABC, 1992.

Television Executive Producer; Awards Presentations:
1996 VH1 Fashion Awards (also known as *The VH1 Fashion Awards*), VH1, 1996.
VH1 97 Fashion Awards, VH1, 1997.
1998 VH1 Fashion Awards, VH1, 1998.
The VH1/Vogue Fashion Awards, VH1, 1999.
My VH1 Music Awards, VH1, 2000.
The VH1/Vogue Fashion Awards, VH1, 2000.

Television Executive Producer; Pilots:
Breakthrough (also known as *break.through*), VH1, 2000.
EveryNight, VH1, 2000.
Fish 'n' Clips, VH1, 2000.
Radical Recut, VH1, 2000.
Reunion, VH1, 2000.
Rock of Ages, VH1, 2000.
Animal Trax, VH1, 2001.

Television Executive in Charge of Production; Pilots:
Strange Frequency, VH1, 2001.

Television Appearances; Miniseries:
Pilot Season, Trio, 2004.

Television Appearances; Episodic:
Herself, *Square Off,* TV Guide Channel, 2006.

Film Executive Producer:
Swoon (also known as *Leopold & Loeb lapsenmurhaajien tarina*), Fine Line Features, 1992.
Zoolander (also known as *Derek Zoolander*), Paramount, 2001.
Final Cut: The Making and Unmaking of "Heaven's Gate" (documentary), Viewfinder Productions/ Specialty Films, 2004.

Film Producer:
Overnight Success (short film), c. 1988.
Associate producer, *Poison* (also known as *Veneno*), Zeitgeist Films, 1991.
Sublet (also known as *Realquiler*), 1991.
Dottie Gets Spanked (short film), Zeitgeist Films, 1993.
(With others) *Kids* (also known as *Dzieciaki, Koelykoek, Miudos,* and *Mularija*), Shining Excalibur Films, 1995.
Safe (also known as *Chemical Syndrome* and *Seguro*), Sony Pictures Classics, 1995.
Girls Town (also known as *Regazze di citta*), October Films, 1996.

Film Line Producer:
Jumpin' at the Boneyard (also known as *Due vitte in pericolo, Manny und Dan—Leben und Sterben in der Bronx,* and *Matkalippu hautausmaalle*), Twentieth Century–Fox, 1992.
Swoon (also known as *Leopold & Loeb lapsenmurhaajien tarina*), Fine Line Features, 1992.
Getting In (also known as *Kamikaze College, Kill Me Tender, Student Body,* and *Vestibular da morte*), Trimark Pictures, 1994.

Film Work; Other:
Assistant, *Compromising Positions* (also known as *Kompromisowe pozycje, Posizioni compromettenti,* and *Todliche Beziehung*), Paramount, 1985.
Location assistant, *Morgan Stewart's Coming Home* (also known as *Home Front, Aelae mokaa Morgan, Kaikki kotiinpaein,* and *Morgan Stewart powraca do domu*), New Century Vista Film Company, 1987.
Production manager, *Poison* (also known as *Veneno*), Zeitgeist Films, 1991.
Video segment editor, *Safe* (also known as *Chemical Syndrome* and *Seguro*), Sony Pictures Classics, 1995.

Film Appearances:
Waitress, *Poison* (also known as *Veneno*), Zeitgeist Films, 1991.

Phrenology head, *Swoon* (also known as *Leopold & Loeb lapsenmurhaajien tarina*), Fine Line Features, 1992.

WRITINGS

Teleplays; with Others; Miniseries:
100 Greatest Teen Stars, VH1, 2006.

OTHER SOURCES

Periodicals:
Broadcasting and Cable, May 2, 2005, p. 24.

ZINBERG, Michael

PERSONAL

Addresses: *Agent*—Robert Broder, International Creative Management, 10250 Constellation Way, 9th Floor, Los Angeles, CA 90067.

Career: Producer, director, and writer. Worked for Talent Associates and Cherokee Productions; National Broadcasting Co., former vice president for West Coast comedy development for NBC–TV.

Member: Directors Guild of America (member of board of directors).

Awards, Honors: Emmy Award nomination (with others), outstanding comedy series, 1977, for *The Bob Newhart Show;* Emmy Award nominations (with others), outstanding drama series, 1990, 1991, 1992, for *Quantum Leap;* Directors Guild of America Award (with others), outstanding directorial achievement in nighttime dramatic shows, 1991, for "Vietnam," *Quantum Leap.*

CREDITS

Television Producer; Series:
Assistant producer, *Nichols* (also known as *James Garner* and *James Garner as Nichols*), 1971.
Assistant producer, *The Mary Tyler Moore Show* (also known as *Mary Tyler Moore*), 1972–73.
Associate producer, *The Bob Newhart Show,* CBS, 1972–75.
Associate producer, *The Mary Tyler Moore Show* (also known as *Mary Tyler Moore*), 1973–74.

Producer, *Paul Sand in "Friends and Lovers"* (also known as *Friends and Lovers* and *The Paul Sand Show*), 1974.

Producer, *The Tony Randall Show,* 1976.

Creator and executive producer, *The Yellow Rose,* NBC, 1983–84.

Creator and producer, *Fathers and Sons,* NBC, 1986.

Executive producer and producer, *Heart of the City* (also known as *Cold Steel and Neon*), ABC, 1986.

Co–executive producer, *Quantum Leap,* NBC, 1990–91.

Executive producer, *Tequila and Bonetti,* CBS, 1992.

Also co–executive producer of *JAG.*

Television Director; Series:

The Bob Newhart Show, CBS, multiple episodes, between 1975 and 1978.

Everybody Loves Raymond (also known as *Raymond*), CBS, multiple episodes, between 1999 and 2002.

The Practice, ABC, multiple episodes, between 1999 and 2004.

Gilmore Girls (also known as *Gilmore Girls: Beginnings*), The WB, multiple episodes, 2004–2005.

Television Director; Movies:

(And executive producer) *For the Very First Time* (also known as *Til I Kissed Ya*), NBC, 1991.

Accidental Meeting, USA Network, 1994.

A Christmas Wedding, Lifetime, 2006.

Television Work; Pilots:

Producer, *The Chopped Liver Brothers,* ABC, 1977.

Executive producer and director, *Not Until Today* (also known as *Home Again*), NBC, 1979.

Executive producer and director, *Mother & Me, M.D.,* NBC, 1979.

Director, *Home Room,* ABC, 1981.

Director, *Whacked Out,* NBC, 1981.

Executive producer and director, *The James Boys,* NBC, 1982.

Executive producer and director, *A Girl's Life,* NBC, 1983.

Executive producer and producer, *W*A*L*T*E*R,* CBS, 1984.

Fathers and Sons, NBC, 1986.

Director, *Together We Stand* (also known as *Nothing Is Easy*), 1986.

Executive producer, *Fathers and Sons,* NBC, 1986.

Director, *Built to Last,* NBC, 1997.

Television Executive Producer; Episodic:

The Bob Newhart Show, CBS, 1973.

Television Director; Episodic:

We've Got Each Other, CBS, 1977.

"Singles," *Lou Grant,* CBS, 1978.

"Pilot: Part 2," *WKRP in Cincinnati,* CBS, 1978.

"Hoodlum Rock," *WKRP in Cincinnati,* CBS, 1978.

"Turkeys Away," *WKRP in Cincinnati,* CBS, 1978.

"Preacher," *WKRP in Cincinnati,* CBS, 1979.

"Double Date," *Who's the Boss?,* 1985.

"Hunk of the Month," *Who's the Boss?,* 1985.

Premiere episode, *Nothing Is Easy,* 1986.

The Tortellis, 1987.

"The Brothers Grimm," *L.A. Law,* 1987.

"Leapin' Lizards," *L.A. Law,* 1988.

"Bank Job," *Midnight Caller,* 1988.

"A Tale of Two Cities," *Cheers,* NBC, 1988.

"Mercy Me," *Midnight Caller,* 1989.

"Kelly and the Professor," *Coach,* ABC, 1989.

"The Loss Weekend," *Coach,* ABC, 1989.

"Good Morning, Peoria—September 9, 1959," *Quantum Leap,* NBC, 1989.

"A Portrait for Troian—February 7, 1971," *Quantum Leap,* NBC, 1989.

"Homewreckers," *Coach,* ABC, 1990.

"Based on a True Story," *Midnight Caller,* 1990.

"The Leap Home: Part 2 (Vietnam)—April 7, 1970," *Quantum Leap,* NBC, 1990.

"One Strobe over the Line—June 15, 1965," *Quantum Leap,* NBC, 1990.

Premiere episode, *Tequila and Bonetti,* CBS, 1992.

"The Coma Episode," *Mr. & Mrs. Smith,* CBS, 1996.

"The Brotherhood," *JAG,* NBC, 1996.

"The Prisoner," *JAG,* NBC, 1996.

"Every Picture Tells a Story," *The Pretender,* NBC, 1996.

"Homefront," *The Pretender,* NBC, 1998.

Maggie, 1998.

"Junk," *The Pretender,* NBC, 2000.

"Contact," *Law & Order: Special Victims Unit* (also known as *Law & Order: SVU* and *Special Victims Unit*), NBC, 2000.

"Heartbreak City," *Charmed,* The WB, 2000.

"Apocalypse, Not," *Charmed,* The WB, 2000.

"Nothing Personal," *Any Day Now,* Lifetime, 2000.

"Bad Will Hunting," *Titans,* NBC, 2000.

"Kim Just Wants to Have Fun," *Yes, Dear,* CBS, 2001.

"Chapter Twenty–one," *Boston Public,* Fox, 2001.

Premiere episode, *She Spies,* NBC, 2002.

"As If by Fate," *Crossing Jordan,* NBC, 2002.

"Conspiracy," *Crossing Jordan,* NBC, 2003.

"Two Rooms," *In–Laws,* NBC, 2003.

"Mr. Monk and the 12th Man," *Monk,* USA Network, 2003.

"Sub Rosa," *Navy NCIS: Naval Criminal Investigative Service* (also known as *NCIS* and *NCIS: Naval Criminal Investigative Service*), CBS, 2003.

"House of the Rising Sun," *Lost,* ABC, 2004.

"Speak Now or Forever Hold Your Piece," *Psych,* USA Network, 2006.

"Manhunt," *The Unit,* CBS, 2006.

"From the Earth to Starbucks," *Psych,* USA Network, 2007.

"Dark of the Moon," *The Unit,* CBS, 2007.

"The Most Beautiful Girl," *The Wedding Bells,* Fox, 2007.

Also directed episodes of *Between Brothers,* UPN; *Bob; Caroline in the City* (also known as *Caroline*), NBC; *Coming of Age,* CBS; *The Commish,* ABC; *Eyes,* ABC; *Family Ties,* NBC; *First Monday,* CBS; *The Guardian,* CBS; *Goode Behavior,* UPN; *Hack,* CBS; *Heart of the City; Holding the Baby,* Fox; *Hooperman; Men Behaving Badly* (also known as *It's a Man's World*), NBC; *Mr. Belvedere; Newhart,* CBS; *9 to 5,* ABC; *Payne,* CBS; *Reasonable Doubts,* NBC; *Single Guy,* NBC; *Taxi; The Tony Randall Show; Where I Live;* and *The White Shadow,* CBS.

Television Work; Other:
Co–executive producer and director, *Wildest Dreams,* 1991.

Television Appearances; Episodic:
"Divided We Fall," *The Yellow Rose,* NBC, 1983.
"When Honor Dies," *The Yellow Rose,* NBC, 1983.
"Sins of the Father," *The Yellow Rose,* NBC, 1983.
(Uncredited) "Homefront," *The Pretender,* NBC, 1998.

Also writer of episodes for *Coming of Age, Duet, Fathers and Sons,* NBC, and *The Tony Randall Show.*

WRITINGS

Television Pilots:
The James Boys, NBC, 1982.

Television Episodes:
"Tobin's Back in Town," *The Bob Newhart Show,* CBS, 1975.
JAG, NBC, 1996.

ADAPTATIONS

The television movie *For the Very First Time* was based on a story by Zinberg.

Cumulative Index

To provide continuity with *Who's Who in the Theatre*, this index interfiles references to *Who's Who in the Theatre*, 1st–17th Editions, and *Who Was Who in the Theatre* (Gale, 1978) with references to *Contemporary Theatre, Film and Television*, Volumes 1–81.

References in the index are identified as follows:

CTFT and volume number—*Contemporary Theatre, Film and Television*, Volumes 1–81
WWT and edition number—*Who's Who in the Theatre*, 1st–17th Editions
WWasWT—*Who Was Who in the Theatre*

Amsterdam, Morey 1914(?)–1996 .... CTFT–9
    Obituary in CTFT–16
Ana–Alicia 1956(?)– CTFT–18
    Earlier sketch in CTFT–8
Anapau, Kristina 1979– CTFT–60
Anchia, Juan Ruiz 1949– CTFT–60
    Earlier sketch in CTFT–28
Ancier, Garth 1958(?)– CTFT–14
Anders, Allison 1954– CTFT–39
    Earlier sketch in CTFT–16
Anders, Glenn 1890– .... WWasWT
Anderson, Andy 1947– CTFT–69
Anderson, Anthony 1970– CTFT–68
    Earlier sketch in CTFT–30
Anderson, Audrey Marie CTFT–76
Anderson, Bob 1922– CTFT–46
Anderson, Brad 1964– CTFT–68
    Earlier sketch in CTFT–30
Anderson, Brent................................. CTFT–57
Anderson, Chow
    See .... Chow Yun–Fat
Anderson, Craig................................. CTFT–1
Anderson, D. C. CTFT–60
Anderson, Daphne 1922– WWT–17
Anderson, Daryl 1951– CTFT–69
Anderson, Dion CTFT–46
Anderson, Donna 1925–..................... CTFT–11
Anderson, Eddie "Rochester"
    1905–1977 .... CTFT–22
Anderson, Erich CTFT–43
Anderson, Gillian 1968– CTFT–46
    Earlier sketches in CTFT–14, 23
Anderson, Gillian Bunshaft
    1943– CTFT–13
Anderson, Harry 1952– CTFT–47
    Earlier sketches in CTFT–6, 13, 23
Anderson, Haskell V. III 1942(?)– CTFT–74
    Earlier sketches in CTFT–4, 33
Anderson, J. Grant 1897–.................... WWT–17
Anderson, Jamie CTFT–56
Anderson, Jo 1958– CTFT–52
Anderson, John 1922– CTFT–9
Anderson, John (Hargis) 1896–1943 ...... WWasWT
Anderson, John Murray 1886–1954 .... WWasWT
Anderson, Judith 1898–1992 .... CTFT–4
    Obituary in CTFT–10
    Earlier sketch in WWT–17
Anderson, Kevin 1960– CTFT–70
    Earlier sketches in CTFT–12, 21, 31
Anderson, Laurie 1947– CTFT–30
    Earlier sketches in CTFT–8, 18
Anderson, Lawrence 1893–1939 .... WWasWT
Anderson, Lindsay 1923–1994 .... CTFT–13
    Earlier sketches in CTFT–2, 6
Anderson, Loni 1945(?)–..................... CTFT–64
    Earlier sketches in CTFT–2, 9, 18, 29
Anderson, Louie 1953– CTFT–43
    Earlier sketches in CTFT–12, 21
Anderson, Marina
    See............................... D'Este, Coco
Anderson, Mary 1859–1940 .... WWasWT
Anderson, Maxwell 1888–1959............. WWasWT
Anderson, Melissa Sue 1962– CTFT–81
    Earlier sketches in CTFT–10, 36
    Brief Entry in CTFT–2
Anderson, Melody CTFT–4
Anderson, Michael 1920– CTFT–27
    Earlier sketch in CTFT–8
Anderson, Michael J. 1953– CTFT–58
Anderson, Michael, Jr. 1943– CTFT–33
    Earlier sketch in CTFT–6
Anderson, Mitchell 1961– CTFT–53
Anderson, Nathan 1969– CTFT–77

Anderson, Neil CTFT–60
Anderson, Pamela 1967– CTFT–41
    Earlier sketch in CTFT–20
Anderson, Paul S. W. 1965(?)– CTFT–63
Anderson, Paul Thomas 1970–................... CTFT–43
    Earlier sketch in CTFT–21
Anderson, Peter 1942– CTFT–11
Anderson, Richard 1926–.......................... CTFT–39
    Earlier sketches in CTFT–1, 17
Anderson, Richard Dean 1950– CTFT–53
    Earlier sketches in CTFT–8, 15, 25
Anderson, Robert Woodruff
    1917–....................................... WWT–17
Anderson, Rona 1928–.............................. WWT–17
Anderson, Sam 1943– CTFT–43
    Earlier sketch in CTFT–21
Anderson, Sarah Pia 1952– CTFT–81
    Earlier sketches in CTFT–12, 37
Anderson, Stanley CTFT–38
Anderson, Steven CTFT–38
Anderson, Tami
    See.................................... Roman, Tami
Anderson, Wes 1969– CTFT–69
    Earlier sketch in CTFT–30
Anderson, William
    See .... West, Adam
Andersson, Bibi 1935– CTFT–33
    Earlier sketch in CTFT–7
Andersson, Harriet 1932–.......................... CTFT–44
    Earlier sketch in CTFT–8
Andoh, Adjoa CTFT–38
Andreeff, Starr 1965(?)– CTFT–31
Andreeva–Babakhan, Anna Misaakovna
    1923–....................................... WWasWT
Andrei, Damir CTFT–78
Andress, Ursula 1936– CTFT–39
    Earlier sketches in CTFT–3, 18
Andreva, Stella
    See .... Browne, Stella
Andrew, Leo 1957– CTFT–8
Andrews, Ann 1895– .... WWasWT
Andrews, Anthony 1948– CTFT–39
    Earlier sketches in CTFT–7, 18
Andrews, Dana 1909–1992......................... CTFT–4
    Obituary in CTFT–11
    Earlier sketch in WWT–17
Andrews, David 1952–.............................. CTFT–81
    Earlier sketches in CTFT–10, 36
Andrews, Dick
    See .... Dick, Andy
Andrews, Eamonn 1922–1987 .... CTFT–2
Andrews, George Lee 1942– CTFT–1
Andrews, Giuseppe 1979– CTFT–51
Andrews, Harry 1911–1989........................ CTFT–7
    Earlier sketches in CTFT–2; WWT–17
Andrews, Jay
    See .... Wynorski, Jim
Andrews, Julie 1935– CTFT–38
    Earlier sketches in CTFT–1, 7, 14; WWasWT
Andrews, Maidie .... WWasWT
Andrews, Nancy 1924–1989....................... CTFT–8
    Earlier sketch in WWT–17
Andrews, Naveen 1969– CTFT–64
    Earlier sketches in CTFT–19, 29
Andrews, Peter
    See .... Soderbergh, Steven
Andrews, Real 1963– CTFT–23
Andrews, Robert 1895– .... WWasWT
Andrews, Tige CTFT–3
Andrews, Tod 1920– .... WWasWT
Andriole, David.. CTFT–71
Andros, Douglas 1931– CTFT–1
Angarano, Michael 1987– CTFT–78

Angel, Heather 1909–1986 .... CTFT–4
    Earlier sketch in WWasWT
Angel, Jack 1931(?)– CTFT–39
Angel, Vanessa 1963– CTFT–39
Angela, June 1959– CTFT–55
    Earlier sketch in CTFT–11
Angelopoulos, Theo 1936(?)– CTFT–22
    Earlier sketch in CTFT–11
Angelou, Maya 1928– CTFT–39
    Earlier sketches in CTFT–10, 17
Angelus, Muriel 1909– .... WWasWT
Angers, Avril 1922–.......................... CTFT–14
    Earlier sketch in WWT–17
Angie
    See.................... Featherstone, Angela
Anglade, Jean–Hugues 1955–.............. CTFT–68
    Earlier sketch in CTFT–30
Angle, Kurt 1968– CTFT–43
Anglim, Philip 1953– CTFT–41
    Earlier sketches in CTFT–20; WWT–17,
    CTFT–4
Anglin, Margaret 1876–1958 .... WWasWT
Anhalt, Edward 1914– CTFT–10
Anholt, Christien 1971– CTFT–40
Aniston, Jennifer 1969– CTFT–53
    Earlier sketches in CTFT–15, 25
Aniston, John 1937–.......................... CTFT–58
    Earlier sketches in CTFT–17, 27
Anka, Paul 1941–.............................. CTFT–60
Annabella 1912– .... WWasWT
Annakin, Ken 1914– CTFT–11
Annals, Michael 1938– WWT–17
Annaud, Jean–Jacques 1943– CTFT–37
    Earlier sketches in CTFT–3, 13
Annis, Francesca 1944(?)–................... CTFT–51
    Earlier sketches in CTFT–8, 15, 25
Ann–Margret 1941–........................... CTFT–60
    Earlier sketches in CTFT–3, 9, 16, 28
Annunzio, Gabriele d' 1863–1938 .... WWasWT
Anouilh, Jean 1910–1987...................... CTFT–5
    Earlier sketch in WWT–17
Anouk
    See................................ Aimee, Anouk
Ansara, Michael 1927(?)–.................... CTFT–33
    Earlier sketch in CTFT–3
Ansell, John 1874–1948 .... WWasWT
Anselmo, Tony CTFT–37
Ansen, David 1945–.......................... CTFT–10
Ansley, Zachary CTFT–34
Anson, A. E. 1879–1936...................... WWasWT
Anson, George William 1847–1920 ...... WWasWT
Anspach, Susan 1939(?)–.................... CTFT–53
    Earlier sketches in CTFT–3, 18
Anspacher, Louis K. 1878–1947 .... WWasWT
Anspaugh, David 1946– CTFT–39
    Earlier sketches in CTFT–8, 15
Anstey, Edgar 1907–1987 .... CTFT–4
    Obituary in CTFT–5
Anstey, F. 1856–1934 .... WWasWT
Anstruther, Harold .... WWasWT
Ant, Adam 1954– CTFT–38
    Earlier sketch in CTFT–14
Anthony, Joseph 1912–....................... WWT–17
Anthony, Lysette 1963– CTFT–80
    Earlier sketches in CTFT–10, 36
Anthony, Marc 1968–......................... CTFT–66
    Earlier sketch in CTFT–30
Anthony, Michael 1920– CTFT–5
Antico, Pete..................................... CTFT–80
Antille, Lisa CTFT–3
Antin, Steve 1956– CTFT–36
Antoine, Andre 1857–1943 .... WWasWT

Cumulative Index

E

Cumulative Index

J

Cumulative Index

P

Cumulative Index

Sakamoto, Junji 1954– CTFT–34
Saker, Annie 1882–1932.................... WWasWT
Saker, Mrs. Edward 1847–1912 .... WWasWT
Saks, Gene 1921– CTFT–21
    Earlier sketches in CTFT–2, 9; WWT–17
Sakuyama, Jimmy
    See .... Mako
Salacrou, Armand 1899–1989 .... WWasWT
Salberg, Derek S. 1912– WWT–17
Saldana, Theresa 1954– CTFT–63
    Earlier sketches in CTFT–15, 28
Saldana, Zoe 1978– CTFT–68
Sale, Richard 1911–1993 .... CTFT–12
Salenger, Meredith 1970– CTFT–57
Sales, Jean
    See .... Vigo, Jean
Sales, Soupy 1926(?)– CTFT–59
Salhany, Lucie 1946(?)– CTFT–12
Salin, Kari Wuhrer
    See .... Wuhrer, Kari
Salinger, Diane CTFT–43
Salinger, Matt 1960– CTFT–63
    Earlier sketches in CTFT–7, 15, 28
Salin–Wuhrer, Kari
    See .... Wuhrer, Kari
Salisbury, Benjamin 1980– CTFT–80
Salisbury, Frank 1930– CTFT–4
Salisbury, John
    See .... Caute, David
Salke, Bert CTFT–62
Salkey, Jason CTFT–76
    Earlier sketch in CTFT–34
Salkind, Alexander 1921–1997 .... CTFT–6
    Obituary in CTFT–17
Salle, Charles (Chic) 1885–1936 .... WWasWT
Sallis, Peter 1921– CTFT–8
    Earlier sketch in WWT–17
Salmi, Albert 1928–1990 .... CTFT–5
Salmon, Colin 1962– CTFT–63
    Earlier sketch in CTFT–28
Salomma, Sonya CTFT–65
Salomon, Mikael 1945– CTFT–10
Salonga, Lea 1971– CTFT–28
    Earlier sketches in CTFT–15, 28
Salt, Charlotte 1985– CTFT–80
Salt, Jennifer 1944– CTFT–7
Salt, Waldo 1914–1987 .... CTFT–6
Saltz, Amy 1946– CTFT–6
    Earlier sketch in CTFT–1
Salvatores, Gabriele 1950– CTFT–34
Salvini, Tomasso 1829–1915 .... WWasWT
Samaha, Elie 1955– CTFT–74
Sammons, Jennifer Dale
    See .... Dale, Jennifer
Samms, Emma 1960– CTFT–44
    Earlier sketch in CTFT–4
Samora, Rogerio 1959– CTFT–34
Sampler, Philece 1953– CTFT–42
Samples, M. David CTFT–4
Sampras, Bridgette Wilson
    See .... Wilson, Bridgette
Samprogna, Dominic
    Zamprogna, Dominic CTFT–74
Sampson, Bill
    See .... Erman, John
Sampson, Will 1935–1987 .... CTFT–17
Sams, Jeffrey D. CTFT–66
    Earlier sketch in CTFT–29
Samson, Ivan 1894–1963 .... WWasWT
Sanada, Hiroyuki 1960– CTFT–77
    Earlier sketch in CTFT–34
Sanchez, Eduardo 1968– CTFT–71
Sanchez, Marco 1970– CTFT–52

Sanchez, Pablo
    See .... Sand, Paul
Sanchez, Penelope Cruz
    See .... Cruz, Penelope
Sanchez, Roselyn 1970(?)– CTFT–61
Sand, Paul 1935– CTFT–62
    Earlier sketches in CTFT–4; WWT–17
Sanda, Dominique 1948– CTFT–45
    Earlier sketches in CTFT–1, 17
Sande, Theo Van de
    See .... van de Sande, Theo
Sander, Casey 1956– CTFT–45
Sanderford, John CTFT–77
Sanders, Alvin CTFT–58
Sanders, Andrew CTFT–68
    Earlier sketch in CTFT–30
Sanders, Brandy
    See .... Ledford, Brandy
Sanders, Chris CTFT–73
Sanders, Henry G. 1942– CTFT–57
    Earlier sketch in CTFT–26
Sanders, Jay O. 1953– CTFT–73
    Earlier sketches in CTFT–12, 21, 32
Sanders, Richard 1940– CTFT–29
    Earlier sketches in CTFT–2, 18
Sanderson, Julia 1887–1975 .... WWasWT
Sanderson, Martyn CTFT–43
Sanderson, William 1948– CTFT–24
Sandford, Marjorie 1910– .... WWasWT
Sandino, Enrique 1951– CTFT–5
Sandison, Gordon 1913–1958 .... WWasWT
Sandler, Adam 1966(?)– CTFT–63
    Earlier sketches in CTFT–15, 28
Sandler, Barry 1947– CTFT–12
Sandor, Victor
    See .... Izay, Victor
Sandoval, Miguel 1951– CTFT–73
    Earlier sketch in CTFT–33
Sandrich, Jay 1932– CTFT–77
    Earlier sketches in CTFT–1, 4, 34
Sands, Diana 1934– .... WWasWT
Sands, Dorothy 1893–1980 .... WWT–17
Sands, Julian 1958– CTFT–39
    Earlier sketches in CTFT–8, 15
Sands, Leslie 1921– WWT–17
Sands, Reni
    See .... Santoni, Reni
Sandstorm, R.O.C.
    See .... Campbell, Bruce
    See .... Raimi, Sam
Sandy, Gary 1946– CTFT–63
    Earlier sketch in CTFT–6
Sanes, Camillia CTFT–64
Sanford, Garwin 1955– CTFT–60
    Earlier sketch in CTFT–27
Sanford, Isabel 1917(?)– CTFT–43
    Earlier sketches in CTFT–2, 21
Sanger, Jonathan 1944– CTFT–1
San Giacomo, Laura 1962(?)– CTFT–45
    Earlier sketches in CTFT–13, 22
Sangster, Alfred 1880–? .... WWasWT
Sano, Shiro 1955– CTFT–33
Sansom, Ken CTFT–37
Santiago–Hudson, Ruben
    1956– CTFT–69
    Earlier sketch in CTFT–30
Santley, Frederic 1887–1953 .... WWasWT
Santley, Joseph 1889–1971 .... WWasWT
Santley, Kate ?–1923 .... WWasWT
Santoni, Reni 1939– CTFT–77
    Earlier sketches in CTFT–1, 4, 34
Santos, Joe 1931(?)– CTFT–41
    Earlier sketches in CTFT–7, 18

Sanz, Horatio 1969(?)– CTFT–76
Saperstein, Harlan CTFT–51
Saphier, Peter 1940– CTFT–1
Sapienza, Al 1956– CTFT–51
Sara, Mia 1967– CTFT–42
    Earlier sketch in CTFT–9
Sarafian, Richard C. 1932(?)– CTFT–38
    Earlier sketch in CTFT–12
Sarandon, Chris 1942– CTFT–60
    Earlier sketches in CTFT–4, 15, 27; WWT–17
Sarandon, Susan 1946– CTFT–40
    Earlier sketches in CTFT–3, 10, 17
Sarde, Philippe 1945– CTFT–37
    Earlier sketch in CTFT–10
Sarducci, Father Guido
    See .... Novello, Don
Sargent, Alvin 1927– CTFT–38
    Earlier sketch in CTFT–12
Sargent, Dick 1930–1994 .... CTFT–24
Sargent, Frederic 1879–? .... WWasWT
Sargent, Herb. CTFT–15
Sargent, Herbert C. 1873–? .... WWasWT
Sargent, Joseph 1925– CTFT–77
    Earlier sketches in CTFT–6, 34
Sargent, Lia CTFT–40
Sarin, Victor CTFT–37
Sarment, Jean 1897–1976 .... WWasWT
Sarna, Michael J. CTFT–37
Sarner, Alexander 1892–1948 .... WWasWT
Sarony, Leslie 1897– WWT–17
    Earlier sketch in WWasWT
Sarossy, Paul 1963– CTFT–79
Saroyan, William 1908–1981 .... WWT–17
Sarpong, Sam 1979(?)– CTFT–60
Sarrazin, Michael 1940– CTFT–43
    Earlier sketches in CTFT–5, 12, 21
Sarsgaard, Peter 1971– CTFT–66
    Earlier sketch in CTFT–29
Sartain, Gailard 1946– CTFT–32
Sartor, Fabio 1954– CTFT–74
    Earlier sketch in CTFT–33
Sartre, Jean–Paul 1905–1980 .... WWT–17
Sass, Edward ?–1916 .... WWasWT
Sass, Enid 1889–1959 .... WWasWT
Sasso, William 1975– CTFT–73
    Earlier sketch in CTFT–33
Sastri, Lina 1953– CTFT–35
Satlof, Ron CTFT–49
Sato, Hiroyuki CTFT–35
Sato, Isao 1949–1990 .... CTFT–9
Sato, Kei CTFT–35
    Earlier sketch in CTFT–1
Satterfield, Paul 1960– CTFT–59
Saucier, Claude–Albert 1953– CTFT–2
Saulnier, Tania 1982– CTFT–71
Saunders, Cliff CTFT–60
Saunders, Derek
    See .... Rubin, Bruce Joel
Saunders, Florence ?–1926 .... WWasWT
Saunders, James 1925– CTFT–6
    Earlier sketch in WWT–17
Saunders, Jennifer 1958– CTFT–77
Saunders, Madge 1894–1967 .... WWasWT
Saunders, Nicholas 1914– CTFT–6
    Earlier sketch in CTFT–1
Saunders, Peter 1911– CTFT–1
    Earlier sketch in WWT–17
Saura, Carlos 1932– CTFT–29
Sautet, Claude 1924– CTFT–26
Savadier, Russel CTFT–77
Savage, Ben 1980– CTFT–50
Savage, Fred 1976– CTFT–59
    Earlier sketches in CTFT–8, 15, 27

Contemporary Theatre, Film and Television • Volume 81

Cumulative Index

Z

Cumulative Index

493